MW00931886

The Early Tales of Snow and Oakham

A Novel by

Philip Chavanne

§

"Isn't it strange how princes and kings,
And clowns that caper in sawdust rings,
and common people, like you and me,
are builders for eternity?

Each is given a list of rules;
a shapeless mass; a bag of tools.
And each must fashion, ere life is flown,
A stumbling block, or a Stepping-Stone."

- RL Sharpe

I wish to dedicate this book to my father, David Chavanne and to Kanakuk Kamps - two of the great stepping-stones in my life. Without them this story never would have been possible.

Table of Contents

Prologue ix

Part I - The Tenpenny Three 45

Chapter 1   Change is in the Air 47
Chapter 2   Melting Snow, Melting Hearts 89
Chapter 3   The Last Hours of Boyhood 101
Chapter 4   The Adventure Begins 133
Chapter 5   The Rojo Prieta 146
Chapter 6   The King of Kamchatka 158
Chapter 7   Feathers and First Blood 178
Chapter 8   Muleshoe 198

Part II - The Wild West End 209

Chapter 1   Back at Tenpenny 211
Chapter 2   Whitehorse 231
Chapter 3   The Birth of Stuart Whitlock 240
Chapter 4   Gathering the Posse 253
Chapter 5   Strangers from Across the Sea 258
Chapter 6   The Student from Gromalsk 272
Chapter 7   Brave Fools and Lucky Branches 278
Chapter 8   The Pritchers 296
Chapter 9   Into the Lion's Den 304
Chapter 10   The Rejuvenation of Unger Soski 323
Chapter 11   Pennies from Heaven 338

Chapter 12   On Their Heals 351
Chapter 13   A Dark Chase Needs a Silent Hound 358
Chapter 14   A Dowry for Mary Mdingwe 366
Chapter 15   A Feather in Their Caps 380

Part III - The Legacy of Thaddeus Parnicca.....391

Chapter 1   Milk and Honey 393
Chapter 2   The Milk of Friendship 413
Chapter 3   A Burial at Sea 422
Chapter 4   The Sons of Otsov Kolschen..................................437
Chapter 5   Arrivals 471
Chapter 6   Sissy's Hurdles...486
Chapter 7   The Western Rim of the World 502
Chapter 8   Six Pigs for the Big Man...................................514
Chapter 9   Secrets of the Mountain 548
Chapter 10   Departures 566
Chapter 11   How Tenpenny Came to Be 585
Chapter 11   The Pickleman 597
Chapter 12   Hands and Feet..608

Prologue

"We orphans we lament to the world: World, why have you taken our soft mothers from us. And the fathers who say: My child, you are like me!"

Nelly Sachs (1891–1970)

1968

Tipper

When Tip Holland turned eighteen he came out in the freedom of the summer heat like a thirsty vessel, a wounded pup, and went searching for his father. Having no other idea where to start he finally asked his mother, there in the sweaty lime green kitchen of the Harlem Heights.

"What you wanna know for, sonny?"

"Other fellas know their pops," he said. "I figure I should get mine."

She turned on him with ailing grief. "Oh, you'll get yours, I figure. Right across the chops. You know it was right here where he done it - with you and your sister inside me he held me down and beat me cause the 'beans are burnin'. I bled right down onto my big round belly. You don't wanna find your father, Tip. He beat me every chance he got."

Just like he'd seen in the movies the boy flicked his cigarette onto the floor and rubbed it out. "You better button that lip, girl. A man like me don't need no advice."

He was a pale boy, with a pot-marked face in the spring and summer but the look of trouble the rest of the year. Like all of his runaround neighbors in the Harlem heights none of his mother's prayers had taken hold.

In that first week of his eighteenth summer his mind began to unravel. The knowledge of his father became the first thought; first, middle and final and he couldn't grasp what ghosts or dreams he would chase if not his father. He couldn't comprehend where the urge had come from, but it was the last innocent pursuit he could envision, the death rattle of his childhood hopes.

He rode the subway to the Upper East Side and found his twin sister, Sissy, baking in the shop where she worked.

"World you want?"

"I'm out to find our father."

"Hah! What for?"

"Other fellas know their pops," he said. "I figure I should get mine."

"Why tell me?"

"Don't know where he is."

"Well like I do. Last I heard he's long gone. Not even his old freight men know him anymore."

"How do you know that?"

"Saw one. Months ago at the laundry. Told me that Pappy hasn't come to the east side since we were kids. Man was huntin dope."

"What man?"

Tipper spent two days searching names of ex-employers, ex-friends and ex- lovers for the man who was his father. Though there was no man to find. The thing that had fathered him wasn't a man, but an eternal child, who was a world away, searching too. All Tip learned was that his old man had left the City years before, taken a freight job oversees, and was last known in a place called Estonia, though Tip had no earthly clue where that was.

The boy had no money and no prospects and the limits of his ambition had been reached. Twice in that first month he was picked up for dope, both times while standing outside a club on Lamar street. Tip had seen a movie where a street-wise kid had gotten the attention of a crime boss by smoking dope in broad daylight. So he dressed in an oversized pinstripe suit his father had left behind, and puffed away as he threw glances inside the club. Both times the police arrived at the owner's request.

After hearing of the second arrest a man named Unger Soski entered the scene. He was a parole officer whose wife went to church with Tip's mother. After the second arrest Unger went down to the station and bailed the boy out, as a favor to his wife.

"You some kinda law?" Tip asked.

"Nope. Just a friend."

"Cause law don't hold me. Twice I been in. Twice I come out."

"I bailed you out, son."

"They seen something in me they was scared of."

As was his custom, Mr. Soski checked up on the boy at his home after a month. He brought flowers for the ladies at his wife's request, and a Bible for the boy on his own accord.

"What have you been doing with yourself, Tip?"

"Oh, you know. This and that. This and that. Got some things going, you know. Working out some plans. Meeting with some people."

"He's been sitting around the house for a month," Sissy said. "On Friday nights he dresses up like he's made or something and talks about his big-shot friends on the east side."

"Big-shot friends, huh?"

"Oh you know," Tip said. "Gotta keep connected. You aren't connected you fall apart."

"Are you connected, Tip?"

"You don't even know," Tip smiled. "Things are happening."

Sissy shook her head. "Nothing's happening. Nothing's ever happening. He just sits around watching mobsters on TV and makes threats and talks about those big-shots on the east side at some club he goes to."

"Why haven't I heard about this?"

"Well I don't want to brag but things are so good right now. So good."

"Sounds like it. I can barely soak it all in the way you tell it."

Tipper got lost, staring out the window. "Yeah I'm getting to be a pretty big deal on the east side."

"No, you're not," Sissy said. "No he's not. He's not even smart enough to hide his lies."

"I'm a big deal on the east side."

"A big deal, huh?"

"People know me."

"No one knows you," Sissy said. "We're the only people that know you."

"Okay. You'll see. I don't mean to brag. I don't want to make no one jealous."

"Jealous? You think we're jealous, Tip?"

"Well you would be if you knew what I know. But that's okay. Things are so good. I don't mean to brag. A man like me doesn't need to brag. It just speaks for itself."

Sissy chuckled into her apron. "You ain't no tough guy, Tipper."

"You wanna bet, little sister? Unger, I don't want to hurt her again like I used to when we were younger. Tell her to stop. She doesn't even know."

"He used to hurt you when you were younger?"

"Yep," she laughed. "We were playing soccer and he tripped me. We were on the yellow team."

"That ain't all," Tip said. "Now you better listen. I asked nicely. I won't ask nicely again. Tell her to stop, Unger. She don't even know what I can do."

Unger sighed, "You ain't no tough guy, Tip. I can't quite figure what you are - but you sure ain't no tough guy."

One afternoon Sissy dropped a letter on his chest while he was sleeping. An hour later Tip sat on the balcony with the letter before him, his eyes dodging, his hands nervously preoccupied. Sissy watched him weeping through her window.

"I've been drafted," he told her.

It was the most beautiful sentence he had ever uttered. "Oh. No."

"Yes, Sissy. It's true. You see I've been drafted. Drafted, drafted, drafted. I don't know how it happened."

"It was fate. They drew your number."

"But why me, Sissy? Why. . . was I. . .drafted?"

"Maybe they heard you were free for the next couple of years. If you'd had a job maybe you wouldn't have been drafted, drafted, drafted." though she knew it wasn't true.

"D'you think they'd let me stay because of my domestic obligations?"

"What are you talking about? That makes me sick."

"You forget that I'm looking for our father."

"I do forget that. How true."

"Maybe they'll give me time to find him. Other fellas know their pops," he said. "I figure, I should get mine."

"You do that, Tip. Tell 'em whose boss. I'm off to work."

In tears he stood to hug her but she weaseled her way out.

The following week Unger paid the family his usual visit. Before dinner was served the boy rang a fork against his glass. "Listen up ladies, hush that talking a minute."

"Oh, Lord," said Sissy.

He spoke proudly and methodically, as if his words were rehearsed. "A strong man leaves nothing to chance. And that's what I've always aimed to be, a strong man."

"You finished?"

"I've decided to enlist," he told them. "Rather than be drafted. I won't let chance decide my fate."

Sissy turned to Unger, generally surprised. "Can he do that?"

"Already did," Tip told her. "Notified my recruiter, got tested and in two weeks I'll join the 82nd Airborne. My bus leaves for Ft. Benton."

"Why wait?" she asked.

"Unger and me gonna go fishing first."

"Fishing?"

"In Alaska," Unger admitted. "I've wanted to go since I was a kid. I've just never had the time or anyone to go with."

"There are bears up there," Tip said. "Big ones. Unger heard that I was a soldier now and asked me to be his bodyguard."

And Unger winked at the women.

It was a week of heavy handshakes, of Priests and dentists calling the boy up to wish, "God speed". For the first time in her life Sissy said openly, "I'm proud of you."

So Tip Holland left his family and fled west for what he called, "My next big adventure." It was an encouragement to his mother to see him spending time with Unger. It was a delight to his sister that he was finally about to leave.

Unger taught Tipper how to fish the big waters, how to pitch a tent, how to fire a pistol. "You'll get plenty of that in basic," he told him. "But it never hurts to come prepared."

They kayaked up the coast, two full days along the beach.

"I sure am glad you chose to enlist," Unger told him. They were cooking their fish along the sand.

"A strong man leaves nothing to chance," Tip said. "And that's what I've always aimed to be, a strong man."

"You think you'll be a career man?"

"I'll give it a few years. Play the field. See what they know."

"They have a lot to offer you."

"I have a lot to offer them, too. Don't forget that, Soski. If I don't like it I'll just come home."

Unger cracked a smile, "I used to be much like you," he told him. "When I was younger. I didn't know my father either so I used to think I could do anything. "

"A man like me doesn't need to think. I just do."

Again, Unger sighed, "We've got to work on that mouth of yours, Tip."

Suddenly the boy was staring off at the sea. He became fixed on the distant trees. Finally he repeated the words, *"We've got to work on that mouth of yours, Tip."*

"That's right. We do."

And again, dead to the world, Tip said, *"We've got to work on that mouth of yours, Tip."*

Unger smiled awkwardly. Try as he might he didn't understand this boy. The distance between them was greater than he had realized. He watched him fidget beneath his blanket, his eye twitching.

Now the boy was speaking in a whisper. *"We've got to work on that mouth of yours, Tip."*

Unger was standing to his feet, still smiling, when Tipper shot him in the back. He had seen it done in a movie - where a double-crosser shoots the boss so he can rise to power. Instantly the big man crashed to the sand. Tipper removed the cash from his pocket, hauled his pack onto his shoulders and kayaked down the beach, afraid to look back at the body twitching in the surf.

That afternoon he arrived at a fishing port, pawned the pistol and the kayak and away he went. He thumbed up the coast, a footpath, then a train. The next day he convinced a Ruski Crab King to let him book passage through the long island chain that connected to the world across the sea. In exchange he agreed to complete petty duties in the galley. The skipper gave him a cot for eight days until, in the midst of a white-capped gale, they made berth on the wild shores of Kamchatka. He buttoned his coat and pointed West towards Estonia. And so went the cowardly travels of Tip Holland. He was neither a volunteer nor a fate-seeker when his journey began.

1982

Sissy had been picky with her suitors and never married. It seems that if you hold out on life, life will return the favor. She soon grew tired of the rabble of the Harlem Heights and began to set her mind to becoming a woman pursuant of noble causes: namely etiquette and fine dining. She enrolled in various courses at the local community college and other etiquette schools in Manhattan, steering her life away from anything to do with her brother's shame. She found that the rigidity of high society fit nicely within her self-perceptions. She preferred to live a beautiful lie than an embarrassing truth.

Sissy continued to live with her mother, who spent her days without asking questions. With her daughter beside her, Sissy's mom baked and chored and kept to herself until finally her mind began to go and the questions returned.

"Where are the men?" she asked her daughter.

"They're gone. All gone."

"Feels different without them."

"How does it feel different?"

"Feels peaceful and boring. Lonely and prosperous."

"Prosperous is good."

"Prosperous is phony, sugar. Only adversity is real. We gals have a monopoly on real."

She spent her long late years scrubbing herself of possible infections and rearranging furniture and died after she split her toe, the second one down from the fatty, on a heavy walnut roll-top she thought should take on more light. And because her incessant scrubbing had left her immune system unpracticed, the little scratch let in toxic invaders that chewed at her from within before her healing agents got the call. She died wishing the coffee table was a bit closer.

Once the furniture was hocked and the deed sold, at the exact moment when Sissy slipped her sunglasses onto her nose and was about to unplug the jack, her last task, there was a knock at the door. Sissy found it difficult to comprehend her mother's choice in light fixtures, or wallpaper, or carpeting that she would never have to see again but even more difficult to understand was the face that greeted her when she opened the door.

"Hello, Sister."

"In God's name."

He had a size and shape that vaguely resembled her long lost brother, a size and shape she had all but forgotten. And seeing him standing there did little to remind her of the boy she used to know.

Tip Holland had been away fourteen years, long enough to escape the war, see five continents, three oceans, fall in love with the poor, amass a wealth of treasure and culture, hear news of his mother's death, and return a changed man. Of the once slack and grease-haired youth who desired moral retreat, there were now few similarities.

"You're prettier than I remember," he told her.

"In God's name."

He had replaced sloth and sarcasm with gentleness and grit. His face had brightened, his eyes had grown lively. Each word that came from him was chosen for its candor. His lingo was a blend of Polynesian/Eastern European and his sister surmised from his palms that he had been an ocean-goer. His clothes were tattered, his sandals and his open collar revealed that the smooth skin of his boyhood had been replaced. He had a wild smell, like that of a man who had been surface traveling the world for over a decade, two parts beach, one part train, scoop of desert, pinch of jungle. He had learned to grow a beard, to cradle his sister's face when he greeted her, to cook with the barest essentials, to use two words instead of three. He began using phrases like "No worries" and calling friends, "good okes" and forever referred to his bathroom as "the lou." Sissy was amazed to see that his new skills included piano playing, storytelling, and an uncanny ability to mop. All of the destructive boyhood quirks that he had amassed in his youth had been evicted from his character. They sat together, outside as Tipper insisted, for a long cloudless afternoon. Like a child with a big screen hero, Sissy began to fall in love with her brother.

"What have you seen? What have you found?"

"Just what I was looking for."

Once the waves had settled Tip told her, "There are some friends I'd like you to meet."

Although empty-handed for souvenirs, Tip Holland brought back six companions from his travels. They followed him like an entourage of the world.

He led his sister to a hotel two blocks away and there in the lobby they greeted her. There was gentle Momma Tom, a mother hen as her name suggested, Doc Zuni - an elderly Persian physician, Padibatakal a kind-hearted crippled girl, Papon - a wild bear of a man from New Guinea, Wonderboy, a tiny African worker who smiled without ceasing, and a huge dog named Putt - a brilliant hunter who had only been with Tipper for the last few weeks of his adventure. During their stay in the hotel they marveled at the luxuries available to them - running water and ice in their glasses but their greatest thrill came when they finally met Tip's only sibling.

"Let's sit down a moment," Tip told her.

Well aware that his life was about to change, Tip hoped that Sissy, the only family he still had, would change with him. So there among his crowd of friends, Tip Holland revealed two things to his sister. He explained that in his travels he had amassed a vast, "Unending fortune. Not a man I know could comprehend it." He described the family's new riches, in vague, confident denominations, but gave no clue of its origin. Sissy looked at him with arched eyebrows.

"Secondly," Tip said, "I've returned with the intent of building a life in the mountains, far from here. I have a dream to pursue, sister, and I want you to be a part of it."

Tip Holland was no longer the kind of man that would lose an audience with empty words. Sissy was captivated by the sheen in his eyes. She wanted to breathe in his determination. A long time passed before she responded to his proposal. What do you say when discovering that you have just inherited a treasure of riches? What do you do when encountering a man with a radiant hope?

The old woman named Momma Tom finally stretched a bony arm across the hickory and said calmly, "Tell her about your dream."

And what began as a vision whispered across the coffee table, turned with the coming years into the mission statement of their lives. Tip had come home boldly, standing for the first time, and Sissy, grateful and inspired, stood beside him. She didn't have a clue what she was in for, but she didn't feel the fright that often comes with change. Her brother had returned home a man and his life was spelled out before her and he wouldn't hesitate to love her, or her him and there was no doubt about whether or not to follow.

"We'll call it Tenpenny," he told her. "Because we're all pennies from Heaven. And 'Ten' because there are ten of us."

The others nodded.

"There are eight of us," Sissy told him, "Only eight."

"Oh yes, Sister, there is something I forgot."

Tipper explained that the present entourage was incomplete. "There are two young boys yet to arrive," he told her. "They belong with us. They just don't know it yet."

"I don't understand. Who are they?"

"Their names are Henry Snow and Jack Oakham. They're very far from here and very far from each other, and they're only small children, but I have to find them."

"Your children?"

"No," he told her. "Not yet."

So what remained of the family's possessions they took with them to their new life. The purchase of land was looked after with care and soon they stood among a meadow, scanning the wood and the stream, the rocky cliffs and the emerald fields with their hands on their hips, imagining what could be.

"It's a good dream, brother."

Tipper pitched a tent and drafted a map of his plan in phases. The ladies left him there with the dog for a week, to begin laying a foundation. He spent his days exploring the terrain, stepping off measurements, building a shelter for his tools. He survived on hares and ptarmigan but left the salmon alone. The others went straight to work felling trees, cutting roads - the Doc designed his infirmary.

For two years they labored, sawed and stacked, hiring a crew of local strongbacks and putting them to the weary. In the evenings they brought ideas to the table at supper, drew up plans after the dishes were done and watched them birth the following morning. Two years and it was started. And no one from the mining flat or the hay town, no one from across the whole of the inlet could understand why Tip Holland had forsaken his lands and decided to build an orphanage.

Henry

They say one man's junk is another man's treasure, and beauty is in the beholder's eye, and don't knock it 'til you've tried it, and all that jazz funk about how there's a star in everyone waiting to be found, a big shining star. And it's all true. Every word of it. "Butterflies" and "cocoons" and

"You could do anything with your life". It must be true because stars are born every day, and firemen burn alive to save a stranger, and because sometimes the future heroes of this world are thrown away as babies.

Henry Snow was dropped in a whicker basket and abandoned cold and hungry on a stone doorstep when he was two months old. His mother fled her home with Henry in tow and journeyed across the ocean to Port Elizabeth, the last place anyone would look. She had hoped that Henry would be raised amidst the color of Africa, with manner and etiquette as priorities. The Nuns at St. Christopher's made sure of it.

"Dear Sisters, The child's name is Henry Snow. My husband is dead. That is why I must give up my son. Little Henry was born on the 1st of March. Teach him to be proper and give him doctrine. Thank you. – His mother."

Through the next six years Henry quickly outgrew all of the black orphans that surrounded him, and was soon big-backed and heavy fisted, with hair wild and curly - the bull moose of a one moose litter. His hands were taller than some of the Sisters, with knotty knuckles and a neck that started at the shoulders. And alongside his stature came a flair for finding the weakness in everyone. He knew when the young nuns were menstruating and if his teachers were lying about God.

But more than his skin, or his size, or his keen eye for people, the characteristic that set Henry Snow apart from every other child at St. Christopher's was that he possessed a general awareness of his surroundings even from his early days of speech. The Africa he saw everyday, poetic and undomesticated, made sense to him, as if he had studied her all his life, as did the Catholic Church, with all of her rigid hurdles to clear.

None of the Sisters could comprehend it. A mysterious white boy, abandoned as an infant, who never asked why was he discarded or why his skin was different became a puzzle to them indeed. Henry seemed to know himself early on, right down to his path. He knew that orphanages were necessary until he reached a certain age. He knew that the world was big and he had eyes to see. But what Henry didn't know was that after six years of waiting the world would be seen much sooner than expected.

On a Thursday morning a man traveled by train from Mussel Bay with nothing but a tattered haversack over his shoulder, chewing biltong throughout his journey and shaking with anticipation. When he arrived at the orphanage he removed a tiny spade from his pack and quickly dug a hole behind the northern wall. When he was finished he found a shady spot and began writing the instant he sat.

"Dear son,

I have an image of you and Jack in my head digging up this box and it makes me smile to think of you among the old and bold. This is your second clue. I've buried it here, Henry, so that in your travels you are forced to come back to where you started. That's always important. Kolschen taught me that. The next stage in your journey will lead you to the high cut of the world. Gimmelwald. There you will find a trail leading east to the green river. Follow it to the timber shelter where travelers have etched their words on the walls for decades. Find my words.

Wish I was there – Pops

The man promptly folded the letter, tucked it into a yellow envelope, which he sealed and placed neatly in a small walnut box. He was careful to fill the hole in such a way that any curious children would be unlikely to discover it. Then the man walked around the outer wall of the shelter, entered through the quad, and wiped his boots on the foot mat as he entered the office.

Sister Katherine looked up at the opening door.

"Can I help you?"

"Yes I have an appointment."

"Are you here about Henry Snow?"

"I am, Miss."

She extended her hand, "I am Sister Katherine."

"Tip Holland."

"Pleased to have you."

When Henry was called out of class Tipper watched the way the boy stood, the way his hair grew curly and wild, and for the rest of his life he described the resemblance as "remarkable".

Once the pair arrived back at Tenpenny, Tip made it clear how the boy should be raised. "Son, you can't have supper until your hands are dirty and your knees are bleeding."

And Henry loved the man immediately.

But Sissy couldn't bear the idea of Tip Holland, a wild man himself, taking full charge of her nephew's development. By that time Tenpenny was well underway, although only a handful of children were being cared for, the orphanage was already equipped with a working schoolhouse and half a dozen teachers. But unlike all of the other children at Tenpenny, Henry Snow was no longer an orphan. Tipper had seen fit to adopt young Henry as a permanent addition to their family and this led Sissy to assume a certain responsibility for his upbringing. She saw to it that Henry was brought up to be an educated young man, tutored not only in the subjects of science, equations, and letters, but in all manner of social graces as well. Sissy began grooming him as an upstart who could excel at everything. He was made to think that anything could be learned yet that not everything should be learned and that to form an impression of someone as either learned or slow-witted, one must merely find out what he knew, and often more importantly, what he didn't.

"If someone knows how to butcher an animal," Sissy told him, "they are certainly not civil. If someone drinks red wine with fish," she continued, "they are certainly not human."

In third grade Sissy had Henry study everything he could read, beginning with the great Greeks, then the Germans, and finally his American free thinkers. With his Aunt's help Henry discovered laws, dogmas, philosophies, myths, religions, goods and evils. There was no limit to his range. One week would end with an exhausting study of carburetor repair and spill over into the next with a romantic interest in cultural geography and ethnic desserts. Instead of eating candy canes and playing baseball Henry Snow soon studied the chemical makeup of red and white food dyes and the force required to launch a successful knuckleball. By the time he was nine, Henry had become pregnant with ideas, fertile with knowledge, and sensitive to sunlight. His father became concerned.

"Let's take a swim," Tip told his son.

"Not now, Father. I've discovered intercourse."

"How bout we close that book?"

Although his Aunt discouraged rugged play, behind her back Henry began to indulge in what his father referred to as "the virtue sports" – those endeavors of contest that sent young men into the woods to find their true selves, shining and brave, or dull and ducking. "There is no greater virtue than humility," his fathevr told him. This was Tip's greatest contribution to his childhood: the absolute wonder of every single thing. "Look at the stars," he would tell him, "They will make you humble. As you shoot a bird on the wing, consider the grand miracle of flight. If you can do that you will respect the provision of food that he brings you, and you will respect our Lord and Savior because he has blessed us with this gift." He often repeated himself. "How better to learn patience than to stalk your prey on a windy afternoon or to tangle your line in the branches at your back? And with these virtues you will find a love for life itself. Can any wisdom be clearer than the kind that grows on trees?" And then he would say to bring his son out of his academic shell, "Sit in those trees, son. Listen to those birds, watch the water. Humility, respect, patience and love. This is what wisdom is made of."

"Thank you, Daddy."

It wasn't long before his father's teaching began to overtake little Henry Snow. The boy found himself romanced by new sounds and smells. Tenpenny provided a beautiful and wild childhood after all, a childhood that was constantly presented with new possibilities - whether it be horses to ride or cabins to build or new orphans to meet. Henry began to read outdoors, to fall asleep against the giant shade trees. Despite his Aunt's vigorous adherence to a "pragmatic interest" Henry began to turn his passion for self- improvement and grand depth of knowledge toward the rugged pursuits of youth. Almost overnight it seemed his heart began to be moved by the wind and the rain.

"I've decided to become a person of virtue, Aunt Sissy."

She nodded blankly. "Okay then, honey, after your studies."

Henry took walks, pictures, liberties. His addiction to answers that was once insatiable had now been cured. The answers were his. He soon journeyed toward a bright, blinding life. He noticed his breathing, how his fingers moved when he told them to, how his toenails grew tirelessly, how his feet stayed on the ground. His mind strayed from the dull and deceitful laws of etiquette and preventative medicine that his Aunt had engraved.

"Have you finished your Scandinavian history?" his Aunt asked.

"It must have slipped my mind."

Henry Snow decided his true tests were yet to come.

One Sunday evening Tipper packed his bag for a long journey. "I'll be back in a week," he told his son. "Do your best to obey your Auntie."

"Where are you going?"

"I'm off to find Jack Oakham."

"Who's that?"

"He'll be your brother, if I ever find him."

With his father absent Henry felt the tug for the wilderness stronger than ever. Once his Aunt was down for a nap Henry stood with conviction, wrapped an apple, some matches, a jug, and a fish knife in a canvas haversack and marched off to the woods.

He went missing for hours.

Of course Sissy was hysterical. She alerted all hands. On Monday morning she began her extensive search along the river. She didn't like dogs so she walked without Putt's nose to guide her. She found Henry that morning beneath his homemade thatched roof. He had gathered the sand he needed for a filter. He was pouring it into an old sock when she arrived.

"I've spoken to your teachers, Henry. They tell me you are falling behind."

"Hello, Aunt Sissy."

"They tell me you haven't been trying."

"I have been trying."

"Mrs. Boijovski said you failed your nutrition exam."

Henry Snow dropped some small pebbles and pieces of glass into the sock. "I don't care what calories are made of, Auntie. I care what I am made of."

"Come home this minute!"

The next morning Henry Snow went back to his lessons but he could no longer concentrate. The schoolhouse was boring. The straight lines infuriated him. Henry felt that the more he learned, the less he knew. Oh how he wanted to be back in his place among the young.

"I see you're back at your studies," his Aunt said sweetly.

"Yes, Ma'am."

"Remember Henry, I'm proud of you. 'The unexamined life is not worth living'."

Humility, respect, patience and love would keep him in his place among the splendid. But the safety of his Aunt's ways was plaguing him.

"Thank you, Auntie."

Yet could he remain dumbfounded? After spending hours in the light could a blind man not remember the colors he had seen? Should Henry Snow lock himself up in a closet and wear gloves and keep his napkin folded neatly, avoiding thorns, brambles, dogs, disease, love, diapers and daylight, or should he sing when knives bled him, girls broke him, and fevers yellowed his resolve? What was he after all, a thing made of soft stuffing, a paper mache hero or the grandest thing in nature, a victorious eagle- a young man?

Until he saw the sunset he couldn't remember the question. But when the colors changed in the west Henry Snow breathed his air again and decided that his youth was too valuable to waste within walls. He would cast aside the benign lessons that bear no fruit and seek out his virtues instead, in the splendor of the field. And so it was. Henry Snow had made a decision, and in doing so, became more of a man than most.

"I've decided to live free, Auntie. Like Thoreau I want to suck out the marrow of life."

"Oh, Henry," she cringed and said slowly, "That's just disgusting."

Gradually he began to sneak away late in the evenings, when his Aunt was off to bed, to build a fire, sleep on leaves, and count the bats. He discovered how to make hackberry butter, to build a sauna, to run a trotline, to mimic eagles. Each morning he would return, unmissed by his Aunt, who assumed he had spent his evenings at his studies. She applauded his efforts as always, thought him a scholar, rubbed his shoulders when he came to dinner. He smiled his suffocated smile.

But no matter how sneaky little Henry was proving to be, when Tipper returned he was immediately wise to his son's plan. He noticed the light that had been bred back into his son's face, a light that no book could have fueled. He knew his son was seeking wisdom in the rocks and the trees. He looked on with silent admiration.

As the weeks passed Henry became more confident, leaving earlier in the evening and returning later the next morning just in time to dress for his pracks and scribble together his lessons. He couldn't breathe in his home, in the schoolhouse, in the soft places where youth was never tested. He found the intoxicant of the water and the wind to be his nourishment. He struggled everyday to make it through his studies, with only the wilderness as a reward. It became unbearable, yet for a time Henry Snow still moved along the creek, snuck in the back door of one of the orphan cabins, and dressed to depart to the prison of his school out of a forced sense of virtue. The most important lessons had not been lost.

Then on the anniversary of his adoption, when he was asked to conjugate the Latin verb "To live" into all six declensions by a benign Professor who had never been in love, who had never been to war, who had never wetted himself because of laughter, Henry Snow knew he had had enough.

That afternoon he went about his after school routine like always, except instead of waiting until evening to break into the wilderness, Henry tore his clothes off as soon as he got home, exposing his chest to the sun, tearing away the threads like chains. His Aunt began to follow him but could barely comprehend the path he had taken. She found him hours later beneath the same tree as the month before and asked him, "What of your studies?"

"These are my studies." He was making soap from ash and fat.

"You're coming back right this minute, Henry."

"But Auntie as I said-"

"Don't you 'but Auntie'. What about your schooling? What about that?"

"Oh, no no," he chuckled. "That no longer matters."

Her mouth was open.

"The *over-examined* life is not worth living," he told her.

"Oh really? No longer matters? Your schooling no longer matters?!" She looked like a woman whose bloom was fading. She was no longer young. Some pedals were dropping, some had fallen off. "Well let me tell you something, young man!"

"My education is all that matters."

"Come down from that tree!"

Later that day when Henry's father stepped along the creek he noticed Henry beneath the brambles. He stood for a moment to admire the little village that his son had created. He knew deep down that every boy wished for such a creation.

"Henry?

"Hello, Father." Then, trying to conceal a smile. "How are you, son?"

"I've decided to take a sabbatical, Father. I'll be living out here for awhile."

And before Henry's father turned and left him he said, "I think that would be wise." That evening his father and Auntie got to talking. "He can't do this!" she said.

"He's thinking for himself."

"But we can't let him!"

"Independence is a virtue."

"His mind will go to waste!"

"Whose mind, Sissy?"

She covered her face in her hands, "Whenever you find Jack is this how you plan on raising him, too? As a wild child in the woods?"

"That will depend on Jack."

She stared blankly. Sadness was coming on. "I couldn't read until I was twelve," she said.

"Instead you played in the street, ran through the fountain in the park," he told her. "You were lucky."

She looked at him and wondered if that was true. She wondered if maybe he had been right. She wondered if her brother was wiser than she. She wondered if virtue, independence, and simplicity were the answer. Then she came to her senses. "You're a crazy man, Tipper!"

After three days without her nephew, Henry's Aunt was threadbare. She had nothing to do, no one to instruct. Her world had fallen apart. So after careful deliberation she decided to assemble an intervention. She knew the people she could count on.

The panel would consist of Henry's Aunt, the Tenpenny Doctor, Momma Tom, little Padibatakal and a group of Henry's schoolteachers. A time was set (before breakfast), a place too (where Henry camped out beneath the brambles) an agenda established, the lawn chairs carried, and the croissants displayed.

As the intervention was about to begin Sissy approached her brother in the hammock. He was holding his nose and looking at his watch, seeing how long he could hold his breath. "I've called everyone together," she said. "I've assembled an intervention for poor Henry."

Her brother nodded. His face was blushing. She looked at him sharply. "I know you probably think it's a mistake. You think I'm silly. But I'm not silly. You're silly! Look at you! Everyone is scared to death for your poor boy and you just celebrate like it's Christmas!"

His cheeks were huge. His face was red.

"You think you're so smart and cool. You think Henry should grow deeper and not wider. I know what you think. And you know what? I don't care what you think!"

He let his breath out and looked at his watch. "Yes you do. Two and a half minutes."

"No I don't!"

"Then why are you standing there?"

"Please promise you won't stop us. Please let us help him."

"I won't stop you."

"And you won't interfere?"

"I won't interfere. He can decide for himself. I'm going for three minutes. Time me."

The interveners sat in a circle along the creek and waited for Henry to arrive. Aunt Sissy joined them. They talked about the knee-high bachelor buttons they were expecting, how the pollen was thick, how the rain was constant. They jellied their croissants. It wasn't long before Henry tiptoed up with a spear.

"Henry!" called little Padibatakal.

Henry's loincloth was wet and he had algae on his belly. "Hello, everyone. I just speared a silver!"

His Aunt launched the boat, "Have a seat, Henry." There was one lawn chair left empty. "We want to help you."

As always Henry smiled back. He looked at the chair strangely and decided to stand. The fish was still flopping on his spear.

"Be humble before us," his Aunt told him.

"Yes, Auntie."

"Say it, please."

"Say what?"

"Say that you will be humble."

"That's absurd."

"Say it, please. Have a seat and say you will listen and be humble before this panel."

"But how can I say it? To say I will be humble would negate the effort to be-"

"Say it! Be humble like me! Be humble like your Auntie!"

Everyone sat blank-faced. The fish was struggling to escape. Aunt Sissy calmed down, closing her eyes. "This is wisdom speaking," she said.

"Listen to yourself, Auntie." Henry then tugged the flopping fish off the spear and laid it on the ground. He pulled an arrowhead from his hip and began to gut it belly up.

"Your school teachers are here," his Aunt said softly. "They came to tell you that you have a great mind. Isn't that right, Mr. Kelvin?"

"You have a great mind, Henry. The finest I've ever seen in gym."

And then Dr. Zuni, "A fine young man."

And the panel, "A son to be proud of."

"See?" his Aunt asked. "Would these people lie? "

Henry sat down and began to fillet his fish. "No," he told her. "I didn't accuse them."

"We are good people, Henry."

"Yes, Aunt Sissy."

"You love us."

"Yes, Aunt Sissy."

"And you will be coming back home."

"No, Auntie. I won't."

Henry's father was watching from a spruce tree, laughing to himself.

Sissy looked at the panel. "You have a great mind, Henry. But there's something wrong with you. You need help."

"There's nothing wrong with me, Auntie."

"Yes there is." Then she smiled and said, "The good news is we've come here to help you. And help you we will. We'll put it to a vote." She cleared her throat, "All those in favor of Henry living out here like an animal, rejecting all of his Aunt's plans and hard work, eating dirty fish, getting sunburned, stung by mosquitoes, and swimming without floaties, say "Aye".

Everyone sat silently, although secretly each of them, because they had once been children, must have wanted to scream.

Aunt Sissy began again. "All those who think Henry should listen to his Aunt because she loves him dearly and wants only the best for him, say "Aye".

"Aye."

Aunt Sissy smiled at her nephew. "You see? The panel has spoken."

Henry shrugged his shoulders. His face was red with coyote blood. "So? The panel has spoken," he said.

Henry's Aunt stood and walked toward her nephew. "You'll need to bathe quickly and throw away that awful necklace. You can have pancakes and butter before school."

"I just speared my first silver salmon, Auntie."

"You may feed it to the dog. It's good to have you back."

"I'll be staying here."

"Oh, sweetie, I'm sorry. The panel has spoken."

"They have no authority on the matter."

"These are your teachers, honey. These are doctors and teachers."

"I see no reason why that gives them authority."

She huffed and puffed, "You always talk about respect! Well show some respect!"

"Alright, Aunt Sissy. With all due respect they aren't very smart."

"Really?"

"They know a great deal, but they're not very smart."

Aunt Sissy shook her head. She looked haggard, shattered. Her poise was a disguise. She waved to the panel, to apologize. "Well, Mister smarty pants," she said slowly to her nephew, "in your infinite wisdom and virtue how do you define 'smart'?"

Henry cleared his throat but didn't take his eyes off the fish. "A smart person; noun – someone who enjoys themselves."

Aunt Sissy seemed ready to cry. She lifted her hands up to her chin. "My boy. Oh poor boy. Will you forget everything I've taught you?"

Henry's father, still perched in the old spruce tree, was spellbound after he heard his son's response.

"No I won't forget, Auntie." he told her. Then Henry began slowly, "Livaris. . . libaris. . .liberis. . .lius es. . .lius eras. . .lius eris. . ."

Aunt Sissy turned to the panel. Her eyes were red. "What is that?" she asked.

Doc Zuni said it was Latin.

"What's he saying?"

Henry continued slowly, "Livas."

"He lives," said Zuni.

"Libas."

"He lived."

"Libis."

"He will live."

"Livisti."

"He has lived."

"Liveras."

"He will have lived."

"Liveris."

"He would have lived."

Jack

Some three years later, and four thousand miles away, Jack Oakham was hanging his mothers paintings on the walls in front of her, and a few even from the ceiling. As she came awake he closed her curtains so the sun wouldn't throw a glare on the paintings. He wanted her to view all the colors her life had made. In her eyes he could see morphine and fatigue and the knowledge that death only made sense if you've loved something.

"I met a woman once who owned the light," she told him.

"Who was she, Momma?"

"She was an orphan. Like you're about to be."

"No, Momma. I'm not."

She did not intend to torture him. "Remember how I told you of the adventures," she asked. "Across the sea?"

"Yes, Momma."

"I met her there, walking down a road and the light was with her."

His mother seemed to see her. Her dark child eyes looked off past the shaded light to a place she had once known. In that moment if Jack's mother had uttered a word the boy would have expected to hear that strange woman answer.

"Who is she, Momma?"

"She is love."

He ran his fingers through her hair. Her eyes were drooping and her words were whispers but when he ran his fingers through her hair it felt alive and full as he had always known it. "I love you, Momma."

He pressed his face into her hair and said, "I love you. I love you. I love you. I love you," over and over like a song.

He began to cry and her hair, coal-colored, long and rich, glistened with the tears. They beaded down her strands and soaked into her pillow and she rested her eyes as he laid his head against her.

"Judith is her name."

"Judith?"

"But you will call her Momma Tom."

The boy put his hand behind her neck and kissed her forehead. "I will call her?"

"She will be your mother, Jack."

He closed his eyes again. "No. No she won't."

"Promise to do that for me."

"Do what?"

"Find her. Do that?"

"But how will I?"

Carefully she took a single sheet of paper from the bedside table and with her frail fingers Jack's mother sketched a diagram of the journey ahead of him. "There you'll find an angel," she pointed.

Then she took an envelope from the tabletop and an old photograph of her and the woman, both knelt beside a gurney. "Give this to her," she told him.

Jack sat with her a long while, falling asleep with her hands in his. They were a mother and son in the wide ranging sort of love, and as long as he could feel her swelling breath he was safe and nothing would ever change. He was safe and nothing would ever change. Then sometime in the night she became a memory.

The funeral was small, the benediction rehearsed. In the coming weeks Jack was ushered from one foster family to another: Deritter, Bogalusa, only to settle with a large family in Terrabonne Parrish. He was allowed to bring with him his knapsack, a suitcase, and any items he could squeeze into his underarms. The paintings were left behind. All that remained from his mother were the contents of the envelope she had given him, which he kept on his person at all times.

When he arrived Jack was given a bed in a crowded room that he shared with his five new sisters, two of which were orphans themselves. The house had the smell of stale cigarettes and thirty year old carpet but that hardly mattered to Jack. What he really missed was the confiding presence of someone who loved and listened. In his new life Jack was never cordially spoken to or prayed over and he found it curious that no one offered any explanation of his future. Was he to go on living here forever?

But Jack soon became accustomed to the changes in his life. It wouldn't be fitting to blame anyone for his circumstances, he thought. Momma would want me to endure.

It was summertime and they lived miles from any neighborhood so Jack had his entire day to himself. His foster parents watched in disbelief as the boy busied himself in the yard, pruning the feral garden, raking the leaves from two seasons before. They thought him crazy, or spoiled to work so hard in the wet heat. "I guess our yard ain't good enough for this one," one of the sisters said to mutual agreement.

But what they didn't know was that throughout his life, Jack Oakham consistently sought out intensive labor. He did so on one hand because not a bone in his body was made for idleness, but the real reason was that when his body was set to a mindless task, his mind was free to pay his mother a visit. And it was to this ultimate purpose that Jack worked from breakfast to suppertime in his new home. It gave him hours to contemplate the only things that mattered to Jack Oakham: his mother, and the promise he had made the day she died. Young Jack thought constantly about how he would set about his journey. Though he didn't have a clue where he would begin. But every time he began to worry he quickly changed his mind. She wouldn't want me to be anxious, he thought. The answer will come.

A month went by. Jack worked all day, never altering his routine until eventually he began to long for something new to read or someone new to talk to. And then, as if his mother was listening, he was given both. One afternoon, along with his daily lemonade, his foster mother handed him a letter. It was unopened, having arrived that afternoon. Overwhelmed with curiosity he rushed into his room and was careful as he removed it.

Dear Jack,

I hope you don't mind me tracking you down. You see I've been looking for you a long time and I've only just found you. We've never met but there's a great deal for us to talk about. I come from a place very different from any place you've ever seen. And there's a spot here for you. A good spot, at the head of the table, if you want it. I know that Momma Tom would love to see you. You know that name, don't you? There's a return address on the envelope. I'll be hoping to hear news of you soon.

Your Friend.

Jack sat deeply confused. There was no signature. He reread it again and again looking for more clues but finding none. He read the address and matched it with the map his mother had given him. All afternoon he pondered what to do.

The following evening Jack's new family traveled to the nearest town with a shopping mall for dinner and a movie. It was the first time he had been out in the world in over a month, and his eyes were hungry for newness.

As they waited on their showtime the family slipped into a bookstore and Jack was quick to find the travel section. He had always been drawn to the wild reaches of the world and to his delight a photo book of continental wildlife was open before him. He flipped through the big colorful pages and stopped when he saw what the insert called "Moose" swimming across a river. Jack had never seen a moose before. He looked wide-eyed at the bears feeding at the river's edge and the lone caribou along the prairie bottom. When he followed his foster family into the theatre all he could think of were wild places.

When Jack told this story to children years later he could never recall what film they were going to see that evening or where they had their meal. All he did remember was that one of the previews played beforehand was a tale called "The Journey of Nattie Gann", the story of a girl who went on a journey to find her father.

She looked brave on the screen and true and Jack had missed those feelings that his mother had given him. He knew that he wouldn't have them again in this new life. Adventure was elsewhere.

And Jack would tell the children that if that preview hadn't played, or if he'd been in the line for popcorn, or if he hadn't just flipped through the photos and seen the great caribou crossing the tundra, he never would have offered to get a drink for his foster father, never would have slipped past the box office and into the parking lot and found the hide-a-key beneath the hitch, never would have confiscated the $350 emergency fund that his foster father kept stashed beneath the floor mat, never would have made his way to the town center and forged a parental consent form in eligible cursive. If that preview hadn't played and his mind hadn't accelerated past the stale bread and the faucet that dripped through the night, and his foster sister's smelly feet, he never would have dreamed of buying a bus ticket. All he had with him were the clothes he was wearing, his knapsack that contained a spare shirt and a few books, an empty bottle, and the money that he hid in his shoes. But he was undaunted. His journey awaited him. On the way to the station all Jack could think on was the old woman's face and the places that surrounded it.

"Would you please have a map?" he asked the man behind the counter. Jack studied the routes for twenty minutes before returning.

"Yes Sir?" the man asked.

Jack pointed at the map. "How much does it cost for me to go to *there*?"

"How old are you?"

"Eleven. I have a note."

"A hundred and twenty."

Jack hesitated. The point of no return. Finally he said, "I'd like one."

He survived on chocolate bars and train coffee and made a habit of sitting beside the largest woman he could find to make himself appear cared for to the other passengers, and to himself. The landscape became his hobby. He watched pines turn to cedars, cedars to mesquites, the Estacado open into a wasteland and close up again as he passed to the east of the Cristos. The cliffs rose out of the sands and when he saw the desert lake he thought it was the sea. The mountains made him feel small and free. He bathed using handfuls of sink water in the stations and saw the ocean for the first time on the third day.

When he arrived at his destination he ate oysters the size of eggs, eighteen of them altogether, stuffed crackers into his pockets along with a stack of napkins and paid the bill, tipping ten percent on instinct. He watched seals basking at dock's end, took his shoes and socks off and ran through the fountain and played hide and seek with children in the park. It didn't take him long to discover that the men and women in the lobbies of hotels have the skinny on everything: each restroom, market, ferry station.

It was a two day wait for the ship to disembark. Jack slept in the park, folding his shirt around his stack of napkins to make a pillow. At one point he entered the Palacio Hotel from the service entrance, took the stairs to the second floor and walked the hall to the main elevator which he rode down to the lobby, but as he approached the front desk and began to request extra soap for his father, he chickened out. Because he was too afraid to lie Jack bathed himself in the river with nothing but the murky water.

On the day that the ferry was to disembark Jack was seated in the shade at the end of a long belt of rose bushes. He had devoured a ripe apple for breakfast that he had found at the market, along with some juice and banana bread that he was nibbling on.

"Don't you have a home to go to?"

Jack was startled. The voice had come from the trees. A young man leaned against the elm beside him and when he saw that the face meant him no harm he answered, "That's where I'm going," he said.

"All by yourself?"

"I'm going to find my new mother."

"Your new mother?"

"Yessir, that's right. A fresh start."

"I can see it in your face - you want her to love you?"

"No sir, I don't think it matters who loves me. It only matters who I love. I can't go round controlling what other people like all the time. I got my hands full just loving them."

And without another word the man was gone, weighing his wisdom against that of a boy.

On the ferry Jack slept in the lounge, twice was woken and asked, "Do your parents know you're here?"

"I'm certain that they don't," and moved to another part of the ship.

Jack enjoyed the water slapping the bow and the fancy waiters with their trays. The first evening he made six trips to the midnight buffet, vomited off the deck, which he later admitted was tons of fun, and after composing himself fixed two more plates of shrimp. He spent most of his hours in the library where he split his time examining maps of his destination and crying quietly. When the ship made berth he only had to wait two hours for the next ferry up the coast. Yet when he boarded he took his shoes off and emptied his pockets on the main deck and discovered that he was down to his last ten dollar bill. He fell asleep in the parlor with a sad, guilt-ridden face, imagining his foster father still waiting in the theatre for his drink.

Green mountains crawled out of the sea and drifting at their shores were pale blue islands of ice, wafting with the tide. The land seemed to know what it was. It called to young Oakham, "Your life has been minor until now. Your eyes have been closed." Gurgling water sounded as the glaciated pieces crashed into the sea. Jack dreamed that his old troubles had let him go.

When he awoke a crowd was lined up against the glass facing the open sea. Jack stood from his chair and made his way to the window. For a moment there was nothing and then with a unanimous breath from the passengers, a giant eruption from the water. The whale breached and crashed and disappeared.

Once he reached the portage town, Jack Oakham walked into the general store and took several small red packets from the bin into his cold hands. In the lavatory he filled his bottle with steaming water. After letting his hands warm he pealed open the packets and squeezed them in. A police officer saw him shaking up the bottle and drinking it in the lot.

"You know that boy?" he asked the clerk.

"Never seen him."

The officer found Jack huddled in the alley.

"What do you have there?"

Jack was frightened and didn't even know why. "Bottle."

"Cold hands?"

Jack looked down at the bottleneck. It was steaming.

"I was hungry."

"You're not in trouble, son. This isn't the first time I've seen poor man's tomato soup."

Jack had never been called "son", not even by his mother. She preferred "sweetheart". When he heard the man say it he began to cry.

The officer, whose name Jack would never learn though he tried to discover it years later, passed him a handkerchief. In exchange young Oakham handed the man the folded photograph that was creased in his back pocket. When he could speak he asked, "Do you know her?"

The man turned the old photograph with his fingers. His face relaxed, "I do, son."

"I'd like to meet her."

Jack explained that he had taken the road as far as he could. That he was near to the woman's home, but that the last leg was a mystery. "I don't know where to find her," he said. "I don't know where to go. All I have is a name and no maps show it anywhere and-" but before he could finish the man said, "I'll take you."

Morning broke as they traveled the hills. The officer gave him a pillow and Jack slept against the window. He missed the brilliant colors that the sun shed on the ocean arm but would see them many times as the years went by. He awoke with a bump as they arrived at the gate - two burled pine pillars.

An old man came out of the gatehouse and nodded to the officer who stepped out of the car. Jack watched as the two stood whispering near the gate.

Finally the man came over to the door. "How did you hear about this place, son?"

"My mother told me."

"Your mother huh?"

"Yessir."

"Well I'm sorry but we don't take walk-ins. Unless you have papers there's nothing I can do."

Jack looked down at his hands. He waited and waited and the two men watched his eyes water. Then he slowly reached into his pocket and took out the envelope with the note inside. "Could you give this," he asked, "to the woman?"

"What woman?"

"Momma Tom."

"Sure. Sure I can do that."

And as the officer was climbing back into the car the gateman said, "But who shall I say gave it to her?"

"Jack."

The old man looked sharply at the boy. "Jack? Jack Oakham?"

Jack was clearly frightened. "Yes."

The gateman opened the door. "Son, you should learn to introduce yourself."

Beyond the gate the old man pointed Jack up a dirt trail and into the forest of Tenpenny. There the trail wound through timber and tamaracks, always climbing, and beyond the bog where the choke cherry shrubs sprouted freely. He crossed over a small bridge as his feet trembled from the shaking grooves in the bridge-boards, and up the dale where his hands shook in the sun. A stone walkway had been cobbled perfectly into the wet emerald grass and meandered through the thick wood. It must have taken years to lay these stones, Jack thought, as he walked across them, trying not to let his feet touch the sprouts between the cobbled pieces.

The deep woods opened revealing a bend in the road and as he stepped out into the meadow the wind settled and Jack Oakham could hear the gentle roar of a river, somewhere beyond the trees. He took the bend and observed before him a huge log home, piney wood stacked high, the chipped bark flaking off, the chirping of laughter, the still-wet grass from the evening rain, and a huge dog on the lawn.

The scent of flatcakes filled the yard under the morning, so heavy that Jack smelled it as he huffed, climbing past the hemlocks and the timber hut that he would someday learn housed the mice in winter.

Putt awoke, picking up a ball and bringing it over, as if to say, "It's about time." and in doing so began one of Jack's fondest friendships. As he rubbed the dog's head young Oakham became aware of the sharp, almost frightening knowledge that he had not touched another living thing in over a week of travel. His elbows had bumped the fat women he sat beside but his hands he had kept to himself. He passed Putt's face from palm to palm, reminded of how fine a thing it is to share the world with others.

He heard laughter again and took long steps up the hill. Putt followed him across the lawn to the cabin, around the piney logs and both turned the corner to the porch. From the screen door the moist aroma of an unspecified taffy batter filled the deck. By the French windows a marvelous rack of delicate ground cinnamon chocolates mixed with the fragrance of baking coffee fruits sat, and with it came an understood awe from the boy. Nutmeg nuts and cocoa nuts, and sweet layered chocolate folded in a circle like a bonbon cake lay covered by the windowsill with wax paper. Jack saw a little girl plop a golden honey-malt fritter into her mouth through the window. He could see beside her, a little oriental boy, standing on his toes, his hands on the countertop above him, hoping to see what the big children were mixing.

A bell chimed from the valley. It rang and each child, young and old put down what they were doing and rushed out to the porch. Jack watched them through the window and, curious, peaked his head around the corner.

From that porch Jack could see a whole new world laying out before him. A wonderland. The river valley accounted for all the colors he had ever known. The cottonwoods were filled with tree-houses and pulleys, cables strung between them. Riverside a long stretch of lanes and sandpits, monkey bars and two ziplines stretched between the towers. From one giant tree a rope had been fastened high in the branches that hung down to a platform at the first fat limbs. To Jack's surprise, the whole troop of children on the porch began singing:

"We children cheer, It's Saturday! It's Saturday! Hooray! Hooray!

Can Johnny Appleseed come out to play?"
We waited through the week to reach today,
We waited in our beds at night for such a holiday,
And now we cheer, It's Saturday! It's Saturday! Hooray!
We sat at our desks for five long days,
Can Johnny Appleseed come out to play?"

The morning was fresh. The light brought a halo to the grass top and the early fog spread itself thinly across the valley that echoed the calls of the children. "Johnny Appleseed!"

Out of the shaded wood a figure came. One strong boy, who seemed to be their leader, a curly-haired youngster, tanned and ruddy-faced, with a bandana around his big head, and armlets tied on, appeared from beneath the shade trees. Voices rallied from the porch, "Hooray! Hooray! He's come out to play!"

The boy king reached the center of the field and gave his crowd a bow. When they roared again he said to them, loud and bold,

"Oh, The Lord is good to me! And so I thank the Lord,
For giving me, the things I need, the sun and the rain and the appleseed.
The Lord is good to me!"

With long steps the boy bounded across the field, and scaled the big tree like an ape. It appeared to Jack that this was something the boy had done many times before. When he reached the platform he spit into his palms and rubbed them together. The children were silent as the boy sprung off the limb into the air. Catching the rope he swung once out, once back, and the crowd was open-eyed as he came high with the sway, let go above the pool, tucked his hands behind his head, like he was napping in mid air, and crashed into the river.

"Hooray!" The children jeered from the porch and all at once they dashed down the steps to the valley. The fireweed and the strawberry stems fell upon themselves from the passing wind. The children scurried across the field, the little ones trailing behind and all flung themselves into the river.

Jack smiled to himself and turned the corner.

A huge table stretched across the porch. A few adults were taking plates and cups off to the kitchen to be washed. There was a humming among them, a quiet tune playing from their lips. "It's Saturday, It's Saturday! Hooray! Hooray!" All of the servers were wearing aprons with painted handprints on them and the word "Tenpenny" across the top.

Beyond them, on a swing worn smooth at the seat, sat an elderly woman. Her skin was like aged raisins. She was no older than in Jack's photograph. Her copper face had hard scars across her cheek. Jack had never seen a woman so old with long hair before. In her arms was a babe.

He stood at the porch edge, his eyes following the movement of the children down below, the servers cleaning up breakfast, the woman rocking at the far end. It was a full minute before anyone noticed him.

But as he was stacking plates, a man with profound dimples and deep-set eyes, noticed that Jack Oakham had arrived. The man gave Jack a curious look, like he had seen him somewhere before. He set the dishes down on the table. The man then cradled his face in his palms. His eyes hopped around. "Hello," he said.

Jack trembled. "Hello."

"What's she doing?" Jack asked looking across the porch.

Tip tightened his eyes to keep the tears from spilling out. "She's praying."

Jack drew a deep breath, "I've taken up praying myself."

Tip spoke in a whisper, the way he liked to speak when he had something strong to say. He would later repeat the tale at large events of how the first words of instruction he ever gave to young Oakham were, "Come, follow me," and that he wouldn't trade them for all the biltong in the world.

As they passed among the servants scurrying about the table, Jack watched the old woman with her head down. For some reason Jack found it easy to walk toward her. His hand trembled as he held the woman's face, kissed the crown of her head, her coal-colored hair.

There were whispers among the kitchen staff. Doc Zuni came onto the porch and moved quickly up to Tipper. "I just got off the two way radio. Is it true? Is that him?"

Tip watched the boy in disbelief. "Yeah. I guess that's him. I was supposed to bring him back. But instead he found us."

The Doc shook his head. "Finally here."

"Finally," Tip echoed. "Five years and just like that the wait is over."

The children were loud as they splashed across the river. The kitchen staff watched silently as the scene unfolded.

"Well, you finally have them both," Doc said. "What will you do now?"

"Raise them together," Tip told him.

"Yes, yes. That was the plan, wasn't it?"

But Tipper seemed not to hear. His eyes were ranging far, through the great branches that cradled the porch and down into the valley where the far off shadowed stream ran to the sea. It was silver and silent and full of second chances.

Part I

The Tenpenny Three

On rare occasions, in remote parts of the world, boys grow into men. For both Henry and Jack it had been an adolescence of freedom and discipline, rough-housing and rigidity, where competition was valued greatly, but character was prized. The highest calling of Tip Holland's life was to ensure that his two adopted sons not only reached manhood, but that they became fully burdened with their role as the gentle warriors Tip had trained them to be.

And by the time he had spent several years raising them together - on the day when the bulk of our story begins, Tip Holland felt confident that he had come dangerously close with one of them.

1993

1. Change is in the Air

When Jack Oakham came out onto the porch the old dog was lapping up the frost from a frozen puddle of hot chocolate. It wasn't a big puddle, probably just what was left at the bottom of the mug when the wind blew it over. But it was big enough to stain the porch rungs that Jack had painted. There were half a dozen mugs on the porch, some on their sides, with the stains of chocolate puddles frozen to the wood. Beside the puddles the pit fire had fizzled in the night and only the coals were glowing in the windburn. Jack could see half a dozen roasting sticks with blackened ends tilted against the pit. Some of the older kids had probably been talking late when the bugle sounded, Jack thought. From the looks of it, Putt, his old dog, had only just discovered the puddle.

"Putt, you know better than to eat chocolate," Jack said. "Even a little makes you gassy."

The old dog licked his chops and looked up at Jack nonchalantly with eyes that seemed to say, "And you know better than to think I mind the gas," as he went back to his licking.

Jack smiled, "Now we all have to suffer," as he closed the door behind him. He stepped out into the cold morning and walked over to the wood wagon and peering inside saw that the bunkhouse stock was getting low. There were wood wagons beside every cabin at Tenpenny and now that spring was coming on all of their wood stocks were dwindling. What frustrated Jack the most was that he blamed himself. With the early snows

47

that winter Jack and his lazy brother Henry hadn't gathered as much wood fuel as Jack would have liked, or as their father had expected. Their wood shortage was a problem he had anticipated all winter. Jack thought the situation over in his head as he watched the sun peek over the eastern slopes and went on to gather a wood stack from the wagon. He thought of the younger children, and of Momma Tom as he continued to remind himself, "Spring is coming, spring is coming."

Of course spring in Tenpenny took a long time to come but when it did come it was well worth the wait. The children rejoiced as the snows thawed, the trees bloomed, but in the meantime their lives were cold and wet. The winter that year had been the hardest of the five that Jack had spent in Tenpenny, and the longest. There were several weeks when the children, who numbered over one hundred and fifty, spent days on end within the four walls of their cabins huddled near a fire, hearing stories, learning to read and write, and eating what meals could be brought from the dining hall in the blizzard. But now there had been no snowfall for over a week and the children were becoming anxious. The sun had come out for three days straight and the porches had thawed, as had the gravel walkways between the cabins, and the afternoon before the icicles that had been growing all winter began to drip and the older children watched with anticipation.

As the sun rose the light hit the peaks first, which were snowcapped year round and then spilled over into the distant hills and the black forest called the Wild West End and the long barren valley that connected it to Tenpenny Hill. Jack looked out upon the west as he carried the wood to the fire pit. He knew that by the time the sun rose high enough out of the trees for the rooftops to catch the light his Aunt Sissy would have collected her thoughts from the evening before and would come storming up the road to have a word with Henry. In the years that Jack had spent at Tenpenny there were only a few things he could depend on day to day. Orphanages are filled with orphans, and orphan problems. Jack often asked himself what could be more complex than a family with one hundred and fifty children who for much of their lives had had no family. His chores had taught him much but their stories had taught him everything. Not one of the children's tales was the same and not one day alongside them like another. Yet there were elements of his day that resembled other days. When he thought about it, and he thought about it whenever he could, he was able to identify only four constants in his life: Momma Tom's love, his father's wisdom, Putt's friendship, and the Biblical struggle between his Aunt and his brother.

Jack Oakham was an orphan in the more visceral sense than Henry, for he had lost his mother, unlike Henry who had grown up without one. In Tenpenny those who are born without families are secretly referred to by the children as "Orphan Born" while those who lost their families are known as "Orphan Grown". Those few who had actually witnessed the death of their parents are the "Orphan Pure" and are highly regarded. Jack being the eldest of the orphan pure needed his mother more and more as he grew into a man and Momma Tom, as promised, had become his mother and her love was constant.

Jack's adopted father, Tip, the first true father he had ever known, had become his pillar for knowledge. As much as Tipper loved his son, it wasn't Tipper's love Jack desired so much as his wisdom. Jack Oakham would always have a hole in his heart in the shape of his real father, a man he had never known, and no amount of Tipper's love could cause his desire to rest.

The one place Jack did rest, however, was with Putt. Soon after his long journey to Tenpenny Jack had discovered that the kind of friend he desired to have, and the kind of friend he desired to be was one who wasn't nosy, was always loyal, and could be trusted. This law was never broken between the two.

And though some days the goings-on at Tenpenny allowed for momentary breaks in the chaos, the only other rule outside of his own relationships that Jack could depend on was that Henry and his Aunt Sissy, by days end, would infuriate each other. The evening before had proved no exception.

Putt had happily disregarded Jack's command to leave the chocolate alone and after warming the patch with his tongue had begun to clean the stain from the decking. Jack set the firewood in the pit, and stirred the coals with a one of the roasting sticks before collecting the rest and stacking them in the wagon. He moved the chairs back into place along the porch and gathered the mugs and went inside to wash them. When he stepped through the door the new light from the eastern windows revealed that Henry's bed was empty.

The cabin was nothing more than a tiny hovel that Henry and Jack and their father had built themselves, with a bunk bed, crude wall shelves, and a collection of boy mess strewn about the single room. In many ways their cabin was inferior to the children's cabins down the road, but this cabin was seen as a sacred dwelling for it was where Henry Snow and Jack Oakham lived, the boy kings of Tenpenny.

The other children on the hill didn't know why Tipper had chosen to adopt these two young men as brothers, for that matter neither did Henry and Jack, but it didn't seem to bother the children in the least. These two "brothers", who shared no physical similarities, were both adored by the orphans of Tenpenny, who followed their every move.

Upon seeing that his brother's bed was empty, Jack ducked to look beneath the bed because Henry had a habit of rolling out and sleeping on the stone floor. But he hadn't this morning. From what Jack could see Henry had risen well before dawn, dressed himself in his heavy coveralls, which had been hanging on a wall peg, and had left with a few loose floor items for the room looked bare compared with the night before. Jack washed the mugs and moved back onto the porch.

"How's the chocolate?" Jack asked.

Putt was finishing the last and didn't reply.

Jack looked east at the sun and the light filling Tenpenny. He looked down the river valley at the cabins and watched for any children rushing out in the cold to use the latrines. The first time his eyes swept over the stables he failed to notice anything unusual but the next time he saw that the two horses he had stabled the night before were missing. He peered inside the cabin to confirm that Henry had taken his bridle and quirt with him. He had in fact.

"You see Henry duck out this morning?" Jack asked the dog.

Putt looked up, but not at Jack. He faced down the road and seemed to give a half snarl that Oakham found amusing when he saw who it was aimed at.

"Morning Sissy," Jack said.

"You still talk to that dog? I'd think you'd have more respect for yourself than to talk to that dog."

"That dog or any dog?"

"Well any dog, but that dog in particular."

"Careful Sissy. My bad side is narrow. Guess I don't need to wonder who you're hunting."

"Is he dressed?"

"I suppose he is."

"Well call him out."

"I'd be happy to but he's already been called out by somethin' else. He left before dawn."

"Where to?"

"He didn't say."

"Well that doesn't sound like Henry."

"No ma'am."

"You got any ideas?"

"Well I don't play favorites with people, Aunt Sissy. Just dogs. So what I can tell you is that two horses are missing and that whatever you have to say to Henry, I'm sure he won't run from hearing. You can expect him soon enough."

"You don't play favorites with people, Jack?"

Jack shook his head.

"Well I know the names of two young ladies who would have a thing or two to say about that."

Jack tightened up and looked down at the snow. She held him in her look and wouldn't let him leave. When it came to matters of the heart Sissy was well known for setting her verbal traps and leaving them until her prey had squirmed a little.

"Do you need any help this morning?" Jack asked her.

She looked satisfied when she said, "No, but the maintenance crew needs a snow shovel. Fetch 'em a shovel and fetch your brother when you see him."

"Yes ma'am."

As was her custom Sissy left without so much as a nod, but did so in an acceptable, almost gentle way. Jack watched her down the road hoping she would avoid the black ice, which she did. He scanned the hills and the riverbed for his brother and the horses again before he rubbed the ears of that old dog.

"Let's see if we can't dig up a snow shovel, eh Putt?"

And the old dog arched his back.

Jack Oakham was rarely hungry in the mornings. He customarily took his breakfasts while working and they were never more than a biscuit or a slice of fruit from the dining hall. But that morning he had awoken hungry as soon as his feet hit the cold stones. He could smell the flatcakes from his porch and even stronger as he walked down the icy road. Jack carried the belief that smells travel best in the mornings, as do memories, and he rarely missed an opportunity to reflect upon his life in the quiet early hours. In that way Jack was much like Tip. They both enjoyed many of the same quiet pursuits but the one they had most in common was reflection. In fact reflection was the only one of Tip's "Five Romantic Virtues" that Jack Oakham ever practiced. It was often said of Jack that he was "born practical and lived to work". He made little time for theory, but instead busied himself with the hands-on struggles of life.

On the other hand reflection was the only virtue on Tip's list that Jack's brother, Henry Snow, didn't practice. "Where I've been doesn't mean a thing compared to where I'm going," Henry once said, before rambling incoherently. He could never justify time spent on the past and he refused to engage those who tried to take him there.

Henry spent all of his time on the rest of Tipper's list: laughter, adventure, appetite and pursuit, yet chose not to reflect on any of them.

Jack was reflecting on his mother and her long dark hair as he walked beside Putt down the road. It was commonly where his day began. It was unusual for his mind to stay there for very long, however. Either he got lost trying to pick out old memories from long ago or he was distracted by his surroundings and his mind drifted to other things. At that moment his mind was drifting towards breakfast. Not only could he smell the flatcakes growing closer with every step but now the scent of cheesy grits and coffee cake came on as well. Putt was moaning and chewing on Jack's coveralls, nudging him towards the aroma.

"You already had breakfast," Jack told Putt. "I'd be a dirty dog if you think I'd let you have chocolate *and* pancakes."

Putt let go Jack's pant leg as if offended, "I don't keep company with dirty dogs," Jack heard him say.

The trees that had drooped with the weight of the snows since the onset of winter were extending their arms out that morning as the sun hit them. Above him the treehouses and rope bridges that had been abandoned these five months seemed to call down to Jack to sweep them clean and invite the children back up into their boughs. He looked the lots over and thought of a young girl he had promised to take riding once the winter broke as he continued to remind himself, "Spring is coming."

Jack stepped off the road and started for the tool house but he wasn't certain the shovel would be there. The afternoon before Henry had taught a pair of Burmese "Henry Snow wannabe's" how to snow shovel race down the slopes at Campbell Field, which had the best grade for racing on Tenpenny hill. Four years earlier Jack and Henry had raced down those very slopes when they were twelve. They had walked away unscathed but the pair of wannabe's had not been so lucky. One of them was knocked out cold and the other lost a little blood. Probably lost the shovels too if I had my guess, Jack thought, as he walked up the path to the tool house.

II.

Momma Tom lived in the heart of Tenpenny in a cabin tucked away in a pocket clearing in the trees. The cabin had once been used to stable the horses before Tip had built the lots surrounding it, but now it was enclosed, with a dusty plank floor, two small beds, a pot-bellied stove, a rocker and a ceiling lantern that gave the only light. When the room was fully lit one could still see the wood scars on the walls where the manger had been pried away.

The room itself was surprisingly warm, even in the cold months, because, as Tip said, the inhabitant was always close to God, and God is never cold. Although she knew better than to argue God with her brother, Sissy suggested that the warmth of the room was a result of the thick timbers and the shortage of windows, being that only a single porthole overlooked the lots, instead of the spiritual temperature of Momma Tom, the old woman who lived there.

Although a practical man, Tip Holland was never one to leave God out of blessing. He suggested to his sister that every good thing comes from somewhere, and it was his belief that it wasn't from thick pine and windowless dwellings.

"Or from the hearts of men," Sissy had said. To which he agreed.

Regardless of the reasons, the small cabin was the warmest room on Tenpenny Hill, making it a fine place for Momma Tom to tell stories to children who longed to forget the winter.

Momma Tom lived alone, but at the time that our story begins she was sharing her space with two young orphans of Tenpenny. She was up well before sunrise with one tattered quilt draped across her shoulders and another wrapped tight around the foal that she was suckling. She had kept her fire going through the night as she gently rocked the foal, which was so small and fragile had it not been for the small white tongue that stirred when Momma Tom fed him, she would have thought he was dead already. Half the reason Momma Tom was feeding him was to see any sign of life because most of the milk was dribbling down the foal's neck anyway. The bottle wasn't made for horses.

Ain't that the way of it, Momma Tom thought. Tenpenny is so full of things used for reasons other than they was made for. Whether it be bottles or people. No matter what it be. So many jobs to do and so few folks to do 'em. But not me, she thought. No that's not my story. Momma Tom is right where she needs to be.

Wonderboy, the top hand on Tenpenny Hill, had found the dead mare two evenings before in the lots and he and Tipper had been quick to cut the foal out of the womb. They had brought a barren mare into the stable to lick away the afterbirth and given the foal over to Momma Tom, knowing that if anything was ever orphaned, Momma Tom would want it.

"Don't fumble it like a pigskin," she had told them. "Momma Tom always says carry an early foal like you'd carry a bucket of runny dynamite. There, there now."

She took the foal without surprise at his appearance and wrapped him in her skirts and rocked him all that morning. When they arrived she said to Henry and Jack, "No matter how strong you become in your own eyes you're blind and helpless to God. Just like this little one."

"He loves blind or not," Henry said, surprising everyone.

At first the foal had been the source of great excitement among the children. Once the news had spread across Tenpenny they came running to the stables to catch a glimpse of the newborn. Those orphans who hadn't been at Tenpenny for long had heard that a foal could walk as soon as it was born and they were disappointed to see that this wasn't the case.

The mare was licking the foal, which looked more like a rubber fetus than a colt, and who had shown no signs of life except a gentle breathing.

Jack and Wonderboy pulled a tarp from the stable bin to cover up the rotting mother, whose entrails were frozen to the ground, but Jack knew even the little orphans of Tenpenny were much accustomed to the knowledge of life and death.

But Henry was more apprehensive. "They shouldn't stay," he had whispered to his father. "If the foal dies the spring will be off to a bad start. We'll be doing damage control."

Tipper knew that the foal had little chance, but he understood the value of teaching the hard lessons early. "They'll stay, Henry. If he dies there will be lessons in that but if he lives the spring will teach them other things."

So the children had crowded in the doorway, waiting for the young colt to stand, or even open his eyes, but it didn't happen. The foal appeared lifeless in Momma Tom's arms, his breathing was so slight. Many of the children began to fear that he was too premature to survive the cold, that if he had come a few days later he may have had a chance. But Momma Tom was quick to say, "Spring's a comin'. You hear? Look out there. Soon you'll see 'em grasses sprout out all over the wide world and I tell you what'll come then; Life. Life is on its way. This stallion'll gallop 'em grasses."

But her words hadn't roused the foal. Now the young colt had been motionless in Momma Tom's arms for two sleepless nights and the children became disenchanted. After giving up hope for a dramatic awakening or a sudden death each of the children had drifted back to their cabins, and soon their minds became fixed on other things.

The only orphan who had stayed was a crippled girl named Padibatakal. She was sleeping in Momma Tom's spare bed beside the rocker and Momma Tom was watching her with the eyes of a mother. The girl had waited patiently through the first night, watching for any signs of life, and she had sat with Momma Tom the next day and finally fell asleep. One of the fundamental differences between Padibatakal and the other children of Tenpenny was that she seemed impossible to discourage. It meant nothing to her that the foal hadn't stirred. She knew that healing was a lengthy process and one she intended to endure.

So now Momma Tom had two orphans in her keep, and it was the happiest she had been in a very long time. Because she had lost her own children, and now she was quite old, Momma Tom cherished any chance she could get to feel like a mother.

"You hear that?" Padibatakal whispered.

"Hear what, Mumsie?"

They were as two shadows whispering in the dark.

"I heard something out there."

As Momma Tom was suckling the foal in the dark of the morning, Padibatakal sat up in the bed beside her.

Now both of them could hear a recurring sound coming from the lots. Padibatakal pulled the covers back and sat up on her knees and shyly she peered out the tiny window into the darkness.

"Don't you hear it?" the girl asked.

But Momma Tom didn't answer. She was looking down at the girl's bare legs. An inch below the ankle both of Padibatakal's legs rounded into a nub where her feet should have started. In the past the girl had always been careful to keep her legs covered with long winter socks, even in the summer. She must have grown too warm in her sleep and stripped them, thought Momma Tom, as she noticed the socks draped across the sheet. Momma Tom eyed the girl's ankles briefly, having never seen them. "Yes I hear it," she said. "But I can't say what it is."

Just then Padibatakal felt a cold shudder and she quickly slipped her legs back beneath the blankets, blushing shyly as Momma Tom pretended not to notice.

When she was very young, before Tipper had brought her to Tenpenny, Padibatakal had lost both of her feet. But despite her rough start she proved to be one of the happiest children Tip had met in his travels. He could see that she was strong and he liked having projects – so long as they were human projects and the two soon found their way back to Tenpenny.

It had taken many years but Padibatakal no longer felt self-pity toward the fact that she was forced to live without feet. Her joys were found in the races she could still run. Of course at first the transition to a place like Tenpenny had been very difficult, despite the standard of living that she now enjoyed. Tenpenny was a place of freedom, and she had been a childhood stranger to freedom. Unlike the children of her homeland, the orphans of Tenpenny enjoyed sports and games of the field every day. When she was a child she would spend whole days alone in the quiet of her bunk thinking long on the wild freedoms of Tenpenny that she had been denied. When she was blue she often thought of things that would bring her out of it, and when she thought of horses, she liked them most of all.

For horses were a way at freedom and freedom was what she wanted most. She wanted to have her own horse and her own saddle to polish. She wanted to stomp around and race her friends and discover the colors beyond the trees. More than anything Padibatakal was born to venture, more perhaps than Henry with his wild ramblings, more than even Tipper could dream. And the sum total of her ventures were consumed in a place she had never seen called the Wild West End.

It was a rumor known throughout Tenpenny and the towns along the inlet that Tip Holland had long ago buried a treasure beyond the deep forest called the Wild West End. Tenpenny legend said that he had buried it high in the mountains and that it would someday be recovered. Padibatakal had thought about the treasure for many years, of where it came from, of why Tipper had buried it, and most often of who would someday dig it up. No one but Tip knew what kind of treasure it was or where it had been laid to rest. All that was known from years of eavesdropping was that far to the west Tip had left a chest for someone to find in the great unknown wilderness, beyond Lah Shakes Lake. Some believed that the story was a hoax while others, like Padibatakal, became obsessed with the mystery. She was a dreamer by nature and her dreams would remain lofty throughout her life. And of all the dreams made available to her in a place like Tenpenny, this was the one she put her hopes in.

Sometimes she would dwell on the great distance she would have to cover to reach the mountains, and of course there was the issue of how she would even get there. She knew she couldn't crutch herself across the valley, and her wheelchair was out of the question. She had concluded years before that horseback was the only way and she set her mind to make it happen. For many years she had spent whatever time she could near the lots, watching the men work. She learned how to shoe a horse from Wonderboy and how to rope from Henry. Other than Tipper, Jack was the best on horseback and she never missed a chance to see him ride.

57

Jack visited Momma Tom in the stables several times a day. And it was for this purpose that Tipper reasoned Padibatakal had chosen to stay with the foal.

Padibatakal was deeply in love with Jack Oakham, though she had never worked up the courage to tell him. She shuttered every time Jack came into her presence and had ever since the day Jack had arrived at Tenpenny, years before.

Padibatakal had been an orphan at Tenpenny before there even was a Tenpenny. She was there when Tipper and Sissy had made their plans, there to watch the roads cut and the wells dug, and the trees hewn down to build the cabins. She was there when the winter came and she remembered the day Henry Snow first arrived. Tipper had left the week before, "On an exciting journey," he told her. "When I return I will have someone very special with me."

Tipper came home with the ruddy-faced Henry Snow and when Padibatakal saw him she felt flushed, went pale. She could tell by the look of him that he was unstoppable. "He might do everything there is to do."

It was a few years later when Jack arrived and she often recalled the way he looked the first time she saw him, with hair a mess, his clothes filthy from travel. They told her he had come a long way to find the place, and that like them he had suffered the loss of his mother. Padibatakal had watched him closely all that day, admiring him from afar, and when he stood up to Henry, a boy twice his size, she immediately fell in love with him.

If it had been almost any other girl on Tenpenny Hill she probably would have fallen in love with Henry instead, but Henry Snow was too loud for the likes of Padibatakal. She didn't care for much talking, or for the drama that came with it. In fact on paper there was very little about Henry that she did value, though she adored him in her own way. She admitted to herself that he was the boldest of all the boys on the hill, if not the bravest, and that no one could match his charm. But ever since Tip had carried her away as a child, Padibatakal had modeled her hopes after Tip's gentle, reliable ways and no boy reminded her of those ways like Jack Oakham did.

He would feed the horses in the mornings and ride in the afternoons. On some days he would teach several of the children how to ride around the paddock and when they did so she stayed away, afraid that her presence would be awkward, or that someone may ask her to try. The fact was that she couldn't try, and she knew it. Every movement she made was a reminder of that. Yet she wanted to, more than anything, and she remained contented to watch the horses, even if that was all she was able to do.

Then one day, at the start of that very winter, Tip saw her sitting on the paddock fence, swinging her footless legs, and he approached her.

"Do you have a favorite?" he asked.

She smiled shyly. "I like the Duke of York."

"Which one is that?"

The girl nodded to the horses. "It's the Philly who always keeps her nose up. She's stuck up but I like her."

Tipper climbed to sit beside her and found the horse in the crowd. "A Philly named Duke? Shouldn't it be a Duchess?"

Once again she ducked shyly away, raising her shoulders and smiling. "I didn't know she was a girl when I named her. I just liked her and thought she was prancy and when Jack told me I could name her I said Duke of York cause it sounded swanky."

"You named her?"

"Yessir."

"You have a real love for horses and real loves never do well riding on a fence. I've been thinking it's time we got you in a saddle, Padi."

The girl put her hands over her face and rolled up like a ball.

"Don't be nervous. Jack and I will work with you everyday. I can make a pair of leg braces that will give you all the control you need. I was thinking we would get started in the spring when the weather breaks."

She began to cry, her face still covered.

"It'll be safer when the snow melts and that'll give me time to build your braces."

"I'd like that," she said.

And he kissed her on the crown of her head.

Lying on the spare bed in Momma Tom's cabin, Padibatakal was anxiously awaiting the arrival of spring. She had always hoped to learn as much about horses, and about her destination as she could. Momma Tom knew much about Mr. Holland, perhaps more than anyone else on Tenpenny Hill. Padibatakal wondered if Momma Tom even knew something about that treasure he was supposed to have buried in the mountains, and why a man would do such a thing. So when Padibatakal heard that the foal had been born, and the opportunity arose to share some time with Momma Tom while learning horses, and being in a place where she could expect to see Jack several times a day, she quickly requested to stay.

"Do you hear footsteps?" Padibatakal whispered.

The sound came from the lots and Momma Tom, despite her age, could hear it clearly. Someone was moving hastily through the snow. But who would be up at this hour? Momma Tom wondered. Mister Holland don't even come down from the chapel quite so early. The only other visitor who they received regularly was Jack, and Jack was even less likely to be up hours before the dawn.

"He's coming closer."

Shadows fell on the snow in the moonlight and she could see through her tiny window a long shape, like that of a man, and in his hands was something tremendous.

"It look like Smithson," Momma Tom said judging from the huge silhouette. "What's he doin' with the horses?"

Huddled near the window they could both see the man loosening the bridles from the hitching posts and leading the mounts out of their stables. He led them each in one hand and in the other hauled up the long object.

"What's that pole in his hands?" she asked.

They could both see him roping something to the mounts and as he turned to lead the horses out the girl unlatched the window and pushed it open, "Smithson! Is that you there?!"

When he put his finger up to his lips and shushed them they could see that it wasn't Smithson, but Henry. His smile shined in the moonlight.

III.

The tool house door was open, which meant Jack knew who the last one was to use it. The tool house was a storage house built into the side of the old gymnasium. Jack and his father had boarded up the building late that autumn like they had every year but as he peered inside he and Putt both knew they had done a poor job of it. Above them they could hear the sounds of a dozen hurried feet shuffling across the gym floor as the tool house door squeaked. The sound circled the gymnasium above them and they both envisioned skunks, or coon pups diving out of the bleachers come thaw. Jack gave a sigh and looked down at Putt. "Might as well have invited the bears to den in the Chapel." the old dog seemed to say.

Jack peered inside the cold dark room and nodded, "I had that one comin'."

It didn't take long for Jack to see that he had been right. Two abandoned tool hooks hung where the shovels should have been. He closed the door and clasped the latch. "Let's hike up to Campbell," Jack said. "Who knows, maybe the elk are running."

The two sank into what was left of the snowpack as they climbed up the hill and when Putt's feet slipped out of the snow they were brown and wet. For the first time in many months, Jack thought.

Tipper had taught Jack never to be impatient for the muddy bottoms. "There is much a young man can learn from the winter," Tipper told him. "There is more a man can learn from the spring. But be patient because the winter's lessons are slow ones, and when the spring comes the lessons come quick and you must pay attention. When you see the muddy bottoms you must start to think in a brand new way."

Jack and Putt stopped suddenly as a sound echoed through the woods. They paused to listen. Jack was almost certain it was the chopping block, which usually came as the sun rose. He did hear a dull thumping, but to his surprise instead of south near Tipper's cabin, the sound came from up the hill, and stranger yet it came in double speed, like the sound of two men chopping.

Putt was slopping the mud across the snow top, angling toward the dining hall and checking back with Jack every few steps to see if he would do the same. Jack moved steadily up the hill ignoring the old dog's request for pancakes.

The sounds grew louder as he climbed and Jack had almost realized what they were when he saw Smithson and Wonderboy digging the ice pack out of the road above him. Smithson was a huge man, tall and shapeless with no eyebrows and almost no teeth. He was the envy of Henry because of all the men he had ever encountered, Smithson had the most flawless, jet-black beard Henry had ever seen. Everything about Smithson was disheveled except for his beard, which seemed to shine on his face like his single accomplishment. Beside him, and working feverishly, was Wonderboy, a much smaller man. The two were breaking the ice pack with a pair of ditch shovels.

"Morning," Jack said.

"Time to break up the pack," Smithson told him. "Your father says the spring is on."

"I was on my way to fetch you a snow shovel."

"Two snow shovels," Smithson said. "We need both. We can't find 'em."

"I know where they are. Have either of you seen my brother?"

Smithson leaned on the handle and spit into the snow. "How can you lose someone as big as Henry?"

"You can't lose Henry Snow. I know. D'you happen to see him?"

Wonderboy smiled as he was in the habit of doing before he spoke, which was rarely. He was a peculiar-looking man, awkward in all occasions except heavy laughter, where he seemed right at home. He was as dark-skinned as any person Jack had ever seen, meaning he was as dark-skinned as they come, for living at Tenpenny Jack had seen it all. Wonderboy's arms seemed a few inches too short and undeveloped, whereas his legs were longer than a man of his height should have been, and much much stronger. He had no shoulders to speak of, but a profound and exaggerated neck leading to his tiny head. It was a common dispute among the children of Tenpenny hill which man, Tip or Wonderboy, was the hardest worker. Jack's brother Henry was the strongest member of the Tenpenny family, but even Henry admitted once, "Pound for pound I will never be as strong as Wonderboy," to which Jack replied, "It would be a waste if you were. He works ten times harder on a bad day than you ever will on a good one."

Wonderboy held his smile with every word he spoke. "Mister Henry went down to the lots," he said. "He took the bigger horses."

"Where did he take them?"

"North."

"Toward the Kopasack?"

He nodded.

"Was the trail horse blanketed?"

"They both were. He was bareback."

"Did he have his rifle?"

Wonderboy shook his head. "Just a box."

"A box?"

"Under his arm," Wonderboy said. "A white box."

With the two men at ease Jack could clearly hear that no wood was being split on the chopping block. He looked north through the trees that were now sunning themselves fully and then peered deep into the timberland for signs of the horse tracks in the snow. But as he began to imagine all of the mayhem his brother might have gotten into, Jack Oakham decided, as he had learned to do since their childhood, not to worry about his brother and to go about his day. "I'll be back with the shovels," he said as he marched on.

Jack was glad not to think about it. Spring was coming, there was work to be done, his belly was rumbling. I don't need to go chasing Henry all across Tenpenny before the sun has even found his way over the trees, he thought. It bothered Jack how much of a distraction his brother could be. He whistled at the old dog who reluctantly left his path down to the dining hall.

The two marched up toward Campbell field but as he was working Smithson called out to the boy. "And Jack?"

"Yessir?"

"You might check on Greer this morning. I know it's early but the nurse says she's worse than ever."

Jack nodded. His eyes were gentle. He tucked his hands in his coat pockets and turned up the hill slower, more careworn than before. Greer Ashby was one of two young ladies who Jack feared he may be in love with, though he hadn't yet decided which.

IV.

Tip Holland often contemplated why God had chosen him to be the caretaker of Tenpenny, when there were so many more capable men around. He had a habit in the dark of the morning of asking God questions concerning his place in the big scheme of things. Of why he had been blessed with so much, he who was so wretched and unworthy. Then again he was a man who had the hours for such questions. As far as Tip Holland was concerned sleeping and eating were each a waste of valuable time.

When he stepped out of the chapel that morning he had already been at work for two full hours and first light was still a long ways off. He had spent the cold dark morning peddling his wood lathe, shaping the birchwood struts that he had in mind for a staircase. He was so carefree he'd given no thoughts to breakfast. When he had finished he worked the struts with a greasy piece of tackcloth, his favorite practice, and ran the names of the children through his mind. He often smiled as he thought of them, marveling at how he had despised children as a young man and at how God had healed his heart.

When he had finished his woodcraft he hung his tools on a coat peg and stood on the threshing floor, staring out at the chapel for a quarter of an hour. To his sons this was his most peculiar habit, and one that he practiced often without even knowing it. He would stand or sit, depending on his mood, and look out upon whichever project he was invested in at the time, some days for over an hour, until suddenly he sprung back into form knowing fully what came next. Like most visionaries he could never explain how the answers came to him, he simply waited patiently until they did.

"I have to see it," he told his boys. "Sometimes it takes awhile."

Sissy once shared the story of how her brother had walked up and down the length of the river for a week when Putt was still a pup, waiting to see where Tenpenny would be built. He would stop and look out at the valley, and back at the trees, then back again until finally on the eighth day he returned to Sissy and Momma Tom and said to them, "There will be two rows of cabins and a road in between, a dining hall where the hill levels out, an upper set of bathrooms, a lower set, a great fountain in the middle, a gymnasium there where the poplars meet. . ."

Although it commonly took hours for Tip to envision a new project, on rare occasions it wasn't a slow process at all. He had once hiked along the hillside south of the lower cabins at dawn in a hurry to play a prank on his sons when he simply glanced down the slope and stopped, and in that moment an idea was instantly planted in his mind.

By day's end a path of trees had been cleared, a slough had been dug, and a long metal wire had been stretched from top to bottom along the hillside. He was the first to try it. As the sun set he was harnessed, with his sons watching, as he glided down the zipline into the slough, to the uproarious cheers of the children.

That was five years ago and his passion for projects had only grown stronger. Tip stepped off of the threshing floor and walked across the room to a workbench in the corner, pulling back a dropcloth that was covering it. It revealed a pair of oak leggings that he had finished shaping just days before. Tip was well-pleased with the result, and was entering into the coming spring with great anticipation. He stashed the leggings into an old tattered haversack and slipped out into the morning.

Outside the chapel he walked along the trail glimpsing the stars through the heavily wooded canopy. Ever since his time on the sea as a younger man Tip had enjoyed the great map of the sky, especially in the last hour before dawn when the stars were on their best behavior.

On the winding trail, which was dimly lit by a long row of lamp-posts, Tip saw where his footprints from hours before had melted for the first time that winter. Like Jack, Tip thought of the muddy bottoms. He marched up the trail keeping a keen eye for the elk that often passed through the trees. When he came to an arbor at the edge of the clearing he dropped to his knees. A small patch of dry winter grass could be seen beneath the arbor and prominent among the grass were the two small barren indentations where his knees rested. Tip could have done his praying in his cabin on the hill, or in the chapel, but he needed to be in a place where he could feel the cold shudder of the wind. For Tip would claim that he was warmed by his prayers.

"Father, we talk often of traits in me that need mending. Make me a patient man. Guide my words when I am weak. I am overwhelmed by your blessings and do not intend to squander them. Bring to full example the lessons of spring, to the little ones most of all who may leave us before another year. May the new families of those who have gone from this place be walking in your will, as we should be daily. I pray for those I have wronged. I ask for your forgiveness and for theirs. I ask for your guidance in fathering children. I pray that my sister know of the peace that surpasses all understanding. I ask that you protect Padi from harm as Jack and I work with her, Lord. I ask that Greer finds hope again. May our words today in this place glorify you in yours. For let nothing—"

Suddenly Tip stopped. He opened his eyes to the sound of heavy footfalls. When he turned to look he could make out the shapes of two horses charging up the slope. As the lights of Tenpenny framed their silhouettes Tip could see snow being thrown from their hooves in the gallop. There appeared to be but one rider, a heavy shape handling both sets of reigns.

In a blink the mounts had reached him. Tip raised a hand in welcome as the figure held his lance overhead. And then he was gone.

The twin chargers could be heard breaking low and hard across the field and into the birchcrest, the snowy boughs snapping as the mounts broke against them.

The hoofsound faded into the dark morning and Tipper stood to his feet, moving out onto Campbell field. When he could no longer make out the faint thuds against the snowcap he closed his eyes again. "And Father, protect Henry from himself."

As was his routine Tip turned to walk down Campbell field. He greatly enjoyed the pale glow of the meadow in the moonlight. Tip passed the fountain and the mat flat and as he stepped onto the road he began reciting one of his favorite passages. "*And if you give yourself to the hungry, and satisfy the desire of the afflicted, then your light will shine in the darkness, and your gloom will become like midday. And the Lord will continually guide you, and satisfy your desire in scorched places, and give strength to your bones and you will be like a watered garden, and like a spring of water whose waters do not fail.*"

He walked up the road. The fire pit in front of High Hopes was still glowing embers in the breeze. Tip ducked to look inside, hoping to catch a glimpse of Jack sleeping.

"*And those from among you will rebuild the ancient ruins; you will raise up the old fashioned foundations, and you will be called the repairer of the breach, the restorer of the streets in which to dwell.*"

Most days Tip went straight from the chapel to his cabin to read until the sun came, but that day a certain child was heavy on his heart. He walked quietly across the hill, through the gravel lots and over the putting green and entered the nurse's office. It was a white room which always felt eerie and clean to the children because every other room in Tenpenny was either masoned from river stones or dark with the oils of old logs. But the nurse's office was white. It was the only time Tip had ever ventured to lay tile, and although Wonderboy had helped him and had enjoyed the work, and although Sissy felt the whole place should be

66

built of something cleaner and neater than logs and stones, Tip resisted, saying that a wilderness place should be built to fit the wilderness and that the only reason he let the tile remain was because the nurses themselves insisted it was much easier to clean. He walked silently down the hallway to a room with metal beds stacked against the walls where kids played card games on their bunks in the daytime. He saw the Burmese twins sleeping on the same twin mattress, their faces bandaged and swollen. Tip closed their door to keep them warm. There were several other rooms on the hallway: a playroom for the young children, an infirmary, a dental room, and a kitchen where Tip would often have his morning tea.

In the last room the door was open. Tip peered inside and saw the silhouette of a girl curled up in the daybed, wrapped tightly in her blanket. "Morning Greer," he whispered. He waited and waited but she didn't stir so he said a brief prayer for her and stepped away. He moved down the hallway on his way to his cabin, to spend the remainder of the early hours splitting wood on the stump.

But when he arrived at the end of the hallway he paused as he reached the door. Before him, on the door back, was the only standing mirror in all of Tenpenny and as Tip opened it, he caught the once daily glimpse of himself.

Tip Holland was a rugged man of forty-two, though not a big man at first glance. He carried an innocence that weighed him smaller and younger than he really was. He wore black and white Chuck Taylor tennis shoes his whole adult life, going through two pairs a year, usually in February and August, and invariably handed over the broken shoes to some lucky child who gave him trouble. His hands were never smooth for he found the actions and the rhythms, the satisfying crack of hewed pine on a chop stump to be the song of his days. He was adorned with bracelets and necklaces that he would hand out to the children. His face was slim and rough, his dimples deep, his smile childlike. He had lost none of his hair, which everyone agreed befit a man of his youthful pursuits. There was nothing about his appearance to suggest his past. His transformation had been so complete that when people met him they believed that the man who stood before them: a quiet, humble, father to the multitudes, was the man he had always been.

V.

The snow shovels were right where Jack thought they'd be, forgotten in the bar ditch at the bottom of Campbell field. He hauled one up onto either shoulder and turned down the hill again. Putt was sniffing the puddle from the Burmese's nosebleed the afternoon before. When he heard Jack turn in the snow he looked up in surprise.

"Where are we goin' now?" Putt asked him.

"I'm going to get some breakfast," Jack said. "And you're gonna watch."

The old dog kept his head low, lumbering as he plodded on. "Careful now," Jack heard him say.

Where the road from Tenpenny meets up with Campbell field there is a solitary oak that grows beautifully among a land of birches and alders. It had always been agreed upon that this oak, with its young slender trunk, fit well among the other unlikely inhabitants of Tenpenny Hill, for it had no earthly business living where it did; hardwoods were rare in those hills and Tip had adored the tree ever since he had discovered it. The belief held by many of the children of Tenpenny, and certainly by Jack, was that this oak, dubbed "the birthing tree" was the true fledgling heart of their homeland. If one were to pass it in the woods without an eye for such treasures, the oak would likely go unnoticed. Except for the small inscription "W.M." at the base of the trunk, there was nothing to mark it.

As he passed through the trees Jack turned to glance at the inscription and nodded in approval at the letters, just as he did nearly every time he read them. With the spring approaching he would have to trim back the sprouts as they rose up to hide the marking.

Putt followed Jack down the hill towards the sound of ditch shovels breaking up the pack. Jack found Wonderboy and Smithson a few yards from where he'd left them, snapping the hard pack and shuffling their feet. He set the shovels down beside them and they nodded silently. Jack nodded back and pointed Putt toward the dining hall where the morning aromas were becoming irresistible.

The two moved through the squeaking double doors that were padded and tarped every September to keep out the winter. We'll need to strip 'em down to screens again in a few weeks, Jack thought, once the melt is over. When the two stepped inside they were standing on a broad rawhide mat and no sooner had Jack begun to wipe his boots then Putt did the same, mimicking the forceful kick that dogs repeat after taking care of their business.

"What's for breakfast?" Jack said as he walked up to the countertop. One of the young cooks was working behind the counter. He was moving with purpose around the kitchen, searching high and low for something he had yet to find. "What d'you care? You never take breakfast."

"I will this morning," Jack told him. "I must have dreamt about food I woke so hungry."

The cook opened the fridge, scanned the shelves and closed it back. "Well I hope you dreamt of coffee cake, or biscuits and eggs."

"Biscuits sound good. What are you lookin' for?"

"A dozen donuts are missing. I had them on the countertop last night and they vanished."

Jack grinned, "I'm sure Momma Tom took 'em. You can't keep her away from the sweets."

The cook scooped three biscuits onto a plate and handed Jack some butter. "How's her foal this morning? Is she drinking?"

"She'll make it. Haven't seen her but she'll make it."

"You're the first to think so."

Jack chewed and shook his head. "No, I ain't."

"Well it's good to see the spring is on. If you're right the spring will help that foal along."

The cook looked down at the biscuits. "Want to jelly those?"

"I would, thanks."

"I'd offer you a jelly donut but the box is officially missing."

"That's alright. Donuts are a dessert. Not a breakfast."

"Which kind you want?"

"What kind you have?"

"Plum and huckleberry."

"Plum."

The cook went to fetch the jelly. "What'd you think Tip will start with this year?"

"Dono. Pine haul. I know that. Maybe finish the climbing wall."

"Will Henry work this year?"

"Depends on what you mean by 'work'."

"Well every spring he manages to find his way out of it."

"He'll work this year," Jack said. "Tipper's had enough."

"Has he?"

"Only excuse Henry could make this year would be-" but Jack cut his sentence short. He sat wide-eyed in his seat.

"What is it?" the cook asked.

But Jack didn't answer. He turned to look out the window with his mouth half-open. Suddenly he stood and took a few steps toward the door, his eyes wild. Jack was thinking about the box of donuts that his brother had stolen.

"What's the date?" Jack asked as he turned back.

"Tenth of March. What's wrong?"

Jack led the old dog toward the door. "I'll be back for the biscuits."

He moved through the double doors and the old dog followed. Putt wiped his feet again when he reached the mat; never able to comprehend that it was an entry-only assignment, and the two moved hastily onto the road.

Jack knew that Henry did a lot of things for selfish gain but all of them had an agenda behind them. Taking a dozen donuts for his own consumption was far too simple an explanation. The theft had been part of a plan and up until that moment, Jack had no idea what the plan was.

All he could assume was that it had something to do with Sissy, for most of Henry's schemes came back on her sooner or later. Jack was quickly reminded of the very public argument that Henry and Sissy had engaged in just days before and Jack felt certain that whatever troubles Henry was going to on Sissy's behalf was a response to their public disagreement.

Jack thought about the argument as he led the dog to the fountain, the central meeting place on the hill surrounded by huge granite stones. Atop the fountain a giant archway extended high into the air with the words "The Four Square Life" etched into the iron, and a pair of wooden spears that criss-crossed behind the lettering. Henry had carved the spears when he was still a boy, working diligently to duplicate the bushman design that Wonderboy had taught him.

When Jack looked up at the arch he immediately saw that one of the spears was missing. He thought about the horses, and the donuts, and the content of the argument as he stared off at the twin sets of hoofprints that trailed out of the lots. "Oh Hell, Henry," he said beneath his breath. And Putt turned on him with a look of disapproval.

The sun was well awake now and young Oakham could see the light spreading out across the cabin-tops and the vast wild kingdom announcing the arrival of spring. The snow covered mountain peaks beyond the West End, the valleys that lulled in the fog, the wild amber forest tops, the rivers and streams that cut across the rocks with their flickering snowmelt, even the unspoken places to the west: all were rising with the light. The land stretched on from the fountainhead in every conceivable direction, an unexplored kingdom, with her great rambling wilderness painted across the distant canvas. There was only one explanation for where Henry had gone and it made Jack feel frustrated and envious all at once. He turned his eyes back to the single lance above the fountain and said, "You thinking what I'm thinking, Putt?"

But before the old dog could respond the clapper of the morning bell began to sound.

VI.

The argument had begun the week before, after Henry had returned a gift that Sissy had given him for his sixteenth birthday. There had been nothing underhanded about the gift, but Henry didn't want it, and he returned it on the spot.

"Now Sissy, I know you don't want to be thick-headed, so when you give me a gift like this you shouldn't be surprised when I refuse it."

The crowded party grew silent. She lowered her glass and honed in. "Why would you refuse it?"

"Thicker than I thought."

Henry had rejected the gift on the moral grounds that it interfered with his simple, unworldly desires. He expressed as much in the letter he wrote to Sissy later that week.

Dear Aunt Sissy,

I want to apologize for the way things went at my birthday party. I meant no disrespect to you or your friends. But now for my side. It seems very foolish to me to collect what we cannot keep, to store up what we never use. If I have a shirt in my closet that I haven't worn in a week I give it to those that have no shirt. Shirts cost money. As you well know they have pockets too, where things can be placed – or in your case – misplaced – lost – which causes frustration, even anger, sometimes that anger causes unkind words to be said among loved ones. For that I am still awaiting an apology. It all could have been avoided if you just didn't have so many shirts.

Some men lose their keys when they throw them on their desks. They become buried in the rubble of paper stacks and bills. I have no desk, no paper stacks, my bills are few and paid immediately. I can't lose my keys because there is nowhere for them to hide.

Some nights I sleep on a couch because it is a great idea. I am not dirty because of it. I am not lowly or foolish. Comfortable places make men soft. What good are they? Whenever I have slept on that couch I have never slept in. An undesirable place of rest makes unnecessary rest uncommon. We are not to live uncooked; we are not to squint when walking barefoot. We are to sweat, to bleed, to laugh without restraint.

"Do, do, do," I've been told. What we need are men that can do. Men with will and confidence. We need proactive men, we need "look you in the eye and know that the job will get done" kind of men. We need men who can. Can fish, hunt, dig, cook, cry, laugh, discipline themselves. We need the lean. We need the tempered men who were given shoulders for a reason. There is true adventure, true courage.

As far as what minimalism is, I will tell you - and you need not shake your head at me again. Let us break things down and return life to its bare minimum before our time is up. Men need food to live – a minimalist knows what food will promote more years with his grandchildren, they buy only what they need, and eat it. They drink juices, and water, and if they can stand it, milk from the soybean. They find themselves in sunlight; they find themselves in unconditioned air. If it is hot they find water to swim in, if it is cold they find fire to warm by. They fall in love with as many things and as many people as possible, and they devote themselves to them. They give themselves over to only one woman, they look people in the eye, they hand out no common compliments, no uncouth rebukes. A minimalist says what he means to say, word for word. He knows how to slow down.

He writes down every active ingredient in his life, every love, pain, gain, or loss, he thinks on these things.

A minimalist never owns what he doesn't need – no radio, no television. He reads the paper and remembers what it says. He recognizes that ownership is impossible.

A minimalist recognizes (and I hope you don't take this personally) that spectator sports are only valuable for father/son, father/daughter outings – that strip joints, Ferrari dealerships, breweries, brothels, pushers, pimps and the pockets of the silly rich are the destination of your dollar. No man I've known could name me three athletes from a century ago and for good reason. They have no lasting impact. A minimalist knows he isn't special because of his body, he isn't special because of his height, he is the crown of creation because he thinks, because he solves, because he learns, because he loves.

If at the end of the week a common man has fifty dollars to spend –he may buy a nice new sweater that matches his nice new pants, adding to his wardrobe. The sweater costs fifty dollars and will go with him as long as style permits, and wear on the threading allows –then he will not wear it again - and his fifty dollar investment will have ceased to be of any worth.

Then there is the minimalist – he also has fifty dollars to spend at the end of the week. He stuffs his pack with all he owns – hikes to the highway – puts his thumb out, gets a ride, has a memorable conversation with an adorable retired couple from Ocalla, Florida who are taking their Airstream to Alaska and back, stops off at the grocery and book stores at the headquarters of Sequoia National Park, buys juice, rice, fly-tying material, a short Steinbeck novel, a collection of stories by Isaac Singer, Soul Mountain by Gao XingJian, and a weekend fishing license, totaling forty-eight dollars and seventy-one cents, hikes into the woods, writes to himself about the pleasures of this grand adventure, catches a few brookies, watches the stars, sees a porcupine, spills his boiling water on the fire by accident and extinguishes it, reads until he falls asleep by one of the biggest trees in the world, hikes twelve miles, strengthens his calves, his lungs, his soul, his memories, takes some notes and heads home. He dies sixty years later. When he goes to heaven, he takes with him the memory

*of a grand weekend. And for an eternity his fifty-dollar investment
continues to pay dividends.*

*Please understand my reasons for not receiving your sweater with
open arms. You nephew, free and clear, Henry*

After reading the letter Sissy marched up to High Hopes where Henry
and Jack were boxing in the snow. Every month the children gathered in
the street for the "Brother Brawl", which was a three round, gloved bout
roped off from the cabins where Henry and Jack were always the main
event. Jack, as usual, was bloodied but standing. Sissy shook the letter at
Henry as he danced around the ring. "You have to answer for this."

"Not now, Sissy. Jack's a jabber."

The fight was appalling to her. Although fresh snow covered the
edges of the ring the boys were dripping with sweat. She could see
blood crystallizing on the ropes. Despite all the hunting and butchering
that took place around Tenpenny, blood was something Sissy had never
grown accustomed to, especially when it came from the young men she
adored. She choked down the sight and interrupted again, "You have no
right, Henry to reject a gift – *any* gift from *any*one. You must be *thankful*.
You must have a *grateful spirit.*"

"I am grateful, Sissy. I'm grateful for my youth, the sports of the field
and the coming warmth. I'm a fountain of gratitude flowing from the
wellspring of undeserved blessing. But I must not forget myself in the
wake of your gift. I have learned to want what cannot be bought or sewn."

"Well I would love it if someone knitted me a sweater. I wouldn't
complain about it. I would just thank them and move on."

"Well, Sissy. . . What *you* want is a sweater," he said, his lips bleeding.
"What *I* want-"

Jack smacked him cleanly across the mouth.

". . .is to be understood."

One of the Burmese twins rang the bell and the other brought the
fighters their towels. Henry pinched his nose and blew out of both nostrils. Two thick streams of blood stained the snow at Sissy's feet. "I mean
it makes sense for me to make you a sweater," Henry said. "But not the
other way around."

Sissy watched the Swedes rub the fighter's shoulders. They were each wearing derby hats they'd stolen from the skit box and were chewing on jerky stubs that were supposed to look like cigars. The Swedes held the buckets for the boys to spit in and Smithson pushed Padibatakal's wheel-chair around the ring as she held up the cue card that read "Round Two".

"The day you make me a sweater is the day I'll quit telling you to grow up," she told him.

Henry smiled at Sissy as he stood, "Who would want to live in a world where Henry Snow grew up?"

The children were cheering for the fight to start again and Sissy abandoned the argument. The bell rang and the two collided. And even though the corners of his eyes were beginning to swell, in his periphery Jack Oakham watched with pity as his defeated Aunt walked down the hill. Jack was always happy to be matching fists and not words with Henry Snow.

When their argument had ended all seemed calm between Henry and Sissy. They ate together and worked among the children and neither one did anything out of the ordinary. It was as if their dispute had been silently settled. That is until that morning arrived when Henry slipped out of bed unannounced.

He had been careful to cross the room silently, lacing his boots on the porch, and walking only across the stones to avoid the crunch of the melting snow. He fetched the spear from the fountain arch, the donuts from the dining hall, and quickly caught the horses in the lots. Then he led them through a skinny swath in the alders, keeping his head low to avoid the melting branches. Henry rode for over an hour in the blackness, the dim glow of the snowpack guiding him through the alderland. He crossed the Kopasack river valley and galloped the geldings parallel across the icy beaches that shattered like pane glass. He fixed a fire within sound of the river to dry the horse's flanks, and he stood well clear of the drift, careful not to let the smoke turn back upon him.

Upwind he smothered the fire and when the embers were lukewarm he rubbed his hands and face with bits of black ash, blackened his bandana, and tied his hair atop his head. He rode the faster mount out of the valley into the birch hills, trailing the heavy gelding behind him, both running for their lives, and his eyes lusty and wild-looking despite the wind. He hadn't been that far north since a year but he steered the geldings through the alders in the dark of the morning from memory. Reaching the summit Henry followed the polestar down towards the ice-covered crags that he and Jack had discovered the winter of their twelfth year.

He dismounted and coursed the horses through the birch vale to a great fallen pine where he hitched them to hollow sockets. He unroped the lance from the fat gelding and turned back into the gorge. The dawn was still an hour out.

The canyon wound icy and dreamlike in the dark and he was a world apart, unaware of his surroundings until after a long march he recognized the faint spotted caves that stood out against the rock face.

Henry took the box from his pack and trailed the donuts along the stones, tearing them in half with his teeth and tossing them to the snow as he sallied on. When he came to a series of rock cliffs that ascended step-like up the face he scaled the crags, leaving the last of the donuts in a pile on a skinny rock trail beneath him. Then, carefully, Henry scaled the rock face and when he reached the top he stripped dwarf birches of their limbs with his skinner and threaded the branches through his clothing.

With the lance in his hands and two rock shelves beneath him, each a man's length above the other, he waited in the dark.

Henry Snow endured the cold and the dead silence as patiently as a cat. His eyes, although slow to move, honed to the yawning canyon, were nevertheless fully luminated by his thoughts. For though he had the appearance of a brute, Henry's mind was never at rest.

Tipper had noted that for most people who met him, Henry's physical presence defined him, and this gave the boy a radical advantage over his brother. Jack left little impression upon visitors for he looked plain enough and said little and quickly it was believed that for Jack Oakham more lie beneath the surface. But with Henry, strangers felt little tug to see past his appearance. "Mark my words," Tip had said. "Henry will be underestimated all his life."

They saw only what Henry could not keep hidden: a heavy jaw, aggressive even as a child - a huge, childlike grin that many mistook for innocence, a strong nose swollen at the bridge, and most memorable - his shaggy curls, auburn and untended, that he wore like a crown of feathers.

Unlike most people who were remembered solely by their faces - Henry Snow could be remembered by one of a dozen features. For just as his nose seemed to be permanently swollen, so too was his neck, which even when the rest of his body was concealed suggested a great athlete.

But little suggestion was necessary. His shoulders, round and broadly cut, his huge, sprawling hands that hinted at future growth, and his powerful height which stood him a full head taller than his father were all noticed at first glance. Young and old watched him mindlessly. He was both heavy and quick, every bit as quick as Jack and Tipper, and stronger than the two of them together. He was what every young man longs to be, unquestionably strong. And to the average onlooker there was little else for a boy of sixteen to wish for.

But to Henry, his physical strength was of little significance. Oh it came in handy when he had a point to prove, or when he felt like working, which was rarely. But most hours of the day his stature never occurred to him. It was merely the shell he had been given. Most men know only what they see, Henry thought. They see it and understand it and it gives them comfort. But it's just dumb matter. Just tissue and bone. Even Henry, strong as he was, knew that his great fleshly strength was fleeting and silly and worth little of his time.

Yet he believed that there was one true advantage to how God made him. So long as men judged him for what they could see, he could outsmart them with what they couldn't. He knew someday he would no longer be the boy king of Tenpenny Hill. Someday he would be out in the world and he must rely on weapons other than his shoulders. So although Henry Snow was apathetic towards his own physical prowess, he more than made up for it with the sharpening of his mind. And his mind was being sharpened with every moment that passed as he sat there on his rock perch, the lance held loosely like a toy within his palms.

He kept a running tally of the trees for the next hour as they slowly sprung to life with the dim morning light. He counted the birdcalls, both male and female, and ranked them by their frequency. In his mind Henry stepped off the paces back to his horses all the while watching the canyon for any hint of movement. His bait was strung out over two hundred feet, west to east, with the final pile scattered beneath him. At one point Henry carefully pulled his heels up, squatting on the stone ledge to get a slightly higher view.

He heard a warbler for the first time as the wind changed. The birds were calling now, all along the canyon as the light continued to rise. The gorge was rich with treasures. So much had Henry missed the spring that his heart began to search for tiny signs of life hidden among the crags.

"Twenty-one minutes to sun up," he thought to himself. "Seventy five until the morning bell. He'll be along shortly," Henry thought. "The smell will surely bring him out." He watched the canyon in silence, waiting to hear the sound of heavy footfalls, or to see his prey moving from the west along the trail.

Still squatting on his heels, Henry continued to examine the shapes of the trees as they grew out of the morning shadows and their branches began to sway. But suddenly, as his eyes shifted, there came a wild and terrifying breath from the ledge above him. The sound grew steadily, a fierce, hungry sound that swelled greater and greater until it spewed forth down his neck.

Henry remained still, even his eyes were frozen like a stone, for he could feel the warm heat of the thing as it breathed down his open collar. Loose rock could be heard scraping above.

But Henry did not flinch. It seemed to him that a dark and dangerous cloud had descended upon him, one that he was determined to shake.

It took all of his will not to turn around but Henry didn't dare for now he knew there was something wild and dangerous behind him and above him, for the breathing was deeper and fuller and heavier than his own. Instead he kept his eyes front watching the gorge, hoping that whatever was upon him could not see him. He set his mind to holding absolutely still, as still as he had ever been, even dimming his eyes to meditate on the beauty of the morning gorge. But Henry knew that whatever was behind him was watching the same gorge he was, scanning the deep fissure for signs of life, and that like him this hunter would notice any movement across the rock crevice, no matter how infinitesimal, and that as reserved as it was Henry could not hold off his own breathing.

He listened intently and heard the faint shifts of a wet tongue behind him. Whatever was above him was cleaning its teeth. Once again the warm breath of the thing came down heavily upon him in a sudden burst, and his neck tingled as he received it. He nearly succumbed to his desire to turn and face the thing that breathed down his back, but his good sense won out.

For above him, eyes squinting to the dawn, a huge black bear was waiting on the cliff edge, doing exactly as Henry was, hunting the canyon for any signs of life. The two were not but four feet apart, the span of one ledge to another, and had it not been for Henry's diligence to blend into his surroundings the bear would have surely discovered him. But fortunately for Henry this bear was smelling other things, things down in the canyon that he had never smelled before.

Henry waited, still on his haunches, for what seemed like hours. His knees were throbbing, his fingertips beginning to tremble from the cold. Suddenly he became aware that if he didn't stretch his legs soon they would begin to grow numb beneath him. Henry contemplated this as he listened to the soft breathing that trickled down his neck. He knew that without his legs he couldn't turn to fight and that if the bear did descend upon him he would be as good as dead.

He weighed his decision heavily, knowing that a charge could come at any time. All he had to do was twitch a muscle and he would be as good as dead. Henry continued to mull over his choices, knowing that the longer he waited the greater his risk. But just as he made up his mind to act, at the exact moment Henry decided to turn to face his fate, the bear rose from his rock perch and walked away.

The sound of his steps could be heard traversing the high ledge to the east above him. Henry could sense that the animal was moving but he remained still, knowing full well that the bear could easily be watching him closely as he traveled. He listened intently, the sound of the steps growing fainter and fainter until despite the straining of his ears Henry heard nothing and was left alone.

As much as he wanted to, Henry resisted the urge to breath a sigh of relief. For all he knew the bear could be thirty feet away, looking down from another rock ledge, waiting for Henry to budge. His knees were aching now but he didn't dare risk it. This was an old bear and a careful hunter, one that Henry had pursued for several springs. One summer this very bear had given Putt a sting across his chops and both Henry and Jack had been hunting him ever since. Now that Henry was so close he wouldn't give up the chance just because his knees were aching. He watched and waited and listened for the old bear's breathing.

Then, suddenly, the heavy shape came into view. For the first time the bear could be seen now, like a black cloud sweeping slowly across the ravine floor, his big head rocking to and fro as he sniffed the cold morning air. Henry was almost directly above him now, his legs beginning to quiver. A giant cottonwood rose out of the ravine and at any moment the bear would pass behind it. Henry knew this would be his only chance. Once the bear was in the open the opportunity would be lost forever. He readied himself to stand and strike.

But just as the bear approached the cottonwood he stopped where he stood, sniffing the pile of crumbs in the ravine floor. Henry waited, his knees beginning to buckle, as the bear held his head high to sniff the trail. The moment seemed to last and last but in reality the great bear waited only a moment before he moved along.

Henry had only that single chance to act. As the bear passed behind the great trunk Henry rose in one stiff motion, the spear head pointed at his feet, and in the next instant the bear had cleared the trunk and his eyes were turned upon Henry. The bear stared for a long time at the tall shape that stood among the trees. He cocked his head curiously and studied it up and down, trying to catch a scent in the cold breeze. Despite the eyes of the great bear honed in on his shape Henry felt relief that his knees were no longer locked. They each waited, eyes focused, for minutes on end, Henry swelling his eyelids gradually to avoid blinking and all the while his hand held tightly to the spear.

Finally the bear broke off his gaze and turned to sniff the pile before him. It had a sweet smell, one he had been hunting all morning and he turned the crumbling bread in his paws over and over before he ventured a lick As the bear tasted the sweet breadcrumbs the world seemed to disappear and all he could see was a long trail of the sweet food laid out for him, a food he had never tasted. And as the bear gobbled the first pieces and moved along the trail a sudden sound came down at him from above, like a limb falling, and at the same instant he absorbed a tremendous blow to his spine. The bear sprung to his haunches but as he did a great weight seemed to lean on him from above. He pinched his shoulders together, twisting and turning, trying to shake the weight from his back, all the while as a burning flame seemed to cut straight through him.

He rocked violently to either side, blood pumping across his coat. He tried to rise again, but this time his knees buckled and he collapsed, crumbling to the trail like a bag of heavy stones.

Slowly the bear's lungs expanded. There was a great hemorrhage that rose up from out of his wound and a gentle hissing that accompanied it. His jowls were dripping with blood as he let out his last slow breath.

A faint sound, like that of a distant whimper could be heard escaping from his body and the sound grew fainter and fainter until his lungs were flattened and his body lay still.

On the bottom ledge now, with a pistol in hand, Henry studied the bear for some time. He wasn't foolish enough to think that it was yet safe to descend into the canyon. He waited and watched the spear for any hint of movement. When he was satisfied Henry put away his pistol and climbed down beside the bear, his hands at the ready, and ran his thumb along the bear's open eye, which was already dry to the touch. He looked at the spear and thought of Wonderboy with silent admiration.

"Are there some among you who live authentic lives?
Worker bees who amidst the drivel do escape their prison hives?
Who bring to mind the way we were when adventure was our friend
And fly the very causeways where our safety does pretend?"

Henry rocked the spear from the bear's back and with all of his strength rolled him over on his side and with his knife spilled his insides onto the sandy stones. This short verse was one Henry had written himself as an ode to Wonderboy after Tipper had told some stories about the little man's early life. He had always planned to kill this bear with the spear that Wonderboy had helped him build, preferably on the first day of spring, and he felt the verse was a fitting tribute both to the danger of the bear, and the danger within himself.

He stripped the branches from his clothes and after his long hike returned with the horses. In the center of the canyon he hobbled the heavy gelding, who was timid near the carcass, and calmed him with his words. Both horses watched intently as he roped the bear around the mid-section and tossed the loose rope over the heavy branches of the cottonwood.

Then he tied the rope to the pommel of the fast gelding and led him on step by step, hoisting the bear up in the air carefully, with melting snow and wet leaves clinging to his open belly. With care he led the heavy horse to stand underneath the carcass. The gelding fought and nickered and once began to buck but with his soothing whispers Henry was able to calm the horse, and once the two mounts were in sync Henry lowered the carcass and draped the bear over the spine of the heavier horse.

VII.

The sun was well out of her den when Wonderboy pulled the long frayed rope of the morning bell, signaling the beginning of the day. The orphanage soon rattled and shook with the scrambling of adolescent traffic. The bell chime was followed by the sounds of screen doors creaking, toilets flushing, feet sloshing over the gravel lots between the cabins, old bunks jarring when children hopped off. Numerous though they numbered as they sprang out of their quarters, there was nothing mob-like about them. They were joyous and well-behaved, all with slickers and ponchos, the girls with their hair pigtailed, the boys with their ball caps backwards. All of Tenpenny was heading to breakfast.

When he heard the bell Tip laid his axe against the chop block and wiped his hands on the old towel he had hanging on the line. Smithson hauled one last load of shattered ice off the road and set aside his shovel. Padibatakal and Greer both peered out their windows as the crowds moved past. And Momma Tom suckled the foal, which lay as still and lifeless as ever.

Ms. Sistine Cornella Holland, or Sissy as she liked to be called, blue parka zipped to the neck, hood covering her hair, walked up toward the fountainhead, beneath the flag, her eyes honed for the arrival of her nephew. As she shivered the children funneled onto the road in every size, shape, and disposition, quietly finding their places in line. Sissy heard little snickers and whispers, a light cry from a babe in the nursery, the motors starting on the carpenter's wood chipper, the gleeful chirping of dovesong and ptarmigan, the crackle of softwood fires in the pits. She could smell the moist aroma of coffee cake, warm bubbling syrup pots, molasses, cornbread, elk sausage, fresh salmon and cream cheese, as well as salmon berries and blue berries, pine bark nuts, the Saskatoon crystal frosted with dew. Like a giant rising after a long winter slumber, the world of Tenpenny was coming awake.

Unlike the children who moved orderly into lines near the fountain pond, Sissy was shivering where she stood, though she tried to conceal it. She stood in a vain attempt to appreciate the beginnings of things – believing that if she soaked up the calm of the morning she would have some on reserve when the day inevitably bombarded her with noise and questions, and unexpected chores that were in part her duty to perform.

The boys were lined up in rows before her, single file facing the fountain, and behind her the girls were doing the same. They stood silently, half awake but filled with anticipation for the warm meal that awaited them, and also for a day of sunny skies and the promise of spring.

"Cabin reports," Sissy requested.

The first child in each line announced the headcount for his or her cabin.

"Cabin one: All accounted for."

"Cabin two: Every man in the foxhole."

"Cabin three: All dogs in the doghouse."

"Cabin four: All cookies in the cookie jar," and so on.

Sissy raised her hand and looked out across the multitude with pride. Together they had traveled from twenty-one countries, were throwaways who had come from tenements and alleyways, mud-huts and haydike block houses. They had lived scattered lives of slow time, played games with rocks in the streets. They'd learned to sing on their own, and to dance. Never tasting candy, never bathing. Their feet had grown wide and leathery and hard and flat and indestructible. The girls had built headdresses out of paper bags and veils out of fishnets. Some turned clusters of corn stalks into bouquets and alleys into aisles. The merchants would run them off, and the soldiers too and they would assemble behind the butchers shop and saunter among the fats and the skins and the flesh, making their living by breeding sympathy with their dirty blouses and trousers, their nimble, dried up fingertips, their tears and their beatdown faces.

At least that was what Sissy liked to think about, how low they had started and how far they had come. Now, Sissy thought, their smiles blend together into one.

Tip knew the joy it gave his sister to begin the morning at Tenpenny, though he didn't share in her illusions. He stood on the short stone wall by the washer pits certain that bread cannot save children and that his job was far from over.

Putt alone heard Tip whisper, "Love them, Sissy. But for their sake and not our own."

It was customary for the final report to come from the oldest cabin, known to the children as High Hopes. When the time came for him to report, Jack looked up at Sissy and said nothing.

Sissy scanned the stables once again, "High Hopes? Cabin report?"

Jack sighed, "One horse in the barn, Ma'am."

"One horse?"

"Yes ma'am."

"Guess you don't want breakfast, Mr. Oakham. Where's your other horse?"

Jack pointed north. "He went off to graze somewhere, Ma'am."

"Well, well, well. Once again no breakfast for High Hopes. One horse in the barn. One jackass in the pasture. Thank you."

Jack couldn't help but smile. In regards to his Aunt Sissy his day was already going according to plan.

One by one Sissy sent each of the cabins to the dining hall. Smithson held the door open for the children to enter and there wasn't a word spoken as each of them found their tables.

The food bins were steaming with bowls of eggs and pans of coffee cake. Gallon jugs of juice and milk were set out on the countertops. Once the crowd had gathered Tip, Jack and Sissy stepped just inside the door.

Sissy leaned in to her brother, "I suppose you don't know where he is either," she said.

Tip looked up. He knew in the springtime Henry was a new problem, a reckless, unpredictable force that, having ebbed in the winter, seemed to grow more roaring and spicy with each new spring. He was like a bull moose in rut in those first days; even when his mind said no his body took him to unguarded territory.

"It's the start of spring," he told her. "Who Henry is and where Henry is go together."

Sissy shook her head and headed off to breakfast, "You always have an answer."

Jack followed his aunt into the dining hall but instead of finding a seat he climbed up on the small stage front and center. The dozen cooks faced him from their stations and the children from their tables and there was no sound among them. When he began singing the children joined in:

"Oh, The Lord is good to me! And so I thank the Lord,
For giving me, the things I need, the sun and the rain and the appleseed.
The Lord is good to me!"

He prayed for the meal and thanked the cooks and when they were all silent Jack released the children to fetch their breakfast. They swarmed the cubbies like locusts. Now the dining hall was loud with chatter. The children were passing biscuits across the tables and singing songs and shoveling triple helpings of greasy bacon into their mouths. They were more joyful than they had been in weeks as they heard the drip drip of the melting ice from the gutters. They feverishly devoured their meals, in hopes of getting on with their day, for the spring would surely open up fields of play they had been missing.

Tipper stood in the doorway. He loved to watch the children scramble in the morning, especially at the start of spring. Behind him the door squeeked open and he didn't seem startled when a hand touched him gently on the elbow. Tip turned to see Wonderboy standing behind him with a gentle expression. He could see that the little man had something important to say. "Hello, Wonderboy."

"Hello, Mister Tipper."

"How do the roads look?"

"They look fine, Mr. Tipper. To be finished by lunch time." Then the tiny man added, "There's a phone for you, Mr. Tipper."

Jack was walking back from the stage and looked up suddenly when he heard the words. The phone never rang at Tenpenny. There was only one receiver on the entire hill and it was hidden in the office closet behind a stack of books. All of the adoptions were completed first by mail and then in person. Two-way radios were used with all of the surrounding work crews and a short wave for special occasions like dentist visits. In fact Jack could not immediately remember a time when the phone had ever rung.

He looked intently at his father who could not conceal the surprise on his face. Tip thanked the little man and smiled at his son who leaned in, hoping to ask his father a question. But before he could speak they were both startled by the sound of Putt howling at the huge shapes that were approaching from the north.

Henry rode up to the fountain with blood on his hands and ash across his face. The head of the bear hopped with the canter and steam rose from the cavity. The great pike was still bloody down the shaft and Henry held it in the crutch of his arm as he reigned the horses. Jack and Tipper stepped out of the dining hall to greet him.

"Well what d'you know? I suppose I was right," Tip stated. "The spring has started!"

"This very morning," Henry agreed. "If I hadn't gotten the jump on him he looked hungry enough to eat me whole."

As Henry dismounted Tip walked up and took the reigns. Then he gripped his son's shoulder in affection. "Congratulations, Henry. I'm glad you're safe."

"Don't go insulting him," Jack suggested. "Henry's anything but safe." To which his father smiled.

Henry loosed the ropes and the bear fell headlong onto the road, the flat thud of his skull sounding on the snow. Jack stood silently, looking on like a dreamer viewing a forgotten piece of time. He and his brother had hunted this bear years before, starting when Jack was thirteen, but since that time his interest in the surrounding wilderness had faded, replaced by the faces on the hill. He couldn't remember that last hunt he had been on, and standing there looking down at the bear Jack couldn't imagine the skill it must have taken to harvest him. Within him rose a humble awe towards his brother.

"D'you see any wolves?" Tip asked.

"I heard some. The elk are moving in."

"I hope you saved your strength. The spring gives us more to chase than bears. Clean this up after you eat. The three of us have to start the spring."

Henry looked his father in the eye. "Yessir."

Tipper handed the horses to Jack and then quickly crossed the road. He stepped inside the office, held the receiver against his chest, and then with a sigh he took the call.

At that moment Sissy stepped up to the scene, an appalled look on her face.

"Ah, Sissy! I was hoping to find you here."

"You ran down our two best horses?" Sissy asked. "On the morning you're to haul the pines?"

"We have others," Henry answered. "Any one is stout enough for the pine haul."

"Others you forgot to feed."

"I'll get around to it. Or you will. Big Sister you're too fond of the way things are suppose to go. Here I chase a plan Jack and I had as kids and all you have to say is, what about them horses? Well I'm proof that the melt has started. I for one have had enough laborin' over details for one winter."

"That isn't proof of nothing except itself."

Henry cut in a circle around the shoulders, leaving a long sleeve of fur on the bear's forelegs. "Jack and me aren't all that different, Sissy. We both wanted this bear. Want's almost everything. Jack would have come along with me if we could get him to act his age."

"Like you do?"

As he spoke Henry straddled the bear and drew his skinner along the pelt. "I'd say that'd be a start. Duty over authenticity is no way to live, Sissy. Jack takes so much responsibility on himself he doesn't have any room left to be himself."

Jack smiled and cleared his throat, "I'd say you're authentic enough for both of us."

Henry rolled the carcass over and was stripping the hide with the bone handle.

Sissy looked at her nephew in disgust. "What on earth are you doing, Henry?"

"What's it look like, Big Sister?"

"Madness," she told him.

Henry worked the skinner around the neck and divided the pelt down the center of the bear, stripping the fat away.

"You know I've been giving our discussion quite a bit of thought lately."

"Have you?"

"We've never been what I'd call 'bosom buddies' but that shouldn't obstruct us from civility. Guys like me don't really have buddies anyway - but civility - now that's something I *can* have."

Angrily she shrugged as Henry pulled the hide clear from the ribs. "What's your point, Henry?"

"The point is you were right and I was wrong. Never look a gift horse in the mouth. Sound wisdom I'd say. Jack could you hold that?" Henry handed his brother the knife.

Once again Henry rolled over the carcass and made one final tug with his shoulders. The hide was torn free, though blood and fatty tissue still clung to the pelt.

"This is my gift to you, Sissy. I made it myself. Here's your sweater."

He presented her the bearskin, a great hole in the spine and before she could respond Henry said, "Imagine how much fun I'll have if you try to return it."

Before she could blink Henry was scaling the archway like a monkey. Sissy held the heavy skin at arms length but didn't drop it, afraid to splatter blood on her shoes. At the top of the archway Henry slipped the spear back in place in the iron fittings. The tip would remain red throughout the spring.

"You're a barbarian, Henry Snow!"

"But an authentic one!" he answered. He leapt down onto the snow. "Deal's a deal, Sissy," and then he winked at her and marched on the dining hall.

"You missed morning flag," she called after him. "You don't get breakfast if you miss morning flag!"

The two of them continued to argue as Henry marched toward the dining hall and Sissy followed him with the bearskin. But Jack was no longer amused. He let their voices fade away. He wanted to follow them inside and steal a quick bite. After all Jack had been thinking about breakfast ever since his feet hit the stone floor that morning. But Jack knew it would set a poor example for the youngsters if he ate right in front of them, even if Henry was doing the same. After all Jack Oakham felt it was his duty to never scar his example. He enjoyed the feeling of being looked up to, if only by children.

He stood with the horses, watching curiously as his father talked on the phone through the office window. The morning was over and any thoughts he had for his mother would have to wait until tomorrow. Now Jack was thinking of Momma Tom, patient for him to bring fresh milk for the foal. He thought of Padibatakal and Greer, the two girls who tugged at his heart. Jack still had to decide which girl would be the first he brought breakfast to that morning.

Jack asked the old dog, "Where to now, Putt?"

But as he asked the question the sound of the words gave Jack a jolt. It was a question Jack knew he would ask himself for many years to come, when he wasn't sure of who he was or when he didn't know if he could handle the life of a shepherd.

2. Melting Snow, Melting Hearts

By the time breakfast had started Tip Holland had already hung up the telephone. He stood silently in the hallway for a moment, cradling his face in his hands. But if someone had been standing there watching the scene unfold the next thing they would have witnessed was something none of them had never seen before: for in the following moment Tip Holland began to sob uncontrollably. His shoulders rose as he took one full breath and on the exhale he seemed to crumble beneath his grief. His body shook against the wall and his tears covered his face until he mopped them away. He remained silent, however, afraid that some loose child may hear his cries and become afraid. They mustn't see this, he thought. It's the first day of spring and they mustn't know anything at all.

He remained idle in his tears for only a moment before he moved back to his office, a place that he rarely visited, and quickly went to work.

Tipper was still shaking as he unlocked a safe beneath his desk and from it removed a stack of letters and a heavy manila folder. Carefully he thumbed through each letter, making certain he hadn't forgotten one and when he was satisfied he stuffed them in his tattered knapsack that hung on the wall.

He placed the folder on his desk and opened it. Tip stood as he read, mulling over the pages with a pen briefly before he smiled and signed his name.

He could hear children's songs coming from the dining hall as he took a single sheet of paper from his desktop. There were sudden tears in his eyes but he managed to sing along.

My Dearest Sistine,

You have found me much changed and I thank you for forgiving the sins of my youth. I assure you none of them were owed you. What I do owe you is an unretreating love for how you have cared for these little ones who have given me so much hope. How marvelous are the young. How unspoiled their appetites for joy and goodness despite their pain and frailty. I wish I had your innocence so I could feel closer to them. What little I ever had I squandered. Sister, there will be many questions brought to you in the coming weeks and few answers to give. I apologize for the inconvenience my absence will bring you. I don't know of what good an explanation would do so I won't attempt to give one. Simply know that you have been an essential ingredient in healing me these many years, and that I leave Tenpenny in your care until further notice. I have taken my dear sons with me so that they may help me see something through to the end. They will inform you as to what comes next. I remain your loving and indebted brother, Tip.

He sealed the envelope and placed it in his knapsack, making sure to set it aside from the rest. He locked the safe with the folder inside and walked out into the morning air with his knapsack over his shoulder.

He took the stack of letters to the mailroom but quickly realized that everyone had headed to breakfast. Tip wrote a note to the mail clerk, a boy named Sulowese, asking him to deliver the letters the following day. Then he left the stack behind, keeping Sissy's note with him as he moved on down the hill.

"What a wild turn," he said aloud. There was no one around. The road, the fields, the cabins were quiet. He looked on them, remembering the placement of each stone. He walked down the road observing every detail of the place, trying to recall how it had come together. When he entered his own cabin, a small single-room dwelling near his sons, the place seemed strangely unfamiliar to him, as if he had never been there, and had no reason to be. Tip moved as in a dream, sluggish from the thoughts in his head. He scanned the tiny cabin, the first he had ever built, and was suddenly visited by a flood of memories. He could see his sister sweeping the floor, and Padibatakal, still a babe, trying to stand in her crib in the corner. There were the long days of the first winter when he thought for hours on how to find Henry and Jack. There were faces that had come and gone, a heartache every time.

Tip shook himself loose of the memories. He knew he had much to do and not much time to do it. He quickly set his pack on his bed and stuffed it with gear he knew he would need. He thought carefully about the journey ahead. This journey is my life's work, he said to himself and he wondered if he was ready.

Lastly he grabbed his travel journal, the one he had written in for many years while on the road. He stuffed it in his pack and turned toward the door and just then he thought of Padibatakal, and her long awaited dream to be in the saddle. He almost began to cry again as he envisioned how disappointed she would be.

As Tip walked up the hill toward the dining hall he could soon smell the food and hear the sounds of the children eating. It wasn't long before they were aware of him. There came a great cry among the crowd, "Tipper! Tipper!" ringing out for him to join them. He smiled gently and came their way.

II.

Jack had decided to go see Momma Tom first. After his brother had ruined his chance at breakfast Jack wanted to calm down and he knew that no one calmed his nerves like Momma Tom.

He asked the cooks to fill up three helpings of eggs and biscuits, but no bacon, for none of the women he was serving enjoyed the crispy taste of hard tack. Jack poured coffee for Greer, tea for Momma Tom, and low pulp juice for the girl. He warmed a bottle of milk for the foal and thanked the cooks. Then he carried the breakfast tray in his hands and Putt stayed close behind.

Jack was never happier than when he was alone in his own thoughts, with the old dog beside him. Every time Jack delivered breakfast to Momma Tom, he thought back on the events of his early life. It was a habit he had only developed recently, but one that he couldn't bring himself to break. His mother had been right; Momma Tom had loved him, and he loved her back. And just like he did every day Jack thought of his mother's hair as he approached the tiny cabin. There was still much that Jack didn't know about his mother's relationship to Momma Tom, in fact he barely knew anything at all. Over the years he had come out and asked her repeatedly, "How did you know my mother?" or "Where did you two meet?" but each time the answer was always the same, "Your father will tell you when the time is right."

Jack wasn't certain when the time would be right, but unlike most of his peers he was a patient boy and he knew Tipper must have his reasons. He stepped up to the tiny cabin just glad to have someone who still reminded him of his mother.

"Open her up, would ya?" Jack whispered to Putt.

Without hesitating the old dog nuzzled the door jamb and pushed his way inside. Momma Tom had the foal across the bed, feeding her from the bottle. The girl was beaming with excitement.

"Good morning, ladies."

"Ah, there you are," Momma Tom smiled. "We were wondrin when you'd get here. We heard the workers a breakin' up the road."

"Yes Ma'am the spring has started. They're breaking up the pack and then we'll be off to the pine haul."

Jack turned towards Padibatakal who looked up at him with full eyes. He could feel her gaze penetrating him, beyond friendship or simple admiration. The girl longed to hear every new word fall from his lips and he could see it in the way she looked at him, and as always it played tricks on his heart.

Jack didn't feel the same tug towards Padibatakal that he felt when Greer was around. This girl was no beauty and she never would be. But what lay beyond the surface always gave him pause. To Jack's mind Padibatakal seemed like the most innocent creation on the face of the earth; innocent and indestructible - like a cherubim sent down to remind men of such qualities. Jack couldn't help but be reminded then and there how much he admired every tender gesture she displayed. He didn't know if his feelings would continue to grow, but Jack sensed that at the very least he and Padibatakal would be dear friends for life.

However every time Jack ran that thought through his head he was reminded of a speech his father had given him. "When a man is married there is little room left for another female companion," Tip told him once. "It blurs the lines for your wife and can be reckless to her heart. Only a rare and unique friendship between a man and a woman can survive one of the two being married. So rare in fact that I can't bring one to mind."

Jack didn't know if he could marry the girl, but her place in his heart was unmistakable and if he did ever marry another, he felt it would be his right to fight year after year for his friendship with Padi.

"Do you have time to play?" asked Momma Tom. On the table beside the bed was a wooden chessboard turned towards him. The two had a habit of playing almost every morning.

"I'd love to," he told her. "But breakfast is almost over and I still have to take Greer her meal. Tomorrow we'll have two games."

"One for me and one for Mumsie," she answered. "I've been teaching her."

"Fair enough," he said. "But you'll have to take it easy on me, Padi."

The girl liked it when he called her Padi. "I will," she said shyly and watched as he turned to go.

"I'll see the two of you tonight at the Pow-Wow. Let's go, Putt," he said and headed out the door.

Padibatakal watched through the small window as Jack walked up the road. "Do you really think the spring is on?" she asked.

Momma Tom was cleaning the foal with a wet rag. She shook her head, knowing she was being baited. Padibatakal would do just about anything to hear someone else say Jack's name. The question was only a ruse. However Momma Tom had no intention of denying her the pleasure.

"Well I'd say so. Jack told us right here that the roads were cleared. You itchin' to do some ridin'?"

Padi looked out the window, her face aglow. She couldn't remember being more excited. All that week she had imagined the coming days and what they would bring. She pictured herself atop Jack's horse, Jack leading the mount through the paddock. She didn't have any illusions about how long it would take for her to adjust to the feeling. She had watched dozens of kids who had learned to ride right before her eyes and she knew it wouldn't all happen in a day or two. Truth was, she didn't want that. She wanted it to last a long, long time.

"Yes, Mumsie, I imagine the spring is here alright. Momma Tom done knew it when Henry stole those horses this mornin'."

"You did?"

"Well sure I did. Henry has a nose for the spring. I knew that and I know me some other things."

Little Padibatakal sat back and rubbed the ears of the colt. The little horse was showing signs of life now, his eyes beginning to follow the conversation.

"What other things do you know?" the girl asked.

"Well it's no mystery. Those eyes of yours go aflutter every time he's here."

"Momma Tom?"

"Yes'm."

"What's in the Wild West End?"

Momma Tom was clearly surprised. It was the last thing she expected the girl to say. After all their time together she had finally mentioned the girl's fondness for Jack and Padi didn't even flinch, instead she wanted to know about some forrest. Suddenly a great many thoughts entered Momma Tom's head, "What do you want to know for?"

"I've just been thinking of it."

"Well it's a strange place to just *think* about, Mumsie."

"Sounds like a wild and beautiful place," she said. "I think I'd like it. I think I'd like to sit beneath those trees and listen to the wind rock the branches."

"Well I think you need to focus on riding that horse, Mumsie. The only thing in the Wild West End is responsibility."

Padibatakal didn't seem to know what that meant, and she didn't really care to. She preferred to think of the place in simple terms. For her it was a gift waiting to be opened and now that the spring was on, she was certain her wait was almost over.

III.

As hard as she tried, Greer could never get excited when Jack came around to see her. She knew without a doubt that Jack Oakham was the best thing for her; he was gentle and encouraging, patient and thoughtful, all of the things that she should have wanted in her life. Greer was still very young, but she had lived enough to know how rare those qualities were in any man, but particularly a young man. However alongside all the rest of it, Jack brought with him a sadness for his mother that Greer couldn't tolerate. The last thing she wanted was to share sad stories. What she needed was to move on, something that was proving difficult in a place like Tenpenny.

Greer was the last surviving member of the Ashby clan, a family that Tipper adored who had lived on Tenpenny Hill for many years. Greer's father had been a dentist and brought his wife and children to live in Tenpenny when Greer was still a child. They had made a happy life together, and Greer, Jack and Henry had all grown up as friends. But just six months prior a heated argument ensued between Greer and her parents and so violent was their disagreement that Greer decided to stay home while her family chartered a plane for their yearly vacation.

The plane crashed shortly before landing, leaving Greer confused and alone to wallow in her grief. For a brief time she had run away to a town north of Tenpenny, hoping that new surroundings would help to ease her burden. But after two days Tipper found her and brought her home and did his best to provide her with the support that she needed.

Now her days were filled with one heartbreaker after another, listening to the little ones cry it out, each one reminding her of the family she had lost. When Jack came around to see her Greer knew that he longed to comfort her, but every time he tried she could see in Jack's eyes a hopefulness that she dreaded. Greer didn't want Jack to be hopeful. She didn't want him to look on her any longer with eyes that said, "I can heal you. You can heal me, too." Truth was Greer had little desire to heal. What she wanted was to move on, to be around people who brought her no questions, who never talked of their past, and never asked about hers. And it was for this reason alone that Henry Snow had won her affections.

The day she arrived back at Tenpenny, after the funeral, she knew within the first hour that Henry would give her what she wanted. The Tenpenny family had embraced her, circling up with words and looks of sympathy, all of them threadbare. Greer felt that such scenes were all an act, that people who absorbed the grief of others were putting forth too much effort. When Henry Snow walked through the door she had expected him to do the same.

Instead Henry paid her no more attention than he would have if he had just passed her in the street. He offered no sympathetic glances, gave no council. He didn't speak softly or hold her hand. Greer noticed immediately that he was the only person on the hill who did nothing out of the ordinary. He actually went as far as to steal food from her plate when he noticed that she wasn't eating.

"Have enough?" she said.

Henry shrugged. "You had your chance."

From day one Henry seemed oblivious to her tragedy, treating her as if nothing had changed. Everyone else had offered their services, and because Henry didn't, his were the ones she wanted. Soon Henry had swept her off her feet without even trying, and without Greer having the chance to put up a fight. By the time Jack arrived with her breakfast that morning, Henry and Greer's love had been lived in secret for many months.

Jack knocked on her door as quietly as he could, in case she had been napping. He knew her to be an early riser, in fact she almost never slept. Still, he didn't want to barge in and risk waking her, or worse disturb her when she wasn't decent. He rapped gently on the door and Greer knew immediately who it was. Only Jack would be so careful.

"I'm here," she told him. "You can just come in."

Jack walked inside, careful with the tray. He was already light in the head. One of the only things that Jack and his brother agreed upon was that Greer was the prettiest gal around - though Tip chose to remain dubious.

"There's a whole world to see," he told them. "A world filled with beautiful things. Don't hang your hat on just one."

Yet despite his council Jack at least admitted that he saw nothing of the world that compared with the blooming girl down the hill. Her sunny hair and late freckles were heartbreaking.

He smiled as he stepped in to see her. The first thing Jack felt whenever he was about to see Greer was excitement. Each feeling that followed was more unpleasant. He was well-aware that he was not to her what she was to him. Jack felt that he needed only to try harder. He couldn't imagine how kindness and gentleness wouldn't win her heart.

"How are you today?" he asked. "Feeling better?"

The girl gave him all the smile she could manage. "That's two questions, Jack. It's better not to start a morning with two questions. Better to spread them out across a day."

Jack delighted at the thought of asking questions of Greer for an entire day, though he knew it wasn't an invitation. "I'm sorry."

"Don't be sorry. Just ask one at a time. For your sake I'll tell you that I *am* feeling better, but as for how I am - I'm still pretty low, Mr. Oakham."

"I'm sorry," Jack said again. He found that he apologized to Greer several times a day, a habit that he was trying to break. "Still I'm glad you're better than before."

But the girl didn't seem glad. She sat with a glossy look.

Jack set the tray on the bedside table. He watched her only briefly before pulling up a chair. Greer made no considerations for his presence. She didn't even glance at him. When enough time had passed Jack told her, "Henry got his bear."

But Greer seemed not to hear him. She sat chewing her fingernails. She had little interest in the adventures that Henry got himself into. It was what he didn't do and didn't say that Greer cared about. There was nothing about the bear that she cared to hear.

"Oh did he?"

"Just as he said he would," Jack told her. "My aunt is in a huff about the whole thing."

Greer knew that Jack wouldn't leave until she engaged him in conversation. He wasn't the type to end a meeting on a bad note. As she sat hearing only the echoes of his words Greer suddenly had an idea. She felt the desire to test a theory she had developed only days before when she and Henry had been talking about Jack.

Henry had succeeded at cheering Greer up ever since they were children because he always ignored her when she turned blue. Henry knew it was the only way. But Jack of course was the opposite. He would go out of his way in his attempts to lift her spirits. It became so plain to her that finally she sat down with Henry and asked him, "What d'you think he'd do if I just played sad all the time?"

"He'd play happy to pull you out of it," Henry told her. "That Oakham doesn't go for sadness. He can't just sit around and watch someone drown."

"Whereas you can?"

"Only if it's you," he admitted. "With you it makes you happy."

Greer was fond of Jack but when it came to making sense of people she believed he was a very slow learner. She decided to see if he could be played as easily as Henry suggested.

Greer turned to Jack seriously, "I wonder if there's any good news anywhere," she said out of nowhere.

Jack looked puzzled. Greer often came up with the strangest things to say. "What d'you mean?"

"I mean I can't imagine it. I can't imagine a bit of good news. What would that news be?"

Jack knew that Greer was near the bottom again. She'd had a habit of getting low from time to time ever since they were children. Now that her parents were gone it was happening with more regularity and it worried Jack more and more.

"There's plenty of good news," Jack said, believing it. "You have to know where to look for it."

"You don't know either."

"I don't?"

"So tell me."

Jack felt deep down that the ability to see life positively was one of his strengths. He believed in his heart that if he tried hard enough he could make anyone look at the bright side, though it had never worked with Greer. It seemed that the harder Jack tried with her, the more negative she became, a habit that he never understood, however it didn't keep Jack from believing in himself.

"Okay I'll tell you this," Jack said. "Momma Tom's foal is getting stronger."

"You and I both know it won't make it."

"I don't *know* that even if you *think* that. I do know that Tip has plans to get Padibatakal in the saddle."

Greer had a great love for Padibatakal, moreso than for anyone else on the hill. She didn't want to say anything ugly about her chance to ride a horse. "It's only good news after it happens," she said.

Jack could see he was getting nowhere. He watched her closely when he said. "I know you'll be glad to know the spring is on."

Greer perked up when she heard that news, though she tried to hide it. This certainly was something she was glad to hear. She had been expecting the spring to arrive every day for the past two weeks. The winter had been so hard and so long that she thought it might never break. In fact she hadn't known a warm day since the death of her family. She turned to peek behind the curtained windows. "Are you sure?" she asked. "How do you know it isn't just a warm spell?"

Well she just asked two questions, Jack thought, but he kept the observation to himself. "There are ways to tell but I don't know them," he admitted. "I think something happens with the trees. Tipper's the one who says when it breaks."

Greer Ashby took a deep breath that ended with a smile. "So it's warming up?" she asked.

Jack was excited by her change of mood. It was the happiest he had seen her in a very long time. "Every day," he said. "They expect the snow will be gone within a week."

"A week?" Greer seemed to dance in her bed. "That means the roads will be cleared well before then?"

"The roads will be cleared today," he told her. "They may be already."

Greer could feel her strength coming back to her. "Oh, how I feel!" she sung. "You wanna know how I feel, Jack? Well now I feel stupendous. As dad used to say, 'WOMP', 'World on my platter'!"

"Well I'm happy that you're happy." Which was true. Jack was very happy all of the sudden. "I guess you can imagine good news after all."

Greer ignored the comment. She ignored her meal as well, one that she had been anxiously awaiting all morning. She couldn't take her mind off the spring. "Oh thank you, thank you, thank you, thank you." She blew Jack kisses and smiled continuously. Before he knew it she had climbed out of bed and began gathering her things.

"What are you doing?"

She dug through a drawer. "I'm getting ready."

Jack had never expected that his news would bring such a reaction. Greer had expressed her love for the spring before, but never like this. "Greer, getting ready for what? The Doc won't let you leave just because the sun comes out."

"When he sees me he will. When he sees me he'll let me go this afternoon. You wait."

Jack was clearly excited by the conversation. He hadn't spoken this much with Greer for several months. He was often frustrated by how much of his heart he shared with her, and how little she gave in return. To see how excited she was, and to know that he was the only one allowed to see it gave Jack a much needed jolt to his confidence. "Well maybe when the Doc lets you out we can go riding together."

"Or maybe I can finally leave Tenpenny for good."

The statement made Jack's spirit's fall to the floor. He thought hc had misheard her.

"What?"

"Oh Jack, I'm sorry. That was rude. I'd love to go riding with you."

"But what d'you mean?"

"Nothing really. I just wanna start a new life. Far from here."

Jack had never considered such a possibility. Tenpenny was his home, and he assumed everyone loved it as much as he did.

"What d'you wanna do that for?" he asked painfully. "Life seems more than fair around here."

"I don't want *fair*, I want *new*."

Jack found it hard to believe that someone would want to leave on their own free will. Yet as he watched Greer stuff her clothes in her handbag Jack had to admit that she looked happy and free. His voice shook. "Where would you go?"

"Anywhere. I'll ask one of the island kids where to go. I can tell you this, though, it'll be somewhere I won't have to wait for the sun to shine half the year."

Jack was clearly upset. He didn't care for her disrespecting his home. "What would you do, then, on your island?"

"I don't know," she admitted. "I'd live. There's more to life than a bunch of sad children, Jack."

Jack knew that Greer didn't mean what she said. She had loved on the orphans for years before she had become one. "They aren't sad, they're broken," he told her. "And as far as finding a happy life, you could do a lot worse than Tenpenny. These kids themselves are proof of that."

"Is that all you think about, Jack? How much worse I could do?"

"That didn't enter my mind," he said. "But I've lived far from this place and you haven't and I think you'll be disappointed when you do."

Jack was bolder than he had ever been with her. She liked it immediately.

"More disappointed than I am now? You came here to get healed Jack, and your wounds have healed. For me Tenpenny is the wound."

Just then Jack heard the bell ring. The children could be heard bursting from the dining hall to their cabins.

"No more ringing bells," she said. "No more stories to hear. Just new faces and new places. Maybe a new name."

Jack turned to leave. Greer couldn't help but watch him suffer. It was the kindest thing he'd ever done.

"I have to go," he whispered.

"Jack, not yet you don't. Tell me about the bear. Tell me about Padi."

"I have to go."

Truth was he was *glad* to go. He didn't know what else to say. He didn't want to listen to any more of her talk. Part of him wished that when he walked out he would never see her again. Jack realized that there was very little about this girl that he understood. He knew that she was heartbroken, and unhappy, and that he was painfully in love with her, but

100

other than that she remained a mystery, one that he now feared he may never get to solve.

"I would still love to ride with you," she told him.

He nodded as though he hardly seemed to care. His mind was elsewhere. It had left him and all that Jack knew was that he had his responsibilities to tend to, his dog waiting outside the door.

"I thank you for breakfast, Jack," she told him. "And the good news, too."

But he didn't say a word. He closed the door behind him and ruffled the ears of the old dog. Jack kept his hand gently on the back of Putt's head, wondering to himself how long he would still have that feeling.

3. The Last Hours of Boyhood

If Tipper had any intention of letting the onset of spring change his schedule, he didn't show it. As soon as the children had finished cleaning their tables Tip was right where he was supposed to be, seated on a low stool, sipping from his mug. It was their custom for the Tenpenny three to circle around the checker tables near the office and discuss their plans for the day over coffee. They called it their Mohican meeting. The children were divided into cabins by their assigned tribe, either Cherokee or Choctaw, but after Tip had been asked countless times by the children which tribe he belonged to, he finally answered, "I am a Mohican," thinking of his two sons as the same.

As the children spread out to their stations the three would gather at the tables and discuss their docket for the day, each with their coffee in hand. Henry rarely drank his, choosing instead to hold it up to his face and smell it as it steamed, but it never stopped Tip from brewing him a cup, and making it up as he liked it just in case he chose to drink.

Jack was already seated beside his father letting the old dog lick coffee from his fingers. Like every other time Henry was late, Putt had been watching Henry's mug carefully, nudging closer and closer in hopes of stealing a lick. Although Jack would have loved to let the dog slobber around the edge of Henry's mug, in revenge for spoiling his breakfast, he knew Tip would disapprove of vengeance, so he dipped his fingers in his own coffee to let Putt have a lick.

"Now don't take my fingers off. They won't taste too good."

Putt seemed to say, "If you gave me the whole cup you wouldn't have to worry."

"No, if I did that you'd expect some every day."

Putt promptly licked his jowls and Jack heard him say, "What's wrong with that?"

To which he answered, "You're spoiled enough as it is, that's what."

Tip watched the exchange curiously, realizing that Jack was fully engaged with the old dog, in word and in action. He couldn't recall knowing anyone else who talked to a dog that way. He wondered when and why it had started.

Henry finally arrived with his hair wet, wearing a fresh set of clothes, something Henry tried to do at least a couple of times a week. In this way he and Tip were very similar. They expressed little concern for maintaining their appearance. That morning Henry was donning an old pair of tattered shorts, something he was known to do the first of every spring, despite the still frigid temperatures. Once he put them on, he usually didn't switch back to long pants until the following winter, unless he knew he was going to be in the saddle for any length of time. Henry found his seat in the circle, and as he lifted the mug up to his face Tip noticed that Henry's knee was badly swollen. Probably got that on his hunt, Tip thought.

"Well the spring is officially on as of this morning," Tip announced, clearly excited. "We may have another snow in the next week but nothing that will set us back too much."

"How we comin' so far?" Jack asked.

"Smithson is about finished with the roads. Wonderboy is rigging the remuda for the pine haul. The rest of the crew is scattered around with their lists."

Henry chimed in, "And the three of us will be moving pines until supper time! So buckle up!"

There was an acceptable contempt in Henry's voice that Tip didn't mind. He ignored his son's remark. He knew that moving felled pines on the first day of spring wasn't the brothers' idea of fun, but that the pine haul was a most necessary beginning to their dry month projects. He also knew that a season of fun was in store for Henry and Jack unlike any they had known before.

"It's progress time, Tip!" Henry continued. "A season of moving forward and taking new ground! Say Talleyho to all the stale ways cause we're pressing on to new country!" Henry rocked in his seat and shook his hands, clearly mocking Tip when he got excited. His father had to admit that it was a much deserved imitation. He had a habit of growing excitable every spring when the pine haul began, mostly because new pines meant new cabins, and new cabins meant progress. And for Tip Holland, nothing motivated him quite as powerfully as progress. He was known to sit awake at night, thinking of ways to take new ground on Tenpenny Hill, and to rise the following morning with a solution. The springtime represented an open floodgate for four months of festering ideas toward progress. His sons consistently noted that as hard-working as Tip was on an average day, when the spring was finally on, his energy level seemed to double.

"So it's go go go, boys! We won't stop til sunset!" Henry said. Then he instantly sat back in his seat, slumped down and transformed his excitable expression to one that was tired and lackluster. "So," he said slowly. "Where are we starting up?"

"Is that me?" Tip asked Jack with a smile. "Do I really say 'talleyho'?"

"Every year."

Tip gave a chuckle. "Well this year we'll start on the westerwing. We may have enough on that side for one cabin."

The boys nodded.

"We *will* be hauling pines for the better part of the morning, but not all day."

The brothers faced each other, clearly surprised.

"I expect we'll finish in the warm of the afternoon," Tip continued. "We'll eat lunch out there and be back in time for afternoon optional."

Jack turned away. The mention of lunch made Jack Oakham light in the head.

"If the melt continues the kids will be sure to want some time on the fields. Jack you're in charge of Campbell with the older guys - Henry I'd like to see you down below with the younger ones."

The boys nodded, Jack fighting his hunger by slurping his coffee.

"There are two new kids arriving this afternoon," Tip said. "Make sure to introduce yourselves, include them if possible."

"Want us to show 'em around?" Henry asked. He loved touring new kids around Tenpenny. It usually took hours and all he had to do was talk.

"No. I've already asked Momma Tom to do it. But keep an eye out. A word from either of you would sure give 'em a boost."

But Tip knew it wasn't a necessary thing to say. One of his favorite traits about these two boys was how welcoming they were to new children, especially Henry. Henry Snow had an undeniable gift for making strangers feel right at home. One could believe after only a minute with Henry that he was on their side, and that their side was finally a safe and happy one.

"Tonight of course we'll have our little spring pow-wow followed by the ice cream social," Tip said. "Henry I want you to wear a shirt this time. Then I need you both to get a full night's sleep. The spring will start early in the morning. Do either of you have anything?"

Henry raised his hand. He didn't look excited for what he was about to say. "I heard some in that soccer bunch talking about the slough lady again. Some of the young-uns seemed pretty scared."

Tip shook his head. It was a rumor that had persisted long enough. He didn't care for rumors of any kind, especially those that frightened children. "I'll address it tonight," he said. "Anything else?"

The brothers shrugged. "Well Wonderboy is already at the westerwing waiting for us so let's get there and give him a hand."

"Yessir."

"Before we do, Henry, I want you to get up to the doc and have that knee looked at."

"It ain't nothin'."

"Maybe so but the spring is on and things are about to get heavy. Come find me at the pine haul when you're done."

"Yessir," he said, retying his hair atop his head and heading towards the nurse's station. He left his full coffee mug steaming on the table.

Tip stood with his hands on his hips. He scanned the land surrounding the overlook to the river. He enjoyed standing quietly with Jack.

"I figure we can fit two more cabins down there by those oaks and a third on the shelf I showed you by the mini-golf. What d'you think?"

Jack puzzled over that for a moment, having never been asked that question before.

"Well I don't know."

Tip walked over to the road. "You think it'll be enough room?"

"I suppose it will."

Then he added, "What are the cabins for?"

"What do you think we need?"

"We need more shovels," Jack said. "We need more fishing poles."

"I was thinking we'd build Momma Tom her own new place, the one there on the shelf. And we'd have a room just for Padi with a view of the river and the horses, with a big low window she could see out from her bed."

"She'd like that," Jack said.

"What would you like, Jack?"

Jack shrugged his shoulders. He rarely gave it any thought. "That'd be all," he told him. "Just that and some lunch I guess."

II.

Henry Snow knew there was nothing wrong with his knee, but he didn't mind moseying down to the Doctor to sneak a peak at Greer. Henry spent very little time in the nurse's station and he knew she would be surprised to see him.

When Henry entered he could see that the Doctor was as busy as ever. The waiting room was filled with cots and chairs, all of them heavy with unhappy children. Those who were aware enough to notice smiled when Henry arrived. The small Burmese boy who had broken his nose was seated before the Doctor with a flashlight up his nose and when Henry entered he almost flopped out of his seat.

"Henry, Henry!"

"Hey, champ."

"Hey so Henry I broke my nose! First broken bone! It hurt real bad but I'm tough so I liked it- there was blood everywhere - I bled on the snow – and and the Doc says my nostrils might not line up right! You ever broke anything?"

"Yep. Hurts doesn't it?"

"Sure does!"

Doctor Zuni turned to look at Henry. "Well Henry, welcome to the slaughterhouse."

"Morning, Doc."

"You a messenger or a patient?"

"Patient."

Zuni saw the boy's knee the moment he said it.

"I see. Well have a seat while I finish with Stuntman Wei."

"Stuntman Wei!!! Stuntman Wei!!! I'm a stuntman and my name is Wei!!!" The Doc didn't realize he had just created a nickname that the boy would take with him long after his adoption. Zuni held the boy still and shushed him.

Doctor Zuni wasn't really a doctor, although everyone called him Doc. He still had several steps to take to officially become a licensed physician, but he had little intention of taking those steps. Tip had met him late in his journey, in a University library in Pakistan. He noticed the man sitting before a stack of novels by Wister, Grey, and Schaefer, and was instantly deep in conversation. Tip was certain that any Pakistani who loved the American west that much was certain to provide a fruitful conversation.

Zuni had for three years studied pediatric medicine and Tip knew he would need someone to administer care for the children – something Zuni was capable of doing. But the whole truth was that Zuni had come to Tenpenny to finally be a part of the American West.

He had spent his childhood in Pakistan, helping his father and brothers steer herds across the desert from village to village. As a boy he watched from beneath his father's hat as the old-timers bartered with nomadic men they rode to meet, armed at all times.

But when he was still quite young, his father joined the war and died of typhus, and Zuni's life in the saddle ended. He was moved from city to city with his mother and brothers, who were much older than Zuni, and soon took up lives of their own.

The rest of his life he dreamed of getting back to a place where he could live as he had as a child; a life of adventure in the natural order. When Zuni was young he had never met anyone whose life wasn't an adventure. Whole families would migrate through sandstorms, and they would hunt and eat kills on the plains. The old timers he rode with spoke of nothing but the life they had known. The older he got, the more Zuni needed to reconnect with that former life.

He remembered reading dime novels as a teenager, about the "Real American West" where the scenery was wild and there was plenty of timber for building cabins and fires. He often recalled those book jackets showing great bears standing on their haunches, towering over mountain men and their trusty dogs. He had always wanted to live in a mountain cabin, surrounded by trees and wild things, a place where he could walk and fish rivers, and be in touch with a vast, mostly secret part of the world.

As the years passed Zuni became increasingly anxious for he heard throughout his adult life that even the wilderness of America was disappearing. Zuni could never understand how something so big could vanish so quickly. By the time he had met Tip Holland Zuni was well into his sixties and had all but given up on recreating the freedoms of his childhood. He still read when the mood hit him, and a couple of times he toyed with visiting America to see the land. What he wanted though was to be a part of something vast again, to freely dream on the land.

For Zuni, the American Dream had little to do with ambition, or bootstrings, or hard work, though he was a hard enough worker to suit most men. For Zuni, the American Dream had always been woven on the fabric of the land. He believed what he knew of the Constitution to be a fine thing, for a man to speak his mind freely, for equal rights to all, "Fine enough," he said often. "But only nice thoughts without the land."

To find a place where a man could think freely was nothing new for Zuni. He had thought freely all his life. No man could own another's thoughts. What Zuni wanted was a place where he could walk freely, have a summer garden where fruits would grow, be shaded from the sun and be surprised by the changing seasons. Even as a boy he was tired of the sand. "America has no wars visit her borders," he told Tip. "This is because their ideas have been put in place and their ideas have worked. But could those ideas have come from a desert? Or from some great city alone? Or from a singular landscape with one type of vegetation? No. The American people are varied because the land is varied. Those people had hope enough to dream uncommonly because they lived on soil of uncommon possibilities. Most island dreams die before you have marched from beach to beach. One of the main reasons this dream has sustained is because for two centuries the land has seemed endless. America is the only place big enough for the American Dream."

A week later, after he asked Zuni to join him, Tip had warned him that what he had heard was true - it was disappearing, that the dream was changing, as was the land. "I'm almost an old man," Zuni had said. "I doubt it will be gone before I am."

Zuni filled the role of physician, nursemaid and counselor to the dozens of knee scrapes and broken hearts that Tenpenny was certain to facilitate. The Doc had an uncanny ability with children, and never grew tired of his new life. He lived in a cozy cabin overlooking the river, had an endless stream of patients, as well as a deeply met hunger for wilderness living. He performed only minor surgeries, and then only with the help of Tip, who himself knew a thing or two about patching holes.

"Henry, do you ever consider how lucky you are?" Zuni said, thinking about his childhood.

"Never gave it much thought, Doc."

Zuni stopped what he was doing and looked the boy up and down. "Shameful. Then what do you think about?"

Henry smiled, "Sorry, Doc. Guess my mind likes to swim around what's coming more than what's already been."

Henry leaned slightly to his side to see around the doorjamb. Greer was sitting there trying not to smile. Her hair was messy and Henry liked that she didn't mind. There was not a nod or a wave or a wink between them. Greer turned her mouth up at the corners just enough for him to notice and he did the same. In a moment his look turned down to her lips, her knees, her ankles. Greer's eyes stayed locked on his.

One of the injured boys with thick glasses looked up shyly at Henry, "Hi, Henry."

Henry ruffled his hair, "Hey, champ."

"I heard you got your blacky," the Doc said. He was shining a light into the boy's nose, which was still swollen and red. It was a well-known fact throughout Tenpenny that Henry Snow was forever on the hunt for a black bear, a brown bear and a wolf. Henry had made is clear to those around him that he would harvest all three that season.

Henry straightened up. "I did. Time dealt me a winner."

Zuni led the boy off the table and ushered Henry to replace him. He immediately began tapping on Henry's knee.

"How far north was he?"

"Not too far. Tenpenny stretches a lot further south and east than it does North."

"West too."

Greer stood silently and came to the door. She slipped her fingers around the doorjamb and peered out at Henry.

"Well I wouldn't know about that," Henry said.

Only a brief moment passed as Henry and Greer looked softly at one another. She slipped her hand down and passed into the back room, closing the door.

Henry leaned to look, seeing that she was gone.

The doctor looked up, "You know you have a gash and a shiner above your eye there. You should probably clean that."

"Thought I cleaned it when I showered."

"Not quite. Wasn't from the bear was it?" The doc began wrapping Henry's knee with a cotton bandage.

"No sir. This was Jack. Compared to Jack that bear's a piece of cake." Henry sat up and scanned out across the desk. "Where's your hand mirror?"

Zuni cocked his head. "They've all gone missing in the past few days. Use the one behind the door. The little handheld ones have disappeared overnight."

Henry squinted, pursing his lips. "How's she feeling, Doc?"

"Who, Greer?"

"Yessir."

"Greer!" he called. "How are we this morning?"

The two men waited for an answer. Finally the Doctor started wrapping the knee again. "She must have stepped out," he said. "She's feeling fine."

"Those mirrors go missing since she moved in?"

"A little after."

Henry nodded. "She's self-conscious about her scar. That's why."

Like crows feet a small scar spread out to the side of Greer's left eye.

With a wink Zuni conceded. "Right right. I should have thought of that. But the scar is so small you'd hardly notice."

"Men won't but she always will."

Zuni paused. He couldn't remember a day on the hill when Henry Snow had not surprised him. He had known many young men who were years ahead of their peers, but never one like Henry. In Zuni's experience the scales that weighed even strong young men were almost always out of balance. Most who were top athletes had little skill for conversation, and most who lived lives of depth had a shallow list of female companions. But Henry was different. He was lazy, and irresponsible - certainly - but Zuni felt this boy's scales were remarkably well-balanced, especially for someone who had been thrown away by his parents.

"How'd she come to get that scar?" Zuni asked.

Henry sighed. "A man at the junction house gave it to her. A very rich man. If you remember she was living up there before the funeral and this man who owned the junction house, he heard about her looks and came down from Stowington or some other."

"Word gets around."

"Fast up there. As she tells it this Joe Forsman, this man I was saying, he comes in with spiked coffee and she didn't like what he whispered so she called him a name and he smacked her across the face and was gone."

At the sound of the man's name Zuni's attention grew. For years the Doc had heard stories of a Forsman who ruled the cattlelands to the north of Tenpenny, along the Cutshank. The man was said to be getting on in years now, and had for some time sought ownership of Tenpenny. He was a wealthy man, and calculating, and every repairman who came to the orphanage from the surrounding villages had either worked for him or had a strong opinion of him. He was said to be of tall, powerful dimensions, not easily forgotten, and was the former sheriff along the Cutshank, still wearing his polished badge illegally. Rumors about the man were never-ending. It seemed to Zuni that outside of Tenpenny the near world revolved around Joe Forsman.

"Is that *the* Joe Forsman? The cattleman?"

"Same one. Drover driver."

"What a cuss," said the Doc. "What a cuss. Bend your knee for me."

Henry winced slightly.

"Is that better?"

"Like new, Doc."

"What'd she call him?"

"An ACOB."

The Doc smiled. "A what?"

"An ACOB. Classic Ashby. Her father was an acronym man." Henry lowered his voice to a whisper. "Stands for "A Castrated Old Bull.""

The Doc laughed. He wrapped the bandages and fastened them. "She just came out and explained it to him?"

"One way or another he got the point."

"I guess. I'd have loved to have heard that. The way I hear it nobody gets the better of Joe Forsman. She probably doesn't know she made history."

What Zuni had heard exactly was that a decade before a pair of men *had* tried to get the better of Joe Forsman, selling him thirty head of cattle and stealing them back that very night. It was a rumor that those cattle turned up back on Forsman's ranch a week later, but the suspected thieves had never turned up, their own cattle business abandoned in the middle of auction month. The rumor only grew when the father of one of the cattlemen came around asking questions. He moved up to the Cutshank when Forsman was still the sheriff and could find no one to answer his questions, least of all Forsman. After a year the old man abandoned his search and now, a decade later no whisper ever came of the suspected thieves.

"What's your father have you doing this afternoon?" Zuni asked.

"We're moving pines all day."

"Oh yes. Well there's nothing' too awful wrong with this knee. Keep it straight when you can. Ice it tonight."

"I will, Doc."

Henry pulled some hard candies from his pocket and tossed them to the children who were awake. As he left he snuck a peak to see if Greer had come out again. There was no one in the adjacent room but as he passed he noticed that her door was cracked. It was open just enough for her to lay in her bed and watch him.

III.

All that morning the sun beat down on the thin layer of snow pack and little streams formed along the roadways, and down the narrow swales in the hillocks. The hours warmed and the little ones climbed on one another's shoulders and brushed the brittle icicles from their porch nests.

Smithson had the road pack cleared almost a full hour before Tip had expected and soon he and the other workmen went to clear the footpath to the river.

Wonderboy had prepared the horses for the pine haul, a Tenpenny tradition on the first day of spring. The pine haul was performed at least twice annually, with the second usually coming in early summer. All winter the men sorted and chopped trees from the surrounding woods to use for the new cabins they would be building when the snow cleared. Throughout the near country fallen pines lay with their limbs stripped and bright flags attached so they could be spotted beneath the snow.

Wonderboy had brought each of the horses up from the lots and paired them two to a rig, with the exception of the broodmares, four of whom were within weeks of foaling, and the three Pritchers. Jack always loved the sight of twenty-five horses swishing among the snowy pines. He stood quietly in the woods to admire them, as did his father.

"Where are the Pritchers?" he asked.

Pritcher was a name Tip used to describe the choice horses for himself and his sons. Although the entire remuda were saddlebroke, Henry and Jack and Tip each had their favorites, collectively referred to as the "Pritchers". The name had an origin from Tip's travels. Tip had once briefly told his sons of the season he spent in some faraway land, one in which he worked with an accomplished horse master named Matthias Pritcher, an ex-patriot who had hired Tip to clean stalls and be a ferrier once he'd learned the trade. Pritcher himself had been killed by a beautiful Criollo filly, his favorite mount, not long after he and Tip had parted company. When the Tenpenny remuda was established Tip instituted the "Pritcher" tradition immediately, so that he and his sons would never underestimate the power of the wild things that surrounded them.

"I gave them a day off," Tip told him. "Henry ran them pretty hard this morning."

"Yours and his he did," Jack said. "Gopher hasn't been worked in days. Lemme get her saddled."

Jack knew that his mare was the alpha of the remuda and among the most dependable horses they had. It didn't make sense for her not to be working the pine haul, especially with the other two Pritchers in the lots.

"Just leave her," Tip told him. "I promised Padi we'd teach her to ride once the spring was on. Gopher's as good as any for her to learn on."

Jack couldn't argue with that. Gopher had been the horse he had learned to ride on about a year after he'd come to Tenpenny, when the mare was still a three-year-old. He smiled at the thought of teaching the girl how to ride on his favorite horse. The spring had always filled him with surprises like this one.

Henry arrived a few minutes later, giving Tip a thumbs up as he pointed at his knee. The men stretched and fitted themselves with heavy gloves and before long each of them were grunting beneath the weight of the trees.

All that morning the four men rolled pine after pine onto the sleds and Jack steered the horses slowly through the trees. It was hard work, and it wasn't long before the boys were sweating lightly, a feeling that told their senses spring had officially begun.

"Ok, so here's a thought," Henry said.

Jack sighed heavily. "Here we go," he said.

Every year at the pine haul, sometime before lunch, Henry Snow made a speech about how smart of an idea cutting a road through the forests would be. "Now here's the thing about it - I'm not trying to get outta work, hear that right off. Put Wonderboy and me on the butt end of the lifting. All I'm sayin' is that with a road you don't need to hitch a dozen pair of horses to homemade sleds ten times a piece and navigate through all these dern stumps. You simply hitch our ten best to one wagon, take half a dozen trips, no navigation required and we're done by lunchtime."

Usually the other workers ignored this speech, which is what frustrated Henry the most, but this time Wonderboy was prepared.

"Sounded better last year," he said, smiling as always.

Jack and Tip stopped to chuckle. "Oh!!"

Wonderboy rarely made a joke, but when he did he was clearly proud of himself for some time after. He held his smile and looked around to the other's faces so that he could take pleasure in the joy he had brought them. He wouldn't know if Henry had found it funny, but he did notice that Henry's speech was cut short, and never resumed again.

Wonderboy wasn't aware of it, but he was the only individual on Tenpenny hill that Henry Snow was afraid to argue with. Henry could never bring himself to risk ruffling the man who he had such an awe-inspiring respect for. He had worked alongside him everyday for over seven years, joshing him and cutting up like he did with everyone, but he never engaged him in a dispute. When the time was right Henry even took the chance to butt heads with Tip, a man who he both feared and respected. Tip was a man Henry felt he understood very well, despite the uncertainty about how he had become who he was. But Henry was never certain what kind of man Wonderboy was. For Henry Snow, knowing what angered someone was the first step in understanding them. "If I know a man's hot spots," he said more than once, "I can usually fill in the blanks."

Wonderboy was far from a passionless man, Henry knew, but he seemed to never show signs of anger, or anxiety over any circumstance in life. Henry knew that Jack's hotspots were disloyalty, bullying, and injustice, whereas Tip's was easily unnerved when machinery failed. "I would pay ten-thousand dollars for a pen that always worked," Henry had heard him say.

But even though Henry had for many years watched Wonderboy in his daily life, waiting to find a chink in his armor, the moment hadn't come and without the knowledge of what would set him off, Henry couldn't work up the nerve to engage him in an argument. He remained content to respect him without debating him, something that Henry Snow found difficult to do.

Before an hour had passed they had already hauled nearly thirty pines to the mill. The horses were well-practiced and the melting snow made for easy pulling.

To the brothers Wonderboy seemed to work without breathing. As soon as they had loaded a sled to capacity he was always the first man saddled, ready to steer the carriers across the westerwing. And true to form, each time they arrived at the mill, he was always the first to dismount. Yet despite the commitment that Wonderboy was giving to his work, both brothers noticed that for a pine haul, Tip was less enthusiastic than usual. He seemed to be going through the motions. It was unheard of for a pine haul to last only half a day. Even Henry was surprised by the announcement. After an hour they both could see that they wouldn't come close to finishing the haul by the afternoon. It struck Jack the most, his father's change in tempo, but it was soon an issue he had forgotten about. To Jack's great satisfaction they took their lunch early.

As they were pulling a load toward the mill one of the sleds was shattered against a standing pine so Tip called the crew to break for lunch. They sat atop the sleds and devoured their sandwiches, all but Wonderboy who ate his meal neat and tidy.

"You barely eat at all," Henry said to him. "As hard as you work I'd think you'd eat two to my one."

Wonderboy grinned, "No one does that."

Henry grinned back. If he couldn't get him to argue Henry would have to try another tactic.

"How old are you, friend?"

Wonderboy shrugged his shoulders, giving Henry much to think about.

"Well it's prolly better you don't know. If you did and you told me I'd only get embarrassed."

"You never get embarrassed," Jack said kindly. "That's your problem."

"I bet Wonderboy could embarrass me."

"How's that?" Tip asked. He was tired of talk but the statement struck him as curious.

"If I challenged him to wrestle," Henry said. "I mean with all my respect he ain't no bigger than a boy, his top half anyway. But there is no way I could outlast him."

It was a well-known fact that all his life Henry Snow had greatly wished to be an underdog. It wasn't uncommon when Henry stumbled upon improbable odds for him to place himself right in the middle of them. At the moment he was truly convinced that the little man could whoop him.

"Every pine haul he just goes and goes," Henry said. "And I'll bet even money he's older than you, Tip. Am I right?"

Tip knew that Henry *was* right. He had met Wonderboy more than twenty years before and though Wonderboy hadn't changed much over the years, at the time of their meeting he was clearly the older man.

"Could be," Tip said. "But you aren't gonna wrestle. We have pines to haul."

"Then after."

"No sir. I'm too scared you'd get hurt."

"Hurt? I get hurt nearly every day."

Tip looked quietly at the pines. Henry Snow was wearing him thin. It was rare for Tip to lose patience with children, especially his own boys, but he greatly wished for the conversation to change course. There was too much on his mind to think of something as silly as two mismatched opponents wrestling in the snow. But before he could say anything, Jack saved him the trouble.

"You *wanna* get embarrassed?" Jack asked.

"Always have."

Jack shook his head. Some days he didn't understand his brother. The one thing Jack lived to avoid was the thing his brother seemed to be chasing.

"Why would you do that?"

"Because it's worth the risk, Jacko."

"What risk?"

"The risk of feeling beaten for once. Living without losing is boring. The hope that there are people and ways to live out there bigger than me gets me all riled up."

"I don't know of anyone out there bigger'n you, Henry," Jack said. Which was true. To Jack, his brother was as big as they come, in every possible way, few of them good ways.

"You know Smithson," Henry told him.

"He's taller - he ain't bigger."

Wonderboy spoke up, "Mr. Forsman is bigger."

Every worker to a man turned on him with wide eyes. The brothers were truly surprised. Hearing Wonderboy mention anyone or anything outside of Tenpenny was a shock, especially Joe Forsman.

"He is?" Tip asked. Tip knew that Wonderboy had once met the man but he never asked for his dimensions. He had always pictured Forsman to be of a smaller stature.

Wonderboy nodded and left it at that.

"Well how do you know?" Jack wondered. He had never known of anyone who had actually met the man.

Tip turned to his sons, relaying the story.

When the boys were too young to remember, Wonderboy went out to find a lost stallion that Tip had bought the week before. Wonderboy had led the remuda to graze in the northern pasture and when one of the cowpokes they'd hired, a man named Tobin, shot a round at a ptarmigan, the new horse bolted across hills and timbers and out of all knowledge. Wonderboy had spent a full day following the horse's track, determined not to come home without Tip's new roan. The tracks led north to their nearest neighbor and when Wonderboy arrived at a juncture he found the horse with Joe Forsman, haltered and hobbled, about to be loaded into a gooseneck.

"What did you do?" Henry asked him.

"What he should have done," Tip told him. "He turned for home and saved his skin. That horse was on Forsman's land."

The brothers were both shocked by such a statement. Neither one made any effort to conceal it. "So you left it?" Jack asked.

"He had to."

"But what did he say to you?"

Wonderboy had thought often about that. He remembered the words well, though he swore to never repeat them.

"I can't remember," he said, which from Wonderboy seemed perfectly believable.

"Well maybe I should go wrestle him," Henry said. "Get that horse back while I'm at it."

"Nah, he sold it the very next day," Tip told them.

"To who?"

"Some family down in Soldotna."

"Why didn't you buy it back?"

"And pay twice for the same horse?"

"Could've talked to the man about it, couldn't you?" Jack said. He was too fond of horses to let the idea of a stolen one drift from his mind. He was also of the mind that his father could talk to anyone.

"Some men can't hear straight talk, Jack."

"Forget talk," Henry suggested. "There are other ways than talk to make your point."

Tip took a deep cold breath. He didn't care for such comments, especially from his son. "Well Henry, just because a man hands you an offense doesn't mean you have to take it."

The whole business seemed like an offense to Henry: no one to fight or argue with, no allowance to take back what was stolen. He considered the offense truly too big to take, so he didn't. "I guess," Henry answered and nothing more was said.

After lunch the crew was at it again. Tip went to hewing loose branches with his axe as the others loaded the remaining pines of the westerwing. There were still dozens more left to haul from other woods of Tenpenny, but Tip didn't seem to have any interest in working further. He appeared increasingly distracted to his sons. Even Wonderboy noticed the change, watching as his dear friend stopped every few minutes to gaze at the nearby forest. Finally Tip put his axe down, his body covered in sweat.

"Henry - why don't ya leave us this one and take the rest down with Wonderboy."

"Yessir. You want us to take their rigs off?"

"No. Just feed the horses and unhitch the sleds. Jack and I will get the rigs."

Henry was quick to obey, saddling one of the steering mounts and turning her towards the remuda. The horses were worn down and he knew they would be happy to be led back to the lots.

"Where should I leave the broken one?" Henry asked. The sled was shattered beyond repair.

Tip had stepped up onto the pine stack and was facing west, toward the purple ranges that rose above the timberland. A valley spread her face out on the land for a considerable distance before reaching those trees, and though the sun was shining fully there was no sign of melt in the valley. Tip kept his eyes on the distant range, unaware of Henry's question. His chest rose and sank with a heavy sigh. It was rare for Tip Holland to become distracted, even by serious disruptions, and when it did happen it was only for a moment and he was back on his feet. Both brothers felt this was something new. The wind shook his clothes but Tip hadn't twitched a muscle. Without consulting his brother Jack stepped up onto the pine stack to see what had consumed him. Oftentimes in the spring the herds were known to migrate across the valley floor and at such times one of the children would call out from the treehouses for the whole of Tenpenny to come and see. Jack and Henry both squinted into the distance, scanning the land, but neither could see what had taken Tip away.

"Just put it behind the gravel lots," Tip said, his eyes still on the ranges.

"Yessir."

The boys looked at one another briefly. The man leaned into the west, his body tilting toward the wind and the ranges. Jack considered climbing back down and finishing his work.

Tip's voice was barely above a whisper and his eyes open wide to the damp colors of the west. "The great struggle," he said, "is not between right and wrong. That is an issue for boys. For men it is to measure what love you have to give and then to dole it out to those who need it. Love is limited but the need is endless." He smiled. "We've panned for gold in many rivers, haven't we?"

"Yessir."

"Yes we have."

Tip held his smile and hopped down off the logs. Before either brother could move their father was handing Jack the axe. "Find me when you have it all done," he told him. "I'm going to see Momma Tom. Leave none for tomorrow! I want a good night's rest so in the morning we can start the spring."

"Yessir," Jack said.

Although they both knew that their father was no stranger to self-examination, they each considered his words to be uncharacteristic, and his actions baffling. Tip never quit a job before he himself saw it finished. They each knew something heavy was driving him. Henry went back to leading the horses and Jack worked steadily in the coming hour, worrying long about Tip the way he often worried about the children.

IV.

To Momma Tom life was most enjoyable when there were no changes or interruptions. For her, a happy day was lived in the order she had planned it. Of course now the birth of the foal had put her plans on hold and her life revolved around keeping the young colt breathing. It was a role she was happy to accept, for Momma Tom was a born nurturer, but she would have had cause for alarm if she knew that an even bigger change was still on its way.

She and Padibatakal were seated quietly over a game of Chess as little Padi scratched the ears of the old dog. Putt was now on the bed with her, licking the foal when it suited him. He wanted nothing to do with the pine haul. Putt had no intention of standing in the snow all morning dodging horses. He would much rather be with Momma Tom and Padi and the colt, in the warmest room on the hill, especially if the girl was kind enough to scratch his ears.

The three sat together quietly, enjoying the thought of the coming spring when suddenly they each looked up and there was Tip Holland, leading a horse by the bit. He had his pack hanging over his shoulder.

"He's got Gopher," Padibatakal said.

"Well then you sure don't have no business thinking about nothing' else."

Tip led the horse up to the fence and tied his lead rope loosely. Each of the gals were leaning out the window when he said, "It's warming up."

"Cause it's springtime," the girl answered.

Padibatakal's hands began to fidget up and down the foal, busying themselves across the downy coat.

"Padi if you aren't too busy I thought I'd start teaching you to ride a horse."

The girl nodded, never taking her eyes off him.

Tip walked inside and opened his haversack. He held her tiny legs in his hands and slipped on her braces one at a time. The girl didn't seem nervous or embarrassed in the least. Her legs tingled at the feeling, which was unlike any she had known.

"You ready?" he asked after strapping her in.

The girl looked on her new braces with wide-eyed fascination. They shined, something she hadn't expected. She nodded with a grin.

Tip let her climb up on his back, her skinny legs dangling over his arms and they all moved out into the lots. Putt stayed on the bed.

"This is a buckskin mare," he told her.

"Gopher."

"That's right. She's about ten years old."

"She's Jack's Pritcher."

"That she is, and for good reason. This is the best horse we've got. It takes a lot to spook her, so I don't want you to worry. What I do ask is that you never forget she's a horse."

Momma Tom watched as Padibatakal was walked up beside the mare. The girl seemed timid but ready.

"See that there?" he asked, meaning his hand on the horse's barrel. "That's a great way to say hello. Let her know you're there. Always keep your hands in the conversation. Kiddo, horses are a little like life, I guess. There is always cause and effect. Even when you think there isn't, turns out there was all along. Every decision you make is either destructive or constructive."

"Constructive is what we're after."

"That's right. Now introduce yourself."

The girl leaned out and brushed her hand along the barrel of the horse, as Tip had done, then the shoulder, the withers, the croup. When the girl was calm Tip lifted her up into the saddle. He marveled at how light she was.

"She's tied, so just make yourself comfortable. I'll have to adjust your stirrups. Jack is a bit taller than you."

Padibatakal flinched when he said it. She had always expected Jack to be there when she started. Nearly all of her anxiety was based on it. "Where is he?" she wondered.

"Jack's at the pine haul," he said. "He'll be around 'fore long."

Tip taught her to drape her reins, to sit upright, what to watch for and most of all to relax. When she was ready he unhitched the mount and led her by the lead ropes around the lots.

"We'll start small today. I'm just gettin' you used to the feeling. I'm gonna lead you around a few times and then you'll have her to yourself. Just keep her easy for a few turns and don't forget to apply the reigns if you need to."

"To show her whose boss."

"Oh no, kiddo. There are no bosses."

"Whose in charge then?"

"Neither. You're partners. Like men. There are no bosses among men."

"There are in other parts of the world."

"No, kiddo. We all belong to each other. Everyone we meet on our journey is a partner. Husbands and wives - sisters and friends. You and I are partners."

"We are?"

"Yes. In conversation. In friendship. In the quest to get you up on a horse. I can't do it without you, kiddo."

"And I can't do it without you."

"And neither without the horse. It is all of us together."

"I see."

"So no bosses. Only teammates."

"Only teammates. I see."

Tip did as he said, leading the mount for a few turns before stepping away. He let go the lead rope and Padibatakal took the mare around the lots. She kept her head up as she had seen Jack doing and her eyes were filled with life.

When Momma Tom could see that the girl was comfortable she walked up and stood next to Tip. When she spoke it was barely above a whisper. "I heard you had you a phone call, Mister Tipper."

He seemed not to hear her. His eyes were fixed on the girl, watching to see how her leggings maneuvered. As the girl turned he said softly, "That's what I came to tell you."

"Always talk to them," Tip called to the girl. "Even if you have nothing to say, tell them a story. Tell them your favorite story. But always keep them listening."

Momma Tom kept her hands on the foal. It was the first time the colt had stood on her own. Momma Tom didn't want her to stumble. "Was it Ruffino on the phone?"

Tip waited. "It was Ruffino."

Other than Tip, Momma Tom was the only person on Tenpenny Hill to know what such a call would mean. Years before Tip had sat her down and told her that eventually this day would come. Yet even though she had waited for it for so long she still felt a great anxiety now that it had finally arrived.

"We'll be leaving first thing in the morning," he told her.

She let the foal stand on her own. "Do those boys know?"

"Hold it firm, now," he told the girl. "A good horse like Gopher will respect you when you do it right. She'll let you try things if she respects you that she wouldn't if she didn't. So keep her head at attention."

At first glance the girl looked to be a natural. She was confident and alert and she sat her mount comfortably. Tip was sad that he would miss out on the coming days of her development.

"No," he said. "I won't tell them until tomorrow."

"They're strong, Tip. They have to be and they are."

"Strong enough?"

"Together they are."

Tip kissed her on the head to thank her.

"I need you to help my sister."

Momma Tom looked surprised. "While you're gone?"

"That's right. A lot happens in the spring. "

"How do I do that?"

It was a question that Tip had thought about a great deal. He knew that Sissy was strong-willed - not easily turned over to instruction. He had doubts that in his absence she would carry things out as he would like. But Tip knew he would have to start accepting the truth that what he liked wasn't at play at the moment. He had to take himself out of Tenpenny altogether.

"Pray with her," he said. "And be her friend. She doesn't think she needs that but she does."

Momma Tom agreed but she didn't say so. "I will," she told him.

Tip walked over and took the mare by the bit. "The trick is to finish every day on a high note," he told her. "That way they look forward to tomorrow."

"What do I learn tomorrow?"

Tip hesitated.

"Now miss Mumsie you know better," Momma Tom said. "That's for tomorrow to know about."

"Rub her along her poll," he told her. "Most horses relax when you do that."

He helped her down from the saddle and kept her on his shoulders again.

"Reach in my pocket there," he told her.

The girl found apple slices and she fed them to Gopher one at a time.

Tip took her back to her room and set her next to Putt. "Good for a first day," he said. "Don't rush things at first. Let yourself ease into it. Before you know it you'll be riding across the land."

To this she smiled. "Where are you going?" she asked.

"On a roundup," he said. "I like to see how everyone is enjoying the spring."

As was always true of Tip Holland there were many children he wanted to see. They were scattered across the hill and he would have to hurry if he wanted to find them all. As much as he would have liked to sit with those two for the afternoon - he knew if he did he would regret it.

Momma Tom was watching him carefully, her hands wrung in her lap. She looked up at him with heartbroken eyes but before she could say anything he told her, "Go on and pray, Momma Tom."

Then he slipped out and walked down the road.

V.

Soon the cresting sun shown bright and full and the air was as warm as the children could remember it. The roads, the pathways, the rooftops draped with sheets of ice - all of them freed of their winter blankets and around them the new golden wood of the high trees was rising. Children were seen scaling recently forbidden branches, priming pump handles that had seemed forever fixed in time. Zuni released the sick ones like dogs into a hunt, their wellness regained. The brothers led scores of them to the fields where boys and girls alike moved as playfully as cubs freed from their dens.

Through the late afternoon the sun continued its search, penetrating the birches, the alders, the tamaracks and the aspens - even some of the pines were thawed at their bases. By light's fading most of the hidden nooks had been warned of winter's end.

All the while Sissy waited at the gatehouse for the two new girls to arrive. They had not come in the early afternoon as expected which ruined Sissy's plans. She had hoped to have them checked in before the afternoon activities so that she could be back up top to see about her baking. Instead she was forced to wait while the orphans of Tenpenny were happily led down to the fields and some time later led reluctantly back up for their supper. Sissy sat through dinner and watched the shadows grow. When the new girls finally did arrive it was near sundown and to Sissy's surprise, there weren't two orphans as expected - but six, two girls and four boys. Each of the children had the proper papers and there was room enough to house them, though Sissy felt slighted that such a mistake had been made.

She led them up the long road, hoping to excite them with new surroundings, but to her dismay they appeared sadly disinterested.

"Anyone hungry?" she asked, expecting an eruption.

But the children just shook their heads. They were each a bit broken and none wished to be talked to very long. Their hearts had been torn here and there and this new orphanage was just another stopping point in a journey they didn't care to take.

When they arrived at the fountain Momma Tom was there waiting for them, a look of great anticipation on her face.

"We've lost the light for a tour," Sissy told her. "Best to go ahead and just take them up."

Just then a crowd of boys were seen migrating up the road, all of them covered in the first sweat of the season. Sissy spotted Henry among the crowd and called him over, even though they hadn't spoken since that morning.

"Yes'm?" he answered with no awkwardness.

"Join Momma Tom and take these boys to the Pow-Wow," she told him. "They just got here. I don't want 'em to sit alone."

"Will do," he said. "You look like warriors," he told to the boys. "Where are you from?"

They led the six shy faces up the road towards the growing commotion that echoed from the top of Tenpenny Hill. The sounds of whoops and jeering and laughter were all heard ringing across the gravel paths and into the distant wood.

"Where are we going?" one of the newbies asked.

"Spring Pow-Wow," said Henry. "It happens on the first night of every spring. You've arrived on a very special day, Champ."

A shy girl asked, "Where are the girls?"

"Oh they're just back at their cabins gettin *all cleaned up*," Momma Tom assured her. "Don't worry. They'll be here. You'll make plenty of friends tonight, you'll see."

Though she remained skeptical.

They soon found themselves walking into an especially large covered court, special in more ways than one. The roof towered over every other structure on Tenpenny Hill, so high in fact that hawks were known to nest there. Balloons were hung on the columns and in each corner of the court a large wheelbarrow had been brought in and a fire was cooking within the open hull.

As they entered the great court each of the newbies secretly marveled at the arching roof that rose forty feet above. Surrounding the court were giant walls with the colorful faces of children painted across them and high above hundreds of flags were hung from the rafters.

As the children began to gather, their songs and cheers soon rang from the great rooftop, growing in volume and frequency as the crowd grew fuller. By the time every orphan from every cabin had gathered inside the courts the cheers had become deafening. The children were so excited for the start of spring that some of them began singing Christmas songs, though there was no logic to it. There was a need for song, that was all, and they belted out every one they could remember.

But the newbies wouldn't have it. They kept their heads down, pretending to ignore the joys that surrounded them. Most of them had been shuffled from orphanage to orphanage, some for many years and if there was one thing they knew it was that all orphanages were the same.

"What are we doing here?" the oldest one called out.

"We're about to start the Pow-Wow!" Henry told him. "But first Tip's gonna say some things about the slough lady."

"What's a Slough Lady?"

Henry instructed the children to take a seat. When the songs died down he turned back toward the children.

"There's a pond down in the valley called the slough," he told them. "The young boys believe its haunted. Some of the older boys tell them, 'Say your prayers and go to sleep. If you don't – the Slough Lady will drown you sure.' The story goes that she rises from the slough after midnight and walks among the cabins and if she finds you waking she rushes in before you can scream and takes you to the slough to drown you."

Half of the children were looking up in mild amusement.

"It's one big lie," Henry told them. "But some of the children taunt each other with the story. This morning I told Tip about it. He'll be coming out any minute to put it to bed."

At eight o'clock exactly the bell chimed from the fountainhead, the bellpull tugged with pride by a boy called Tigger the Greek, and the echoes rang up the hill through the boy's gym and the matflat with their newly opened windows and along the thawing roadway, and up and up the slow ascent of trees to the domed court where the children were gathered, seated and huddled close, jammering and yammering as they waited with fidgets of anticipation. In an instant the quick bell chime sent a shiver of excitement through their bones, the shiver they knew would come. But the knowing didn't dim their excitement - instead it increased it, and the new lot of six, still crowded close together, were soon met with whispers from their neighbors in the huddle, "Shhh! Tipper is on his way!"

But the name meant nothing to them. The six didn't know a thing of Tipper, nor did they care to know. They quickly returned to their sullen expressions, knowing that it wasn't a song or a dance or a cheer that they needed. To their minds all they needed was each other. Their boycott remained unspoken but none of them would dare show a moment's enjoyment amidst this charade.

These "orphans" in this snowy land were foolish, they thought. Every single one of them. With their cheers and their wildness. And though in their minds they tried to ignore the needless excitement, soon they found it impossible to ignore. Now the crowd had grown completely silent. Henry snuck away behind the stage without a sound and shushed them as he left. One of the six yawned loudly and was turned on with scornful glances. The silence grew thicker, even more difficult to ignore than the pounding cheers that had preceded it, and all six, though subtly, raised their eyes as Tipper appeared on the stage.

He jogged up the stairs and when he reached the stagefront he jogged in place, always smiling and waving his hat.

"Ladies!"

"And we are ladies!"

"And Gentlemen!"

"And we are gentlemen!"

"Good evening," he said.

"Good evening, Tipper!"

He was all smiles but there was a sadness underneath it who Jack, hidden behind the stage, could see clearly. Tip was slow to start as if he had a great weight on his mind. For a moment he simply watched the crowd, all of them hungry for what awaited them.

Let my words be your words, Father, he said to himself. My thoughts, your thoughts.

"Did we have a good day today?"

"Yeah!!!!"

"Before we start our celebration this evening we have something that needs to be discussed. Something small but serious. I'm the first to admit that I make mistakes all the time. Say things I shouldn't say. But I'm asking something of you now. I am asking you to do something for me. We have always had our traditions here and we don't want to lose them. They remind us all of good times, right, ladies?"

"And we are ladies!"

"But we have one tradition that doesn't remind us of good times. We have a tradition that does not represent ourselves, our home, our God in a respectful way. This tradition stops today.

'Many rumors are spread across this hill. The rest of your lives you will live with rumors. The rest of your lives you will live with gossip. Gossip is no good, gentlemen."

"And we are gentlemen!"

"Gossip is like confessing other people's sins. Gossip and rumors blind us to the truth. So I say to you my brothers and sisters we must all stop the rumors that spread across the hill. Many of you may talk about a ghost that roams the land of Tenpenny. Most of these things are said in harmless fun. But sometimes it frightens people, it causes fights. Some of you can't go to sleep. Is that what we want? Do we want to frighten our fellow man or build him up? Of course we build him up. Of course we shouldn't spread scary, made up stories.

So I'm here to tell you all, here and now, that the Slough Lady isn't real. She was made up a long time ago and somehow she's grown into a Tenpenny legend. And now it is time we put it to rest. From this day forward anyone heard by their counselors scaring others with stories of the Slough Lady will have to see me personally. Understood?"

"We got it, Tipper!" they cheered.

"Good," Tip said, "Now for more important matters," as he ducked behind the stage and disappeared.

There was a web of whispers among the children as they rocked with anticipation.

The newbies were all watching now, careful to keep their heads down but far too curious to miss what was coming.

To their great delight fireworks burst outside the court in the next moment like a thunderclap! Soon the singing voices of the counselors and the kitchees rang clear and true from where they were seated.

"Spring! Spring! Merry old spring. . . .
Come again and sing!

Just then Henry, Jack and Tipper, each dressed as wild Indians, sprung out from behind the stage. The children smiled as they whooped and danced with their warpaint shining. They circled each other with their plastic tomahawks, squawking and rousing the crowd. Finally they stopped in unison and began singing:

"We are the warchiefs!!! Proud and true,
And making rules is what we do,
Clean your plates, wash your hands!
Turn off your porch lights and your fans!"

"We, the War chiefs, proud and mighty!
Always make sure that your cabins are tidy!

The war chiefs called out, *"Clear off the snow with the big fat shovel!"* And the children answered, *"Off to the field and on the double!"*

Warchiefs: *"Put out your fires before you sleep. . ."*
Children: *"Dry your woodstack in your keep!"*

Now the newbies were watching with fascination as the scene unfolded. The crowd was electric. Tipper sat down in a big chair on the stage, crossing his arms with a solemn expression. Henry and Jack turned to plead with him.

Henry:	*"Brave War Chief, proud and true,"*
Jack:	*"We have a favor to ask of you."*
Tipper:	*"Speak!"*

Henry:	*"For months the children are locked away,"*
Jack:	*"Can they finally come outside to play?*
Tipper:	*"No!"*

Henry:	*"But they want to run and jump, to climb and hide!"*
Jack:	*"They want to zoom along the water slide!"*
Henry:	*"They want to swim the lake, to race the track,"*

And the children yelled, *"We want to have our freedom back!"*

| Tipper | *"No!"* |

| Jack | *"They need some room to breathe, my friend,"* |
| Children | *"To taste the rain and feel the wind!"* |

Jack:	*"Is it too much to ask that these slaves be free?"*
Henry:	*"Too much to hope that these blind may see?"*
Jack:	*"Too much to dream that a day will come,"*
Children:	*"When the birds will sing and the bees will hum?"*

Now Tipper scratched his head and every face in the crowd was smiling. He rubbed his chin and nodded and made whispers to his Chiefs. They discussed amongst themselves and all the while the children began to chant, "Free-Dom! Free-Dom! Free-Dom!" louder and louder with every word.

Finally Tipper raised his tomahawk and held his hand out to the crowd. He stood to quiet them and as they grew silent he raised his voice,

"We are the war chiefs, proud and true!
And making rules is what we do!
So now the first rule - it's time to bring,
Awaken, oh sleepers, stand and sing
Rise from your slumber, the fog has been lifted
Open your eyes to the gift you've been gifted

Thank God above for the blessings he brings,
As we say in one voice,
   "It's time for spring!!!"

"Yeah!!!" The children cried and cheered. Henry jumped into the crowd and threw a pair of them on his shoulders. In an instant the lights went out and the music started.

Behind the scenes the counselors had dressed as knights and cow-boys, court jesters and wild beasts. The Kitchees were princesses, elves and Viking queens. Once the first song had played through most of the children were dancing. But Jack and Henry weaved through the crowd to find any younger girls who needed partners, on their father's instruction, and whisked them away in their laughter.

The dancing carried on for half an hour, but there was still one more surprise for the children of Tenpenny, one that would excite them more the others, if Tipper had his way. As a song ended the lights were dimmed and a trumpet sounded and the great curtain behind the stage was pulled back revealing white cloths draped over a dozen tabletops. A line of cooks had been assembled for the occasion and they stood each one to a table, their desserts displayed in huge portions above heated trays. The children salivated over the steaming cobblers and pies, and the warm strudels and foster. They longed to guzzle the chocolate fondue and caramel sauces straight from the bowl.

Sissy had overseen the whole affair. She stood by eyeing her creation proudly, pleased to be out among the children again. In fact by that time everyone on the hill was in attendance. Zuni stood alongside the crowd, marveling at the sudden health the spring had brought his patients. Putt laid his nose atop the tablecloth, nudging the tray of chocolate fondue and silently judging the cooks. Even Wonderboy stopped working for a moment on his way to the toolhouse, and gave dancing an awkward try before carrying on about his labors.

The celebration carried on well into the night and it was all Tipper had hoped for. He stood alone and watched as the ragamuffins of the world danced and sang and forgot their troubles. His heart began to overflow. At one point Jack walked by and Tipper turned him from the crowd, "Did the new kids arrive?"

"Yessir. Momma Tom and Henry were with them. Why the long face?"

"Oh, this crazy get-up. I don't like it."

"The war chief? You don't like it? You never said anything before."

"It's just not how I see myself," Tip told him. "Get a good night sleep tonight, Jack. An early sleep."

"Long day tomorrow?"

"Long few days," Tipper said and slipped off toward the newbies.

Jack watched as he left. There was the same sadness in the man that he had seen throughout the day and Jack knew it had nothing to do with the war chief. His instinct was to ask Tipper about it but before he could he spotted Padibatakal sitting alone in the upper bleachers. She had the foal in a large basket near the barrow fire and sat with her legs covered beneath the blanket. The site of her looking down among the dancers nearly brought Jack to tears. But in the next moment his heart gave a jump as Greer stepped up and sat beside her. She appeared to be in the rarest if moods, laughing at everything she saw. The two of them were getting along, as they always had, and Jack longed to sit among them. But he knew his heart couldn't take it. He wouldn't know what to say or who to say it to, and he remained fearful that his heart was splitting down the middle. He gave them one last look and took his father's advice, slipping silently away to his cabin.

Tipper found Henry and Momma Tom in the crowd and nearby were six new faces, shiny and sweaty and full of life. He introduced himself, shaking each of the children's hands and asking about their travels.

"D'you see the ocean today?" Each one of them nodded.

"D'you eat some goodies?" And this time with vigor.

"Good. Good."

Then he welcomed them further by taking two bracelets he was wearing, a wristwatch, his ball cap, a rope necklace and a pin and handed them out. They thanked him and he smiled and headed off to bed.

"Who is he?" one of the newbies asked.

Henry looked at the boy curiously, "*Who is he?*"

"Yeah, *who* is he?"

"Who is *who?*"

"One of the children cracked a smile, "Who is *Tip*, silly?"

"Oh, Tip! For a minute there I didn't know who you meant. Sorry bout that," and Henry turned around to face the music.

The children waited, "Well?"

"Well what?" Henry shrugged.

Momma Tom was watching with a big smile on her face. Several of the children were grinning now. They could see Henry was on their side.

One of them smiled big and bright and almost yelled, "*Tell us who he is!*"

And oh how Henry loved the task. He leaned toward the children and brightened his eyes. "He will greet you slow and clear, 'Hello, brother,' you'll hear him say. And when he does he sounds identical to every man you've ever met and yet somewhere in the eyes and behind you don't hear, 'Hello, brother.' Instead you hear, 'When hard winds blow, Henry – you'll be left standing,' as he walks on to solve every problem in Tenpenny. For me he's a measuring rod for all other men to stretch against."

"He's the man who done built this place," said Momma Tom. "And we love him. That's an easier way to say it."

4. The Adventure Begins

The next morning Tip Holland rose from his bed at 5 A.M. and headed straight for his closet. There he found the same tattered shirt that he had worn while traveling the world that great season long ago. Although twelve years had come and gone since Tip had thumbed his last highway and settled on a dream, he still kept the memories of his travels whole in his heart. The shirt smelled surprisingly fresh as if it too had woken that morning ready for one more adventure. He tied up his old boots, double knotting the laces, hauled his pack onto his bed and stowed the last remaining items into the pockets before turning off the light.

Tip walked up the hill in the moonlight. The cabins were facing each other from both sides of the road and he had always enjoyed the quiet evening thought of children sleeping in their beds, of the morning and breakfast, and the day to come. The lower cabins were where the young ones slept. He liked to keep them close in case a bed-wetter needed him. The girls and the boys were on opposite sides of the road, with separate bathrooms for each. The cabins were built uniformly up the hill, all with porches and a single swing with a two child limit, and no high swinging. There were drinking fountains spaced out along the road and gravel spread between the cabins that sloshed beneath their feet. It had been Sissy's idea to bring in the gravel. "It cuts down on maintenance and the children can't sneak around in the dark," she said. On top of that Tip enjoyed hearing the children's feet crunch the ground when they ran, like music for their steps. The windows all had rope-rolled curtains, with stripes red, yellow and blue running vertically and the children were required to keep them closed in the evenings, in case the rowdy ones hoped to get a peak at someone undressing across the road. There were two fireplaces in each cabin for the winters were cruel. A giant wall fan, like the kind found in a gymnasium, was used in the summertime to keep the children cool.

As he moved further up the hill Tip passed the older cabins, where the twelve and thirteen year-olds slept. All was silent as he thought of their faces. The road he took up the hill that morning was dimly lit and had been named "Memory Lane," by the first orphan that ever came to live there. Not only was Tenpenny the kind of place where cliché phrases were commonplace, it was to Tip's thinking the only name for such a road. For along it lived the once waiting to be found, the ragamuffins, the cast-abouts, the beautiful abandoned, and their place was now on that road and their old sorrows only memories. There would be no more sifting through city garbage to find unclaimed meat for these children, nor would they ever be sold to men again in the neon streets. In Tenpenny they were captains and heroes, artists and all-stars. They were adored as children of light.

When he arrived at the lots Tip saddled the three Pritchers, each one fitted with their rider's favorite rig and quickly he led them up the hill. He came to a ramshackle bungalow that the two brothers had built themselves and tied the horses to the hitching post. As he stepped up to the cabin he smelled the grit of sweat and wet shoes, laundry hanging on the line, a dirty mop, pine bark, dew. On the stone porch a collection of baseball mitts and swim trunks, cleats and racquets and fishing rods were left wet from the evening rain. Above the door was a hand-painted sign with the words "High Hopes" carved in the face. Tip shook his head and carefully slipped inside, the screen door squeaking at the rusted spring. And there they lay.

If the boys had known what was coming they wouldn't have been asleep I can assure you. Their father had yet to tell them what was in store that Wednesday morning. He wanted one last chance to look on them as children, to watch them resting; the marvel of boyhood: Henry and Jack.

Tip's two sons slept in their bunks by the fire with their legs bare, their scrapes and bruises exposed from any assortment of wild horseplay. He let his deep voice rise above the light snores and the whispers of sleep, "Mornin', ladies!"

At first there wasn't a sound. If Tip had been of a mind to play a prank on them, which he often was, now would have been the time. But there was a more pressing reason for his arrival. He stepped up to the bunk, leaning in with his full voice, "Henry. . . Jack. Enough dreamin' 'bout stealin' kisses, sons. Wake up."

A hoarse grumbling rose from beneath the blankets; a rustle, a toss and a moan, "Go way." It was Henry growling.

Jack peeked up at Tip's silhouette and covered his head in his pillow.

Their father turned on the bedside lamp, having planned for such a reaction. He walked over to the door and hauled up a bucket that was heavy with cloudy mop water. He approached his sons again, "Wake up, O Sleeper, rise from the dead and Christ will shine on you!"

And then there was a Crash! In one toss their father hurled the soggy water across their beds, spraying the log walls and bedposts. Instantly Jack threw back his covers, swung his legs round to the cold wood floor. He spit and buzzed his lips and wiped the dirty water from his face. "Gross," he said. He squinted through the moisture, "Did you do that for a reason or just to amuse yourself?"

"Well, I'm amused. So both. Help your brother."

The water had run off Henry and dripped onto the bed beneath him. He laid still in the soggy puddle, though he looked as comfortable as he had before Tip had splashed him. His face was dug cozily into his pillow. Until he wiped the water from his lips he hadn't moved. "I don't need help with anything but going back to sleep," he said muffled into his waterlogged pillow, "If either of you old men try and pry me from this feathered foundation I'll be forced to give you your appropriate beating."

Tip and Jack looked sharply at one another and shared a devilish grin. Before the echoes of the word "beating" had disappeared they both pounced down upon Henry. Tip dropped the bucket and charged in with his hands ready. Jack ripped the wet blankets from the bed and Tip grabbed his son's ankles, yanking him to the floor. Henry's knees hit hard and he yelped and smiled and turned to defend himself. His brother began punching him lightly in the chest and laughing and Henry stood quickly, his feet wet from the splash. The boys exchanged slaps, wrestled on the floor as they rolled, writhed and thrashed about like all boys should until Tip said, "Enough! Time for breakfast!"

"Breakfast?" they asked, still wrestling. "It's five a.m."

Tip slipped out the door. "Make it quick."

They took the opportunity to slap each other across the face twice more before either one stood up. Their bodies were wet and they had to use loose items around the room to dry off with. Jack found a crusty towel in his trunk. Henry didn't care to stumble around in the dark so he used a pair of boxers that were hanging from his bedpost.

"What's going on?" Jack asked his brother.

"Hell if I know. Maybe he's got us cutting down trees again. Maybe another horse is calving."

"We wouldn't stop for breakfast if a horse was calving."

"I would," Henry said.

Snow and Oakham descended the hill with nothing but their shorts on. When they reached the big cabin they walked inside and slumped into their seats at the table. What signs of life they had shown while tussling about had left them. Henry put both arms flat on the placemat and rested his face between them. Jack sat with his eyes squinting at the light, his hair wild and wet across his head. Because the brothers were still living in a dream at the time, stumbling out of their aborted sleep, for years afterwards they couldn't remember what they'd had for breakfast that morning. All they do remember is an extravagant spread of fresh fruits and pastries, juices and sliced meats, biscuits and honey dishes with small spoons for serving.

"What's all this?" Jack asked.

Momma Tom smiled at them from the kitchen. She had been baking and frying the eggs with extra pepper the way Henry liked it. Their plates were ready when they sat.

"Something special," Tip told him.

Henry seemed unimpressed by the elaborate table settings and the sterling silver trays and mugs before him. He rubbed his eyes.

"You know where we're going today?" Tip asked as he set their food down before them.

Henry grumbled, "Back to bed?"

"Please?" Jack asked.

Their father shook his head as he swallowed a raspberry, "That would be a mistake, boys. You'd miss all the fun."

Henry spoke deep and slow like Frankenstein, "No fun. Sleep only. Fun later. Sleep now."

Momma Tom draped the kitchen rag over her shoulder and smiled.

"You should eat," Tip said, looking at the clock, "You're wastin' time."

Neither of them could hear the urgency in his voice.

Jack looked at his fork. "I'm not hungry." He hated to say it because he couldn't remember ever seeing such an elegant presentation. There were three kinds of sugar in tiny teapots near his plate.

"You *will* be," his father said, "And by then there won't be any food and you'll come cryin'."

Tipper felt strange making the statement because in all his years with Jack the boy had never to his knowledge made a complaint.

The boys didn't heed the warning. They sat, dumb-faced, motionless. "Momma Tom do we have any coffee? Boys are thirsty."

"No coffee, Dad," Henry grumbled. "Coffee bad."

"Coffee *good*," his father told him. "Coffee wakes up the nose. Makes you a better hunter. I never met a travelin' man that didn't like his coffee."

By then Jack was awake enough to enjoy himself. He made the most pathetic face he could, hoping Tip would see it, and he lifted the fork as slowly as possible without shaking, all the way to his mouth where he let the eggs dribble off his fork.

Henry had a savage face; A hawk's face. Not pointed and bird-like in that sense – but wild in the way his curly feathers lay thick against his crown, the way his big eyes, always alert, saw before they were seen. And like the feeling one has when catching a hawk's glance just for an instant, so Henry's strong gaze made young and old feel lucky to have captured him, if only with their eyes. When Henry raised his head his appearance had changed. He had become fully awake, scanning the room, watching

Momma Tom and his father. "We're going somewhere," he said with a heavy voice.

His father had been watching him carefully. "We are." Tip whispered, quite happy.

Jack chewed nonchalantly. "Fish the Lake?"

"That would be too easy. This trip will take everything you've got."

From the kitchen Momma Tom looked like a child about to open a long awaited gift. She almost burst into tears. Henry saw her face and he instantly knew this was no day trip they were about to take, no stroll to a local museum or even a ride in a helicopter. Never had there been such a production made of breakfast. He began to watch his father, noticing the tattered brown shirt he had never seen him wear.

"Skydiving?" Jack asked, half afraid. "Is it skydiving?"

As Tipper shook his head Henry saw in his father the same anticipation that he had seen in Momma Tom. It was as if the dinosaurs were walking the land again and Tip was about to take his sons off to hunt them. Henry stood from his seat.

Jack pealed a banana carefully and stuffed it into his mouth. He looked down at his plate and shook his head. "Moose season isn't for a few more months," then his eyes went wide. "Ah! We're getting the dune buggy! It's the dune buggy isn't it?"

"No!" Henry said.

Jack looked up at his brother, "Don't you want the dune buggy?"

"Of course I do, you *wombat*! It was *my idea!*"

Then with a verve that only Henry Snow could produce he began to slap his bare chest with his palms, building a rhythm and humming along. Jack watched him, unsure of what was happening. His brother began to speed up the beat and the humming along with it and before Jack could predict it Henry started to sing:

"Down the dagger to the broken road,
Across the big red wind. . .

Jack's eyebrows raised high. Wrinkles appeared on his forehead. He wore an open, astonished face; the look of a boy with a gun pointed at him. He began to sing along:

Ne'er before have I heard told,
The tales of the Wild West End!"

This time Jack Oakham's eyes were wide with surprise. He looked to Tip, "*We're going to the Wild West End? You're taking us to the Wild West End?*"

Henry pounded his chest with his fists and hopping up and down like a boxer warming up.

Because no one was telling them otherwise the brothers both knew it was the truth. They were finally going on the journey that they thought would never come. There had been no warning, no notice given. Tip had simply woken them in the dark.

"Think you're ready?" he asked them.

"I've been for years," Henry said.

"And you, Jack?"

Jack couldn't believe what he was hearing. "If you say so."

The reality of the moment hit Jack like a jolt. The rumors of the treasure buried upriver were now becoming a reality. Of course no one but Tipper knew what kind of treasure it was or where it had been laid to rest but that hadn't stopped speculations from forming.

All the information that had been collected from years of eavesdropping was that far to the west, further than anyone cared to go, Tip had left a treasure for his sons to find in the great unknown wilderness, beyond Lah Shakes Lake. Some believed that the story was a hoax and others thought the road was far too dangerous to risk for unknown riches. "Troublesome Creek is home to a thousand northern bears and two thousand from the south," they'd say. "And even if you kill every one you see, and the storms don't flood the basin and you avoid the razor sharp thorns on the Rojo Prieta and if the ice melts early in the springtime and the mountains are passable, even then you don't know where he buried it."

But most of the old-timers who heard the stories envied the journey and stated they would make the trip regardless of any pot of gold at the end of it, especially those whose traveling days had come and gone. They said this and remembered their childhoods along that river. "Oh, Troublesome Creek! A happy land! A place where you could live a hundred years worth in a day, a place filled with appetites: unspoilable, unending appetites, all of them pure, like the rain, and with no unwanted citizens at all."

And when he was of a mind to titillate his listeners the father of Tenpenny would strum the table with his fists and sing,

"Over the hills to the big dark trees!
With dirty hands and bloody knees,
I've seen the sky and
Off off you fools,
Let's off to the red sky deep in the hills,
Let's off to the Wild West End"

Neither of the brothers could say what the rainbow end was exactly, but it was believed to be a vast, unending wealth. No man they knew of, other than their father, had ever been there. And because of this, what lay behind the forest to the west had remained a mystery all their lives. They could see the purple hills from the high dive, the blank outline of the valley behind it called the Rojo Prieta, and what they could only view from the top zipline in the cottonwoods was the dark, formless shadow of the mountains. Each of them felt like a man the moment Tip asked them to go. Neither one was a man themselves, but together. . . well together one could line up all the Hucks and Toms in the world against them and find no equal.

"When are we going?" Henry asked.

Henry Snow was not a person that took long to get around to the topic at hand.

"Eat something first," Tip told them.

Henry sat up quickly, stuffing various foods into his mouth as fast as he could. Then through a mouthful of fruit and pastries Henry asked again, *"When we going?"*

Tip looked at his watch, "If we don't dilly dally we'll be on our way by sunrise."

The brothers faced each other, seeing the world for the first time. "We haven't packed," Jack mumbled.

Henry swallowed. "We're leaving this morning?" he asked, clearly excited.

Tip stood and wiped his hands. He brushed his hair back and rested his hands in his pockets. "At forty minutes after five I will start for the west, with or without you."

The boys squinted at the clock in the dark.

"It's five thirty-seven," Tip told them.

Neither boy could make his throat work long enough to speak.

Tip dipped his biscuit in the honey and said casually, "That leaves you three minutes."

"What do we bring?"

Their father said seriously, "Hurry."

"But Dad. We just can't—"

"Go!"

The boys sprang to their feet and fought one another for position. "Miracles are waiting to be handed out," Tip said as he watched them race out the door. The table was left filthy: grease drippings were on the tablecloth; the plates were covered in tomato blood and seeds, biscuit crumbs and coffee droplets were scattered.

Momma Tom pushed herself up against the sink to let them pass. As the sounds of the heavy footsteps were heard thumping along the deck Tip moved into the kitchen. He took Momma Tom by the hands and then rocked her in his arms. A sadness filled the room then and though neither of them spoke of it, it was there and it was heavy and Tip rocked her like it was the last time. "You'd better wake up my sister," he said.

Both brothers were wearing frightful smiles as they crashed into the cabin. Henry was the first to reach the door. They stomped into their boots without tying them, buttoned their shirts unevenly, leaving them untucked, threw back pillows and comforters to find what they needed for the journey.

Tip followed the boys up to the cabin to observe their packing. For him it was like watching two treasure hunters digging through everything they owned to find the pot of gold. They scuttled through the drawers and shelves, pitching wet towels and dirty linens across the room as they searched. They began to collect their gear and stuff it into their packs.

Although equivalent in their anticipation, Jack and Henry differed greatly in the way they prepared for a journey. Henry carried a tiny canvas haversack with frayed stitching that had loose torn pockets popping out all over the face. Inside he barely had enough equipment to survive on.

Jack was unlike his brother in many ways and the manner in which he packed was certainly one of them. He lugged around an Alice pack, fully loaded with straps and snaps for every pocket and three times the size of his brother's. In it he kept every bit of survival gear a person could gather, including a full rain poncho that weighed a solid half-pound. Henry kidded him often about the burden. "That yellow raincoat is impractical, Jack. It's so heavy it could be made of gold." Jack had ignored the remark. He found it irresponsible that his brother carried only a folded trash bag as a slicker. "Works just as good and cost me just twelve cents a piece," Henry told him. Though Jack was unconvinced. He sorted out his few remaining items as his father watched from the doorway.

"Leave your watch behind, Jack."

"Yessir. Why?"

"No time where we're goin'."

As the brothers were packing frantically their Aunt Sissy stormed up the hill with nearly the speed that the boys had. Before Momma Tom had even reached the door to her room in the big cabin Sissy came stomping into the hallway. "I'm up, Momma Tom," she said. "No need barging in!" She had heard the ruckus and when she met the old woman at the door she asked Momma Tom two questions and before anyone knew it she had burst into the boy's cabin to protest.

"Going adventuring?!" Sissy yelled. "Going adventuring?! Off to the Wild West End? You call yourself adventurers? Tip look at you," she smiled. "You haven't changed shirts in a week, your neck is untrimmed, you have blood on your collar."

"Who cares, Aunt Sissy?" Henry said. "We're going west."

"Yah who cares?"

The brothers ignored her, keeping to their packing and racing against the clock.

It was true, however that Tip as a rancher made a habit of keeping himself unkept. His appearance had been a topic of scrutiny for years. He would often cook breakfast for the family before sunrise only to discover later that he had wood chips in his hair from the afternoon before. He kept his nails short, which pleased everyone, and his breath maintained, and tried to wash everyday to fend off any unwanted comments, but the riding he received for bad dress or shaggy grooming he had tolerated for life.

Once, after performing a wedding ceremony for a local couple, Tip opened his jacket and Sissy immediately observed that the skinny end of his tie was longer than the fat. "You may want to be like John the Baptist, but for Pete's sake you don't have to *look* like him," his sister said, on account of his wildness.

It was considered a truly bold thing to say in public, especially to someone who was commonly regarded as the most capable and unpredictable man that anyone could remember. "Sister, pardon thee – I have so much to learn."

But if anyone could get away with turning Tip Holland's other cheek it was his Sissy. She was looked upon as the ultimate litmus test for strengths of a man. Her hairstylist said of her, to his regret, "To sit beside her is to understand mad cow disease."

Both of her nephews said of her often, "She is the reason God invented patience." Little phrases like that were common in Tenpenny. And this one in particular became a blanket at the end of every conversation the boys put over her. In fact the little cliché was such a common subtitle for Sissy that an anonymous five-year old once repeated it at a brunch straight to Sissy's face. After a brief interrogation the wailing child revealed the culprits. Sissy slammed several doors.

"*Patients*," Henry said laughing. "Like in an office. What a misguided child that must have been."

Jack sprinted to catch up, "That's right, Aunt Sissy, *patients*." He almost burst. "You, oh nursemaid, are the reason God invented *patients*."

Tip refused to punish them. He did, however, laugh harmoniously.

It was now almost dawn and no matter how she tried Tip wouldn't listen to his sister's plea for them to stay. "Fools! Expeditions should be planned out. Do you even know where you're going?"

"The Wild West End!"

"Do you know how *far* that is?"

"*Over the Hills to the Big Dark Trees. . .*"

"Stop Singing!"

"How far *is it*, Dad?" Jack asked, curious.

"Far enough to leave early if we ever want to get there. You ready, Jack?"

"No, Sir. Can't find my sandals."

"What for?" Henry asked him, "You're not hiking in *sandals*."

"I like them at night by the fire."

"Go barefoot," Henry smiled. He was packed.

"I like my sandals." Jack told him, knowing full well that it was impossible to discuss luxury packing with his brother. Henry rarely packed more than a few pounds of gear to take with him on a long journey: pair of dry socks, matches, a toothbrush with the handle sawed off, small canteen that fit inside his cook pot, Swiss army knife, ground pad, small tarp, fishing line with flies and a harmonica. Once Jack had tried to argue with his brother that a harmonica was as luxurious as it gets. "It won't get you from here to there," he said. At which point Henry strummed a mighty tune, and his father started whistling and Momma Tom, who was known as far away as Pontotoc for her pipes started singing "Amazing Grace". When it was done and Henry was red-faced and everyone smiled across the room, Jack knew full well the rest of his life that music was never meant to be a luxury.

While Jack was burrowing beneath the bed Tip said to both of them, "You have thirty seconds." And when he was out the door he added, "Bring your rods and bows along."

Henry looked up with a sudden thrill. "Rods and bows?" he thought. Of course hunting and fishing excited Henry. He scrambled to find his arrows. The idea that they would be surviving on the river by their own means alone was like a dream. He slipped his little fly rod over his shoulder and dumped his reel in his haversack along with his tackle bag. Then he realized he had nowhere to strap his bow. It frustrated him that his romantic way of packing wasn't practical for the trip they were about to take. Jack, on the other hand, had a pack with a frame, filled with every known bit of gear from a cooking grill to a weather filter, with straps for everything. He pulled his dusty flyrod down off the wall and shoved his tackle box into his pack and then snatched his bow from the hooks on the wall and fastened it to the pack with ease. Jack then scrambled to the porch, found his sandals, wet from the melting snow, stuffed them in his pack and hurried down the hill.

Henry felt rushed. His little pack was no more than a dirty haversack. He felt the urge to hustle so he grabbed his tips and arrows and his bow and a shoelace from a loose boot on the floor and raced out the door, down the hill and onto the porch at the big cabin, ready as he would ever be.

When the boys arrived, breathing heavily from the fast packing, Sissy and Momma Tom were waiting for them. Tip came from his room and swung his backpack onto his shoulders. "We're all here," he said gladly.

"You're crazy children," Sissy told them. "You'll freeze to death. Or starve. Why not do your stupid adventuring in the summertime?"

Henry burst out, "Ah nuts, Dad. I forgot my bad attitude back at the cabin. Aunt Sissy, can I borrow yours?"

Tip cut in, clearing his throat loudly. He held his hands out at his sides, his palms up and everyone saw him. The murmuring ended suddenly. Everything became solemn and the smiles were washed from their faces. Momma Tom and Sissy each took one of Tip's hands and left the other open for the boys. Each of the brothers was wearing a hat and they both took them off as they joined the circle with their hands, their eyes closed.

Tip spoke softly and it was a comfort to them as always to hear only his prayer, "Guide us across the Rojo Prieta, Lord. Lead us through to the Wild West End and home again. Keep all the children on this hill safe and loved. Thank you for your Son. I pray that it will be evident by how we leave and live that we love you."

And everyone said "Amen".

Tip kissed Sissy and Momma Tom on the crown of their heads. He cradled their faces as he always did and rubbed their fingertips as he stepped away. Henry and Jack said quick goodbyes and hurried after their father.

"That wasn't much of a farewell," Sissy said quietly to her old friend.

With their packs hoisted high the two brothers followed Tip down the wide steps from the woodland cabin to the river where they took wet strides along the bank. The rain was light but the tall grasses were heavy with morning water as they mounted the horses. The troupe turned and waved at the two women, who watched from the porch as the three men in their lives began the long ride west.

And if you were to ask her even now, how she ever allowed her globetrotting brother to take her two nephews out into the cold morning without a map or schedule, conditioner or first aid, leaving the kitchen table looking like a Sunday morning frat house, Sissy would be reminded of the sharp truth that some men, however few, cannot be stopped.

And that was how the journey began.

5. The Rojo Prieta

They rode in single-file along the saddleback, following the deep cut trail that ran through the alders; the same path they had taken all their lives. The rains fell gently. Their necks were soaked, their eyes half-closed, their toes already numbing to the cold. Henry was rigging his bow to his haversack with the shoestring he had grabbed on his way out of the cabin. He fastened it as tight as he could but it still flopped on his pack like a tail wagging.

"Aren't we bringing Putt?" he asked his father.

Tip measured the journey in his mind and the years on the dog. He wondered to himself if the old dog had it in him. But he quickly decided that it wasn't his choice to make. Might be his last big adventure, Tip thought. "If you want," he told them.

Before Henry could, Jack turned sharply, ashamed that he hadn't thought of it himself. He cupped his mouth and called out the dog's name over the hilltop.

Putt awoke stiff-jointed, limping to see why Jack was on the river. The light rains wetted his coat as he came to the edge of the great porch. The voice came again and though the old dog couldn't see the caller through the high branches he scrambled down the steps and charged through the birches. Sissy moved aside as the dog galloped past her and she was glad to see him go. Now all the wildness has left the hill, she told herself.

When they met in the dark Jack hung from the saddle and ruffled Putt's ears in excitement. The dog looked up at the Pritchers, the loaded saddlebags, the heavy packs. He seemed to squint at each of the riders. "You didn't tell me we were traveling," Jack heard him say.

"Well it's a surprise," he told him.

Putt licked his chops and slipped in among the Pritchers. "I might have packed a lunch."

Following the moonlit trail the party of four set out for the Wild West End. West of the cabins the riverbank was covered with mighty trees: tamaracks, pines, quaking aspens and the white pulpwood of the spruces.

They coursed quickly beneath the branches of the familiar country on the well-worn path; the only such trails in Tenpenny, for it was the only place visited with enough frequency to create a path. The horses tossed loose snow across the still-white slopes and as they thundered near the riverbank pieces of snowpack crashed into the icy water, splashing and spinning as they were swept into the current.

By the time the party crossed Nippintuck Creek Henry was humming the melody of the Wild West End. The heavy hooves shattered the icy breaks in the slow current and even in the darkness the party could see the big sockeye taking flight from their dens. Tip and Henry stretched up the dell with their horse's fetlocks wet from the crossing, steering carefully around the rock ledge and ducking beneath the branches of the bog spruce. Jack and his dog trotted along the bank, making a new trail. "No need for showmanship, eh boy?" Jack said.

To which Putt replied, "Who they kiddin?"

They rode up into the hillocks of the westerwing over trails still distinguishable by the moon. The passing was made easy by the sparse forest thinned from years of the pine haul. But after no more than a mile's ride the trees thickened with low branches and the trail retreated to the unspoiled banks along the river, and snow flung from the muddy-bottomed hooves of the Pritchers.

They rode over beds of pine-bark that shattered like crispy flakes beneath the snow and over moldering logs and great sprouting sages that flourished despite the winter. Soon they came to the last familiar sight on their journey: a pass where the rock cliffs closed in on a narrow gap along the riverbank. There the trail ended abruptly and standing a man's height from the snow was a wooden signpost with a phrase carved into the face. For many years the brothers had pondered the meaning of the words that were etched there. All that was known for certain was that the signpost was the definitive boundary of the west, one that neither brother had ever crossed, even to test their fates, a fact that Henry was still proud of. Putt had crossed the boundary many times over the years, always disappointed that Jack wouldn't follow him. As the horses approached the signpost all three Pritchers began to circle back, as they were accustomed to doing, but Tip quickly led them on. "Not this time, Satchbo," he assured his mount. As he passed the signpost Tip slapped the sign face with his gloved hand, shaking ice from the lettering. The brothers consulted each other with their eyes, each taking a deep breath as they led their horses past the boundary. They too gave the signpost a slap and the remaining ice fell away. Even there in the dark the sign was legible: "No one passes but the Picklemen."

They rode half the morning in that splendid mood, beside the river all the while into new country, the cold wind rustling the trees. They rode up into the hills again when the banks became rocky and jagged and impassable. They crossed a meadow and it was unlike anything the brothers had ever seen, wholly unadulterated until the horses and the old dog cut a path across her shallow snows.

The only time they stopped was when Tipper stood in his stirrups and looked back at Tenpenny. The bell would be ringing within the hour, he thought. The fast-paced orphan world would carry on without him. Tip knew that from the moment he had hung up the phone his life had been different. He had abandoned his former self and now his soul was weary from the change.

The brothers watched as the sun's rays flooded the ridge top, filling the rolling country with whites and yellows and greens and the wet rock shined. The bed of the river shook with prism light, the colors spreading on the water like a puff of smoke. And with the clearing of the sky came the open-colored view of timber country. The party turned back to the west.

"Out there," Tipper nodded. "Where the trees rise to a point, that's where we enter the forest."

The boys straightened, craning their necks and setting their eyes on the horizon. They could see before them, dark and hungry against the sky the purple forest far away. All their lives those hills had been like a promise since they were little, a gift waiting to be opened.

But the promise would not come true today. The party had a long journey before they reached the tall timbers. They would still have to cross the dry valley that lay ahead if they were to reach the edge of the great forest. But they knew that even that was only the beginning. They would still have to pass through the woodlands and reach the mountain hills before their travels ended, a thought that suddenly exhausted young Oakham.

"How deep is the forest?" Jack asked.

Tip looked over the dusty plain, "As deep again as this thirst land."

"How long will it take us to get where we're going?"

"You mean to dig up your birthright?"

"Yessir."

"We must be through the forest, beyond those trees, and to the base of the mountains in three days. There's little time to waste."

At which point Jack gave a sigh. He had never anticipated the crossing to be so broad. He turned to look over his shoulder, hoping to catch one last look at the orphanage on the hill. His heart sank as he thought of Padibatakal waiting that very morning for a riding lesson that wouldn't come. He tried to push the sad thought from his mind but as he did, another thought even more heartbreaking took its place. He wondered if Greer would even be there by the time he returned. The spring would be in full force within a few days and there would be nothing to stop her. Jack was flooded with regret as he turned back to lead his mount down the trail. He tried to catch his breath as the thought of losing her crept deeper and deeper into his mind. But the thought didn't have long to settle. Jack soon realized that he would have to keep sharp if he wanted to carry his weight throughout the journey. The trail wound through wild country and he didn't know what challenges lay before him. As they set out on their travels that morning Jack's only hope was to travel without making himself a fool. Unlike Tipper and Henry Jack didn't feel up to snuff as an adventurer. With the exception of his journey to Tenpenny as a boy he had never done much traveling - unlike his brother who rambled day and night and Tip who had walked the globe full round it seemed. Certainly he was excited to be in the saddle, but Jack was beginning to dread the scope of their upcoming adventure.

But not Henry. For Henry Snow that forest was rooted and shaded in unmade memories, too proud of itself to wait another day. And he wanted it; wanted to light a torch and carry it high above his head, to watch the light and the shadow dance together on the rooftop branches. He wanted to be swallowed by the forest, to sit with his father and hear the old tales, to close his eyes in the dark and listen for the wild game that lurked there, to catch a glimpse of the wolves as they passed soundless between the distant cottonwoods, to live out the great journey of his youth.

This is a story about Henry and Jack after all; of how they came to the end of their childhood, found adventure and learned what stuffing they were made of.

As he looked upon his sons it was clear to Tipper what each of the boys were feeling. Henry wore his excitement like a crown while Jack was clearly anxious in the saddle. His heart appeared torn from the moment of their departure.

"It's different out here, you know?" Tip told them.

Jack asked quickly, "Different how?"

"The rules are changed. There are differences in a man's walk and talk when he's shepherding. But when a shepherd has no flock he isn't a shepherd anymore. He isn't looking for what's coming. He's just a kid. There are different rules for kids."

Henry knotted his bandana tightly behind his head and looked out at the valley. "I myself can't feel the difference."

"Big surprise," Jack said.

"Henry be honest with yourself," Tip told him.

"I don't look for what's coming," Henry told his father. "I doubt I ever will."

"Yes you do, and you do it well."

Henry sighed. "Well I'm no shepherd."

"No?"

"I enjoy kids. That doesn't make me a shepherd."

"It doesn't?" Tip said.

"Not as I see it."

"Well what would?"

"What would make me a shepherd?"

"That's what I'm asking."

"The choice to be a shepherd."

"Oh I see."

"You've said that all our lives. One either chooses to love or not to. I believe all that. I'm choosing not to take on the burdens of a shepherd."

"Can your actions override your choices?" Tip asked.

"How do you mean?"

"Can what you do make your choice irrelevant?"

"I don't follow you, counselor."

Tip squinted and brushed his hair flat down the side of his head. "Henry, a Private is in the trenches and his natural courage influences his men. Is he a leader?"

"If he chooses to be."

"You don't think he just is?"

"It takes more than influence to be a leader."

"Wrong. If a frat boy impregnates a girl, is he that child's father?"

Henry didn't say a word. The pause seemed endless as the three men trotted, and even Putt looked back, feeling the difference.

"He is," Jack said.

"He is?" Tip asked.

"I think so."

"Why do you think that?"

"Well, like you asked it. He doesn't have to choose. He is."

"That's right, Jack. He is. You are Jack Oakham. You are Henry Snow. We can sharpen ourselves but we still are ourselves. And whether you like it or not we, all three of us - are shepherds. We are born that way. Wonderboy isn't a shepherd. But Henry when you spit - kids learn your style, so spit well."

Tip choked off the rest of what he was about to say, realizing he was in no mood for a sermon. "But, aha, we're not leading now," he said with a smile. "This place is different. The rules have changed. You can go back to accepting all the responsibilities once we return to Tenpenny. This is a journey for boys."

Jack looked at his father curiously, not expecting that last statement. Tip seemed more free than he had ever seen him, it was true. Maybe his burdens have truly been lifted, he thought.

But Jack couldn't help but think of Padibatakal and Greer, and the laundry list of springtime chores that would mount up as he rode across the wilderness. He was down on himself for worrying about life on the hill, while real adventure lay before him. But he couldn't shake it. It seemed unnatural to cast aside his responsibilities so quickly, as his father seemed to be able to do.

As for Henry his thoughts were turning back to responsible things as well, but for the first time in a long time. His father's words turned over in his head again and again and he glanced at Tip with unknowing eyes. He couldn't be sure of his father's knowledge, but even the thought worried him, the thought of betraying Tip's trust, and now more than ever the thought of shepherding, and all the weight that came with taking on and taking on. Truth was Henry Snow could bear a great deal, but his heart cried out to bear nothing at all. No ending this boyhood, he thought. Just run, and extend it. Let this journey just be another chapter, and let all the rest be just like it.

Within only a few moments Henry had blocked the thoughts of duty from his mind and carried on, thinking of the west and how things would never change.

When Jack finally looked at him his brother seemed reduced, his face and eyes heavy. Henry looked away so his brother couldn't see his shame and neither Tip nor Jack heard him when he whispered, "I am Henry Snow".

They rode through country that swallowed them up within her wild reaches. Each of the riders scanned the unfolding canvas with eyes wide to their adventure. Jack felt his stomach grumble from all the bouncing and the bobbing in the saddle but true to his character he said nothing and watched the land unfold. To be perfectly fair Jack didn't know how meals were to be handled on such a journey - and he was beginning to wonder. But just about that time they came to a deep pool where the tamaracks grew tall, shading the riverbanks and her rocky holes. Perfect, Tipper thought. He dismounted quickly and began assembling his gear and soon the boys did the same, needing no instruction.

Once he was on the ground Henry sat immediately and crossed his legs, leaning back on his elbows with the morning sun on his face as he threaded the line. It was commonly how he stretched after a long ride. Jack began to search through his clothes for his tackle. His extra shirt and socks were clumped together across his gear. He thought to himself how shameful his packing had been.

Before either of the boys had even cast a line Tipper was slipping a grayling on the stringer. It was a decent catch, enough body to make brunch for one of the boys. Tip kept the fish alive on the twine and Putt watched the fish fighting the water.

As Tip began casting again the brothers watched him like they would watch beautiful girls sunning themselves by a pool. Like they were lucky.

For despite the adequate training both brothers had received, neither had any doubts that Tip was the strongest fisherman.

Henry moved upriver but Jack stayed behind, taking a longer moment to observe his father's skill. Jack loved to sit silently and enjoy what others hadn't seen. Jack's love was subtle, not big and bold like Henry's. Henry could talk day and night about the wind and the trees and fishing but mostly it was just talk. He fished, but he never stopped to enjoy it for what it really was.

Jack's love was subtle, but it was there. If one were lucky one could catch Jack loving life. It may be seeing him holding his hand gently above the water to feel the temperature rise from the rapids, the spray tickling his fingertips. It could be seeing him before dawn collecting firewood and stopping to watch Momma Tom's sleeping face as she sat dozing on her porch swing. That was how Jack Oakham loved things. He loved them gently. He loved them without their consent.

Henry rarely made allowances for such things. He could speak with confidence about every pattern, every cast, and every hole in the Papersack River with unmatched authority and did so whenever the moment arose. He could draw a star chart from memory, whereas Jack couldn't sketch a constellation. He could advise men twice his age on the wonders of a beautiful woman, of the poetic smell of still-wet hair. But never could you catch him whispering those sermons to Greer, or staring big-eyed at the clear night sky. His work was done when he mastered the technique. The practice never played a role.

The family laughed about it. Guests would often ask, "Ducks on that river?"

"Oh, sure," Henry would say.

"Y'ever hunt 'em?"

"All the time in the winter, all the time."

Henry loved to chatter and it was fine if he wanted to carry on about fishing and hunting like an expert. But once Henry's habit for verbal liberties got him in trouble. When Henry and Jack were twelve Greer Ashby and her family came across the river for a brunch and with them they brought their spaniel, which followed Greer everywhere. When Henry saw the lovely girl's affection for the animal he found Putt behind the tack room and called him over. Greer cheered for him, asking his name.

"Putt," Henry told her.

"He's beautiful," she said as Putt licked her neck. "Is he yours?"

"He's mostly mine," Henry nodded.

Jack had never been one to overlook injustice, despite his quiet ways. So when he heard his brother claim a dog that he hadn't spent any time with in a month Jack stood from the porch swing, took two steps toward his brother and punched him in the mouth. Henry crumbled down the steps and came up swinging.

Jack's love was subtle.

After tossing out no more than a dozen casts Henry was soon resting against a wide flat rock overlooking the river. He was wondering how marshmallows were made. He no longer had the patience for fishing. Awhile later Jack hiked upriver, shook his wet boots on the bank, and approached his brother, "How'd you do?" Jack asked, clearly mocking.

"Too nice a day to fish," Henry said. "You need more practice anyway."

Jack held up his catch. "Got any floatant?" he asked. Henry pulled the little bottle from his vest, "Keep it. I'll fish with sinkers."

"Where do you figure we're going?" Jack asked.

"Out west."

"But what for?"

"Hell if I know. I'm just glad to be going. You think love is a real thing or just an idea?" Henry asked.

Jack looked away like he was thinking about the question. "It's real."

"Aren't all ideas real?" Jack added.

"They say they are. You can find some people who will say that two plus two is as real as my hand here. But two plus two never comes and goes like love does. So I have my doubts."

"You can find people who will say anything," Oakham said. "I bet everything's been said. When was the last time you went fishing?"

"Before today?"

"Yeah."

"It's like riding a bike."

"*When?*"

"Who can say?"

"I can."

"Please don't."

Jack bit the extra tippet that hung from his knot. "It's embarrassing when you tell people you're a fisherman."

"I know more about fishing than any two people on this river."

Jack spit out the tippet and shook his head. "Nope, *now* everything's been said."

Henry sat up and began talking with his hands. "About this time of year the mayflies spawn and the grayling always feed on the east bank because the west wind drives down the flies. That brings the silvers out of the shade in midday to look for baitfish. That and the waxing moon."

Henry tipped his hat forward and shaded himself.

Jack tediously examined his fly, holding it up to the light and squinting, "You made that up, Henry."

"Every word."

Jack shook his head in shame and walked back to the river.

Henry called out from beneath his hat, "I'm still a better poker player than you!"

After a short nap Henry gathered his bow and arrows from the saddle and headed further upriver. Soon one of Henry's arrows pinned a duck to the bank, and another dragged a rabbit through the melting snow. Jack and Tipper had strung a half-dozen grayling by that time and once the fish and duck and rabbit were plucked and gutted the brothers tied cords around their necks and through their gills and hung them from low branches along the river.

Tip gathered dead-gray sticks and nettles and crispy dry leaves to make a fire. They relieved the mounts of their burdens and let them graze along the river.

Soon the sweet hiss and crackle of wood was filling their ears and the warmth was pulling them in. The wood fire blazed the high boughs, shook air light ashes from the flame and carried them up to the damp branches above. Jack watched the orange specks rise and stick and evaporate.

Lunch consisted of fish steaks, duck and rabbit cooked over Tip's fire. Jack filleted enough for the party to be stuffed until suppertime. The pink fish steaks curled black around their skewers.

Tip and Jack each ate half the bird while Henry had the rabbit to himself. And although Henry hadn't caught a single fish he'd eaten more than either his brother or Tip had. When they fed Putt some scraps from the grayling he swallowed the fish without chewing.

The boys belched heavy and often and dunked their heads in the river to have a drink. "I wish I could eat like that," Henry said watching the dog. "All I'd do is eat if I could take it down like that."

"All you do *is* eat."

"No, I complain as well." Part of the charm that allowed Henry Snow to hitch-hike through life without paying his dues was his accurate impression of himself. "That's really all I have. I bet he doesn't taste much swallowing it whole."

"Makes up for it with what he smells."

Henry took his boots off and rubbed his toes near the fire. Their father sat puffing his little antler pipe. He was thinking back on the first morning, and how fine it was to be in the saddle with his sons. "Marvelous," he continued to say while riding. "Marvelous."

As they sat burping against the white aspens, Tip began to whistle. The song didn't have a name, at least not one the boys knew, but Henry enjoyed the melody so much he began to wonder where Tip had learned it, for it was too sweet a tune to conjure on the spot.

When the song stopped Tipper looked lovingly at his sons by the fire. He crossed his fingers and set his hands atop his lap. "Now we come to the purpose of our journey," he said.

Each of the boys sat up straight, waiting with anticipation as their father looked heavily upon them. Tip Holland was known for his dramatic transitions.

"To tell a story well is a *serious* business," he assured them. "There are dozens of ways to do it right, but tens of thousands of ways to do it wrong."

He took a contemplative breath. "It matters where a man gets his start," Tip said. "If a man's story is his home then his beginning is the foundation."

It is important to note that on Tenpenny Hill, storytelling is something taught with as much importance as history or algebra in the local school. What began as a pastime for Tip and his sons soon flourished into the guarantee stamped on every visit made there: Stories would be told. Everyone was welcome as long as they loved to tell, or loved to listen. At the time of their little journey to the Wild West End, Henry Snow and Jack Oakham hadn't yet perfected the art of storytelling. It was a study that they would only sharpen years later. But that season of their lives doesn't find its way into our little story.

"You may both be wondering," their father said. "'What's this all about? Why the fanfare? Well, my brothers I have saved this time for a specific purpose: To tell my sons my story.

"To tell you *the* story. The one I have been keeping hidden in my heart these many years. And though it wasn't the time then, it is now," he said. "It needed to be told, and the two of you, most of all, needed to hear it. So listen well. Don't laugh at what you hear. Don't ask me what comes next. Some of this will be painful for me." he sighed, "But what I tell you in the coming days is meant to guide you on. To help you understand some things you don't. To help you see how I change from the boy I was into the man I have become."

"Should we start writing?" Jack asked.

"No not yet. Put your pencils down." Their father's lips quivered.

"Yessir."

Tip sighed again and closed his eyes. He wrung his hands together. When he looked up he wore a face they had never seen. "I shot a man when I was younger," he told them. His eyes were filling with tears. "When I was your age. I shot him in the back and ran away."

There was a dead stillness then for Jack Oakham. As if Act One of his life had ended. He knew his father to be a serious man. He would never prank them on such a horrifying note.

Both brothers felt tempted to look at the other, anxious to see a reaction, but neither would dare. Their eyes remained fixed on their father.

Tipper wiped away his tears. "I shot him as a means to run away. I had been drafted and it was a cowards way out. And running begets itself. No, no. Don't ask any questions. A question would take me by surprise and I'm not sure I could tell the story like that."

Snow and Oakham found their storybooks. Both were worn and scuffed, with a tight band around the outer cover. Tip tried to smile through his tears, "Yes, yes. Now you two can start writing," he told them.

As the story unfolded Putt slept peacefully beneath the sound of the chatter.

6. The King of Kamchatka

By Henry Snow

The trawler had been at sea for over a week when the deckhands caught sight of the shoreline. A bell rang from the nest and men poured out of the hold wearing parkas with sheepskin boots and fur caps, and goulashes to fight the bite. Before them, spread across the quarterdeck were a dozen giant cages, stacked two high. The hands moved alongside them, watching with pride as four- thousand king crab snapped at them from the inside.

Below deck Mushkin, the Captain, was in his quarters, his ledger open. He was a round man with graying sidelocks and the smell of coffee grounds. The old man scanned the ink-smudged pages scribbling notes on little slips of paper across his desk. When he had finished adding the rubles, he slipped his spectacles off his bald head and ran his wrinkled palm across the back of the last page of his ledger, enjoying the tiny dimples that his ink pen had imprinted in the paper. He stacked the crew's wages and stowed them in his top desk drawer. Then he loaded his bundle with his personal effects and as he did so, he began to sing a song he had been holding off on for many years. He hummed the tune and began singing as he moved toward the deck.

Mushkin stopped. He stood like a statue with his hands on the taffrail, his chin turned down toward his boots. Beneath his slicker he wore a suit of long cotton johns faded from years in the cutting tides and his sleeves were curled up past his elbows. His forearms, each tattooed, could be seen flexing as he gripped the rail. He stood there for only a moment before he threw back the door beside him.

In the last cabin a boy was sleeping in his clothes. He looked to be in his late teens, but the bruises on his face disguised his age. His right eye was swollen shut, his lip bloody.

"Get up."

"I want some lager first," the boy said.

The Captain slapped him. "That's not what we call it."

"Well I want some. You've got plenty. And I'm hungry."

Mushkin cuffed the boy across the face but he wasn't pleased so he pulled him by the hair from beneath his blanket and cuffed him again, this time with the back of his hand. The boy's face thudded dully into the iron walls. The boy rubbed his jaw briefly, and curled back into his bed, neither angered nor injured by the blows.

"If I were in a sailor's mood," the Captain said. "I'd drag you up on deck, let you see the land, and tie anchor to your sad heap and drown you on the drags."

"There's no land," the boy said, though his eyes had hope in them.

The Captain rubbed his knuckles. He had believed his own words – he hated this lazy boy – he wanted him to suffer, but his good mood overtook him. "When we dock I want you off and gone. I want you to go and keep going. I don't expect you'll survive a month here. Your card cheating has lost you everything and no one here will hire you, and you can't go back." Mushkin smiled. "Best catch hop I've taken in nine years and you could've had a cut. But now you'll die in the street."

"Is there really land?" the boy asked.

Without looking at him the Captain kicked the boys pack beneath the bed, slammed the door behind him and went up on deck with his men.

When he could hear the Captain reach the quarter deck the boy sprung to his feet, scrambling to the cabin window to catch sight of the shore. This hell is over, he thought, and began collecting his belongings.

The deckhands were preparing to tether the trawler. They had ropes ready – watching the men on the shore with their cranes. Mushkin joined them on the deck and all around him his men were joyful, smoking as they waited to share the news with their wives. There were already women on the dock, some with bottles, some with children. As Mushkin passed his men they shook hands and slapped one another on their shoulders and there was a unanimous laughter among them.

Everyone grew quiet as the boy stepped around the taffrail. He eyed them nervously and turned his head toward the deck. Some of the men used words to curse the boy, while the few who were closest spit at him. The boy spread a little evil smile across his face as he walked toward the ramp.

Mushkin set the tether ropes and stood uncomfortably by the boy. He didn't want to look at him. As he stood along the rail one of his crewmen noticed Mushkin's bag. It was full, much fuller than it had been when they had departed a month before. "What did you get yourself, Captain?" the crewman asked with a smile, his hands creeping up the bag.

Mushkin turned on the man sharply, a violent expression on his face. "Never touch that!" he said. The crew was startled instantly. They each stopped what they were doing. The Skipper's reaction all but shattered the man's mood, causing him to back away apologizing. If he had known that the reason his Captain was so upset was because in his bag he was carrying dozens of colorful braziers, at his wife's request, he would have been laughing heartily instead of standing there in fear.

They docked and tethered the trawler. The first mate stood near the cages, waving the crane in. "Bring the splits with you tonight," Mushkin said to him in Russian. "Last time Pavel had to run me a tab."

It was a tradition to hand out the men's wages over drinks that evening.

"Not this time, Skipper," the first mate said, trying to calm his Captain. "This time we'll buy *you* the drinks."

Mushkin moved onto the ramp smiling. For once he looked forward to drinking with his crew. He would have brought the money himself, but he always felt ill at ease carrying that kind of cash around, especially with his wife knowing. She was a leech, that woman, or so he thought. It wasn't enough that he had to buy her lingerie, but if he ever brought cash around she would surely skim some from both ends of the stack.

The rest of the crew went to work, but Tip was free to go. It was late afternoon and they still had much work to do before they divided the hop. They wouldn't have accepted his help if he'd offered it. The boy kept his head down as he crossed onto the ramp, trying to avoid the looks of the crew. But the crew was now only part of Tip's problem. The sight before him was daunting.

The village was small, but the mountains tumbled west all around it. He looked up and down the coastline for any sign of roads, or other villages, but saw nothing. He knew very little about where he was, how far north he had landed. All he knew was that he had in fact landed, into a new life, and he had no direction in which to take, no path to call his way. He simply knew that east was the sea, east was the way he had come from, east was a place he could never see again. He knew that in front of him, from the edge of the dock onward was a land so vast and incomprehensible that the very thought of it made him shudder. He knew it was a cold land, a hard country, and a place not welcoming of his people.

He looked out upon the rickety tack shacks, stumps for benches, clotheslines for the fish. The gulls were squawking on the ash gray sand. He could see birch firewood stacks and old wheels, picks and ploughs and steel sleighs. He wandered aimlessly through the streets. Twice women looked upon him with fear when they saw his swollen face. He disappeared into alleys, reemerging moments later. He wandered for over an hour without a word to anyone – until he finally realized that there were no roads leading into the mountains, or anywhere else, just a small village alone on the shore.

Tip Holland sat in the street to weep. But soon it began to rain and the boy found shelter in an open room in the alleyway. The room was a storage unit of some kind, filled with empty shelves, a wall lantern, and stacks of newspapers and dry wood. He didn't understand the room's purpose but it was dry, and quiet, and he could be alone there with his sorrows.

Some time passed before he heard a whistling in the street. Tip ignored it at first. There was nothing he cared about, least of all whistling. But soon the tune was so strong that Tip found himself leaning to peak out the doorway, down the alley, where he saw a man walking cheerfully in the rain. The boy kept his head down, but beneath his hat brim he watched him carefully, though he didn't know why.

The man was dressed in the pants of a pauper, frayed at the trousers, and his plaited shoes had soles that had rubbed thin at the edges so that he walked on the outside of his feet. He had withered mustaches that grew out past his smile, which was gentle, and eyes so blue and startling they were remarked upon for years after his death. His face, unlike the other villagers who carried an emaciated look, seemed to be pumping with the blood of a young man. He was so large and independent that he seemed to fill the alley he was walking in, both with his stature and his liberty. The moment the man saw the boy alone in the room he stopped. The man looked kindly at him, asking a question - though the boy didn't understand.

Tip leaned back into the poorly lit room.

When the man stepped closer he asked the question again. Tip raised his head and saw that in close quarters the man was so large that he couldn't keep him in focus. He waved him off.

The man ignored this and spoke again, this time with a raised hand, like he was giving the boy a blessing. Then to Tip's great surprise the man left some money at the door and was gone.

Tip could hear the man whistling to himself as he carried on down the street. Quickly he collected the money, stuffing it in his pockets.

The sunset came shortly thereafter, as did a hunger like none the boy had ever known. They hadn't fed him since they caught him at cheating. It had been two days and he was already light in the head. The hunger came in waves and his wave was reaching its peak. He rose to his feet and walked the alley, no more hopeful than he had been before the man's gift. The dusk light was the only thing that gave him comfort. He was happy to stay in the dark as long as he could. He had traded hell at sea for hell on land, with little hope of escape, and even that hope was dangerous. The boy was certain that if he did ever leave this place it would be by boat again, something he dreaded more than death. All he could think about was one warm meal, whatever he could find, and as many drinks as he could consume. Beyond that he had no plans. The boy's road seemed at a certain end. He thought of killing the Captain and then himself, though he doubted he had fight enough for either.

As he came to the square he could hear strange music playing inside the only shop with lit windows. There were curtains preventing him from seeing inside and a sign hanging over the door that he couldn't read. For all he knew the Captain could be sitting inside, but he smelled food and he knew he had to risk it.

Tip walked in. It was a tavern but to his surprise the place was nearly empty.

Seated before him was the man who had greeted him in the alley. He sat silently at the head table, watching the door as if he was waiting for something. Tip nodded at him, but could think of nothing else. The man nodded back, his face heavy with concern when he saw his bruises.

With the exception of a barkeep and the old woman he was talking to, the only other occupants were a pair of lumbermen sitting near the corner. Tip thought he knew why the place was vacant. The tavern was a mess, with open cupboard shelves, loose magazines, a pot-bellied stove lit with driftwood sticks, a row of caps on the walls hanging on cork bulges, fishing vests hung from the rafters, rag baskets, slickers, pitchers, paddles, ladles, nets, hip boots, bibs, a whole store of provisions, sugar jars. The boy didn't like the idea of taking a meal in such a place - but he had no other choice. He found a poorly lit seat in the corner beside the lumbermen and turned his chair in such a way that it looked like he was with them. A moment later he took a ball cap off the wall, and switched it with his own cap, to hide his face.

When the barkeep came around the boy took a menu. The man asked if he was alright when he saw the boy's chin but Tip simply pointed to the first meal he saw and said, "And a Vodka."

The barkeep hesitated then headed back to the kitchen. The kind man at the table was listening to the exchange.

In the next moment the door to the dusty tavern swung open and the new guests arrived to an uproarious reception. Tip kept his head down and he was soon glad that he had. The entire crew stepped in. The barkeep and the old woman celebrated. The lumbermen lifted their drinks. The huge man seated at the head table stood to his feet, raising his hands in the air, "Vashya Drovye!" he called out.

The crew echoed the blessing, each one of them embracing the man.

They filed in, every one in a chuckle, and found a seat at the long center table near the door. Mushkin was the last of the crew to enter. When he did he greeted the man with laughter, though none of their words the boy could understand.

"Otsov Kolschen," said Mushkin. "Back after so long away from us."

"And just in time, Mushkin!"

"Just in time, Kolschen! Time for a drink and a tale I say."

Kolschen was a name each of the shoremen said with delight. The big man owned the tavern and was known to buy vodka for all of the tavern dwellers when the catch hop came in.

He and the Captain found their own table, not far from the boy, though Tip was pleased to see that Mushkin sat with his back to him. The crew hadn't noticed either. They were too busy drinking away the pay that they hadn't yet received to notice anything but Kolschen and their drinks.

However Kolschen was not so easily distracted. As he sat Kolschen noticed the boy again sitting alone in the corner.

"I see you've brought the lot," laughed Otsov.

"I have, Kolschen."

"Who's the new hand?"

The Captain said, "Don't have one," without looking up.

"How long have you been at sea? I'm old and I'll drink to oldness, my memory is fading."

"To oldness!"

"I hear you had a catch hop to beat all."

"Otsov Kolschen, I did at that." He pulled his friend up close. "This one has saved me, old friend. All these days with nothing to show. I tell you Otsov, it's dreadfully boring. Of all the trades God cast me as a fisherman, and I'll never understand. How many long summers, Otsov, have I pined and toiled?"

"Too many to know!"

"Too many!" and Mushkin took a long drink.

"But now I am here, and a what a hop! Tell me I don't look younger. You can't, Kolschen. You can't do it. I feel like a young man, like a starling even."

"You look a week old at most, I'd say. No hair on top like a babe."

"A week? Kolschen what a pity! I feel like I have only lived in the light of day! I am but a day, Kolschen. Today is my first day! To my first day!"

Kolschen was all smiles. He couldn't recall a time when Mushkin's crew had been in a better mood. "Well no one deserves it more. What was your good luck charm, Mushkin?"

The skipper shrugged. "Don't know," he told him. "Maybe it was fate. I have found favor with the weather gods."

Kolschen ignored this. "Did Lubochka cook you something fine, perhaps, to send you to sea?"

Mushkin buzzed his lips, "Blah! My wife cooks for herself alone. There is no room at the table for the two of us. She is so fat, you know."

"I know better than that, Mushkin. She cooks you fine meals but you never eat them. And your wife is lovely in her skin. Maybe she alone was your good luck charm."

"Nah, I've had her forever. If she were really a charm she would have kicked in sooner. Maybe it was how much I drank the day I left. If I could only remember."

"Same crew?" Kolschen said.

"Very same. As noble a cast of sealubbers as I've known. You know them all, Kolschen. You saw them as they came in."

"Well I haven't seen *that* one before."

Mushkin turned with his wooden mug. When he saw the boy behind him his upper lip seemed to vanish. He ducked his head to be certain of what he saw but there was no need. The boy's bruises alone gave him away. Mushkin slowly stood to his feet and sent curses across the room.

Beneath his hat brim the boy saw Mushkin coming. He feverishly began to devour his meal. Tip soon had rice on his shirt and in his beard. In an instant the Captain grabbed the boy's plate and pushed it from the table. It rattled on the floor.

"Pavel?"

The barkeep was nearby. "Captain."

"Never serve this pup again," he said.

"Sir?"

The boy looked down at his meal and Mushkin put his boot in it. The boy rolled his eyes.

"His money is no good here, Pavel. Nor is any man who hires him. It's a cheat, this one. It's a coward. Let him beg for food behind the can at Lady Iraina's."

Kolschen spoke up, "Watch your tongue, Mushkin, It's bleeding all over the place."

"Let it bleed. I don't care. This boy isn't welcome in my tavern."

Kolschen reached out for his friend. He didn't know who the boy was or how he had come to drive Mushkin to such anger, but such things were irrelevant to Otsov Kolschen. He took the Skipper gently by the wrist.

Mushkin stared down at the boy with his drink in his hand, and pulled his wrist free. "Are you hungry, pup?" he said, twisting his boot.

Soon Kolschen was standing over the Skipper. He laid his big hand on the Captain's shoulder and when Mushkin looked up he seemed reduced in stature. He turned away. "Sit, down, friend," Kolschen said gently.

The Captain looked up and nodded. He bowed to the boy and walked across the room to join his crew.

Kolschen remained standing alongside the boy. He noticed that he looked white as a cloud, his hands hidden beneath the table. Instantly

Kolschen called Pavel to replace his meal. But before the cook could even fill a plate the boy slipped out from his seat, his pack in his arms as he moved awkwardly past the men into the street. The boy had left some of Kolschen's money on the table, but not enough. The man paid out the rest of the bill, leaving Pavel a tip.

The Captain joined his men and they each had a second round and a third. Dinner was brought out for them by Pavel and the old woman. They devoured their meals and spilled their drinks and replaced them with new ones. Even Kolschen, who looked harshly upon drunkenness, could not deny how long it had been since the tavern had witnessed such a celebration. These men in their wild excitement were the picture of peace towards one another. Every word they spoke was one of affirmation.

The party continued until the beginning of the fourth round of drinks when suddenly the door to the tavern swung open again. Mushkin looked up. The last two members of his crew were standing in the door - Gosha his first mate, and Georgiy, one of the older hands.

"Vashya Drovye!" Mushkin called out.

But the two crewmen didn't return the blessing. Instead they stood with contempt in their faces, each of them breathing heavily and staring him down. The Skipper turned his head in confusion and lowered his glass. He was still in a fine mood, but he could feel it slipping away. First the boy had showed himself in the tavern and now his first mate was openly insubordinate. He looked around the table at the rest of his men. Each of them sat at full attention.

"Explain yourself, Gosha," he said.

"Myself? Have it your way all along then. Myself? What of *your* self, Mushkin? What have you done for *your self?*" The man was barely able to contain his anger.

Mushkin smiled. He thought this was some kind of joke to celebrate the hop. He didn't find it funny, though he rarely did find much funny with his crew. He decided to play along with his men.

"Why don't you drink and let go the joke, Gosha? Every moment we waste on stunts is one less we spend celebrating our hop. To our hop!"

Only half the men echoed, "To our hop!"

"The hop is gone!" said the first mate.

Mushkin leaned in and weighed the man carefully. His eyes were small and his fists were shaking at his sides. He decided that this was no joke at all. He stood up and stumbled through his thoughts. "Gone? Have you lost it, Gosha?"

"Hah! What a fine con! We swept the drags and loaded up and the rest of them finished too. Georgiy and I went down together. No man went below deck before us."

"No one?" said Mushkin. His eyes were still small. "Are you—"

"No one but you, Skipper." There was insult in the man's voice.

Mushkin could hear the implication. He widened his eyes and cocked his bald head at his first mate, but before he could speak one of the crew stopped him, "What was in your pack, Skipper? What were you hiding?"

It was the man who had been embarrassed by the Captain on deck that afternoon. He wasn't embarrassed then. He was angry. All of the men were growing more angry with every moment.

"Now you listen, boy," Mushkin said. "I won't have my catch hop drinks pissed away by some rabble."

"These aren't your catch hop drinks!" Gosha said. He was edging towards his Captain. "There is no catch hop now!"

Mushkin could feel the crowd growing closer. For an instant he looked over to his friend.

The first mate was quick to say, "Stay out of this, Kolschen. I ask you kindly."

"And I ask you to calm yourself," he answered. "But we both know there are some things words won't buy."

The first mate's smile was ugly. He has honed in on the Skipper.

One of the older sailors asked, "What was in the pack, Mushkin?"

The Captain hesitated. He knew his wife would curse him for telling the truth.

"We checked his pack," Gosha said.

The Captain looked surprised.

"When?" asked one of the men.

"Just now, in his home."

The men were silent.

"Whatever had filled it was gone when we got there."

The Captain showed no fear and admitted nothing. He wouldn't have his men see him bow.

"You did what, Gosha? In my home you searched and what did you find? Nothing! There is nothing *to* find!"

"Not in your home perhaps."

"Not anywhere!"

Ever since he and Kolschen were young Mushkin had been a violent man. He had never cared much for digging himself out of a hole with his words. He would find whoever had taken his catch hop, and he would enjoy it, but Gosha had insulted him. He was old and heavy but when he struck Gosha a blow it knocked him back so hard he fell through the door and into the street. The Skipper followed to finish the job.

What happened next, however, surprised him greatly. The remainder of his crew swarmed upon him before he could turn around. They burst through the door and smothered him, each pounding him with their fists. A moment later Kolschen was right behind them, flinging them aside by their coats and into the street. They turned and he stared them down.

The Skipper was bloodied top to bottom, his face beginning to swell. Gosha picked himself up and knelt beside his Captain. He wouldn't strike him again with Kolschen standing there. None of them would. But he still wanted answers.

"You may question him, but let him breathe," Kolschen told them.

Gosha and three others sat on his arms and his knees to hold him down.

"We have you, Skipper," Gosha said. "You'll never leave port unless you tell us where it is."

Mushkin was spitting up blood but he looked strangely content, like he had a great journey ahead of him. His men loosened their hold.

The Captain sat up like he had something to say. His eyes were rolling in his head. He would soon fall asleep.

"Gosha," he said. "Georgiy. All of you sad heaps." He turned to look at them. "Don't you see it? "Best catch hop I've ever had." And moments before he passed out he said fully, "That boy. That devil below deck. Don't kill that boy without me."

With a jolt Gosha realized his mistake. Of course the boy had been below deck all along. Instantly the crew looked down the alley. In a moment they were in frantic discussion. What happened next was a wild panic among the crew.

As the crowd grew louder and more violent Kolschen slipped away silently into the street. He hated to leave his friend but broken and bruised was nothing new for Mushkin. He had lived the life he wished for. The boy was another matter. They would kill the boy. Kolschen knew right where to look. Night had fallen and the streets were black but he could still see enough to find his way through the alleys. He turned the corners of the village like he had done all his life, hustling to beat the crew that would surely be scattered throughout the streets within minutes.

He came upon the alley where he had met the boy late that afternoon. Quickly he stepped into the room. It was total darkness. He kept his hands before him and his eyes keen but there was nothing for him to see but blackness. Kolschen could already hear sounds of men running over puddles in the next alley so he closed the door behind him and bolted it from the inside.

He looked across the darkness and cleared his throat. "What do you want?" he said in English.

Silence followed. There was nothing but dead, still air. Kolschen listened for breathing but heard none. He expected that the boy was against the far wall.

"There are men outside looking for you," he said, hoping for an answer.

His ear was turned toward the far wall, listening for a breath, a rustle. "I mean no harm and have no hatred," he said. "I own the boat you traveled on and the crew and her Captain are loyal—"

A loud banging came against the door. The sounds of two men could be heard rattling the metal frame on its hinges. There was an argument in the street, each man's voice was raised. This must have been the first place they looked, he thought. Nothing else is ever left open. There was a single stroke against the door again, and Kolschen could hear their steps trailing away down the alley. They would be back, he knew. They would be back with means to open it.

When the sound was gone Kolschen took a breath. He kept his hands out in case the boy had a weapon.

"If I knew what you wanted I could help you. I have my ideas of how to help you but they are mine and not yours. What do you want?"

Kolschen heard nothing. There were sounds of men passing through the street again.

When they were gone Kolschen repeated himself, "What do you want?"

"To go west," came an answer.

Kolschen nodded. He could hear the fear in the boy's voice. "It isn't easy. There is a wilderness all around us."

The boy readied himself as he heard footsteps crossing through the streets. Kolschen stood calmly. When they had faded Tip whispered, "I was hoping to find my way to the trains."

Kolschen lit a match. It did little to light the room but he could see the boy, in the corner squatted down, a broken bottle held in his hands.

The old man began to whisper himself, "Once you've mended wounds you can barely think of other things."

"What?"

Kolschen stepped aside with his match and lit a lantern on the north wall. "When the captain couldn't pay them – they beat him," Kolschen said. "He's outside all a mess."

The boy looked away.

"They'll do worse to you when they find you."

The boy started to cry, "I know."

Kolschen lifted his hand, to calm him, and stepped forward as he did.

But the boy stopped him, "If you give them the money will they let me go?"

Kolschen shook his head. He had thought of that himself. "With the crew it's a gamble. They may be drunk enough to let it pass. But when the Captain finds you I have no doubt what he'll do. Even I won't be able to stop him."

The boy wiped his tears. "I could pay you," he said.

"Pay me for what?"

"You could kill him."

Kolschen found a chair by the door. He sat down heavily. When he thought about what the boy had said he could barely contain the tears himself. "God help me, I don't know you, but you're hardly a buck. Whatever you've done you're young, and no one in my circle hurts the young. You'll come with me. You'll come tonight. You'll keep quiet, and when I say, you do. Look up now if you agree."

The boy didn't hesitate. He stared heavily at the old man.

Kolschen rose and quietly they left the small dark room. The two moved through the alley. Kolschen crossed each street before he called the boy to follow. They moved westward out of the village all the while hearing the roaming party kicking in doors and calling out threats in the dark.

They slipped unnoticed up into the hills through a winding trail. Kolschen kept the boy in sight, always mindful of his hands. After a short distance they stopped.

"These men will hunt you," he said. "They will bring dogs up into these hills and your death will be unspeakable. Once they start there is little I can do to stop them – so I'm going to stop them before it starts. Do you understand?"

The boy nodded.

"Where did you hide the money?"

The boy sat in silence. "How do you know I hid it?"

"It doesn't matter. I know you did. If you tell me then I can help you." The boy backed away. He shook his fist as he spoke. "You're no saint! You're gonna keep the money for yourself! You're doing this for yourself! You can go to hell before I tell you—"

"Keep your voice down!" Kolschen sighed. He never enjoyed raising his voice. He took out his wallet and emptied it on the ground. "The money you hid in the village doesn't belong to you. Neither does this. This is a gift – the other was a sin. Where did you hide the money?"

The boy scooped up the bills from the ground and began to count them. When he was finished he stuffed the wad in his pocket. He couldn't be certain but it seemed the man had given him a small fortune. "I hid it under a mop in the street."

"A mop?"

"You know a mop," the boy motioned with his hands like he was sweeping. "Wet for cleaning?"

Kolschen ignored the insolence in the boy's tone. "Near the tavern or where I found you?"

"Around the corner from the room I was in."

Kolschen stood up to return to the village but he stopped only a few feet away. "If you run you'll die," he said. "It's two-hundred kilometers to the nearest town if you know where you're going."

171

The boy nodded and Kolschen descended down the hill. As he did the boy whispered, "Thanks, dummy."

The men were searching the beachfront cottages and the shanties one by one, just as Kolschen had thought they would. Several of them had brought dogs along, all Samoyeds with heavy collars and long leashes. Members of the crew had torn the bed sheet from the cabin where the boy had slept and held it over each dog's muzzle. Soon the Samoyeds were scrambling through the streets.

They roamed up and down the docks, searching every boat, then the tack house, the bakery, the market, the fin shed. Kolschen could hear them hunting as he moved through the streets.

The catch hop was right where Tip had left it, crumpled beneath a mop in the alley. It was wrapped in a paper sack and Kolschen stuffed it in his coat. As he moved back towards the square he could hear the dogs growing closer.

It was lightly raining when Kolschen found the Captain unconscious in the street. He lifted him in his arms and carried him back inside, setting him on one of the tables. Beside him Kolschen laid the catch hop. The money had already been divided. There were eight envelopes in the sack, with a crew member's name and his wage scribbled on each. Kolschen counted the Captain's share and divided it up among the rest of the crew. The barkeep walked in just in time to see Kolschen stuff the paper sack in his coat, but before he could ask him anything Kolschen was back out the door, with Mushkin asleep on the table.

Outside the dogs were sniffing furiously down the boat dock. The crew was traveling as one party now, searching rubbish bins, wagons, open doors. They moved with purpose through the streets cursing and whooping and calling out threats until they met Kolschen in the square. He was standing like a great statue with his arms raised. The crowd slowed when they saw him. Kolschen was not a man to be ignored, even by a drunken crew of sailors who had been robbed of a month's wage. They gathered together, the first mate in the lead, around Kolschen whose arms lowered gently as the crowd grew silent.

"What do you want?" Kolschen asked them. There was no fury in his voice.

Some in the back kept their eyes to the street. They knew Kolschen was a peaceful man. The cruel weapons in their hands caused them shame.

The first mate stepped up. He was an angry man, but when he saw Kolschen in the street he doubted that his anger would find any satisfaction that evening. Thirty years before Kolschen had taught him in grammar school - he had yet to know a challenge that the old man couldn't handle. "These men were robbed, Marshall. Robbed blind."

Kolschen nodded to the men, each and every one. "What do you want?" He asked again.

"We want our catch hop."

Kolschen produced the paper sack and passed each man his wages. No questions were asked. Some of the crew rejoiced, a few were silent. The first mate was the only man counting, "There is more here than there should be," said the first mate.

"With interest," Kolschen said. "Overtime for the hunting party. I expect you to spend every ruble of it on your skipper."

The first mate was pleased with the wage. It would have been hard not to, it was the biggest hop of his life. And though the crowd was calming, Kolschen could still see the anger brimming from a few. The three dogs still sniffed against a tight reign.

"This puts an end to it, then," Kolschen said. "Now leave the stow-away to me. You must forget him."

"He stole our hop!" said one of the crew.

"And you've been compensated."

"By you, not by him."

"We all belong to each other."

Each of the men seemed to stumble when they heard this. Not a one of them could find a response.

Kolschen knew he had them. He gathered the men together with his arms. "Men, your hop is bountiful," he said. "Your wives are waiting in your beds - dolled up no doubt for your return. Do you want to let them sleep cold and lonely another night?" Kolschen leveled his eyes on them. "Just because someone hands you an offense - doesn't mean you have to take it."

Kolschen's talent was in disarmament. It never took him long to collect everyone's bullets.

Suddenly they all felt very tired. Some of the men were still angry, and many of them drunk, but not a one of them was awake enough to argue. They had their catch hop after all. The thought of a mattress that didn't rock involuntarily sounded wonderful.

Kolschen looked over the faces of the men. Only a handful avoided him.

"One more thing, Gosha," he said. "I'd like to rent your dogs."

Several men sprung to attention. "What?"

"I'll pay top dollar for their company. Just one night - then you can have them back."

The first mate smiled. "They aren't mine to rent."

"Then why are they here?"

The first mate signaled his men to hand over the dogs, which Kolschen handled like pups.

Kolschen watched as the men wavered. Some were too tired to stand with any decency. "No more drinks, tonight," Kolschen said. "You can celebrate the hop tomorrow." The men were strangely mellow. Some were silent, some thanked him, all took the catch hops back to their homes and tucked them beneath their beds.

After Kolschen had dealt with the dogs he hurried back inside the tavern. He was too excited to remain still. The barkeep was standing over Mushkin, a wet towel draped across his forehead.

"Has he woken?" Kolschen asked.

"No. He's sleeping better than you do."

"Good. Let's hope he stays that way."

Kolschen went to the kitchen and filled his coat pockets with bread, apples, and link sausage. He worked quickly. "I have a favor to ask of you."

The barkeep looked up from his bar. He was wetting another towel. "What do you want me to do?"

Kolschen took off one of his shoes. He removed the insole and produced another stack of bills. "Give this to Mushkin when he wakes up."

The barkeep looked at the money and took it.

Kolschen leaned across the bar. "I know to a ruble how much I just handed you, Pavel. I'll be back in a few months and when I do I'm going to sit down with my friend Luka Mushkin and ask him how much the biggest catch hop of his life added up to. He better have been pleased."

The barkeep nodded uncomfortably.

"In the meantime I need to pay you for a service."

Kolschen unfolded a few bills from his shirt pocket. "What service?"

"Tend him as best you can for tonight only. I've no doubt he'll be good as new by the day after tomorrow. He's had worse."

"Where are you going, Marshal?"

"Oh, friend, please don't call me that. On an errand, Pavel. Oh what a joy! Is there something you would like me to bring back? Perhaps a new record for your wife?"

"No. Thank you, Kolschen. My wife has enough records."

"Oh well. There are three dogs locked in the cooler. Let them out in an hour and in the morning give them over to their owners. They'll come looking for them."

"In the cooler?" Pavel said. "Won't they freeze?"

"Only if you leave them longer than an hour. If men come asking for them before then, tell them nothing."

"What if they ask in two hours, Marshal?"

"They won't. By then they'll be asleep. I will see you in the fall, Pavel."

*   *   *

Kolschen found Tip huddled right where he had left him. He was hugging his knees behind the shadow of a tree.

"Well?" Tip asked.

"Now you're with me," Kolschen told him. "If you value your skin you should never set foot in that village again. Some men have long memories even when they're drunk."

"I don't want to. I just want to go west to the trains."

"Then that's where we're going, and quickly," he said. "Mushkin will be back on his feet before long and you must be far from here whenever he does."

He led the boy out of the village up a long sheep trail that wound into the hills through trees and wild places. They hiked two full miles in the dark until they reached an abandoned cabin, bolt locked with a room full of gear and a fireplace. The boy saw a gravestone in the trees near the cabin – and a portrait of two sons and a wife on the mantle. Once inside Kolschen quickly packed two bags, both laden with warm clothes and fishing gear, tarps, tents. The boy watched the packing with fascination. It seemed that the man had done this before – left suddenly in the night and headed west into the wilderness. As he waited Tip noticed a world map on the wall, covered in pins of three colors, representing the travels of Kolschen and his sons, he supposed.

The man gave the boy all the food he had, filled a canteen, found him a good hat, handed him his pack, a canvas haversack that he would keep nearly all his life. Lastly Kolschen moved to the closet where he took out a bow with a full quiver and a Rettig rifle and a bearskin coat. Tip stared at the rifle.

"God gave us the great commission and I, Otsov Kolschen am his servant. With Ruffino there were no questions. He followed me. I cannot lead if you do not follow."

"Who is Ruffino?"

"Ruffino was the first. Fled his country because the war killed his brother. Came across the sea and I fed him, and I led him west. And he followed. We are all disciples of someone. Now we must go."

Outside Kolschen saddled two horses in a stabled clearing. The boy had never been on a horse though he thought there was nothing to it. He mounted from the right and Kolschen corrected him. As the old man adjusted the stirrups the boy eyed the rifle carefully, just inches out of reach, holstered on Kolschen's saddle. The boy knew he couldn't overpower the man, despite his age, but he felt confident that he was quicker. He kept his eyes nervously on the rifle, losing all interest in what Kolschen was doing. The old man sensed the change.

"Have you ever fired a gun like that?" Kolschen asked.

The boy was dumbstruck, staring wide-eyed at the man. "No."

"Ever fired a gun at all?"

When he answered it was in a whisper. "Just once."

"That will change," Kolschen said. "To survive out here I'll have to teach you." Then he stepped away to collect their packs.

It was the perfect opportunity to steal the man's rifle, but at that very moment the boy lost interest. If Kolschen was trusting enough to let him shoot, the boy knew it would be much easier to kill him when he handed the gun over himself. The boy thought it wiser to wait.

Kolschen helped him with his pack. When they were loaded the old man laid a hand on the boy's shoulder and prayed for him – and his family. If he had any God knew. The boy sat awkwardly with his eyes open – having never been loved like that. When Kolschen was finished he saddled up and led the boy deep into the wilds before the sun rose.

The two said nothing through the first hour of their journey. The boy grew tired and uncomfortable, but kept his complaints to himself. They rode west through the wild lands up into the hills until the sun rose at their backs when Kolschen pulled reign and awkwardly the boy did the same.

"Have you ever been baptized?" the man said.

The boy answered with a pop. "Nope."

Kolschen smiled, "What is your word for cured food?"

"Cured food?"

"Yes, cured. Like in vinegar? I can never remember the word."

"I don't know. I don't think we have one."

"Do you know what I'm saying, a food that is kept? Food that is preserved in vinegar? We do it with onions and cucumber."

The boy didn't give it any thought. "We don't do that."

Kolschen sat in silence, trying to recall his time in the States. He rarely grew frustrated, usually only when his memory failed him. "What do you call a cucumber in a jar? In green water?"

"A pickle?"

"Ah!! Yes, a pickle! That's the word! A pickle!"

The boy frowned awkwardly. He had never known anyone who didn't know the word for pickle.

"Later today I'm going to teach you how to fish," Kolschen told him.

"I already know how to fish."

"And tomorrow I'm going to teach you how to ride."

"What d'you call what I'm doing?"

"And then after that you will prepare for the life ahead of you."

Tip had given the life ahead of him little thought. The fact that some strange old man was thinking about it for him made him uncomfortable. "I just want to find the trains," he said. "I thank you for your help."

Kolschen nodded. He leaned out across his saddle and fed his horse some apple slices. "Yes. And when we're done – you'll be a pickleman."

Tip decided that the old man was crazy. He didn't know what a pickleman was, and he didn't want to. He was glad for the food in his belly, and the old man *had* helped him, though he couldn't understand why, but he didn't intend to be anyone's pupil. He thought saying so up front was the well-meaning thing to do.

"Sir, I didn't ask for anything from you. You wanna go on some pilgrimage – it's your country. I'm just a coward who's running for his life. You can keep your lessons."

Kolschen watched the sunrise and the boy watched it too, the first he could remember. The man passed Tip some bread. "The point isn't to become a butterfly overnight," Kolschen told him. "It's to agree that a cocoon is necessary."

They rode all that morning until they came to a great rushing river where they stopped to fish. Kolschen watched as Tip fumbled with the line.

"Stop pretending," he said. "Do. To make new who you are, you must first make new what you think. To start from the outside is backwards."

"What the hell should I think, then?" Tip asked, but before Kolschen could answer the boy added, "Don't you even want to know my name?"

The old man put the rod down in his lap and smiled. "You're right," Kolschen said. "That's a better place to start."

7. Feathers and First Blood

When he had finished telling his story, Tip gathered up their gear into the saddlebags while the boys continued scribbling.

"How long did it take to reach the trains? Henry asked.

"Two weeks," Tip told him. "Two wonderful weeks. And by the end of that time he was everything to me."

"Really?"

Tip nodded. "There wasn't a moment in those two week when we were apart. We rode across the wilderness and he taught me every kind of skill. He told me stories and listened, really listened to me for the first time in my life. Once we arrived in a town I was already feeling the change. I remember feeling invincible - like there was nothing to fear. I knew how to ride, how to shoot, how to make a fire. I had a friend. Piece by piece my world was coming together. Then we arrived at a town and the changes continued. Kolschen bought me new clothes. He sold his horses and we rode the trains west from city to city. He worked with me through the language and some days he made me do the talking. I hated it at first but little by little my confidence grew, only because of his patience. Town by town we went, always westward, until we finally reached my father."

"Your *father?*" They asked in unison.

"Yes. My father. We went to find my father."

Tip rose and caught his horse and as he mounted he looked worn-thin from telling the story. "Let's get."

"Already?" Henry wondered. "Thought you might tell another."

"I'll tell them along the way," Tip assured him. "You've got three days of stories to hear. So let's get going."

"What's the rush?" Jack asked, clearly frustrated. He was finishing up his notes about Mushkin.

"Don't worry," Tip told him. "You'll have more time tonight after we make camp."

Henry closed his storybook, stowed it in his saddlebag and mounted quickly. But Jack didn't stop. He scribbled away until his father spoke with his silence.

"I wish I could dry my boots a little," Jack said. "They're slipping off my feet."

"It wouldn't matter," Tip told him. "We're crossing the river."

"We are?"

"We're heading north to Muleshoe."

The brothers looked at one another. "Muleshoe, where's that?" Jack asked.

"It's a township on the Cutshank. They have a saloon there. Thought we could break some rules."

What was left of the ducks and the fish were hung from Tipper's saddlehorn. Putt moved alongside the party, watching the bodies bounce. As they followed their father across the river, Henry and Jack looked at one another repeatedly. Both brothers wondered what came next in both journeys: Tipper's and their own.

Once across the river a blanket of cold came upon the land. The hooves of the Pritchers soon skipped across hatches of black ice and the riders were forced to breathe from the side of their mouths so they could watch the land unfold. It came dotted with small frozen millponds, a thousand in number, which steamed with the rising sun. They rode among the muddy banks, kicking up tufts of tundra until the horse's fetlocks were appropriately browned.

Tip and Henry thought to themselves how fine the party looked as they traveled: fresh mounts, young riders, gunned in the saddle, riding towards points west unknown to them. Tip half expected the eyes of the land to open just for them, to see such a convoy one last time.

But Jack was too distracted for such thinking. His shoulders were white with sleet and he couldn't shake his father's story from his mind. He stayed turned in his saddle, looking back for Putt, thinking how close his father had come to death in that small town years ago. Jack couldn't help but wonder what his life would be like if Tipper hadn't made it out of that village in one piece. It was a thought that troubled him during their long riding hours.

But he soon admitted to himself that he liked his father's story, regardless of how improbable it seemed. Jack couldn't imagine Tip Holland the way he was described as a younger man. For the Tip that Jack saw in the saddle was nothing like the boy from the story. It made his heart long to know what had changed him. It caused him to catalog the things he wished to change in himself.

By the noon hour the party came to the end of the rolling country and descended into a great valley that stretched north to no end. The wind howled across the land.

"I farted a second ago and I'll bet you it's hundred miles away by now," Henry said.

"No, it's still here," Tip assured him.

The dead grass danced where it stood, twisting wildly when the wind began to whine across the land. "At least it's flat enough to cross," Jack said gladly.

Tip called it the "Varem Merkakem" and said nothing more.

"Is that Yiddish?" Jack asked.

"Ye zun."

"'Yes, son.' Henry told him. "What's the other mean?"

"The endless valley," he told them. "Arayngeyn leoylem-vod."

Jack turned back, "What?"

"It goes on forever," Henry whispered.

Tip smiled as Jack admitted, "I hope not."

The thoughts of home were weighing heavily on young Oakham. Jack was accustomed to the sounds of Tenpenny: the ringing bell at mealtimes, the accumulated laughter of the children as they ran out into the fields. He knew that the bell must ring and that the children still cheered and that they would be overjoyed to see he and Henry and Tip when they returned, but that their lives would carry on. He thought of Sissy and Momma Tom carrying on a conversation for several days, the subject no doubt being the condition of the missing. But mostly Jack thought of Greer and Padibatakal. Jack wondered if Greer would miss Henry. He hoped she would. He worried too. But the feeling didn't last long. Jack and his brother each marveled at the new landscape. The valley was painted with ash-grey stones and emerging grasslands that sprung like emerald ponds from the powder. Near the valley center a large stretch of untouched powder swelled and around her edges were the only trees in sight.

"Coulda built your orphanage out here," Henry suggested. "Could build a ballpark in that field there."

Tip didn't answer. Something in the valley had attracted him. He drove the horses down the slope.

On the snowy field a blackened figure lay, resting near her center. The dark shape against the powder was unmistakable. No bigger than a packsaddle, Tipper thought. But he could see that it clearly had the look of the living.

The riders crisscrossed down the slope, cutting their own switchbacks, until they could see the edges of the shape stirring with the wind.

Henry dismissed the sight, thinking it to be the carcass of a vulture, something he had seen many times. As Tipper rode ahead the brothers parked in the saddle and waited on the dog.

"What do ya think?" Henry asked beneath his breath.

Jack kept his eyes back as the dog approached; completely ignoring his brother, a habit that he knew infuriated him.

Finally he said, "About what?"

"About this whole business."

"You don't want to know what *I think*. You just want *me* to know what *you* think."

Their first few years together, as they squared off as competitors, Jack had always been the one to initiate conversation, but time after time Henry made a fool of him, until their very words became a competition. Soon Jack had had enough, and sought his conversation elsewhere, usually with kind listeners like Zuni or Momma Tom. Jack didn't need another battle to fight with his brother. For young Oakham, Henry Snow was his battle, one he waged daily. And though Tip had taught him that every young man needs one, and even though he knew that going toe to toe with Henry ultimately made him stronger, Jack wouldn't allow for something of dignity like his words to become a pitch for his brother to swing at.

Henry chuckled. "I let you hit me the other day so you wouldn't lose face. The least you can do is talk."

"You wouldn't let a five year old hit you. And I wasn't the one who lost face."

Jack was turned away so Henry felt it was safe to smile. He knew his brother was right.

"We're the only two in this thing," he said. "You must have something to say."

"You don't care what I think, Henry. You just want someone to argue with."

"Not this time, brother."

Jack turned to see if Henry was just having fun with him. Henry Snow had a talent for getting what he wanted. If what Henry wanted was for Jack to engage, he was playing his cards beautifully. Jack couldn't recall an instance in their years together when Henry had referred to him as his brother. The word gave him pause like no other could.

"What d'you want to talk about?" Jack asked.

"D'you ever wonder who your father is?"

"What?"

"I do. Twenty minutes a day I do."

Jack was silent. These were not the words he was expecting. Henry was known to be apathetic about his past, or so Jack thought. He waited for Henry to finish.

"I like that you knew your mother," Henry said after a pause. "I like that about you. You've always seemed more complete to me. For me there's no place to start. I'll just sit there and wonder what my old man looks like. I never wonder about my mom – though I guess I should."

"Why'd you ask that now?"

"I don't know. This all seems to me about passing down the wisdom torch. An old Russian to Tipper and Tipper to us. Made me think about progeny and succession and all that. I just wondered if you think about that kinda thing. "

"I know who my father is," Jack said.

Then he added. "So do you."

Henry nodded, out of character, "In that case my mother must have been *good*-lookin'." Then he winked at his brother and rode on.

When they arrived at the flat of the snowy field Tipper was carefully eyeing the black shape from a distance. He motioned for the brothers to dismount, an action that Henry knew was coming, but frustrated him all the same. All his life Henry had been forced to stop for Tip. The man investigated every burrow or moose rub they came across, no matter how insignificant it seemed. The moment Henry spotted the bird he knew they would have to stop, even though he was clearly disinterested in the whole affair. "What does it matter how the bird died or what it looks like?" he thought. "It's dead, we're not – let's go find the treasure."

But Tip thought it mattered so the brothers dismounted near the trees surrounding the field, letting the Pritchers graze what little grass sprouted along the shore.

"What d'you hope to learn from that vulture, Tip?" Henry asked.

"What vulture?"

"That'n yonder. The one we're crossing this field to look at."

"Oh my mistake. I saw the plumage on his chest and thought he was an eagle."

"An eagle!" Jack called. "How bout that!" He had wanted to see one since he was a boy. "What kind is it?"

Eagles were among the great treasures of Tenpenny, giving her inhabitants pause every time they were spotted. Tip had always claimed the eagle as his favorite of God's creatures, especially the Goldens, which he had never seen up close. From the shoreline Tip knew that he finally had his chance.

"Alright here's the thing about it," Henry started up. "So you trumped me. You're old eyes can still see. I'm just sayin' it's a whole lot of ground to cover for just one bird."

"You're a bag of hot air, Henry."

"I might be. But a dead eagle isn't worth popping it."

The party treaded across the melting snow and Putt followed close behind - though his paws continued to slip, giving this strong, sure-footed dog a clumsy appearance.

As they made their way across, the surface cracked repeatedly, making each of them nervous - but nothing was said until out of the blue Henry declared, "Hey, today's my half-birthday. How bout that?"

The others chuckled and carried on.

Putt had never smelled a bird like this before. When Tip opened up the wings to lay them flat on the ice the old dog licked the feathers. The brothers had never anticipated that any bird could be so large. Its great wings spanned more than the length of a man and the colors along its breast were deep, dazzling even at further glance.

They could all see that the bird hadn't been dead very long, a few hours at the most. The eyes were still intact and the wings flexible.

"You know what killed it?" Jack asked his father.

"Don't know," he said. "These don't come this far north except to breed."

"Is that why he's swollen?" Jack wondered. "Because of breeding?" The first thing that had caught Jack's eye was how round the bird looked.

"He's swollen cause he's dead," Henry said.

Tip shook his head. "He isn't swollen, not yet anyway. He's fat."

"Birds don't get fat."

Tip flipped open his knife and slit the bird apart at the breast. To his son's surprise the eagle indeed held a heavy layer of fat beneath his feathers.

"Well they aren't supposed to," Tip agreed. "All that flying should keep 'em lean. "But this one did."

184

Tip checked the bird's feet, his wings, anything that would have kept him from flying, but he found nothing. All he could see was that the bird's throat was engorged.

"He choked or what?"

Tip opened up the throat and reached inside, finding a collared pika, still warm inside the gullet. The small rodent had pale grey eyes and was crushed from side to side.

"I'd say so. Doesn't tell us why he was fat, though." Henry said as he tossed the pika across the field.

Henry stood to his feet, making his case once again to get back in the saddle, yet for once he was silent about it. Jack found himself in agreement. Like his brother he became impatient to get back to the trail, though he was well-pleased that Putt had been given a chance to rest.

It was at that moment when Jack realized that Putt was gone. The dog had slipped away when Henry tossed the pika and Jack spotted him off a ways licking the dead rodent. The thought of his dog eating a half-digested rat and sharing a tent with him that evening was unsettling. "Come on, Putt," Jack said. "Leave it alone."

"What's the harm in a light snack," Henry jabbed. "If I was a dog I'd love a warm treat about now."

Jack curved his fingers into his mouth a made a whistle. "I'm surprised you didn't eat it yourself. Come on, Putt!" he whistled. "We're off to the Cutshank."

What Jack saw next was one of the most frightening moments of his life. Putt was beginning his return when the ground beneath his feet suddenly broke open underneath him. There was a tremendous pop heard across the valley and Tip, Henry and Jack each watched as the dog clawed across the snow and disappeared.

Before he could grab a thought in his head Jack pushed past his father and charged across the snow, his hands catching him as he stumbled. He tossed his pack from his shoulders and waited for whimpers or for Putt to spring out of whatever hole he had slipped through. But there was nothing.

Jack soon began to hear pop! pop! pop! beneath his own feet as he ran and in that moment Tipper called out, "Jack! Stop!"

Jack could feel the ground cracking and popping underneath him. He slowed to a walk and turned his head.

"What?!" Jack yelled frantically.

"It's a lake!" his father warned him.

Jack turned to face the horrifying truth. What he had believed were icy puddles on the smooth valley were actually bare spots in the snow. The entire valley was a huge frozen lake covered in snow drift! No sooner had Jack realized this than the ground beneath his own feet began to crumble. Tipper and Henry looked on in horror as a light mist erupted from the crevice, an icy trapdoor opened, and Jack disappeared.

There was no pause between them.

"Rope!" Tipper called out.

But Henry was already working. They both knew they only had seconds, not minutes, without a moment to think. Henry and Tipper worked the rope quickly without a word and soon were tying one loop to each of their waists. In no time the two began to move across the laketop as one, fully expecting to see Jack and the dog rise to the surface at any moment.

Tip knew they were both excellent swimmers and felt certain they would find their way back to the breach. But to his surprise Jack and the dog didn't resurface. They simply slipped through the ice and disappeared.

Tip could see the openings where the pair had vanished but there were no splashes. They edged cautiously towards the breach, with Tip out front and Henry close behind. "Hold back," Tip told him. "Dig in and hold the rope!"

Henry dug his boots in as best he could, but the ground was icy and there was little to brace himself against. Tip moved steadily out towards the breach, all the while waiting for his son to resurface. With every step they could hear soft cracks popping but they kept their eyes front and their steps light. There was no other sound. Tip hoped that by the time he came to the breach that Jack would have resurfaced. But it didn't happen. The breach remained still; no movement or splashing water and he could not understand it. When he came within a few steps of the breach, there was one crisp pop. The ground shook beneath them. In the next instant a hollow voice called out from below, "Don't move!"

Henry and Tip stopped suddenly. The voice was like an echo.

"Jack?"

"Back up," came the voice.

Tip and Henry did as they were told. Henry shook his head, "What're you doing?"

"I'm sittin' in the mud," Jack said in a hollow voice. "Lake's dried up."

Tip chuckled. "Are you hurt?"

"Just a little. I wouldn't come closer. I can see her cracking beneath you."

Tip had heard of winter lakes drying up before, but this was the first time he had ever known one himself.

"The dog alright?"

"He is," said Jack. "Licking his paws."

"How deep are you?"

"I'd say twelve feet. You wouldn't believe this."

"You aren't hurt?" he said disbelieving.

"I broke some fingers I think."

Henry and Tip consulted one another with their eyes. They tried to peer over the lip of the ice but when he did all he could see was the darkness below.

"I'm gonna send the rope down," Tip called. "Tie the dog on first."

He pitched the rope and watched it snake across the ice, shaking it until the tip slipped through. "Dad?!" Jack called.

When Jack spoke Henry and Tip began to feel the slow crackle of the laketop, splitting where they stood. They spread their arms out to keep their balance. "What is it?"

"I think we'll walk out, if that's alright?"

Tip hesitated. "Is there a way?"

"I think so. I can see light. We'll meet you near the lake rim."

"What if you can't get out?"

"We will," Jack assured him and nothing more was said.

After Tip thought about it, hauling out a young man and an old dog as the ice cracked didn't strike of wisdom. "Be careful," he told his son, though he felt that he and Henry were in more danger than Jack.

Henry watched as his father tiptoed across the ice, "The spring is on," Tipper said with a chuckle. Though Henry was too nervous to reply.

*   *   *

Jack sat upright on the lake bottom. He checked his dog for injuries a second time and rose to his feet. Two of his fingers were broken, but they were of little concern. Jack was overwhelmed by his surroundings.

Before him in all directions stretched a great cavernous hall of glowing blue light.

The roof was a canopy of polished crystal. A filtered glow shown on them like flamelight, dimming and bursting with the passing of unseen clouds. Jack watched as the glow drizzled down upon them; the very earth blued by the vacillating light. He turned to find his bearings - his only landmark the open breach where he had fallen. It looked small and of little interest in that moment, as did what lay above it.

Jack turned in a circle, squinting across the icy sea until it faded to black, like he was looking through deep water. He knew the ground must rise in a grade to the shoreline, though he couldn't see it. All Jack could see was an endless flow of blue vapor between him and the distant black.

But then, faintly, Jack began to spot flickering hints of light in the distance. Immediately he raised his compass but in the next moment the light was gone. He watched and waited but only darkness remained. The clouds above the lake have parted, Jack thought, letting the light stream in for an instant. He knew that if he was patient the light would come again.

The great hall grew dim and Jack waited. He paid little attention to the soil beneath his feet, which was dark and surprisingly dry at places. His senses were consumed with new sights and sounds and smells. All around him the lake rocks lay thinly clothed in blankets of silt. He could hear it flake away beneath his feet. The air was thick with a musty smell, a filthy, rotten stench that Jack had never known. The longer he lingered, the stronger it became.

Jack could hear the echoes of his breathing playing back from the darkness. At one point he faintly heard the echoes of those echoes, gently whispering softer and softer with every note. He had never known of a place that whispered his every sound back to him and in the years to come whenever Jack found occasion to be in an opera house or a symphony hall he was brought back with a cold shutter to that whispering cavern. There was a great stirring all around him when he tugged his boots from the mud - when Putt huffed, when he closed the lid of his compass by mistake.

"Hello!" he called. The notes seemed to rhyme with one another as they grew further and further away.

Despite his broken fingers, Jack was well-pleased that the ice had split, and even more that his father had given up on the rescue. For Jack Oakham was wise enough to realize that what he was seeing was a rare spectacle, one that very few were blessed with. Jack wished his mother was there with him. He closed his eyes and imagined her staring up at the blue heavens alongside him.

"How am I doing, Mother?"

"You'll be fine."

"But am I doing well?"

"More than well. You're growing up."

"Do I have what it takes?"

She smiled at him. "That isn't for me to say."

Jack was surprised to realize that he wasn't cold anymore - as he had been all that morning. He was warmer in the belly of the lake than he had been minutes before riding in the sun. He could still feel the coolness of the ice above him but it was merely that: coolness – Jack was far from cold. He reasoned that the icy roof, a foot thick at places, was a splendid insulator and with no wind the room became quite comfortable – even cozy. Jack agreed with Henry that Tip should have built the orphanage on the shores of this lake. Surely this cavern would inspire wonder among the little ones. He knew that when Tip found his way down into the hold of the lake he would have a dozen ideas to improve upon it. No doubt he would set up obstacle courses and treasure hunts in this new underground dreamland and each child would be equipped with lanterns and helmets and the leaders given maps and quests to complete. And of course the place would certainly have a name. Jack smiled to himself then, remembering how Tip had always let the children name the landscapes they discovered. On several occasions during their childhood he had led Henry and Jack on adventures across unknown corners of Tenpenny – all except the west of course – and in their travels Tip had let them name many of the sights that they had seen – but only if they had a story. "You want something to have value," he had said, "Give it a name. You want something to be remembered – have a story to go with it."

There in the blue glow of the lake-bottom Jack was already thinking of possible names for his discovery.

"Whispering Cave," he said aloud. "Or Oakham's Oceans? No that's no good."

"Maybe we should mark the spot where we came through, Putt – like an historical marker on the highway."

Suddenly the light rose out of the darkness again. Jack raised his compass. "Southeast," he said aloud. "Follow me. I know the way out, Putt."

Putt seemed to ignore him. He sniffed the moist earth and appeared to be following the trail of an animal, as he often did on the surface. But Jack knew better, "There's nothing to hunt down here, Putt," he said with an echo. "Just soak it all in."

Putt continued his hunt, ignoring Jack completely. "You do your job and I'll do mine," he seemed to say.

Jack was enjoying talking aloud with the old dog. In fact he was enjoying himself altogether. Most of Jack's favorite times were spent alone with his dog. He had known little excitement without him. It was a welcome surprise to share something so unique with his old friend, and he was particularly delighted to freely think as a child does, of fantasy names for his wild discoveries. His father had instructed him repeatedly on the value of a well-oiled imagination, and though Jack had done well to keep it in practice, he rarely walked along speaking aloud his dreams. The act in his mind seemed juvenile, but in practice was sensational. It gave him great comfort to know that he and Putt were alone in the blue cavern, that he could speak openly without concern for any ears picking up his silly talk.

Steadily the two of them walked through the mud until the clouds moved in again and the light dimmed across the cavern. Jack watched as the blue glow faded until he could only see a short distance. He opened his compass just inches before his face and they moved steadily to the southeast.

Wild fractures ran throughout the canopy like veins of silver. Pockets of air seemed lodged like gemstones in the ice. Suddenly Jack felt a soft crunch beneath his feet. He stopped only to find that he had shattered the skeleton of a small fish, a young char he believed. As he carried on he began to see dozens of similar dead, scattered across the lake floor, dead many months, no doubt since the lake dried.

Jack thought of the slow death all of the lake-dwellers must have suffered, day after day sinking deeper until their bellies flopped on the muddy bottoms.

"Now we know what a lake full of dead fish smells like," he said aloud. Though as he said it, it seemed hard for him to believe that he was smelling dead fish. The air is just heavy, he decided, which must make smells heavy, too.

Putt moved from fish to fish, nudging them softly as he sniffed.

"My apologies," Jack told him. "You were right and I was wrong. Search away, good hunter. We have an exit to find." The dog paid him little attention. He was too busy chasing the trail.

Jack was leading them closer and closer to the exit but in truth, he didn't want to leave. He wished he and Tipper and his brother could carve an entrance big enough to lead the horses down into the cavern and build a fire under the blue glow of the icy canvas. When Tip sees this, he just might agree, the boy thought. But he knew there was much to see in the Westland. A whole journey ahead of him. He didn't know what lay in store for him, but he couldn't imagine it would be anything as beautiful as this whispering wonderland.

The ground grew dryer and fish bodies thicker until suddenly Jack became aware of a sound in the dark. He stopped where he stood. But when he did all he could hear was the sound of their breathing. The cavern was silent. Jack held his breath but Putt huffed away, and Jack was surprised by how loud the dog was breathing. The sound echoed across the whole of the dark. It seemed to Jack that the echoes were growing louder the further they walked. The same was true of the smell, he thought. The odor was becoming unbearable.

The cave had grown dark again, so dark that Jack could barely read his compass. He knew his exit wouldn't be far now. The ceiling was gradually growing lower and he could feel the temperature rising higher as he steadily approached the door in the ice.

He kept his eyes up to the light, thinking about Tip and Henry, hoping they had reached the shoreline safely. He couldn't wait for them to see what he had seen.

Just then Jack felt his foot brush something in the mud. Thinking it was Putt he reached down and patted him, but then he saw Putt standing still behind him. Jack looked down at his feet.

What Jack saw there on the bottom of the frozen lake frightened him so much he stood like a stone. He covered his mouth with his broken fingers. His eyes opened so wide it was like he was trying to push them from their sockets. All around him, snoring deeply, at the end of their long winter sleep, was an enormous den of bears, too many to count.

As the light streamed into the cavern Jack was amazed to find that he was surrounded in all directions. Huge woolly mounds sprung out of the mud around him. He could see the great heaps swelling as they breathed, their cubs nuzzled at their breasts. What he felt against his boot was a great male that stirred when he kicked him.

Jack stood terrified. He could think only of backing up without a sound. He would turn back the way he came and disappear into the dark and search for hours if he had to until he found another exit. But before he could even take a step Putt let out a growl. The dog was nose to nose with the bear at Jack's feet and he seemed to want to challenge him to a fight. Quickly Jack grabbed Putt by the muzzle, clamping his jaws together. He wrapped his knees around the old dog and pinched them tight, applying all of his strength to restrain him.

Now Jack and the dog both stood facing the bear, who laid soundly in the mud, snoring away. Never in his life had Jack been so angry, or frightened, or confused about what to do. But he knew he must do something, and quickly. At any moment the bear would come awake.

When Putt settled down Jack took one of his hands away. His broken fingers were throbbing. He reached for his pistol, but then thought better of it. He knew he would have to unload every round into just one bear to have any chance of killing it. The others would have him torn apart long before he could escape. Jack soon realized that his only chance lay in slipping out without a sound, a prospect that proved much more difficult with Putt at his side.

The dog stood still but Jack didn't trust him to remain that way. Silently he slipped his belt from his pant loops. He could hardly believe what he was doing. The bear was stirring, as if he smelled something foreign in his den. Jack watched him, his fingers shaking as he looped the belt around Putt's muzzle, cinched it down, and pulled the old dog back.

Then he looked up. Jack could see that the exit was no more than seventy feet away. The bears lay all across the floor - some to his right and his left, even some behind where he had come from. Jack had stumbled straight into their den. He would have to travel just as far among the bears if he headed back the way he came as he would be if he pressed on toward the light. The decision was simple, the situation impossible.

So off they went, walking among the bears. Jack tiptoed through the mud, though he could not prevent his spurs from jingling softly. He moved as nimble as a cat, one step at a time, the snores and the suckling all around him.

Jack's heart thumped so loudly in his chest that he could hear it playing just for him, like a wild chorus as it joined the sounds of the bears. The snores, his beating heart, his broken fingers, even the beautiful vacillating light raining down through the silver canopy all came together and brought anguish upon him. Jack nearly crumbled to the ground. But he pressed on. One step at a time, he said to himself. He thought of his mother with every moment. He was the type that believed her eyes were upon him. At one point he even looked up to apologize, trying to convince her that he would be alright.

But Jack was the one who needed convincing. His brother was well-known for saying that decisive action could get a man out of anything, whereas Tip believed in prayer. In most situations Jack prescribed to the notion that a cool head, the head of a thinking man was what was needed in a panic. He knew as he walked among the great shadows of the bears that there was no decisive action to be taken, and that no thinking man would have ever found himself where he was. Jack moved silently as he prayed and prayed and prayed.

The biggest bear was ahead of him, off to herself. She lay with her back to them, three cubs milking at her teats. To Jack's great relief he found that he and the dog had passed among half a dozen of the bears already, some only inches from his boots and none had stirred. He knew with any luck he might survive to tell Tip a story of his own.

Jack and the dog continued slowly across the open ground. They could hear the soft squeals of the three cubs as they fed. The bear rocked in place.

Jack stopped where he stood. The mother was nursing, though Jack couldn't tell if she was sleeping.

After a long, dead silence the bear remained still and Jack led the dog out away from her. They moved silently to her right, always watching, until they passed her, and all the while she lay still.

Jack could clearly see the breech and the open sky beyond it. It looked barely big enough for a man to squeeze through. He didn't think Henry could have done it. The canopy was only a foot above his head now and he knew he would have to duck as he covered the last twenty feet. The two moved steadily, gaining ground, until one last time, as a precaution, Jack looked over his shoulder. In that moment the clouds seemed to part just in time. The room was aglow with a pale blue light and Jack watched silently as her eyes came open. They were small and locked upon him.

In that instant Jack gave little thought to what he must do. He knew what to do, and exactly how to do it. Before he could think he gathered the dog in his arms, something he had never done, and raced across the lake bottom toward the light.

He could hear a horrible groaning rise in the cavern behind him, like nothing of this earth. Soon the sounds of heavy footfalls were slapping the mud and the ground was shaking.

Jack looked up. The exit was no more than a dozen feet away but the sounds of the bear was growing stronger. Suddenly Putt began to growl, watching as she charged across the mud. Like a great dark mass she ran. If he had had it his way Putt would have been dropped right there and left to fight. Jack could have his escape, Putt thought. But the idea never occurred to Jack Oakham. He ran as fast as his legs would take him.

The bear came to full sprint as Jack reached the opening. Like a heavenly beam the sun peaked out through the breech.

Jack scaled up the incline and feverishly pushed Putt up into the light. The dog sprung onto the shore and Jack scrambled through the breech and onto the snow and as he came free he felt a mighty tug on his boot. His leg flopped wildly. The bear had him around his ankle and Jack could already feel something sinking into his heel. Jack kicked and thrashed as the bear dragged his body through the snow.

He braced his free leg against the canopy and squared his boot up against it, trying to hold back the weight that was pulling him. But it was no use. Jack could feel his body being sucked into the hold. The weight became unbearable, his leg buckling, and just as he felt himself slipping into the dark cavern - his boot was torn free.

Jack scrambled crabwise to his feet and stood lopsided. Quickly he drew his pistol. Putt was at the rim snarling; his face painted with mud.

"Get back!" Jack said. At the sight of the gun Putt cleared away.

Jack could hear an unseen jingling in the hold of the lake, his boot ripped apart no doubt, his spur torn loose. He kept his pistol up.

The Pritchers could be heard then, bearing down the shoreline. Tip and Henry were riding hard through the snowpack. They hadn't seen the bear but once they came upon Jack with his stocking foot bloodied and pistol drawn, Henry was quick to call out. "Is it a brown?"

When his brother spoke, Jack hesitated. He even glanced at the mounts to see if Tip was ready with the rifle.

"Yeah!"

"Any cubs?" Tip asked.

Before he could answer Jack shot the bear. Her head had burst through the canopy as her shoulders shattered the ice and Jack fired the moment he saw her. The bullet caught her around the collar.

Jack lined up to shoot a second time but before he could fire the bear was gone. Blood was splattered across the ice.

Tip and Henry flurried to calm the horses and when they were turned the two sat with rifle and bow ready from the saddle.

And there they waited, all four of them poised for the charge. Henry moved to his right, at full draw, ready to knock a second arrow when needed. Tip kept his eyes honed on the bear's exit. He knew it was his rifle alone that would stop a brown. Jack took a knee and leveled his pistol at the splattered canopy. Putt had been on enough hunts to know that after the first volley was fired whatever they shot at would be fair game for him to finish. He stood beside Jack with his weight on his forelegs.

They waited - only the swishing of the horsetails could be heard on the lakeshore.

Twice the party heard a faint rustling beneath the lake, like the sound of a great weight slapping at the earth. But even though Jack felt certain that his bullet had barely wounded the big brown - the charge didn't come. After a couple of minutes Tip led Jack's horse up to the boy. The Pritcher turned to receive him.

"Eyes front, walk back to me," Tip told him.

Tip was quick to get Jack in the saddle. He knew the horses would bolt if the bear showed herself again. Jack limped backwards across the snow - his heel bleeding through the sock. Putt licked it up as he followed.

They rode out of the trees and up onto a snowy hogback all the while looking over their shoulders for the bear. When they came to the high knoll, a quarter mile above the lakeshore, Tip called them to stop. He dismounted and looked over Jack's injuries, handing Henry his big rifle. "Don't take your eyes from that spot. Not for a moment," Tip pointed. "Things could still get western."

The boy's heel was bleeding badly. Tip helped him down onto the snow. "How well did you hit her, Jack?"

Jack looked startled. Life seemed to be moving in fast forward. For a moment he couldn't recall if he had escaped the bear, or if he'd been pulled down into her den and torn apart. But then his throbbing heel reminded him of the truth. "Not very," he said finally. "May have clipped her collar."

Tip removed the boy's sock and made a quick bandage with it. Then he went to his saddlebag for a needle. "Well, you clipped something alright. I saw that myself. You stopped a charging brown with that pea whistle of yours." Tip shook his head and looked at the boy's pistol, still in Jack's hand. "I wouldn't have thought that was possible."

Henry knew his father was right. By all odds his brother should be dead. Even if Tip had gotten off a lucky shot the bear would have already taken Jack apart.

As Tip cleaned and stitched the wound he asked Jack many questions, wanting to know all about the experience, mostly to calm him down. But what Jack told his father was so far from what he had expected that no one in the party could remain calm. Henry was as astonished by the story as Tip was, but for different reasons. Tipper thought it a fantastic experience, one his son would never forget, but Henry looked on his brother's injuries with pure jealousy, knowing that the scar on his heel would be worn like a badge of honor throughout his life.

At one point Henry looked down at the bear hollow and thought of charging in with his father's rifle. A crowded den of bears was something Henry had never even found in all of his wild ramblings. It was impossible for Henry not to feel envy toward his brother's chance discovery.

He rubbed the ears of the old dog and said, "Putt - You're lucky to be alive."

Putt was already asleep but he opened his eyes long enough for Jack to hear him say, "Says you, lazybones."

In the next moment Henry turned and gave Jack a smile. Henry knew that the moment had been real and that his brother had stumbled upon it out of bravery. He left his post for a quick moment and addressed Jack with a handshake, "It's a great story, brother."

Jack nodded but made no reply. He was still shocked by the attention that his adventure had brought him. He decided that he didn't care for the feeling. Jack had never been the man of action. That was his brother's role. It felt strange to hear such praise coming from the mouth of Henry Snow. It was as much a surprise as the bears had been.

Henry sensed his brother's hesitation. He knew nervous eyes when he saw them.

As he turned back to his lookout Henry pondered his brother. How little we really talk, he thought. He knew they both were clueless about the other's story. It shamed him in a way. He dwelled on the prediction that Tip would likely tell him many stories about Jack, and it excited him enough to smile. The story of the bear's den set Henry's mind to know more about his good, kind brother.

But for Tip something about Jack's story didn't ring true. Bears didn't den in packs, he knew. They were solitary creatures, especially a mother with her cubs. Jack had never been known to embellish a tale like Henry often did, though the idea of more than twenty bears wintering in one den seemed like fantasy to Tip. He wore a look of skepticism as Jack told that part of the story. It wasn't until years later that he came to understand how true Jack's tall tale had been.

It wasn't long before they set off again. Jack couldn't be in the saddle long without a good pair of boots, Tipper knew. He set a toothbrush splint on Jack's fingers and stitched his foot and built a makeshift boot from one of Jack's spare sandals, surrounding it with a canvas flap from his pack and sewing it together to keep his foot warm.

"We'll get you a new pair of boots in Whitehorse," Tip suggested.

"What's the place where we're drinking?" Henry asked. He had been excited about the drink all morning.

"Never been. But I know there is one. It's in Muleshoe. The first town on the Cutshank. "We'll have our drinks then ride west to get Jack his boots."

As soon as he had Jack in the saddle – Tip gave a whistle. Henry sadly left his post and handed the rifle back to his father. Then he gave Jack's pack to him. He had retrieved it for his brother and was wearing it himself. His own tiny haversack was hanging from his saddle. "This pack of yours is heavy," Henry told his brother. "I was worried that if we lost you I'd have to carry it all the way home."

"Lucky for you," Jack said.

"For all of us."

Tip looked his sons over and sighed. One helluva beginning, he thought.

The party turned north. They rode on until they saw before them a pale grey plateau rising out of the plain that Tip called the Cutshank. The boys

197

had only seen it on rare clear winter mornings and even then her edges were blurry.

Tip turned back to look at the lake only once. Even amidst such high action Tip's mind returned to the sight of the eagle on the ice. The look of it filled him with sadness. His entire adult life he had been hoping to see one. Now the image was imprinted on his mind: a bloated corpse, dead even as it flew, fattened and unmentionable to him, having choked to death on some unneeded meal. He knew it meant nothing. But nevertheless he couldn't shake it. He thought on it for days and days.

Meanwhile Jack was thinking of home as he leaned back in his saddle. He wanted to laugh and cry at once. Laugh because he had lived a fine adventure and cry because he likely had many more to come before he saw his home again.

It took the riders an hour to reach the Cutshank. The land grew increasingly dry and barren to the north. The wind and the sun and the white land were blinding them and they preferred to ride with their eyes to the snow at their feet. They cut back and forth up the great plateau and when they reached the top they could each see the cubes of a small town cut into the white prairie.

8. Muleshoe

Joe Forsman sat in the corner smoking, his hat low on his face. He was surrounded with men who bored him, and who he could never seem to shake. Forsman held the belief that life changed only when he permitted it to, and he hadn't given life permission to change in twenty years. For Forsman, what happened in Muleshoe was what had always happened, and would keep on happening as long as he wore the biggest boots.

Muleshoe was the chief village along the Cutshank, a snowy plateau inhabited by hay farmers, cattlemen, and drovers who drifted east and west along the train bearings when the work was available. From Muleshoe the tracks pointed west to the melancholy towns in the valley: Whitehorse, Tallow, Stowington, and east back to lesser villages on Lah Shakes Lake.

The men along the Cutshank were quiet men, of few stories and little worldly education; they were an independent sort, not accustomed to outsiders, nor very interested in the shape of things off the Cutshank. They concerned themselves with what they could see.

A single road led down to the tracks from the north and at the junction, emerging like scars on the land, were a handful of weather-beaten structures: a train station, a petrol pump, and a tiny general store with a bar and a post office tucked behind.

To the south there were no settlements of any kind, nor any homesteaders or ranchmen, or hayfields, or roads leading in or out. The villagers talked of the land to the south as if it were a great mystery, and they did so with much interest, sharing tales about what they had seen of the landscape, either from their shallow trespasses or from flights above her, on their way to the sea. What little was actually known about the land south of Muleshoe was that it is for the most part a barren countryside. To the southeast a great sandy valley lay open-faced against the sun and to the southwest a wild timberland stretched out of reach to the mountains and the sea. Occasionally a pilot who stopped in the Muleshoe Tavern would share news of what he had seen of the southland when he warmed himself at the bar.

The Muleshoe Tavern can seat ten when it's crowded, but it is almost never crowded. Once, a few years earlier there had been a strange norther that blew in late that spring and the trail riders and hayfarmers, all unprepared for the winter bite, were stranded in muleshoe for two days, many of them drinking non-stop and some paying to sleep on the barroom floor. But most days there were no crowds. Most days the only men who visited the Muleshoe Tavern were lone drifters, with the exception of the same four locals who arrived every day after lunch.

Pulley was in the seat beside Forsman, a fat man from his childhood who was commonly silent and perpetually drunk. Joe Forsman didn't care to think of how many years he had watched Pulley fall asleep in that same roundback rocker, with a cigar in his mouth, wearing that worn-out souvenir hat from the Hayfarmer's Union rally of 1980. Some days he wanted to spit in the man's face and tell him to shadow someone else for a few years, but Joe Forsman was short on companions, and he needed men around to feel bigger than, even if they were just boring drunks like old Pulley.

At the bar Frank Creed was divvying up the mail for the hay farmers who would be in to collect by the end of the day. Forsman knew that he treated Frank unfairly, but he wasn't of a mind to do anything different. Years before Frank had come back to Muleshoe after a semester at college when his mother fell ill. She had worked for Joe Forsman for twenty years and her dying wish was that Forsman would find him work until he got on his feet. Forsman had never been far out of Muleshoe. He had lived on the plateau all his life and he harbored a jealous streak toward men who had seen college and the world outside. He had kept Frank Creed on a leash for eighteen years, serving drinks, dividing mail, missing out on his twenties and thirties. Frank was the only man Joe Forsman spoke to in a given day with any brains at all, and he knew it, and it satisfied him to mistreat an educated man.

The only other man in the room was Forsman's only son, Danny, who was whittling a piece of birch just to keep his mind occupied. He was Forsman's favorite, not because he was his son, but because he was a young man, and the presence of young men always made Joe Forsman feel young himself.

"Dad, d'you get the paper?" his son asked him.

"Did."

"What's the war doin'?"

Joe Forsman had listened to his son talk of the new war, which he considered of little significance, for over three months, always gathering news when he wasn't diligent enough to read for himself.

"What it does. It wages."

"Is there anything new you can tell me?"

Forsman poured himself a drink. He shook the glass in his hand and looked long at his son. Finally Forsman took a drink. "There's no war up here on the flats, and there won't be. Life isn't about to change anytime soon."

"You shouldn't drink so early."

Forsman stared down his son. "If you read on your own you'll get better at it. Instead you're a leech." The man paused and squinted at his son. "Are you a leech, Danny?"

Frank Creed walked out from behind the bar and brought Danny a drink. "Don't answer that, son. He's just trying to pick a fight," he said. "It's been a slow week for the war. All they're doin' is talkin'. Nothing but a bunch of old men talkin'. You know why old men try to pick a fight, don't you, Danny?"

Danny was slow to respond, "Why, Frank?"

"Because they aren't in one."

Danny avoided the eyes of his father, instead he turned down to his drink.

But Forsman kept his eyes on the barkeep. He knew Frank was getting bolder every year. It wouldn't be long before he said something that Forsman would have to cut him for. Forsman had known Frank since he was a boy and he knew Frank had never been in a fight in his life. He took comfort in the belief that he could still whip the younger man, though he hoped it would happen sooner than later. He was a cattleman and lately he felt like an old cattleman. I'll probably never see another fight myself, he thought, as he turned his eyes away from the barkeep and stared long at his drink.

The bar was quiet only for a moment until each man heard the hinges squeal. Forsman looked up to see three figures huddled in the doorway. Each man wiped his boots at the door and fluffed the rain from their collars and they were strangers to his eyes. As they stepped inside they began taking their coats and their gloves off and as the door closed behind them Forsman could see that they had reached Muleshoe by horseback.

"Afternoon," Tipper said.

"Afternoon," said Danny and Frank. Pulley was in a daze.

The party put their hats on the bar and ordered a round and Frank worked the beerpulls and set the mugs down before them. Forsman watched the travelers carefully from beneath his brim. The men in the party appeared to be well-suited for travel, all with good coats and boots, except for the smallest who had a makeshift bandage around one foot. Their hands were black, from this morning's fire, Forsman thought. Their lips were all numb and chapped, as if they had been in the wind all day but there was an air of anticipation about them, a wide-eyed excitement as the two younger men in particular reached the bar.

The oldest of the three raised his glass, "Here's to adventure," Tip said, "And here's to Jack, who lived to tell about it."

"To Jack," Henry said and all took a swig.

Forsman's eyes brightened. He leaned forward in his seat. The other men in the bar paid the comment no attention. They carried about their business. But Forsman lowered his hat and watched the three strangers closely.

"And to your health, gentlemen." Tip continued.

The men in the corner raised their glasses as the Tenpenny three drank a round. When they did the smaller one had trouble keeping it down, but the other young man swallowed it easily.

Forsman paid Henry special attention. The older man who had toasted them was nondescript, as was his dark-headed son. But the big one was unique. He was wild-looking, like the one he had heard so much about. Forsman had a hatred for the wealthy and had spent years pondering the possible faces of the rich family who lived south of him. No one knew the owner, though he was believed to be a quiet man who never left his ranch. Those who had been to Tenpenny to do special repairs had been screened before entering, and never knew who the owner was, for everyone there referred to one another in equal terms. All that Forsman had learned through years of questioning was that it was a beautifully maintained place, with dozens upon dozens of children living there, and that one of them was a wild eagle with curly red feathers. He had heard about the boy on two occasions. The first was when his neighbor, Charlie Granstaff had spotted a lone rider trespassing bareback across his southern boundary. Charlie had said the boy appeared to be feral and no more than twelve, but strong with crazy red hair. Charlie said when he told the boy to leave he had only chuckled at him, as if he wasn't even there. The next time was only a few months past, when Al Sallie, a bush pilot out of Dillinger, had to put down on an uncharted lake to the east during an electrical storm. Al had told Forsman at that very bar about the three hours he waited out the lightning on the shoreline, and of the horseman he saw crossing the alder vale in the flashes of light. The rider had approached the lake and circled his mount on the bank. When he stood on his wing in the rain Al could see that it was a huge boy, red-headed, atop a grey Appaloosa with WM branded near the withers. The boy had offered Al a lift back to shelter, which he graciously refused.

Forsman looked Henry up and down there at the bar and whispered something to his son. Danny stood and walked to the end of the bar by the window and ordered another beer. While he was waiting Henry noticed him glance at their mounts. Danny took his beer back to the table and a moment later Henry saw him whisper something to his father.

"You boys ain't old enough for your liquor," Forsman said with a friendly laugh.

"No we ain't." Henry told him. "Not by years."

The man squinted at Henry.

"Someone should put a stop to it," Henry told him as he took another drink.

Forsman looked at his son and at the barkeep, and lastly at the quiet man at the bar who refused to engage.

"There's no harm in having a drink with your father, son. If he's your father then he has every right to buy his sons a drink."

Henry watched Forsman's companions carefully when he said. "He's my father. His name is Stuart Whitlock. I'm Henry and this is my brother, Jack."

"Enjoy your drink then. Anyone who's been out in this wild parcel should expect a drink. I'm Joe Forsman."

Jack at least almost dropped his drink. The sound of the man's name gave him a cold shutter to his bones. Beneath his breath he barely uttered the word, "howdy". Tipper gave the man a nod, and a good careful look, having never seen him before - but then dismissed the whole encounter. Tip Holland wasn't the sort to be very interested in a man like Joe Forsman.

Meanwhile Henry gave Forsman a thorough look and smiled to himself. Wonderboy was right, he thought. When it came to sheer size Forsman had him beat, but that wasn't all. The man had the same wildness in him that Henry had, though not as cheerful. He was distinguished in his dress, his boots polished, his shirt and trousers neatly pressed, his badge still worn for all to see. But there was nothing wrinkle-free about this man, Henry thought. Behind his smile he seemed stained and battered. Henry propped his leg up on his knee and slipped off his boot spur. He turned the rowel with his fingers, placed it on a napkin, and began wiping it clean.

When the party went back to their drinks Forsman kept his eyes honed on them. He was hoping they would give him a reason to strike up a conversation, but all of the sudden they didn't seem interested in chatter.

"It's a rare thing to see such a wild bunch rising out of the wilderness," Forsman charmed them. "Are you goin' upriver?"

Tipper spoke quickly, preventing Henry from saying another word. "We might. It's such a wild parcel we don't know where we'll end up."

Forsman squinted at the men again. "A trio of wild adventurers," he said as he nudged his boy. "You see that, son. That's something you don't see these days. Intentional men. This country used to be full of them, but now they are hard to find. I'd like to buy a drink, Frank, for three intentional men."

The barkeep popped the bottles and slid them before the party.

"Here's to safety wherever you're going," Forsman smiled.

Henry, Jack, and Tip raised their glasses and took another drink. Jack could already feel his stomach turning over. He watched his brother down the bottle, took a deep breath and drank it quickly himself. Henry put his glass down and spit on his boot spur, still rubbing it with the napkin.

"D'you fellas see any wolves over there?" Forsman said.

"Over where?" asked Henry anxious to be in the conversation.

"Well, from wherever you came from. Rumor is they've been seen from the south and the east. I was hoping you might help the rumors, one way or another."

"No sir," Henry said rudely.

Forsman cocked his head.

"By 'No Sir', he means 'No Sir we didn't see any wolves'." Tip suggested. "We crossed a river this morning and saw some elk but that was all."

"What river was it?"

Henry looked at his father, "Is there more than one?"

"More than one?" Frank said. "There are hundreds."

"Hundreds? Well I'm glad we warmed up when we did. I meant no disrespect, sir," Henry said." I am naturally suspicious of strangers and I apologize for being short. I must be a bit bold after those drinks."

"No offense taken, son. I like a young man who is honest about his mistakes." Which was true. Joe Forsman valued men who took an accurate stock of themselves. "Let me buy you the next one."

Henry smiled again. He appeared to be warming up to Joe Forsman.

"Thank you, no." Tip told him as he patted his son on the shoulder. "These boys have had one too many, as it is. We thank you for the warm bar and the drinks."

When they had finished their drinks Tip paid the barkeep and stood up and his sons did the same. "Good afternoon," he told the men.

What Forsman said was, "And good afternoon to you, gentlemen." But what he was wondering was, "What did you bury out there?"

Henry put his hat on and walked over to Joe Forsman and shook his hand and thanked him for the drinks again.

Tip and Jack nodded to the men and then all three slipped out the bar and mounted their horses and rode east. Forsman stared blankly at the table. He could still hear the footfalls on the snow. "How fast are they ridin', Frank?"

The barkeep looked back at the travelers. "Not too fast. They have a dog with 'em."

Forsman lit a smoke. He looked hazily at the match as it fizzled.

"Strange them just poppin in like that," Frank said. "They were barely here ten minutes."

Pulley awoke for a moment and mumbled, "Maybe they aren't people of conversation."

"I guess," Frank agreed. "But I wish they had been. Those three looked like they had some stories."

Joe Forsman looked up. "Some stories, eh Frank? Is that what they had?"

"I'd say they looked like it."

"And that's all you have to say? 'They had some stories'."

"That' all, Joe. Stories is all they got as far as I know. I'd of liked to have heard one. Mine is dead." Frank tossed a match.

Forsman pointed at the door with his cigarette. "I tell you that was the one. Just as I've heard it," he said. "And that was the father too."

"The one what?" Pulley asked.

"Go back to sleep."

Frank spoke up, "You don't know those guys more than I do. Those fellas could be anyone."

"*Anyone* riding in *this country* with two boys, one a wild-looking red on a gray Appaloosa? And Danny saw the brand. That was our man."

Frank followed the party with his eyes until they dipped into a valley out of sight.

"You want another round, Joe?"

Joe Forsman looked sharply at the barkeep and knocked his bottle off the table, breaking the glass.

"Another round? That was our man."

"So you found your man. You know his face. Good. He seemed regular to me. Don't know what difference it makes to know his face. You'll likely never see him again."

"Don't you see, Frank? Mounts on the river, heading west at the beginning of spring? Three men tell us nothing in this country and you don't get curious?"

"Curious about what? No I don't. They paid for their drinks and they rode away peaceful. Curious about what?"

Forsman threw one of the other half-full bottles at the barkeep, cracking the mirror behind him. "D'you get a good look at those mounts, boy?"

With fear in his eyes Danny looked up. "I did."

"How were they rigged?"

"The dun and the Appy both had long saddle flaps like bow-hunters use. The buckskin held a rifle. Each had packs tied to the saddles, some bigger than others."

"Any shovels?"

"I did see a shovel."

"You're damned right you saw a shovel. Could be anyone, eh Frank? Horseback, armed, carrying shovels, one of them is a red top, and their tracks come from the east."

"Don't forget the brands," Pulley said.

"I ain't forgettin' the brands, Pulley. A man can be sure just cause I ain't mentioning the brands that I ain't ever forgetting the brands. They were branded, Frank. Branded like the pilot said they were. Branded like Doctor Ewen said they were when he went out to geld the studs. Branded beneath the withers. Like they do it in Spain."

"You may be right, Joe. I'm not saying either way."

"You don't get a say. This is my bar and that was our man. Danny wherever they're headed can't be more than a few days with that old dog. If they think we're tracking 'em they'll double back and come later in the spring and we'll miss 'em. So we have to give 'em room. The last of the snow will be gone in a few days so we can't wait long. We'll need four good horses and another man."

"Another man?" Danny said truly frightened by the conversation.

Then Pulley added, "Only one of them was armed."

"We don't know that. I didn't like the look of those boys. We'll bring another man. We'll send Wade to follow their tracks back to the south. I have a feeling they stayed along the river to fish. Did you see any poles or tackle?"

"Nope."

"Well I'll bet it was there. If he tracks their trail a day back to the south Wade'll be able to tell us how they made their living. Chances are they'll do the same thing comin' as they did goin'. My guess is they'll stick to the river."

"If you're lucky the horses'll lead 'em back the way they came," Pulley said. "If we're dumb lucky they'll stop in for a drink on the way home."

"Nah on the way home they'll be too scared to stop. They'll know what they have even if we don't, and they won't risk stopping for anything. They had their drinks to celebrate. From here on they'll stick to the river. Danny, once Wade has a look back south you and I and a third man need to pick a spot to come at 'em. As close to their property line as possible. They'll be relaxed by then."

"Do you mean to rob them blind?" Danny asked. "I still don't know what you mean to do. You 'Think we need another man'? Well I think it's better if we talk some sense before it's—"

The door swung open. The four men looked up to see Henry standing in the doorway. He wore a half smile and walked across the room. "I forgot my boot spur," he said.

Forsman corrected his posture and smiled around his cigarette. "Well, welcome back. Pull up a chair and we'll have another round."

Quickly Henry crossed the room - and went in with his boot. He broke Forsman's jaw in such a way that he never closed it again. Then, when he broke the man's nose with his fist, blood pumped into his open mouth, nearly drowning him. In a panic the son grabbed Henry by the shirt collar, but he had no plan. He was swung around the room like a horsetail, and ended up fetal by the bar. Pulley kept his hands up through the whole thing, a cigar drooping from his lips. Before the barkeep could load the shotgun Henry had him belly down on the bar, and went to work with his knee.

All of the men were conscious but the only one who saw Henry grab Danny by the hair was Pulley. Pulley was afraid of what he might do. But when Henry grabbed the man and rolled him over he didn't do anything. Danny had been laid out in such a way that he could see his father on the floor beside him, blowing bubbles from his gaping mouth. When Henry saw his face he let him go. "D'you get a good look at my horse?"

Then he turned to Forsman. The man was pumping blood down his throat and across his shirt, his crotch, the floor. His hands were holding his jaw in place. Henry knelt beside him and gave Forsman a good look.

A look without judgement or pity. Then he gripped the man kindly on the shoulder and waited until he could catch his breath.

He spoke proudly. "My father told me once that a good nickname and a worthy adversary are the two things you just can't give yourself. You sorta have to stumble upon 'em." His eyes watered. "My name is Henry Snow. Thanks for making my childhood interesting. I welcome whatever retribution you can muster."

Frank the barkeep was breathing heavily as Henry stood and took his boot spur off the napkin and slipped it back in place. He covered his bloody knuckles in his gloves, took the shotgun apart and stuffed it in his saddlebag, so Pulley wouldn't shoot him off his horse. He washed the bloodstains from his boots and his trousers with his canteen and mounted up. He thought about killing the men's horses so they couldn't follow him but he knew it was an ugly thought. Much uglier than what he had done. He turned his mount back into his tracks and caught up with his party a short ride later. The horses were grazing along the snowy creek.

"D'you find it?" Tip said.

Henry held his boot up and shook his spur at his father. "It was right where I left it. That barkeep must have been deep in conversation. Did I miss anything?"

Tip smiled at Jack. "You missed the great Jack Oakham almost getting thrown."

"Really?"

Tip stood by the creek with a half-grin. "We came on a lynx when we cleared the bank," he said. "And that dun almost threw him. Putt chased the cat for a quarter mile. I've never seen Jack make that face before."

The two men laughed and Jack admitted his mistake. "She almost tossed me," he said. "Those drinks got me tipsy."

Henry shook his head. He was completely convincing when he told them, "I always miss the good stuff."

Part II

The Wild West End

Kolschen always said of justice, "Your sins will hunt you down."

1. Back at Tenpenny

"The plane went down on a Friday and after that the pictures in the frames didn't seem real. I kept sayin' to myself, "Momma Tom, now they in a place you never been. No use worryin' bout 'em now. Too many other worries now. They done left behind a fine girl for you to help along. I think I'll worry for myself someday but right now it's Greer we gotta fix.""

Momma Tom was seated before the half dozen newbies in the dining hall. Behind her Wonderboy and Smithson were doing their best to remove the nine foot mounted shark that hung over the stage.

"So where did the shark come from?" one of the newbies asked.

"Well I'm gettin' to that. I made a funnel cake for Greer while I was worryin' and left it on the bench beside her seat where she was starin' at the river. She wasn't cryin' that I could tell but she weren't talkin' neither. She left the funnel cake without touchin' it and walked down to the river and stared at the ripples and smoked. She smoked all the cigarettes until the sun went down without eatin' and stayed down there in the dark all night. That was on a Tuesday. Day of the funeral."

The next morning I found Greer there on the porch in her big cowboy hat but she didn't hear me cause she was chewin' her ice. She had a stroke of bad luck turning out so pretty. She couldn't hear me so I stepped up slow like, still trying to hoparound on my hoparound and whispered, "Greer, me and Mister Tipper been talkin'. We wants to take you fishin'.""

Little Greer just nodded and smoked her cigarette and didn't say nothin' or turn around – just tossed her cigarette and snuffed it out with her foot.

The day after Tip packed a bag for her, and held her in his arms and rocked her, and cried.

So Greer and me and Mister Tipper took a little plane to the Keyes where all the enlightened live and where people take pictures of Jesus and Elvis and put them on their bodies. Then they do the needles and make art. Crazy people that don't cut their hair and smell like B.O. and don't share. Mister Tipper was worried about a plane trip so soon after the tragedy and that Greer would hallucinogen and have the fits but I didn't think so.

When we got there Mr. Tipper rented this boat that he called a "schooner" but Greer made a face when she heard the word "schooner" like she didn't know what a schooner was but she couldn't ask cause she still weren't talkin'.

She was wearin' this fat floppy hat – that looked like a pancake on her head. I wondered where she got it but I didn't ask cause she don't have to talk. Not for a while. Still that hat looked like the kind the painters wear to go with their little mustaches. Elvis was special for a while with those glasses with the big bug eyes and the cape but Jesus is King.

The boat captain was this big man with wavy buffalo hair and a smile that didn't match from top to bottom. He was excited that Mister Tipper had rented the boat and he came out greetin' us, but when he saw all us walking slowly like in a dream, aware and unaware of each and every thing at once, his crooked smile settled down.

And then, when Mister Tipper shook his hand and whispered somethin' to him – that big boat captain seemed scared to death and looked at the ground and I could tell he wanted to look at Greer but maybe he was scared. Greer just rubbed the dock with her sandals. She knew better what was goin' on than I did. She was so sly pretendin' not to notice, pretendin' she was just a shy kid with nothin' wrong. I watched her standin' against the railin' with her big floppy pancake hat and her short pipe and the blue sunglasses and it made me wanna hug her and rock her until her family came back to life.

Oh well, the boat done rocked her instead. The boat was big and cute and sturdy but it was still a boat and boats shouldn't be trusted. The captain must have known how foolish it all was cause he put us all in these highchairs and strapped us in and gave us our own big fishin' rod that looked like a flagpole. The chairs didn't swivel like a barstool do. They just sits there. Then he gave us this big blue bottle of suntan cream he called "Crazy Love". All of us passed around the Crazy Love, sharing the Crazy Love and rubbing the Crazy Love all over our bodies. I watched as Greer poured some Crazy Love on her arms and strapped herself in, Mister Tipper was watchin' too. Greer was on the opposite side of the boat away from the rest of us and the waves was heavy and she was rockin' in her chair.

The big captain was careful when he baited Greer's hook – he just looked at the girl and was careful not to bump into her or nothin'. He put this fish on a hook and when Greer held it up she nodded to the Captain like a 'thank you'. She was holdin' the fish and twirlin' it in her fingers and seein' how the eye moved when she wiggled the hook. While she was doin' it the sharp barb stabbed her in the finger. She didn't make a sound. She sucked on it to stop the bleedin'. Then she just cast the fish but never turned around. I think she was afraid to ask for help. That's what I think. I think everybody needs a little help sometimes- even children.

The big Captain put on some music to cover up the sound of Mister Tipper and me catchin' all the fish. It was trumpets. I wanted to smile cause it was like this Captain was a sudden angel but I couldn't smile cause Greer couldn't smile. She couldn't talk neither. Greer was tryin' but hadn't caught nothin'. Not a thing. The girl was hidin' her face she was so sad.

Mister Tipper got to talkin' with the big boat Captain about planes and boats and his experiences with both. I'd been thinkin' a lot about planes and what I'd learned about lift from all the travelin' Mr. Tipper done. He told me how the air glides over the top of the wing faster than it glides beneath it and that's why there's the lift above the wing. That's what makes the plane rise up. That and speed. Speed can be dangerous, in planes, in cars, in boats.

One thing about planes is that they don't crash like cars crash. Cars stop on a tree or another car. But planes glide right on through. They so heavy. That's what I learned from the tragedy. I had expected it to just be over but apparently they sailed on once they hit for a long time. They tell me Greer's little sister Phoebe lost her voice she screamed so long. She had that much time to scream.

When we was on that boat I woulda settled for hearin' Greer scream if I could get one out of her. I shoulda screamed too. I shoulda called to the Lord in my biggest voice, "Which side shall Greer cast the net, Dear Lord? Where the fish, Oh Lord? Where's Greer's bountiful provision, Father?"

But I had no doubts.

The Lord was on her side. If He hadn't been Greer's heart woulda stopped beatin' when she got the news. She woulda dropped dead from the shock. The Lord was on her side. And Greer would reach out to us. Greer would seek shelter. Greer would open up her little lovely heart. The Lord was on her side.

But even though the big Captain and the Lord was both on Greer's side it didn't change the fact that Greer hadn't caught no fish. Mister Tipper and the Captain both had lots of the red ones and I was doin' okay. Greer just sat there – there's a catch – and there's a catch. All she needed was a little bite - a little tug to feel better. But Greer hadn't caught none. Not even a bite.

Finally Mister Tipper took his bait off the hook and just cast the lead weight. Then he whispered to me, "Take yours off too, Momma Tom. Just to be safe."

'I had hardly given that a thought when I saw the most incredible thing since the plane went down. With her bad posture and funky outfit, covering up the most shattered heart a kid could have, Greer was strainin' to hold her seat. Her fishin' pole was bent over, like a rainbow that bounced up and down. But nobody had noticed nothin' but me. The big captain was pullin' in a black net while Mister Zuni was fiddlin' with his line.

Greer was bent double holdin' up her rod, her seatbelt stretched tight. I watched her strugglin' to hold on, her hands shakin'. I waitin' for her. I could see it comin'. I could see it in her face. I almost turned to say somethin' to Mister Zuni but luckily I hooked a fish in the nick of time. Otherwise I mighta spoiled the whole trip. My line struck and I pulled my rod up tight and started reelin'.

Greer looked as nervous as I'd ever seen, like she had the whole weight of mankind on her line and it were up to her to reel it in alone.

Don't tell me it wasn't no shark cause I saw it with my own eyes. A big shark. And that's the one - hangin' there.

I saw the big fin floppin' before she caught it. It tore the water all up. My line was spinnin' with my tiny fish but my eyes was on Greer. Her hands were shinin' and slippin' tryin' to hold the pole. Finally she turned round, half hung over the railin' from the weight of the fish. Her knees was shakin'. She looked just like a little girl beside that big pole, that big shark, that big ocean. I watched her like I'd watch a movie picture – as if it weren't really happenin' and I could rewind it and watch it again any time I felt like. She began to turn towards us. Or me – cause everyone else was off doin' their thing. When she did turn I started twirlin' my reel the wrong way, pretendin' not to notice nothin'. Greer started standin' up in her chair. I could see her from the side of my eyes.

She bent over that great weight and her sunglasses fell to the deck. Then she arched her neck and started to speak. She had to been thinkin', 'If I refuse this instant, I'll never re-enter the human race. I'll be astray, pass along, fall apart, run alone.' And with her throat tight she groaned like an old woman out of breath, " Uh, uh. . .a little help!"

"We was all over her like Crazy Love."

Then Momma Tom sighed, letting the children know the story was over. "So that's the story of the where the shark came from," she said.

The shark looked ominous as it hung over the stage. Smithson's hands were balancing the mount as Wonderboy stood beside him on a ladder of his own.

"Why are they taking it down?" one of the newbies asked.

Momma Tom had been wondering the same thing herself, for she loved the memories of her day at sea. But when she answered the children it was in a whisper for Sissy had just stepped inside the dining hall.

"Because Miss Sissy don't like it," she told them. "She say it's frightening to you kids."

Sissy walked up to the stage and twirled the long string of her whistle around her finger, watching as the men balanced the shark. "I wanted it moved before lunch," she told the workers. "I told you that very thing."

Wonderboy smiled, "Mister Tip wouldn't like this," he said, surprising her. "He hung the fish himself."

"Mister Tipper isn't here. And he's been wrong a time or two, if you'd recall."

Smithson unscrewed the final bolt and lowered the tail fin. Then two workers stepped down their ladders and hoisted the shark onto their shoulders.

Momma Tom looked away sadly as the shark was moved out of sight. "Go on, find a table," she told the newbies. "Lunch about to start. I'll see you round."

Sissy turned to face her. "You're not eating with them?"

Momma Tom was sad for the change to the dining hall. She was sad for all the changes taking place across the hill. "No, Miss Sissy," she said, not hiding her angst. "I ain't gonna. I'm gonna to see bout Padibatakal," a statement for which even Sissy had no argument.

Momma Tom filled a tray with salad and fruit and hot tea. Quietly she snuck it out the side door, anxious that the crowd of hungry children might see her. When she stopped to think about it the old woman was anxious about many things; for Tip and his sons to return, to see Padibatakal and the foal, anxious to be back in her own room, in her own bed, the one place Sissy wasn't likely to make any changes.

II.

That morning Sissy had sprung out of bed determined to make Tenpenny run smoother than it ever had before. She didn't expect her brother to be gone more than a few days, despite what his letter suggested. Maybe he would stop at the West Village and maybe he wouldn't; either way she didn't think she had any time to waste. With one side of her shirt collar still turned up Sissy had burst out of her cabin and marched down the hill, paying no attention to the amber of the sunrise.

Truth was she had little time for sunrises. Sissy's mind dwelled solely on the future of Tenpenny, and how she could effect it. She gave little thought to her brother, and even less to her nephews, and none at all to the old dog they took with them. When she did think of them it was a feeling of relief that they were gone. Over the years Sissy had watched both of her nephews slip further and further from the high hopes she had for them. The young men they had become seemed such a disappointment to her now that it was a great relief not to see them everyday. She set her mind to other things, to the wheels she could turn around her; wheels that didn't have minds of their own. Sissy had complained about her brother's management since the whole thing started and now that she was in charge, she immediately began making changes.

On her first day she had eliminated spanking as a last resort and had required Doc Zuni to attend to all patients, regardless of how minor their infractions. The good Doctor had spent that whole day surrounded with hangnails and chapped lips as he muttered the words, "We are now in a wussy paradise."

That afternoon Sissy required curtains to be put up in between the toilets in the boy's bathrooms, calling their lack of privacy shameful. What proved shameful was in fact the shameless display of torn toilet curtains, each used to wipe the bottoms of some unruly rabble, who had no doubt been emboldened by the impossibility of spanking.

Knowing that Sissy would punish the messenger, Smithson never gave word of the incident, causing her to think her plan a success, although by then the curtains had all been discarded.

That evening she required the boys to wear shirts with sleeves to the dining hall as they ate over their meals, and all of the children to keep their bike helmets on, even when walking the bike trail. Sissy was convinced that by the time her brother returned he would be so impressed with the streamlined changes that he would adopt them himself.

Tenpenny is broken, she thought. It always has been and unless something changes before my brother returns, it always will be.

"Some of these kids are tougher than dirt," The Doc tried to persuade her. "They've lived in places you couldn't walk through. It's silly to treat them soft."

"Respect is a stronger stuff than toughness, Doctor," she said confidently. "And they will respect me for keeping them safe."

"They will despise you for keeping them neutered," he grumbled.

To which she gave a rich chuckle, her first in days. "No ideas now, Doctor."

When the clapper of the lunch bell sounded Wonderboy and Smithson were still carrying the shark out of the dining hall. Sissy watched as the doors swung open and the great hall was flooded with chatter. The children broke through in a fever, their hair electric atop their heads, their aroma like a great moving cloud of stench both charming and repulsive. Sissy bit her lip as she watched them rush the food to their tables.

It was common for her to feel nervous at the onset of spring but her apprehension was never stronger than on that day as she looked ahead without the strength of her brother beside her. She questioned whether or not she had the stamina for another year chasing children who were here today and gone tomorrow.

Sissy had no longing for her old life, one she was thankful to be done with, but she did often wonder what kind of toll these children were taking on her future, a future that she still envisioned would include a family of her own. As she stood watching the beginning of another spring she began to question again whether she had the endurance to see it through to the end.

The children were passing biscuits across the tables and singing songs and shoveling triple helpings of beans into their mouths. They were as noisy as ever, but more joyful than they had been in weeks as they heard the drip drip of the melting ice from the gutters. Feverishly they devoured their meals, in hopes of getting on with their day, for the spring would surely open up fields of play they had been missing.

Sissy panned across their faces, seeing the needs of so many that she didn't know how to fill. Her brother would tell her that she didn't feel capable of filling needs because she wasn't capable of any such thing. "None of us are," he would say. "To meet our needs we must always rely on a higher power."

His words echoed through her head as the children fed themselves, but they gave her little comfort. She knew that Tip believed those words, and took strength from them, but to her they were only words.

III.

But Sissy Holland wasn't the only woman on the hill with a mission. Just one day after the Tenpenny Three had set out on their adventure all four of the women in their lives had each devised plans of their own.

Greer, for one, was already setting her plot in motion. Her ideas, however, were as far from improving life on Tenpenny Hill as they could get. Greer was determined to *leave* the orphanage as soon as possible. All she needed was her backpack, her mother's necklace she'd left in the infirmary, and the cover of darkness. And a note, she thought. She couldn't go without at least telling Henry where to find her.

Twice she had considered waiting for the boy to return, knowing that he may want to come with her, or, at the very least help map out her travels. But after reading Tipper's letter she was certain that the Tenpenny Three would be missing for several days or even longer and instantly her heart sank. If she waited for him she may be waiting for a long long time and she didn't know if her heart could take it.

All that night she pondered what to do, hoping that Henry would surprise her and come strolling up the hill. But it never happened. Until she entered the dining hall for lunch the next day she had yet to make up her mind. But when she saw that her shark had been removed Greer came to the quick conclusion that she'd had enough of Tenpenny Hill. Enough of the children and the singing, enough of the sermons and the skits and the God-awful reminders of her tragedy. Before lunch had ended she marched out of the dining hall determined to leave that very day.

She slipped away to her cabin, which she shared with a dozen other girls, and immediately began packing her belongings. The little stone house was a disgrace by Tenpenny standards, where a mandatory ten-point cleanup was practiced by every orphan each morning. But that day her cabin hadn't been touched. At morning flag the children had all been detained for half an hour so Sissy could instruct them on the new traditions. From there the melting snow consumed Tenpenny Hill and everyone forgot about cabin cleanup.

As Greer stuffed her backpack a little smile spread across her face. She knew that the spring was on everyone's minds. It would surely take longer for her cabinmates to notice her disappearance than if she had skipped out in the dead of winter. The stars have finally aligned, she thought.

As she stuffed her pack Greer tried to envision what the road would look like, and where her journey would take her. It was a strange and exotic thought, the open road. But despite her great desire to be free the thought of heading out on her own still terrified her. She knew nothing of what lay south of Tenpenny Hill, and it was the south she was determined to seek. To a warm place where she could keep the boy's attention year round.

When she had finished packing she slammed the lid of her trunk and burst out of the filthy cabin, hearing the squeak of the springs as the door slammed shut. For the last time, she thought.

Greer walked up the road toward High Hopes where she would write her letter quickly and move along. As she hurried she noticed the smell of the hill and the melting snow, and all the grandeur of the place that she had ignored these past six months. She found that it was easier to love Tenpenny now that she was leaving.

She entered through the squeaky screen door of High Hopes and stood looking out upon the vast disaster of Henry and Jack's belongings. No one had cleaned their cabin since they had scrambled to pack their bags and their room was evidence of their departure. She tiptoed over piles of boxer shorts and old socks, loose arrows and fishing tackle, and a pair of gloves that Henry would greatly need in the days to come. There were photos on the walls, curled and warped from weather, of the many trophies the boys had taken from the woods: beaver, salmon, lynx, many when Jack and Henry were still children.

Greer shook her head, thinking of the brothers out in the wilderness, knowing she may never see them again. She regretted being so cold with Jack the day before he left. He had done nothing to deserve that and she had regretted it ever since. She thought of writing him a note as well, but quickly dismissed it.

All I have to do is leave Henry a note, she thought. Then grab the necklace from the infirmary and I'm free. No more cold days and no more orphans. Just the open road and a life far away from here.

She sat on Henry's bed and pulled a notepad and a pen from her pack. Greer scribbled away as fast as she could, telling Henry everything she thought he needed to know. When she had finished Greer tucked the note beneath his pillow and as she stood to leave she noticed Wonderboy through the window walking up the road.

The little man was on his way somewhere, picking up pieces of fallen branches as he walked. He piled them inside one of the wood wagons when he passed. As was his nature he never missed a chance to improve the place. Greer's father had been the very same way.

Greer watched the workman amble down the road and the girl knew she would miss him. She was in a fine mood when she entered the cabin but as she thought of Wonderboy's work ethic her mood continued to improve.

But when she looked up the road through the window her mood changed suddenly. She saw that the infirmary was crowded with children. Greer still had to go to the bedside drawer in the infirmary to fetch the necklace that her mother had given her. The thought of visiting the infirmary frustrated her more than ever.

Now that the spring had started the injuries had begun to mount up and Greer knew she would likely have to wait by the door. Of course waiting was something Greer had grown well- accustomed to on Tenpenny Hill. As she started to write the letter all she could think about was how much waiting she had done since she had been orphaned. She had waited for days for news of her family's death, and she had waited weeks to arrive back at Tenpenny. Then for six long months she had waited for the winter to melt away. Little trickles of snowmelt ran down the rickety roof, having been set free at last. She watched the streams puddle in the gravel through the window and she tried to smile. Soon Greer would be free, when darkness fell, but for now all she could do was wait.

IV.

When Momma Tom entered her cabin with the lunchtray she was both surprised and excited by what she saw. The girl was standing up on her crutches, a gentle smile on her face. Ever since he had left Tenpenny Hill, Padi had been forming a plan to surprise Jack Oakham whenever he returned. She woke up several times a night thinking of it, hoping that he would come home sooner than later. *Every moment my heart grows closer, but the further he goes away*, the girl thought. A shiver ran down her spine as she imagined the next time she would see him, and the plans she had made for when the moment arrived.

As Momma Tom entered with the lunch tray Padibatakal knew that part of her plan was about to be set in motion.

"What's a birthright?" the girl asked.

Momma Tom stood and pondered. The question seemed to rise out of thin air.

"A birthright is a promise, Mumsie. It is a gift left behind."

Padi smiled then. The very thought of someone leaving Jack a gift was well-pleasing to the girl.

"When did Tip bury the birthright?"

Momma Tom set the tray on the bedside table. "Before Henry and Jack ever came upon this hill," she told her. "Mister Tipper buried that promise high in those mountains way out there."

"In the Wild West End?"

"Even further."

When Padi heard that the Tenpenny Three had set out before dark and were heading west on horseback she immediately suspected that the forbidden forest was their destination. Later that afternoon when her mail was delivered all of her fears were confirmed. She read Tip's letter and her heart turned sad immediately.

Padibatakal had been within days of learning how to ride when they had left without her. All she wanted was to go on an adventure. But now the adventure was going on without her and there was nothing she could do to stop it.

But before long her sadness had melted away. She decided not to focus on her own disappointment, but instead on the thought of Jack riding high in the saddle. It was a wonderful place for her heart to rest. I will have other chances for adventure, she knew. Henry and Jack were chosen to find the treasure. I was chosen for other things.

"I've decided Jack is my birthright," she said to Momma Tom.

The old woman sat down upon the bed and looked long at the girl. There was so much joy in her eyes that she couldn't think of words careful enough to say.

The girl seemed to have a new lease on life. Her attitude was bright and airy. "Will you come out today?" Padibatakal asked.

Since their departure, Momma Tom had devoted her time solely to prayer for Sissy and the adventurers. Other than that morning's story-telling she didn't even leave her little room to watch the spring unravel. Smithson brought her food for lunch and dinner, and she brewed her own tea in the morning, but beyond that her life became a constant prayer for Tipper, Sissy and the boys.

"No today I'll be stayin' right here," she said kindly. "Askin' the Lord for their safety. Oh oh oh they out in the middle of it, you know?"

"But Tip will care for them, won't he?"

"Yes, yes, course he will. He'll go protecting 'em with that earthly hand of his as our Father protects with that heavenly. Now I'm gonna pray now, Mumsie," the old woman said. "You go on and have your fun."

Despite the fact that she respected Momma Tom's piety, Padibatakal knew she couldn't sit in that little house all day praying for the boys. The spring had awakened her. She had a mission of her own and she didn't have a moment to spare.

She crutched herself out the door and turned toward the lots. She could hear the sounds of someone working near the stables and when she turned the corner she saw Smithson standing beside a gentle gelding. The girl took a deep breath as she approached them. For after a long, almost sleepless night, Padibatakal had decided to tell Jack Oakham how she felt about him, and to do so in a way that he wouldn't soon forget.

The first thing she decided was that it must be from horseback. It wouldn't make sense any other way. She had waited for years to be in the saddle and she set her mind to impress Jack with her riding whenever he returned. And then I'll tell him, she thought. I'll ride alongside him, down to the river as the evening comes, and I'll share my heart and he'll hear it.

Padibatakal had thoughts of writing Jack a letter, but she couldn't conceive of reading anything from horseback. She knew whatever she had to say must be from memory, and from her heart.

But first the horse, she told herself. My heart will come easily. My heart has had years of practice. But getting my legs beneath me may take some time.

Standing in the lots, haltered to the post, was the gentle mount that Tipper had picked out for her. The horse and the girl acknowledged one another and Padibatakal crutched herself through the gate. Smithson was waiting in the shade, a pair of braces in his hands. He too had received a letter from Tip Holland and his mission was simple: Teach the girl to ride.

He looked on as she approached the mare, her eyes wide with excitement. She sat upon the low bench and with great anticipation the girl watched as Smithson knelt before her, his giant hands fumbling with the buckles to her shiny new braces. The cold metal and the leather bindings tickled her legs and she thought of Tip and how much he would love to be there. She couldn't deny that he owned her with his love. He owned all of them with his wondrous spell: his sister, his sons and the orphans, the old dog and the workers. With his slow and steady love he possessed the world.

And it was his love that she felt as the braces swallowed her ankles. Smithson smiled silently as they fit snug against her skin. Other than socks the girl had never worn anything against her legs and the feeling was strange and wonderful.

She raised her legs to shoulder level, admiring the workmanship, but then suddenly her eyes were stolen away by a passing shape. Walking up the road, with a twinkle in her eye, was Greer Ashby.

"Going to lunch?" Padi called out.

Greer turned to find the voice and was clearly surprised to see Padibatakal sitting in the lots.

"No, to the Doc's," she answered. "What are you doing?"

Padibatakal stretched her legs out with pride, hoping Greer would notice her braces. "Today I'm learning how to ride," she said before her smile faded away. "But I thought you were feeling better."

"I am," Greer told her. "I just left my mother's jewelry in the cubby. I hope no one took it."

"Let's hope not," Padi said sincerely and Greer gave a gentle wave goodbye, looking happier than she had in months, Padi thought.

Despite Jack's feelings, Padibatakal felt no jealousy whatsoever toward the girl. The thought hadn't occurred to her. To Padi, Greer was just another orphan who had lost her family, and that thought would always trump the others. She knew that Greer was beautiful but that her beauty came naturally, unlike Jack's that had been earned with every inch. Padibatakal was frightened that Jack may not yet know the difference. He was still too much of a boy to take accurate stock of himself, she thought, and he may have missed the source of lasting beauty, as most boys are destined to do. Maybe he doesn't know her, she wondered. Maybe he doesn't know himself, she feared.

Smithson hauled the saddle off of the pony and carried it away. Beneath the shade of the run-in shed laid a sturdy crossbeam, raised on two great sawhorses four feet off the ground. Smithson carried the girl's saddle into the shed, resting it securely on the beam and strapped it down. Then without a word he lifted her up like a babe with his giant fingers and set her upon the saddle.

The girl swung her legs gently at the knee, feeling the weight of the braces tight against her skin. She enjoyed the weight. She enjoyed the look as well. If I squint it looks like real legs down there, she thought.

"Can you hand me the reins?" she asked sweetly.

Smithson happily did as he was told. The girl held them together in her right hand and crossed them flipwise over her knuckles, just as Jack had taught her. She was just about to ask Smithson if she was doing it correctly when they both looked up and saw another visitor moving hastily towards the lots. Sissy carried a frazzled, beaten expression as she approached them, and a clipboard in one hand.

Ever since her brother had left her in charge Sissy was constantly fearful that the lots would become filled with the Pritchers once again. Several times a day Sissy scanned the paddock to assure herself. As she walked up she was relieved to see that the prized horses were still missing, however when she spotting Smithson and the girl her easy feeling disappeared.

"What are you doing here?"

"I'm teaching the girl to ride," Smithson said, surprising himself.

Sissy was aghast. To her mind it was reckless to put any child on the horse, but especially this child. The thought of the crippled girl in the saddle was irresponsible.

"To *ride*?"

"Yes ma'am," he told her. "Mister Tipper asked me to."

Sissy was instantly frustrated. It was just this kind of behavior that had caused friction between her and her brother for so many years.

"I'm sorry," she told the girl. "There's no time for that today. We have work that needs doing before my brother returns. Go on and have your lunch, Smithson. Your list awaits you."

Sissy smiled and stomped away, her breath blowing out like smoke from her lungs.

The girl smiled to Smithson. "It's alright," she said. "Tomorrow won't be so busy. We'll do it when your work is done."

He nodded and said okay.

But when she heard the words Sissy Holland stopped in the road. She knew she couldn't spare Smithson. There was so much for him to do. She took a breath, performed an about-face and gracefully approached the girl. She knelt down by the paddock and smiled at the girl's braces.

"Where did you get those, Padi? They look spectacular."

"Tip made them for me."

Of course he did, she thought. "They're very nice. Was he going to teach you?"

"Yes ma'am. He carved them for a week and he and Jack were gonna teach me to ride on this horse."

"They were?" she asked with wonderment.

"Yes Ma'am."

"Well why didn't they?"

"Because they didn't have time before they left."

"Oh I see. How sad. But then again, if it was their wish to teach you, I think you should wait to ride until they get back. You see Padi, their plans changed, so your plans need to change as well. You understand."

"But I was gonna surprise them. Smithson can teach me just fine. I wanted to ride up and surprise them as they came home."

Sissy chuckled. She stood and wiped her hands on her pantlegs. "They'll have enough surprises when they come home," she told them. And with a half-smile Sissy Holland ended the conversation, turning for the final time down the road.

The big man sat heavily on the low bench, hearing only the knickers of the horses and half-muted sounds of Momma Tom's prayers. He had been honored by the assignment and had looked forward to it all morning. Padibatakal could see that he was devastated.

"It's alright," the girl told him. "At least I have the braces. They sure look pretty don't they?"

He smiled but still looked sad when he told her that they did.

V.

Even from the road the infirmary was loud with children, which meant Greer knew she would have to wait. She slipped quietly inside the door, welcomed by the mindless chatter of the rabble who were almost as unhappy to be there as she was.

As he moved down the line pulling teeth Doc Zuni stood calming the children with his stories of adventure. Throughout the day Zuni told many tales of the Wild West End and especially of the hosts of bears that awaited anyone who traveled there. The children listened with attentive ears, for they longed to hear news of the Tenpenny Three, even if the news was mere speculation.

The ploy was working so well that Doc Zuni had already pulled three teeth that day without a single teardrop and now he only had two more to go.

"In the bed or in the can?" he asked his patient, a heavyset ginger named Bawner.

"In the can!" the boy shouted.

In his first year on Tenpenny Hill Doc Zuni had pulled so many teeth that he began giving his patients the choice of trying their luck with the tooth fairy or donating their teeth to science. "In the Can," he called it. The plan was made in an effort to lower orphanage costs and curb potential theft from neighboring pillow barons. When the children learned that tossing their tooth, "In the Can" guaranteed them a lollypop upon each subsequent visit it became rare for the any of the children to test their fate on fairy tales.

With great exuberance Zuni told the boy of a bear named Esperanza, a great bear that had lived in the forest since the dawn of time. She is the mightiest of all the bears, enormous and a fearless pursuer, he told him, and only a bold and powerful hunter could ever face her. But if the hunter hoped to survive he must know Esperanza's secret.

There was actually a great deal of truth behind Zuni's story. In the heart of the Wild West End lies a place unlike any other on the planet, a place where bears and men walk together and live side by side, a place Zuni had visited many times. And although brown bears and black bears show no fear in their wild surroundings, the great she-bear named Esperanza they were afraid of.

She had been given her name some ten years before by a friend of Zuni's who lived beyond the Wild West End. If the bear was still living she would be very old now, but likely as fierce and restless as ever. But Zuni assumed that Esperanza had died. Bears past their prime didn't last long in the Wild West End and he hadn't heard news of her in some time. But Zuni didn't mind that the great bear was probably dead, her story still distracted the children as he closed in to pull their teeth.

"Do you want to know Esperanza's secret?" he asked in a whisper.

Wide-eyed the boy nodded. And with ease Zuni plucked the tooth cleanly from his gums and tossed it in the Can. The Can was actually a huge glass jar filled with hundreds and hundreds of teeth that Zuni had collected over the years. It was a sight that had always disgusted Sissy and all that day Zuni had waited, hoping that she would have the nerve to try and remove it, but so far it hadn't happened.

He swabbed the boy's mouth and gave him a cotton ball to chew and when he was finished he handed him a lollypop. "But not until after supper," he said.

"What about Esperanza's secret?" the boy mumbled.

"I'll finish the story the next time."

As the boy jumped from his seat Zuni noticed Greer standing in the doorway. His eyes were tired as he took her in.

"Hello, Greer," he said solemnly. "I've been looking for you."

This surprised her. "Good afternoon," she answered, but with a question in her voice. Why was he looking for me? she wondered. She crossed her hands behind her back so he wouldn't notice her nervous fingers.

Zuni held his look a long time, "Have a seat with the others," he told her.

At that moment Greer felt a cold rush of doubt overtake her. Zuni had never looked at her that way. He seemed ready to accuse her of something. But what? she wondered. I haven't done anything yet. At that moment Greer felt a sharp pain in her gut. She was certain that the Doctor knew something about her plans to run away. Now he was waiting to spring the news. But how could he know? She wondered. He couldn't. He couldn't possibly know, she thought.

She stood in silence for what seemed like ages until Zuni said, "Who is next in line, soldiers?"

Greer could understand at least part of the Doc's exasperation as she looked across the bench. The room was overflowing with unmet needs. The children sat along the window, some with fevers and rashes, others merely homesick or heartsick. At the end of the bench two of the children had bandages wrapped tightly around their foreheads that they had applied themselves to make-believe wounds as they waited. Greer wanted to smile, for it was something she would have tried herself in her younger years. But in that moment she was too ill at ease to smile. There was a significance in the way Zuni had welcomed her and she couldn't shake the notion that she was caught.

Perhaps the Doctor had heard her conversation with Jack before they left, or maybe he had seen her sneaking away. Greer couldn't bear the thought of being trapped in Tenpenny, and if they knew she was about to run away, they would keep a close eye on her, making her exit next to impossible. She wrung her hands across her lap, ready for the line to dwindle, to face the Doc with whatever he knew.

He leaned over his patient. "All it takes is one brave moment," he told the tomboy. "If you toss out the possibility of the pain and the fear," he told her, "All you can see is the happy ending."

When she heard the words Greer sat up tall in her seat. Zuni's pep talk had caused her to summon a strange burst of courage within herself.

Maybe I shouldn't wait, she thought. My mother's necklace isn't worth risking my freedom for. I'll just go, right now and start a new life. I'll stand up and walk out and never return.

With Tip gone Greer knew that the only real leader on the hill was Doc Zuni and she could see that the Doctor was overrun. There may never be a better time to slip away, she thought. I could grab my pack and march down this hill and through the trees and to the highway with my thumb out before anyone would know, she thought. She watched as the Doctor pulled the girl's loose tooth, swabbed it clean, and then Greer braced herself to depart.

But just as she was beginning her escape the Doctor looked up and their eyes met. The tomboy took her lollypop and rushed out the door as Zuni gave Greer a gentle smile. "We'll start with you," he told her.

"I just need to fetch something from my old room," she told him. "They can go first. I'm not in any hurry."

There were half a dozen minor injuries, scrapes and gashes, two down with cough, but Zuni ignored them. "They're fine to wait," he answered. "Come back to your room. I've been needing to see you."

The girl rose from her seat and followed him sadly. When they had entered the room Zuni pointed at the bed and she sat without questions, thinking to herself, "He knows, Greer. He knows. You don't have a prayer."

"I'm not feeling so sick anymore," she told him.

"No?"

"Really I've been feeling better since the thaw. The spring is good for me."

Zuni closed the door. "That's good to hear. And you're right, the spring is good for everyone."

Greer was nervous. She watched his every move. He sat beside her and took a deep breath and looked down at his chart. She couldn't bear the silence.

"I'm thrilled to get out and do some things," she told him, which was true.

The Doc eyed her carefully. He knows, she thought. It'll come any second.

"What things would you like to do?" he asked.

Greer hadn't really thought about it. "I want to try the new ropes course that Jack and Tipper are setting up. And the trampolines. I've always liked trampolines. My family had one when I was little."

"Your family had a trampoline?"

"Yessir, in Westchester. All of us would nap on it."

"Really? I've never tried that."

Greer was nervously trying to delay the inevitable. "Sometimes we would eat on it, too. My little brother Rygh wanted to be like his big sisters and would bring his tea and crackers to eat and drink on the trampoline with us. He was jealous of our tea parties. But we would bounce him until his tea spilled so he would leave us alone."

"Why'd you do that?"

Slowly Greer admitted. "Because we didn't know anything."

Zuni nodded to the girl. She could tell that he was sad for her. "Would you change that story if you could?" he asked.

"If I could, Doc, there isn't much about my life I wouldn't change."

Zuni softened his gaze. "I understand. It's quite a hand you've been dealt. But still I'm afraid that this won't be a season for trampolines."

Greer sighed and put her head in her hands. She could feel freedom's door slamming in her face and all she wanted to do was scream. When she spoke her voice was already breaking. "Are you gonna put me under house arrest?"

Zuni's face turned in a question. "Why would we do that?"

She shook her head until he asked again, "Why would we do that, *Greer*?"

"I don't know," she admitted, her hands shaking. "Sometimes I just say things. Things I shouldn't say."

Then Zuni assured her, "Well Greer, we don't *have* house arrest. So whatever your reasons were you don't have to worry."

The girl breathed a sigh of belief. They were silent for a moment before she asked him, "But it isn't a season for trampolines?"

"No, it isn't."

"Tell me why."

"Because I did your bloodwork."

"My bloodwork?"

"You're pregnant, kiddo."

Greer was swallowed up in a dark, fearful dream. For the second time she felt the door slamming shut. But this time her freedom was closing off all around her, and with no windows for her to look through. She thought of Henry and it was a long while before she spoke. "Then it isn't a season for much of anything."

"Just new life," he told her.

2. Whitehorse

A half-day's travel across thinly wooded game trails brought them to the Rojo Prieta, a strange land filled with colored sands and rock faces merging on the river. The party of four, bearing what was left of the fish they had taken, led the horses all that day at a gentle clip, always westward, and all the while Henry kept a watchful eye to the east.

As they traveled the spring faded out of memory and was replaced with a brittle snowcap. The patches of winter grass that still sprouted from the clefts became less frequent and the winds howled across the open country. But the riders were comfortable and content, especially Jack, whose new boots were finally warming his feet.

That afternoon they had stopped in Whitehorse where Tipper had picked up a new pair of boots from the general store. The clerk eyed the troupe with subtle fascination, having never seen a traveling trio like that one before.

They headed southwest and they didn't stop until late afternoon and then it was only to give Putt a breather. Within a few minutes they had a fire going and the old dog was fast asleep. Beside him Henry and Jack were each seated beneath a single paper birch, shivering as their father told his story.

"For two weeks we crossed the mountains by horseback and he taught me to fish, to ride, to shoot," Tip told them. "He made me keep a journal of my travels every day. I was miserable at first. I resented him for everything I had to do. Terrible things like saddling the horses and leading them to the river for a drink. Catching my share of the fish or starting a fire. I was a real piece of work. But Kolschen just smiled and carried on," Tip assured them looking sad. "We stayed at a farmhouse where the owner's daughter was very sick. For days Kolschen prayed for her and did his share of doctoring too. While we were there I learned to milk cows and chop wood. Things I hated at first but learned to love. The day we departed Kolschen gave away our horses to the farmer to sell so he could take better care of his girl. The farmer could never quite believe what Kolschen had done. Soon we crossed a great river into a city called Yakutsk and for two days Kolschen worked to get me a passport. He seemed to know half the people in every town we came to. I almost forgot that part. He knew everyone. Before I knew it I was a Canadian named Stuart Whitlock. Kolschen bought me books to read and I had to order food at restaurants in his language. I learned that he had been a soldier once and before we left he visited the gravesite of his wife, who had died many years before. The two of us hitchhiked south from town to town. He owned a boarding house in every place we stopped at. We talked all day and he laughed more than any man I'd ever known. He prayed for me shamelessly. Finally when we reached the trains we rode five thousand miles toward my father."

Although their hands were shaking from the cold the boys were scribbling notes as fast as they could. Each of them longed to hear of Tipper's father.

"That must have been strange to see him for the first time," Jack said.

"Yes, it was. Very strange."

"How'd you find him?" Henry asked.

"I didn't find him," Tip answered. "I didn't know how. But Kolschen could find anyone. All day long he lived with the assurance that anything, no matter how unlikely, could be accomplished. He asked for the same confidence in me, which I had trouble finding." As he listened Jack picked through Putt's belly for sticker burrs and down his legs for nettles that had become planted in the trek. Then and there Jack decided that Kolschen was the kind of man that he longed to be. A man of possibility, like Tipper and Henry were. Jack couldn't think of a single thing that his brother wasn't capable of. Instantly he longed for that kind of strength. As he searched Putt's belly he found a winter tick as big as a thimble and removed it, rubbing the ears of the old dog for comfort.

As he continued Tipper watched his son and smiled gently. "All it took was two months with the man and already I could see how wrong I'd been, aware of all of the lies I had believed."

"Like what?"

"Like how small and insignificant I really was. Like how to treat people. How to treat myself. Kolschen was making quick work of me."

Tip told them of his father, of the great journey west to Estonia and the lessons that he learned. When they were warm and cozy the party mounted up and Tip spouted off more stories as they traveled west. Sometimes the brothers brought out their books and scribbled a quick note, and other times they just listened, but all along they stuck close to their father so they could hear his words above the wind.

Putt however, stayed out front, feeling rested. He kept his nose down, sniffing the Arctic bell heather and the roseroot, but mostly looking for birds. As they crossed the broad valley he stopped sharp and tiered forward on his toes, pointing like he had as a young man, with his raw tail out straight and his mouth tight until the grouse gave up hiding. It was a female spruce, fat with almost no color. Putt watched her flutter with his tired eyes open wide, until she disappeared through a patch of briar. The old dog turned to Jack then, relaxing his face, his tongue hung happy, with the look of success as if to say, "You were sleeping, Oakham. That was a fine shot I handed you."

"We're not shootin' right now, Putt," Jack said aloud. "Keep leading the way."

Putt tightened his face again with his ears forward as he waddled through the snow, "You would have missed her anyway," he seemed to whisper.

Jack smiled and looked over at his brother. Now Tip was riding a bit ahead of them and Henry was at the rear. It was then that Jack noticed Henry's mood had changed. Ever since they had left the saloon his brother had grown more quiet with every hour and continued to look over his shoulder, at the tracks he had made in the snow.

There was a great deal that Jack didn't understand about his brother, but his habit of mood swings seemed to be his strangest trait of all. It wasn't uncommon for Henry to fall into a quiet mood for long spells, oftentimes spending the better part of a day in silence.

Over the years Jack had reasoned that it was always brought on by adrenaline, like the calm after a storm, though he couldn't decide what excitement might have caused his brother to turn so blue at that moment. Perhaps it was just the excitement of the journey, he thought, or perhaps something else altogether. Whatever it was Jack knew that those sad spells were just a part of Henry, part of being strong. Jack also learned that the moods never lasted long and that when Henry snapped out of it, he snapped out fully. But as Henry sat in the saddle that afternoon he seemed to hold on to the sadness more tightly than usual, his eyes glossed over, a blank expression on his face. Jack realized something as he sat in his saddle. "How little my brother and I really talk," he thought. He knew they both were clueless about the other's story. It shamed him in a way. He dwelled on the prediction that he would likely learn a great deal about his brother on his journey, and it excited him enough to smile. He set his mind to know more about his brother.

Jack leaned over in his saddle. "I've got a tough question, Henry."

"What is it, Jacko?"

"What is harder on the heart: Love or family?"

Henry rolled his eyes and drummed his fingers on the saddle horn, but he didn't speak. He knew that simply thinking about that question for too long would make him lonesome. "Love or family, huh?"

"That's right, love or family?"

Henry patted his pockets, in search of his gum. "I'll think about it, Jack."

Then Jack watched as Henry distanced himself from the party, leading his mount out ahead a short ways. From time to time he turned back to the east.

Jack was sad that his brother was feeling low. Their day seemed to have been designed for someone like Henry Snow and he couldn't understand his heavy heart.

But as Henry rode on ahead he talked only to his mount. The sunlight was warm and a cool soft breeze blew from the Cutshank. Henry knew of course that it was for each man to decide what is harder: love or family, and for each man the answer is different. For some both may be equally impossible and for others equally plausible, yet love is certainly hard, for who wants to be vulnerable? And family, oh family, what a heartbreak, with all those different sorts to please, or so Henry thought.

Then he thought of Tenpenny. He thought of leaving once he returned home. He could ride day and night until he reached the sea. He could sell his horse and saddle and take the train, or he could keep his mount and ride along the beach for a full year, all the sand until Tierra Del Fuego. He thought Tenpenny would get the best of him if he didn't go soon, and then he would never leave. There he would always be just a boy king. There he would get trapped in a world of orphans and responsibilities and there he would die. He thought to himself, "When this journey is done, I'll go. I'll leave a note and slip away and start my life." Then Henry sighed. He looked sadly down at his stirrups. He knew he needed to see Greer again.

He knew that. Henry knew that his childhood would never be over, ever, as long as any wound he had dealt was still bleeding on the Hill.

Soon it was nearing suppertime and the boys could see as clearly as a hawk that there were no fish to be caught. The party boiled some of the poverty weed that they found along the bank, eating the stems as they steamed.

"At least it isn't the end of winter and we aren't hungry," Henry said. "I look at things happy. That's what I do."

"We're gonna have to hunt if we want to eat anything," Jack said.

"Hunt what? There's nothing out here but chiggers and ticks. Maybe we could brew a soup of 'em if you want. I could get us started. I've got a dozen in my pits already."

"That may do for you but I need food I can chew," Jack answered.

"You see any?"

It was true that no life moved across the Prieta. They were cold and their calves were sore and neither could recall a time when they had been more hungry.

"No worries," Tip assured them. "There's plenty to hunt in the West End."

Jack had heard of men treading upriver before, as far as the valley, but the forbidden forest he considered in his heart to be the boundary of the world. Although he had heard tales and songs of the faraway woodland it wasn't clear to Jack exactly where they were headed. He had spent very little time away from Tenpenny in the past few years and almost no time at all exploring the wild woodlands. Jack's brother, however, seemed to have been born for such an adventure and the contrast was showing with every mile they covered. Try as he might Jack Oakham couldn't seem to overcome the fears that he would somehow disappoint his father and Putt and Henry with his own inabilities.

"What is the Wild West End?" he asked finally.

"The forest," Tip pointed, "That one there."

"But what is it?" Henry jumped in. "I don't imagine you'd build up all this mystery just for a forest."

"Too impatient to see for yourselves? This is a teachable moment."

Henry spit. "Tipper, are we gonna see more than a forest?"

"Much more."

"Any hints?"

Tip had been careful with his language for many years and he didn't intend to give away any details this late in the game. Finally he said, "The Wild West End holds something that we are seeking."

"And you know where it is?"

Tip nodded.

"What's our birthright anyway? Is it just the treasure?"

"Could be a treasure, perhaps a story, or an adventure, the end of one thing and the beginning of another. It may be an idea, or a door, could be a puzzle. It could be the rest of your life."

"But you won't tell us?"

"That's the rules."

It was a well-known fact that Tip Holland was fickle about rules. He seemed to respect the way things had been laid out before he was born, like taxes and responsibilities: "Render unto Caesar" was not a thing he forgot. But Tip was also never prone to go too far obeying a rule if it didn't suit him.

"Since when do you give a flip about rules?" Henry asked, just ahead of Jack.

But Tipper just smiled and led the party on. No matter how many questions the two sons had for their father Tipper gave nothing away. Instead he remained silent, marching them westward with the knowledge that the answers would come with each unfolding hill.

The valley was giving birth to things now. What had been a dense nothing reaching to the west was now speckled with giant tamaracks a half-mile or more from each other across the valley floor. They had come off of the knoll, deeper into the wide Rojo Prieta when the sun finally cleared the cloudpath and shined the road ahead.

"There it is," Tip said finally.

From the top of the plateau the valley looked like a sea of snowcapped hills rolling west into the birches. At the end of the long valley, a mountain wall of ancient trees cut across the Prieta, its forest spires shading the grasses, the tallest giants stretching to the clouds. They saw the kindled bowers of honey colored branches, the brilliant boughs that absorbed the light. The forest top swayed and the party could hear the rustle.

For centuries the windgap had carried the seedstems across the Prieta to the coal-colored soil of the Wild West End, a shadowland, trees as thick as honey poured on the earth, as if the gods had seen fit to cover the desert edge with life-giving oil, for the branched giants were as black as the soil that nourished them.

"We should be there by nightfall," Tip assured them. "We'll slip into the forest at first light."

"It'll be nice to get out of the wind," Jack admitted.

Soon the party approached the great woodland and smelled the wild scent of the hemlocks. Henry and Jack rode wide-eyed as the great trees rose like towers before them. A cool pink sky lit a haze upon the valley and the air was kind, living a life of its own.

"We'll camp here," Tipper said as he led his mount to the river. Putt followed them willingly, eager to stretch their backs and sleep off the day.

It is important to note that a feeling of rest and renewal came over the party as they reached the forest. The first thing they did was fix a fire and place round greystones beneath the burning logs to keep them hot for hours. Next Tip sent the boys looking for bedstraw near the edge of the woodland and they came back with a bundle. They picked the tiny fruits and bagged them; the leaves they stripped and steamed over the boiling pot.

They filled their canteens, sharpened their knives and their arrows. Tip and Henry sat about tying flies from the duck feathers and hackle that remained. Henry brought in enough brook trout that night to feed them all. They dried the meat out on the rocks, gutted the fish and kept the offal to use as bait.

An hour later, when they were sparkling, Tip shoveled the greystones out of the embers into a hole he had dug nearby. Without a word of instruction the party stripped down to their skivvies and sat around the stones. They covered themselves tightly with a tarp they had stowed in their saddlebag and dribbled water from their canteens onto the scalding rocks. Soon the three were swallowed by the rising steam. Tipper called it a "river sweat": an Indian sauna and each of the brothers loved it, though neither could remember one as intense as the one that night. They remained there until the greystones had cooled when all three sprung from beneath the tarp and dove into the river, and soon they each felt cleaner than they had in years.

Next they washed their clothes in the streambed and stood naked before the fire, watching their clothes dry on old logs near the flamelight. Tip explained the forest to his sons more like an idea than a place and the two brothers each created their own predictions as to what the idea would be. They talked far into the night of the expectations they held in their hearts.

Soon the brothers were stuffed and satisfied. The fire was crackling and hissing, "Pop, sizzle!" went the flame in a careless rhythm. Their feet were warm, their belly's full, their storyboards crowded with ideas.

By then of course Henry's mood had shifted. He no longer felt low about what he had done to Forsman. Bright were the high forest walls that kept him from the wind and bright were the thoughts that his day had raised. He curled up on the soft ground and prepared for a grand sleep, his face turned in a smile.

Meanwhile Jack was dwelling on the bears in the lakebed that he had encountered. The very thought of them made him shudder. He knew that with one wrong step things could have gone differently. He thought of Momma Tom and Padibatakal and Greer and how close he had come to never seeing them again. Then he looked out at the dark forest. The spring was coming, and Jack knew the dens would come awake and the hungry giants would rise and march across the woodland. He fell asleep wishing for a taller horse.

But it was Tipper who was up well into the night. Despite the long day's ride and the great journey ahead his heart was still unsettled and he needed time to think. He stared into the fire as he listened to the tails of the Pritchers swishing by the river. Once he turned to look proudly upon his sons and tears filled his eyes.

"I pray they're ready for this," he whispered. "I pray I've done all that was necessary." He watched them as they slept beside the fire. The thought of the pain and the joy that awaited them waged a war in his heart.

The next morning he woke the party before dawn. Both of the boys sprung up instantly but Putt was slow to rise.

"Get up, old man," Jack said when he saw the old dog laying still. "We have a forest to see."

The old dog was stiff-jointed, his body raw from the day before. "I've seen forests before," Putt seemed to say.

"Maybe so, but not like this one," Jack answered.

"You've seen one you've seen 'em all."

They didn't linger for breakfast but quickly gathered their belongings. Tip had just finished cooking his Tule. The long slim stocks, Kolschen had taught him, could be stripped to find a powdery sugar source. Tip removed the fruiting bulbs, pealed the young rootstocks, and after bruising the stocks he boiled the stems.

Henry looked ahead with great anticipation. "What will we find in there?" he asked.

Tip breathed into his hands, his eyes lighted with the flame. "Life and death."

"Let's hope more of one than the other," Jack smiled.

The wind wandered among the treetops and the leaves rained down. With the lanterns held above them the flamelight lit the branches and the trees seemed to glow.

"Now, for the forest and the west," Tip told them. Henry and Jack's eyes dimmed as they scanned the line. A vale cut deep into the forest like an underpass, a hollow cutting of earth that opened the woodlands.

"First light, Henry, see if we can't pull in some fish for breakfast."

"And rabbits," Henry said, "I've already seen a dozen."

"Rabbits would be good for lunch."

Tip led them down with his rifle ready. "And now begins our wild adventure. But beware, this leg is treacherous."

Henry felt so excited that he could hardly breathe. He wondered if what he felt was the same feeling Tipper had the first time he met his father.

As the daylight reappeared behind them a little afterglow spread itself thinly across the sky and the Tenpenny journeymakers, four strong, entered the heavy wood with lanterns lit.

So ended the voyage across the Rojo Prieta.

3. *The Birth of Stuart Whitlock*

By Jack Oakham

It was still the first day of their journey together when Tip got his hands on Kolschen's rifle. They had sat down to lunch and the big man was preparing fresh fish for the boy when suddenly Tip swung the rifle up and aimed it at Kolschen.

Kolschen's face remained calm and attentive, and only a quick flash of anger poured out of his eyes. "Here is what we will do," the big man said. "You will follow me to the west across those hills. Very dangerous. But your best hope, I assure you. Without me you will die."

"We'll see."

"What will you do when you reach the trains?" he asked.

"That's my business."

"Ah yes. Indeed. I don't intend to rummage through your business. But I do mean to prepare you for your journey."

Tip was growing tired of the man's talk. He didn't know what he meant by "prepare" but he wanted no part of it. Instead Tip prepared to pull the trigger.

"You see the trains require a ticket," Kolschen said evenly, "and the ticket master requires a passport. And I can assume you don't have a good one."

"I have a passport."

"No, you don't. What you have is a prison sentence. Photo proof of who you are, where you're from, and with one phone call what crime you've committed. What you carry is all the evidence that any local magistrate will need to lock you up."

"I can blend in. I can stay hidden."

Carefully Kolschen shook his head. "You are not one of us. Anyone can see it."

Tip's face began to unfold into a trembling gaze. "Then what do I do, smart guy?"

"You follow me. Men will never question you when you're with me. The moment you're out of my sight the clock will be ticking. So you must never leave my sight. I won't ask you why you're running. I won't turn you in. If you do what I require."

Tip sat in thought. His head was pounding. "What do I have to do?"

"Follow me. In every way follow me. If you can follow me until we reach the trains I will hand you a working passport."

"How do I know you won't just kill me for trying that?"

"I don't kill people. Maybe that's the first lesson you need to follow."

And it *was* the first. Tip lowered the rifle.

Kolschen patted the ground beside him and offered the boy some fish. "You will have to go through four stages if you want to become a man," Kolschen told him.

"I've been a man for years, Mister."

"The first stage is to know yourself. Most men never get past the first stage. It can take years and many hurdles to take accurate stock of who you are."

"Know myself how?"

"Know your strengths. Know your weak points. Know who you were born to be."

Tipper looked off somewhere, seeming disinterested. "What are the other stages?"

"The second stage is to know a friend. True friendship. Sharing your pains and struggles. Listening and giving advice. Sacrificing and understanding."

The thought of Unger Soski passed through Tipper's mind. He lowered his head, rubbing his temples. "And the next?"

"Stage three is to know your mission. Not just who you were born to be, but what you were born to do. Every man was born for something."

Tipper didn't disagree, though he couldn't imagine what he was born for. Born to run he predicted. Run away from his troubles and never look back. He was feeling overwhelmed. He breathed deeply and tried to listen. "What's the last stage?"

"The last stage is to know heartbreak."

"Heartbreak?"

"That's right. No strong man has done without it. You must be broken to be rebuilt."

Now Tipper had a smug smile across his face. "So what you're telling me is that if I follow you I'll get to know myself, I'll make a friend, I'll find my mission, and when I've done all that I'll get shattered to pieces. Is that what you're telling me?"

"Shattered and rebuilt."

"And then what?"

"You'll be a pickleman."

"Sounds great, friend. Sounds like a real vacation."

Kolschen smiled. "I will escort you to the trains, I will provide you with a working passport. I will stick with you until you know who you are."

The boy huffed, "What do I have to do?" he asked sullenly, though in truth he found the thought to be fascinating.

"Whatever I ask of you," Kolschen said.

In the coming days Tip was made to fix a fire, right beside Kolschen's, and to build it as instructed. The big man taught him how to shoot, to fish, to cut lumber, to cook their food. Sometimes as they rode through the jackpines Kolschen recited poems and stories like none the boy had ever heard and in the evenings he would ask Tip to close his eyes and tell of their journey, in every detail he could voice. Good as his word Kolschen led them across the vast wilderness to safety and never left the boy's side.

II.

It was three weeks of hard travel before the two finally arrived at the next village and the road was unlike anything Tipper had imagined. The wild places unfolded before him like a dream, much of it overwhelming his young heart. Yes despite his comfort in the saddle and his new-found confidence, when Tipper spotted the small village in the distant hills the sight came as a welcome relief. By that time Tipper was weary of travel and longing for a bed, though he wasn't weary of Kolschen's company, as he once had been. The boy still despised any notion of authority, but the man had given him a horse, and kept him well-fed on their journey, and even Tipper couldn't deny that he had learned a great deal since he landed in Kamchatka.

The boy had spent many nights imagining what their destination would look like but that evening, as they rode into the hamlet, Tip could quickly see that none of his predictions were coming true. The houses in the village were small and strangely configured, looking more like chicken coops than homes. The lanterns were the only lights on the street, with the exception of a few lit candles in the front windows of the houses. The town was silent but as Kolschen tethered their horses to a pair of fence posts they soon began to hear sounds of life from the top of the hill. As the two weary travelers approached it the sounds grew richer and smell of warm food spilled onto the street.

Much like the port they had fled the month before there was a single tavern in the heart of the village that glowed from within, pouring the only bright light upon the street and casting shadows of patrons as they mingled. On one side of the building, a few feet from the windows, was a tiny wooden door with a lock hanging from the hinge. Kolschen moved past the door and peered through the window into the tavern. Then he gave a smile, "Fiodr is at it again," he said.

Although exhausted, Tip glanced through the glass at the gathering crowd. A man who appeared drunk was trying to stand on his head. But Tip's eyes were stolen away when he heard the sound of jingling keys. Kolschen had drawn out a key ring from his pack and was opening the padlock that was latched to the wooden door. He struck a match on the doorframe and lit a lantern that hung from the low ceiling.

"Follow me."

They stepped inside and Tip looked on with quiet fascination. It was only a small room, likely used for storage at one time, but now it was a rest stop for Kolschen. On a great desk were piled an assortment of colored envelopes, small and large, a few paper packages, and a pair of tiny boxes, all addressed to Kolschen. From months ago, Tip thought. Along the wall were two large cots, covered in bearskins, and a wide range of supplies on the wall shelves, maps, books, and a faded portrait of Kolschen's family from long ago - a wife and two sons. Tip soon realized that this was a duplicate of the room they had departed from weeks before, only smaller, and not nearly as secluded. But like the other it serves a temporary purpose, Tip thought. But what purpose he could not decide.

They let their packs fall to the floor and Kolschen set his rifle beneath the desk. They each washed their hands and faces in a corner basin and as quickly as they had entered they were out in the street again.

"We are here for a warm meal," Kolschen said as they stepped up to the door of the tavern. "If you keep quiet no one will press you for questions. So don't ask any of your own."

243

Tip nodded, his stomach rumbling. All he wanted was a full belly and a warm bed, nothing else.

"Find a seat in the corner and wait," Kolschen told him. "I will come in shortly and buy you a drink. Pretend we haven't met."

Tipper did as he was told, happy to be back in a warm, dry setting, but slightly fearful of the place, for it reminded so much of the tavern on the sea. The room was dark and scattered with ragtag workers from the surrounding farmlands, some of them with miner's hands, their palms stained from the work. Later that evening Tip would learn that Kolschen had owned both taverns for many years. In fact there were more than a dozen such establishments throughout the world in Kolschen's name, although none knew of the other's existence.

As Tipper entered the tenants at the bar paid him no mind. He kept his hat low across his face and found a seat in the corner.

But a minute later when Kolschen ducked through the door there came an explosive chorus of welcome from the villagers. The crowd turned with eyes wide and a loud and unanimous "Voshye Drovye!" rung out from the tenants. All who were seated sprung to their feet and those already standing rushed the doorway to embrace him.

"Welcome friends, welcome! How long has it been?"

Tip couldn't conceal his surprise. He squinted at his mentor. Immediately the barkeep began working the beerpull, preparing a large frosted mug for the new arrival.

As the owner of the house, Kolschen felt it was his duty to greet each of the guests by hand and did so with great enthusiasm, and some of the guests were confused by the uproar, for they had no knowledge of the man. But the local villagers knew him and their joy was painted on their faces.

Although each of the small hamlets where Kolschen had settled welcomed him fondly, this village in particular looked upon the man with wonder and delight. His fame was attributed to his skill as a surgeon, and a caregiver to the needy, both reputations he had gained by saving the lives of twin infants years before who had nearly succumbed to pneumonia. However, to the villager's memory little else was known for certain about their Otsov Kolschen. They thought of him as a jolly figure who came and went as he chose, never visiting for long; a simple man with a simple smile. But what they didn't know was that the scope of his life was far beyond the village, in places they would never see or hear of or even understand, places where very few would risk to travel.

On a few occasions he stayed away so long that some of the chattier inhabitants spread rumors among the village that he had passed away, only to see him walking down the street a few weeks later, a smile on his face as he said, "How lovely your garden grows!"

And when pressed by the locals Kolschen never discussed his own affairs or whereabouts, but instead turned the conversation full circle, inquiring of the lives of the people and encouraging them through their troubles, all the while keeping the details of his own life a mystery. But as the years had passed and his mystery grew, so did their suspicions.

Once the room had settled Kolschen ordered a round for everyone, to much delight, and delivered a drink and a meal to Tipper himself, who still sat alone, enjoying the welcome that his mentor had received. The scene raised many questions in his heart about Kolschen, who he still knew little about. In time he opened his journal and began recalling his days in the saddle.

Kolschen ate at the bar and from time to time he glanced over at Tip and gave a gentle nod. Several times the big man thought of joining him, but he knew it wasn't necessary. He didn't intend to linger long. Soon he was paying his bill and saying his goodbyes and before the crowd thinned out he shook everyone's hand throughout the tavern.

When Kolschen finally stepped across the room and stood beside Tip, the boy had his journal open-faced on the table and was still nursing his beer.

"I'm settling in," Kolschen said in a whisper.

Tip nodded to his journal. "I'll be right behind you."

Kolschen hesitated, thinking it unwise to leave the boy alone, but then thought better of it. "We start early in the morning," he told him.

And as he stepped away he proclaimed loudly in his language, "Nice to meet you, my friend!"

He wished the tenants goodnight as he crossed the room. They returned his blessings and toasted his health and Kolschen slipped out into the street with a full smile.

But to Tip's surprise, the moment Kolschen was out of sight the crowd swarmed the bar and soon the room was deep in talk; the history and character of old Kolschen becoming the topic of conversation.

There was Fiodr, the outspoken drunkard, and Berin the barkeep, and various other inhabitants, all of whom were soon discussing the mystery of the gentle giant. The men were each leaning across the bar, careful to keep their voices low, but not too low for Tip to hear them.

"I have an uncle who saw him in Yakutsk. 'A man twice the size of a normal man,' he says. And he was dining with the Prince of Vestok.'"

"The Prince of Vestok?"

"So my uncle says."

"I have heard another story," one of the men told them. "A banker in Alosk says Otsov Kolschen is the wealthiest man in the district. He was a Marshall in Kluchi and a surgeon in Yakutsk until his wife died."

"I heard he was a hero in the war," said another.

Now the stories were pouring in from one man to the next, and many didn't know which to believe.

"He has some past he must keep hidden," Fiodr suggested. "That is why he comes and goes. He has a secret he is running from. A crime perhaps."

Berin the barkeep waved the man off. "Don't go listening to that nonsense," he said. "The man has a heart of gold. I'll swear it."

"A heart of gold maybe, but he's a fool for carrying it," Fiodr suggested. "A heart of gold is too heavy a thing. It's some guilt that drives him."

"That's a lie," Berin told him. "I know the man. He is far from guilty. He is kind."

But Fiodr the drunk wouldn't be persuaded. "He's a phony, I tell you. And a crazy man. I too hear stories of famous men seeking your Otsov. Prince's and Captains and the wealthy men of Moscow. Now what interest would they have in such a man, dressed as he is?"

The barkeep yawned. "What are you suggesting, Fiodr?"

"I'm suggesting he isn't who he says he is. No poor man has friends like this."

"No one said he was poor."

"He dresses poor. Like a commoner."

"If he dressed like a rich man would you trust him?"

"No. I would trust him less."

"Ah! Then there's no winning with you, Fiodr."

"You may be right. But I tell you he's hiding something, that one."

Berin shook his head, disliking the drunkard more than ever. "We're all hiding something, Fiodr."

Tip Holland thought long of the words of the strangers, and wondered which to believe. He wondered if guilt did indeed drive Kolschen's actions, for they seemed motivated by some powerful force. But even as he thought back on the drunkard's words they did not convince Tip of any such thing. His fondness was too fixed to be shaken by the idle words of a drunkard. Tip saw no guilt in Kolschen's life, only a joy that bewildered and astonished him.

The men of the tavern carried on their talk for hours, predicting and speculating about various things but Tipper had heard enough. When he left the tavern and retired to the little room Kolschen was already fast asleep - snoring deeply on his cot. Tip curled up and listened, feeling a deep pride to have met the man. Throughout his life Tipper had given very little thought to his future, but now that he was seeing a man's life lived before him he couldn't help but wonder who he would become.

The boy was only hours from the trains now and only a few weeks from finding his father. The next day Kolschen would sell the horses and purchase young Tip a new passport with the money he received. The boy would have a new name. Stuart Whitlock, and new freedom in his lungs. Then the pair would make their way together across the vast land to the west.

But despite his anticipation Tip's mind was consumed with other things as he lay there on the cot. He couldn't deny that he hoped to have what Kolschen had someday, in however small a measure. For the first time in his life he was dreaming of something to become.

III.

A month later was the first day of fall in Estonia. At the kitchen table a hunting guide was working to clean the dishes. Tip sat on the kitchen bed with the wool shawl wrapped around him and his eyes tight. In his mind he could see the water waking through the screen window and could hear bare feet stepping across old boards above him. His father's feet.

"Hello, Tipper."

Tip opened his eyes to see a man standing there half asleep. "Hello, Kolschen."

The man poured himself a soda and stood sipping by the window. Tip could tell he had something to say. "Did you enjoy the moose hunt?" he whispered.

"Sure."

"I'd hoped you would."

Tip felt quiet. He was thinking on the story of his day. He thought how strange it had been to meet his father for the first time and of how hard he had tried to make his father love him. He thought the story to be a strange one and he didn't understand all of it. He knew that his father was a drunk on his last leg, and that after Kolschen adopted him that he wanted to take him to meet him. "It will be good for you to meet your father," Kolschen told him. But he could not begin to understand the whole story and it kept him awake. "Why do you like to tell stories so much, Kolschen?" he asked.

The kitchen was loud with the dishes.

Kolschen was so surprised to hear the question that all he found himself doing for some moments was breathing. His eyes rested as he answered. "Tip you can tell a lot about people by the kinds of stories that they tell. You can tell a lot about yourself too. It's a reflection mostly. Telling stories is a reflection of the world that men choose to see. They leave out all that fluff and when they just stop to tell what it is they are thinking and feeling, you can really get down to it. To what aches them. And that's the bottom line – that aching in each and every one of us to tell."

"Is it?"

Kolschen nodded. He was sure of himself but Tip said nothing.

"Tip do you remember when I would take you through the jackpine groves along the rivers and I'd ask you to close your eyes and tell me about what the grove looked like?"

"Yessir. You wanted me to describe the trees and grass."

"Yes. But that wasn't just good practice, you know? That was my way of learning about the aches and hurts of a fine young man."

Many times in their journey Kolschen had sensed a sadness in the boy and that moment was no different. Often he would observe him from horseback, staring off at the passing trees, glossy-eyed and heavy of heart. There in the dimly-lit room Kolschen watched as the boy continued to battle the forces within himself, rocking like a tiny skiff on the sea.

"I just read my journal," Tip admitted. "I can't believe the person I was when I met you."

Kolschen nodded. "I understand."

"Well I don't," Tip said heavily. "Where did those feelings come from? How could I feel those things?"

"Because you're a slave to yourself."

Tip felt an anger rise up from within; the same anger he had felt before shooting Unger Soski.

"Kolschen, there's something you don't know."

"I may know it, Tip."

"I killed someone. D'you know that?"

Kolschen nodded. "Someone close to you, I think."

Tip caressed his temples gently with his thumbs and put his face in his hands. Despite two months alongside Kolschen the boy remained surprised by his every word. He gave a heavy sigh. "The only one close."

Kolschen leaned down to pick up Tip's boots that were on the floor before him. Immediately he began to give them a polish.

"Now that you know that," Tip asked, "Aren't you afraid I'll try to kill you too?"

"You've already tried to kill me."

"I could try again."

"You won't."

Tip searched the man's eyes. "You aren't afraid to die, are you?"

"I'll never die," Kolschen told him, polishing away. "I'll live beyond those mountains, live longer than the sea."

"Because you have a heaven?"

"We each do."

The boy turned back to the water light. He could see the tint of the leaves above the lake beginning their transition. Tipper knew little of heaven. But he believed that if heaven existed this old man belonged there. He belongs at the head of the masses with a front row seat. But you don't, he told himself. If there was one thing Tip did know it was that there was no room in heaven for murderers.

"Now that you know that you may not fear me," Tip admitted. "But you *must* think less of me."

Again Kolschen shook his head. "All men are guilty. No man is good. All fall short."

"But not all are murderers."

Kolschen put down the shoes and polish. He reached out and placed his hands gently on the boy's shoulders. "Hear me now. Nothing you could ever do would make me love you less."

"What about.-"

"There's *nothing*," the man said. "*Nothing* you could do."

For over a month the guilt in Tip's heart had grown and grown until he ached to confess what he had done. And now that he had told Kolschen of his crime the man had forgiven him without a passing thought.

"Kolschen?"

"Yes?"

"I have something to say."

"Good. Say it."

"I'm afraid that if I say it then I'll never be able to take it back again."

Kolschen nodded. "Then don't. Never say what you'll have to take back."

"My mother told me once that she had a miscarriage before I was born. Not with my real father but with another man."

"I didn't know that."

"If the baby had lived then I would have had an older brother."

"Or sister."

"Or sister, yes. Most of the my school friends didn't like their older brothers and sisters but I would have forgiven them for doing all the things that they would do to me. Like bully me or leave me out. I think I'd just love 'em because it's a pretty cool thing to have someone that is related to you. Didn't I ever tell you that my mother had a miscarriage?"

"No, Tip, you never did."

Tip Holland fumbled with the journal that lay in his lap. He looked up to see the guide in the other room doing the dishes. The guide's son followed his father when he stepped from place to place. "I would have made my brother, if I had a brother, a little fold-up knife like the one you made for me with a hickory grip but mine would have said 'From your little brother, Tip' if the baby had lived."

"This is nice to think about."

"You've been away from your sons a long time?"

Kolschen didn't answer, but turned away. Then he said slowly, "A long time."

"What happened? Was it the war? Is that what broke their friendship?"

"They've never stopped being friends, Tipper – there is love there. But sometimes, two brothers want to have the same thing and it breaks them apart. As far as I can tell wanting to have the only thing that your closest friend wants is the only moral way to lose them. And it was something like that that brought all of us apart."

"I feel guilty."

"Why is that?"

"I can't say."

Kolschen waited. "Then don't."

A sound of heavy feet was heard above them. Kolschen knew it was the sound of Tip's father. Tip looked up at the sound and rolled his eyes. "Kolschen?"

"Yes, Tip."

"You told me that we were going moose hunting out here because there weren't enough moose back east but I think that was all an excuse to get me to meet my real father because he lives here and if he won't come to see me then we should go to see him."

"That's all true."

"But I don't think that you did it so much to save him. You did it to save me because I need saving as much as he does."

In all the years that followed, Kolschen never thought of Tip the same way.

"Do you want to tell me why you feel guilty, Tip?"

"I love you, Kolschen."

"Oh." Then he sighed again but in a new, easy way. "Well I love you too, Tip. And I understand."

Tip wrapped the blanket tighter around himself and waited. He could no longer hear the sound of his father stirring on the floor above him.

And then they were just two people sitting on a kitchen bed in the forest of Lapland with nothing more to say. It was a fine quiet and they both knew it and neither one wanted to do anything to shake it but Tip was about to explode so he just went ahead and asked.

"Kolschen? Does my father need me? Is that what he needs?"

"I hope so. . . but you never know what another man needs, Tip. Most of us end up knowing only that we need, but never discover what or who that need is."

"That's too bad," Tip said.

Kolschen listened to the pure sound of the water running and he felt a calm come back to him that had drifted away for centuries, it seemed. They were quiet again, twice in a row like they were always supposed to be quiet and they were the first people ever to figure that out. Kolschen looked carefully at the perfect face of the boy he loved and knew clearly that young people feel more than the rest of us, hold tighter to the things they love, and understand all, but rarely have the language to describe that understanding. It overjoyed him to be sitting with one. It upset him to speak but he knew that silence was no answer at all.

"I want to ask you to close your eyes and tell me what you see."

"Like the jackpines. Why?"

"So I can see what is worrying you. So I can understand a boy as he becomes a man. Scan the room, go back to when you were still vulnerable, capable of living in the moment, then scan the room and tell me."

"Tell you what?"

"Close your eyes, Tip."

He did. "And now?"

"What do you see?"

Tip Holland looked in his head a long time. He liked how long he could be silent without being forced to hurry up and answer. He could still see some of the images of the room, left over in his imagination. He rocked beneath the wool shawl and finally he spoke slowly, while panning across the room in his head.

"One of the guides has brought his son to work and the boy is standing beside his father in the kitchen. They are doing the dishes together. Next to him is an old fire stove, boots drying beside it. And they are using loose pots that are hanging from long pipes on the walls. There is a whiskey barrel rubbish bin, long worn cutting boards slanted on their shelves. And then there is loose food on the open cupboard shelves. Spice and oil and fish pepper, lemon salt. The pots on the wall are still wet from the washing. The high stairs slant up into the trap door roof. There are books too that I can see. Dubliners, and an American Dream by Norman Mailer. And there are whole stacks of cooking books. With titles I cannot read. And there are worn guitars with old strings, and soft beds with lumpy mattresses, like the oatmeal on the stove. An old iron-cast sink, curtained windows and closed doors with old games. Pictures of killer whales and the bayou, fish charts and seashells and thirty-year old couches. The waterlight comes in through the windows. And the boy, just look at the boy. Just look at him and smile as he calls out 'Papa'."

4. Gathering the Posse

Joe Forsman didn't wake for over an hour and when he did his men had to help him to the truck. Forsman's in-house veterinarian iced his face and pulled a pair of bottom teeth and cleaned his gums and his nose and wrapped his face from top to bottom. The painkillers worked quickly and he had spent the night sleeping on a old couch in one of his barns.

The next morning there were five fresh horses saddled outside the bar loaded with rifles, ropes and bedrolls. Most of Forsman's men were already mounted. His son sat a horse before the mount line, doling out envelopes to every man.

"Quarter now," Danny said.

"Why not half?"

"If we don't find him in two days it'll be half."

Forsman headed into the bar for one last drink. He didn't want to listen to any talk before they rode. He didn't want to listen to any talk *while* they rode, either. The truth was Joe Forsman hadn't wanted much of anything in a very long time. The boy had blessed him, in a way, and his heart was thankful for a chance at vengeance. He called for a drink. Frank Creed had tape over his nose, a purple mouth. He eyed Forsman up and down as he served him.

Forsman drank his drink and called for another and dribbled it in. His mouth wouldn't open enough to sip so he had to tilt his head back and pour the whiskey down. All the while Frank watched him, and he watched the men outside.

"This isn't the old days," Frank said.

"Looks the same to me."

"But it isn't."

"So you said."

Frank looked out the foggy window. The three men were with their horses, waiting for Forsman to finish his drink.

"You know the law, Joe."

"I know the law. What law do I know?"

When Forsman spoke it was in a gurgle, his tongue dancing at the back of his throat. His jaw was locked in place but his voice was still strong.

"Can't go after no kid with a gun. Can't do that."

"You're the one who doesn't know."

"I know it. And I won't let this pass."

Joe stood up, "You're a great mystery to me, boy."

He turned and walked to the door but Frank stopped him. He stood in the doorframe. "You should listen up, Joe. I'd rethink a great many things if I were you."

"If you were me?"

"That's right. You should sit back down and let me tend you. You aren't a young man."

Forsman managed a smile."I'm surprised by this, I must say."

"By that kid?"

"By you. Losing all of your dignity."

"I'm losing nothing but my patience. You should listen to me. My dignity is intact. You can't rise above this. You have a responsibility. We aren't lawless even up on the Cutshank."

Forsman said nothing. He looked past Frank at the slow tumbling hills and the tracks leading west. Frank watched him curiously. The man's whole frame came instantly into focus. Other than the tall body that stood before him Frank had no reason to believe the man was even there.

"Do you not think the law will come for you? They will."

"Who do you mean exactly?"

Frank was waiting for Forsman to push his way through the door. He fully expected him to try it. "You lived for the law once."

"I've lived for life. Everything else fits within it."

"Huntin' down a kid fits within it?"

"Where else would it fit?"

Frank laid a hand on Forsman's shoulder. "Nowhere at all. I won't let it pass."

"So you've chosen to stand in the door there?"

"Those others won't go if you don't. "

"They have their own minds to make. I've made mine."

"And I won't let it happen."

Frank had waited all his life to stand up to Joe Forsman. Despite his great stature the man before him seemed to Frank like the smaller man.

Forsman edged forward, his patience expended. "There's a mount ready on the hitch if you change your mind."

But Frank didn't budge. Instead he gripped both sides of the doorframe with his palms and watched the old man carefully, keeping his hands in focus. "Nothing could change my mind. I'd rather die than hunt a boy. I won't let you write a boy's death sentence, or harm your own son. That's your son. Are you gonna lead your own son into this?"

"I told you. His mind to make."

"And I told you, I won't let it pass."

Forsman didn't feel like cutting the man. He tended bar and made him feel young, and a promise had been given to Frank's mother years ago. Forsman had always been a man to stick to a task when his mind took hold of something and that morning his task was to hunt down the boy, not to carve up Frank Creed. He had already wasted enough time getting back on his feet and he didn't intend to waste any more in conversation.

But as he looked to the south at the rolling hills he realized he wouldn't get past Frank unless the proper pressure was applied.

"While you're telling me things, maybe there's something I should tell you," Forsman said fully.

"Why don't you do that, Joe?"

The riders watched as Forsman whispered close in Frank's ear, his hand gently on the man's shoulder. Frank still gripped the door, his body strong within the frame, but as the moment lingered he seemed to shrink back as Forsman whispered.

With every word Frank Creed grew more and more deflated, and with every word Forsman grew fuller and fuller until he seemed like a figure back in his prime. Now Forsman was speaking quickly and Frank's hands began to tremble. His weight shifted. Frank turned his head away from the words but Forsman wouldn't stop. He wore a half-smile that only the riders could see as he patted the man in the shoulder. His words came gently, and from the looks of his hands no threats were being made.

Danny knew of Frank's plans to stand up to his father, and hoped he would succeed, but as he watched the bartender's hands release the doorframe and his body shrink back, Danny knew that his hopes were dashed.

Frank backed out of the door completely and kept Forsman at arm's length. In a moment he had dropped to his knees and was covering his face.

Forsman was quick to approach him, still whispering. The only words the riders could hear were the last few the big man spoke. As Frank lay crumpled on the wood porch, his face covered in his hands, Forsman said sharply, "That's your heritage, Frank."

Frank was weeping uncontrollably now, his legs dancing wildly before him as Forsman slipped by.

Two of the men, Wade and Culpin sat motionless on their horses. They paid the incident little attention. But Danny tipped his hat forward so his father couldn't see his face. He didn't know what the words meant but he had known Frank Creed all his life and longed to help him, but lacked the courage. He watched sadly as Frank wept heavily across the wooden porch.

When Forsman mounted he looked exhausted and let out a heavy groan. They rode west northwest and they rode hard and Forsman stayed in the lead, unaware when the others fell behind.

They arrived at Whitehorse, following the tracks to the station. Forsman stayed in his saddle but the rest barged inside like some bygone rabble, their urgency in every word.

"What did he buy?"

"Boots."

"What size?"

"A nine. Danners."

"You remember what time a day it was?"

"Yesterday about lunchtime I figure."

"D'you see 'em leave?"

"I didn't see em leave. But I never saw 'em again."

"You ever seen 'em before?"

"No Sir. None of us had. Those fellas were real friendly. What happened to the Sheriff there?"

"Don't call him that, Wilks."

Outside the station Forsman saw a girl seated on one of the benches near the tracks. There was nothing extraordinary about her. She was the only person at the station and she looked off at the hills, squinting as she wrung her hands together. Forsman watched her casually from the saddle. When she saw his face she turned away and never looked back. But Forsman didn't turn away. He looked hard upon her and didn't let go his gaze for minutes on end.

The riders came out together and the clerk named Wilks was with them.

"Joe?"

"Uhm humn."

"I heard news yesterday that I thought you should hear."

Forsman spit. "From that son of yours?"

"Yes, from that son of mine. From him and about him. Him and your daughter, too."

"Uhm humn."

"They lost the little one after all. I figure you hadn't heard."

Forsman gave a shrug. "The little one?"

The clerk stepped back."God man, didn't you know? Their little girl went sick a month ago. Bad sick."

"Which'n?"

"Little Eleanor."

"Uhm humn."

Wilks waited for the man to say more but Forsman showed no sign. He simply patted his mount. The clerk began to tremble as he searched the faces of the riders, but none gave him any relief. Last of all he turned to Danny but his eyes were hidden beneath his hat brim, his hands working up around his face. Finally the man turned back to Forsman.

"So I thought you needed to know."

"Uhm humn."

"She was sleeping when she went they say."

"Uhm humn."

"The funeral will be in Stowington."

Forsman didn't say anything and slowly Wilks backed away. He noticed the rifles and the long cartridge belts hanging from their rigs. When they turned reign and kicked along Danny gave Wilks a wave that his father didn't see but kept his face hidden by his hat. They rode south from the station and the tracks weren't hard to follow but the sun was beating down on the snowpack and in less than a day their trail would have been lost. They rode until they came to a huge valley where the snow had all but melted and the trail had nearly disappeared. They spread across the land, hanging from their saddle horns, their eyes to the ground. They spotted horse scat and rode on. They found no sign for hours. They rode in the direction of the trail, weaving a thread across the land. They found signs of fisherman on a riverbank and a cold ring of embers above a long prairie. Each time they mounted quickly and pointed for the western forest and they didn't stop until it was too dark to see.

5. Strangers from Across the Sea

When they were twelve years old it was the custom for Henry Snow and Jack Oakham to hunt the great woodlands that surrounded them, often from horseback, and always with great anticipation, the kind only boys can feel. For it was in the wilds, Tipper taught them, that each of them would temper their patience and courage; in the wilds where their eyes and ears would become accustomed, even in their first spring, to the sensation of glorious dangers. They had met the pursuit like savage kings and it wasn't long before their expeditions found them burdened with great slabs of meat bound for the kitchen fires of Tenpenny. They came home in the evening not as children, but as great providers feeding the masses. And now that the two of them were crossing the Wild West End they were wishing for burdens of a similar stock, for they were hungry, and it was meat they favored.

However the Wild West End was proving to be less generous than the woodlands that surrounded their home. All that morning they had scoured the forest for an assortment of game meats but all they had found were a handful of nuts and unripe berries.

After hunting for hours the party stopped to let the Pritchers graze. They didn't speak of it, but by that time all four of our travelers were painfully hungry. Henry tore a tuft of grass from the path and chewed it, hoping he could create a cud in his mouth like the cattle do to help fend off his appetite. Jack began gnawing on a leather strap that hung from his pack and Putt ate the great leaves of the Saskatoon bushes. None were producing the desired effect.

The brothers each sat frustrated beside the fire, wishing for some luck to come their way. But as they rested, Tip, in his warm voice told many tales to keep their minds occupied; stories of the teachings Kolschen had given, of his adventures across the sea, of the spectacles he had witnessed, the wild lands and the walled cities, where strange peoples lived, some who had never seen a white face.

Henry listened carefully, longing for the kind of journey that his father had taken. He began to feel that there was no limit to what a man could see or smell or taste, in a life lived freely.

"To travel is to be released from manmade bondage," Tip said. "One must never spread their roots too deep in their youth, but go, go far, meet many and see much, sift through the raw hovels until you are left with only shiny stone gems in your crown of memories. Then come back to your favorites.

"Arumforn iber," he would say, again and again.

"Which is Yiddish for what?" Jack asked.

Before Henry could answer Tip said, "Your travels! In one river a man may pan for gold and find a nugget, but in fifty, he will find a storehouse."

As he was accustomed to doing, Henry listened for only a few minutes before his hunger overwhelmed him. Soon he took to the river with his rod and reel.

When he was gone Tip faced Jack and circled the rim of his pipe with the lit match. "What do you miss most from back home?" he asked.

"Momma Tom," Jack answered, the moment the question came to him.

"Really? I woulda thought Greer."

Jack shook his head. He was surprised that his feelings were so widely known. "No. She isn't mine," he said.

Tip Holland, rarely startled, nearly dropped his pipe. "Then whose is she?"

"No ones. But everyone wants to be close to a beauty. And she's a girl and Momma Tom's a woman and I like the differences."

Having two sons was all Tip could have hoped for. He too sat admiring the differences.

"Jack I want to talk to you about you and your brother."

"Yessir."

"I'm concerned, Jack, that Henry's boyhood is far from over."

"I see."

"And that yours has been dead for awhile."

Jack nodded as if in agreement. It was something he had considered himself. "Mom told me once that I didn't know how to be young. We traveled all the time. Town to town and I never made any friends. It wasn't until I came here that I really had a buddy."

"I'm not worried for you, Jack. Only for your brother."

"I don't understand."

Tip moved closer to his son. "Jack when Kolschen took me on the road he introduced me to cultures and peoples you couldn't dream of.

And sometimes he put me to the test, making me defend what I believed against the strongest and wisest men we encountered. One person that he introduced me to was a strange man named Patris Cammobi. He was a former Stavrophore monk living as a peddler. He was a small and sickly man, Jack, but of all the men I've ever known he had the most brilliant of minds. Kolschen said he had never heard of another like him. No matter the language or the concept this man could grasp it, almost instantaneously. And he was a born leader. Men and women alike came to him for answers. But he was a solitary man with no roots and no compass. He had no wife, no family, no commitments, and little education. He was addicted to his freedoms. If he had been born to a loving father, or married to a righteous woman his country may be a very different place today. But he died a week after I met him, of consumption. He was thirty-three."

Jack scribbled a few notes in his journal and it wasn't until he stopped that Tip continued.

"Now you know how proud I am of you, Jack. Make no mistake you are my wise and diligent son. But you must also know that Henry is unique. He isn't like you or me or even Otsov Kolschen. Henry Snow is like Patris Cammobi. He is a phenomenon. And like Cammobi, Henry Snow has no roots to hold him down. I fear that Henry may prolong his boyhood for the remainder of his life. A young man like him could do mighty things with his gifts. But I assure you he won't so long as he doesn't have a reason to."

"You are a loving father. You are the reason."

"No, Jack. It isn't me. It must be you."

Jack turned his head in confusion. "Why me?"

"Because to Henry, I'm a figurehead. But *you* are an equal. Henry needs an equal. He needs a friend to walk beside."

Jack thought long on his father's words, both startled and encouraged by them. Of course Jack knew his brother was extraordinary. So did everyone else. And he understood his father's challenge, though he didn't know what to do about it. They sat long in the small clearing, Jack rubbing the ears of the old dog thinking of what to say. But he found no answers. Soon Jack and Tipper joined the dog in a short rest. They were well-shaded and the embers warmed them as they slept and they weren't woken until a half hour later when Henry came marching back through the thicket.

"Better start up the fire," he said.

Jack awoke suddenly, "Why?"

Henry was smiling. "How else could we cook the steaks?"

Along with his fishing rod Henry had carried his bow off into the woods as well, in hopes of trailing a snowshoe hare. When he returned, however, it was with a much larger prize. In his right hand Henry presented them with a moose tongue, from a young calf and instantly Tipper sprung to life.

"The hunter's life is filled with danger!
The hunter's life is wild and free!
You can have your streets and your soft soles, stranger. . .
But save the woods and the hills for me!"

Everything was done with speed and precision for their hunger consumed them. Henry and Jack found the moose in the woods, dressed him quickly and dragged him to a clearing. Henry butchered the calf while Tip collected twigs and kindled the fire, stacking softwood branches nearby. When Henry had the steaks stripped Jack washed them and plopped them down on the hot skillet. To the sound of cooking meat Henry played his little pocket harp and the party sang songs and Putt looked out with lust in his heart for the fresh warm cutlets.

But as Jack watched the meat sizzle all he could think of were the pleasures of home. He imagined Putt asleep in the corner and Momma Tom playing him a long game of chess. His feet were bare and it would have been cold in the room save for the crackling fire, so he snuggled up beneath the quilt blanket. The image of Greer and Padi passed through his mind as the two of them waged war with his heart. For despite the drama they brought him Jack adored both of them equally and didn't feel whole without them near. Ah to be back back home again, away from this murky forest, away from all of the filth just for a moment, to eat some of Sissy's sweet chocolates, to hear the children running outside, to take a hot shower.

"Jack!"

Jack awoke from his daydream to see his father and brother squatted down near the fire, scanning the woods. Tip was looking off at the tall grass, his rifle in hand. "What is it?" Jack asked as he squatted.

"They're hiding in the saskatoon."

"Can you still see them?" Henry whispered.

"Yes," Tip said. "The big red cedar is hanging over the one on the right."

"How many?"

"What is it?" Jack again.

"Drifters."

Now Jack could see several low shadows. They looked like children to his eyes.

All the members of the party were wondering what these men were doing in the wild wood.

Finally Tip squinted off into the woods and whispered. "Henry, where'd you kill the calf?"

The boy pointed at a patch of sedges by the spring. "Right out there."

"You dragged her from there?"

"Yah."

"Where d'you gut her?"

Henry and Jack looked toward the red cedar where the drifters were cowered. "Right where they're hiding."

Tip rubbed his face with his palm. He shook his head slightly. "You know what they're doing, men?"

Henry chewed his moose steak, "Having lunch?"

"That's right," Tip told them. "They're having lunch on us."

Henry shrugged, "They must have heard us singing."

The boys struggled to imagine who could be living in these lands, and how they had grown so hungry that they had swarmed the gutpile for their supper. Both brothers had read that primitive people throughout the world eat the intestines of large mammals on special occasions. Despite his wild ways even Henry couldn't imagine enjoying such a meal.

Tip stood up, lowering his rifle, his hand raised in the air. Jack and Henry were surprised that their father had stood in full view of the strangers. Men that would come so close unannounced could be dangerous men, Jack thought. Yet before they could question him, Tip called out to the strangers but sounded friendly and gentle when he did so. "Not to worry, men. We're friends here. You're welcome to some steaks, if you're hungry."

There was a long pause until out of the brush came a murmuring. It sounded like one voice to the party. The voices continued to rise until four men and a boy stood out of the grasses. They seemed to be carrying little or no gear.

Jack let his jaw drop when he saw them. Henry continued to chew chunks of steak from the pan. The troupe was a collection of small, dark men with squinty faces. An old gruff one with a patchy beard and dark fingers stepped forward. He had deep scars on his face, dimpled all over. Henry called it "hail damage" in his mind. He appeared to be the only one with a pack. The others had little knapsacks that looked half empty to our heroes. The man raised his hands, making peace, "We are sorry. These men were very hungry."

Tip noticed that his rifle made the man nervous. He propped it against the tree beside him. "Don't apologize for hunger," Tip said and smiled. Tip Holland had a talent for smiles. "I'm Tipper. These are my sons, Jack and Henry."

Both brothers stood, nodding awkwardly to the stranger.

Their leader crossed over the grasses and shook hands. "My name is Ibrahim. I have been leading these men for two days."

"You're doing a fine job." Tip answered to his son's surprise. Not only was Tip not offended by their trespass, he appeared approving, and almost familiar with their travels.

The other men walked up and all shook hands. Henry and Jack later agreed that with the exception of Ibrahim, all of these men looked like the photos they had seen of the people that lived above the clouds, in the high peaks across the sea. They had leathery faces and dark, lithe bodies. Their eyes were small and squinty, from years too close to the sun. Even their colorful shirts and big, constant smiles reminded Henry and Jack of all they had ever learned about such people. Bhotiyas they were called. Their names were Yigal, Radim, Chhedup and the boy's was Immanuel.

The little boy didn't look like any of the men he was traveling with. He had a round face, with a short neck and stubby fingers. To the boys from Tenpenny he looked like a portly little gentlemen. They didn't know that he would be a giant someday.

Tip offered the men the three canteens and they passed them from man to man.

Meanwhile Ibrahim looked long at our heroes. Their gear was tattered, their faces filthy. *These are the poor of this land,* he thought. *Only the dog looks healthy.*

263

"Why are you all the way out here?" he asked.

"Enjoying the scenery."

"Don't you have homes?"

"We do."

"Cozy ones with warm fires?"

"Yes."

"And you sleep in the forest with the bears?"

Tip's face brightened. His sons had seen this look before, usually when Sissy had a complaint about the manner in which he was raising her nephews. "I don't want a wrinkle-free life," he told the man. "I won't stand for comfort-friendly footwear. Give me a horse and the force it takes to tame him, give me the wisdom of fire and ice, bring me a boy and seven years to claim him, and I'll hand you a man both naughty and nice."

"I'd prefer a bed," Ibrahim said.

Tip winked at the boy, "Right about now," he said, "So would I."

The men laughed and toasted one another with their canteens.

Ibrahim was surprised to see that the two young boys could fish so well. He had trekked a long time on these waters and was silent as he realized these boys were more productive than he was. When they camped together that night each boy had plenty of trout for themselves and the Bhotiyas too, and they were gracious with the food, and gathered the wood unselfishly, and one offered his coat to Immanuel Labor, who accepted timidly.

The father of the two boys brought a ptarmigan to the camp that he had killed with a smooth stone and plucked it and cleaned it with his fingers, and cooked it slowly, giving it to the men as a gift. He let the strangers lay their bedrolls in the space nearest the fire as his big son played his little pocket harp.

Ibrahim believed this to be a very unusual gang of travelers. They ate sparingly and crossed a great deal of harsh country with few supplies. They sang songs. One of the things that always bothered Ibrahim about the men in this land was that they never sang. But these three sang. Even the dog bayed when the pocket harp was played. They sang so beautifully that some of the refugees fell asleep sitting up listening to the sounds, and others hummed along. The second oldest man, Yigal, thanked them for the song, he said it was good luck to have met them, said it was an omen for a new life. Tip understood the talk and explained it to his sons and they laughed gently.

"Do you know whose land this is?" Ibrahim asked Tip.

Henry answered, "Heard his name," as he glanced at his father.

"They say he buried a treasure somewhere upriver."

"We heard about it."

"I don't believe it."

"Why not?"

"Rich men have banks. The banks are good. Why would a rich man bury a treasure?"

Henry shrugged. "Maybe it isn't true."

The men looked very happy and thankful as they ate the moose steaks. Jack watched them carefully, curious what their story might be.

"What are you doing all the way out here?" Jack asked.

Already Ibrahim had a strange admiration for the boy so he chose to answer, "I am leading these men to a new life."

"Where?"

"Through the forest for awhile."

"Then?"

"The man that owns this land."

"Yes?"

"These men are going to work for him."

Henry and Jack came to attention. "Work for who?" Henry asked.

"The man who owns this land. Do you know it? Says he needs men to work and pays me to bring them across the sea and guide them there."

Jack turned to look at Tip who was digging in his pack, pretending to have no interest in the conversation. Jack smiled. "You don't say. What kind of work is it?"

"Good work. Above ground work. You know who owns this land?"

Jack and Henry both nodded smugly.

Ibrahim wondered why Tip hadn't answered. He said clearly, "And you? Do you know the man?"

Tip bowed his head slightly without looking up, "I do."

"Is he an honest man? A good man?"

"I've known better."

The young boy, Immanuel, was frightened at the sight of the brother's injuries. Jack's broken fingers made it difficult for him to cook and when

Henry removed the bandages around his knee the boy became very afraid of what lay ahead. The old ones too had noticed the wound, and shocked that the party of white men continued to travel despite warm homes to return to. Their father must be a cruel and selfish man, they thought.

"How far do you have to go?" Henry asked, fascinated.

"If we cross this forest to the east then a long desert valley then up into some hills where their new home will be."

"If the bears don't kill us," Chhedup said in his own language.

Until then Henry and Jack had yet to hear this man speak. Both his voice and his language were each a strange surprise that they both enjoyed.

But Yigal began to spit angrily when he heard the words. It was not good to speak of bad things. His wife's appendix ruptured while she was pregnant, poisoning the baby and finally herself, and he found her lying arched on her belly, the big hump supporting her. He never spoke of it or thought of it for it was a bad thing he knew, and he knew better than to speak by the fire of the bad things. Such things are made real by thinking of them, he knew.

"They worry about the bears," Ibrahim said. "But I tell them we've come through the worst of it."

Jack asked, "Have you seen some?"

"If you stay along this river to the west, you will see the bears," Ibrahim answered. "I swear it."

Henry spoke up again, "How do you know where you're going?"

"I have taken men there many times."

The brothers turned when they heard the heavy clumping of feet behind him and were greatly surprised by the site of Radim leading five dun ponies across the clearing. The mounts were worn and slender, but fine horses all the same.

Jack and Henry began sharing the warmth with the boy, who put his palms up to the tiny flame. Without saying so the brothers were both clearly fond of the little one. They were both hoping to claim him like a prize once they had come back to Tenpenny.

In time the two groups of travelers drifted off to sleep, warmed by the fire and the food in their bellies. The Bhotiyas had only small blankets to wrap around themselves but none appeared to be shivering. They must be accustomed to the cold where they come from, Jack thought.

266

Jack was doing a lot of thinking that night, about the nature of these men, and of course wondering where they had come from. They must have a port, he figured, and a stable for the horses. He couldn't imagine what lengths Tipper must have gone through to bring them across. And why, he wondered? For what purpose were they traveling? But despite the great mystery that the Bhotiyas presented Jack's mind soon began to drift to other things. He was glad to see that he was the final member of either party to stay awake that night for he longed for some peace and quiet. That afternoon when he realized the Bhotiyas would be traveling to Tenpenny Jack had decided to write a letter, and the quiet moments around the fire gave him just the chance he needed.

Carefully Jack told Greer all the things he wished he had said before he left, being completely honest with the girl for the first time. He knew if she followed through with her plans to leave Tenpenny she would never receive the letter, and that if he didn't send the note immediately and she did leave, he would always regret it. These two possible outcomes gave Jack a dose of courage he didn't know he had. He fell asleep emboldened and proud of his words to her.

The following morning Ibrahim arose to find Tipper skinning more of the moose so the Bhotiyas could have meat for their journey. The other men were still sleeping but Ibrahim just stood watching Tip curiously.

"You are hurt?" he asked.

Tip looked up. The question surprised him. Then he thought about the appearance of his sons who were feeding the fire nearby. He turned to look at Henry. The bandages around his knee was dirty. "He'll be alright," he said. "And Jack has broken fingers before. He doesn't play piano."

The little man smiled, "You're the one I mean."

"Sorry?"

"You're hurt worse than them. Am I right?"

"I'm fine."

"You're not fine. I can't tell if it's a woman or something else but you're a bit more frightened than you've been in a long, long time and it has something to do with where you're headed. Am I right?"

Tip didn't respond to the question. He knew it was a mistake to let the discussion continue. He looked heavily at the little man and went back to sorting out the meats.

The young morning still clung to the damp chill. The ground was frosted over. Immanuel's arms, from supporting his head throughout the night, had both fallen asleep at the elbow. As he shook them from the shoulder the travelers watched and laughed so hard that Yigal rushed in from squatting in the bushes to join them in their jeering. "Shake them alive," they told him. Little Immanuel was embarrassed from all the mocking. Old Radim and Chhedup were imitating the boy by standing dumb-faced and flopping their arms about like dead snakes. But the boy couldn't help but smile for it had been a long time since he had been presented with such attention. When his blood worked its way down to his fingertips he tried to keep flopping, but the men grew tired of the joke and went back to their quiet ways.

"The forest is long," Yigal said finally in his own language. "When is the next sunshine?"

"This afternoon," Ibrahim assured him for the second time.

The strange guide named Ibrahim handled the meats and stowed them in paper, stuffing them into their saddlebags. Stranger or not, from a world far away this traveler had clearly seen in a few glances what Tip's sons hadn't noticed through many days of travel. That Tip Holland was carrying a heavy burden on his heart.

Tip leaned in to the stranger and whispered, "A week ago you met a man across the sea who welcomed you to his home, fed you, took you across the water?"

The man wore a startled face, his eyes large, "You mean Ruffino?"

"How is he?"

"He is well," the man said, still surprised.

The Bhotiyas finished off their moose steaks and before long the four man troupe and the one shy child were saddling their ponies and packing to leave. Discreetly Jack stepped up to Ibrahim and handed him the letter. "I have a friend where you are going," he whispered. "Could you see that she gets this?" The old guide agreed and they nodded their goodbyes.

As the men mounted and were turning to the east Tip called out to them.

"Before you go," Tipper said. "There is something I want you to have."

To everyone's great surprise, especially Henry and Jack's Tipper led the Pritchers across the clearing and handed the man the reigns.

"We don't need them anymore," he said. "Take them to the place you are going. Ride them if you like. They are good horses. We'll come to get them later. When you arrive give them to a man named Wonderboy."

"Wonderboy?"

"Yes. He is a friend of ours."

Each of the travelers were astonished by the gift, especially the child. They nodded their appreciation and said prayers over the Tenpenny Three.

The parties exchanged glances before the little men trickled through the thicket one by one.

"Tell us about them," Henry said as he watched them go. "Why are they here?"

"We need a few more cabins built."

"The three of us could have built them."

"We could use some help. The older you get the more I have for you to do."

"Do they know what they're in for?"

"Not really," Tip said. "Their lives were pretty hard on the other side and they all have sad stories. To drifters like that almost any change is good change."

"So you bring them across the sea?" Jack asked.

"Sissy's idea. 'We'll become a gateway,' she said."

"Best idea she ever had," Henry suggested.

Tip turned to Henry, his blunt son, and smiled. "It wouldn't kill you to be kinder to my sister."

"She hates me."

"Yes, she does."

"And I don't mean man hate that happens before a scuffle and is over when you're done trading licks. I mean woman hate. She'll hate me forever."

"Probably."

"Now can anybody tell me what I did to deserve that? Anybody?"

"You designed a pistol target with her face on it."

"I meant in the last few minutes."

They all chuckled as they watched the ponies pick their way through the forest, one step at a time across the spongy turf. Jack turned to his father and said with a scratchy whisper, "Why d'you do it, dad?" he asked.

All the while Henry and Tip and Jack and the dog kept their eyes on the horses as they slipped away.

"Do what?"

"Couldn't have been easy. Sometimes I think about it. All night I just sit there thinking about it, of how the kids have come from all over, and the workers, and you and me and Henry. Sometimes I think you went out of your way to find all the beat-up and left-behinds of the world, and of how you brought us all together. It's good that you did and I love all of them, but sometimes it's just a little hard for me to understand. Why you wanted it? You could have done anything."

Tip rubbed his worn leather boot on the turf and rested his eyes on the far off places of the world. "I'm as beat up as anybody, Jack. I'm just like those wobbly-kneed children that show up scared at the gate, from one hell or another. If I had "wanted" Tenpenny it would have ended up a joke. Tenpenny wasn't a wish. For me Tenpenny was a conviction. I was a coward, sent across the sea by my own cowardice, and from the moment I landed in the new world I began to find things no one had ever told me about. I had been living a make believe life. And all the while true life was going on and I had managed to miss it, I'd managed to think what I was living was life, that life was what I saw before me everyday, that there was nothing else. I had no idea that the whole world wasn't made up of spoiled crooks like me. The world is made up of the poor and the hungry, boys, much stronger than the three of us.

No. Tenpenny was my job to do. And I pray that now I've done it, my name will disappear for good."

There was a silence then. Jack was certain that something had happened, that something was suddenly understood. He wanted the moment to last and last.

"It couldn't be a big treasure we're hunting," Henry said.

Tip frowned at his son, "Why not?"

"Even when you were younger you couldn't have carried anything much bigger than your pack through this forest or across that dern valley and I hear there's some hills on the other side of this everlasting wood and you couldn't have lugged anything too big up that either."

Jack shook his head, frustrated that such a moment could be overlooked by his brother.

Tip asked, "What's your point, Henry?"

"Henry has a point?" Jack asked.

"He started speaking practically so for a moment there I thought he was approaching a point. He's made points before."

"Good points?"

"Oh no."

The Tenpenny three stood upon the verandah, shaded pleasantly, and watched the wood. The crackle of high flames blazed the trail and little eyes in the dark sparkled with the light. The trees leaned into one another like a canopy across the path. There they saw the Bhotiyas, the only true travelers they would ever meet disappear into the black holds of the forest and their horses with them.

And Henry said, "There's something tragic about a tramp."

When they returned to their campsite Henry and Jack, still hungry, were suddenly struck by the sight before them. The moose was gone! Every tasty morsel had been cleaned from the carcass! Without telling them Tipper had stripped all the meat that remained and given it to the Bhotiyas. All that lay before the brothers was bare bones and the calf's head. Both of them turned to voice their complaints but they wouldn't get the chance. Tipper hauled his pack onto his shoulders as he knelt down to address them.

"Listen now, there is much to discuss." From his pocket Tipper unfolded a small map made of parchment paper and set in at his feet. For an instant each of the brothers forgot their hunger pains.

"Here is a map of the great wood. I made it for just such an occasion. It will lead you on for the next leg of the journey."

Jack was quick to comment. "Lead *us* on?"

"That's right, Jack. Putt and I are going to take a different road, for a while. I leave the two of you alone to face the river."

Jack stood up. The idea of being left in the deep woods without his father was terrifying business. "Where do we go?"

Tip pointed at the map. "Keep west along the river. You will come to the iron hills within the hour and you'll cover them until dark. Make camp along Troublesome Gully. And keep your fires large. Don't cross the river for any reason."

Henry was clearly excited, "And then?"

"Tomorrow morning you will arrive at a wide clearing six miles west called the "Window in the Meadow." Pay close attention. *You must arrive at dawn.* Don't be late and don't be early. Arrive at first light. Sit at the edge of the clearing and wait. Don't make a sound and don't fall asleep. Just keep your eyes on the meadow. If you are even moments late you will be in great danger. The map shows everything."

Without a moment's hesitation Tipper stood to leave. He nodded to his sons. "Promise me you won't cross the river."

And they did.

Then he shook their hands, turned and left, leading the old dog by the collar.

Jack was as sad to see Putt leaving as he was his father, though he knew it was a foolish thought. Putt was a fine companion but as Tip departed so did the only shreds of security Jack had left. Never in his life would he feel more homesick than he did in that moment. To make matters worse he heard his father whistling as he slipped into the wood and out of sight.

"Never forget. The two of you were chosen!" Tip called. "It was not at random. You were hand-picked for a purpose!"

"What purpose?" Jack asked.

They could hear Tip chuckle as he disappeared into the woods. "Allohim layhim!"

Jack shook his head and turned to face his brother. "What's that mean?"

Henry gave a little sigh. "It means, 'All in good time'."

6. The Student From Gromalsk

By Henry Snow

With the Sabbath came all sorts of smells and sounds that, among certain nights, reminded the Rabbi that the traditions, although bland and humdrum, were familiar. As the first stars appeared in the sky he always finished the Sabbath meal with a song from the fathers regarding such traditions. It too was both common and familiar as were all the goings-on on most any Sabbath evening. The mysteries of the Torah were discussed at length, the hurricane lamps and the valedictory candle were lit, and he said grace over the wine and dipped his fingers in it and sprinkled droplets on his eyes to insure good fortune, for the beloved Sabbath was ending and another week beginning.

There were no changes in their traditions throughout the fall until the night when a student from Gromalsk entered. When the song had been sung, he burst through the door with his brow seared to interrupt, "Rabbi?"

He was dressed like most students, ragged, smelling like a pauper with only a chin beard beginning to sprout, his caftan torn, his cap patched. He put his books down by his side quickly, nodded to the Rabbi's wife graciously and with a sturdy "Good Sabbath" to his sons and daughter asked again, "Rabbi?"

"I am the Rabbi," the man said, noticing a slim yellow envelope in the boy's hand.

"A good week to you."

"And to you, good Sabbath, what is it?"

"Rabbi?" And when he could see that the young man was nervous before the children with the dinnerware still fresh on the table he said, "Come join me in the study."

He walked with a fever, quickly as if chased. He held tightly to his patched pack that was in his hands and moved beside the Rabbi into the small room. It was unlit. He set down his books and the bright envelope. He slipped into the seat before the fire and removed his cap.

"Rabbi?"

The Rabbi found his seat. "Yes speak up, what is it you have to say?"

"I have a question, Rabbi."

"Well, ask it."

"Do you think the devil is a genius?" he said.

A silence followed that cannot be described. What only can be said is that the Rabbi smiled then frowned and thought for a long while before he ever spoke.

"A genius? He is no genius. Who are you?"

The young man hesitated then spoke strongly, "I am Stuart Whitlock, a student from Gromalsk. It is a question that has been posed to me so I ask of you, a Rabbi."

"And I tell you 'no'."

For a moment there was nothing. The student looked at the fire and said with his eyes empty like a blind beggar, "I myself was led to believe that one so evil could not receive such a compliment but on further-"

"Young man."

"Rabbi then what is he if not a genius?"

"He is the great deceiver – driven to corrupt."

"Can a common man not corrupt? Can an adulterous woman not corrupt if she wishes to?"

"He is no genius," the Rabbi told him. Then for the first time the Rabbi thought about the question the student had asked him. "He is fallen."

But the student was not satisfied.

"Look what he has done, Rabbi. I can break bread and wheels of cheese but not families."

"He is our enemy. That is all we need to know. He can break more than families. Do not be corrupted yourself and you will defeat him."

"To take what is pure and to turn it around is not merely corruption is it? Look what has happened in your lifetime!"

"You came from Gromalsk to ask? What a student! What a question to travel for! It has been my lifetime, do you think I have not seen?"

"If you have, Rabbi, let me know. I wish to know of his corruption and defend myself."

"He corrupts that is all. He is the deceiver. He turns the hearts of weak men towards evil. He has many methods, many demons and imps of persuasion but the true repentant heart has no fear of him. Defend yourself by dwelling on the things he hasn't corrupted. Let no more words describe him on this Sabbath!"

"But Rabbi, how clever! Let us feel guilty to describe him you say? What an idea. We must define what it is. We must know!"

"Calm yourself. This is the Sabbath."

"Women are no longer women, Rabbi. They are something new. Have you seen? Men cannot decide what they are. So much pride, no time for anything. How busy he has made us. Sin is in the streets, Rabbi. We are watching his victory. Families-"

"Enough, I need no lessons!"

"Rabbi, I saw this darkness as I entered the city. It is all around this very house. Families are broken, children lose value in themselves. They look up to imps in disguise writhing around together in dance. Women

274

perceive what they are to be from the lies men tell. Men discern what they want from the lies they tell themselves. Little whispers, little whispers always spoken in the dark. Today a little whisper reaches everyone, the devil uses our things. He is organized by our inventions. Good ideas are smothered."

"Young men interrupt dinners."

"Rabbi, my apologies. But I believe the devil to be a genius."

"No!"

It seemed then to the Rabbi that the young student from Gromalsk and he were fighting with their words and he could not understand it. The way the student looked had changed and the way the Rabbi was speaking was not patient but forced, bullish. The student looked older, thinner, more pointed and gaunt. He leaned into his questions.

The Rabbi stood with a stern expression and moved toward the door to close it. He looked in on his family and waved them off. As he did so, the student took the yellow envelope and quietly slipped it beneath the great bookshelf beside him and returned to his position. The Rabbi didn't notice. He found his seat and looked long at his visitor.

"Forgive me, Rabbi," the young man said.

The Rabbi felt unwilled to speak. He could see that he could not merely wish this student from Gromalsk good Sabbath, scoot him out the door and carry on with his ritual bath and start the new week. This student seemed to have come to his study not merely to convince himself, but to convince the Rabbi. He needed a pair of ears and nothing more. Then as the Rabbi was about to suggest he return to his Sabbath meal that he must have interrupted to find him, he started again, "Rabbi what troubles me is that the sanctity of marriage has been lost most recently, and what has followed is disastrous. I could not have planned such a thing! Isn't that tragic! He poisons the fishbowl before dropping in the fish."

The Rabbi felt himself reentering the discussion. After all this young man was nothing more than a curious student on leave from his studies who needed a Rabbi's advice. His inquiries were challenging and youthful and unfamiliar. He may have been impatient in his questions but the Rabbi was simply that, a Rabbi, not the young man's father.

"It is true. It is worth considering," the Rabbi told him. "We have a great enemy."

"You agree with me then?"

"I will say nothing of the kind. What difference would it make? The Torah defines what he is and what he will do and how he will lose, don't forget. He is more cunning than the worst of men but nothing more."

The Rabbi stood and moved toward him. "What is the cost of following the holy book?" he asked. The Rabbi placed his hand on the student's shoulder. "For you, to be troubled by your enemy who has no power, the cost is small. What is his cost? What is the cost of turning from truth, falling to the earth and condemning oneself forever to corrupting the hearts of men. The cost is too great to measure. He made a foolish choice. A foolish choice. A fool himself. A fool who preys on others, eating the weak. You give him too much credit, young man."

The student from Gromalsk seemed satisfied at last. He took a long breath and drew his eyes away from the fire. "Thank you, Rabbi," he said.

He stood and handled his books tightly. "What is the cost, Rabbi?"

"For a Sabbath dinner twenty kopecks."

He handed over the coins and nodded graciously as he had when he interrupted the dinner moments before. He seemed ready to speak but hesitant.

"Be diligent in your studies," the Rabbi told him. "Never forget the example you set."

The student smiled and turned toward the door. He put his patched cap back on his head and said without looking up, "I will Rabbi. I will be diligent. Out of respect for the devil I will study more thoroughly."

"Respect?! The devil has corrupted you surely! Respect?"

The Rabbi knew at that moment that his ears were red with fury and his voice loud like thunder. "Does your feeling of respect for him dim the Torah? To come from Gromalsk with such a proclamation seems treason for a student."

The Rabbi was calmed then, for it did seem foolish to bring such a statement after all.

"Respect in his evil, Rabbi," he said, shocked and afraid. "There is a difference. A man may be impressed by evil without being corrupted by it, may he not? He is impressed because the evil makes a dent but he is not proud of it."

"Repent young Stuart Whitlock for the devil has made a dent," he answered slowly. "He is making his dent bigger with every word you speak."

And it was quiet again. The Rabbi could hear his family listening over their Sabbath meal. The young student from Gromalsk stood tall and lowered his head. He said then with no emotion or doubt, "Rabbi, genius seems too small a word."

"Go from this house! Go repent this Sabbath!"

"Rabbi."

"Go!"

And the young man with many questions and a torn caftan moved from the study through the house with his books. He passed by the sons and the daughter and the wife and stepped into the street and did not return. The Rabbi watched him through the window come alongside another man, enormous and bearded, and the two crossed the street.

In the street the Rabbi glanced the vendors over but the women he could not look at. He still was not a part of the street. The street in no way resembled a garden. The market was filling as the two men disappeared into the crowd.

The two of them moved silently down the long street. The boy took off his caftan and skullcap and placed his books in his haversack.

"He is a wise man, the Rabbi," Kolschen said.

Tipper nodded.

"Did he argue with you?"

"Vigorously."

"A good man. A man filled with goodness. Ah, how I love him. But did you see him? So frail and poor? These people here do not see his goodness. They see only his frailty. His poverty. They do not see the hands that reach out to them."

The street grew dark as they crossed the great bridge that divided the city. The lights flickered as they came awake.

"Where are we going now?" Tip asked.

"There is evil in the world. You know that?"

"I've been it."

"Sadly, we all have."

Then he added. "Now we go to meet a very different kind of man. A man on the other side of things. He is an evil man. Much loved among his people. What they fail to see in the Rabbi they also fail to see in this one. For they look upon him with envy. To them he is strong. A great man."

"But not to you?"

"Not to me. To me he is not a man at all. There are but a handful of fully-formed men in this world."

"Do you want me to argue with him too?"

Kolschen stopped to address him. "Yes I do. Are you afraid to?"

"Should I be?"

"In the world's eyes you may never meet a stronger one than this. He scares most men right out of their boots."

"Does he scare you?"

Kolschen smiled. "He used to. But not anymore."

Suddenly Tipper felt a wave of terror pass right through him. He couldn't imagine what sort of person would frighten Otsov Kolschen.

They carried on across the bridge, the boy sweating at the palms. Finally he asked, "What would you like us to argue about?"

Kolschen smiled proudly on the boy. "Well let's think about that, Tip," he chuckled. "What does an evil man hate to hear?"

Back in his home the Rabbi waited in his study by the dying fire for the sound of the student's return. He desired to hear more questions. He wanted to be tested once again. Never had he spoken out in anger in any room of the house and his wife and children were silent as they removed what remained of the Sabbath meal. He repented but felt no peace.

The Rabbi brooded then and he smoked his long pipe, and he did not eat or drink or speak. He did not move. He only thought. And the only two things he knew for certain throughout the coming week until the traditions of the Sabbath began the following Saturday were that students were a dangerous kind and that the devil was a genius.

7. Brave Fools and Lucky Branches

Esperanza had laid there for a full day, licking her wound as the cubs grew restless. The bullet had entered at the shoulder and was imbedded in the bone. She could hear the ice atop the pond pop pop popping as the surface swelled with the coming spring and all along her cubs nudged her, anxious to be in the light.

Up top on the Cutshank the heat came swiftly and the sun lay on the snow until it softened and trickled. For a full day the land along the open valley took her first drink of spring until the puddles swelled within the tiny dimples on the land, and then the puddles spilled over, doubling onto one another like a floodland. Soon the rolling hillocks were dotted with shallow blue pools dripping into one another until the streams cut through the swales and ran restlessly toward lower country: the lowing plains were saturated, the crags gurgled with swift water, and a great lake, nestled in the bosom of the land and frozen at the surface, began to fill like a thirsty basin.

With every passing hour the cubs nudged her but the bear only ignored them. Now that she was injured she knew more rest would be needed for her journey ahead. She curled in her moist bedding and ran her long tongue across the wound and when her cubs approached the lighted entrance she hissed to draw them away.

After half a day the bullet had bled out and the wound was sealed and the bear went to rolling her shoulder into the softening mud. But hour by hour the den continued to fill with snowmelt and the cubs had trouble sleeping as the streams cut the mud beneath them.

They stayed that night but after a long day tending her wound the water pooling beneath her finally became intolerable for the bear. In the early afternoon she rose from her burrow and limped heavily toward the light.

When she climbed out into the sun, she squinted at the pale blue sky like she had days before when the boy had shot her. The bear had denned beneath the lake for over twenty years, throwing triplet cubs every fourth season, but now she would have to find a new place to winter for her den was no longer clandestine.

The bear had lost her footing when he shot her, slipping into her den, and there were bloodstains splashed across the melting snow at the foot of the burrow. The bear ignored it, knowing her scent too well, and plodded up the bank for a better view.

But her cubs didn't follow. They stopped to sniff the strong aroma and soon were licking her blood from the melting snowpack. Other than milk it was the first taste they'd known in many months.

The old bear stammered up the lakeshore, still icy, and when she reached the bank she raised her head to peer across the rim. All she could hear was the wind over the pale valley. All she could see was the cool white light of the early afternoon shining down amidst the open country.

She turned and stood on her haunches and gave a quick stretch in the sun. Her gnarled legs were threadbare at the knees, as were patches along her rump where her sitting had long ago worn her blonde hide bare. When she yawned her row of top teeth shown, yellow and incomplete, just as several of her claws were shattered. But her nose was still in tune to dangers and her body strong despite the years, and there was nothing about her that reeked of pity.

The Rojo Prieta and the forbidden forest to the west were each filled with peril and rooted in dangerous things, but none were more wicked that the mighty Esperanza, for her heart had turned hard and sour toward the children of all living things, accept her own. Her form was diminished but her strength was mighty and she was still the most cunning of bears, and a master of the hunt, and her legend had spread to the peoples on both sides of the forest. Her dark and hungry spirit coursed like great veins into the hearts of her young and seemed to puff out with each breath like a cloud of trembling for all who drew her scent, until she had every living thing, from the Rojo Prieta to the mountains beyond the forest held firmly within her spell.

As her cubs fought over the bloodstains the bear called out to them, her hoarse bellows echoing off the laketop. Quickly they followed her, their eyes throbbing as they squinted into the light. They were large cubs on their second spring, the size of great mastiffs, but not yet practiced enough to hunt on their own.

The great bear's gnarled legs ached as she led them over the escarpment and each of the cubs looked about curiously as they saw the long land ahead. Deep to the west a densely hanging fog drew a veil across the land, removing any memory the cubs had of the forest and the mountains. All they could see was an endless territory of millponds and snowcapped hillocks and the sea of fog to the west.

Their mother stopped at the first pool they came to. All three of her cubs were soon copying the way she knelt and drank, but when she rose they followed, and they didn't stop for many hours.

The bear labored wearily over the Cutshank, leaving a deep trail through the chutes of grass and the moist prairie loam and what was left of the snow she flung aside with her lumbering paws.

The violent wind bent the low forbs flat on their stems and the bears kept their eyes small as they fought it. Little by little the army of life crossed the lifeless prairie until they came upon a freshly-beaten trail that wandered to the west, marked by the repeating depression of heavily circled hooves. And although the trail led toward the great forest, the bear ignored it, keeping instead to the path she had cut the previous winter; a path she could still smell despite the snowdrifts that had covered and recovered it throughout the cold dark months.

With every mile the bear ignored the wound within her shoulder. She had taken many wounds across the years and soon the bullet was just another ache she grew accustomed to. But what she couldn't ignore was the growing tightness in her belly.

In the hours since the bear had emerged from her winter den, her thoughts were on nothing but food. The wound had sapped her strength and her cubs had been late to emerge. From years of treading the same path across the Cutshank the bear knew there was no food to be found for miles and miles. If they didn't reach the forest quickly she would be too weak to hunt for her cubs.

But soon they craned their necks to look out upon the western clouds, draped low across the Cutshank, and at last the mountains with their dark spires spread before them like a banner to their homecoming. Now the trees were dripping down their backs and the low branches ran across their hindcoats like combing fingers. Within moments of entering the forest the great feast began. The bear and her cubs fed on sedges and salamanders, skunk cabbage and glacier lilies, forbs and bearberry. The cranberries had yet to bud. The bear showed the cubs how to suck the new spring wasps from their nests and near the river she found the remains of six dead trout discarded near a ring of stones. They were mostly-eaten and skewered to blackened twigs. One of her cubs, the biggest, began gnawing on the fatty end of the fish, tearing the leftover meat from the bones. When his sisters pounced on him, he easily overpowered them, hoarding the trout for himself. The two cubs hissed at him and taunted him again but he ignored them, sucking down every last morsel by himself. Their mother stripped the bark from one of the great pines and when she had raked the bark flakes from the trunk she began licking the thick sap from the wound. Soon her cubs had done the same.

The bear constantly sniffed the dead forest air for any scent of carrion, sticking close to the river, chewing up the thirsty cabbage, hoping to find a fat-rich meal. The southern cutbank rose above a sandbar and the cubs walked carelessly along the edge, peering over the sides into the water searching for fish.

As they passed a row of paper birches the great bear's head suddenly rose up and she drew in a quick breath. Her nostrils were quaking now as she charged down into the draw. Deep beneath the birches the great bear tilled the earth. The cubs watched as their mother tugged out the deep roots, flinging out a mound of cool, moist soil. Within minutes the giant patch of sweet vetch had been uncovered and the mother and her cubs were feasting on the heavy starches. The two runts nuzzled up behind their brother but again he snapped at them, keeping the food to himself. The pair of smaller cubs hissed at him and turned away.

Now the going was easy, and the great bear's blood was pumping well. The forest was how she remembered it. Her neck waggled and spun with the anticipation of the hunt.

*   *   *

According to the map the Irons Hills weren't but a few hours away and with any luck the brothers could arrive near the Meadow by nightfall. That morning both boys had prepared their hearts for what lie ahead. Henry carved himself a new spear from a piney branch while Jack reorganized his pack and prayed for safety.

Now that they were on their way the brothers took deep breaths of anticipation, keeping their eyes sharp and their noses up, drawing in the damp breath of the woodland. The wild smells were so strange and fantastic that it seemed the boy kings were traveling in a dream. The aroma of newly melted snow and musty old middens hung in the air and the giant ferns shook dew from their leaves like dripping emeralds when the brothers passed.

They had to step along one foot in front of the other if they wanted to keep their feet upon the path, ducking trees that had been felled, their arrows before them resting on their knocks. The surface of the woodland was covered with a soft turf that sank with the weight of the traveler's feet. And although it was a curious sensation to have the ground adjust to their steps, the low brushwood made their walking tiresome.

From time to time Jack tilted his head back, his eyes in search of the heavens. But they couldn't be seen. For the boughs which reached high above him, tangled as they were throughout the old wood trunks, were as thick between the high conifers as the undergrowth was on the forest floor. Even the ancient, shaggy hemlocks, with their blackened vines that clung tightly to the stalks, grew so tall that their tops couldn't be seen through the softwood canopy.

As Henry went before him, Jack kept his bow raised, pausing only to listen to the silence. The winds that had howled at their backs the day before had now been absorbed by the heavy conifers of the West End, leaving the woodland almost eery in its stillness. Even the river, not a short walk to the north was silent. All they could hear was the sound of their breathing and the creak of forgotten birchwoods snapping beneath their feet.

Jack had always found silence to be an invitation to reflect on the questions of his life so as he crossed the soft turf he began to dwell on matters of the heart and where his affections rested. Jack wished that before they had departed he had had a few short days to teach Padibatakal how to ride, something she had longed for all winter. He also wished for another chance to speak to Greer, but the note would have to do. Ah in that moment how he wished to be home again. But Jack knew it would be days and days before they returned to Tenpenny. They still had the heavy forest to pass through and the hills to venture up, and who knows what at the top. Jack couldn't imagine climbing any mountains in the condition he was in. The dark holds of timber and vine had begun to take their toll on young Oakham, and the battle waging within his heart was growing more and more distracting the further he traveled.

Beside him Henry smacked his chops loudly with distaste. Minute by minute he was growing more and more hungry until finally he turned off towards the river.

"I'm gonna go fishing in the river. Nude."

"I wouldn't," Jack said.

"Doin' it."

"What about hypothermia?"

"Not doin' it."

Henry returned to the path and the pair covered the woodland in silence.

"Gosh, I can't believe we missed that marmot," Jack said.

"My wrist is broken, I think."

"D'you wanna try again?"

"Nope."

"Well Henry you did say you were hungry."

"Hungry for moose, not for marmot. We can kill a moose and crawl inside it to keep warm. Boom."

"Or we could cook up a fire."

Henry farts.

"There's literally never a moment when farts aren't funny," Henry said.

"Never?"

"Think about it."

"Done."

"Now think about it again."

"Done."

"Jack, smell the roses."

"When do I stop thinking about it?"

"When I say so. They're always funny. Old ladies, little kids, always funny. There is a chigger bite in my navel that is swelling it shut."

"D'you kill it?"

"Yesterday."

"You killed it yesterday?"

"I couldn't be certain."

"So it could still be biting you?"

"It could still be biting me. I should set it on fire."

Jack chuckled. "You should. Whatcha got to lose?"

"Dead chigger."

"Dead navel."

"Doin' it."

"No matches."

"Not doin it."

Henry suspected strongly that if they didn't stop to catch some fish he would drop dead from hunger. He believed he could live the rest of his life on only a few hours of sleep a night, and never indulge in any luxuries but one pleasure Henry could never refuse himself was full stomach. Back on the hill he ate constantly throughout the day, but the night before his supper had been shared with the Bhotiyas, and now he had missed his breakfast, and soon lunchtime would come along. All he could think about was sizzled meat roasting on a stick. His hunger overtook him and again he turned back toward the river.

"Where are you going now?" Jack asked him.

"Fishing. Now I'm going fishing. Still early enough to trick the silvers."

"I thought you said we were hunting moose?"

"I never said any - such - thing. Absolutely never. And even if I had I've just changed my mind. It takes too long. There's too much meat to carry. I could go on and on."

"But lucky for me you won't."

"No, I won't. I'll spare you the gospel truth when it comes to moose. Some things you just have to learn on your own."

"Anything else you can spare me?"

"Not right now. But you can go after all the moose you want if it keeps you happy."

"Keeps me *fed* is what it does," Jack said, proud of his answer. "All the way to that mountaintop."

Then he added, "I'm gonna get up in one of these conifers," Jack said. "I'll hunt the moose if you won't."

Henry smiled and shook his head. "You sure you remember how?" And without another word the brothers parted ways.

Jack gave the thought a half smile, but silently he knew his brother was right. He couldn't remember the last time he had been on a hunt, least of all with a bow. He hoped his aim was still what it used to be, and it had never been that special.

Jack trekked into the shallow forest, knowing that the moose would stick close to the river. Twice that morning the brothers had heard the sound of unseen hooves thundering through the distant softwoods and Jack felt certain that these acres were thick with game. He had to pull back his bow just to remember the feeling but even though the bow behaved as he had expected it to he wasn't comfortable hunting alone. He thought of his old dog, roaming at Tipper's side deep in the forest somewhere, and Jack wished to have him back.

He found a suitable spot in one of the conifers and planted himself there with his arrow well-intended. Soon Jack smiled as he looked down upon his field. Beneath him a series of intersecting trails were laid out, coursing through the woodland. The sign along the pathways was thick, with some tracks only hours old. To his north Jack could see the river, gleaming like burnished silver, his ears turned toward the hope of hoof beats. He wondered how the work was coming, and how the winter orphans were adjusting to the melt. He smiled at the thought of their first game of football played on Campbell field, whenever Sissy decided the time was right.

His longing for home became so strong that Jack turned his eyes back to the east, hoping to catch the impossible sight of his home on the hill. Had it not been for his deep hunger Jack could have imagined he was home.

Meanwhile Henry's hunger was as big as his brother's, if not bigger, but his patience was inferior. Henry was already at the water's edge, overlooking the deep, thundering belt of river that cut the forest in two. He tied a fly to his line, dropping his pack and his spear near the beach, and soon with legs shivering Henry was out atop a great stone, whipping his fly across the watertop. Henry's hope was to have a trout in his belly within the hour. If it took any longer than that he didn't think he would survive.

*   *   *

The moose watched her calf as she searched among the frosted leaves. The light rains had come and gone and now the trail was quiet. The mother preferred to feed at night now that the spring had broken, but the cloud cover and the thick forest canopy gave her comfort.

Slowly, Jack drew up his bow. The fletchings shook between his fingers. He had waited in the trees for two full hours and now he was watching the moose duck her head to suck the forage from the earth. Jack's arrow held steady. Sixty paces, he thought to himself, a shot he should never take.

Quietly Jack let off his bowstring and rested his arrow across his lap, unwilling to take a poor shot. He knew his brother would be furious at his decision for Jack had been watching him from his perch and so far Henry hadn't caught a single fish. But Jack didn't care. Men have gone weeks on end without food, he thought.

Jack watched the mother and her calf forage the trail before him for half an hour, and he knew he would never have a better look as long as he lived. They circled beneath the birches, chewing noisily the long chutes. Naturally the sight of them brought to mind the image of his own mother when he was young.

The pair ambled down the trail to the south, and were just edging out of sight when Jack felt something stir in the shadows behind him. There was no sound. Nothing but an overwhelming feeling he couldn't ignore. Carefully Jack turned his head and what he saw was one of the wild shocks of his life. Creeping low on her belly was a great bear! with a wide square head like the one he had shot days before. The moose and her calf were grazing along the trail, still chewing, when the bear sprung from the trees and came after them.

Suddenly the moose fled into the forest and Jack could hear the popping of old branches and the thunder of unseen hooves. The bear followed close behind and Jack was awed by how quickly she moved. She passed beneath him and disappeared through the forest.

A moment later the boy heard a rustling far behind him and he turned, seeing two large bear cubs trailing their mother down the path. Both were fierce looking and Jack kept his bow ready. His heart was racing from the sight of the hunt but he knew he must keep his head about him for either of the two cubs were big enough to drag him from the tree.

Back at the river the remaining cub, the male, tore at the loose soil like he had seen his mother doing, and chewed the roots, the dirty vines hanging from his jaws. Moths fluttered out of their nests and the little cub tried to swallow them mid-flight. He was hidden between the bank rocks, nosing among sandy bits and pebbles until his snout was filthy. The slugs were diving to deeper soil as the dirt shook above them. But cubs are clever things, and this one in particular was a relentless pursuer, nosing clumps of loose soil until his head was submerged.

Henry dragged himself silently through the current. He knew he would have to be quick. If it had been a shallow, roaring piece of river he could have rushed the cub. But the river ran deep and quiet so Henry moved slowly, holding his spear above his head.

The little bear tore at the ground, loosing the soil from the den. His paws were caked with mudpack, and his whiskers wet and filthy from the dig. The moths fluttered and he swatted at them, chomping noisily on the fat-rich roots.

Henry moved toward the bank as quickly as he dared. The floodwaters had brought hundreds of loose branches up to the shore, which would make for noisy steps. He would need to run the spear straight through before the cub turned to meet him. It was a great risk, Henry knew, and one that wasn't likely to play out as he had planned. But Henry took confidence in the fact that the cub had nowhere to go. He was half buried before a wall of rock and to each side of the cub were boulders. One way or another, the bear would have to face him.

The young bear didn't hear him but the spear came all the same. The point of the lance slipped cleanly through, surprising Henry by how easily it penetrated. The spear tip was now protruding from his belly and in an instant the bear wheeled around, yanking the lance from Henry's hands. It swung behind him like a tail wagging.

When the cub saw Henry, he let out a low growl. The boy raised his hands before him and backed away, surprised the cub was still standing.

In an instant the cub was on him.

He fell to all fours and his jaws almost caught Henry round the knee, tearing through his trousers. Henry beat his fists against the cub's face, to no effect, and kicked at him with his steel toe. The lance rocked atop the bear like a pendulum.

In the next moment the bear ripped through the boy's clothes and across his chest. Henry continued to pound his face, holding back his cries, for he knew he had met his match. Even skewered as he was the young bear was much stronger than the boy, and although he would die within minutes, Henry wouldn't last but a few seconds unless he acted quickly.

The cub wrapped his jaws around Henry's forearm and the boy fell to a knee. If the cub had been a few months older he could have snapped the limb cleanly, but his teeth caught bone, and the boy didn't scream.

Henry had but one chance. He lowered himself flat against the sand and with all of his strength hauled the cub's hindquarters off of the bank. Instantly he stumbled, the bear's weight nearly buckling him, as he brought him up onto his shoulders. Warm blood pumped down the spear onto Henry's chest as the cub thrashed and hissed. The spear slipped through the wound in the next moment, barely missing Henry, and fell to the sand as the boy stumbled backwards. The cub was still locked to his forearm when he turned at the river's edge and violently brought him down. A great stone rose sharply out of the current and Henry wheeled him on his side and slammed his weight upon it.

Instantly the cub set him free, his body quivering as he slapped the rapids. The force of the impact brought Henry down beside him and the two of them tumbled into the current and were quickly swept away.

The world spun and turned as the cold shock of the water stirred Henry to the bone. Both bodies drifted on their backs, the cold water stinging their open wounds. As they floated together the boy watched curiously as the cub licked the sides of his mouth. He could smell his warm breath across the water as he turned again to face him.

*   *   *

Jack always feared his brother would die a young man. Henry wasn't just hard and quick, he was reckless, and Jack was certain that whatever luck had kept Henry unharmed up until that point would someday run out. Jack was determined to save him whenever it happened.

He had turned his head to the river, shortly after the bears had passed, only to see Henry with his lance high above him. Jack wore a look of terror as he watched the event unfold and by the time he realized what was happening Henry had already tumbled into the river and was quickly whisked away.

Instantly Jack scaled down the tree, hauling his quiver onto his shoulders and galloping toward the river. He cut a path across the forest floor, his breath rising in his lungs. Suddenly a wild sound rolled in from the forest like an echo, low and hollow, repeating off the trees to Jack's astonishment. The boy stopped, turning his ear back to the forest. Even as he stood the wild call was answered by a second and then a third voice, both much closer than the first.

The bears are calling one another! Jack thought as he trembled. The voices repeated from among the trees, and then instantly it grew quiet and all that remained was the churning of the river.

A great anger stirred in Jack's bones in that moment. Of course Henry had speared the cub, he thought. He was hungry so he speared it. That was the way of him. But now Jack was alone in the forest and the great bear close behind. He knew the cub's mother would scour the land in search of him and that he and his brother would have to be on the lookout for the remainder of their journey. He felt a fury rise in his heart against his brother.

But despite his anger Jack pressed on at a great pace, ducking the low woods and hurdling the fallen pines that criss-crossed the trail. When he reached the river, Jack instantly spotted the bloodstains along the sandbank and the bloody lance resting against the stones. He leapt down and stumbled to the river's edge. Standing on his toes with his neck craned Jack feverishly searched the rapids for the floating figures.

He knew he had to act quickly. It wouldn't be long before the bear came searching for her cub. He began to hunt for a shallow crossing but the river flowed deep and cold and Jack knew he wouldn't be much help to his brother if he plunged into her waters.

The bank was narrow but Jack scrambled along the sandy walls, gripping the loose roots that sprouted. When he found a crossing Jack instantly thought of the promise he had made to his father, and then pushed it from his mind.

He leapt from one stone to another, stumbling once, and soon crossed the river, slipping into the forest with wet trousers. He covered a quarter mile with his bow in hand and like the bear, his voice rang from tree to tree.

A strange thing happened then. As he moved through the thickly wooded riverbank Jack came quickly from one stone to another and caught a glimpse of what he thought was a man, swift and agile, moving in the same direction through the woods. It came and went in a flash. But because he called out and received no answer he wrote the sighting off as imagination and never mentioned it.

Soon Jack's heart was covered up in fear. As he searched frantically along the bank he began to think that his brother may not have escaped into the woods at all. He may in fact have been torn limb from limb or drowned in the river. He felt that each scenario was unlikely, for the bear had been speared clean through. However Jack had learned that nothing in the wilds was ever certain. A bloody fate *may have* fallen upon his brother. But he pushed the thought from his mind, however, focusing instead on the riverbank, and listening for the sound of his brother's call.

But it wasn't his brother he heard. As Jack approached the river bend it was the unmistakable sound of a wounded bear that echoed through the trees. He rushed upon the bank and when he arrived Jack Oakham stood like a statue.

Before him lay the cub, a trail of blood draining from his gut. Henry was on the beach bleeding as well, and shivering in the sand. His shirt was torn open and he was trying to rise to his feet. Jack watched as the bear came up on all fours, his legs quivering. The boy could see a rib protruding from the bear's back and a heavy mass spilling slowly from the wound in his gut. Henry lifted himself onto one leg and then the other and scrambled to unearth a large stone from the beach sand. When he lifted it over his head Henry's hands were shaking so violently that he fumbled the stone into the river.

In the next moment what remained of the bear rushed upon him. Henry's hands were too numb to close into fists so he pounded the face of the bear with his palms. The bruin hardly seemed to notice. He wagged his head back and forth, and a deep moan echoed from his throat as his mouth bled. Henry pounded and kicked but soon he realized that he had no hope of overpowering the brute. His hands were numb, his legs were shaking. He didn't have the strength to toss him as before. As a last resort Henry turned to scale the bank, hoping to slip away and let the bear bleed out on the sand. But the bank proved more difficult to scale than he had imagined. All his life Henry had hurdled whatever wall stood before him but now he was retreating and his wall nothing more than a sandy piece of earth six feet in height. Again the bear moaned and was slow to approach; still wagging his great head back and forth but Henry's hands failed to pull him onto the bankwall. Soon, like his brother, Henry's boot was gripped within the bear's great jaws. He kicked and flailed still trying to pull himself onto the grassy shelf. The moment seemed endless as the bear tugged him loose. For a third time Henry heard a deep moan bellowing from behind him and with it Henry could feel the bear's grip loosen on his heal. He's dying, Henry thought. Just survive for sixty seconds more.

The boy dug his elbows into the sand and pulled himself forward with all his strength. The bear shook his boot casually until Henry heard a pop on his heal and suddenly the bear loosened his grip. Henry's boot was let go. He could hear the great body slump to the sand. Instantly he turned back and what he saw bewildered him. For across the cub's body, ranging from the bear's haunches to his neck were the fletchings of three arrows, bloody and protruding from the fur. Henry breathed a deep sigh of relief as he saw his brother.

"S-s-s-omedays I want to be just like you," Henry mumbled. "You b-b-elieve that?"

Jack was quick to help Henry to his feet. "Not really."

Once he saw the bear was dead Jack leapt down to the sandbar and cut away two great slabs of meat along the backstrap. What remained of Henry's shirt he wrapped around the meat, tying the sleeves together and hanging it over his shoulder. Then he turned back to the bear and with all of his strength Jack rolled the carcass into the rushing river and in a moment the heavy shape was whisked away.

"Can you walk?"

Henry looked up, his heart still racing. "I can run," he told him with teeth chattering. "Just don't ask me to play no piano."

Jack was slow to get the joke until he saw his brother's hands shaking violently. His knees were knocking too. Jack scaled the bank and approached Henry with open arms, wrapping him in his coat. The two stumbled through the woods, ever westward.

Jack listened for the sounds of the bear who was certain to be hunting them. He knew their time was running out. Jack could see that his brother was growing numb below the knees and his face was pale. All Jack could think about was his gear - his dry clothes, his sleeping bag, his cookpot.

"I need to cross the river and fetch my pack," Jack said.

"Th-th-th-th-the she-bear is on the other side."

"How do you know that?"

"I-I-I-I-I don't. N-n-n-n-n-no telling w-w-w-w-w-what a bear might do."

Jack agreed with his brother. 'No telling' was right. They may never see her again, or she may spring on them in the night. Either way Jack knew he couldn't leave his brother in the state he was in.

"Then we need to get up in the trees," he suggested.

Henry didn't argue. But he did raise his hands to eye level, to show his brother that each of them were shaking violently.

He won't be climbing any trees, Jack knew. At least not yet.

Jack found a clearing and began to fix a fire as fast as he could. He pulled his brother's flintstone off his necklace and scraped the spark fire onto the tinder. Soon the flame was crackling against the pine nettles and he fed it quickly. Henry was curled up against a great tamarack, shaking violently, his hands extended as he watched the fire grow.

Jack was a few feet from the flame, gathering a pile of drywood when he heard the great bear bellow through the forest. He looked up suddenly."D'you hear that?"

Henry nodded. "S-s-s-south."

Feverishly Jack fed the fire. He searched for the driest branches he could find and tossed them into the flames. At one point Jack took his brothers hands and rubbed them together, then rubbed his shoulders and his neck and encouraged him like he would a child.

Again Jack heard the sound of the bear's call ringing through the trees. This time they were closer than before but still across the river, he thought.

The fire was growing strong now and Henry's hands began to still. His shivering slowed and his color was returning. His body was wrapped around the flames.

Moment by moment Jack could see his brother's strength returning. He handed Henry his pistol. "Take this up the tree," he told him. It was the first order he had given his brother in his life.

"Wh-Wh-Where are you going?"

Jack was suddenly struck by the fear in his brother's eyes. "I'm gonna fetch our packs. We'll need them to survive the night."

Henry sighed and carefully scaled the mighty tree, his wounds tearing at him with every move. When he was high in the branches Henry leaned against the trunk and took a deep breath. Instantly he tore open his undershirt and looked down at his wounds, smiling when he saw the claw marks across his chest.

Jack charged toward the river with his bow ready. He only had three arrows left but the thought never occurred to him. If the bear discovered him Jack knew it was unlikely that he would get a shot off before he was torn to pieces.

When he arrived at the river Jack froze the instant he looked down the bank. The great bear and her two cubs were sniffing the trail a short ways downriver. They were turned from him and traveling at speed. With his eyes watching them Jack cautiously crossed at the shallow passage and was quick to charge into the forest to fetch his brother's pack and then his own.

When he returned Jack checked the river and the bears were gone. He crossed, holding his pack above his head and his brother's on his shoulders. Near the bank he opened his pack and sprinkled pepper on the earth along with a few loose items: his sandals, a mug, and a small jar of honey that Sissy had given him.

Jack criss-crossed up and down the river with the pepper, surprised by his quick thinking, until he dumped what remained in a burrow.

When he reached the clearing in the trees Jack was quick to tie a knot to his pack and toss the rope to his brother. Soon both of them were situated high in the branches, each with arrows knocked to their bows and their ears to the forest.

They heard the sound of distant bellows rolling through the timber as they waited. But then for over an hour there was nothing. They waited and waited and yet the silence continued. Finally Jack looked over at his brother who was still pale with cold. His eyes were dim with hunger and his face was colorless. Silently Jack stood atop the high branches, opened their packs, and brought out his cook pan, some dry clothes, and what remained of his spices. He was careful as he broke off a few small branches nearby and crossed them over the great bowers they sat upon. In that way Jack made a grill for his cook pan and set it carefully on top. He then set about making a small fire in the pan, all the while with his ears to the river. He tore the bear steaks into small pieces with his teeth and skewered them on long straight branches that he stripped from the great tree. And there he cooked shish kabob for his brother who was starting to shiver.

"I want you to have some," Henry told him.

"I think there's enough for us both."

And Jack's words proved true. The first backstrap was devoured quickly, most of it burned at the edges from their nervous shaky fingers. But when Henry was warm he salted the second round of meat and prepared it evenly over the fire; the fat dripping off the roasting steak. The two of them savored the feast silently in the high branches. Henry sat back on his elbows, his wounds glistening in the firelight. His boots were drying near the flame and his socks too. He liked the feel of the cold air hitting his toes. He liked rubbing his fingers across his wounds and wincing. He liked the prickle on his heels, the numbing of his skin, the dirt beneath his toenails. It's good this way, he thought. I'm better off barefoot.

Jack marveled at his brother. He had washed his wounds with his canteen and at one point climbed down to the forest floor to cake mud across the deeper cuts. He used his brother's kit to bandage himself across his chest and his knees and finally he changed into his spare pants and shirt and cut his bloody clothes into strips with his pocket knife and burned them in the fire. Despite the broken sight of him, Jack was struck by the gleam in his eyes. Moments before he was at death's door and now he was made whole again. More than once in the years to come Jack Oakham would go back in his mind to that image of his brother.

But to Jack's surprise, and even his own, when Henry Snow had finished patching himself up, he began to cry. His face squeezed up tightly until he burst. Jack had never seen him weep so heavily. Jack fetched the harmonica and played a soft melody, the only one he knew. But as he watched his brother, shaking and sobbing in the branches of the great tree, Jack began to cry beside him. All young Oakham needed to bring about tears, or laughter, was to be among others who needed the same.

All during the killing Henry had tried to collect the moments and store them away like keepsakes. Adventure, solitary and bloody, had found him. It was what he'd longed for but now it was over and he knew nothing would match it, possibly for many years. Henry knew that at least one of the glory days had come and gone and a sad, lonely sorrow filled him and his eyes burst with tears. Now I don't know if Jack understood those tears, I doubt very much if he did. But certainly he understood the importance of them and asked no questions. After he had done his best to console him, Henry waved him off and sat alone in his thoughts.

Darkness fell and through the night the brothers could hear the bellows of the old bear ringing through the trees, although never too close for comfort. Soon they wrapped themselves in their sleeping bags, their bows and the pistol close at hand. Jack gauged that they still had several miles to travel before sunrise, if they hoped to reach the Window in the Meadow on time. But he wasn't concerned about sleeping through it. If he could catch any rest in the high boughs he doubted it would be very much. They sat a long while thinking back on their adventure and it was Henry who finally broke the silence.

"I mean it. Sometimes I want what you have, Jack. After a long look you're an easy guy to love."

Jack shook his head, "The children love you, Henry. Everyone loves you."

But Henry wasn't only smart, he was wise when he wanted to be. "It's *you* they truly love," Henry told his brother. "With me they're just afraid I won't return it."

8. The Pritchers

The Bhotiyas all agreed that the Pritchers were the finest horses they'd ever seen. They led the party on a perfect course to the southeast and were always well-behaved and each of them were a joy to look at, even amidst the marvelous surroundings.

Once the boy became accustomed to them he asked in his language if he could lead them, though Ibrahim refused. "When you arrive to your new home there will be a great many horses and many children to ride with. Someday you may even have a pony of your own."

I don't want a pony, the boy thought. A pony would be too small. You have to train a pony. I like this one. He is already trained.

Immanuel had taken a liking to Henry's horse, a dappled Appaloosa named Morrison. And the boy was right, the horse had been well-trained. Immanuel knew the horse belonged to the big boy with the wild hair and that someday the boy would come back to claim it, but he didn't care. It was the prettiest one he had ever seen, though he had only seen a few. He decided that while they traveled on their journey he would claim the horse as his own.

"Will we ride horses there, like we are now?" the boy asked.

Ibrahim shrugged. He had never been up on Tenpenny Hill himself. It was not his job to know what happened day to day. When he had taken the job of bringing men across the sea it had been explicitly stated that he was never to wander onto the hill, but for what reason he didn't know. As much as he wanted to comfort the Bhotiyas in their future life there was little he knew to tell them.

"I don't know," he admitted. "There are many fine things for a boy to do though. I know the place was made for children."

"Only for children? What about us?" Yigal wondered. "We are not children. Is this place not made for us as well?"

"This is a good place," Ibrahim suggested. "You will work for a man who will treat you fairly and you will have your own bed and all the food you like and you will never have to worry about banditos or gangs or any other evil thing."

"Will there be bath huts?" the boy wondered.

"Yes there will. They call them 'toilets'."

Each of the men were well-pleased with this news.

"And we won't have to get our food."

"No. Someone else does that."

"Who does it?"

"It just comes. They bring in a camion with your food and there it is. You don't have to buy it or pick it or grow it."

Chhedup was wide-eyed with excitement. He had a multitude of questions. "We work everyday?"

"No, not everyday. You will have days when you don't work. There is time to rest as well."

"Who else will there be? Will there be other men like us and men like you, or only children? Will there be any women there like in the last place?"

But the conversation was cut short. Ibrahim squinted across the open plain at the sight of riders from the north. There were four men that he could see. The Pritchers began to whinny as they saw the new horses approaching.

"More friends?" Chhedup asked him.

"I don't know."

In all his time on that country Ibrahim had never once come across a man he hadn't expected. On this trip he could count seven, and they still had a half day's ride ahead of them. His experience taught him that one party almost certainly had to do with the other. Ibrahim looked across the great valley. He had no reason to believe they had anything to fear, and nowhere to hide if they had.

Immanuel watched the riders approach. The thought of new faces excited the boy. So far in his journey the boy had enjoyed every person he had met. He had been well taken care of and especially enjoyed the old dog from the forest and the new horses trailing behind them. He rubbed their ears whenever they came by. This new life had brought many joys with it and one that he enjoyed the most was seeing faces he had never seen before.

"We're still on the land?" Cheddup asked.

"Yes we're still on it," Ibrahim told him. "So are they. This land stretches almost a day to the north."

Yigal flinched when he saw the men. "They are unfriendly," he said. "I feel it."

"You thought the men in the forest were unfriendly," Chhedup told him. "They fed us and welcomed us. They were the most friendly people I have ever known."

"These are not the same men," Yigal told him.

Ibrahim rode ahead to meet them and the Bhotiyas stayed close behind. When they came within sight of the riders the boy's easy feeling went away, and was replaced with a shuttering fear. Yigal is right, he thought. These men didn't look kind or gentle. The lead rider was a huge man atop a tall roan who kept his eyes on the horses. His face had been battered to the color of a plum, a fruit the boy had eaten only once, just days before, and his head was bandaged so tightly it seemed it was there to hold his jaw onto his face. Some of the other riders didn't look much better. Two of them had bottles in their hands. Another, a young man, was bruised around the face and neck. The boy watched each of them carefully. He was beginning to see how dissimilar white men looked from one another. A strange looking one took the lead as they approached. He was a squatty man with bulldog features, short arms, a pug nose, and fingers that seemed to have been stopped growing when he was a boy. Those hands were accentuated all the more because they danced before him as he spoke. "My name is Culpin Stanley," the man said as the parties met. "How the hell are you boys?"

Ibrahim raised a hand to say hello.

The man called Culpin slipped off his saddle and stretched his back. Wade and Danny did the same and the three men approached the Bhotiyas. They paid special attention to the Pritchers.

Ibrahim climbed down off his saddle to shake Culpin's hand. He knew it was a risk to dismount, but by the looks of these men, rude behavior may have been a greater risk.

Culpin smiled and gave his hand a shake. He nodded to the Bhotiyas who smiled back at him, all except the boy. Once Culpin had a good look he turned to his saddle and pulled a rifle from the scabbard, aiming it carelessly at the ground. "I reckon you better get off those horses," he told them casually.

Ibrahim never took his eyes from the man. He had stood before a hundred men holding guns, and a dozen who had pointed them at him. So far this man hadn't. Until he did Ibrahim chose to remain reasonable. He signaled with his hands for his party to dismount and all the while he watched the stubby man with the rifle.

"They're A-rab rats," Wade whispered to Danny. They were looking on the Bhotiyas with curiosity. "Just like those mice we're at war with."

"No they ain't. I don't know what they are. But they ain't that."

"They look like it to me. They look like half chinese, half mexican," Wade said. "Bet they can cook. Any of you rats speak English?"

Ibrahim disregarded the man, looking instead to Forsman. "I am no rat."

Culpin turned to the old guide. He looked him up and down. "We'll see. Do you know who owns this land?"

Ibrahim remained calm. "I do not."

"Then what are you doing out here?"

In all his years crossing that country Ibrahim had never forgotten what to say if he was ever asked that question. "I am an employee of the Coastal Counties Tribes Act, the CCTA. I deliver Inuit natives to shelters where they can be given a new start. In my shirt pocket I have documentation."

"These aren't Inuit," Culpin said. "I've lived here all my life."

"The Alchos are all descendants from one mother," Ibrahim told him. "Have you ever seen an Alcho Inuit?"

"No."

"Neither had I until last week. Now you have. You're looking at a rare breed."

Culpin opened the man's shirt pocket, pulled out the contents, and began shuffling through it. "I don't care how rare they are," Culpin said, "I care about their horses." He gripped the reigns from the lead grey and turned her, revealing her brand beneath the withers. "A day and a half ago these horses came from the southeast, where you're headed, except they had different riders. We'd like to have a word with one of em. How d'you come to have his horse?"

Ibrahim was not one to bite the hand that fed him. "I bought the mounts. They now belong to the CCTA."

"Bought 'em? You don't look like you could afford a bath."

Ibrahim ignored him. Instead he turned his eyes to Forsman. He was the only man who wasn't drunk or scared. It was clear to Ibrahim that this was the man he was truly dealing with. He believed the others would do nothing without his say so.

"Speak up, " Culpin said. "When did you buy these horses?"

"I don't like your tone or your questions. In fact this land is big enough for us to remain strangers."

The little man tipped his hat to Forsman and turned to leave. Quickly Culpin leveled his rifle at him. Wade took out his pistol and did the same. "Where ya goin'?"

"I have these men to deliver and I've wasted enough time talking to you."

Culpin hesitated. He looked up at Forsman who seemed disinterested in the whole affair. "You just ran upon a horsetrader out on these flats?" Culpin said. "What do you think I am?"

"I'd say you're a coward, pulling guns with this boy here."

Culpin looked around at the other riders. "All I see is boys. This is boy business."

"Then I'd say you're in good company."

"Well you're saying a lot of things for a man in your position. You're saying you bought these horses on the flats?"

"No sir. I didn't say that. You listen about as well as you think."

Culpin was growing more perturbed with every moment. The little old man didn't seem to be afraid of their words or their guns. Both surprised him. "Then where?"

"Near the treeline. A place you'd be advised to stay far from."

Wade found the shotgun in the saddlebag and tossed it to Forsman, who caught it without even looking.

"That shotgun there belongs to us," Culpin said. "It was stolen yesterday."

"Tell your friend to stay clear of these horses," Ibrahim said calmly, though he was surprised to see a gun hidden in the saddlebags.

"You better answer for this."

"Unlike you I have nothing to answer for. Keep that shotgun," he said to Forsman. "We didn't know we had it. And keep this wildcard at home next time. All he knows how to do is drink."

Culpin tossed the papers to the ground and aimed the rifle at the boy.

In that moment Ibrahim thought of his only son, who had died thirty years before. He had had the same kind of pride as these men.

"The fellas you bought these horses from," Culpin said, "What did they look like?"

"Go home, son."

"We're looking for three riders with a dog. Is that who sold you these horses?"

The old man sighed. "I see you've already found their tracks so if you want them, go get them," he said. "I can't stop you. They'll probably kill you if you do. They don't drink in the saddle and they know this country up and down. From the looks of things they got the better of you already. And they aren't alone."

Culpin was beginning to boil with anger. "You're a stubborn little man. Those riders you met aren't worth protecting."

Ibrahim turned to leave. He signaled for the men and the boy to mount up.

"If you're lying to us we'll find you," Culpin said.

Ibrahim laughed, "You'd do better to drink it off. That's my opinion."

Culpin spit his beechnut onto the snow and squinted at the sorry looking troupe. "I don't want the opinion of an old runt."

"Good. I'm tired of giving it. I'll hand you some advice, though. You go in those woods drunk and you won't come out. You go in those woods you better think straight. There's a lot more in there than three riders."

The Bhotiyas were soon back in the saddle. Ibrahim walked his horse over to Danny and reached out to take the reigns of the Pritchers.

"How much did you pay for the horses?" It was Forsman who spoke, his broken voice startling the riders.

"Porque?" said Ibrahim.

Forsman wouldn't repeat himself. He took his wallet out of his coat and waited.

Ibrahim gave a gentle sigh. "One thousand for the geldings. Twelve hundred for the mare."

Forsman licked his thumb and handed the man a stack of bills. The Bhotiyas stared at the money with great interest. They had never seen so much wealth in their lives.

"Saddles too?" Forsman said.

Culpin was annoyed at the situation, but especially that Forsman was being so polite to a man who had openly insulted him.

Ibrahim was annoyed as well. He didn't like the idea of selling off the horses. It felt like a sin to let down the men in the forest. He thought he might bargain with the man but when he looked up he could see the big man would accept no negotiations. "The saddles were included," Ibrahim told him.

Wade led the Pritchers away from the party and handed Forsman the reigns. He stared dead-eyed at the mounts.

"I would expect they'll want to buy them back from you," Ibrahim said. "They're fine horses."

"Very fine," Forsman answered. But before anyone could protest the big man leveled his rifle at the horses and fired three times, braining each of the Pritchers.

A wild panic spread among the Bhotiyas. Their mounts skittered and bucked.

The Pritchers flopped before them, their blood running black against the snow.

Ibrahim threw a glance at the big rider, but the man had already spurred his horse, holstering his rifle as he rode.

Culpin took a gulp of beechnut, hiding the shock on his face, and then he and Wade mounted and followed Forsman without a word. They each took long swigs as they caught up to him.

But Danny remained frozen where he stood, with a look of terror on his face. His eyes were wide with fear. Just moments before Danny had a great many things to say to his father but now he couldn't remember what they were.

By now the boy had his head down and was crying hysterically. The eye of Henry's Pritcher protruded from the skull.

Yigal covered his mouth and turned away spitting. He cursed the men beneath his breath and asked his spirits to take them away, these evil men.

Ibrahim looked on helplessly as the beautiful mounts swished their tails across the snow. But within moments all of them were still.

Soon Ibrahim and the Bhotiyas dismounted and began to unsaddle the Pritcher's, which proved difficult, and loaded the saddles onto their mounts as cargo. Danny tried to help but their stares drove him away. Soon he left the scene without a word.

The poor travelers watched as all of the riders headed into the west, the heavy wood a short distance across the plain. When they were gone Ibrahim led them southeast to the sound of the boy's weeping.

"There will be other horses," Ibrahim told him finally, though he himself was almost unable to speak. Despite his words the boy just wept with his head down. They rode for hours and none of them spoke.

It was a long, quiet afternoon, their hearts filled with terror. None of them spoke of the scene and each of the Bhotiyas soon wished to be home again. Within a few short days their desire for a new home had faded and now they wished only to be back across the sea.

When they reached the hogback, Ibrahim rested his hands on the saddlehorn and pointed for the other men to see. "There is the place," he told them. "You can walk the rest of the way."

The men turned to their guide in surprise. "Won't you come?" they asked.

Given the circumstances Ibrahim felt that he should lead these men onto the hill, at the very least to explain the dead horses. But his instructions were clear.

He handed over their papers.

"I agreed never to see the place," he explained. "But I was told there is a man here who understands your language. Take the saddles, walk up those steps and ask for a man named Stuart Whitlock. Give him those papers. Tell him about the horses. Tell him everything you have seen."

Sullen, each man slipped down from their mounts and Chhedup helped the boy. The Bhotiyas carried off the saddles and nodded to their guide and handed him the reigns.

"And give him these," he told them. Ibrahim handed the men two letters, the one Jack had given him and the other that Ibrahim had written himself. Before they could thank him he had spurred the stud into a trot down the hogback, going over the tracks he had just made.

9. Into the Lion's Den

When Henry and Jack arrived at the Window in the Meadow, they were late, the one thing Tipper warned them *not* to be. The evening before they had sat high in the trees with the bear steaks roasting and had bundled within their sleeping bags even as they ate. It isn't hard to predict what happened next. Each brother lay near the fire and they remained there through the night and into the cold of the morning until Jack suddenly awoke with a start and scrambled to rouse his brother.

"We're late!" Jack called out.

"For what?"

"For *what*?" Jack asked. "For the "*Window in the Meadow*"! Look at the hour! We have miles to go!"

Henry was quick to strip his sleeping bag and stuff his gear within his pack, so quick in fact that it frustrated young Oakham. He was never able to assemble his gear with haste the way his brother did. By the time Jack had collected his cookware and begun to gather his bundle, Henry was already standing with his pack high on his shoulders, giving no sign that his wounds were troubling him.

"For a man in a hurry, you sure do take your time," Henry said.

Even in the dark of the morning, Jack was already worn thin by his brother.

"See this cook pot, Henry? Who was the *one* who carried it? See these spices you loved? Who brought *them* along?"

Henry chuckled, scratching at his wounds. "And what about them steaks you devoured, Jack? You sleep well last night with that full belly? If there's a mooch around this fire, I'd say I'm looking at him."

"You'd say a lot of things," Jack admitted, rubbing the bear claw between his fingers.

As they clambered down the tree they were both still weary of the great bear hunting across the forest. But for hours that night there had been no bellows in the dark, no sounds of heavy feet. As they sprinted toward the river they each prayed that the she-bear had lost their trail.

They sallied through the den of the forest at great speed in the dark of the morning, making up time with every step. Their way led them through a maze of mighty tamaracks rising out of sight in the darkness and around

304

great rock portraits passing judgement as they were woken, and then over the swells of distant hillocks and with great haste down their broken escarpments choosing paths along the spines of fallen birch trunks that built bridges to the lower lands.

On occasion Henry checked the map for clues of their location but their path proved even more confusing in the dark of the morning. There was no sign of a clearing and though Jack checked his compass regularly he remained concerned that they weren't on the right path at all.

"We could still be hours away," he admitted.

There was no sound except their panting and the river which seemed at times to be far away, perhaps turning north out of sight. Jack was certain they were lost in the darkness and would find the meadow too late that morning, missing what awaited them. The idea of letting Tipper down weighed heavily on his heart. But then to make matters worse, dawn came and a deep blue-green haze opened across the sky above them. They raced harder and faster but their spirits sunk as they began to see the sky unfold through the thinning trees. They were to be a hundred paces from the meadow's edge by first light, but one by one the stars were vanishing from the sky as the brothers raced, watching as the world came awake.

"We're late!"

"Late for what?" Henry wondered.

"I dunno," he caught his breath. "All I know is. . . Tipper said to wait one hundred paces from the meadow at first light. . .and we ain't a hundred paces. . . and it's already gettin' light."

Henry shook his head. "Never any harm in being a little late."

The first of the birdsong began high in the birches. Then suddenly the golden light of the sun struck the highest clouds. As they sprinted each brother looked out through the open sky and at once their eyes turned to the rising formations beyond the treetops. Now for the first time they could see that surrounding the pinnacle shaped trees were mountains! Snow-topped mountains, a sterling white against the forest top! Through the thick forest the sawtooth peaks climbed into the sky like white daggers reaching the heavens. The western slopes were capped in golden light.

"We're nearly there!" Jack said.

Before them they could see where the land opened up revealing what could only be the meadow. The smell of conifers filled their lungs and the smell of change followed close behind, for they were weary of the heavy forest.

They peered out across the sparse wood, their eyes sharp to the coming light. Jack could see that the meadow was close. He focused on the high spires, "Is that it?" Jack asked his brother.

Henry smiled. "I reckon it is," Henry told him. "Just a jog past those trees and I'll race you to the top."

Of course what they saw were the far mountains of Tenpenny, where the treasure was believed to be hidden.

"We've come to the heart of the forest," Henry claimed. "We're on our way to Luleo."

"What's Luleo?" Jack asked. "Is it the mountains?"

"No," Henry said as he handed his brother the map. "Some place called Luleo is at the edge of the forest. The mountains are past it."

Jack searched the map as he ran. "More than a jog, I'd say."

When they approached the meadow Henry began to long for the open view. The light could be seen high in the clouds and on the mountain peaks but the meadow itself was still covered in darkness. It was Jack who called them to stop.

"I think we've done it," Jack said. "We're only a little late. We should wait here for whatever happens."

"*You* can wait," Henry said, clearly winded. "I'm gonna creep a little closer."

"We're close enough," Jack told him. "We have instructions, or don't you listen?"

"Not if I can help it," Henry said as he crept off for a closer look.

Jack watched as his brother disappeared. It seems there's no teaching that one, he said softly. He remembered thinking the evening before how much different his brother was likely to act after receiving his injuries. Henry's tears had convinced him that change was coming. But now, after one hard sleep his brother was just as he had always been, proud and impatient, and the thought of chasing after him again made Jack want to sleep himself.

The light was slowly giving shape to his surroundings and whatever Tipper had planned for them would be coming within minutes. As he rested beside the trail Jack noticed the wear the wood had taken. The old logs that laid across the trail were so worn in fact that Jack turned and followed the trail with his eyes. He knew it was far too wide to be an animal trail. The channel was broad enough for five men, walking shoulder to shoulder to pass through. As he searched among the ferns he noticed heavy animal prints sunk in the trail and large clumps of scat scattered about. The sign was sparse at first but grew thicker as the trail approached the meadow.

"Brother," Jack said. But he heard no response.

Quickly Jack drew two arrows from his quiver and slipped his bow from his pack. Saskatoon shaded the trail. Jack kept his eyes on the great ferns. They could spring on us from anywhere, he thought.

Just as Jack was about to call out to his brother, Henry suddenly returned.

"There are bears all around us!" he whispered.

"I thought so. I think we're on one of their trails. D'you see 'em?"

"No, but I heard them gurgling. This was what that old tramp was talking about. Keep up," he said as he disappeared into the trees.

This time Jack didn't hesitate. He knew they were moving closer to the meadow than they were supposed to be, but he didn't feel safe on the bear trail, and it couldn't be denied that Henry had more experience hunting bears than he did. They kept low as they moved through the heavy ferns.

"Where d'you hear 'em?" Jack asked as they knelt beside the meadow.

But Henry never looked at him. He wore the face of a serious hunter. Jack had seen his brother wear that face many times, and it was never in vain.

A high breeze swept over the clearing and they heard the grasses rustle. The first light rained down across the skylight and Henry admired the faint colors of the treetops. He had missed the breeze and the colors of the new birth. "God has married the fall and winter," Tip had always said, "so they may give birth to the spring. For the spring is the world in bloom," he told them, "Pregnant no longer. She wears in these months her Sabbath dress, fertile with generous fruits and alive with many dangers." Henry could hear his father saying it as he looked upon the meadow. For Henry the spring was a time of great torment in his heart.

"Look there."

Across the rolling grasses a blanket of fog had spilled in but through it Henry noticed a strange shape resting at the heart of the field.

"Where?" Jack asked.

"Don't you see it? There, in the lowing."

At first all Jack saw was a rolling wave of grasses and the black veil of trees beyond the pasturage but as the light crept in Jack made out a figure in the meadow. It was shapeless at first, but soon his eyes made out the distant frame rising out of the fog.

"A chair?" Jack asked.

"A rocker."

Soon Jack was certain of it. A rocking chair stood alone in the heart of the meadow, the fog surrounding it.

"Now what?"

But before Henry could answer their eyes were drawn away. Moving toward the center of the field was a wild looking man, burly and dark skinned, with strange markings. He had curly silver hair that had grown bushy and he was dressed in nothing but a set of tattered trousers. The man carried two heavy sacks across his shoulders and most of his lower half was concealed by the fog.

Even Henry couldn't hide his surprise. The man didn't seem to pose a threat to the brothers, but they watched him cautiously, their bows ready before them.

"What's he carrying?" Jack whispered.

Though it was still too dark to see when the man reached the rocker he opened the bags and spilled the contents across the earth. He made a wide circle across the heart of the pasturage, emptying each bag as he lumbered. Henry leaned his head back and drew in a full breath, trying to sniff the air, but all he could smell was his brother beside him.

When the bags were empty the man was seated in the chair and was searching beneath it. The brothers heard the squeak of hinges.

In the next moment the forest man crossed his legs and leaned his huge head back. Then a song played off of the old timber, filling the air, and it wasn't long before Jack and Henry were lost in the melody. Instantly both brothers knew it was a mandolin. Other than Henry's harmonica, it was the first music the boys had heard since their departure.

As he listened Henry thought back on the events of the past few days, the words spoken from the Bhotiyas and from Tipper when he left them. Their words played back for him more clearly than ever as he noticed the branches of distant tree begin to rattle.

"Jack?"

"What?"

"Button up your shirt."

"Why?"

Out of the woods came a rustling. It was as if the trees were rubbing against each another. At first the sound was merely a faint swish but soon the whole of the meadow seemed to tremble.

The brothers scanned the treeline, their palms sweating down their fletchings. The pasture, which had now filled with a spring fog, lay dormant like a millpond, until from the distant trees two dark, fog-shaded figures appeared, and then a third, and all of them crept along the earth as silent as black cats. They moved like whalehumps across the pasturage with only their great shoulders cresting the fogline.

The mandolin played and the brothers watched as the forest spilled more headless shapes onto the lawn, some larger than others, and lighter in color, all encircling the man on the rocker.

The creatures remained veiled in a blanket of fog, until one, a tall auburn, rose high on his haunches near the meadow's heart and it was then that both brothers saw what it was.

"Oh, God," Jack said in fear, for the first time in his life.

It was a great brown bear, standing with his paws up before the wild stranger. Henry and Jack watched in astonishment as more bears came out, one after another: ten, then fifteen, then twenty! They gathered from all directions like an army of soldiers. The man sat calmly on his perch, the host of killers surrounding him, as the bears began to devour the fodder at his feet. As they searched the grasses some of the bears brushed up against the man and all along the song played, and not a note was missed and both Jack and Henry thought it a dream.

"Where are we?" Jack wondered.

His brother smiled. "Right where we're supposed to be."

Just then there was a stirring in the nearby trees. Out of the thick, palm-leafed branches came the arrival of a dozen more heavy figures, shapeless through the fog causing both brothers to spring to their defense. The beasts were black or auburn-colored, and each moved with speed onto the pasturage. Some emerged just feet from where the brothers were hiding, and oh, to have seen their faces.

Jack trembled behind his arrow, watching as the bears multiplied before him. One of them, a grizzled black, stopped at the meadow edge and glared at the brothers. Instantly Jack raised his arrows but the bear soon ignored him, huffing indignantly as he crossed the field toward his breakfast.

Soon the entire congress had gathered around their king, some standing tall on their haunches, while others rubbed their ribs across his knees as he sat. Once all had arrived the man put his mandolin away and ruffled the ears of the bears, talking to them in his strange language as they nibbled food straight from his palm.

In that moment Henry's feeling of awe was replaced with a jealousy for the man. Whoever he is, he's in touch, Henry thought, and the reality of that thought caused a great envy in his heart. He could only imagine what came next.

When the strange man walked among them, the crowd of bears paid him little mind as they went about their feeding. Some stood in his path but he pushed their heads away as he crossed the pasture. He was moving south now, clear of the bruins, and to the great confusion of the brothers the wild man looked up from the meadow and waved them on. "Come!" he called, and his accent was strange to them.

Without consulting his brother, Henry stepped out, leaving Jack like a stone behind his bow. Henry reasoned this was likely the most surprising moment of his life, and being no stranger to surprises he had no intention of missing it.

But Jack stood dumbfounded, both by the man's invitation and his brother's departure, neither of which gave him comfort. The man seemed to have known of their presence all along, but Tipper hadn't said anything about strangers they might meet, and such a man as this hardly seemed like one to put his trust in. However Jack soon realized that following the strange man was the only option that remained. We can't turn back, he thought to himself, (though with each hour he wanted to) and he wouldn't dare remain in such a place, surrounded by killers on all sides.

In the next moment Jack found himself marching on a congress of bears, something he could have never imagined. They were spread out across the enclosure, numbering more than thirty by his count. Yet despite his mounting fears Jack willed his legs to carry him. His hand continued to tremble on the arrow and his eyes were wide to the ghostly dream.

He told himself, all you have to do is follow Henry. Keep your eyes on Henry and do as he does. Jack kept a steady gaze upon his brother, who was quickly approaching the crowd of beasts.

The bears, assembled as they were in their wild pageantry, carried a fierce aroma across the meadow. Each brother noticed the assortment of open wounds that each bear had received, some across the faces, others with patches of pink flesh torn free from their hides.

As he walked across the pasture Henry came within reach of one of the bears, a great brown. He let his bow rest at his side and then did something his brother would never forgive him for. Without a word of warning Henry ran his free hand across her powerful shoulders.

Jack saw neither fear nor concern painted across his face, instead Henry wore the look of elevation and again Jack wished to have Tipper and Putt back among their party.

As they approached the strange man he turned to face them, and when he did each brother took a moment to size him up. The man was no giant, though he appeared as fierce as the bears surrounding him. He was of a sturdy build and his face was marked with strange spiraling tattoos. He too was adorned with scars of every dimension, across his chest and forearms, and one running the length of his hand to a nub where a finger should have been. When they approached him he turned and led them away from the feast. "Bahulogine," the man said. Then he turned and pointed off into the trees.

Both brothers were surprised to see that on the far end of the meadow, draped in heavy shadow, a tiny cabin appeared against the western forest. A thin stream of smoke puffed from the chimney.

The day is young, Henry thought.

Jack kept his bow up as a precaution, but the bears gave no sign of interest in him, choosing instead to devour their meals. He walked past them cautiously, his fate in every step he took. The meadow was quite large, much larger than either brother had first realized and soon Jack turned, walking backwards down the thin trail, his eyes always on the beasts as he ambled through the grasses.

When they approached the cabin Jack breathed a heavy a sigh of relief. He turned and saw that surrounding the lawn was a thin wire fence with white knobs spread between the posts.

"Mind," the man said as they approached it.

And they knew what he meant. They each crossed over the fencing, careful not to let their legs brush the electric current.

Now they were removed from the bears and it wasn't until that moment when Jack gave the cabin more than a passing glance.

Stretching across the thatched rooftop were several ivy-covered trees that swallowed the little porch with her black veil of branches. There were two small windows along the face, one a thick rectangle pane framed in cast iron, with windshield wipers braced to the bottom. From an old jeep, Jack thought. The other was a tiny circular sheet of glass, like a porthole from a sailing yawl.

The cabin was so well-hidden that Henry and Jack both realized they could have easily marched across that meadow many times without ever having noticed it.

In the yard they observed large holes dug near the trees and sections of bark scraped bare from the pines. Along the northern face a wall of firewood was stacked between two tremendous cottonwoods and a chopping block balanced an old, smooth-handled axe.

As they climbed the porch steps they noticed that the front door was a cut strip of heavy lumber, unusually thick, with claw marks scarring the surface. The old hinges creaked as the strange man opened it.

"No after you," Henry suggested.

But the man pointed forcefully for them to enter.

As the brothers stood peering at the open doorway the man crossed the porch again, having done his job, and returned to join the bears. Some of the astonishment had left their faces, but was quickly replaced with curiosity.

"Whoever's in there," Henry said. "They sure know how to roll out the red carpet."

Jack gulped, still shaken from the morning. It was frightening to enter a hovel of that kind in such a wild place, though not as frightening as what awaited them on the lawn. Each brother ducked inside the small doorframe, squinting as they entered.

They were now in a warm dark den, lit only by a great fire at the far end. The porthole windows were shaded with wooden barreltops and the candles with their puddled bottoms stood unlit atop their sconces.

"I could stay here for a week," Henry said, a smile on his face.

Jack covered the room with his gaze. "I doubt we'll stay the night," he answered, but truly it was his hope that they wouldn't. He doubted he could find rest in such a place.

The floor was covered with strips of animal hide, loose grass and scattered trash. A wood stump made a chair by the door. Lipton bags and empty cigarette packets and Swiss Mocha and a torn couch were scattered about.

At the center of the room was a rough-cut timber table with countless scars on the tableface. From cutting up steaks, Henry thought. Initials were carved there, and on the walls as well, with dates etched beside them.

The brothers tip-toed across the room, feeling the floorboards creak. Their feet half-expected to sink as they crossed the timber. Soon their eyes adjusted to the darkness.

At the head of the table near the fire rested a great high-backed arm chair, and almost invisible within its shadow, sat a woman. Her eyes were closed and her hands crossed atop her lap.

Both brothers watched her carefully. Her head stood upright, perfectly still which gave the impression that she was still awake, but she made no motion when they addressed her.

"Howdy," Henry said.

The soft-wood logs were crackling in the fireplace. A kettle was hung above the flames, beginning to whistle, but the woman gave no sound. She sat, her mahogany skin shaded to the flamelight.

Jack didn't know where they were, or what to expect, but he knew he had never been to a stranger place in his life. On the walls were furs from animals he didn't recognize and antlers from the moose and the caribou carved into tools for some unknown purpose. There were dozens of wood carvings as well, of great trees and the sun, of children and birds and frogs. In the corner near the door stood a pair of homemade fishing rods, fashioned out of some kind of beech wood, and what resembled a woomerah, the kind Tipper had taught him about. There were small seashells everywhere - piled in boxes, on hanging necklaces, covering the face of the creel that hung from one of the chairs. Even on the wall, coal sketches of children showed them barefoot on the beach, with those same necklaces hung around their necks. Jack expected that like himself, Henry would be eyeing the artifacts, but when he looked up his brother was giving them no attention. Instead Henry was running his fingers along the grooves in the tabletop, curious who the visitors had been.

The floor continued to bend with every movement, until they felt their silence was hopeless. Don't know why we'd be quiet to begin with, Henry thought. Seems as though they've been expecting us.

"You two are far, far from Tenpenny Hill," the woman said.

The sudden words gave Jack a shock. Quickly he turned to look at her, a gentle smile on her face. "I see you've left Putt with your father."

Jack was certain he had never seen this woman before, on Tenpenny Hill or in any other place, yet she seemed to be expecting them, and knew Putt and Tip like she *had* been to Tenpenny Hill.

Henry scratched vigorously at the wounds across his chest. He yawned, "No place for a watchdog," he suggested. "Quite a greeting that fella gave us. Felt like a royal welcome. I'm Henry Snow," he said nodding, "This is my brother, Jack."

The woman rose to her feet, a surprisingly tiny and youthful appearance, and spoke with bright eyes. "I am Pasismanua. The man that greeted you was my husband. You must forgive him, he has only small pieces of English."

"Fair enough," Henry told her. "He speaks better *bear* than either of us."

At that moment, from the dark hallway, three small children peaked their heads from around the doorframe. The brothers each gave the children a smile, and in an instant their faces had ducked away; the sounds of their laughing was heard echoing through the den.

"Our children," Pasismanua said. "They only wake for strangers."

Henry chuckled, "That's alright. Where we come from, the children only wake for bears." To which she smiled.

It pained Jack to see the children. His mind was already holding tightly to Tenpenny and the sight of colorful children playing nearby only added to his longing to be home. He knew the sun was rising by now and that the morning bell would be coming within the hour. He thought of Greer, and wondered if she still planned to run away to her new life, wherever that was. It was a thought that had been visiting Jack for many days, and one he was certain would return to him again and again, until he had no reason left to wonder. Jack began to worry that some great danger, like the one that had just visited him, would soon go overlooked due to his daydreaming. It won't do to get killed either, will it Putt? Jack thought, wishing his friend was with him. I can't see her again if I'm dead, now can I?

Jack was determined to see Greer again, before she left, but he couldn't let Tipper or Henry down in the process. He set his mind to staying focused on his journey, though more and more his heart ached for home, and the children in the hallway only added to his homesickness. He looked away and gave the strange woman a smile.

"They're beautiful," he told her.

"Please sit," she said. "It should be a welcome feeling."

The old chairs were stiff and cold, but Pasismanua was right. As they sat their backs gave a sigh of relief.

To their great surprise the children brought out two steaming bowls of oats and set them down before the brothers. Before the brothers could thank them the woman stretched her hands out for each of them to hold. After a long silence she closed her eyes and prayed.

"Great Father, these two once journeyed to be among their earthly father, and now a new journey has taken them here and their answers are not long to wait. Give them strength. May this food help them and may You bless it. My prayer is for their obedience. Hold us together, we the poor and wounded at your feet. "

"Amen."

Immediately Henry dove into his oats. Jack, on the other hand, watched the woman. She kept her hands crossed and wore a gentle light in her eyes. Before he started eating Jack listened to the echoes of her prayers and ran them through his mind, as he would for years to come.

"Did your husband carve these?" Henry asked pointing at the walls, "And trap the furs?"

Pasismanua's eyes lighted with surprise. As the brothers would learn her eyes were never idle. Like her spirit they were living a life of their own.

"Papon does the trapping," she told him. "The carvings were given by our families, when we left our home."

Henry looked long at her, putting his spoon down as he examined her features. "If I had a guess I'd say you're from one of the Sepiks. Am I right?"

To this question, however, Pasismanua didn't seem surprised, Jack thought. She was probably told all about Henry's broad range of knowledge long ago.

"No," she answered. "In Chimbu. Though the Sepiks are lovely lands. Our neighbor lands."

As was customary in these moments Jack sat baffled. He had studied geography alongside his brother, but wherever the places were that Pasismanua and Henry were speaking of, Jack hadn't heard of any of them.

"Your husband is a hunting man I take it?" Henry asked.

"Among other things."

"Ever seen any wolves?" Henry asked.

"No," she told him.

"Never?"

"We might see a lynx or a bearcat, but the wolves are gone from here. We have never seen one. We have never heard their cries either and we have listened."

Henry winked. "So what'll you bet I see one fore this trip is through."

Pasismanua closed her eyes and gave a shy whimper. "I don't take bets."

"Hard case. I'll bet I'll have a wolf's winter coat wrapped around me by season's end. The journey back if I'm lucky."

The woman sighed and stretched her back. Like before she looked off at nothing, "No. Not much left in the way of wolves," she told him. "None in Tenpenny."

"There are some," Henry assured her. "They may be but a few but there's some. I've never seen them either but I've heard them howl and once I found their tracks. Tenpenny is a vast open land, don't forget. I doubt any man knows *all* about her."

Jack felt certain that Henry was right. No man knew this wild land entirely. Each hillock revealed more of herself, and she seemed to stretch on endlessly to the west, letting on more and more for so long that Jack began to wonder if the land would ever end. The thought reminded him of when he was a boy and he had traveled on horseback for hours to the north in search of Putt, after the dog had run after some quarry in the night. Jack could still recall riding over wild hills of Tenpenny North and discovering the skeletons of two great moose locked together at the antlers, there bodies frozen in a perpetual draw. They've been in open sight for years, he thought. Perhaps a generation, yet not a man alive has seen them.

There *may be* wolves in Tenpenny after all, Jack thought. He didn't know. What he did know was that it wasn't wise to put limits on the land. The land was revealing new secrets every day.

"What is this place?" Jack asked kindly.

She answered with a proud smile, "This is the *Window in the Meadow*."

Jack looked around, "Yes, but *what* window?"

And again a smile, "The meadow *is* the window. The window across the forest. Didn't your father tell you?"

Henry spoke with a mouthful of oats, "Our old man loves his secrets."

"It's his right," she suggested. "This meadow is the window across the forest. It is the only safe way to pass. Any other path chosen may find you face to face with the bears. But come through the window at dusk or dawn and you will find a safe passage, free of danger. At those moments, as you have seen, the bears are very busy."

Both brothers noticed that Pasismanua's speech had changed, sounding smoother, more rehearsed. She has given this explanation many times, they thought.

"The recent travelers were told the same?" Jack asked.

"Yes. They were told to mind the meadow. Ibrahim is well-acquainted. You see?" And Pasismanua pointed where the man's name was carved.

Jack and Henry moved their eyes across the tableface and began to recognize many names stenciled in the wood. The names "Smithson" and "Zuni" were among them as well as dozens of other workers they remembered through the years.

Immediately Jack began to feel homesick and looked away, keeping his eyes on the strange woman, whose gentleness was comforting after so many hard days of travel. She was the most surprising part of their journey thus far; and he couldn't deny how her presence effected him. For Jack Oakham had always been more deeply moved by people than by circumstance. The parade of bears they had just passed through was a creation of men, and their delivery was one of timely circumstance. Even his discovery in the den beneath the frozen lake had been a chance happening, if not an extremely unlikely one.

Jack then thought back on the Bhotiyas, looking toward a new life, and of Immanuel, a boy so much like himself. He remembered too the broken sight of Joe Forsman, a figure through his youth he had come to pity and to fear, now drinking himself away in a cave of his own making.

Jack had never expected to see him, and upon seeing him, did not expect they would meet again. For years the harms the man had done, to Greer more than the rest, had swelled up thoughts of vengeance in Jack's heart. But upon seeing him, Jack knew that no vengeance was necessary. The room where Jack found Forsman had a vengeance of its own.

Jack had already seen more in their journey then he had ever expected, but as he looked at Pasismanua, her presence stirred him further than the rest of their adventures combined. Her story surrounded him, on the walls and the meadow, in the ways of the wild man she called her husband. Jack felt certain that this woman had been expecting them for many years, and appeared to know a great deal about he and Henry, more perhaps than they knew about themselves. Jack even wondered if she knew the nature of their journey. He half-doubted it, remembering that Tipper *did* love his secrets. But then, like the woman could read his thoughts, Pasismanua said those very words.

"You are traveling to find your birthright," she said. It was not a question, but a statement.

Henry, whose hands were nimbly dancing across the names in the hardwood, looked up suddenly and said through his oats, "We are."

"Your father is a good man."

The brothers nodded. There was a heavy weight of anticipation spread throughout the room.

"Not good because he is taking you to find it, but good because he *has* *it* to give."

"Yes ma'am," Henry said. "Like you, we know our Father."

But how *well* do you know him, is the question, the woman wondered before she smiled. She had small hands, strong and veiny. She wrung them together. "Father's are not commonly good. Most know little of their children, and even less of themselves."

"Was that the way with your father?" Jack asked softly.

"*My* father was *your* father," she told them. "In many ways."

"Our father?"

"Tip Holland. Yes. He is to *you* what he *was* to me. You're father got me out of prison," she said strongly, her eyes filling. "I was imprisoned and he set me free."

"Prison, literally?"

"Again in many ways."

Simultaneously each of the brothers reached for their storybooks. They waited patiently with pencils ready.

"He set many of us free," she continued. "He's a good man, your father."

Jack could see the woman's eyes darting, her hands fighting nervously with one another. He knew his question must come gently. "Where did this happen?" he asked.

Pasismanua gave a timid smile, "What are those for?"

Henry glanced down at his storybook. "They're for your story," he told her.

Pasismanua looked long at each of their books, filled with long pages of notes and pencil smudges. "No," she waved them off. "You won't hear my story today."

"Hogwash," Henry told her. "Isn't that what we're here for?"

Pasismanua stretched her palms out toward them, a strong gesture from a strong woman. "No. That is not the reason," she said, and instantly they believed her. "It is not my story that matters. It is your father's story. Do you know your father's story?"

"Some of it. He's been telling us along the way."

She watched them closely. "What then, do you know of Unger Soski?"

The boys hesitated. "Tip shot him," Henry said. "He was his only friend and he shot him dead on the beach."

Quickly Pasismanua collected her thoughts and watched both of the boys with the eyes of a mother. "Shot him, yes. But not dead," she told them. "You see, like the rest of us, Unger got a second chance."

Jack and Henry both rose in their seats, as if a great opportunity had just been given them. Each were well-pleased with the news. It erased the pain of believing their father a murderer. Jack beamed with curiosity. "What second chance?"

"After nearly a year with Kolschen your father longed to turn himself in and beg forgiveness to Unger's wife. But when he called overseas to the Precinct he found out that Unger was very much alive."

"But that wasn't the end of it, was it?" Henry asked.

She shook her head. "You must know by now that Kolschen made it his mission to change the life of your father. He knew Tip would never be completely healed without the forgiveness of Unger Soski and Kolschen had always set out to heal your father completely."

The boys nodded, for the statement made perfect sense.

"What happened next?"

The woman placed her hands on the tabletop and kept her eyes closed as she told the story. She never paused for questions, telling it straight through from start to finish with a gentle smile at times, for the boys could see she relished the tale. When she was finished she finally opened her eyes and watched as the brothers scribbled from page to page.

"I call it, 'The Rejuvenation of Unger Soski' she told them. "But you can call it whatever you like."

Neither brother gave a suggestion. They were both so pleased with the story and its implications that they didn't want to speak, for the story was warming to their hearts.

Finally, when they were finished the woman asked. "Do you know your story, Jack?"

"Some of it."

"How you came to the orphanage?"

"Yes."

"Then maybe *your* story is *my* story. Maybe the story is the coming here. You found a family, you started again, you have a second chance and now you must—"

But her words were choked off. She shook her head and looked up at the ceiling. "Excuse me."

"Must *what*?"

Pasismanua dropped her smile. For the first time she looked at them with careful, weary eyes, "You don't know what your birthright is, do you?"

"No, ma'am. We have no idea."

She watched every move they made.

"This evening you will arrive at lands beyond your knowledge and tomorrow your life will change."

Henry leaned in to her. "What's beyond the trees?"

"You should wait and see."

"Then tell us what you would tell the others."

The woman could see the anticipation on their faces. She leaned in and whispered. "When you leave here you will pass through the trees and carry on to the west for half a day."

Henry nodded excitedly.

"It is not a simple passage like your road has been so far. The forest grows even thicker. Take care where you wander. Do not go off alone."

"And what happens after half a day?" Jack wondered.

"Ah. Then you will begin to see light peaking through the trees and the world will open and before you, you will see the end of your journey."

"The mountains?"

"Beyond that I cannot help you. All I can say is that you will need to be strong on the road ahead for much will be asked of you. Your hearts may grow heavy, but do not despair. Stay close to your father and listen well and he will guide, as he always has."

When they had finished their breakfast Pasismanua led them down the hallway. On the walls were old wood shelves and on the shelves were rows of tattered books. Books about the apartheid, and flyfishing, and home repair. Some were hand-written novels that Pasismanua herself had penned that no one would ever read.

Henry longed to pull any one of the books off the shelves and read it through. quickly, so hungry he was for the written word. But instead the brothers moved down the rickety hallway past a large, well- lit bedroom. They each felt the same tingle rush through their bodies as they peered inside. For in the room were three perfect bunkbeds with heavy quilts folded neatly. The floor was covered with a thick rug and on the bedside table rested a faded leather guestbook and a lamp. The room appeared so well-kept and inviting that the only thought in either brother's head was of a long winter sleep.

She led them down the hall, through the door, and onto the back porch where they saw in the yard a dozen bears waiting for their breakfast. At least half of the bruins that had filled the meadow had now migrated into the woods and Papon was feeding them from his hands. Soon the children spilled out onto the porch and said their hellos to the cubs as if they were members of the family. Young Oakham still wore a startled face of fear and wonder, afraid to speak, but he couldn't deny the exhilaration as such deadly beasts befriended him.

Soon Jack grew accustomed to their fantastic situation. He fed a cub from his bare hand and Henry ruffled the ears of a mighty black.

"You have the same bears every year?" Henry asked.

"The very same. The blacks come first," the woman nodded. "They're poor fishermen so they get very hungry."

"They come the same time every year?"

"With the snowmelt. All have come in the past week."

"So have they all arrived?"

"All but one," she told them, "There's a huge brown who dens in the east somewhere. She throws three cubs every time. I expect her any day now. We call her Esperanza."

Jack's thoughts returned to the bear he had shot, just days before. He turned his eyes back toward the east, to the deep den of the forest. When he did he noticed a well-trod swath that had been cut through the fan plants.

"What's the trail from?" he asked.

"He walks them," said Pasismanua.

"Walks 'em?"

"Every morning an hour after breakfast. On a trail back to the east."

"Why does he walk them?"

But before she could answer a heavy voice thundered from the porch behind them, "Because he's crazy!" the voice laughed.

The brothers turned and saw Tipper standing in the doorway.

"Tipper!" Henry called out. "You missed your breakfast!"

Their father chuckled as he looked at Henry. He didn't seem to notice his sleeves rolled down or the new limp in his gait. "She fed you breakfast? She won't even give me a place to sleep."

Pasismanua smiled shyly.

"Her oats were top notch," Henry smiled. "Much better than anything you've whipped up this trip."

"Well, if your bellies are warm I'd say it's time to go."

"Time to go?" Henry gawked. "Shoot we were just settling in."

"You've done well on your own," he told them. "But we still have some ground to cover."

As he stepped up to his sons they both could see a sadness in his face, and his eyes were bloodshot, as if he'd been crying.

Jack felt a sigh of relief wash over him as he shook his father's hand. He looked on him differently now that he knew Unger had survived, though he knew he shouldn't. He was the same man as before.

But when Henry embraced his father Tipper watched the boy closely, seeing him flinch. Henry was quick to turn away, feeling certain that his father was more aware of his injuries than he let on.

"Where were ya?" Jack asked.

"Handling some chores of mine."

"Where's Putt?"

"Chores?!" Henry wondered. "You *would* find work to do in the forest."

"But they're done now."

"Good," Henry said. "You're awful slow when you're distracted."

Tipper turned back to Jack, "Putt's tied up in the woods a ways. I never bring him here."

Papon and Pasismanua stepped up to greet Tip, a look of wonder on their faces. "G'morning Mr. Tipper," she said.

"Good morning, sweet sister. Good morning, Mr. Wan Wokabaut."

The man laughed for the first time that morning, revealing only a handful of teeth.

"I see you've been introduced."

"Oh yes," she assured him. "Very well. But I've decided Henry is not as smart as he's famed to be."

Tipper laughed, "Why is that?"

"He believes you will find the wolves on your journey. Do you believe that? The wolves?"

Tipper smirked, rolling his eyes. "I don't believe in chasing wild geese or, fairy tales."

"Then what are we doing out here?" Henry asked him.

Tip looked long at his son, so long that the boy smarted, "Here we're catching 'em."

And secretly Jack smiled in his heart. He was glad to have his father back.

10. The Rejuvenation of Unger Soski

By Jack Oakham

All that week as they kayaked up the coast Unger had dreamed of his retirement, a time that he imagined would be filled with trips like this one. Unger Soski had been a dreamer all his life, and now that his career was ending he felt that his dreams would soon be realized.

But as he paddled down the beach for help, his yellow kayak streaked with blood, he knew that his dreams would have to wait. However he couldn't help but think of them.

Unger had always held to the belief that his dreams would save him someday, and as he passed in and out of consciousness, he hoped that dwelling on his dreams would keep him awake.

But instead he passed out and was strapped to a gurney and flown three hundred miles to emergency surgery where he was put on a ventilator for seven days. It was a retired nurse, and not his dreams, at least this time, that saved Unger's life.

When he woke Unger felt his dreams fade further as the extent of his injuries were finally felt. He waited an hour for the surgeon to fill him in.

"What's the damage, Doc?"

"The bullet punctured your lung, shattered two ribs and a bit of it splintered into your shoulder girdle."

"And my chin is broken."

"That was from the fall."

Unger chuckled, "I know. What d'you do to patch me up?"

"We had to remove the two ribs that were shattered."

"I can feel that."

"And we performed a lobectomy. Which means a third of your lung is gone."

"A third?"

"If it had been your left lung it would have been more. The right is a bit higher."

"Because of the liver?"

The Doc nodded, "I read you were a medic."

"That's right I was. What should I expect, Doc?"

"You'll be fairly short of breath the rest of your life. You may experience decreased function in your shoulder and more than likely have some arthritis pain. I wouldn't be surprised to see your stamina effected. Perhaps significantly."

Unger began to sigh but stopped himself just in time.

The next day he developed a soft tissue infection and was fighting it in the ICU for a week. After that he spent another two weeks in general care and a month in therapy. When he finally did arrive home he was welcomed by a convoy of his peers, all with vengeance in their hearts. But soon the fanfare had ended and his life became a slow and steady regiment of codeine and outpatient therapy. Within six month he and his wife had moved out of Manhattan to a small farming community a few hours upstate. Within a year Unger Soski's youth was just a memory and his dreams had been forgotten.

He had given up exercise, dancing, playing chess with his neighbor. He paid a kid to mow his lawn and a widow to clean his trailer home. Unger sat with his horseman magazines and slept with his crosswords.

His wife soon mimicked his habits.

"I've decided not to renew our passports, dear," she said. "I've decided to sell the bike."

And so it may have gone on like that forever. For many men it does. Yet along with all of the other things that Unger Soski was unaware of, he didn't realize he had many battles yet to fight.

II.

Outside Outshoorn the sun raced up the hill, past the dun heaps and the roll scratches that the horses made, above the fence tops that cast shadows beyond the landing, to the last of the dark spaces, nestled on lonely rocks atop the Outeniqua pass. It was a crowded ride, but a pleasant one, one of the most pleasant they had had in days. The blacks were lined against the flapping canvas, a crowded mass of faces that smiled whenever they faced them. Both men sat with their packs across their laps, breathing an air of quiet satisfaction, the smells of Africa all around them as they let their legs dangle over the open road. Kolschen went as far as to remove his socks and shoes so that his feet could swing bare against the wind. Tipper may have done the same if he hadn't been lulled to sleep by the dim light and the flapping of the canvas.

Kolschen sat still watching him, marveling at how far the boy had come. He wore no pride or jealousy, he had no temper to speak of. He was loyal and gentle and joyful in his freedoms. He knew himself completely. Kolschen knew he would miss him dearly. He leaned his head out of the bakkie and saw the road ahead.

Quickly he woke the boy, "Do you know what today is, Tip?"

Tip roused gracefully and after a gentle shrug he said, "No sir."

"Today is our anniversary," the man told him. "A year ago this evening I met you in the alleyway."

In an instant Tip came fully awake. The previous year of his life rolled backwards through his mind until he saw the alley, dark and painful before him. Finally he turned his head. "I try not to think about that."

Kolschen faced him. "No, no. *Think* about it, Tovarisch. Even write about it. Your story won't keep in a bottle."

"*My* story?"

"It isn't mine. You could have given up on this journey long ago. But you stayed so the path is yours."

Tip leaned in and whispered. He smiled with every word. "How do you know it isn't just *your* story I'm living. Like maybe I'm just a passenger on a ship."

"Maybe," Kolschen said, seeming surprised. "But I don't think so. You're a man now, Tip. Your heart is your own."

When he heard the words Tip nearly fell out of the bakkie. A tremendous weight had been lifted. He realized he had just been knighted by his king. For Kolschen was very careful with his words and Tip had often pondered how the man would measure him. And now the weight of not knowing had vanished. A moment later, however, a new one took its place.

Tenderly Kolschen leaned in and whispered, "When we arrive at the crossroads, Tip, our long journey together has ended. I have to say goodbye."

Tip turned cold and fearful. The words circled around him like a cell. When Kolschen patted him with his giant hand, as a comfort, Tip hardly seemed to notice.

"Now?"

"Every boy needs a wilderness experience and you've had yours," Kolschen said. "But every man needs his wings. And that is what I'm giving you."

Kolschen tried to reassure him, "No. No. Don't say anything. You will understand. A young man cannot cleave forever. You will see that when you go out on your own."

"Go out?"

"To make your own path."

Tip imagined the lonely road ahead of him. While they sat in silence tears soon filled his eyes. "Will we meet again?"

Kolschen chuckled. "Of course, Tovarisch! Of course we will! But only if you choose it." Then he smacked him across the shoulder. "How many Tip Holland's do you think I have? We are lifelong friends, you and I."

The road carried on, with the smell of three-awn licking off the sides of the tarp. There was so much Tip wished to say, so many questions he still had before he was alone in the world. But before he had time to let his mind settle the humming of the road slowed to a gentle beat.

Soon the driver steered the bakkie onto the shoulder and slowed to a stop. Then he turned to the truck bed and called through the window.

"Knysna is that way," he said. "This is as far west as we're going."

Kolschen nodded and slumped off the stanchion. "Thank you, my brother," he said to the driver. "If it's alright Stuart here will go with you to Knysna."

The driver nodded, "No worries."

Without warning Kolschen turned and swallowed Tip in his arms, praying a blessing over his life. Before Tip could respond the man let him go and was walking backwards along the shoulder.

"So we'll meet again?" Tipper asked with a nervous smile.

"Yes," Kolschen assured him. "But not for a year. If you choose to return I will be waiting for you one year from tonight."

"Where?"

The driver punched the gas and the bakkie started off. But they were still at an intersection, moving at a snail's pace behind several other cars.

"A place called Uttar Pradesh. A place where we'll both learn some *new* things. If you join me. But I warn you it will only be harder. Don't find me if you are looking for a vacation."

"Uttar Pradesh?"

"I left a note in your journal."

Tip shook his head. "Are you going home?"

Now the bakkie was picking up speed and Kolschen's voice was raised.

"First I have matters that need tending to! See that the children at the school are well taken care of!"

Until that moment Tipper had forgotten the reason they were traveling to Knysna in the first place. He was breathing deeply with every moment, as he watched his savior, his only friend, slipping out of his life.

"Where should I go?" he called.

"What would you like to see?"

Tipper was smiling through his tears. Kolschen was slipping away. "I'd like to see someplace wild! Like our time in the forest!"

Kolschen was walking slowly now, following the truck as it pulled away. "Now you begin phase number two. You must find a friend! Every young man needs a friend!"

Then he lifted both of his giant hands to wave as the bakkie sped across the intersection. In a moment he had was too far away to answer.

One of the blacks who spoke English watched the big man on the horizon and turned back to Tip.

"So he just left?"

Tip answered through his tears. "He did."

"Just like that?"

"Just like that."

"What school are you going to?"

Tip's eyes were lost to the horizon. He could still see his friend carrying the same weightless freedom that he'd possessed the night they met.

"A school for orphans," Tip told him. "We were going there for a month to teach them English."

"Will you still go?"

Tipper had never considered going anywhere without Kolschen. But now he supposed that he must.

"If they'll have me."

"Where will he go?" the worker asked him.

Tip looked at the long road cutting east across the continent, and where the road crested he caught his final glimpse of Otsov Kolschen and all he carried as he disappeared beyond the flats. Tip smiled. "Who knows?" he said beneath his breath.

III.

At ten o'clock in the morning Unger Soski had united with the cushions of his lazyboy when the doorbell rang. He hadn't shaved, hadn't eaten, his shirt was covered with a mustard stain from the night before. And if that doorbell hadn't rung, this image of him would have been faxed, over and over, every day for the next seventeen years of his life, until he died. Unger grumbled as he stood up to answer.

At the doorstep stood a huge man about his age. He carried a canvas haversack and his boots were falling apart from wear. He was seeking day work as he hitch-hiked up country.

"What sort of work?" Unger asked him.

"I'll do yard work, engine repair, cut logs, paint houses. I can plumb. I'm here to serve," he said. "Christ was a servant. That's what I want to be. Forgive my English it isn't so good."

He was about to dismiss the man but the mention of Christ's service revived something within him. Unger hadn't heard words like that in some time.

"I can't pay much," he warned.

"Good," Kolschen answered. "I wouldn't take much if you offered it."

Kolschen spent all that morning cutting a french drain in their driveway and that afternoon cleaning out the gutters.

Unger helped when he could, but if he exerted himself his breathing grew short. After a day's work Kolschen asked about his condition.

"A year ago I had an accident. Pretty bad one. It's taken me some time to get back on my feet."

"Now that you're healed have you made any plans?"

Unger shrugged, "No plans," he told him. "I used to be a dreamer but this roadblock has set me back."

"What did you dream of?"

Unger took a deep, but careful breath as he answered. He hadn't spoken of it in some time.

"When I was a boy my grandfather had a farm. In this very county. My father grew up there. He always wished to take it over and whip it into shape but he and my grandfather died in the same winter. The land has been mine for thirty years now and I always planned to fix it up when I retired, like my father wanted."

"Now you don't think you will?"

"With this lung I wouldn't know where to start."

Kolschen gave a nod of understanding. "You live in a fine country. A country where a man can build his dreams without fear of having them stripped away. A country where a young man's hopes can be realized in his twilight years. That is a mighty thing. Please forgive me but it is much mightier that your roadblock."

Unger listened in astonishment. It had been a long time since any man had spoken to him in such a way. Not only was he being challenged by this stranger but this stranger was a foreigner, and yet spoke so highly of his country. He was searching for a response when the man stopped him in his tracks.

"If the service taught me one thing," Kolschen said. "It's that there's nothing more shameful than a man without a mission."

He worked alongside Kolschen when he could, day after day straining harder than one day before. For three days Unger kept the man busy with every task he could think of. Soon Unger found himself inventing tasks just to keep the man around, but before long the work had dried up, even petty jobs that his wife was willing to do.

"It's time I should be heading on," Kolschen told him.

"I know it, though I'm sad to see you go."

The traveler shook hands but refused his wage, even though Unger insisted.

"No, no," Kolschen said. "I enjoyed it too much. But a friend of mine who will be passing this way some day. I wonder if I could trade my wage for you to house him for the night?"

Unger thought it a strange request, but then most of the things Kolschen said were a bit strange, if not bursting with truth.

"If he is a friend of yours he'll always have a place here."

After a prayer for his new friend Kolschen headed west again, toward the warming summer.

As the weeks passed Unger heard Kolschen's words in his heart yet all the while his breath was shallow. Oh how I wish I was whole again, he thought. What an ending I could have had.

One afternoon as he scrubbed the dishes he looked at an old horseshoe that dangled by a nail in his kitchen. It was a rusted shoe that he had found as a boy, on the old farm where he had spent his childhood. It had been on his wall for years, and had always reminded him of his ramblings as a child, of his early dream to mend old planks of the forgotten farm, to observe daily the labor of his hands. And like so many times before, Unger let the thought fester for but a moment, until he imagined all the hard work it would take, all the sacrifice he would have to make. "Who ever heard of an old man starting a farm?" he asked himself and shook his head.

But this time as he said it, Kolschen's words echoed in his heart. He missed those challenging words. He missed the work even more. Just thinking of it caused him to hunger for a project.

"I'm driving out to farm," he told his wife.

"What for?"

"Some air is all," he assured her. "I just need some air."

It had been six months since Unger had looked over his abandoned fields. The springtime had been a wet one and he knew the pasture would be overgrown. It had always caused Unger great dismay to see the farm in the growing season, when there should have been cattle grazing the lush grasses. As always he prepared himself for the bewilderment of his forgotten dream.

But when he arrived at the gate what he saw bewildered him more than ever. The tall field of grass, overgrown these many years, had been cut. The road which had been swallowed by fallen trees wound clearly through the pasture. The tractor, long abandoned, was resting near the gate with new tires and implements, and a fresh engine.

On the gate an envelope had been clipped. His name marked across the face. When he opened it Unger found that he was having trouble breathing.

My Friend Unger,

Please forgive me for taking such liberties. But sometimes all a man needs to get a fresh start is a clear view of the ground before him. You'll find that your dream is ripe for the taking. I do wish you much success. In your mailbox I have enclosed a check with the money the boy stole from you last year, with interest of course. Someday I will visit you, in hopes that your dream is realized. Until then, ignore the roadblocks.

Your Friend,
Otsov Kolschen

Now Unger was no fool. He knew that moments like this one come along too rarely to mention. For now his mission was clear. He drove across the farm, already unrecognizable, and as he paced the fields his heart was racing with exhilaration. But he didn't linger. Unger was quick to load back in the car and drove home again. It wasn't long before his heart was full again. Not long before he marched into his wife to slay his apathy. "Get dressed while I pack the car."

At 61 years old, Unger Soski set out to rebuild his father's farm. It was hidden deep in the bushy forest of his childhood and the roads were poor. But that didn't cast a shadow on his dream. He looked at the rundown property with a young man's sense of purpose.

"I won't grow idle," he told his wife. "A man must dream until his breath has left him."

"We're too old for all that, Unger."

And all he could do was smile.

The farm had no irrigation, a forty year old tractor, and only one working hand, Unger himself, but the foundation was sound and the field unspoiled. Yet for a man Unger's age, the workload was intense.

The farmhouse had dry rot and a rusted roof. In the yard lay scattered bottles, woodcrates, deer skeletons, and tin. The barn was unpainted, the fence unposted. But Unger had always believed that it was better to clean up a dream already dreamed then to begin a new one from scratch. He could not imagine laying a foundation, or designing a structure, but the notion of taking his father's dream and rebuilding it was warming to his heart.

"You see this land?" he asked his wife. "This land was my old man's childhood. My old man's dream. Now it's become our dream. I feel like a kid again, Betta."

Unger's wife looked haggard and worn. Cinderblocks and egg crates and beer bottles filled the house. A possum had made its home inside the woodbox. "It seems a lot of work," she said.

But despite Betta's apprehension, Unger Soski saw no reason why his spread should not be the best dairy farm in the whole county. "We'll rename it the "Unworked Soil of All.""

He and his wife made a list of chores to be completed before summer's end. He dictated the list to her as they laid in separate beds, "Seed the fields, cut the firewood, build a swing."

"Oh, yes. How nice."

The challenge of turning an abandoned cattle farm into a well-oiled machine consumed old Unger Soski. Throughout the coming months he carried the folded list in his back pocket wherever he went. It was seven pages long. He believed his dream would come true. He told his neighbor that very thing.

"Come by when I've fixed her," Unger said. "You won't recognize the place."

"Don't fix that barn, Soski."

"What?"

"If you do, the appraiser will come. Your taxes will skyrocket."

"I'm building it with my own hands. They can't tax that, Hoyt."

"They'll tax you to death, Unger. These kidney stones are giving me hell."

The next morning work began at dawn. Unger Soski knew this to be a noble project. A project to end with. His wife helped him with the details. "I'll handle the kitchen and the furniture," she told him. "And the flower beds and the weeded walkway."

"Thank you, Betta." He held her hand.

It felt strange to her. "Mark them off your list."

Unger started with the rock-picking. He laid a length of chain-linked fence in his truck bed, and pitched the lawn rocks into the truck. Then he drove to a bare spot on the farm where he tied the fence to the cedar and drove off. The rocks dumped themselves.

Once the field was picked Unger painted the cowpins, the fenceposts, the gates, the porch. He rented a bushhog and cleared out the small trees. He bought a wheelbarrow, a mailbox, a feeder for the birds.

He began to think and pray and sweat again. His goal had made him younger.

Unger worked whole days throughout the summer, breaking only for lunch and falling asleep at sunset. His wife hadn't seen him so excited since their son was born.

"It's coming along well," she told him as he undressed.

"Tomorrow I have the stock tank to clean and the plumbing to fix."

By June the feed bins had been washed and sanded, the dung stalls raked, the hay ordered. Unger had painted the metal roof silver, stretched a clothesline between the oaks, laid a firepit in the yard. The farm had taken shape.

In the evenings he would shower and a eat a bowl of kashi in bed as he looked at his list. His work had brought back a feeling of youth. He gave himself a close haircut. He gave his wife a kiss.

"What was that for, Unger?"

He was awake now, in more ways than one. "That, my dear, was because I love you."

When it rained, Unger studied, reading notes in the twilight hours. He learned woodcarving, seed timing, masonry, and plumbing. He read outdoor tales, and dreamed big dreams.

"Why Unger I never. You haven't read in years."

After a hard days work he would look at his list, and recopy the undone chores onto a new sheet, wanting his list to be fresh.

"We're down to three hundred chores," he told his wife.

She clapped her hands together like a spectator.

Unger felt a quiet satisfaction when he was alone in the field. He began to notice the leaves hanging on, the birdsong, the sounds of the day waking.

In July he bought buckets, coyote traps and overalls. He set up a weathervane, watered the lawn, built a cattle ramp. He bought a sheep dog named Uncle Sam. His pants no longer fit him.

"Thank you, Lord, for the rain, the work, the health and strength you've given me."

The labor continued, and the progress as well. He tilled the soil, cleaned the pipes, watered the beds. Unger trimmed limbs, piled leaves and burned them, hung signs to discourage trespassers. Every dusk he looked at the lawn with pride.

"Thank you, Lord, for the grass, the colors, the dew of the morning."

His wife bought curtains, silverware, and bedding. She too had been romanced by her husband's reinvention. She liked his suntan. She held his calloused hands.

"The place looks wonderful."

Unger chopped trees, and dragged them to be sawed. Yet there was one tree he left alone. A family of eagles had lived there for years. There they felt protected. There they would be untouched. "Thank you, Father, for such a gift. A powerful gift, a powerful symbol, a beautiful thing."

One evening his wife returned from the local grocery with a look of concern. She had spoken to someone in town. "The taxes will go up?" she asked her husband.

"Yes."

"We won't have the money?"

"No, we won't."

"You can't repair the barn?"

He shook his head. "I don't know."

"Oh, Unger," she whimpered.

That night they looked at cattle prices, their savings, the cost of living. They crunched the numbers, added up receipts, assumed the worst. "We'll never make it, Betta."

"But your dream? You're living it. What else are we to do?"

Then Unger said something she remembered for the rest of her life. He looked happy and sad all at once. "It's an unfinished dream, that's true," he told her. "But you're my wife. That dream has already come true."

When they were finished making love Unger thought long about his dream. He knew it had been a good one. Someday he might still finish the barn. In a year, two years, whenever the money was good. Then he sat up in bed shaking his fists. "I won't fade to grey!" he said.

He was no longer the sort of man to sit on a porch with his abandoned dream staring him in the face. He wasn't a young man anymore, no matter how good he felt. There were no guarantees of another year or another dream.

Despite the warnings Unger Soski went to work on the last leg of his project. The words "Fix barn" were all that remained of his list. He knew that he had come a long way, but that his last task was the hardest project of all.

He began the next morning by buying a lathe, cutting down cedars, making measurements. Unger sliced the boards and stacked them neatly. He sandblasted the doors, the walls, the bins with the wood flooring. The townsfolk watched the work from the Paper Sack River Road. He stained the wood, replaced the mortices to the door hinges, sanded the roof, masoned the steps. He set rat traps, shot pigeons, swept the floor, replaced the fixtures.

The second week he draped two ladders on either side of the roof, thirty feet up, and used them as handles as he sanded the tin. The rust was thick but the next day he started to paint.

"Mustn't we pay our taxes?" his wife asked.

"We must. We must always render unto Caesar what is his."

"Oh, I don't understand," she smiled.

In late August, when the barn was near completion, Unger went to town to buy a white stag vest for the coming fall. At the checkout some officials approached him. "Hello, Mr. Soski."

"Gentlemen."

"We've seen you working. That's a fine place you've got out there."

"Do I know you?"

"We need to appraise your land," they smiled.

Thank you, Father for government, for laws, for checks and balances. Unger smiled back. "Come by Tuesday," he said. "I'll unlock the gate."

On Tuesday at sunrise Unger took his tractor and dumped twelve logs at his gateway. When they arrived he called from the porch, "I'm sorry gentlemen. I've had an accident. Come back next week."

The officials smiled at the thought of their new adversary (everyone wants one) and climbed back into the car.

The next week Unger left a note on the gate. The officials arrived and read it aloud. "Please feed the dog, Sadie. He likes tug'o'war. We'll be back on Sunday, Unger and Betta."

Unger and his wife giggled from behind the silo. They watched the officials drive off and then necked for half an hour.

The following week the officials arrived at eight in the morning, this time with a police escort.

"Hello, gentlemen," Unger said. "What brings you this way?"

"How was your vacation, Soski?"

Unger smiled. "With a wife like Betta and a place like this, I'm always on vacation."

"We have a warrant."

Unger opened the gate and led the men up to the barn. It looked incredible. There had not been a renovated barn in the county for ten years. They looked at the paneling, the paint, the stonework and the pins. Above the double doors a white sheet was draped and folded, covering something.

Mr. Soski led them inside and was quite cordial as they questioned him. "Is that double paneled roofing? Is the power up and running?"

When they had finished the survey the officials made some notes and walked with Unger out the door. "You know, Mr. Soski, with this added value the worth of the farm has increased considerably."

"It has?"

"That means higher taxes," they smiled.

"Does it?"

"If you were smart you would have considered that."

"I considered it. I won't pay higher taxes."

An awkward pause and then, "I'm sorry?"

"I decided the taxes were fine as they are. I've decided that they won't go up."

Then speaking slowly one of the officials said, "Mr. Soski. . . by state law-"

Unger interrupted, "It's more of a state suggestion, actually. See I've found a loophole."

The officials began to grow agitated. "Mr. Soski there are no loopholes in our government. It's the law. When your barn is improved, the farm has more value. A more valuable farm has higher taxes. It's the law."

Unger Soski looked at his barn, his field, his home. Then he said, "If everyone listened to *that* law, there would be no reason to improve. Dreams would die, gentlemen. So I found a solution. I built a post office."

As the officials looked at each other Unger reached up and pulled down on the white sheet. Beneath it was a large wooden sign. It read: County Post Office.

There are of course too few dramatic victories in life and as Unger knew, when they come it is best not to gloat. . . but to simply enjoy them.

One official smiled. "You think you're very smart."

"You pompous old man." the other told him.

The cop looked dumbfounded. "I don't understand what difference that sign makes. So what if he made a sign?"

One of the officials said scratching his baldhead, "By law, if Mr. Soski turns his barn into a government building, then the government cannot tax him for his improvements. He's wasted our time."

The cop was still confused. "Is that it?" he asked.

They nodded. "Afraid so. We can't do a thing. To stay legal Mr. Soski is only required to send one parcel of mail through his post office across county lines every year."

Unger's wife stepped off the porch with a tray of lemon tea.

The old official turned to Unger. "And I must assume that it took Mr. Soski some time to handle the paperwork for such an arrangement."

Unger spoke up, "Three weeks," he smiled. "Three Tuesdays to be exact."

The policeman stood with his hands on his hips. "It's a fine barn, Unger."

"A fine farm, Soski."

"When are you bringing in the stock?"

And Unger looked at his wife as she approached them with the tea. She nodded to the officials and handed them the glasses. The field was clean and green, the farm freshly painted, his wife smiling with her hair down. He could see the eagle's nest in the tall oak, untouchable. He thought to himself, "What a beautiful dream. This country."

11. Pennies from Heaven

Greer rung her bell. "I want to talk to the Doc!" she sung from her bed. " Hello! I have a question for the Doc!"

Doc Zuni awoke from his nap and walked in a daze through the infirmary and into the girl's room. The place was empty except for her. Zuni's hair was smeared atop his head. "I'm here," he told her.

"I want to see a calendar. I want to see when the baby will come."

Zuni rubbed his eyes. "It will come next winter. At the start of the season."

Greer dropped her face in her hands. The thought of another winter, this time with a child to tend was too much for her to comprehend.

She hadn't stepped foot outside the infirmary since Zuni had told her the news. The idea of celebrating the spring when her freedoms had been stripped seemed a hopeless endeavor. She had spent the better part of the first day in silence, going over her options in her head. But Greer knew her options were dwindling. She felt an anger rise in her heart when Henry came to mind, an anger that Zuni was doing his best to squelch.

"Did you sleep?" he asked her.

"When I have this baby, can I leave it here?"

"Is that what you want?"

"What I want is to go," she told him. "I was on my way out when you roped me back in."

"I didn't rope you," he said. "This isn't a prison. You're free to go if you like."

For the past two days Greer had thought about nothing but leaving, but always her heart turned back to the child. She knew she could never care for a baby on her own, with no money and no home and no idea of the world. Since the news of the child came the girl's mind settled not on the freedom of the road, not on Henry Snow and his boyish charms, but on the weight of a responsibility that was growing inside her.

"But I'm not free," she told him. "Zuni I'm not free and I never will be again."

He sat beside her. "Would you tell that to every mother that ever lived?" he asked. "I think you'd lose that battle."

"Not if they were *single* mothers," she said.

Zuni shook his head. "No one says you have to be a single mother, Greer. This place takes care of its own. Not to mention the father, which I could narrow down pretty quick."

"I have no feelings for the father," she told him. "Whoever he is."

Just then a great commotion was heard outside the infirmary. Zuni took his eyes off the girl, for what he saw stole his attention. Up the old stone steps came the shapes of three men and a boy, appearing out of the wilderness. His heart began to celebrate for he thought the Tenpenny Three had returned. But almost immediately he realized that this was a party of strangers and furthermore from the timid looks that they carried they appeared lost, or worse. Doc Zuni begged the girl's pardon and stepped onto the porch.

The men did not appear dangerous or hostile but the sight of several wild men rising out of the wilderness was enough to make anyone cautious. The boy with them put the Doc at ease. "Hello," he said, his hand raised. To his great pleasure every traveler, to a man, smiled back, some of them with rotten teeth, and in unison gave a, "Hello."

They were small men, all with thick hair except the old one who was bald. Every man had tattered trousers and dirty hands, and only one of them, the man out front was wearing a pack. The others seemed to have nothing except for the saddles in their arms. Doc Zuni stood, sizing the party up and the silence was prolonged as the Doctor searched for something to say. Before he could speak, however, the one with the pack asked, "Stuart Whitlock?"

*   *   *

When paying Sissy a visit, it was customary for Wonderboy to gauge her mood before he interrupted her, for Sissy had her moods. There was no better student of Sissy's intemperate behavior than Jack Oakham, who could spot her tells almost immediately. Even Tip was impressed by how well his son could read his sister. But Wonderboy was close behind and often had more reason to fear her moodswings than any other man on Tenpenny Hill for his job required many untimely interruptions. That afternoon he found himself particularly distressed by the thought of confronting her, because she was in the chocolate house, her favorite place, and one she visited only when she was stressed herself. He stood quietly with his ear turned to the door, listening to the soft sweet notes of her singing.

Sissy was seated at a huge table covered in wax paper. She had dozens of candies laid out and a soft song playing from the stereo. All of the curtains were drawn and she was wearing a wide colored apron and a net to keep her hair up.

Wonderboy cracked the door open. "Miss Sissy?"

She didn't look up. Instead Sissy began to dapple the small chocolates with drops of caramel.

"Miss Sissy there are men—"

"One day is all I ask, my friend. Can't there be just one?" she wondered as she swallowed a chocolate. "A day? When everything runs on time and I'm left alone? Can there be such a day?"

Wonderboy smiled, "No, Miss Sissy. There cannot."

The man's honesty caused her to smile herself. "So I'm learning. And what is it that interrupts me today?"

"There are men with the Doctor. New men come from the village."

She looked down at her chocolates. "They haven't seen my brother have they?"

"They didn't say, Miss Sissy."

She rose from her table in the chocolate house. "Did they have their papers?"

"They did," he told her.

In a huff Sissy stormed out the chocolate house and headed up the road. Wonderboy always found it difficult to keep up with Sissy when she walked, for she moved with great intention. She marched without stopping and when she burst inside the infirmary she was quick to look over the dirty travelers.

"You men seen three horsemen on your journey?"

Their eyes were blank.

"They don't have any English," the Doc said.

"Well what do they have?" she asked, "Besides filthy hands and bad teeth."

"They have jobs," the Doc told her. "Tip wrote them in as 'labormen' a week ago."

"Is that what their papers say?"

"I haven't read their papers," he told her as he handed her the envelope. "I thought *you* should read them."

Sissy looked down at the boy and managed a smile.

"If you didn't read their papers how did you know they had jobs?" she asked.

"Tip told me when he hired them."

A flurry of anger rose within her. For years her brother had made decisions on Tenpenny Hill without her consent, something she had come to accept. What she could never accept was that others on the hill knew more of the goings on then she did, especially Doc Zuni who, other than Henry, seemed the one person in her life least concerned with her opinion. The thought that Zuni had been expecting these new workmen without her knowledge infuriated her.

"Tip wrote them in as 'labormen', you say?"

"Yes ma'am."

"Tip has gone off to endanger his sons, in case you've forgotten. Tip doesn't know what's happened here for days and when he wrote them on he couldn't have known what we'd need them for."

"Couple of cabins that need going. That's what we need. That's why he wrote them on."

"There's other things need going besides cabins! These men might be digging graves for my nephews if my brother has his way!"

"Bull!," the Doc said, waving her off. "The children don't need to hear such talk. Henry and Jack know what they're doing."

Sissy turned sharply. "They don't have the *first idea* what they're doing. They're boys, in case you've forgotten."

"Maybe in years. But I say I've known few men that compare."

"And I say only a fool would put those precious boys in harm's way. Or a pair of fools! They're miles from home with no food and the bears are well out of their dens."

"Well they're fine hunters. I'd say Tipper chose his timing well."

"And I'd say you're hopeless as them. But it won't be you who gets hurt out there."

"*Hopeful* is what I am. One's early years should not be wasted in soft pursuits."

To that she chuckled, "And one's *old years* shouldn't be spent quoting my brother,' she told him. She sighed then and looked back at the travelers.

"Wonderboy, take them up to the Roost for now. Make certain they shower and have a warm meal."

Sissy handed the envelope back to Wonderboy. "I'll let you two go over their papers," she told them. "Zuni have a look at them when they're cleaned up. I'll decide tomorrow what work we can give them."

Without another word she turned away and headed back down to the chocolate house, content with her decision. She was pleased that the interruption was over. Sissy kept her eyes out ahead of her, careful not to glance upon any of the children, for fear that their troubles may distract her. The Bhotiyas watched silently as the scene came and went, weary already of this fast talking woman.

Wonderboy did as he was told. The Bhotiyas were led towards Rocky's Roost, the guest house on the hilltop as many of the children came onto their porches to have a look at the travelers. The boy especially seemed pleased to see the young faces. It had been many weeks since he had been among children and the equality brought him comfort.

As they walked up the hill the four Bhotiyas stared at their new home with disbelief. The grounds were immaculate. Immanuel had seen postcards once of a golf course and the sight before him was the only place he could compare it to. All along the river the trees had been pruned, leaving no branches low enough to interfere with running children.

Down the road they saw the shapes of many cabins, dark-logged with flagpoles, and some of them built high up in the trees. They looked up at the treehouses with wonder, watching as a small child emerged to cross a bridge.

The men glanced briefly at the huge plaque labeled the "Map of Records". It was a wooden display built to celebrate the record holder for both swimming and track and field events on Tenpenny Hill. On the wood face dozens of names were inscribed and around the border were a hundred or more framed pictures. Although the names meant nothing to the Bhotiyas, they paid special attention to the photographs. The men looked over the pictures and Chhedup's eyes widened as he approached the plaque. Jack Oakham's was the first face he saw. There were other pictures of Jack there, and one of Henry on a stage with a black wig, his body painted green. Chhedup thought back to the forest and wondered who the man was with these two boys. Had he taken them away? But before he was able to run wild with his thoughts Chhedup caught a glimpse of a small face among a crowd of children. The man was wearing a ball cap and he seemed to be soaking wet. It was a shy smile, the kind one wears just before bursting into tears of joy.

"Tipper," The man pointed.

The others stepped forward and gawked when they saw him, repeating the name once again.

Wonderboy turned around. He held a strange smile on his face. There was no inscription beneath the photo, nor any nameplate that could be seen.

"How do you know Tipper?" he asked them.

But the travelers only looked at him, then turned back to the pictures.

Wonderboy was certain of what he had heard, what he wasn't certain of was how these men could know such a name. Wonderboy had welcomed many workers to the hill over the years but none had any knowledge of Tip Holland when they arrived, as was intended.

He asked again, this time pointing at the photo. "Did you see Tip Holland?"

Each of the men nodded. "Tip-per," they said slowly.

The name Tip Holland wasn't known off of Tenpenny Hill, causing Wonderboy to conclude that these men must have met Tipper in their travels. Instantly he looked down at the envelope in his hands. These papers may have been signed by Tip himself, he thought, and if so these travelers might shed some light on their progress, for Wonderboy was anxious for their return.

Immediately he tore open the envelope, something Wonderboy had never done. He flipped through the pages quickly, hoping to find the proper documentation, but as the little man saw the contents within he felt a wave of confusion rise inside of him. The papers were in order but along with them was a thick stack of bills and two notes paper-clipped to the top. Wonderboy pulled the first note from the envelope and read it slowly, as was his way.

Receipt for the horses: $3200 Now deceased. Saddles to be left. Please advise on the mounts. Met many travelers - Please advise. Workers to explain. Ibrahim - Luleo - 4-14

Wonderboy read the note a second time and begged pardon of the men, leading them across the road and back down Tenpenny hill. When he reached the trailhead he found the saddles that the Bhotiyas had laid there. Even from a distance he could see the leather splattered with blood. He hauled one of the saddles up in his arms and they moved quickly down the road, the children watching with interest.

When he returned to the nurse's office Wonderboy took the Doctor by the shoulder, out of character, and pulled him to one side of the room. For once he wasn't smiling.

"Doctor I have a report to give."

"Go on, man."

"Someone killed the Pritchers."

Zuni stood in shock.

"I think the new ones saw them do it."

"Why, killed them? Why would anyone do that?"

"Don't know, Doctor. They couldn't say."

Doctor Zuni eyed the run-down looking party, searching from man to man. "Is it true?" he asked. "Did you see this?"

The men stared back at him blankly.

Zuni turned to Wonderboy. "Did they tell you this?"

"No. They had this saddle with them. They had this money with them and a letter." Wonderboy handed the Doctor the note, which he read quickly.

"Run fetch Padibatakal," the Doc said.

When Wonderboy hesitated the Doc told him, "She speaks their language, run get her."

Wonderboy hustled to the lots where he found Momma Tom and the girl praying over the foal. He grabbed Padibatakal in his arms and without saying a word he ran her back to the nurse's station. The doctor brushed back her hair and leaned in gently.

"Padi, how is your riding coming?"

She looked at the strange men. Each of them gave a passing glance at her feetless legs. She was ashamed that Sissy had kept her from learning to ride, but too considerate to speak ill of the woman in front of strangers.

"I'm excited for Jack to to get back," she said.

"We all are," he assured her. "That's part of why you're here. Do you know who these men are?"

"No sir."

"They're from Luleo. The west village. They are new workers on the hill."

She smiled at them.

"You speak their language, if I'm not mistaken."

The girl tensed up. Padibatakal hadn't spoken her first language since she was a child and the thought of those words brought on the thought of those years.

"I'm gonna have you ask them some questions and when they tell you the answers you have to promise to only tell them to me and Wonderboy. Do you understand?"

"What do I have to ask them?"

"I don't want you to worry. Jack, Tipper and Henry are fine. But these questions concern them and they may frighten you. Can you remember those old words well enough?"

She nodded. Even if it meant speaking a language that she hated, Padibatakal desperately wanted news of the travelers. "Can I tell the answers to Momma Tom?"

Doc Zuni knew it was no use asking the girl to keep anything from Momma Tom. The two did little but talk to one another.

"But only her," he said.

On the surgeon's table in the light of the doctor's lamp Wonderboy laid the saddle seat up, blood clear on the saddle horn. The Doctor leered at the leather through his glasses. "This is new since they left," he said looking at the bloodstain. He turned to Wonderboy, "What d'you think?"

The little man looked at the stain only once but was instantly certain of his answer. "Not a man's blood," he said.

"You sure?"

Wonderboy nodded.

Padibatakal looked curiously at the men, wondering why the Doctor would seek advice from the Wonderboy on such matters. The Doctor turned again to his translator.

"Ask them if they saw Tipper." The men looked down at the girl in surprise as she spoke to them. Immanuel smiled up at her, delighted by her sound. When she had asked her question the old one, Yigal, was the man to answer, "Yes they saw him," she said.

"Where?"

"The trees," Chhedup said, looking frightened.

"Were there two boys with him?"

"Yes, one of the boys was. . .," and he looked for help.

"Was what?"

Chhedup turned to the other men and began discussing the word he wanted. They gestured with their hands and spoke softly.

The Doc gave them some options which Padi repeated, "Loud? Rowdy? Funny? Quiet? Sweet? Gentle?"

The men watched her and waited, shaking their heads. "Tall, short?"

Finally Immanuel ran his hand across his body like he was scraping it, making a painful face.

"They were hurt?" The Doc asked.

"Yes," Chhedup told her, satisfied.

"What was wrong with them?"

The men then proceeded to indicate the injuries that Jack had sustained with a series of hand gestures, showing Jack as shorter and Henry as tall. Padibatakal was so nervous she could barely translate.

"Ask them where the blood came from," Zuni said.

She looked afraid. "What blood?"

Doc Zuni looked down at the girl with all of his compassion. "Padi, these men brought back the saddles of the Pritchers and we don't know why. One of the saddles, this one here, has blood on it. I don't want you to be afraid. But I need to know where the blood on the saddle came from."

She nodded and asked the men. They answered with solemn faces.

"From the horses," Padi said, a look of terror on her face.

"What else can they tell me?"

The girl nervously spit out question after question. Wonderboy and Zuni waited for the Bhotiyas to respond.

"There were four of them on horses," she said finally.

"Four of who?"

"Bad men."

"What kind of horses were they?"

"And one of them wore something on his face."

The Doctor looked sharply at Wonderboy. "What does Forsman look like?"

"Like any man, only big."

"Did he wear glasses?"

"No glasses," Wonderboy said.

"What was it on his face?" the Doc asked the girl. "Glasses?"

The Bhotiyas shook their heads.

"Not glasses," she told them.

"A mask?" asked the Doctor.

The Bhotiyas hesitated and shook their heads.

"No, not that. Something I don't know. A scarf maybe." Padibatakal reached out to grab Dr. Zuni's loose scarf from the coat rack, and wrapped it around her neck.

Again the Bhotiyas shook their heads.

"Not a mask, not a scarf. What else?" wondered the Doctor. "Have they tried to tell you?"

"They've tried. A 'priyote', they called it. I don't know what it means."

"Ask him again."

The girl expressed how important the man was and asked them again.

"Tell him to describe what it looked like," the Doc told her.

Finally Chhedup made a motion like he was wrapping something around his face. He did so feverishly and with great expression.

Wonderboy and the Doctor squinted at the man.

"Like a noose?"

"No. I don't know."

"'A covering,' he says."

"Like a mask?"

"No, it was *no* mask. They could see his face. 'His face was dark,' they say."

The Doctor shrugged. "Not Forsman."

"'His face was broken,' they say."

"Broken?" Suddenly the Doctor's face turned grave. Thoughts of Henry filled his mind. He reached across the table and grabbed an ace bandage. He unraveled it and wrapped it around his face.

"Was it this?" he asked them.

In unison the Bhotiyas nodded happily.

"A bandage," the Doc said, worry painted across his face. "Man took a beating. Had he been beaten?"

The Bhotiyas shuttered as they confirmed it.

"How did the others look? Were they all hurt?"

"They say one of them was."

They relayed the story to the little workman, who listened patiently and with great interest.

"Who killed the horses?" he asked.

The men faced each other.

"Was he a big man," Wonderboy asked "A very big man? Going old?"

They nodded excitedly.

"Was he the man in the 'priyote'?"

And every man said it was.

Now began a great fever on the hill, like nothing ever seen before. Wonderboy swung Padibatakal on his back and the Bhotiyas led him and the Doctor to the bottom of the hill where they confirmed the two remaining saddles, one with bloodstains across the stirrups.

"Where were they shot?" the Doc asked.

"'On their trail', he says."

"How far?"

"He says, 'Almost to the trees'."

"Did you cross any fences?"

"No, sir, they didn't."

"When did he kill them?"

"This morning. Late this morning. The sun was well up."

Wonderboy leaned in to Zuni. "Ask her where the horsemen came from."

"Which way did they come from?"

"They say, 'From the North'."

Wonderboy immediately went to work, gathering what he needed for his journey. Many times he had seen Tip act quickly in stressful situations, and each time the little man had been overwhelmed by how calm he remained.

But now Wonderboy was in just such a situation. He had no time to think. He grabbed a canteen and a bottle of oil for his lantern and rushed to the toolhouse.

When he arrived back at the lots Doc Zuni had the rifles ready and their calibers to match. He led two mounts out of the paddock.

"I'll try to get the village on the radio," Zuni said.

Wonderboy nodded. "Will they be listening?"

"I don't know."

It was then that Wonderboy noticed the mounts. One was rigged for riding and the other had only been haltered. Zuni watched as the little man paid close attention to the mounts.

"The Doctor will be staying?"

Zuni was standing on the line between bravery and shame. There was nothing in his life that he wanted more than to ride off on an adventure, but his age had made him conscientious. At first Doc Zuni seemed not to hear the question, his eyes drifting off. Then he answered, "Someone has to tend the children."

The words were tender but the moment was anything but. Wonderboy led the horses away from the lots, careful not to look too heavily upon the doctor, for fear that his gaze would shame him.

He wore a heavy expression. "Should we tell Miss Sissy?"

"Lord, No!" The Doctor barked. "Go! Ride!"

Padibatakal watched from the tabletop of the infirmary as the little man turned the mounts. She could clearly see that Wonderboy wasn't comfortable with horses. He mounted with haste but was awkward as he turned down the trail, leaning too far back in the saddle, his reigns held far too loosely. She wondered to herself what good it would do to send such a man on the journey. She couldn't imagine him finding the party in the woods.

The doctor hurried back up the hill and sat near the girl.

"If anyone asks you must tell them Wonderboy went off to hunt."

"What d'you think is happening out there?" she asked.

"Nothing they can't handle," he assured her.

But the girl didn't believe him. Padi didn't know who the bad men were, but anyone who would shoot a horse is evil, she thought. The thought of never being able to ride the Pritchers with Jack caused her heart to crack open.

She could hear Wonderboy cutting a path with the horses over the foothills and into the valley with great haste. Tip Holland is the man who saved my life, she thought, and Jack Oakham is the boy who will be the man who will love me. Try as she did the girl couldn't make peace with the idea that all was well, not with the little man riding off armed and hurried as he was.

Doc Zuni opened the envelope again, to give Ibrahim's note a second look. The girl watched as he read it and pondered every word. When he was finished Zuni pulled out the stack of bills and only then did he notice a second note, folded neatly and addressed to Greer in Jack's handwriting. Padi looked up at Zuni, a great confusion on her face.

"What's that for?" she asked.

But the Doctor was quick to step away. He didn't know what the letter was for but oh how he wished the girl hadn't seen it. He remembered Greer then, still in the back, the door cracked open and he stepped across the room to see her.

But even before he entered the room he knew what was coming, for he could hear her gentle sounds leaking through the cracked door.

When he entered Zuni was certain from the look on her face that she had heard every detail. She was shaking with fear at the foot of her bed. Her cries were not the ones of a fearful single mother but new tears, tears of young heartbreaking love. She feels for them after all, Zuni thought, as he watched the girl tremble.

12. On Their Heals

The campfire they discovered was a day old, but much fresher than the previous ones had been. A moose carcass, some roasting sticks and the bones of a brook trout were all that remained. But close by they spotted the tracks of four horses coming in from the west and seven leading out to the east.

"This was where they sold the mounts," Culpin suggested.

They ranged far that morning, sticking close to the river, and always their eyes were upstream. For hours they searched the sky for any plumes that may have drifted but all that morning there was nothing to suggest their quarry, save for a few shallow boot prints along the bank.

Soon they discovered that they were trailing two men instead of three, and now the dog was gone. Wade wanted to double back to find where the trail had forked, but Forsman wouldn't have it. One of the two boot prints they tracked was large and unmistakable, clearly that of the red top.

As they led their mounts through the forest in single file, their bodies were low against the saddlehorns. But when they arrived at a great bend in the river and peered over the bank their eyes widened and every man dismounted.

Frozen stiff in the shallow water was the carcass of the cub. He had a gaping wound near his spine and his backstraps had been stripped. They rolled him over and his cold entrails swayed in the current. The trout darted from their meal.

Soon they came to another sandbar where blood was splattered along the bank. A series of heavy footprints ranged up and down the river and surrounding them were bear tracks, adult and cub sized numbering a hundred or more.

"Looks like that bear killed someone," Danny suggested.

And at first glance Culpin agreed. The high sandbar showed boot scrapes along the wall and hand prints on the shelf. There were shreds of clothing near the water, more than enough to suggest a casualty. But for the moment Wade remained silent. If the bear had killed the boy on the river his body would still be there.

"Bears don't drag away their kills," he said.

They crossed the river and ranged throughout the forest, finding a small ash pile among the trees. The horses went into fits as they sniffed the pepper but soon they had arrived at the site of the spearing, where blood was still visible on the jagged rocks.

It was a hard hour through the timber. Forsman led the way as Culpin and Wade stuck close behind, still drinking in the saddle, but Danny stayed back, waiting for the worst.

Long before he reached the forest, Danny felt great distress over the fact that he hadn't stayed home, leaving the vengeance to his father and the others. Danny had never felt any love for Joe Forsman, though he had learned to endure him through the years. The great trick about the man, Danny always thought, was to never interrupt, to pretend to listen, and laugh at the end of every joke. As long as the man was of a mind to talk, Danny knew he could steer clear of his father's anger.

Of course to Danny's mind the only thing worse than his father talking all the time, was when his father wouldn't talk at all. It was a challenge the boy had never faced, and never intended to. But now they had been in the saddle for more than a full day and in all that time his father hadn't spoken a word to him.

Danny watched him as they rode, waiting for Forsman to glance back, even for an instant, but it never happened. He slowed his mount only to study the tracks and a few times a day Forsman would raise his canteen, only to have half of his desired ration spill from his mouth that was too swollen to close.

When his father did face him Danny had trouble recognizing the man. Forsman's eyes had glossed over, the whites now crimson, and his face was swollen and disfigured. But it wasn't the man's injuries that concerned Danny most. For the most part, those wounds will heal, he thought. It was the horrible silence that gave him pause.

The previous night Danny had tried to coax his father into conversation, but with no effect. The man sat alone in his thoughts. At one point for his own amusement Wade stood high on his saddle, testing to see how far he could make water. The other men watched as the horse bucked him and Wade was thrown with his pants around his ankles, covered in his own spray. As he collected himself Culpin and Danny laughed hysterically but Forsman didn't even turn to see what had caused the racket. He simply stared at the fire and when it died he kept staring until the others were sound asleep. His back was to them throughout the night.

Danny made his own fire away from his father's and the others spoke in a whisper as not to disturb him. In the morning Forsman was still there, wrapped in his blanket with his eyes small. When there was enough light he mounted and followed the tracks to the southwest. The others caught up to him at sunrise and Forsman hardly seemed to notice.

All his life Danny had known his father to be a drinker and a talker, and now the man seemed to be neither. When his father was drunk, Danny had always counted on the hours to cure any anger he had, but now that he was sober, Danny knew of no remedy for Forsman's rage. And it was rage, to be sure. The man was boiling silently just below the surface. The thought of following such a man into his violent revenge didn't sit well with the boy.

He was frightened by what lay in the forest, by the words of the old man, but he was more frightened by the men he rode with. He had no idea what would be asked of him if they *did* find the red top they were hunting, but whatever it was he wanted no part of it. He felt he deserved a chance to make a different path, in another place, away from such hard dealings. He began to scan the woods for a place where he could slip away unnoticed. But Danny knew his escape would have to come soon for with every hour they seemed to be gaining ground.

"How far ahead are they?" he asked, out of earshot of his father.

"Not more than a few miles now," Culpin said. "They're on foot. Tracks are fresher with every yard." Later Culpin added with a smile, "Looks to me your father is still cozy in his saddle. That boy got lucky is all. Took him for a blindside. For a while I was worried your father was over the hill, but he just got blindsided. But he's lost none of his fight, as we're about to see."

Danny looked distraught, "I'd hoped he would cool off after a awhile, but he hasn't."

"Why would you want *that?*" Wade asked. "That boy we're after robbed his face."

"I didn't forget."

"And gave you a slap or two from the looks."

"I'm no stranger to a slap."

"Well your father is," Culpin said. "Your father won't abide a cross look if he ever gets one. You could learn something from that kinda man."

"I figure I've learned all there is to learn," Danny said, feeling bold.

The men both eyed Danny curiously, hearing indignation in the boy's tone. Culpin was about to correct him but when he looked up the trail he stopped suddenly.

Forsman had pulled reign. His head was turned to the side, listening to the woodland. The other riders did the same, tilting forward across their mounts. They didn't know what they were listening for but they waited silently, poised for anything.

Ahead of them the trail was wide, cut by some unknown force. As they waited, a wild, hollow sound rolled in from the forest, repeating off the trees for all to hear. It grew with every note. Even as they waited the call was answered by a second, even fuller voice, and then another cry responding to the first. Soon the murmuring chatter was spread wide before them, not human sounds, but those of wild things in their wild speech. The riders listened as it rang from among the trees like a great chorus of unknown evil. Then instantly it grew quiet and all that remained was the sound of their breathing.

"The hell was that?" Danny asked, though not a man among them knew what they had heard.

"Dunno," Culpin admitted, his voice rattled. "Maybe they've spotted us and are havin' some fun."

"Those weren't human sounds," Wade told them. "No man made them. Whatever did there were plenty of."

But then their ears were drawn back to the forest. Through the wild calls came a whistling. Not that of a bird chirping, but a man's melody.

Forsman drew out his rifle. Through the thick forest he could see a blackened silhouette slipping in and out among the trees. One figure passed, then a second and a third. As they peered through the dimly lit branches the strange sounds were growing closer.

"Is it them?" Danny asked.

Before anyone could answer the shape of a man came walking up the trail. His hair was woolen and he was dressed in nothing but a pair of pantaloons, his feet bare, and from top to bottom he was like nothing they had ever seen. The horsemen gave the man little thought, however, for behind him, with their heads wagging, were a great host of bears, too many to count, walking the trail from shoulder to shoulder.

Instantly each of the horses began to buck violently and Danny was thrown. There was a general panic among the party, the horses skittering as they fought the reigns. Forsman wrapped his coat across the face of his mount and steadied her. Soon the others did the same. Danny's horse turned to flee and by sheer luck Culpin was able to catch the mare and bring her round but when she saw the line of bears on the trail she broke loose again and charged back through the forest. She had been a gift from Danny's only uncle, a brother to Forsman, twenty years his senior, and when she fled into the forest she was never seen again by the party, nor by anyone at all, only the beasts of the west end and the wild trees that swallowed her. Her story was lost forever.

Danny scaled atop Wade's mount, and sat pale-faced at the rear. Papon cocked his head and faced the riders with little expression.

The riders, each one, looked down upon the scene in disbelief.

"The hell is this?" Culpin said.

"Hell itself!" Wade suggested.

Many of the bears were standing on their haunches, talking to one another with their wild voices. A pair even brushed against their master when they rocked.

Culpin said, "I mean the hell is this place? I'm dreaming or drunker'n I thought."

"Whatever it is," Wade answered. "I'd say it's *his*. Doesn't look to be a man who just turns around."

Culpin could see that his partner was right. Nothing about the man seemed to shy from four armed riders.

"Mister, who the hell are you?"

Papon kept his hands at his sides. The bears had their ears back but none of them moved.

"Speak up, man!"

Papon spoke slowly, whistling to the bears between words.

"Take your fire go," he told them.

None of the riders could find a word to speak. They kept their rifles on him.

"To save for you," he said at the end of a whistle. "To save, I say. Take fire go."

Culpin and Wade glanced at each other. Forsman at least understood what the man had meant. He edged his mount forward two steps and when he did the bears tightened around Papon.

"They're protecting him," he told the riders, though they could barely understand. "They'll charge if we provoke."

It was an easy thing to believe. The lead pair, both black bears, were now pacing back and forth before the man, their eyes locked on the party. Papon smiled and whistled.

"I ain't getting tossed to a team of smokies!" Wade told them. "Any more and I'm ridin on!"

Forsman could see that the situation was impossible. The trail was filled with bears and there could be no negotiation, and no force could let them pass. The very thought of threatening the strange little man seemed ludicrous.

"Get on," he ordered, and the riders turned into the woods.

Of course getting on was easier said than done. Away to the west, as far as he could see were blackened nets of vines and trees, stretching out from one to another. The horses were more than willing to flee, but the low growth slapped them as they picked through the thicket. The forest was reluctant to make passage as the men dismounted and led their horses through.

In that way they traveled for over a mile, all the while at the ready for some other strange sport to find them in the forest. Forsman knew they could easily wander for hours in such a place. The groves were black and endless and nearly impassable. But just as they felt they would never be set loose the sun fired down and they broke into a rolling grassland. The horsemen squinted and crossed the meadow with their rifles up. Trails threaded out across the open country. The tracks of the two boys were clearly marked in the muddy path, as were those of countless bears, old and new ranging across the meadow.

The riders followed the tracks to a cabin with thatched roofing. They raised their rifles, believing the party to be inside, but soon saw more prints leading away to the west.

Wade and Culpin searched the cabin with their guns drawn, rifling through what food they could find. A child looked on from the hallway.

It was a crisp, fine day in the meadow, with the sun glowing around them, but Danny felt anything but fine as he sat beside his father. He guessed he might throw up his breakfast if they went on any further. He knew the party couldn't be far ahead now, as they were still afoot, and he measured they would come upon them before sundown, if not sooner, and the thought made his stomach turn.

"What do you intend to do?" Danny said finally to his father, feeling brave.

Forsman had taken off his hat and was retying his dressing. He ignored his son and patted his horse's flank with his boot.

"These men will be missed," Danny suggested. "And you'll answer for 'em missing. The old man and those Alchos have seen you, and now that other one. These men out here came from somewhere and will go somewhere and you can't know who'll listen. And you ain't done nothing yet."

Danny couldn't believe his own words. It was the bravest moment of his life. "So far you ain't done nothing at all. 'Cept stare down all those bears back there and live to tell about it. There's no shame in that."

Forsman cinched his jaw down and pulled his hat tight atop his head. He turned back to Danny and rested on the saddle horn. "My only shame is you."

Danny didn't look at his father anymore. He tried not to think of anything save the grass that swayed around him and the new spring that awaited him back on the Cutshank.

Wade come onto the porch "There are kids inside," he said. "That bear tamer's. You should've seen those angry little eyes."

"They say anything?" Danny asked.

"Nope. But they wanted to."

When they were mounted Forsman followed the tracks of three men leading west that weren't yet dried in the sun. The path through the tall grass cut like a vein and he kicked his stud into a gallop. But as they turned west to leave the meadow they were each surprised to see an enormous bear appear from the east woods and race across the clearing. She had two cubs trailing behind her, and a heavy limp in her gait and it was the largest bear any of the men had ever seen. Each of the riders raised their barrels but in an instant she covered the whole of the meadow, showing no interest in the riders, and disappeared into the folds of the western trees.

Each of them lowered their barrels. The bear's path was the same one they were trailing. Curiously they turned in behind her and followed the bear, setting out across the sunlit meadow where the tracks were fresh and clear. Danny shuttered at the thought that they didn't know what would be coming. Now that he was sharing his horse his hopes of escaping had been thwarted.

They rode at a quicker clip than they had since they'd started. They rode until the forest grew so thick that they had to dismount again and lead the horses on foot. They traveled the most dense woodland any of them had seen, and the trail wound and snaked through the walls of blackened trees. They rode across middens and moldering logs, and down a dark path that swelled and receded, always with eyes to the trail. For some while there was nothing, just the sound of hooves on cold wet earth. But as they passed a mighty tamarack, blackened in the shade of the woodland, an echo sounded through the darkness.

Forsman dismounted, distancing himself from his horse's breathing.

"D'you hear that?" Culpin said to the others.

"What?"

He waited. "Gunfire."

The men paused to listen and in that moment came the second shot, a muffled report, not a mile deep.

Forsman turned to address them. Danny shied away at the sight of his face. "It'll happen within the hour," he said. "Stay close and not another man takes a drink. Danny, kill that dog when you see it. None of you bat a lash."

"Do we shoot if they shoot?" Wade asked.

Forsman turned his mount and checked his rifle, "They won't shoot." he decided, and led them further in.

13. A Dark Chase Needs a Silent Hound

There were only three times in Jack Oakham's life when he was covered in blood. The second time came while he was carrying the worst man he'd ever met to safety through the streets of Riyadh, years later, and the third is too horrible to mention. But the first came that afternoon, as the party was picking its way through the thickets along the river.

It had begun just after lunch as Tip was scrubbing their pan of the beaver fat from the steaks they had eaten. They had started early, covering a wide spread of country, stopping neither to rest or to eat until nooning. Tip was clearly pleased with their progress. With any luck they would come to the end of the forest by nightfall, having crossed the dense black woodland with only minor injuries.

"How much further until we break out of this madness?" Henry asked.

"Not but a bit. Soon the trees begin to red and the forest turns into groves and we're set free. As you can see the trees are already changing."

The three spread their hands out before the fire; Henry closed his eyes and carefully set his knee to the ground and then braced himself as he sat. His wounds were tender from the fight with the cub but he didn't want his father to notice. In the days of trekking across the soft turf his feet too had grown blistery and tender, giving him an excuse for wincing if his father took notice.

"We break free of the forest," Henry said. "Then what?"

Tip took a small piece of wood from the fire and lit his tobacco with the burning end. He puffed a few times before tossing the flaming stick onto the embers. "I don't think you like adventure," he said to Henry. "No. I'm certain it's not for you."

"Cattlepatties! There's me and there's you. And you're an old lady! Pass me your canteen."

As Tip handed his son the screwtop he said, "Then enjoy not knowing. This trip is a long time comin' and there are many surprises yet to be had. Don't ask too many questions, unless they pertain to the nature of men. In fact any topic of discussion is open except the ones in the proximity of 'Where are we going?' he said in a whiny voice. "Or, 'How much further, Daddy?' or 'Where's my diaper, I need a wet wipe?'"

"Do that again," Henry said.

"What?"

"That face. Make that face and do that pathetic thing with your hands like you're an infant who doesn't get his way."

"It's an impression of you."

"It's a good one. I wish you'd do it again. Here's a question. Why don't they make adultery illegal?"

"They did," Tip said. " 'Scarlet Letter', which you read as I recall."

"But why'd they change the law?"

"Because of church and state. Marriage is God's institution. Not the country's. Now the government won't interfere."

Henry nodded. "Unkay. What's the best way to gain a friend's trust?"

"Be vulnerable. Ask their advice about something important. The act of asking will bond them to you immediately."

"Why does love die?"

"It doesn't. Love isn't an emotion like anger or sadness that fades or changes with time. Love is a choice. You get up in the morning and you choose to love. Every single day. Emotions don't last sixty years. But love can."

Henry rocked in his seat. It was rare that someone answered hard questions as fast as he could ask them. He enjoyed it. He licked his fingers of the beaver blood and wiped them on his trousers, "Who was smarter," he wondered, "Einstein or Shakespeare? And why?"

Before he answered Tip puffed his little antler pipe.

The old bear kept her nose down. Some of the footprints were still deep in the turf. As soon as she could smell the fire and the warm meats, she knew she must be close. She followed the scent through the sedge-plants that cluttered the forest floor.

At normal speeds a sow with her cubs can travel six miles in a day. In the long hours since her cub had gone missing this old bear had covered nearly twice that. The evening before she found the carcass of her cub in the sandbar and the scent trail continued upriver. By that time her remaining cubs were too exhausted to hunt and had chewed on the flesh of their dead brother when they found him. Esperanza growled at them and they hurried along. Whatever had killed the cub had been smart to cross the stream for it took a long time for her to find the trail again.

She moved through the heavy trees for hours, stopping only to nurse her young. At one point she heard strange sounds in the deep wood, high in the trees, but decided not to follow them.

Instead she stuck to the bank where she found the trail scent and followed it up river. There she caught wind of a pungent odor and her nose was filled with a violent scent. All three of the bears walked in fits trying to shake it.

She crossed the river and moved back and forth, frantically searching in the moonlight. The long winter rest had taken much of her strength and she couldn't continue through the night. She fell in slumber between two fallen logs and her cubs didn't wake every few hours as they were accustomed to doing. They slept hard, motionless sleep.

The next morning she roused them and their pace took them quickly through the black forest. She trekked for hours that morning, finding no sign, and almost gave up the hunt when footprints appeared on the trail, seen even by the cubs, and they each could smell the constant scent of meats and spices, and dried blood filling the air.

When Esperanza arrived at the wide meadow she crossed the pasture traveling at great speed, and charged back into the woodland on the heals of her quarry. The tracks of the creature she was trailing soon merged with two other walkers of equal size and one wolf with light feet. Soon she discovered a patch of wet earth pungent with the smell of her prey and great ferns still dripping.

She trailed them through the heavy green ferns that shook as she passed them. She trailed them through the understory that sprouted thick on the forest's west end. She trailed them until she could smell the chocolate boiling on the fire and could hear the old one talking. There were three of them she could see. As she kept watch she lowered her head again, her mouth frothing, her ears back, and dug her claws into the crumbled bark at her feet.

The hot chocolate was warm inside the kettle. The old dog was sleeping. Tip had his pipe tight in his mouth, and as he spoke, the tobacco bowl bobbed up and down.

"That's a good one," Tip assured him. "I tend to think that relativity would have been discovered regardless of Einstein. But Shakespeare's gifts could only come from Shakespeare. But maybe that's no judge of genius."

Jack leaned forward, not to warm himself, but to be nearer to those he loved. That was the most important thing. He ran his hand along the dog's back, took a sip of his cocoa and wiped his eyes.

There was a strange silence then, like something was coming. It filled the woods. Even the fire seemed silent as Jack leaned into it, the steam of his cocoa rising before his face. Henry and Tip knew that Jack had something to say. Anytime young Oakham leaned forward as the quiet settled in, it was clear to everyone that his heart was heavy.

"There's something I'd like to know," Jack said.

Henry and Tip shared the moment. There was something tender and honest about Jack that neither one of them could ever duplicate. Henry continued to admire it for years to come.

"I'll do my best."

Jack took a long, cool breath. And when Jack spoke, Henry rested his eyes on the embers.

"A lot of children born with nothin', and I get this," Jack said. "I get to swing round like a monkey and do flips in the air and we hunt and we fish and there's never any worry. 'Want to learn something new?', you say. 'Take your pick, and I'll teach you.' And so we box, and we read, and we're heroes to children, and we sharpen against each other, and you teach us the disciplines. You teach us the things only a few men know. Before long the world has become like some ongoing playground. We live like kings, claiming the mountains we find. And now adults look to us as men. Misers in the woods know us by reputation. You decide one morning that it's time, so you roll out of bed and you present us with a journey, a chance for adventure. No one goes on adventures anymore, but we think nothing of it. We saddle up and follow. We follow you because you've claimed us as your own. Because long ago you buried a treasure in the west, and of all the world's children you've picked the two of us to find it. And all the while a question waits to be answered. My heart goes out to a girl on the hill and sometimes when I look at her that question comes up. Momma Tom sits with me over chess, and the kings and queens ask it again. I feel that I've been ungrateful. I haven't thanked you," Jack said. "So I'm thanking you, and at the same time I'm asking you."

Tip took a long puff on the pipe and waited, for the moment was made for waiting. "What exactly," he said.

Young Oakham looked long at his brother, until it seemed that they were both asking. And when he said it, he said it grateful, "Why us?"

Esperanza crept silently over the forest nettles and was just beginning her charge when Tip, still smoking, brought up his rifle and shot her through the mouth. Her head shook so heavily from the force of the bullet that she sagged back onto her haunches.

Henry was so amazed by what he saw that he stood, upright for all to see, and didn't reach for his weapon or look for cover. He stood, facing down the heavy bear, in awe.

Jack backpeddled a few paces. He knocked his arrow to his bow. He was several feet away from Tip now. Out of the corner of his eye he saw his father with the rifle up, waiting for the bear to spring out again.

Only her eyes were visible over the fan plants as she charged a second time. The ferns snapped, shaking droplets from the broad leaves as she tore through the brush, her heavy body rumbling towards them.

A feeling arrived. A horrible, beautiful feeling. One of those reasons to breathe. A moment Tip would forever keep on file.

"It was one of those razor-sharp sensations, boys," he would later say. "Like the first time you ever slice yourself open with a kitchen knife, or see a woman naked."

Tip Holland, that boiling hot blend of good and evil fired on impulse. "And I got lucky," he later said.

The crack of the big rifle could be heard across the forest, but to the Tenpenny Three is was an echo, faded and faraway. Time stopped as Tip squeezed the trigger. All the smells and shapes of the Wild West End seemed to swell before them. Everything was closer than ever, and at the same time, farther and farther away. The bear was just a few feet from them and when the crack came the smoke puffed from the barrel, reaching out to touch the great bear.

They couldn't see where the bullet had entered, but all three of them were certain that it had. The bear's head had jolted and with a moan steam rose out of her nostrils.

Some men are never good when it counts. They practice well, they make fine coaches, and their words are what they are known for. Yet when the solid stuff of life comes their way, their words fall short, they back-peddle and re-evaluate, instead of remaining calm, taking careful aim and putting a hole right where they want it to go.

The bullet sliced between the bear's nostrils, cutting a path through her sinuses and up into the bridge of her nose. A flash of white heat burned behind the great bear's eyes and like a blinding light the pain shot through her and she let out a moan as smoke drifted from the wound.

The bear continued to run but the bullet had turned her in a new direction, her shoulder brushing Tip's elbow. She could feel her mouth filling with warm blood and her throat clogging as she charged haphazardly into the forest.

There were two quick barks from the dog and something sharp slid deep into her hind leg. She had lost her sense of smell and her eyes were boiling. The bullet had divided her nose and ran along the bridge, slowing to a stop on the hard shell between her eyes. They were swelling with fluid. The first shot had cut through her jaw and her wide pink tongue was severed, flopping from her mouth. She swallowed blood as she ran. Twice she had crashed into standing trees.

By now both brothers had their bows up and had gathered near the fire. Jack was knocking a second arrow. A crash was heard as the bear stumbled through the thicket. Tip reloaded his rifle and looked his sons over. All three of the party members were breathing heavily and both boys looked on their father in a new way. There was a silent understanding. Like life had just paid them a special visit. The distant sounds of the dying bear could be heard galloping through the forest. A sigh of relief was breathed by all.

That should have been the end of the episode. Esperanza was blinded. She wouldn't return. The bullet that had entered through her mouth was now crushed against the back of her throat and the bleeding was heavy. The lucky arrow had cut an artery in the hind leg. Within hours the wounds would have killed her.

So if Putt hadn't intervened that would have been the end of it. But the old dog, who had been hard asleep during the charge, had caught wind of the bear and when she stumbled through the fan plants Putt charged after her, sniffing the blood trail as he ran. In a moment the dog slipped through the thick ferns in her direction and his light colors disappeared into the brush.

"Get back!" Jack called.

Henry and Tip turned, watching as the old dog vanished into the forest.

What happened next filled only a few moments in time. Tip fetched a box of bullets and the first aid kit from his pack. Jack and Henry grabbed their quivers and were already running through the woods when their father started after him.

He leapt over the small campfire and followed the path of swaying ferns. The blood was splattered across the greenery and he trailed the bright colors as he ran. The brothers charged through the foliage, leaping over the small turf humps and ducking the boughs that dipped along the path. Jack was in the lead, sweating for the first time in weeks. He kept his bow tight to his body and his quiver ready. They could still hear the distant snap of breaking branches and the faraway rustle of leaves and nettles but the ferns had stopped swaying. There was no sign of movement across the forest. They listened to the baying of the Malamute as they ran and followed through the heavy brush.

In a deep, dark place of the forest Henry caught a glimpse of something hanging from a nub on an old pine. It was evidence that someone had once been there, ages ago. What appeared to be letters etched in the trunk and a long belt of rusted bullets and a sword in its scabbard all hung in plain sight. He saw the treasures only for a moment as they charged through the wood but they were unmistakable. He cursed his judgement for not retrieving the items the moment he saw them and reading whatever clue had been etched upon the tree, but in all fairness those were not to be his adventures. Those belonged to other boys of Tenpenny, even stronger and wiser than Henry and Jack, and they would come for other reasons, and find not only those treasures but many more across the world. But theirs is another story altogether.

They came to an open patch in the forest that was shaded so completely that they couldn't see any blood. The sounds had died down in the distance. They huffed as they searched the ground for sign.

Tip caught up to them and the three breathed heavily as they scanned the turf.

"She'll kill him," Henry said.

Tip knelt down over the earth and scooted along. He thumbed two small branches that had snapped.

Jack watched his father, then looked off into the thick. "Maybe she's already dead."

But then Tip saw what he was looking for and stood quickly, starting for the trees. His breath had come back to him and he had his rifle raised. "She isn't dead," he said softly as he moved through the ferns.

Jack started for the woods, "How do you know?"

Tip ran with his rifle ready, following the trail. "Because I do," he said. "If we don't kill her, she'll kill him."

Jack and Henry followed, their eyes on their father, until they felt a shudder run down their backs. They could hear the dog baying at the bear, deep in the forest.

14. A Dowry for Mary Mdingwe

By Henry Snow

When Koba Shenzi was a child he was given the nickname "ugalo", which means "teeth", by the old ones because he was always smiling. He communicated with his eyes and his hands and smiled as if it was the only face he had. But if asked, no one could remember a word he had spoken in his first eleven years.

He moved about the village sharing his smile with everyone. He smiled to the animals that roamed the great plains, and to the sun and the moon. He listened to talk of the rains, he learned the life of the bloodletters, and smiled as he fell asleep and smiled when someone woke him. Koba Shenzi's smile seemed to be enough to get him by, for he kept his thoughts to himself. He preferred to listen to the words of others, to the stories and the laughter. It never occurred to him to share his thoughts with anyone until one day he was overcome with the need to speak and he immediately approached the village elder.

A young girl named Mary Mdingwe lived in an indlu a few down from his own. She was a round-faced girl, not a beauty, with big eyes and a tooth that protruded from her lips. She had an amiable, tender disposition that lent great weight to the attraction. But more than anything when Koba Shenzi smiled, Mary Mdingwe smiled back.

He approached the elder, gently caressed the man's hand, his eyes serious, his smile sure, and said, "I wish to marry your daughter."

The elder Mdingwe told him, containing a smirk, "You must have a dowry."

"Ndugu?"

"When you have a worthy gift you may ask again."

Without another word Koba Shenzi left the elder and went to collect dried dung for the afternoon fires. He gathered water at the shallow well and ate among his brothers and for days he was deep in thought. Despite his life of silence, if one had watched him, the way he moved and breathed and stared, one would have felt the torment in his heart. After much deliberation he concluded that he had no suitable offering to give. A child may not own livestock unless ill-fortune befalls his father and he had no wives to trade, for it was a wife he was after. Such was the quandary of his romantic expectations.

He reasoned that in time he would be granted his own cattle and could begin trading for huts and hides. Yet before long Koba Shenzi reasoned any suitable barter for such a wife would take years to accumulate. The men of his village married women much younger than themselves, and Koba Shenzi knew she would be betrothed and wedded long before he was able to amass such collateral. The slow fire that love burns in the belly of the young was cooling in the breeze of tradition.

About that time, a traveling band of adventurers arrived after several days of trekking through the featherhead. They were thirsty and had been following a wounded tsessebe for a full day. Koba Shenzi ignored them. Such men often appeared out of the hills and always they were taking lives.

Despite his own disinterest the villagers welcomed them. "We need food," they said.

The band of drifters ate all of the food the villagers offered and slept in the huts that had been built for such guests.

Koba Shenzi sat awake near the boma, looking up at the stars. He had never been taught how to pray, for it was not a trade his people practiced, but as he sat in the sand with his legs bent tightly against his chest, his body warming by the dungfire, he said softly, but clearly to the maker of the stars, "Might I have her?"

That evening a strange winter rain fell upon the land. The villagers scrambled to collect the dung and keep it dry. No one could remember such a downpour in the dry season. The following morning when the band of hunting men awoke they set out after their wounded tsessebe but found no sign. The tracks had been washed away.

Jobé, the tracker, gave up the trail after half a day and the troupe returned to the village empty-handed. They slept in the huts that the villagers opened for them. The boy looked at their wristwatches and their great trunks and their fine heavy clothing and almost at once his destiny became like a mesmerizing song of assurance. These were the men that would grant him answers.

In the night Koba Shenzi found a faint trail in the dark where he had seen the old tracker searching. He was able to pick up the trail immediately, following it through the thorn lands and the winding hills with ease, something he had been able to do ever since he was a small child.

If Koba Shenzi were ever to be questioned regarding his ability to follow a quarry across open country, his silence would not have been what prevented him from explaining. Truth was he never understood it himself. The genius is the man that can do without training or effort the things most men cannot do with a lifetime of both.

In the morning the boy returned with the tsessebe's tongue.

The traveling men demanded an explanation. No one blamed Jobé for abandoning the search. How can a tracker do his job without a trail to follow? And it was that very question they asked themselves as they watched young Koba Shenzi move quickly from grassy patch to loose stone to the still-fresh carcass of the tsessebe, not two kilometers from the village. The whites congratulated him with handshakes and spirits. The head white, the Kitzi Waitzi, hired him immediately.

Koba Shenzi was led by the band of hunting men out of his village and, although she never turned to look, he waved at young Mary Mdingwe, and whispered soft promises across the herringbone.

The safari troupe was made up of a variety of castabouts from all corners of the globe. One must be a bit crazy or estranged to live the life of a land pirate and once living it one becomes even more so. They roam for days on end, and bring back meats and marula fruits so the cooks would prepare them and the whites would rejoice. All three of the women were fat in a land filled with slim figures. They danced and talked about their husbands and laughed about their husband's wives and bathed in the clear pool near the camp and ate throughout the day.

The head man was the Kitzi Waitzi. He owned the company. The Kitzi Waitzi kept the hunters happy. He was in charge of paying the cooks and the professional hunters and the gunbearers and the skinners and the trackers and making certain everyone did their job. He was an enormous bearded man, consumptive and overjoyed. He smoked even as he ate and had to crawl out of bed three times a night to puff two cigarettes in a row, before he could fall back asleep. In the midst of the bloody business he was above all things a gentleman.

"Peace is not the absence of something," he told the cooks. "It is the presence of something."

"What though?" they wondered.

"Could be as simple as love."

The gunbearer carried the guns and caped out the kills and if there were any grasses obstructing the view of the dead animal for a photograph he hacked it down with his long bladed panga. His name was Metinga. He had three wives and nine children and the whites kidded him because he had once been given a long coat by one of the hunters and the first night he wore it he stood too close to the fire and it burned up the back. Metinga still wore the coat with the edges black. When they kidded him he danced around to show off the burn scars and he smiled, revealing a mouth of golden teeth.

The professional hunter's name was Paul Lawrence Day. His duty was to guide the whites across the land. Paul Lawrence Day had lived and worked in the southern half of the continent since his wife left him fifteen years earlier. He smoked Stuyvesant cigarettes continually throughout the day, stopping only to eat. He spoke with joy of his University days, of how he and his mates had eaten mushrooms until their heads started dancing and how they watched Smurf reruns and served one another Five Roses tea. He had once been a promising litigator and a brilliant chemist and swore to Metinga that someday he would take him back to Cork and they would be done with the killing.

"It's green and your wives will grow fat and happy and I will teach you cribbage."

For years these safarimen had traveled across the plains seeking adventures. They had known the Masai well and roamed alongside them. They had known Swedish trackers and Zulu trackers and trackers with no tribes at all, bushmen beholden to the land, but never had they seen a one such as Koba Shenzi. He moved nearly twice as fast as men with a lifetime of experience, and never with the need to double back. For two weeks Paul Lawrence Day bet against him and lost every time. The Kitzi Waitzi was becoming a wealthy man. Within two years the boy was as trusted as any member of the traveling family.

In those years Koba Shenzi witnessed every caliber of man, saw the great divisions. He was there when lightning struck a giraffe and he watched as her daughter circled the dead mother in the rain. He was there when the band of lions devoured a newborn elephant as it burst from the womb. He watched Paul Lawrence Day shoot that bloody newborn to shorten a life made only of bad memories. He stared down the mambas and followed hippos across swamplands. He carried the burden of tusks and hides, of more death than life.

He watched Metinga, who was terrified of snakes and evil spirits, fall into convulsions as Paul Lawrence Day jumped out of the brush with his hands and face painted glow-in-the-dark colors and as the Kitzi Waitzi dropped a dead python on him from a tree. You could have lit your way home with Koba Shenzi's smile that night.

He met wealthy eccentrics from all over the world, some of whom, it seemed, desired to watch him track as much as they desired blood.

Through his first year as an apprentice Koba Shenzi took up many trails that Jobé had abandoned. Each time he returned with a smile. Though Jobé was envious, he loved the boy too much to complain. He was old and his eyes were fading and his knees didn't like the long walks. He had been chasing death across his country for thirty years and the boy was better. He had always wanted to go back to where he was happiest, as a child. Perhaps he could still find a wife or two, barren or not. At the end of the season Jobé went back to the forest to be with his brothers.

Before anyone knew it, the boy began to grow, thickened muscles swelled like ropes beneath his skin.

"He'll be the greatest of the Zulu trackers," Paul Lawrence Day said, counting his money. "He's a fine boy! Cheers! A wonderboy! Call him Wonderboy, Metinga! He'll be our ticket home!"

"To Wonderboy!"

Metinga and Paul Lawrence Day drank to him often. They would sit beside the fire at night and sing endless rambling songs of the hunts. To Wonderboy the songs were like their days, aimless and unpredictable. He liked the life he had found, but a greater part of him missed the life of the village, the old men, the calm days. He thought often of Mary Mdingwe.

Wonderboy's fame grew wildly in his third year. When he saved the life of a surgeon his boyish physique made his heroism even more remarkable.

They had been hunting for twelve days when the surgeon shot the buffalo near the chimcherinchee. Metinga and Paul Lawrence Day and the surgeon and Wonderboy all followed the big-hearted buffalo into the tall prairieland. Wonderboy was certain from the pulpy grasses dribbling out of the animal that the Buffalo was very much alive.

"Mhora mopeli."

The Professional Hunter looked at his gunbearer and both wore worried faces, "Wonderboy says he's gut shot."

Of all God's creatures it may be hard to find one with a more stubborn heart than a Cape Buffalo, especially with a bullet in his belly. Paul Lawrence Day instructed Metinga to give the Rettig rifle back to the surgeon and to fetch the two spare rifles from the jeep. When he returned the three men checked their loads and followed Wonderboy who moved cautiously toward the chimcherinchee.

Wonderboy didn't even bend at the waist to look at the prints he was following. Some said it was because his vision was so good that he didn't need to be any closer to see, and others thought he didn't really look at the tracks at all, but could envision the path the creature had taken like he was watching a reel of film playing just for him.

The grasses at the edge of the chimcherinchee were no higher than a tree stump so not even Wonderboy expected the animal to be hiding so close. When the buffalo charged out of the short grass the surgeon lifted his rifle and fired in a panic. He was standing behind the others. The first shot killed Metinga instantly. The surgeon fumbled with the bolt as the buffalo grew closer. The second shot came slower than the first but by now the big Cape was almost on them and the surgeon's hands were shaking, and when the bullet blew a hole through the lungs of Paul Lawrence Day, his fingers were trembling so violently that he dropped his rifle to the sand. The buffalo gored the surgeon, his bladder torn. His body was tossed and dragged across the earth.

Wonderboy obtained the white man's rifle, and after discerning how it functioned, killed the buffalo with a bullet through his brain. It took him some time to learn how to operate the jeep but he soon steered his way across the featherhead, moving the gearshift as he had seen Paul Lawrence Day do for many years. One at a time he loaded the bodies into the seats and drove through his tears. When his dead friend Metinga fell out of the jeep on a sharp turn Wonderboy stopped and hauled him up again. Then he fastened him and Paul Lawrence Day and the surgeon tightly with their seatbelts. The surgeon survived in a coma and to my knowledge is still dreaming, I hope of things other than his cowardice.

Because the nature of safari and the nature of man are one, men will always take them, and always praise them, and always hope for one better than the last. As long as there are beasts to kill and fires to sit by, as long as some parts of the world aren't shielded by glass then men will find adventure, men will eat the fresh flesh of cats, will follow dark men into dark places with sweat soaking their open shirts, their lives heavy in their hands. For the franchise of living and dying has always been in business and wherever Wonderboy went, business was good.

Although his name was connected across the land with tales of tracking and adventure Wonderboy knew nothing of his fame. To him the world was a continual duplication of what he saw every day, more hills and genets, fruit bats and wild whites traveling across the plains in search of adventure. He had heard that there was a great mountain to the north with a cloud that clung to the top, but he didn't believe it. Mountains and fame were the white man's concern. His concern was for a woman.

One day a caravan stopped at camp and the Kitzi Waitzi gave each of the travelers frosted Windhoek beers. A young man among them, a shaggy drifter, shook the Kitzi Waitzi's hand.

"That's him?" the drifter asked, looking off at Wonderboy.

"That's him," the Waitzi said. "He's a good oke."

The drifter ate biltong and had deep set eyes and a quiet humility that the Waitzi liked. He was hired to replace Paul Lawrence Day.

"Do you smoke?" the Kitzi Waitzi asked as he offered him a cigarette.

"No," he answered.

The Kitzi Waitzi handed over the pack. "You better start."

Wonderboy worked alongside the young white for half a season. He had never known one like this before. The young man carried a tattered knapsack cluttered with old garments and several well-used books with faded pages and notes scattered throughout. At night by the fire the new man read by the flamelight and scribbled notes in the margins and kept a thick journal in his pantlegs that he marked in throughout the day. Somedays the young man drew sketches of the wild land and her inhabitants.

Wonderboy taught the white many things: lung blood and liver, the running step, the dying step. Before long the white was tracking across the plains. In return the young man instructed Wonderboy how to follow the tracks of the letters on the page, a difficult task, even for a tracker such as Wonderboy. Tip could sound out words from symbols on paper and soon enough so could the little Zulu tracker. Within weeks the white showed him how to use his Rolliflex camera to keep the memories alive on paper and was telling him the Gospel of Grace. Wonderboy greatly enjoyed them both.

Although their friendship was growing it was a hard season to endure. They traveled high into the mountains, their way hard and twisting through the canyons, the water cuttings, the great stone clefts. They spent evenings skinning and eating within scent of the viscera, their eyes dead on the night fire. They sang dark songs of ongoing prairie death to come, took bloodoaths, and painted their faces with the warm runnings. When they came after the spotted cats they would make no fires for weeks, eating dried biltong, and the smokers would suffer, and they would bury their scat beneath the sand and speak only of necessity and then only in a whisper.

The troupe moved like a pack of wild dogs, neither noble or sporting, laden with every needed instrument for long range killing, their vests fastened of homemade hides of aardwolf, hartebeast, their collars and hatbands adorned with claws and tusks, quills, feathers, their snakeskin belts heavy with thick-bored pistols, bone-helved skinners, black-bladed pangas, they wore greasy, oilcloth slickers and leggings hand-sewn with long strands of unknown hair, bone bracelets around their wrists and ankles, strange particolored tattoos across their hands and bodies, their clavicles bruised from the weight of cartridge belts filled with solids, their hearts dull to death quick or slow.

They pursued and overcame and pursued again. In the slack time between journeys their conversations halted as if when they had nothing to pursue they had nothing to say.

The game was varied and continuous. The kudu furied through the thorns like some grey devil apparition with their swords black and spiraling and laid down upon their backs as if a warning to their pursuers. They listened with their ridiculous ears, pink and enormous for the footfalls of the stalkers and their huge bodies seemed to hang, suspended on giant puppet stings as they made impossible leaps through the thistlelands. Zebra in the white sun seemed to shimmer and melt into the great plain like a breathing mirage, their swishing tail their only betrayal.

The killers splattered bushbabies when they emerged from their burrows and hung them and the dik-diks they had killed from the syringas and the tambotis for the cats to find and then they killed them too.

The eland moved like great migrating clouds across the grasses, the droop of their frontcoats slapping as they trundled. Oftentimes they would be lungstruck by the big bore rifles and go on for hours, only to be found and summarily brained by the professionals, their eyes spewing from their heads like corks.

Around the kills the natives would dip their hands into the warm pile of viscera, squeeze the pulp through the tubing, and eat it uncooked when it was washed.

On reaching lands end where the rock-bowled hilltops threaded out into slow, prehistoric dunes, the party made their final chase corralling the last of the trophy stock in the drinking nooks, clouding the small clear puddles of water with arterial blood and when they had finished carving the kills they cupped handfuls for themselves with their palms and slurped it despite the pink.

They hauled the stripped carcasses and saved the back meats for themselves and piled the naked cages moist and warm on the dry sand, salting the hides, packing them tightly around the skulls with the twin prizes protruding.

On mornings as they returned they would see like a blur the shapes of wild pack dogs fighting over the crinkled meats sun-drying and the dogs would come together to fend off the hyenas until the hyenas were too many in number and then they too would feast quickly until the lions came one at a time until their numbers became too great and they would hold until their bellies sagged and the vultures came last and stayed until the bones were suckled.

When they needed rest or a boma they traveled to the edge of their territory and stopped in native villages and shared biltong and bushveld fruits as an offering and the natives built great fires and danced around them and each other and they sang low rhythm hummings to gods and the moon and the rainmaker and always Wonderboy wondered of his home.

"You should go back to her," Tip told him. "If you stay out here this place will kill you or your heart will die and you will forget your cares. You should go back to her soon."

And Wonderboy whispered, "A tula bebe?" Which means "With what?"

Tipper knew that his heart was changing too. He no longer felt the glow of hope that Kolschen had given him. It saddened him that such joy could simmer so quickly. He longed to flee these wild men and return to his chosen path. But not without Wonderboy, he thought. Wonderboy had become the friend he was sent to find. Together they would leave. They would head south and be through with the hunts. Tipper's only thought through those long nights was how the two of them would break away. But there was no simple solution. Neither had enough money to go far and Wonderboy's heart was in his village. He would never leave without a dowry. Tipper pondered the problem and prayed that an answer would come.

Because old men were once young men whose appetites had grown, because fortunes and boredom allowed for wild undertakings, because life and death remain at the forefront of the human question, men beyond their prime are known to suit up for bold escapades, to answer the unanswered questions.

It's not important to use the man's name or even his title. This story isn't about that kind of power. It's enough to say that in the winter of Wonderboy's nineteenth year, after he had served the Kitzi Waitzi for seven years, a tremendously famous and untrustworthy leader of the world came across the lands between to have one last adventure.

Wonderboy had no knowledge of the man, nor could he comprehend the impact of his actions. But Tip kept his eyes keen on the old, short official, eyeing him nervously. The man seemed normal enough to Wonderboy, even a little more. Most of the whites that he worked for had the gunbearers carry their rifles. They dressed like soldiers with their boots shiny and their earthtone shirts and matching hats. This man was old but one could see that he had been a great lion himself once, and there was no doubt that in his mind he still was.

It took only two days to harvest the leopard. The old man blew a hole through her backbone and the cat fell from the tree. They spent the next days stalking the buffalo, then the lion. He wanted a hyena and a baboon for his collection.

"You want a baboon?" the Kitzi Waitzi asked.

"That's right. ."

Tip spoke up, being brave, "What for?"

"I'm gonna mount him sitting down with his hands up above his head and his palms facing each other and I'll set him in my bathroom and I'll put a roll of toilet paper between his palms."

The big five were taken within two weeks. The old man shot well. Each of the animals fell instantly except for the lion that dragged himself into the thick so there was no tracking for Wonderboy to do. The elephant was out in the open when the bullet found him and although he ran wildly everyone except the Kitzi Waitzi had eyes strong enough to see the land whale in the shadows of the boabab where he fell.

"Maybe I'll shoot the next one through the kidneys and give you a chance to prove yourself," the old hunter said to Wonderboy. To which the little tracker answered with a smile.

On the last day they hiked through the black monkey thorn after the kudu and the hiking was hard. Black monkey thorns are shaped like fish hooks and they hide among the harmless leaves of the flowering shrubs. The hunter's trousers were torn around his bloody knees.

Wonderboy stopped suddenly and pointed off at the valley. "Kudu."

The Kitzi Waitzi, the old hunter and Tip all looked across the thick basin with their glasses up to their eyes. "I don't see it, Wonderboy."

Again the tracker pointed, "Uwalo," he said.

"Ear," Tip told the hunter.

"Ear?"

"That's right. Wonderboy sees an ear."

The little man pointed for the hunter, lining up his child fingers until the old man glassed the fat ear, a half mile away. With glasses down, "Kudu," he said, clearly impressed.

They stalked the animal an hour through the num nums and the koeleria, rolling their pant legs up as to not let the black monkey thorns catch the fabric. "If the bushes shake he'll see us coming," said the Waitzi.

They moved as one through the cruel thicket and each of their legs were bleeding. When they came to the crest they spotted the kudu again and as the hunter lifted his rifle, his last trophy, that wild, elusive lord of all antelope laid his horns back and fled through the brush. As the big bull turned in a gallop the faces of the hunting troupe all went limp as the kudu jumped through the thornlands, but then, quite unexpected, the loud crack of the gunshot came like a thunderclap. Each of the men ducked and threw razor-sharp stares at the old hunter. Before the Waitzi confronted him the man said with confidence, "I got him."

Wonderboy found the patch of sand where the kudu had stumbled and there were three tiny drops of blood visible on the trail. The troupe followed the tracks which were clear for all to see, across Doornlaagte, through the false barley grass, but no more blood was found.

After some time the tracks merged with the prints of forty other kudu, who had each cut across the valley that day. Wonderboy examined the ground as he moved quickly across the valley, staying only with the single kudu he had been tracking. When the old man saw that they were standing among a field of tracks, each identical to the one beside it, he asked the Waitzi, "How can he tell one track from another?"

Tip spread a cocky smile across his face and asked Wonderboy, "Kolebe kudu kulumane bul?"

Wonderboy answered as if the question annoyed him, "Uwayo mhora besi mbi mhora."

The Waitzi puffed his cigarette, "He says, 'The same way I know your face from the rich man's'."

A short time later the tracks split off in two directions. Only six of them turned to the south but Wonderboy turned with them. The old hunter doubted they were on the trail at all now, for they had not seen blood in several hours.

"How long will we follow him?"

"How long?" the Waitzi asked his tracker.

Wonderboy didn't stop to answer. He moved along at a steady clip across the valley, "Kudu mbi maral. Kudu kalo bom."

"Says he'll go off alone soon and die. Says his front legs are numbing."

The day was long and the old hunter shook his head. "Either he will or he won't," he said. "I already have my vote."

An hour later one of the kudu trails turned south and by that time the troupe had been following the bloodless tracks for almost a full day. The legs of the old man wobbled.

They were starving when they came to the edge of the great precipice. Their legs were pink from the blood that their sweat had washed away. But when he peered over the rim they could see Wonderboy's face rise with a smile. "Abalo kudu mimbe."

The Kitzi Waitizi couldn't remember a more difficult trail or a bigger kudu ever taken on the Doornlaagte. No doubt this tale would cause the boy's fame to grow even more. He could raise his rates again.

Wonderboy and Tip spent an hour carefully taking the kudu apart. The big animal was drenched in blood. When he was finished the boy's hands were dried with it and his little knife too. The old hunter approached Wonderboy.

He looked at his tracker briefly before removing a large knife from his belt. "Have a look at that," he said.

The old white handed his knife to Wonderboy, who looked it over. It was a spectacular piece. Wonderboy was not expected to appreciate the quality of such ornaments but over the years he had come to admire the workmanship required. He knew gold when he saw it and felt balance when it was placed in his hands and understood that it must have taken talented men to carve bone into such designs. His smile was genuine and his eyes wide as he handed the knife back to the white.

The old man slipped it into an ornate leather sheath and then wrapped it tightly in a canvas pouch. "This is yours," he said. "I've given it to you. The doctor you saved was a friend of mine. He owes me money, if he ever wakes up."

The face Wonderboy wore would best be described as terrified, a face no one had ever seen. He held the knife like a treasure in his arms, nodding blankly at the old man. Immediately he stepped across the sand and found his boss.

"Waitzi," he said looking at the ground. His smile was gone.

"Good work today."

"Ktsimi selebalo nkulumane mut," Wonderboy said shyly, showing the boss his new knife. "Andaza halanbangana choo, Mary sha bezi bon."

The safari man stood up straight. The dusk light was brilliant on his face and so is this man, the Kitzi Waitzi thought. This man is what I should have been. Of course the answer was yes.

He didn't know if he would ever see Wonderboy again and there was so much he thought to say later, when it was too late, when the boy was gone from him. But at that moment he said the only thing that came into his mind. Words he would later describe as absurd.

"Do you need any help?" he asked his tracker.

Wonderboy thanked him, "No."

"Alright, friend. Go well. We'll finish the kudu."

The little tracker didn't have to look to the horizon to find his bearings. He always knew his way. He shook Tipper's hand firmly but other than that he said no good-byes.

There was no sense in building on what wasn't there. What made sense was toward the sunset and he would find it as fast as he could.

The old safari man watched a long time, so long that the moment seemed to infect the rest of the troupe with the stillness of important air. So long that they all stood beside him to see the little child warrior, with nothing but the knife in his belt, set out across the Doornlaagte, through the chimcherinchee where the leopards lived, across the cooling sands that had the prints of the big paws, and into the empty, deadly, unsentimental places where only fools go walking.

"Where's he going?" the old official asked.

"Do you know what you just did?"

"I gave the boy a knife."

"No. You changed his life."

"I did?"

The Waitzi passed the flame from one cigarette to another. "In a few days when he reaches his village that knife will become a dowry for his bride. If she's still there after all these years."

Tip could see beyond the milkwoods the shape of the little Zulu tracker moving along at a steady clip. The plovers stirred from their day-time drinking as the tracker faded. The dusk was coming on and the long shadows fell across the flat-flowered aloe and the sandy breaks.

The old official had the look of a boy discovering his own strength. "And just like that?"

"Just like that. Changed his life forever."

In the pink of the dusk they watched the little tracker slip beyond the hills and disappear. They thought of the beasts that would be hunting him in the dark, the thorns and the winter. And though he would never see her, the old hunter believed the woman to be the most beautiful in the world.

"There is so much for a man to feel," Tip said, "Seeing that makes we wonder if one life will be enough."

The Kitzi Waitzi tightened his eyes to the thought of life and death and his face lit up when he drew back on the cigarette. "Oh yes," he said. "More than enough. Every life is an enormous thing."

15. A Feather in their Caps

Down the trail they charged, sprinting through the thicketland. They burst from hollow to hollow and the hunt seemed to allow them speed they would have otherwise been denied, for they were now moving through the dense forest at the same clip as the great bear, as if the hunt itself had given them haste. For all the honor in the world I could never run this fast, Jack thought. It was strange to him how the chase willed him through the thistles.

He had never felt more alive. He darted through the thoroughfares the rabbits took, leaping from rise to fall. If he kept his speed up he could see the trail the bear had taken by the swaying limbs across the thick of the forest. Jack slapped the branches away as they blocked his path.

So light were the steps they sprinted that a heaven sweat seemed to pour out of them, that their lungs filled with luck, that from them came all the bulletproof thoughts of young men, of eagles on first flight. The chase was torture for their feet, which were raw from the days of hauling heavy packs but onward they raced down the slopes, their heals thudding the gullies as they sprung up the grassy humps and continued from rise to rise.

Tip knew that in most cases chasing an injured bear through the thick was the last thing a hunter should do. A wounded animal is a desperate animal, and even more dangerous. But he also knew that this bear's wounds were fatal, but not immediately so, and that it would simply be a matter of time before Putt found her. His hope was to catch the bear in the forest and finish the job.

It seemed that the sores and the wounds of the party had disappeared. Branches slapped across Henry's chest and Jack's fingers continued to be squeezed as he pushed away the boughs but neither could feel a thing.

As they ran through the thick of the forest all the members of the party began to sweat from their brow and from the balls of their feet. If they hadn't been running they would have noticed the trembling of one another's hands, their gazes glossed over, heard the certain death in their voices. When Jack brushed the saskatoon he thought about how the leaves looked like spades, the stems like honey suckles. He saw squirrel's tails shake high up in the trees and heard the little chirpings of the birds.

They scrambled through the lengthy belt of poplars that grew near the path. The tracks were deep in the turf and the blood was splattered broadly. Jack was out front, sprinting with his eyes down, following the trail, pointing and calling as the others followed. It was something Tip had never done, running and tracking at once, and he found it satisfying.

They dodged through the timber, panting as they leapt from rock to root to dusty earth. I should not have liked to be that great bear on the river that day. Her life until then may have been fat and easy, but her death was hard. In most ways I would not have traded places with the brothers either. It was not a hunt for tenderfoots, as you will see.

Esperanza's lungs spilled onto the ground. Her heavy legs crashed into the small trees and thudded the fallen birches with a crack like breaking bones. She chewed her tongue, the blood drenching her frontcoat. She had abandoned the trail long ago and was now running wildly, trying to build a breath. She rested near a clearing, her body heaving. She had not run through the timber at such a speed since she was young. Her lungs were burning with the cold air and the thick flow of blood draining into them. She turned when she heard the sounds of approaching feet. She could hear voices calling. They were fearful, excited sounds. She heard the brush shake and twigs snap and fast footfalls slapping the crackling carpet of the forest. The wound along the bridge of her nose had pooled inside her head, and her vision began to redden, and she stared at the glaze the blood made. One of her hind legs began to numb and she could hear the constant dripping when she slowed. She doubled back toward the path and slipped behind the tall ferns until she was hidden.

The Malamute, a solid white flash through the forest, charged down the trail. Even Wonderboy was no match for Putt when it came to tracking at speed. The old dog raced through the shrubs as if they weren't even there, leaping over the fallen logs and the small knolls, sniffing the blood scent as he ran. When he came near the clearing he smelled the bear. A pool of blood had gathered in a low spot on the turf. With blood crusted along her snout and down her thick beard, the bear rushed into the clearing. Putt's shoulders puffed up, his coat stood on end, his tail high, spinning, his legs locked. He met her with his mouth open.

Jack swore he could hear the sounds of those he loved cheering him on, willing him faster, saying his name over and over, "Jack Oakham! Kill her, end her, run her through, skin her living, eat her raw."

There came the sound of a wild breathing, a hoarse, dying wind. If he had turned his ear to the sound he would have heard the wind choking around the bear's throat, the garbled bubble of blood seeping into the lungs and coughing out again, and the sound of a single whelping cry. Jack continued to run, his bow ready, as he heard a snarl, a roar, the rustle of wild combat just beyond the trees. He steadied his nerve and noticed the sweat running down his hands.

When Jack came into the clearing what he saw caused his heart to stop. Putt was standing before the bear. The dog's front leg was dangling limply and his face was smeared with blood. On the ground beneath him, Putt's entrails were hanging out, dragging on the turf. Jack stopped suddenly and the forward motion caused his feet to skid across the wet ground and he found himself in the open.

He fumbled with his bow.

Esperanza limped toward the dog. Jack could see that one of the bear's paws was bleeding. To walk, the giant had to stand on her hind legs every other step, and crash down again on her healthy foreleg with the next. Later when he had time to think Jack said it was like a brick scooting along on it's belly, then standing on end, then falling forward with a crash and scooting along again.

And that was how the great thing closed in on the old dog, with a limp and a hop, rising and falling towards him, causing all of Jack's virtues and vices to rise in his throat, to race down his arms to his fingertips.

Jack's knees were knocking and his fingers shaking and the husky shape was moving closer, not running, but clumping heavily with every step. Jack drew back and raised his bow and didn't stop to aim, just let the arrow swim across the clearing, and through the belly of the bear.

Jack didn't wait to see where he'd hit her. He still had three arrows remaining and he knocked the next one and drew the arrow back. As he lifted his bow to shoot he heard the whistle of an arrow shot from behind him, past his shoulder where it hummed through the air. Jack had his eyes on the bear as he watched the long dart sink cleanly through her throat. Jack didn't turn. He squinted and aimed but as he was about to let the arrow fly Putt charged the big bear, his guts scraping along the forest floor, his hair standing on end. "Get outta the way!"

Henry stepped beside Jack and both had their bows up. They were squinting and sliding their aim left and right, waiting for Putt to move. The bear was open-mouthed. She and Putt snarled at one another. The two were at a standstill. The bear had only one mangled paw to fight with. The other was holding her up. The bleeding had become so heavy that she constantly had to spit out waves of blood to keep it from choking her. She could only see a few feet.

Both brothers held their aim as the bear coughed again, throwing blood across the dog's face. Then in a flash a hand grabbed Jack's arm, and then Henry's, and lowered their bows. Tip brushed past them and charged across the clearing. When he reached the dog he sidestepped through the brush with his rifle ready. He was only five feet from the bear when he fired but she had never seen him. He walked toward her and shot Esperanza through one eye and yanked the lever, and fired again.

Esperanza stood tall and as she did another needle slipped through her hide and beneath her ribs and high into her lungs. Her eyes and her lungs and her nose and her mouth were each like scalding hot coals burning from within. She had yet to feel the arrow in her belly and she never would.

Another crack sounded and this time she saw the shape on two legs, just a few feet in front of her, breathing up and down. Then another shot came and the world went black.

Jack leaned forward and shot the bear easily. The arrow sunk into the sternum but it didn't matter now. Soon Esperanza's legs went numb and she fell back against the giant poplar. Her chest continued to heave, her mouth continued to bubble. When she hit the ground Putt limped toward her, pulling his insides behind him. Jack threw away his bow and ran up to the dog, grabbing him by the neck and holding him down.

The beast looked almost handicapped by her round heaviness. The foam in her mouth dribbled from her lips when she breathed. Tip had seen many bears fattened before the winter but never one so full and overbuilt after the long cold sleep. It was hard for him to remember a time when this bear had galloped through the forest, cutting like a train through the very trees.

"Sounds like she's in labor," Henry said.

The bear took short, sharp breaths, one after another and with every one a gurgle.

When Henry mentioned labor it reminded him of little Immanuel and the travelers from across the sea. He began to contemplate the fate of their silent companeros, beyond the earth's curve somewhere, lost to them.

"I'd like to know how Ibrahim is doing. And the others. I hope they found their way."

When he noticed that her arms were limp, Henry approached her, setting his bow on the ground. He came alongside her and knelt down at her feet. Her eyes were gone and her nose continued to bubble but she could still smell him through the fury. Henry patted her on the leg, "Go on," he said.

Tip locked the breech and the crack of the bullet sounded through the forest. The boom slumped her head to the turf. At the sight of the old bear, the faces of Henry and Tip both went limp. There is something heartbreaking about witnessing the end of something wild and free. And it was more of that heartbreak that our party wished to avoid.

At first glance Putt appeared to be dead already. He had only a gentle breath left in him, his body swelling slightly. Jack could see where a single claw had scraped across the dog's face. It was deep, but Putt had been cut worse in the past.

The leg was shattered. When they moved him it flopped like a snake. Tip knew, at least, that the old dog would lose his leg. As hard as this was for the party to stomach, losing a leg wouldn't kill him. Having his insides emptied onto the ground, however, was a different sort of wound.

"I don't see any holes in his guts," Jack said holding the dog's entrails in his palms.

Tip put his hands around them, feeling up and down for a trickle. *She just unzipped him,* he thought. *If he stops bleeding we can fix it.*

The brothers looked at each other and waited.

Their father spoke calmly but firmly and displayed confidence with his words, "Henry I need you to fill your canteen at the river as fast as you can and come straight back. When you're through you'll need to fill it again." Without another word Henry Snow patted the bear on the knee, like he was saying good-bye to an old friend, and sprinted off into the woods, unscrewing the canteen.

Tip took his coat off and laid it on the ground near the old dog. He set Putt's insides on the fabric and began to pick off the leaves and loose grasses that had become stuck to the organs in the running.

"You're doin' fine, old timer," he said, his hand on the dog's neck, "You're doin' fine."

Tip opened the kit and removed a small bottle of saline and some antibiotics. The bandages and the tape he set aside.

"Jack?"

"Yessir?"

"You have your knife with you?"

"Yessir."

"I need you to skin that old bear as fast as you can. Just take enough to wrap around Putt and make a gurney for him so he can move. You have to do it quickly but I know you can. First find a sturdy piece of wood for us to carry him with."

Jack was covered in blood. When he had held the old dog down the open wound had continued to pour onto Jack's trousers and forearms. He was already frantically searching the forest for a gurney pole when Henry arrived with the water, and handed it to his father. Tip knew that Jack couldn't skin the old bear by himself, she was too big to move alone. He knew it would take both brothers even to roll her over, so he suggested that Jack find the wood pole first, giving Henry time to fetch the water that he needed.

Tip squirted some saline inside the old dog and then dumped one of the canteens of water in, washing the grime from the entrails with his fingers. "Go," he said to Henry who took the canteen to fill again.

Tip repeated this process three times, mixing the saline and the fresh water inside the body and washing the old dog out. He wished the water hadn't been so cold but there was nothing he could do. After three trips to and from the river the dog was clean.

The weight of Jack's body bore down on a small birch until it snapped. He had to press his feet against the cottonwood beside it and it took all of his strength to bend it but the small tree broke surprisingly and he carried it back to the clearing.

When he arrived his brother was already knelt beside the big bear. "Here," Henry said. Jack took his knife out and squatted beside him.

Jack made long strokes with his knife and as he did Henry took the edges of the hide in his hands and pulled with all his strength, watching as the heavy coat ripped away from the muscle.

Meanwhile Tip was tending to Putt. By now the blood had been rubbed deep into the old dog's fur and his white coat was a sticky pink color across his belly. Tip struggled to keep the dog from squirming so Jack came alongside his father to help him.

With their fingers they pushed the dog's entrails gently back inside the cavity. Both men had opened up enough animals in their lives to know the high from the low. Jack carefully held the dog open as they worked. "You're doing fine, Pop," the boy said to him. "How'd that old bear taste, huh? You took a chunk out of him, didn't you, Putt? We got him good didn't we, you and me? Just hold still and we'll fix you up like new."

As they gently positioned the organs Tip Holland felt a wave of pride come over him for his son. There was no question Jack loved the dog. He spent the better part of every day with Putt, and now he was trying to save him, holding his warm stomach in his hands and petting his back leg softly to calm him, and his hands were steady, his eyes were clear. Jack had run after a wounded bear and killed it, as much as anyone, and the moment it was done he had begun the task of mending his old friend with the steady hand of a surgeon. Tip wiped his eyes.

Putt seemed calm and content. His tongue sagged out of his lips and his breathing was slow and easy. If it weren't for his wounds one might have thought the old dog was just catching a breather after chasing a frisbee across the yard. He closed his eyes and took a deep breath. His breathing was stronger now. As he lay waiting, Putt dreamed he was curled up with his sisters again. All of the pups in his litter had been girls except for him. He dreamed he was suckling his mother in the short grass. He remembered the sun hurting his eyes as he fed so he kept them closed. He remembered his mouth moving with his mother's breathing. Later he chased a butterfly with his small sister, the one he preferred, across the lawn and tore a wing by sheer misfortune.

"Hand me the antibiotics," Tip said.

When he had them in hand Tip dumped them into the cavity and rubbed them along the tissue. "How's that gurney coming, Henry?"

Henry Snow was quickly stripping the last bit of hide he needed. His lips were curled up in a little ball like he was whistling but Tip couldn't be certain.

"Almost got her. You wanna hang him in the fur side, right?"

"Right."

Tip pointed for the bandages and Jack grabbed them. Then he placed them over the wound and taped them down. The cotton was soaked red the instant he applied it. He laid out two more thick strips of bandages, all that remained, and then pulled his shirt, that still lay nearby, around the dog as tight as he could stretch it. His son began to wrap the tape round and round the shirt, fitting it snugly to the dog's body. The shirt and the bandages began to fill with blood but the flow had nearly stopped.

Henry and Tip began cutting holes in the hide for the birch to slide through. Jack still had his hand on the old dog, rubbing his ears.

When they had a hole cut in every corner Tip and his son laid the heavy bearskin on the ground beside the dog and lifted Putt carefully in one movement onto the center.

The boys had been quick to strip the hide from the bear and the speed with which they had skinned her was obvious. Chunks of meat and fat still hung from the fleshy side.

Jack rubbed the dog's ears as Henry and his father wrapped the bearskin around him, lined the holes up, and slipped the birchwood through the grommets. Lucky it fit, Henry thought.

They lifted together and let the birch rest on their shoulders, Tip at the back end and Jack at the front. Putt awoke as they lifted him, looking around for someone to protect or something to attack but could find neither, so he fell back asleep, saving Henry and Jack in his dreams.

"Where to?" Henry asked.

Tip nodded to the southwest and as soon as the brothers turned in that direction Henry took his hat off, "Look," he said.

The party had been so concerned with the kill that they had failed to realize at the time what they had broken into. Ahead of them to the south the three began to see faint glimmers of gold light through the forest. Even to their weary hearts the sight of sunlight raining down gave them comfort. Open air began to fill their lungs.

Carefully Tip searched the trees for some sign of their destination. His eyes grew tight against the shafts of light entering the forest and in a moment they gave him the answer he was looking for. He said to his sons, "We're going past those trees into open country," he pointed. "Henry, when we get there I'm gonna send you out ahead, to go for help."

"Help from who?"

"There's a ranch. And a man you'll need to find."

"How far is it?"

Now they began walking. They each stepped over the stripped carcass of the bear that looked almost human without her skin, and began trekking at a steady clip with the old dog bouncing in the gurney.

"It's close," Tip said. "We're lucky. It's only a few miles."

As he held the dog up, Jack's eyes swelled with coming tears. And with the sudden suffering of a good friend, he realized that this was the second time heartache had paid him a visit, and it brought to sharp attention the first.

"Will he make it?" Jack asked finally. His eyes were swollen.

Tip looked down at the old dog breathing steadily. "He won't bleed to death but shock might kill him."

"What does that mean?"

"His body is trying to preserve his vital organs," Henry told him. "The vessels have shut down to the extremities. That's why his legs are cold. Soon his eyes will begin to dialate and he'll start shivering. Then his breathing will increase and things will begin to fail. He'll become unresponsive and his blood pressure will rise."

"How long?" Jack asked quickly.

Henry didn't answer. He turned back and led the way.

"We have an hour," Tip told him.

They marched on through the high ferns, swaying the dog above the growth line. They marched on through the last of the thick groves and the tangled, vine-covered, chest high shrubs with berries just now budding. They marched through the last trees of the Wild West End, and good riddance, they thought, dreading the fact that they would still have to slop back through on their long road home. They marched as quick as they could, trying not to keep record of time, but there is nothing except death which is quick in the Wild West End, and their going was slower than they'd hoped. At last the sun began to bleed through the high boughs and the colors of the trees glowed onward and westward. Ahead they could see where the great giants spread out, could hear the faint whisper of a wind they had forgotten.

"I didn't intend to dodge your question, Jack," Tip told him, giving each of the boys a start. "I will explain soon enough why I chose the two of you. After we find some help for Putt here. I'll answer that and some other naggings that I'm certain you have."

"Who is the man we're looking for?" Henry asked.

Tip squinted, his head ducking and turning slightly as he peered through the high boughs. "His name is Unger Soski."

Part III

The Legacy Of Thaddeus Parnicca

"I was born to a woman I never knew and raised by another who took in orphans. I do not know my background, my lineage, my biological or cultural heritage. But when I meet someone new, I treat them with respect. . . . For after all, they could be my people."

- James Michener

§

1. Milk and Honey

The party burst out of the trees and spilled onto an emerald meadow. Each of the boys had to squint to see what lie ahead. Before them hundreds of stumps, many of them freshly clipped, swelled like grave-stones out of the grass. What surrounded them now wasn't a forest at all, but open country tumbling like a vast lawn to the west. Tip had foretold that they would soon reach the end of the forest but neither brother had expected the change to come so quickly. A broad swath had been hacked through the tall spires and all that remained were the greying leftovers, the "nubs of the lumberjacks" as Tip called them. Even the fallen limbs that had cluttered the floor of the Wild West End had been plucked from the meadow, as if a gardener that tended these lands had seen fit to tidy up the grounds.

The travelers filtered through the last of the standing trees and there they began their race across the prairieland. The sun was setting on their faces, making the land in the distance difficult to see. But as their eyes adjusted both brothers watched as the grassland stretched out across a great expanse and at its end were tall black trees, and beyond them swelled the sight most connected with wonderlust - the sea!

It was a cold grey sea, blackening with the setting sun but bronze and inviting where the sunlight touched it. Many days at march across the Wild West End had engulfed the party within a claustrophobic shell, a shell that was broken the moment they saw the line of watery glass.

"The ocean!" Henry gasped.

It rocked before them and reflected the crisp mountaintops across the inlet, at the western edge of the world. The view was so magnificent that even Putt, cleaved and travel beaten as he was, his body sagging in the

393

gurney, raised his head to have a look. All of them peered over the watertop to the wood of the far shore, and beyond to the rising glens, the highland green, and up to the crags with their speckled rock tops where the snow seemed blue-gold in the evening sun. Jack patted Putt on his neck as they ran, his worried face searching the horizon for their destination. Tip had said there was a ranch close by, but even that hadn't prepared him for what he spotted in the distance.

As his eyes adjusted to the light Jack began to see on the shoreline, in the far shadows beneath the trees, a great host of structures: cabins, barns and workshops, and some buildings of unknown use. More than a dozen smokestacks rose up from chimneys and forges, and cooking pits beside the homes. They could now see stables and two men on horseback, and others passing in and out between the cabins, some carrying burdens, while others still worked with tools on high scaffolds, one man atop the barn was painting the cupola.

As they grew closer Jack began to appear hopeful. The place was far too vast to be a ranch or even a farm, he knew, but instead had the look and feel of a hamlet upon the sea. They could now see dozens of workers moving along the far edge of the meadow. A row of pine cabins with screen porches extended along the beach as far as the trees. Each had stone chimneys puffing smoke and lanterns illuminating the porches and the pathways between them.

And as they steadily approached the brother's astonishment only grew. In a flat field before them was what appeared to be a runway. Yes, a bare lane had been worn down, not as a road would with connecting points, but merely a worn stretch of earth beginning and ending, a few hundred yards in length. Jack's suspicions were confirmed when he noticed that well-hidden in the shadows were the shapes of what could only be single engine airplanes! At least half a dozen parked beneath the far trees. And nearby was the scattered wreckage of dozens more; wings and doors and scrap metal crumbled and twisted, a single fuselage with the paint peeling off.

"What is this place?" Jack asked, breathing heavily.

Tip moved the gurney pole from one shoulder to another. "This is Luleo," he told him. "We're beyond the Wild West End."

The brother's eyes were wide to the mystery that surrounded them and they each had many questions, but their questions would have to wait.

"Henry?"

"Yessir?"

"Look at the trees by the water," Tip said. "D'you see a long building against the beach?"

As he squinted Henry began to see deep among the faint corner of the trees, a large shape emerging from the shadows. He tilted his hat down as he marched, shielding his eyes to the light. "I see it."

"That's a hangar," Tip said. "The ranch foreman will be inside. I want you to find him as fast as you can. Have him meet us in the galley. Go!"

Henry rested the gurney pole on his brother's shoulder and charged across the field. Jack and his father watched as the boy high-stepped over the tree stumps, across the meadow a half-mile wide, until he was but a speck in the distance.

"You're doing good, Putt," Jack said. "Keep breathin'." He placed a hand on the old dog's side. "Just a few more minutes."

As Henry crossed the great field he could soon see women and children, whole families spread throughout the village. When he came within site they stopped where they stood and watched him with knowing eyes. Some of them were smiling widely, especially the elder citizens, but Henry was too concerned about Putt to inquire.

However as he raced toward the southern hangar more questions mounted in his mind. Inside the building, which was an enormously framed wooden structure, rested five additional airplanes. They were all in different stages of disrepair, some with only naked frames assembled, and others needing propellors, or engines, or windows for the cockpit. The great room was crowded with torches and picks and a dozen or more oak-handled hammers. There were table saws and engines disassembled on the work desks, all grease covered and caked in sawdust and paint. Young men were working. They had filthy hands and grease smeared across their shirts.

As Henry entered the hangar several of the mechanics looked up without a word. The boy had the look of a wild animal emerging from the forest, his boots and pantlegs caked with blood and dirt clods. His face was sallow, as were his coat and shirt, each a washed-out tattered remnant. Immediately the workers noticed the off-white strips of cloth and the heavy bandages fastened to his arms.

"The straw boss?" Henry asked, breathing heavily.

It took a moment for the question to register. Perhaps these men didn't expect such a wild boy to have yet harnessed the power of speech. To hear a question put to them so directly without introduction struck them as both rude, and bold. They admired the boy for it. Without a word all of them pointed toward the back.

The workers couldn't help but remain fixed on him as he passed, the forceful way he carried himself, the slight limp in his step and the bloody hole around the knee of his trousers. Henry passed them and moved across the hangar.

He ducked beneath a pair of wings and at the back saw the silhouette of a man in the only plane that appeared ready to fly. Dressed in overalls, it was Unger Soski, of course, and it was in his home that Tip and his sons would stay.

His appearance hadn't changed a great deal since the last time we saw him, though many years had passed. He still wore a crewed haircut, which he had never abandoned since adopting it back on the farm, and continued to dress in a manner befitting a man of the field. He took a breath and looked the boy up and down. "Henry, from the looks of things I'd say you just walked a hundred miles through the woods."

Henry didn't respond.

"I'm Unger Soski," he said strongly. "But I'm sure you already knew that."

"It's good you know me," Henry answered. "We need your help."

With haste Henry led Unger out of the hangar and pointed across the greenway. When he came into the light Unger spotted three shapes on the horizon. "Tell me that isn't Putt in the gurney."

"It is," Henry told him, "We need to patch him up."

They began jogging toward the galley. "What happened?"

"He got after a bear. A few miles back."

"A black?"

"No, Sir. A *big* brown. Dad called her Esperanza."

Mr. Soski gawked and slowed his pace. "Esperanza?! Then Putt's lucky all she did was maul him. What'd that bear do then?"

"Nuthin'."

"Nuthin, huh? Well I bet she did somethin'."

"No sir," Henry told him. "We killed her before she could."

Unger Soski tried not to show too much surprise, but for his own sake he wanted to find somewhere to sit. He slowed his pace just to give Henry a serious look. Unger could have written a collection of stories about that old bear over the years. He looked down at Henry's hands with the blood dried beneath his untrimmed nails. There was nothing proud about the way the boy had told him, and he knew it was the truth.

"Putt's the only one hurt?"

"Yessir. The bear opened him up along the belly."

"His belly?" Unger asked.

But just then Henry caught sight of something that caused his bones to quake. Not far beyond his father and brother, in the shadow of the forest, were the shapes of three horses, one with two riders, and another carrying a huge figure out front. The horses burst into the clearing at a fast clip but stopped at the edge of the field. The riders were turned in their saddles now, having halted their pursuit. Henry watched them carefully, though Unger's eyes were too old to see.

"That's right," Henry answered, his voice quaking. "The bear unzipped him."

The pair was approaching the galley now. Unger waved Tipper and Jack to meet them. He looked up at Putt and said, "I'll see what I can do."

As they burst through the door Tip and Jack were breathing heavily. Tip set his rifle behind the door as Jack and Henry lifted the old dog onto the countertop. Around them were tools and charts similar to those one might find in a veterinary office.

Unger ran his fingers nimbly across the dog's face and the crude array of bandages. When he looked up Unger eyed Jack briefly, his shirt and arms covered in blood.

"When did it happen?" he asked.

"An hour ago."

"Antibiotics?"

"All we had."

Unger checked the dog's pulse and held up his broken leg, running his thumb along the length of it. The old farmer squinted at Tip, but as he felt the brother's gaze he turned back, opening Putt's eyes with his fingers. The dog's breathing was growing softer.

"How old is he now?"

"Couldn't say."

Unger nodded. "Jack Oakham."

"Yessir?" he said, finding it odd that the man knew his name.

"I need you to wet his face and keep talking to him."

Jack nodded and grabbed a rag from the sink.

Next Unger instructed Henry to loosen two bags of ice from the freezer. The boy worked quickly, keeping one eye on his father's rifle and the other out the window.

"We'll need cortisone and valium," Unger said to Tip, rolling up his sleeves. To Jack's surprise Tipper knew right where to look.

Unger sorted through the cabinets, finding sutures and needles, and heavy bandages. He took out two long syringes, plunging them into the jars.

"What do those do?" Jack asked.

"Cordizon stops the shock," Unger said. "Valium knocks him out and helps with seizures."

Putt was shaking violently now, his good legs quivering, a puddle of drool forming on the countertop. Unger injected him along the spine and as the needle slipped in Putt's eyes moved from man to man.

Jack's fears began to overwhelm him. He wanted nothing more than to be back at his home on Tenpenny Hill sitting beside Momma Tom and Padi, playing chess and the old dog snoring beside him.

"You're looking good, Pop," Jack whispered. "Not long now and we'll have you patched."

Putt's face was warm to the touch but as Jack brushed his leg to comfort him he felt that it was cold and lifeless. He struggled to fight back his tears, as he prayed for the dog's life.

Putt widened his eyes. His jowls shook and Jack heard him whisper, "Promise me, Jack."

"Promise you what, buddy?"

Putt's eyes rolled back and forth in his head. "Promise you'll let me have the next bear all to myself."

Jack smiled. "Anything you say."

The dog's entrails sagged from the wound when Unger removed the wrapping. He dabbed them clean and opened the cavity to have a look. Henry took a look as well, but not at Putt, at Unger Soski, the paradox that stood before him. His arms were tanned and grizzled, his face beaten by years in the wind, and his shoulder, when relaxed, hung strangely to one side. This is the man that Tipper shot, Henry thought. Shot him and left for dead. As the two men worked together the reality of the moment consumed him.

"He didn't lose anything," Unger said as he swished the saline around with his hand. "Easy big fella. Here we go." Then he rolled the heavy dog on his side.

Unger let the solution dump out, the pink fluid spilling onto the floorboards.

"Sutures."

Tip handed him the pack of threading. The first of the sutures was already swedged to the needle and Unger worked quickly, running the needle through one lip of the wound and back through the other, rejoining the muscle walls. He repeated the process down the length of his body as Tip held the two sides of Putt's belly together.

Jack noticed that the bites where the needle came through were only bleeding slightly, which raised a question in his head.

"Why didn't he bleed to death? I would've thought with a wound that big—"

"Best place to have a wound," Unger said as he swabbed the stitching. "No arteries down there. If you have to get opened up, that's the place."

Jack could see through his tears that Putt was breathing normally. They applied a new set of bandages and the cuts on the dog's face were treated. But as relieved as Jack felt, what came next caused his heart to jump. Unger Soski came out of the closet with a bone-saw.

The feeling in Jack's throat was one he had known before; a palpable, heartbreaking fear. Jack had felt the same anguish as he watched his mother fade away on the bed right before his eyes. The sight of Putt on the countertop only brought her to mind so he closed his eyes and rubbed the dog's ears with his fingers. He kept his eyes closed throughout the process, keeping record of Putt's breathing with his hand. But the sounds that Jack heard were some of the most painful of his life. He hadn't considered that the darkness would only amplify them. By the time the cut was made, Jack himself began to shake, imagining all the limits that would now be placed on the old dog.

Even Henry tightened his face in discomfort as the sawyer worked. It was hard for him to witness the injuries that the bear inflicted, but it soon became nearly impossible for him to observe the treatment that Unger and Tip had to administer. It's enough to say that both men knew what they were doing, that each of the vessels were tied off, the nerves and the arteries both, and that the muscles were dissented appropriately, and that the cut was clean.

When the amputation was complete Unger Soski did his best to comfort the brothers. He told them of a hound he'd once had that still hunted long after losing a leg. "We have the antibiotics," he explained. "He could be standing in four or five days."

Tipper shaved down the thick fur near the wound and patched him up with fresh bandages. When it was done he wiped his eyes and held the dog in his arms. "Lots of miles. Lots of years."

Then he added, "Boys there may never be a more strained introduction. This as you know, is my dear friend, Unger Soski."

The boys nodded and offered their thanks.

"My honor to help," Unger told them. "And to finally meet you both."

Then Tipper and Unger embraced and a great heaviness came with it, a heaviness that Henry believed came not only from the surgery but from something else altogether. However before he could inquire Tipper squinted at Jack and unbuttoned his shirt.

"You look a mess," Tip said. "Take mine while we get that shirt cleaned up. You can't walk around this place covered in blood."

Jack was slow to respond. His heart was still busy sorting out his feelings. "Thanks," he said finally as he began to undress. He washed his arms and his face in the sink and stood over the sleeping dog.

For some minutes the men stood in silence. There was a somber understanding that each of them felt as they watched the old dog sleep.

"Boy's the mess hall is up the road," Tip said finally, surprising them. "Round up some food for yourselves and meet me here when you're done. I need to talk something over with Unger."

Jack didn't want to leave. For that matter neither did Henry, but for other reasons. Casually he eyed his father's rifle. But they knew he was right. It had been a long time since they'd eaten. Henry swung the rifle over his shoulder and reached for the door. "Come on, brother," Henry said. "He's sleeping well."

Jack nodded gently and followed his brother.

"You can leave the rifle," Tip said.

"No," Henry smiled. "I'll keep it with me. In case another bear gets after us."

Tip questioned the boy with his eyes. But he felt no desire to argue and had no reason to deny him. With a wave he sent them off and, heavy-hearted, the brothers slipped through the door.

They stepped out of the little building and met up with the dusk light. Despite their heavy hearts, Henry and Jack remained amazed by what they saw. Nearby was a workshop with a single fire burning. Men were smelting horseshoes and iron tools. The roof of the hangar was being completed by workers on scaffolds; the sounds were of hammers falling. Everything appeared to have been freshly built from the trees surrounding them.

The brothers agreed that there must have been at least a hundred people living in Luleo. They were tall and short, black and white, with wide pug noses or small sharp ones. Their clothes were uniform work attire but their skin tones were varied. Suddenly a sawman's wagon, towed by heavy horses, trundled over the humps in the muddy road that had been cut by wagon tracks and rolled to a stop with a "Whoa!" The wagon seemed to have arrived from the trees to the north and in her carry were heavy logs. The driver began unhitching the horses as two workmen slipped out and called for others to begin unloading. When the driver had the horses unhitched, Jack watched as the man led the heavy Morgans away from the wagon to a clearing behind the workshop. There a paddock had been laid. The stables, with loose hay scattered inside the trough, seemed hidden out of sight. Jack saw a number of draft horses feeding on the muddy sod.

To his further surprise these horses were branded in the same way as the remuda back at Tenpenny. "What is this place?" Jack whispered as they both grew steadily closer to the bustle.

But Henry didn't hear him. His eyes were locked on the eastern trees. Faintly, through the tall spires, he could see four riders standing beside their mounts, and the tails of their horses swishing in the shadows.

"Yeah," Henry said. "Some place, huh?"

And Jack could only nod.

As they walked the brothers saw beyond the village center, and only visible through a window between the cabins, three distinct structures which had been placed near the sea. The first was an anchor house, as Tip later called it, which housed the spare nets, the anchor line, pulleys and buoys, buckets for chumming, wood boxes filled with hooks, assorted reels and slickers, two old rudders that needed mending and a wide variety of heavy tackle. It rested near the foot of the dock.

The second was the dock itself, a long, wide platform which extended from the shaded beachhead out into the open sea, pointing like an arrow toward the mountains. Despite the mosses that had already collected among the posts it had been built quite recently. The plank boards showed no sign of sea rot and the grooves had not begun to ricket.

The "Arch Angel" was a steam trawler tethered to the dock. It was the third structure they spotted on the water. She was a heavy vessel, and not a young sea bird by any stretch of the imagination. Over the years the barnacles had collected so thickly across her hull that to see her, one might have thought she was built of coral instead of steel. Her ropework was sound, her engine well-tended. She was gaff-rigged and her deck was open, as if she was intended to haul in heavy cargo. She was fitted for whaling but couldn't maintain the speed. The harpoons and haul nets were only kept aboard in case the swabbies came upon caribou, which often crossed the cove in spring and early summer. From the look of her she was well-used.

Jack assumed that the inhabitants of Luleo must have depended heavily upon the sea for their resources. He smiled at the thought of the leathernecks bringing back king salmon every evening, the deckhands singing songs.

It was then that the scope of the place came in to view for Jack Oakham. His eyes were sad, his heart full, but the marked curiosity of boyhood still lived within them, no matter how small a dose at that moment. Jack loved knowing what made things work, the more complex the better. As he pondered Luleo he estimated that it was more complex than he had first imagined. He didn't know where these people had come from but he assumed that they had not arrived all at once. Wood has a certain way of settling, both in its color as well as its form, and these cabins, which at first appeared uniform, proved to be staggered in age upon closer examination. The ones nearest the workshop had been built several years before the ones beside the hangar.

The picture Jack formed in his head was of a handful of men, in the beginning, arriving and setting about the task of building a single structure out of the timber. He believed they had no mill at the time, nor a dock or trawler to haul in materials. He envisioned them tented near the beach, one hunting for provisions, the others chopping wood. Before long they had a cabin, most likely the present workshop, where they slept and ate and stored their tools. Next, he imagined, they constructed a dock. Although the present dock was new, Jack believed it had been rebuilt, after the original dock, like the workshop, had begun to crumble.

Next they had brought in the trawler, and more hands to labor. They must have unloaded the mill and with it, the first cabin had been quickly built. Then the second, and more hands arrived. They soon had need for horses because the hunting was growing scarce. The men had to travel several miles from camp to find moose to bring back. Horses needed stables so they built those too.

Jack had yet to discover how the wreckage of the airplanes had arrived, or where it had been gathered in the first place, or what purpose the constructed fleet would serve. There must have been a purpose, for more hands were needed to do the work. More hands meant more food so they planted a garden and rigged the trawler for fishing. They built the anchor house to store supplies. They built a kitchen. A huge cooler for the game meats and the frozen foods was brought in by the trawler from some unknown shore. Now Luleo was working, Jack thought.

All the people had jobs to do and they did them to survive. They worked among one another and for one another toward some unnamed objective. This was just one more question Jack couldn't answer. What were these people doing here?

What had summoned them to live at the end of the world? Had they simply given up on their old lives and started over? If so, where had they come from and why were mechanics slaving round the clock, transforming scrap heaps into working planes again?

Jack didn't know. But for the first time since his father had woken him with the wash bucket all those mornings ago, Jack Oakham had a goal other than digging up a buried treasure. He desired to know the secrets of Luleo.

Henry noticed a small crew of workers carrying a huge log to the mill. He and Jack hurried to help. When they arrived, both of the young boys slipped their shoulders beneath the log and shared the burden with the workers. Everyone worked silently, moving the log towards the mill and setting it down as one. It seemed that the brother's arrival was somehow expected, and none of the crew appeared surprised by their assistance.

But when a small woman in the lead turned to face him, Henry's heart almost stopped, from the wild smile she wore and the light burning in her eyes. As Henry looked away he noticed that a similar expression was across the faces of the others. They were each glaring at the two, as if they were looking through them.

"Hello, Henry," the woman said through the habits of her language.

"Hi," he said meekly.

Although the brothers didn't know it at the time, each of the workers were very much aware of the journey the brothers had taken, as well as the one they were yet to complete. They gave the boys a careful look – knowing their appearance and their wounds would be a topic of discussion for years to come.

The woman held her smile. "And hello, Jack."

Jack said hello, a curious look on his face. "We're looking for the mess hall," he told her.

The woman pointed down the road, "The house with the open door," she said. "In a moment the bell will ring."

Jack and Henry nodded their thanks but as they did, the little woman lifted a wide necklace from her shoulders while another worker untied a simple bracelet that he wore upon his wrist. Both pieces of jewelry were fashioned of simple hemp and each had a colorful stone at the center, with strange engravings on the face. The necklace was handed to Henry and the bracelet to Jack.

"So wonderful to finally see you," the woman said and a flood of tears filled her eyes.

Henry and Jack watched awkwardly, not knowing what action to take. They thanked the workers and waited for a response, but the crew simply nodded and within a few moments they drifted away.

The brothers gave one another curious glances. "What was all that about?" Jack whispered. And all Henry did was shake his head. His eyes were turned back to the distant trees, where the shapes of horses and riders were now gone from his sight.

As they moved toward the mess hall Jack noticed that inside the cabins men and women were working, sorting out clothes or building trusses. Others were cooking halibut steaks and caribou over grills built into stone platforms. One of the small cabins, an open room which appeared to be a warehouse, housed boxes that the boys could see stacked from floor to ceiling. On the side of the boxes was the sketched image of a open book. They're building a library, Jack thought.

Near the crates, and clearly visible through the open doorway, were rows and rows of dog food in fifty pound bags. Several men were inside with clipboards, talking something over.

Halfway down the road the brothers found themselves passing through a new garden, quite large, and yet to be seeded. This garden was oval-shaped with the road cutting through, and at her perimeter were small vine stalks scaling the tidy wooden fencing. Huckleberries and salmonberries that at the time were only tender stalks would bud and ripen in the coming weeks. There were small fruit trees, too, that would never grow large but would yield enough for pies and jams. The long beds were being tended. Two women were plowing them with hoes and rakes. I'll bet that's for the spring vegetables, Jack was thinking.

After passing through the garden they saw an old well, the kind they had always dreamed of, with smooth river stones for it's wall and a sloping rooftop made of dark planks. The bucket, faded and well-used, hung from the pulley.

Beside the well the ground sloped up into a hillock. Both brothers, upon seeing what was carved into the face of the hill, turned towards one another in astonishment. An amphitheater, made of stone and mortar, had been built. There were rows and rows of stone benches, built in a curving semi-crescent. Two aisles had been left to allow easy passage and at the forefront a pulpit and a towering cross. It was a perfect duplicate of the boy's church back at Tenpenny.

Before they could speak they heard the sounds of women singing and turned their heads to find them. From within the wide cabin near the end of the road a chorus of six women of all sizes were chanting a tune that, upon hearing it, made Henry's skin tighten around his body, and Jack's eyes swell with tears.

Oh the Lord is good to me!
And so I thank the Lord
For giving me, the things I need,
The sun and the rain and the appleseed,
The Lord is good to me!

This, of course, had been Henry Snow's song for over a decade and upon hearing it, his heart began to ache. The women, whose voices carried the notes like an ensemble of heavenly birds, reminded him how far he was from home. The surf and the soft light, blended with the quiet manner of the workers carrying timber and finishing off their labors, created a magical sensation. The light was dimming all around them and it was the time of day that romantics and poets wished they could pause and live within their entire lives. The sky was aglow with pinks where the clouds were catching the last of the failing light. The breeze was so gentle that they were only just aware of it, not turned cold as they might have been with stronger gusts. They could hear the faint crash of the ocean tide against the sand and the quiet murmurs of the workmen finishing up. They could feel the warmth of the nearby fire, the humming of the ladies over their cooking. They could smell the spruce smoke the chimneys made and the fresh, grassy aroma of the wild land, the scent of an unknown stew bubbling in some unseen pot, the halibut and the sizzling steaks of the caribou on the outdoor pits. If they had closed their eyes and removed the sound of the ocean slapping the shore and replaced it with the chatter of one hundred and fifty children, their laughter ringing, then Snow and Oakham would have believed that they were home. It was in that moment alone that if Henry Snow had been asked to abandon his adventure and rejoin the safety of his peers on Tenpenny Hill, he would have shyly nodded. But he was spared such an admission for Jack was far too consumed by his own emotion to speak.

Both travelers took gentle steps toward the mess hall. The door was open and a glowing light poured out of her windows onto the lawn. There was a bell dangling from the porch roof, and Jack said, "My God it smells like home."

Inside were rows and rows of tables, with roughly sanded tops, and on the tops were rolls of towels and dull tableware and glasses filled with ice. Under the tables were sturdy wooden benches with bark still on them and beyond the tables was a long boarded countertop spanning the length of the room. Cast-iron pots, steaming from beneath the lids were set out before half a dozen women in dirty white aprons humming little tunes as they cooked. They could smell sauces and soups and warm vegetables. They could see baskets of figs and huckleberries and fresh produce by the bushel. On the far ends of the long countertop were jars of jams and apple butter.

When one of the cooks looked up she let out a gentle gasp as she saw the brothers standing there and soon all of the women were motionless and the whistling had stopped.

For a moment Henry and Jack stood idling, not knowing what all the fuss was about. But soon they approached the women, as a pair of inmates might approach a parole board, begging for a pardon.

"We were told we might have something to eat," Henry said, humbly.

Instantly all of the cooks scrabbled to prepare. They brought out pots and trays and racks of meats and fruit baskets. Behind the countertop the brothers saw an elaborate kitchen, with an entire wall adorned with spice glasses of various shapes and sizes, from all over the world. On the opposite wall was a huge deep bookcase with cookbooks numbering in the hundreds, written in a half dozen languages by Henry's count.

But it was the sign above them that ultimately drew the brothers attention. From a pair of light chains a small plaque hung from the ceiling that read:

"Here there are no hungry and no poor,
No famine and no war
No renegades, no foes,
No cause to count your woes
Here there are but people, broken and unworthy
A sum greater than her parts
A commonwealth of hearts
Who know that duty is volition
And our cause the Great Commission"

"Potatoes?" the young cook asked, a bit nervous.

The brothers remained speechless as they smelled the food spread out before them. Finally Jack nodded. "Thank you. Yes. What is this place?"

She stopped, rubbing her hands on her apron. "Didn't your father tell you?"

"No, Ma'am."

The woman hesitated, and then shoveled out the spuds. "We call it Luleo. But that's all I should say."

The brothers were blessed with more food than they could handle, each carrying two full plates back to their table. Two of the cooks brought them drinks and spices and Henry lifted them both in his arms to hug them. They shuffled away, smiling.

Neither of the brothers spoke as they devoured their food, taking little time to enjoy it. Both thought to themselves how nice it felt to have a table to set their plates on and to have a hand available to drink with. Henry was so careless with the food that he let the milk trickle down his chin, wiping it with his sleeve.

Just then one of the elder cooks walked across the mess hall and disappeared through the front door. She crossed the porch and as Jack was about to clean his first plate he was startled by the ringing of a bell.

Soon voices were heard out on the lawn and then footfalls sounded as the citizens of Luleo came thudding up the steps. They entered as one long continuous line, and were careful to wipe their feet, and the men took off their caps and hung them on the rack beside the door, and the ladies, numbering fifteen altogether, were allowed to pass to the front.

Each of the men had laborers hands, dirty palms with black nails and calloused fingers, and their faces were all sun-beaten, and their clothes were charmingly tattered. Three of the men, some of the last to enter, had huge pistols holstered on their hips with belted bullets. They were wearing worn chaps, boots, knives. They must be the hunters, Henry thought.

The brothers marveled at the assortment of faces. Not one of them looked alike. Some had dark, sealed-shut eyes, with wrinkles surrounding them, while others looked out with round, pale stares, eyes of possibility. Two of the men were no bigger than children, but their beards gave them away. One man, the oldest, was quiet and enormous. When he entered the cabin he had to turn sideways and duck beneath the door jam. He nodded shyly to the brothers.

All of the people of Luleo were polite as they watched their young visitors eat, many of them marveling at Henry's stature. In describing him later one woman called him "a kind-faced brute", while another said he had the look of a young viking. But there was no doubt in their mind to his identity and none of them needed to ask his name. They all knew that Henry Snow had finally arrived.

One mother with her child whispered for the little one to wave. Everyone smiled graciously and several came over to shake their hands, though little was said. That is until one young worker, a stout carpenter with wood chips on his sleeves approached them from the back of the line.

"They said you were here."

Henry nodded. "We're here."

"Goin' to the mountain, are ya?"

The man's language was raw, unbridled. He pronounced his words with a heavy lilt that neither brother recognized, but that both admired immediately.

"We don't know where we're goin'," Jack said.

"Well, you will soon enough. I'll venture that."

"What is this place?" Henry asked with frustration.

"Don't ya know, okes? You've found heaven. No not really, but it fooled me the first few months."

"How long ya been here?"

"Two years now. Goin' on three. But I won't make it. They'll send me back at summer's end. I'll be ready by summer's end."

"Ready?"

The man smiled and patted Jack on the shoulder. "There's a lot you don't know."

"Apparently."

"No worries. There's time. You have a good guide. The two of you have a world of work ahead of ya and there's plenty of time for the details. Eat well and take some rest. Where you're going you'll need your strength. The wilds make a measure of a man."

They shook the young man's hand and he stepped back into line.

But then came a pair of women, dark-skinned and full of life who seemed like twins to the brothers, though in truth they were only sisters.

"Would you be so kind as to solve a discussion we were having?" the older one said.

Jack shrugged and smiled. "We'll certainly try."

But the women nodded awkwardly, and looked instead to Henry.

Henry understood their hesitation, and leaned in and smiled, "What is it ladies?"

The women told him that they'd had an argument over a passage of scripture. "A very difficult text," they called it. Henry agreed and translated the text immediately. "But I'm sure I got lucky."

Next came questions of photosynthesis and Homer and the breeding of draft horses; things they had been pondering.

"Luleo is a hard place for a scholar," they explained.

Henry answered their questions one after another, careful not to seem too brash.

"But don't trust me," Henry told them. "I could always be wrong."

"You're not," one told him. "We looked up the answers when we heard you were coming."

Henry cocked his head. "Then why ask them?"

"We wanted to be sure it was you."

The women smiled, thankfully, and the pair could be heard whispering to one another as they walked away.

Jack enjoyed the exchange, though it surprised him. "Knowing you as well as I do it's very easy to forget you're a genius," Jack told him.

Henry chuckled, "Genius or not, I can't explain what all these people are doing here."

"Me neither," Jack admitted.

The faces that surrounded him each had a story, a story Jack yearned to know, but his heart couldn't handle any more information. He felt overwhelmed as he sat there, for Putt and his survival, for the vast surprise of Luleo, for the apparent friendship that Unger and Tipper shared. To cope with the weariness Jack sat in silence, pretending to be half asleep while chewing his food.

Henry on the other hand appeared to have plenty of room in his heart for the strangers that surrounded him. He was not careworn for the old dog the way his brother was. He knew that all must die, and that Putt had lived his share. In fact he felt connected to the dog in that moment, and admired him greatly, but out of respect for his wildness would not let his thoughts linger on sentiment. Nor did his heart resign to ponder the mysteries of Luleo, although he knew them to be of great significance.

Henry felt certain that answers would come, about the nature of this place, and about Unger Soski and Tip and their untold story, a story he had already begun to predict. No, in that moment none of the events of the last hours overwhelmed his heart, instead his eyes were open to the new world around him, to her people and their stories and a chance at some adult interaction, something he rarely experienced.

To his delight when everyone was well-fed the crowd gathered on the lawn at a great fire ring and it was there that Henry and Jack introduced themselves. There were dozens of nods and hellos and little whisperings until finally one member of the crowd urged Henry and Jack to tell the story of their adventure.

It was a task perfectly-suited for Henry Snow.

The boy stood, his wounds exposed to the firelight, as he toasted his new friends and told roaring tales of their adventure with great charm on his lips. The stories delighted everyone and Jack even laughed at his jokes, well told. Yet even though it was a great pleasure to hear told an account of their journey, Jack couldn't help but notice that his brother changed some of the details to suit his whimsies.

But the crowd was entranced. At first, their eyes were fixed upon his every word, but before long they watched only his great movements, his lively eyes, until his spell was cast so completely that his words no longer mattered. He could have said anything and they would have listened. When a drink was handed him Henry thanked the server in their native language and everyone stood in amazement. They smiled at him and nodded with approval. At one point from across the crowd Jack saw an old man look firmly at Henry and he thought he heard the man whisper, "It is him, after all."

An electricity was spreading among the villagers, as if a pair of miracles were unfolding before their eyes. But it couldn't be denied that they were more interested in Henry, who seemed to them like an old friend stopping by for a visit, and whose appearance was so remarkable that even the oldest women seemed to gawk.

"Hurrah! A toast to Henry Snow!" One of them called. "A son of thunder and celebration!"

"Here, here!"

"To Henry Snow!" And all drank.

There was a brief silence.

"And to Jack Oakham!" another called and for an instant the crowd seemed at a loss for words.

"A son of humility and strength!"

"Here, here!"

"Three Cheers for Snow and Oakham!"

Soon Henry was chuckling loudly, and rousing laughter as he carried on about their wild adventure. But all along he kept his eyes honed to the great field they had crossed that afternoon, his rifle ready, and ever watchful for the riders to approach, but nothing came.

"Then, all of the sudden, Jack's boot sprung off with a pop!" Henry told them. "And we could hear the spurs jingling beneath the ice!"

Even though the crowd remained entranced by the tale some of the villagers soon began to rise and drift off to work: stringing up lanterns and strands of lights, carrying out long pews for what looked to be a festive celebration. Henry was engaged in telling his tales but Jack watched the people curiously. There was so much he didn't understand.

Long afterwards young Oakham thought back on that evening with wonder and amazement. Through those hours he absorbed so many faces and voices that at the time he felt he must be dreaming. He was so fatigued that the thought did not seem far from the truth.

After their story was told the boy kings shook many hands and by then their minds were crowded with questions. They left their new friends to their labors, nodded goodnight, and their bellies were tight as they walked down the road to Unger's cabin.

As before Tip and Unger were seated together, though this time each had tears in their eyes.

"From now on send them with more supplies in the springtime," Tip said. "The hunting is hard this early."

Unger accepted the order and nodded in agreement. "Bigger saddle-bags will do it."

Tip offered an exhausted half smile to his sons and wiped his eyes. "Were you well-fed?"

"It was life's great feast," Henry stated and Jack agreed. "You have a lot to answer for, old man. This place is full of mysteries."

"I know, I know. Tomorrow," Tip promised. "But for now you two must get some sleep."

"How's Putt?" Jack asked.

"He's fine," Tip encouraged. "Look in on him. But don't linger. It's late and tomorrow is the longest day."

The brothers were made comfortable in the country home of Unger Soski, although the accommodations were far from elegant. The spare bedroom had one small mattress that the brothers shared. Tip volunteered for the floor beside them.

Almost instantly the brothers fell into a black, consuming sleep. Once Henry found the bed he let his coat drop to the floor, dirt shaking from the stitching, and crashed onto the mattress. He fell asleep with his boots still tight around his feet and his father's rifle beside him. Not long after, Jack curled up next to him and neither moved through the night, their bodies frozen in slumber.

They slept all evening and across the dark of the morning before either stirred from their bed. But Tip was up before dawn. He was dressed almost immediately, not out of some half-zealous attempt to salvage his day, but because he had urgent business to attend to.

2. The Milk of Friendship

When Wonderboy found the Pritchers there wasn't much left to find. It had only been half a day since the horses had been shot but already the wolves had devoured most of the choice flesh. From the looks of things it had been the feast of a lifetime.

The first pack had arrived from the south, circling a mile out before swarming in mid afternoon. They were soon joined by a big pack from the northwest, nine by his count, and a short time later by a third pack from the southwest. Under different circumstances Wonderboy would have relished such a discovery. In powder like that he and Henry would have had an excuse to chase the wolves for a week. But Wonderboy didn't relish anything about his present situation. The three spent cartridges he found were from a large bored rifle, typical for great ranges, and the shots were placed knowingly. The tracks of the wolves that circled, some with blood trails of their own, were of little concern to him but what did concern him were the westbound tracks, the tracks of fine mounts, four of them, tall by his measure, and all carrying riders who were confident in the saddle.

413

The trail cut a line across the western hillocks toward the purple rise of the Wild West End and didn't break formation for miles. Before he rode on he thought to collect the three bridles still worn by the Pritchers, a pair Tipper had made himself for his sons, but he was overtaken by his haste.

As he rode a strange fear swelled inside him. The rifle that rested in his scabbard was weighing heavily on his mind. He hadn't fired it, nor even loaded it in many years and the truth that his ability to use it, and use it well may soon be of great importance caused Wonderboy to sweat lightly from his brow. His fears lingered for some hours until he came across a single tree growing alone on the plain, the only shape in a rolling sea of melting snow.

The tree grew on a gentle slope, it's silhouette painted against the pale colors of the open landscape. Wonderboy wasted no time dismounting the horse and tugging the rifle from the scabbard. He stood with the big gun to his shoulder, his hands shaking from fear of the recoil. And when he fired a single round at the lonely trunk, soon his arms were shaking from the recoil itself.

The shot covered a fair distance, more than he hoped would be required of him, but Wonderboy had little certainty about what lie ahead. Quickly he scoped the trunk, checking his aim on the wood face. Satisfied, he saddled his horse and rode on.

As he turned he caught a breath of the wild and familiar smell of the spent cartridge, and Wonderboy tried to recall the last time he had fired the gun. Tipper had given it to him as a gift, upon his arrival at Tenpenny, a decade before. Shortly after Wonderboy's wife had died in the heat of the summer, Tip Holland, now a man of great resolve, rejoined his old friend and mourned his loss beside him. Less than a year later Wonderboy was given a new home on Tenpenny Hill, one he grew to love immediately, for it was a peaceful place, unlike the life of his younger years. He found that the years with his wife had been a peaceful, gentle time, the kind he preferred, and finding a similar home on Tenpenny Hill was a great comfort to his mending heart.

But Tip soon told him, "It is still a wild place, my friend," when he presented him the rifle, and Tipper struggled with the words.

"You are the kind of man that great gifts fall to. This is for you," he smiled. "If there is ever any danger I'll need a man I can trust."

The rifle had been kept on hand for hunting, or if something fierce came wandering up the hill, but in truth Wonderboy had little intention of ever using it. He never felt a kinship with any weapon, great or small and he knew Tip or Henry were both more likely to bring down any beast that might threaten the children.

But upon its presentation Tipper had taken him to the flats to give the rifle a try, and Henry was there beside them, still a boy at the time.

Timidly the little man aimed and fired and the recoil was so powerful that little Wonderboy nearly let the rifle fall from his hands. He smiled nervously and shook his head, trying to return the gift.

"It's yours," Tip told him. "We'll try it again."

Reluctantly the little man aimed at the river, picking a wide flat target, and although his aim proved true his arms and hands began to shake so violently after the second shot that he set the rifle down on the snow.

"Please no more shooting," he said.

"No more shooting?"

Wonderboy smiled awkwardly. "Please no more."

Tip chuckled, unloading the rifle. "But you might need it. If a bear comes after me."

Wonderboy shook his head, his smile wiped away. "It will be a bad day when I need to use this rifle."

Tip gripped the neck of his old friend. "Fine. Fine. You stick to the tracking - I'll stick to the shooting."

"That's what comes natural," Wonderboy had said. And like always his smile led the way.

And now, many years later, the tracking was still what came naturally. Before long Wonderboy barely had to think about what he saw to know which way to lead. But what didn't come naturally was the riding. He had never been confident in the saddle and the mount he had a chosen, Sissy's blue roan she called Monk, was far too tall a horse for such a small rider. She was much too tall for Sissy in fact, but that was beside the point. What Sissy looked for in a pony was much different from what the working men on the hill were looking for.

Wonderboy spent much of the day bent across that high saddle, his eyes following the tracks to see how the path diverted. If he had a shorter mount he could go faster, he knew. And when he caught them he wouldn't be so easy to spot in the forest.

It was a thought that came and went throughout the day and into the night. What would he do when he found these men? Wonderboy had never been a man of action, though he had led many such men, sometimes to their deaths. He knew too well the nature of such business, and that it never went as one anticipated. He also knew that killing horses was one thing, but killing a man was another.

When he was a boy, the elders of his village had declared war against a neighboring tribe of bloodletters. They had stolen three of their goats in the night and after hunting the men for two days the tribe's war party had only caught one of the thieves. One was enough for his eyes, Wonderboy remembered.

They dragged him far outside the safety of the boma and after driving four stakes into the ground they tied down his ankles and his wrists with goats hide and sprinkled blood on his thighs and left him for the night. The next morning the children of the village were led out to the spot where the stakes had been laid. Wonderboy and all of the other young ones were forced to look down at the scene. The man's wrists were still tied, but his top half was all that remained. The lionesses had consumed him, starting with his feet, and were halfway past his ribs when the sun rose.

Wonderboy had seen many other men laying dead on the soil at his feet, but despite how often he had seen it, the sight of a dead man, even the *thought* of a dead man, always chilled his blood. It called to mind many deep ponderings that Wonderboy had dwelled on in his bed late at night, one of them being the comfort and certainty that he would never have to take another man's life.

He rode faster and harder than he could remember, oftentimes gripping his hat for fear of losing it. But no faster than the ones I'm after, he thought. He could see from the digs that his quarry was moving with great haste, and may have already come across Tip and his sons. It was a constant fear in his heart that he would ride upon three dead friends at any moment; or three mounds of fresh soil covering up their bodies. But such thoughts never lingered in his mind. He simply reminded himself of who he was trying to save - knowing them to be worthy, capable men. It wouldn't be Tip's way to die out here with his sons, he told himself. Tip has a job to do and he hasn't finished doing it. He couldn't imagine the world without Tip Holland and that gave him great comfort as he cleared another hillock.

At dusk he reached the forest and as expected he was soon surrounded by darkness. He found a ring of stones in the clearing, but it was too dark to tell much about it. He fetched the lantern from his saddlebag and held it above the stones and lit it. Instantly he noticed the bootprints of his friends, and the flattened ferns where the party had made camp.

There were fish bones scattered about and he could see the tracks of Ibrahim turning into the forest, choosing another path. To Wonderboy, Ibrahim's trail was of little concern. He would have liked to speak briefly to the man about the four riders he was trailing. But time spent finding him in the forest was time he didn't have. He knew that his trail would slow greatly in the Wild West End and he could only hope to gain ground by his own efficiency.

He pursued the two parties throughout the night, never stopping to rest, his eyes locked on the trail beneath the glow of the lantern light. He found more abandoned firesides, one with the coals still sparkling. He found the site where the horses were traded, where the Bhotiyas turned east. Soon he discovered the point where Tipper and Putt had turned north, crossing the river, and the brothers had traveled on a path of their own.

He decided to follow the brother's trail, for Henry's large boots and heavy steps were the easiest to track at night. The brothers remained on the beaten path, heading west and after miles of steady work he discovered the sign of several bears, sniffing the earth, and the carcass of a cub with three of Jack's arrows raised from his back. The brothers were across the river now, one of them bleeding lightly. They found refuge in the arms of a great tree and some hours later their trail began to race along the river.

Soon he reached a great circling of horses - all of them from Forsman's troupe. There were cigarette butts left on the trail and the riders were moving with haste for some miles. But then, to his surprise, he crossed the track of a horse pointing east and he quickly dismounted. It was the track of one of Forsman's horses, the rear mount for most of the journey, but the track was now astray and from the lighter print he could see that the mount no longer carried a rider. The reigns hung underneath and snaked across the path, leaving their own trail, and from time to time Wonderboy could see a scrape where the horse had stumbled.

The discovery left him puzzled. Now the horses were three in number, and the rear horse carried two. He came to a place where the trail widened and a great host of bears had circled around the prints of a man in sandals.

Then the horses turned north through heavy timber, but Wonderboy had no intention of following them. Despite the bear traffic he could still see the cut of the brothers boot soles marching along the trail. It was their path he would follow. As the soft rains came down finding his friends was the only thing Wonderboy could think about.

The Window in the Meadow was growing close, which raised an anxious excitement in his heart. The excitement came because he hoped to question the couple who lived there. But at the same time his fear swelled within him, for he knew that in the near shadows of the forest there was an unseen host of bears surrounding him. Through the darkness, at the far end of the meadow he could barely see the shape of the tiny cabin, and the glow of the lantern in the window. He didn't like the idea of approaching the place gingerly, for he would feel too much like hunted prey. Best to announce your arrival, he thought. He raised his rifle and fired into the air. Having known the couple that lived there for many years, Wonderboy felt confident that his shot would make for a suitable greeting.

He waited beneath the moonlight, his rifle ready as the sound echoed through the trees.

Wonderboy had often thought of the family out here in this dark hollow. *Woodsies,* they were called by the people in the west village. What he thought about most was how lonely they must be out in this wild place. Wonderboy was no stranger himself to wild places but always they were peopled. He couldn't sort out what kind of days this family spent here, what filled their hours but silence. But Wonderboy was never one for idleness so the very thought of it perturbed him. He believed a man must have something, or especially someone to keep his mind occupied or else he'll grow sick with boredom. Even the brief moments he spent there irked him later on. If Wonderboy didn't have people to look after, he thought it would drive him crazy.

As Wonderboy waited in the saddle, Pasismanua came to the door. Papon stood silently by.

"It is Koba Shenzi," Wonderboy announced, riding closer. "I have ridden from Tenpenny Hill. Have you seen Tipper and his sons?"

"Yes," she answered. "They arrived yesterday morning. But then-"

Cautiously Wonderboy rode closer. "What?"

"Then riders came into our home and frightened the children. They had guns. They were looking for someone."

"They rode west?"

"Yes. Toward the west village. Who were the men?"

"Did you hear shooting?"

She looked at her husband. "We did."

"When?"

"Just after they passed. But too far away to be the riders."

Wonderboy cocked his head, surprised by these words.

"Too far. Too far," Papon called.

"I don't understand."

"We think it's Mister Tip who did the shooting."

Wonderboy had many more questions but the Woodsies had told him what he needed to know. He nodded and mounted his horse and rode on nervously, all along weary of the bears lurking about.

He rode west all that dark morning and there was no more tracking to do. The trail was cut deep before him and he began to see Putt's paws and the bootprints of his friends imprinted in the path. Soon the tracks were joined by the marks of a great bear, and two cubs behind her, and then by the horseman. The Tenpenny Three were traveling leisurely but the horsemen and the bears were moving with great haste.

Wonderboy was puzzled by the presence of the bears for he couldn't understand how the three parties worked together. But no sooner had he pondered this then he stumbled onto a bigger mystery. He came upon a small camp where Tipper and his sons had stopped for lunch and Wonderboy felt a cold shutter sweep over him when he looked down at the campsite. The backpacks of the travelers had been abandoned by the fire.

The belongings had been tossed from the packs and strewn about. From the looks of things, two small bear cubs had eaten what remained. Their mother's prints ran west and the others followed, including the horsemen. A great anxiety rose up within him for Wonderboy knew that Tipper would never have advised them to abandon their packs. His fears were confirmed as he examined the campsite. Nearby were two shell casings from Tipper's rifle, and ranging across the clearing, was a wide splattering of arterial blood.

The party was shot and fled, he believed, and the horsemen followed. A short time later a host of bear cubs came along and rummaged their gear.

Fast tracks led away from the clearing and Wonderboy found a trail of blood leading west across the forest. His heart sank as he followed it, knowing he would likely discover the remains of his friends at any moment.

But soon he began to see that the running prints of the old dog were covering the bloodstains, and over Putt's prints were those of the Tenpenny Three, who followed close behind. The bloodstains had been sprayed across a wide berth down the path, like a head wagging and there were dozens of small saplings that had been split with a tremendous weight, heavier even than a horse. Soon he began to spot the prints of a great bear galloping a trail all her own.

What happened here? He wondered. It seemed to him there was a great chase between the Tenpenny three, the old dog, a bear, and four riders. He couldn't make sense of it. He spent much of his pursuit on foot, peering closely at the tracks beneath the lantern light.

He moved with speed, racing from one clue to the next. But just as his mind was rattling he peered through a patch of tall ferns, holding his lantern high, and before him was a horrifying scene. His nostrils were filled with a wave of rotting flesh and a huge carcass, bloated and fly-ridden, was splayed out before him.

At first glance Wonderboy didn't know what he was looking at. In the lantern light all he could see was a swollen and shiny mass of fatty flesh.

He approached the shape cautiously in the dark, and it wasn't until he stood alongside it that he could see the head of the great bear, her mouth agape, her eyes blown out.

Wonderboy was quick to examine the scene, knowing he was closing in on the west village. A tree had been hastily snapped off near a pool of blood and there was a half-empty canteen with the screw top left open. Strands of Putt's hair were clumped on the ground and near the bear's head were two cigarette butts, barely smoked. There were bandage strips strewn about, and dozens of boot prints of all sizes, some of them Forsman's. With his horses in tow Wonderboy followed Henry's boot prints clearly pointing west.

Their pace grew slower as their trail led on and the old dog was no longer with them. The felled tree, the skinned bear, the bandages: as Wonderboy rode the evidence began to unfold. He knew it was Putt's blood he had found, and the old bear's he had been trailing. Tipper and his sons had skinned the bear and hung Putt in a tree-poled gurney and carried him west. It was a trick one of the Professional hunters had taught Wonderboy and Tip, when they were in the field together.

As he carried on his pace quickened and he felt a wave of relief come over him. Wonderboy was sad to think that the old dog was injured, but just moments before he was nearly certain that one of the Tenpenny three had been shot.

Now he had a good feeling in his heart. The trail of the horses hadn't doubled back and the distance to the west village was growing close. Forsman must have lost them to the village. Otherwise he would have buried them and headed east. Forsman had brass, Wonderboy knew, but he couldn't imagine any man riding into a place like the west village with but four riders. Every man in Luleo had arms.

No, Wonderboy believed the riders were circling north, watching and waiting. The little tracker held on to hope that he may still have time to warn his friends.

The sun was rising now. Even beneath the shadows cast by the great trees he could see faint hints of light growing around him. His pace quickened as he swept through the giant trunks and all along his eyes were honed to the trail. Soon the lantern wasn't needed and he traveled by dawn light, watching as the path coursed through the grassland that was opening up around him.

With the beauty of the morning swallowing him up Wonderboy thought of the early spring atop Tenpenny Hill, and the work to be done. The children would be rising soon and it would be another day in the warming sun.

He was mid stride with a gentle smile on his face when the crack of a bullet sliced through his horse's mane and killed her instantly. The mount flopped only once, and fell dead as her blood pumped across the saddlehorn.

In a blur Wonderboy was thrown from the saddle, tossing his lantern into the forest. He had been lucky with the fall, still within reach of the horse but hidden by the giant ferns. More bullets struck the trees that surrounded him as he gripped the rifle stock and pulled it from the scabbard.

Now he was alone on the forest floor, holding his rifle snug against his body, with four men perched somewhere nearby. The bullets continued to whistle by and twice he was struck by pieces of deadwood that shattered like shrapnel.

He had only eight rounds loaded in his rifle. The ammo belt that hung from his saddle was now crushed beneath the weight of Sissy's horse.

Hidden behind a great tree, Wonderboy breathed heavily. He knew that his size was his only advantage. He was so small and dark that when he slipped away into the shadows he was undetected in the half-light of the morning.

3. A Burial at Sea

When the brothers awoke it was not to the sound of the river, as was their custom now, nor to the snores of the old dog and his whimpers, but to the quick shuffling of feet throughout their little room - a hurried bustle, the sounds of tardiness and haste.

Jack woke immediately, stirred and embarrassed by what he saw. At the foot of his bed two young ladies were laying out newly shined shoes and fitted shirts and trousers, draping them over the footboard.

"Good morning," one of them said as the other nodded.

"Well hi," whispered Jack, a little unsure of himself. The sun had not yet risen and the room was lit only by candlelight. "What's all this?"

"Your father asked us to get you going. You must get dressed at once."

"What for?" Jack wondered.

"No questions," she told him expectedly, "Rouse Henry and ready yourself fast as you can."

Jack looked over at his brother, who lay with one eye open and cleared his throat. "Who dares disturb me on this holy day of repose?" Henry said high and mighty into his pillow, receiving a chuckle. "'Tis early yet and nay not enough hours have passed since last I fell to slumber."

The ladies were laughing heartily. "Would you rather we threw water on his face?" they asked Jack.

"It wouldn't help."

"Go from me *now!* You *thieving* harpies!" Henry ordered with both eyes closed, "Go from me or I will banish you from all of my houses!"

Jack looked on in amazement as the two young women sparked at his jabs. Each one absorbed his threats with haughty delight. "Then banish us!" the spicier of the two called out. "Your Lordship is wild looking and smells of brook trout."

Henry shifted on his pillow. "This is Jack Yellowbelly, my trusting squire and servant. He will see to your banishment. Off you go. Away with them."

Jack smiled, "I resign my position."

Henry buzzed his lips against his pillow case, "Have I not *one* worthy servant who will defend my noble right to respite? Must I live in this bored and crowded realm with no one to aid me? Nay but my kingdom is filled with none but noisy harpies and sons of betrayal to rouse me to arbitrary meetings. That is the state of things."

The two young ladies turned serious in an instant, remembering once again the purpose of their haste. One of them said with no jeering in her voice, "This is no arbitrary meeting, Henry Snow. No, that joke won't do at all."

Henry rubbed his eyes and pushed himself up from the mattress. His voice had returned to its usual morning timber. "Then not just another breakfast feast?" he wondered.

"You could have a breakfast feast back at Tenpenny," she answered. "You didn't come all this way for food."

Jack looked up curiously. For the first time he paid close attention to the clothes at his feet.

The young ladies solemnly walked toward the door. They were both quite serious when one of them said. "Like we told you there isn't much time. The sun is rising soon. Come out to the dock when you are dressed. And come with a more serious tone," she warned.

"Are we dressing for a wedding, sister?"

"A funeral, Henry." And then she closed the door.

The faint light of the cold spring morning was now beginning to break upon the sea. As they stepped out from their cabin all of Luleo's bustle and toil that had charmed the brothers the night before vanished instantly, having been replaced with silence and stillness. Not a footstep, or a door creak, nor the cry of babes or women's laughter were heard across the tiny village; nothing but a gentle breeze tumbling off the sea.

Like his brother beside him, Jack was certain that answers were coming. He assured himself that the questions that had been strung out across many years were certain to be answered, answered in Luleo, before they pressed on any further, and he hoped answered that very morning, before the rising sun.

Henry proved to be in tune with his brother's thoughts when he said, "I for one am not a patient man, and never aim to be. But what patience I do have has just about run out."

Jack smiled. "Do you consider yourself a man, Henry?"

Henry Snow gave his brother a curious glance, as if the question was silly. "Oh, no. Not where it counts I don't. And patience is one of those places where it counts."

The vast lawn was vacant, save for two long rows of lanterns erected sometime in the night that stretched across the green field all the way to the dock. The lanternlight flickered and glowed down the trail to the sea, inviting them on. Snow and Oakham followed the path silently, their eyes ahead for what awaited.

"What about you?" Henry wondered. "I respect you as a patient observer. Maybe a bit too careful for my taste."

"Was that a question?"

"Do you consider yourself a man?" Henry continued. "Or have you not been *burdened* with enough yet to call yourself one?"

Jack liked his brother in these moments. Authentic and vulnerable were badges Henry wore quite well, if rarely. "I don't know when the burden will be enough for that," Jack admitted. "I do know I want to be remembered as someone who carried my share of the water."

"That's all?"

"That's enough."

Henry gave his brother a serious look. "When you say it I believe you."

They could now see before them a yawl tethered to the dockposts at the end of the long lantern rows. Both brothers were certain that it hadn't been docked there the night before.

But ahead of the yawl, on the last stretch of lawn before the dock, surrounded by a circle of lanterns, were rows and rows of pews, thirty or more, facing the sea, and at its rear was built a small stone pit, glowing above the dawnlight.

It was there where Henry and Jack saw three men knelt deep in talk beside a fire. They were but glowing figures at that distance and their words were but faint whispers. But as they approached the brothers could soon see that it was their father and Unger, and a third man they hadn't met. All three were well-dressed in clothes cut for such an occasion, by the same tailor, Jack predicted. Though that was the only prediction he would risk.

The third man, a grave and quiet statue, was built like a set of twigs and his hair was long and worn back to his shoulders. Each of his eyes struggled to peer through the sad and tired sockets that drooped like deflated tires. But unlike his companions he watched with interest as the brothers approached.

What circled before them was the talk of serious men, Jack knew, and a cold shutter ran over him as his father raised his eyes to greet them. This *was* to be a funeral, Jack knew, for he had never seen such a weighty look worn by Tip Holland, and there had been many sad days on Tenpenny Hill. As the brothers arrived the circle opened to receive them.

"Morning," Unger began.

"Morning, Sir. How's Putt?"

"He's sleeping fine. I just checked him."

The stranger nodded to the brothers, "I am LaMont," he said in a nearly indiscernible smoker's rasp. "I was at sea with your father."

The brothers offered their names.

"Take a seat," Tipper said, and they did. "I want you to listen carefully. This is the turning point in our journey and we have only moments before it begins."

"Yessir."

"A man very dear to all in Luleo has died. The father of this place. Last night he was brought here from across the sea and this morning his funeral will be held. It is important that you be here to see it. I know how tired you both are but you must stay awake and pay attention. These details may only come once."

"What day did he die?" Henry said, startling his brother.

Tipper seemed surprised as well, "Three days ago. Wednesday."

"So this is why we've come." Henry said.

"Yes," Tipper told him.

"The first of a number of reasons," Unger added.

The fire crackled as Jack thought back to Wednesday, his last full day on Tenpenny Hill, to the phone call, to the changes in Tip's disposition, and the hurried departure. Finally everything came together.

"Is it someone we knew?" Jack asked.

Tipper breathed deeply. "No. Unfortunately not," he told them. "Though I desired that for many years."

"For many years?"

"More than anything."

"Dern that's not like you, Tipper," Henry suggested. "To want something and not get it. Something grand must have blocked it from going off."

Tears filled their father's eyes. "He had been in prison since I've known you."

"Good reason."

"The only possible reason." And the other men nodded.

The sparkle of the flamelight glistened on Tipper's face. He seemed ready to speak again but his voice crumbled at the start of every word.

Suddenly as they were watching the fire a single bellchime rang clearly from the dock. The three men stood quietly as Henry and Jack squinted toward the sea. "That is the calling bell," Unger told them. "We're to be silent from here on."

The brothers turned their attention back to Luleo. Beyond the glow of the lanterns they could now hear doors creaking open and soon could see shadows spilling onto the lawn. One after another all of the villagers emerged from their seaside cabins, some families holding hands and some singing gentle songs. All of them were dressed in heavy white fashions similar to the style Jack and Henry had been presented. Within a few moments the crowd funneled down between the lanterns and met in unison like a great procession. The brothers watched the crowd as they trickled silently into the pews. Unger and LaMont found their seats but Tipper held his sons back, waiting for the remainder of the crowd to pass.

Jack noted new faces, some with wildly extravagant features that he was certain weren't present the evening before. Each one seemed alarmed by the presence of the brothers, as Jack and Henry were both now accustomed to.

When all had passed Tipper waved the brothers on. They each stepped cautiously, both a bit timid, until their eyes were drawn to the end of the aisle.

Standing at the head of the dock, alongside the podium, was a tall, noble character if Jack had ever seen one. Dark features with eyes of grey silver, strong proportions and a weathered brow, with the dark mane of a man half his age, and a steady glance of virtue and reassurance. He calmed all who looked for answers with his great, restful dignity. Both brothers assumed he had emerged from the yawl and rung the bell, for neither had seen him pass in the crowd.

The great figure was robed for a funeral, with sharp, simple lines - a silk scarf draping to his knees; and though he was richly adorned his boots betrayed him for a sailor. Indeed his hands did the same as he raised them to welcome the gathering crowd, his palms the picture of the sea's restless toil. Around his neck was a single black Tahitian pearl roped with common thread and he wore a silver rosary ring on each hand. He waited patiently as the crowd found their seats, nodding in silent recognition to each man and woman as if a great span of time had passed since last he had seen these friends.

But when Jack and Henry came into view he didn't offer any sign of welcome, but instead stared upon them with instant wonder.

"Who's he?" Henry whispered as they sat on the front pew.

Tipper hesitated. Finally he answered, "He is presiding."

No answer at all, Henry thought. But he knew there must be reason for his father's hesitation.

As they waited Jack and Henry looked beyond the pews to the yawl where for the first time they noticed a coffin resting atop the port deck. They each wondered where the coffin would be buried, for there was no gravesite cut before them. But their questions would have to wait. Before they could ask anything the man at the pulpit was addressing the crowd, a book open in his hands.

"'When God made His promise to Abraham, since there was no one greater for Him to swear by, he swore by himself, saying, "I will surely bless you and give you many descendants." And so after waiting patiently, Abraham received what was promised.'

The man took a deep breath.

'You see every man must choose either to take God's gracious blessing or to shun it. Every man must choose to rid himself of calling or follow the call. All choices lie within. And if we are loyal to the call we shall receive what has been promised. This gathering here, my friends, is what was promised to our blessed Otsov Kolschen."

Briefly Jack and Henry faced one another.

"Each of us here have a story to tell of the man. Some sad, some funny, but all of them reflect the man in the same light - for he was the same man to each of us - there was only one side to him. His love came for us all."

The man's eyes passed over the brothers. "My story is laid at sea, in the Maldives, in the most beautiful season of my life. But for many of you your stories are much different. He appears to you now during times of great anguish, reminding you of your story with him, and how he comforted then. He comforts still, does he not?

Some of you were but children when he found you, some old men, even older than he, though it's hard to imagine being older than Kolschen. Or younger really. But I assure you he had a mother and a father - and they bore a great likeness in spirit. They were reproducers. And they reproduced a reproducer. And so did he; that was his gift to us. And so on and so on - and now a crowd is gathered beside the sea.

And this crowd has the same calling - made by example, a calling that doesn't taint with time or tarry when urgent - but ticks away with every chance meeting, every teachable instant, reminding the easily distracted heart of the reproducing we must do.

In my story he came gently when life called for gentleness and he carried justice when it was ordered. But even then - he wore an invincible love. A love that made me, this rebuked man, feel neither judgement nor ridicule for a moment, but instead held by a father that I had never had. And now I want to reproduce that story in my own life.

For Kolschen was a man of stories. There was nothing recreational that he would rather do than listen to the stories of others. In this way he served us all. An old man in a train station asks you where you're from and in a blink it's been half a day and he's bought you a meal and two coffees and all the while it's like you've known him your whole life, and he barely says a word. He just listens, indestructible. Undistractible. For all of us long to be known. Did anyone really know us like Kolschen? This prisoner to listening. How fantastic, how enduring were his ears?

There should be no tears today - not for a man who lived like this. It would seem a disgrace to his memory to wish his life even a bit different - even if that wish was for him to have lived a little longer, or for him to have smelled the sweet air of freedom one more time. Yet even though it seems a disgrace - I wish those things. I wish for more of the world to know him. But for now let us remember him with our stories. . . before we return his body to the sea."

And the great figure stepped down from the pulpit and found a seat at the end of the front pew. All was silent in the crowd.

The first to stand was a woman, young and brazen, telling her story of her triumphant escape from an abusive father, and how Kolschen walked her through it. She was followed by a little Filipino man, who muttered only a few words before breaking down.

One by one the citizens of Luleo approached the podium to tell their stories. All were favorites of the tellers, some involving Tipper and Unger, and the man in all of them seemed like a legend to Jack and a myth to Henry, a man who had survived impossible things and loved dearly those surrounding him. The wondrous tales poured out like tears.

When it was Tip's turn he rose to the podium as the first hints of sunlight were breaking on the water. All was silent as he unfolded a paper sheet from his shirt pocket.

"He always encouraged me to write," Tip explained. "So I chose to write this - as a tribute."

Then he cleared his throat.

"There are many men I love - but your father alone I respected."
Said a friend to me the other day when she heard the unexpected
"Kolschen was the only man I knew with shoulders wide enough
To love boys when times were easy and lead men when times were tough."

He spent a lifetime giving gifts - keeping no receipts along the way
Because the treasures he handed us were the kind we never can repay
He never learned how to lie and he rarely told a joke.
But his laughter was like a freight train and his word was like an oak

The statement often came from men who met him only once,
"Your father has all the character," they'd say, "without any of the fronts."
And we often pondered what it was that made the big man bond
To hearts of strangers when they met and many years beyond

He looked his neighbors in the eye and loved them where they were
He listened well, with open arms and their hearts began to stir.
He never missed a single chance to cherish and to serve
And when someone wronged him deeply he never gave back what
they deserved

He had a way of welcoming, even when he was your guest
His love was slow and steady - but was never laid to rest
He made all who were to meet him feel a little taller still
And he never preached a sermon that his life could not fulfill

I've never known a gentler man - though not afraid to live.
He was not afraid to die as well - the last lesson he had to give
I was told there was no fear in him - his assurance like a wing.
That shaded his guards from all the doubt that loss and pain can bring.

They watched him smile at the thought of what awaited him
For he knew his life was fading fast and his time was growing thin
So in the end as they sang a tune he winked at them for fun
"Who would you like to see?" they asked, and he told them,
"Everyone."

And in walked his cellmates expecting him to be some other man
But instead he gave his listening ear and the welcome of his hand
By his side some asked him if he had more he wished to say
But he had said it with his life, they knew, and he's still saying it today

He's telling us to love our children, to be faithful to our wives
He's telling us that to live for Christ means to give our very lives
He's telling stories of forgiveness now, love in its finest form
Of how there is nothing left to fear, of hope amidst the storm

Forever more Kolschen will shout the echo of his story
That he lived a life from start to end for his savior's glory
He was taken home on a Wednesday morning without a worry
on his heart
And together he is with his King and they will never be apart

And even though his voice is gone, he'll always have a say
In how we raise our children - in how we love and how we pray
In how we imitate the manner in which he held us in his arms
How he prayed for our departures, how he shielded us from harm

And now we all feel the weight of the council he won't give
There are questions that need answering, and roles he used to live
But some of us would never know how to trust in God alone
If he hadn't left each of us to steer these waters on our own

For though I have a hole in my heart in the shape of my dear dad
It serves as a reminder of the blessing that we had
When he was walking here among us - a shepherd to us all
Faithfully pursuant of his family and his call

And now the orchard that he left us grows from the very seed
That he scattered on the ground until everyone agreed
That the fertile soil that he tilled will forever hold her roots
Yielding bushels for generations of the first and ripest fruits

I sit and wonder about him now - Of the choices he would make
I didn't deserve to be his son - I only rode upon his wake
But I know his life was simple - he loved his neighbor until his rest
And I think it would be hard to find a man who was as blessed.

My life is on a mission now to carry on my father's torch
Handled with clumsy awkwardness - my fingers sure to scorch
But a torch is meant to light a path and on this mission I will strive
For I would rather walk my father's path, then of any other man alive

Tipper stepped away from the podium to the sounds of quiet gasps throughout the crowd. Henry and Jack were each growing tearful as they watched him move down to find his seat with his sons. It was Henry, so moved, who leaned in to his father and whispered. "When did you write that?"

Tip wiped his eyes. "This was my chore in the forest."

Before either of the brothers could ask any more questions another disciple of Kolschen stepped up behind the podium and began his story. His was a long parable, told over the course of many years, broken apart by mighty laughter and gentle tears, and ending with the great man's imprisonment.

"He dealt justly so he will be remembered justly."

Next was a tiny woman, middle aged, who stuttered through her thoughts and seemed to tremble with every word. She told of much different circumstances, a single day on a ferryboat, when she was traveling home, heartbroken, planning to end her life when a gentle giant a few seats down had found the words that no one else could.

There were tales of great valor told by men who had witnessed it first hand, two of whom chose to honor Kolschen with song, while another prayed and others still told word for word of their deliverance, some at sea, some in cities, while others simply cried.

But the story Jack listened to the closest was about a Province called Uttar Pradesh and a young girl who lived there. At first Jack listened vaguely, having absorbed so much that morning that he could hardly open his eyes, but when he learned that the girl's name was Padibatakal, Jack nearly sprung from his seat. His eyes danced back and forth as he heard her story, and the teller's as well, both delivered from a world of servitude.

When the young man had finished his tale Jack longed to ask questions of Padi's life, but the moment would have to wait, for others were still waiting to pay their respects.

The talk continued through the rising sun and not all of their words bear repeating. It is enough to say that Kolschen was honored well, and remembered precisely as he was. When the line had ended and all had spoken, several of the deck hands untied the trawler, boarded her, and steered the vessel out to sea. For minutes on end the crowd watched in silence as the sun continued her climb and when the trawler was deep offshore the huge weighted coffin was dropped into the sea, sinking immediately.

The somber scene turned joyful as the citizens of Luleo rose and embraced one another. Henry and Jack watched as some in the crowd mingled and laughed, while others sat alone to weep. The pair stood away from the gathering, watching as Tipper left their sides and greeted one guest after another.

The brothers both felt overwhelmed by the weight of the morning. Jack hadn't been to a funeral since his own mother's and Henry could not remember one in his life. The sun was up now, full enough to show the forest all around them and the sea and the mountains beyond but it was the beauty of a life well-lived that flooded their thoughts. We must have some hours to talk, Jack thought. Just sit and talk with Tip and set all of this straight.

Henry, always in tune, must have been thinking that very thing for in the next moment he whispered to his brother. "I think it's time we cleared the fog. Have a chat with the old man."

They followed Tipper through the crowd, hoping to pull him aside. Jack for one felt that if one more question was posed before he found some answers he would surely collapse. But Henry believed that he already had the answers, at least some of them.

But all of his confidence was whisked away as he heard the sudden crackle of gunfire beyond the tree line. His eyes turned toward the forest as more shots came, one after another, before all fell quiet. The chatter of the crowd was surrounding him, drowning out all sounds from the distance, but he knew what he had heard. He turned his head to watch his brother, but Jack gave the sounds no more than a passing glance.

When they approached Tipper he too was distracted by the crack of gunfire in the distance. Strange, Tip thought, for he believed that every man of Luleo had been present at the funeral. More than once he looked back to the tree line, puzzled, but as he turned toward the faces in the crowd it seemed that no one else had noticed.

As Henry and Jack reached their father, Unger was standing beside him. "Is anyone out in the forest?" Tip asked.

Unger shrugged. "No. Everyone's here. Why?"

"I heard some shots past the trees."

Unger faced the forest and cocked his head. "Maybe Ibrahim coming back. Or the Woodsies."

"Maybe," Tip said, though he couldn't hide his doubts.

Just then Unger turned to the brothers. "I'm sure this all must seem a bit overwhelming."

Henry nodded. "Unless there's more to come we'd like some time to talk."

"No, no, Henry. We understand. But I'm afraid there is more to come. This very instant. A matter for the two of you that's a bit more pressing than casual conversation." Unger looked at Tip. "Are we ready?"

Tip Holland looked carefully at his sons and then over his shoulder at a cabin in the distance. Then he nodded, "Yes, we are."

"Ready for what?" Jack asked.

They were led away from the procession and across the great lawn into a log cabin with a giant pair of open bay doors, inviting them in. The room was filled with world maps and charts on the walls and a library of old texts alphabetized on the shelves.

Both brothers could see from the scuffs on the floor that the room had been used to store huge crates, or some supply at one time. But now the room was empty except for half a dozen chairs that were circled up at the center. Already seated were Unger and the frail man called LaMont, and in between them was the robed figure who had overseen the funeral. He sat with a pair of decorative boxes at his feet, and as the brothers entered he rose slowly to greet them.

"My name is Ruffino," he said, shaking their hands.

"Pleased to know you."

"Have a seat," the man told them, pointing to the chairs.

Each brother found their seat quickly and soon Tipper had joined them and all six were circled up facing one another. The man named Ruffino looked at each of the brothers carefully.

"These are for you," the man said, lifting the two decorative boxes onto his lap. "I have been holding onto them for many years."

Each of the boxes were intricately carved, a cherry wood finish, the brother's names engraved on the top.

"What did we do to deserve these?" Henry asked.

"Whether you deserve them or not is yet to be seen, Henry. But they're yours," Ruffino said, handing over the boxes.

"You act as if you know us."

"We've met before," he assured them. "But you were only infants then."

Jack flinched when he heard this, his mind spinning with questions.

"That may be," Henry said. "But the people here don't know us as infants. They know much more than that. Things we don't even know. They know who we are."

"Some of them do."

"Do *you* know that?"

Ruffino looked long at him before answering.

"Henry Snow."

"Yes?"

"You were born in Chattisgaarh District, India - July 17, 1977."

Henry answered smugly. "Was I?"

"To mother Phillippa and father Alexander. Your father passed away August 9th of the same year. Soon after you moved to live with the sisters of St. Benedict's Orphanage and School on August 21, 1977 near Kimberley, South Africa."

Now Henry was staring down at the floor. His eyes dancing back and forth.

"You remained there for five years until you were adopted by Stuart Whitlock, also known as Tip Holland - May 21st, 1983 and moved again to Tenpenny a week later. You've been living with the orphans ever since."

Henry took a deep breath and looked up again at Ruffino. "Was that a question?" Henry mused.

"No. Do *you* have any questions?"

"No," Henry admitted. "Phillippa and Alexander. July 17th. Chattisgaarh. That about does it."

Ruffino shook his head, "That doesn't even break the surface."

"If you say so," Henry told him.

Confused by the boy's words, Ruffino turned to Jack, who waited longingly in his chair.

"Jack Oakham?"

"Yessir?"

"Jack you were born in Pokhara, Nepal, January 4th, 1977 to father Peter and mother Sierra Jo."

"Peter?"

"Yes. He was a fine man."

With every word Jack's heart seemed to rise in his chest.

"Then you moved to live in Chattisgaarh District, India, early March, 1977. Your father passed away on August 9th, 1977. It was then that you and your mother traveled back across the sea and were not found until May of 1988, in Calcasieu, Louisiana, three weeks after your mother's death. Jack, then by your own reconnaissance you made your way to

Tenpenny, arriving at the age of eleven on June 23rd, 1988 where you too have been living with the orphans ever since."

Henry and Jack faced one another.

"I think we knew one another as babies," Henry suggested.

"Is that true?" Jack asked. "Were we in Chattis. . . .?"

"*Chattisgaarh.*"

"Were we in Chattisgaarh at the same time?"

The four men nodded. "You were," Tip told them. "Some days you even slept in the same crib."

Jack's head was spinning now. He couldn't contain his frustration. He was thinking of old Putt on the mend, and the story of Padibatakal, and the mysteries of Luleo, and now, after all these years he had been given clues to his identity. It all seemed too much for the boy to handle.

Ruffino started again. "I know this is a great deal to absorb. And I know you are weary from your journey. But—"

"Dad," Jack said, interrupting. The circle of men looked up in surprise.

"Yes, Jack?"

"Is he about to tell us something?"

Ruffino leaned back in his chair and smiled.

"Yes, Jack. He is."

"Why don't *you* do it? No offense, Sir, but we just met. If it's all the same, Dad I'd rather hear it from you."

Tip turned to Ruffino and asked politely. Ruffino nodded back, giving Tipper the floor. It was the first instance in either brother's life where Tip Holland asked for permission.

Suddenly Tip was in a strange mood, one neither brother recognized. He was never a man for giving speeches, nor did he enjoy having the floor, but he seemed in the lightest of moods as he spoke, as if some new freedom had been granted him.

"Yes Jack, we are here to tell you something. Something you've waited many years to hear."

"Why here? Why now?"

"Firstly because I wanted you to know who Kolschen was. Not just from me but from so many who knew him. You were denied a precious gift of his friendship."

"I wish we had known him," Jack nodded. "I can see what you loved about him."

Henry agreed, though only with his eyes. He was certain he knew what was coming.

Tip leaned in to the brothers and wiped his tears. "Jack do you remember the question you asked back in the woods?"

Surprised, Jack said, "Yessir."

Tipper gave a long heavy sigh. The other men were silent and all eyes were on the brothers. "The reason I have brought you all this way," Tip told them. "And the reason you live in Tenpenny, and the reason I chose you - was because Otsov Kolschen was your grandfather."

4. The Sons of Otsov Kolschen

by Jack Oakham

After a year had passed Kolschen told him they could meet again, if Tip wished it. But Tipper was quick to discover that a year was passing too slowly for his taste. Just days after Wonderboy walked across the wilds to find his wife, Tip too, was finished as a safari man. He collected his wages and struck east across the continent, taking an overland passage through the rugged plains, among savannahs and foothills to the floor of the great mountain.

Throughout that summer he threaded among the herds of the wild migration like a bird of prey and when he reached the great desert Tip dressed himself in white and traveled among the Tuaregs for the autumn of that year.

The great caravans moved like restless vagrants, their only purpose striking out for water, and Tip watched as the dunes tumbled and silvered beneath the glistening moon. But no matter the company he kept or the language they spoke, not an evening would pass when he didn't envision his destination, or wonder of Kolschen's place in the world.

"At whose door are you standing, friend? Whose heart are you making well?"

Tip remembered Kolschen as he had last seen him, his pack worn like a knapsack across his great shoulders, his hair and his mustache filthy from travel, but his great laugh echoing through whatever space he filled.

From hamlet to village to salty sea Tip Holland traveled a thousand miles if it was one and never saw joy like Otsov Kolschen's.

What will he say when we come together? Tip wondered. Will he still be as proud as he once had been?

After months apart a shadow of doubt was cast across his memories, and he thought it had all been a dream. Kolschen told him once that men are fragile beasts. "Leave them unwatered and they grow to doubt themselves."

Those words had echoed through Tip's heart over many lands. But he wasn't about to forget the lessons he had learned, or the man he hoped to be, no matter how many unwatered miles he traveled. Tip's bond to Kolschen was sealed for life.

When he reached lands end he dunked his head in the salty sea and booked passage across it, and by the time he made berth on the western shore he was hungry for crowds and fruits and the colors of his world. He was weary of the road by that time, but Tip still had a great journey ahead of him.

He found a curio shop in a bazaar and spent his last dollars on a warm meal and a pocket harp and quietly taught himself songs in the alleyways. He slept in roadside ditches, in empty train cars, on the rooftops of buildings, wherever he could find rest. He traveled in the mornings and stopped on street corners when he grew too hungry to walk. He busked for hours with his pocket harp, playing exotic songs from the west like Amazing Grace and Davey Crockett that the locals had never heard of and when his purse was heavy he pointed east and traveled any way he could manage.

He measured his days in miles and his months by countries until it was all like some hazy dream of crowds and streets, of blisters and chatter that he couldn't understand nor did he wish to. All he wanted was to reach the end of his road, to hear a familiar voice. His heart ached and moaned for the comfort of friendship.

He reached Uttar Pradesh the evening before his deadline and in all his travels he had never known a more filthy land. By then he had no money and little food. His clothes were beginning to flake off at places, his shirt pocket ripped away, his socks and shoes threadbare and rank-smelling. His hair was long, his beard patchy and dark.

The crowds and the stench filled him with disappointment as he moved aimlessly through the streets. He kept a look-out for new birds and trees like Kolschen had taught him, but it was too dark to see and there were none to find in the heart of the city. There was nothing at all but people; masses of people moving and dealing and shouting their lives away. What Kolschen wanted there Tipper could only guess.

The hour was late and he found a slum on the western side of the city where crowds of children had gathered to sleep in the streets. They laid hip to hip atop the trash-beaten brick sidewalks near a long row of shanties; Some of the lucky ones had blankets, while others curled with the street dogs to feel their warmth.

Tip curled up beside an abandoned news kiosk, still within sight of the children, and once again read the instructions that Kolschen had left him. When he was finished he wrote in his journal beneath the flickering street lamp and watched the swarming moths circle above him, listening to the labored breaths and snores of the children until he fell asleep.

It rained in the night and he woke to see the children migrating calmly to the walls beneath the gutters and Tip hurried to do the same. The following morning the sound of a train car as she shook was what finally stirred him. When he sat up the children were already sifting through the rubbish heaps that their mothers had searched the day before. They found bits of bone for chewing or fruit cores if they were lucky. Others were making water in the street and chasing their sisters and brothers and dogs down the sidewalks.

Tip watched them painfully. Their feet were wide and disfigured, calcified by the urine puddles they soaked in. Darkened by the rain, the vomit, the scat the livestock left, stained forever with the filth of tradition. The peanut roasters hissed at them when thcy strayed too close.

Tip was glad he had finished what little food he had in the night, for eating in sight of them seemed to him a great sin. He rose and nodded his hellos and all that morning ranged the sweaty streets, grey with gloom, and found them dimmer and more depressing than the night before. There was no color to the brick or the clay, the walls, the street, the children's faces. The color belonged only to the trees, ashosha, bouganvillea, banyon, coconut, and the crisp laundry which glowed an array of miraculous yellows and pinks, reds and limes, and flapped from the windows like flags of prosperity.

Tip thought of his mother then, who had hung similar displays from her balcony window. Somewhere in those rain-soaked streets the boy realized he couldn't remember her face. He felt certain that her features would eventually spring to mind but they never did. Two years to the month had passed since he had left his mother and sister and already their faces were gone. He hardened his heart with the knowledge that he would never likely see them again.

His instructions were to "Convene on Baiga Boksas Street, at the northwest corner near the grocer, at 7a.m. on the twenty-fifth of July."

He checked his watch and quickened his pace. Many of the streets had no names and those that did were not well-marked. Twice he had to seek directions from the only men who spoke his language. There were hundreds of faces coming and going, some of them children, others peddlers. They rode bikes and rickshas and cabbies and dodged the strange beasts that roamed freely throughout the city. But to his delight he reached his destination sooner than expected.

Tip took a deep breath as he tucked the instructions back in his pocket, and a strange floating sensation overtook him as he crossed the street. Before him stood a building, long abandoned. Beside it was a line of seamstresses working in the shade and a raw foods market with vendors shouting and laughing and inviting him to buy. He reached out for the only door he could see, a heavy wooden frame with no windows, stiff to the push, and when he moved inside he saw a huge empty warehouse and a stairwell with fresh footprints shining in the dust.

His heart raced as he scaled the stairs. Voices could be heard faintly on the second floor and they grew clearer as he reached the top. He turned one corner and then another and when he arrived at the end of the hall he stood in the shadows of a doorway, looking in on a great circle of men.

They were seated before him, deep in talk, and even from behind Kolschen was unmistakable, rising out of his chair like an imposing figure. The men surrounding him were all strangers to Tip's eyes and when he walked through the door they rose to their feet in unison.

Kolschen turned, a laughing smile spread across his face as he threw his arms in the air and kept them high as he crossed the room. Tip grinned as the big man hauled him into his arms and hugged him fiercely.

"Alive and well!" Kolschen said.

The boy was overjoyed of course, though he felt a bit self-conscious about his stench. But Kolschen didn't notice. There was a great lightness in his eyes; a genuine delight as he scanned Tipper from head to toe.

"My dear friend," he whispered. "A grateful man I am!" Then he slapped him on both shoulders and turned to address the men.

"My friends, *this* is our young Tovarisch. As most of you know Tip was my understudy, and my bodyguard, all the way from Kluchi to Mussell Bay."

Every man among them had a strange joy painted across his face, as if they too had once received a similar introduction. It was only then that Tip fully absorbed the men who stood before him. They each had the look of capability, though Tipper could not decide what gave it away. They ranged in age from their mid-twenties all the way to Kolschen himself, who must have been near to seventy by then. On either side of him were two men who looked like twins.

"These are my boys," Kolschen told him.

His sons were proudly named Pietr and Alexei and both had inherited the pale blue eyes of their father. Yet it was hardly Kolschen's only legacy to his boys. Each brother spoke with authority and displayed gentleness in their actions and though neither were quite so large as their father, they each brought weight and influence into every room they entered. Pietr was the older brother, a carpenter by trade, but so were all of the Kolschen men. He was quiet and reliable, and less apt to joking than his brother was, though it would be hard to find a more patient man. Alexei favored his father more than Pietr did, though both bore a sudden likeness. He was jovial and tender, and apt to talk for long stretches, and to listen even longer.

After Tip shook each brother's hand the other men approached him, and graciously introduced themselves. There was Brett Myles Emerick, an engineer from Lancaster. Derealdjon Polle, a squat dentist who along with his assistant, Yancey LaMont, were the only non-whites. Among them stood Ruffino, who, although the youngest among them, was heading up the operation in Uttar Pradesh whenever Kolschen was absent.

Ruffino was a well-structured man, who although not much older than himself, possessed a strength that Tipper had rarely seen in any of his countrymen. Tip eyed him curiously. He seemed tempered beyond his years and had none of the ignorance and bravado that often comes with youth. Kolschen and all of his men held his opinion close to their hearts and trusted them as they did one another.

There were seven men altogether. "Kaleos" they were named. Called men with a called purpose. They had each committed their lives to the service of their fellow man and Kolschen was their captain, the first among equals.

They sat together and within minutes Kolschen requested tales of his travels and when they had sung many songs they celebrated Tip's arrival and toasted his health. Despite his best efforts to hold it back, soon Tipper was weeping. The boy had never received such a welcome in his life.

But to his relief not a word of shame was given. Tipper was to learn that compassionate eyes and patient ears were two talents that came with the trade.

In time the Kaleos began to tell tales of their own - tales of heroic men and evil dealings, of rare things altogether holy, and common things altogether wicked. They too shared of their comings and goings, great tales of weary travel that brought them to Uttar Pradesh. Tip learned quickly that every man in the party had sacrificed much to be there and he would soon learn that they knew his story well.

"Wwwwhat are we doing here?" Tip asked shyly.

"Ah!" Kolschen said, wrapping his great arm around Tipper's shoulder. "Derealdjon, bring us the map."

Derealdjon Polle unrolled a map of the district over the table. The Kaleos sat listening as Kolschen went on to describe their plan.

"The greatest number are to the North. *Here* and *here*," he said pointing. "But there are traders working all along the border. They contain the greatest number *here*, near the heart of the slums."

Tip looked up, searching the eyes of the men, especially Ruffino's before returning to the map.

"Our hope is to build at three key intersections," Kolschen explained. "The first will be along this thoroughfare where the crowds filter down from the slums."

Ruffino stood and moved alongside Kolschen. He too pointed for Tip to see. "This one will give us the most visibility and therefore legitimacy, but once the other two are integrated we expect them both to serve a greater need."

Tip looked up again, but this time with a strained smile. "I'm sorry," he said. "I must be dense."

The men looked at him blankly.

Tip waited through an awkward silence but when no one spoke he was forced to admit, "I have no idea what we're talking about."

Kolschen chuckled, "Forgive me!" the big man roared. "So many miles and so many words. I often forget what hasn't been said."

He gestured for Tip to sit. "You have journeyed far and are now at home among new friends."

Tip smiled.

"What are we doing here? You ask." Otsov Kolschen grew suddenly serious."Tip, these six men and myself, along with a great many helpers, are committed with all of our resources to strike at the heart of the *slave trade*."

Their headquarters was positioned upstairs, in the very room where the men had reunited. The Kaleos felt no need to paint the walls or dress the windows for fear of standing out. The entire facility remained run down, and their efforts were directed elsewhere.

"Whether you knew it or not," Kolschen explained to Tip. "You have jumped headlong into a harsh reality. Throughout this district, millions of men and women, young and old, who appear merely poor, are actually slaves. They are held as collateral. In bondage against a debt that is owed. And there they will remain until the debt has been paid. Most of them are completely unaware of the loan that they are paying off. They were born into it, from some age-old agreement that their father or grandfather failed to uphold. But whether they are aware of the reasons or not, they are forced to pay off the loan, a loan which accrues interest at an astronomical rate, and alongside the debt comes the cost of paying back their owners for the expense of feeding them and housing them for life.

'If they flee, which is rare, their children are often killed. If they don't flee their children are beaten to remind them not to flee. The debt continues to accumulate throughout their lives and will likely be inherited by their children. Most children who are born as slaves will die as slaves, one way or another."

Tip felt overwhelmed, his heart racing. "Well what can *we* do?"

Tip watched in amazement as the Kaleos went about their work. From meeting places to codewords, everything was handled in secret. When the Kaleos crossed paths in public they didn't exchange as much as a word of greeting. Due to the nature of their jobs, Kolschen's sons were rarely seen, and the only scheduled appearance they made was at their secret weekly meeting. But to avoid being noticed the brothers arrived hours before the others and departed in the dark of night, long after the meeting adjourned.

Each member of the team was given a specific role to fill. Brett Myles Emerick designed and built the facilities. There were three stations in mind and all of them required an engineer, an architect, and a general contractor. Emerick was all three. He completed basic renovations of the warehouse and once the supplies arrived Derealdjon Polle and Yancey LaMont began practicing general dentistry from the aid station.

Soon the station was flooded with visitors, hundreds of children a day, and it was all Ruffino could do to manage the chaos. They required their names and date of birth and always Tipper was there, helping keep the records.

"Why dentistry?" Tip asked Derealdjon.

"Because we are at one of the great crossroads of human trafficking, picked specifically for this purpose. Some are trafficked in while others are trafficked out. Some traders don't care who they're selling, or who is buying. But others do. Some are particular about the little things. Like the health of the child. Like their teeth."

Tip dwelled on his words.

"Another reason is time. If we had time with each child, time to explain their reality, to teach them of freedom, a great victory would be at hand. Sitting in a dentist's chair, even for a few minutes, gives us some time."

"Then why not a doctor? Why not build a clinic too?"

"And we are. Very good. Emerick will have it built within the year and Mr. Kolschen is on the road in search of a doctor."

Tip knew that Kolschen traveled often, but he didn't know the reason. When the big man arrived he went straight to work as if no time had passed. He came alongside Ruffino, ordering supplies, asking questions, and making decisions that Ruffino wasn't prepared to make.

And just as quickly as he arrived Kolschen would slip off again, for months at a time, on some faraway mission that only Kolschen knew. When he returned he would often have some new protege in tow - not one intended for Uttar Pradesh, but instead some distant destination that Kolschen oversaw. Tipper wasn't privileged with the details and few questions were ever asked. All he knew was that Kolschen bore a great burden of responsibility everywhere he went, and that he was fearless in pursuit of his mission.

But of all the men that worked to break the slave trade of Uttar Pradesh, Tipper believed that it was Kolschen's sons who had the most challenging duties of all.

Each morning the brothers set off into the slums, Pietre to one side and Alexei to the other. They walked the streets, finding vendors and asking them kindly, "Do you know a child's marketplace? I need to make a purchase."

Some ignored them while others grew angry, but all it took was one to point the way. They followed vague descriptions but soon each of the brothers were introduced to a trader and their conversations were almost identical.

"My friend, I need to make a purchase right away. Big hurry. Very desperate. I won't argue about the price."

"Do you have an age in mind?"

"No older then ten. Seven or eight, if possible. My clients like to train them young. For help around the house. You understand."

"Ten I can do. Seven or eight is harder.

"No matter. So long as it could be today. "

The trader frowned. "No, my friend. Not today. Tomorrow at best."

"I was told I could finish everything by today. My client is very impatient. Is there someone else I can speak with?"

"No, no, my friend. I will help you. Tomorrow is fair. I must clear things with the family. You understand. What do you prefer, boy or girl?"

"It doesn't matter."

"And when I ask the family, where should I tell them the child will live? They want to know these things. You understand."

"A good home. Very nice. They will have schooling and three meals a day."

And then the cash came out. "Will you bring the child here or must I travel to get them?"

"I will bring them here. I will find you just what you like. Don't worry."

The next day a child was brought to each of the meeting places but for both brothers the story was the same. "I am sorry for your trouble, friend, but my client has withdrawn."

Like a script the trader grew angry, cursing the buyer. His words spewed like venom until Alexei and Pietre leafed through a stack of bills.

"For your trouble," they had said. "Perhaps we will have more dealings very soon."

And in this way trust was established.

When they met up that evening Tip asked. *"Why not just buy them out?* You had a child *right there.* She could have been free. Why didn't you just *buy her?"*

"Tip, we don't buy children," Ruffino said. "No matter the seller, no matter the reason, children should not be bought."

Tip stumbled on his words. "Then can we do anything? Can we pay off their debt?"

"In some cases we can. So long as the money doesn't end up in the hands of the traders."

"The *traders?* They're just bums on the street. Isn't there any police in this country?"

Collectively the Kaleos shook their heads. "We've tried that. But like any impoverished country money does the talking. Bums maybe. But the police receive regular bribes from the traders."

Tip was visibly discouraged. In his heart the situation was hopeless. "If we can't buy them then what are we doing here?"

Alexie gripped the shoulder of the boy to calm him. "There are some who slip through the cracks. Sometimes a child is orphaned and forced into debt bondage. Later she might be sold into prostitution. Line up a hundred child prostitutes in a dentist's chair and tell they can be free. Maybe ten will listen. Maybe two will come. But that's two lives you saved in less that a week. Tip it may take years for you to understand this, but we can't end slavery. We can't save even one percent of the children in these slums. We don't have the means to pass a law or to reverse traditions and the vast majority of our work will end in failure. But at the end of it there's life. For a few hundred children there's life. Now my father has been out there, looking all his long years, and he hasn't found a better way to spend his life or mine than by saving a few hundred children."

"Why can't we just steal them when they slip down into the village?"

"We could never steal them all, Tip. And the ones left behind would pay an awful price."

Tip chewed on the words. "So stealing them is never an option?"

"No, Tip. Stealing them teaches them nothing. You first have to convince them that they *can* be made free. It isn't easy. No one has ever told them of freedom. They have been seasoned to believe they can never leave. They don't know that they are slaves. But if freedom becomes *their* idea, then we're getting somewhere."

"But they just could run away. Couldn't they? They could just start walking and go somewhere else."

"But where?"

"Anywhere. Somewhere."

"Tip, I understand how you feel. But each of these children is overseen by a trader and each of the traders is overseen by a head Dalal. A pimp. And the main job of every Dalal is to teach his slaves that they can never be free. That even if they were to run like you said, a great host of his subordinates would be sent to find them and once they were found their sisters and brothers would be made slaves too, or worse."

"Or worse?"

"Sometimes they rape them and kill them in front of their parents."

A great fire churned in Tipper's belly. He found that he could hardly breathe. "I want to go up there. I want to see these men. I want to grab those children and take them away. Take them as far from this place as I could get."

Alexei nodded. "I understand that too. Believe me. But your place is here. Take my advice and steer clear of the slums, Tip. If you go up there - they'll grow suspicious."

"But how do *you* do it? Keep them from growing suspicious?"

"Being Russian helps. Among my countrymen there is a great market for child slaves. The traders know this. That's how trust is established."

"Do they take that into account when they set the prices?"

"The traders don't set the prices. The prices are set by one man and all the traders report to him. He is the Dalal. He takes a cut of every child sold. He wants to know everything. Who is doing the buying, where they came from, how many children are moved by each trader. Not a trade takes place up there without his knowledge."

"Well who is he?"

"I don't know much. His name is Golgol. He is very careful about his business."

"Have you seen him?"

"No one has seen Golgol. He lives up there, in the Pradesh district, though no one knows where. The traders speak of him rarely."

"Well he couldn't be too hard to find. Make a deal with a trader and follow the trader. You said nothing happens without Golgol's knowledge so they must go up to see him."

"Tip if I follow a trader up there all of our trust will have ended. No more trades. No more children."

"Then send your father, or one of the others."

"To find Golgol?"

"Yes."

"And what'll they do when they find him?"

Tip listened to the words with a breaking heart. If his travels across Kamchatka had been his boyhood and his wild ranges with Wonderboy his adolescence, then Uttar Pradesh would surely mold him into a man.

And so began the most refining season of his life. For years he lived among them, and his life was born of service. Tipper's duties consisted only of labor and maintenance. He cooked for the Kaleos, and cleaned their bedchambers and tended the building daily. But he felt no shame in his duties. He was proud to play any part at all.

Tip resigned himself to the frustrations of their work, serving the cause silently, watching the Kaleos like a child, hungry for knowledge. He was invited to their meetings and listened to their prayers, but rarely spoke a word, choosing instead to observe and reflect, to humble himself through his silence. In his second year he chose to be baptized, and in keeping with tradition each of the Kaleos, including Kolschen himself, came together and washed his feet.

And Alexei was right. The children began to slip through the cracks. The Kaleos shared in the celebration as a child or two every week, sometimes more, decided to break free. They too were baptized and moved far from the slums to a faraway orphange that Kolschen oversaw.

In the third year Kolschen purchased one of the local banks and instructed the team accordingly. Each Kaleo, Tip included, was charged with gathering a dozen community fathers, all under bondage, and helping them form a self-governing credit union. Each of the slaves were asked to collect a single rupee by any honest means and soon over one hundred rupees were gathered, enough to take out a loan at Kolschen's bank. The loan was then applied to the debt of a single slave, buying him freedom, and Kolschen himself paid off the balance. It was a time-consuming means to an end, but it taught one hundred men that, with enough diligence, freedom could be gained.

The freed slaves often came to work for the Kaleos, and soon their families joined them. Emerick now had hands to lay brick and Ruffino kept a secretary. In fact every Kaleo but Tipper had an assitant of some kind, and most had more than one.

Kolschen hired a dozen local boys, all of them slaves, to deliver medicine to the elderly. They were too old to be sold by the traders but they could only break away from their debtors for an hour or two a week so he paid them ten times what their hours were worth and taught them every session about their bondage and what the money meant. Since they couldn't escape their oppressors it was Kolschen's hope that they could slowly pay them off.

With the exception of Golgol, Kolschen's sons knew every trader and pimp in the slums and when their father brought a new protege to Baiga Backsas, they always used them for a stand in. Alexei and Pietre would lead the new recruit up the hill to visit a pimp and upon arrival their act began. There was a great market, they would say, for such children in the east. Boys or girls it didn't matter - but they must have porcelain teeth.

The act was always the same and soon the pimps brought the prostitutes down to the clinic in mass. They assumed by Golgol's instruction. Bit by bit the Kaloes got their hooks in.

The work was taxing, and some days Tip's heart couldn't bear it, knowing how many were left behind. But once a week they would sit on the rooftop of the clinic and drink Kalyani Black Label and try to relax.

On one such evening, as Kolschen was preparing to depart, Tip asked him, "How do you measure a man?"

Kolschen answered simply. "By his burden."

"His burden?"

"What he can undertake. That's always been my measuring rod."

Kolschen smiled then, and spoke his gentle farewells. He reminded them of the need in every man to fight for something he believes in, and the cold truth that most men never find it, and that many never look. Then he was off on the road once more, back to the coastal village where they had met, Tip supposed, or off to some half-way house to recruit a new disciple. Tip didn't know the details and it hardly mattered. He knew the man's nature. Wherever Kolschen went goodness was sure to follow.

"I want to be a man like he is," Tip said to Alexei. For of all the Kaleos it was Alexei he favored most.

Alexei smoked his great pipe. "Maybe you will be."

Tip scanned the faces of the children passing below. He wondered if one of them was a slave to Golgol and his traders.

"How will I know when I'm a man?"

Alexei nodded. "There will come a moment when your loved ones will look upon you in a different light. I cannot say when it will come. But they will see that you can bear the burdens that have been handed you. They will know you are able to face the life before you. And they will feel safe."

Tipper looked longingly up the hill, at the dark slums that seemed to cover his every thought.

"I think my burden is what's up *there*," Tip said pointing.

Alexei puffed his pipe. "Is it?"

"I think of it every night. Some kid on the bad end of a lie, hungry or beaten, abandoned. And they're just kids. Their faceless in my mind, but they're kids every one. God it bothers me that we can't get them out. "

Alexei sighed in agreement, a great truth on his face. "There will always be a child who needs help on that hill."

II.

Padibatakal stood by the open window, raised on her tip toes, trying to remember the last time she had stepped outside. It was a quiet morning and the wind from the city lifted the scent of some wild lilac or azalea up through the window. She closed her eyes and drifted off into a dream that she was somewhere else.

She wished she could break out of those walls to get to the street, or jump to her death, either one. But the windows all had bars, she knew. So was her life: the stale walls of that apartment and only the smell of lilacs if she was lucky.

The small apartment would have been comfortable, had it not been for the sins the walls contained. At some point, long before Padibatakal was sold by her family, the room had been chosen solely for the view. Built on the top street on the hill, three stories high with wide windows, this particular apartment provided the best view of the slums money could buy. The furniture too had been carefully picked. Every piece was dark wood or leather. The doorknobs and other ironworks were all artistically crafted. By design there were no rugs, or carpet, only a shiny wood-patterned linoleum that Padibatakal cleaned each day. Nor were there any mirrors or glass. The only photos on the walls were of horses in pursuit, framed in rope work. In the corner by the door were rolls of blank carpet, cut in sections and above them was a poster of James Arness.

Padi took another deep breath, hoping to hold the scent of the flowers as long as she could. But the moment didn't last. She exhaled slowly and her eyes opened as a voice called her from the kitchen.

"Are you mine and mine alone?"

It was a deep, hollow voice. The only one she heard on any given day.

She stepped away from the window and walked into the kitchen, her head down. "Yours and yours alone," she said.

Golgol sat on his kitchen stool, humming to himself. He had spent all that morning baking pastries and pies and mixing pudding in a huge wooden bowl.

He wore a pistol on his hip, held in a leather holster with bright sequins, the kind a child would wear. In fact his whole arrangement was a comical display. He wore tight pinstriped pants that he starched each morning, and bright boots beneath them that he shined every night. His shirt was a checkered pearl snap, worn loose to conceal his belly, which grew every year with the mounting pastries. His hair was thick with jelly, combed and coifed. But his hair lip was his most distinguishing feature. The cut was so ill-centered and predominate that his teeth shown even when his lips were sealed.

But his lips weren't sealed at the moment. As he gripped the girl's chin in his hands his smile was spread out broadly.

"Little Padi bones. My Padi bones. What did you see out in the street?"

"Nothing," she said. "I smelled some flowers."

"The streets are soooooo filthy, you know? They are mine, all mine, but I want nothing to do with them. Are the streets soooooo filthy, Padi?"

For the first year Padi had planned to run away. But she knew that if Golgol found her he would kill her, like he had with all the others. There was no chance to run away. They were confined to the kitchen, the small sitting room, the bathroom, and the bedroom that they shared. Neither Padibatakal or Golgol had left the apartment in over two years. Yet even though she could never escape, in the first months she still dreamed of being rescued. She woke in the night, beside Golgol, with the image of her savior painted across the ceiling. He was a young man, with dimples and deep set eyes. She had the dream every night for many months, but eventually they faded.

Golgol was still waiting on his answer and Padi knew the answer he wanted. The answer he wanted was always the answer he gave. She repeated his words. "The streets are sooooooo filthy."

And Golgol nodded in approval. He stirred his pudding and whispered in her ear. "And what will you do today to make Golgol happy?"

But before Padi could answer there came a knock at the door. It was a rhythmic knock, the pattern required to enter. Golgol turned toward the door and coughed loudly in response. Instantly the door swung open.

A shy boy was ushered inside by the skinny man behind him. The man was not very old - and he wore a wisp of a mustache half grown across his lip. He kept his hands tight around the boy's shoulders.

The man was a trader, Padi knew. She had never seen this one before, but he looked like all the others she had seen. He wore a gold watch and several rings, all dazzling, like nothing else in the slums. She was very young but her experience with traders was already extensive.

After Padibatakal's mother contracted polio, one of Golgol's traders approached her father immediately. He was given the choice between watching his wife die slowly, leaving him alone to provide for his children, or selling Padibatakal to a trader to pay for a doctor. The girl had a splendid voice and was considered a great beauty, even as an eight year old. "When she arrives she can begin to send you money," he was told. "She will fly to America and be seen by the multitudes."

But she hadn't flown anywhere and she couldn't send money. She lived just minutes away from her family and the only people who ever saw her were Golgol and his traders, and the occasional child who was brought up to be punished.

The moment the boy stepped inside Padibatakal knew he was about to die. There was a wild fear in his eyes, a guilty fear, and more than anyone Padibatakal knew what Golgol did to the guilty.

Golgol was still humming to himself when the boy stepped up. The child was shivering with fright, his head darting from one wall to another. Golgol smacked his food and looked the boy over and when he was satisfied he returned to his baking.

"I see you've come back to me, Zu."

The boy was motionless. "Back to you?"

"Yes. Yes. Back to *me*. I am Golgol. I am the King of the Mountain. I am the Lord of the Hill. You run away from my trader and you run away from me."

The boy's blood went cold. He knew the name Golgol and what Golgol did to boy's who run away.

"Shall I be merciful?" Golgol said to his trader.

The man smiled and shrugged his shoulders.

"Shall I be merciful?" Golgol said again, this time to Padibatakal.

She looked up, the only time she looked up. "Golgol will be what Golgol will be."

And he grinned, his hair lip opening like a curtain over his gums. "So it is," he said.

Just then two young girls were brought in behind the boy, both in homespun dresses. Golgol nodded to a second trader and the girls were moved to the sofa.

"These are your sisters, is that right, Zu?"

The boy turned to look at them and his eyes grew wide. Now he was more afraid than ever.

"*I said, 'Are these your sisters'?*"

"Yes," the boy whispered. He was trembling now.

Golgol lifted the pudding bowl and stood before the child. Gratuitously Golgol dipped his short polished fingers into the pudding and pulled them out again, a great lump of chocolate dangling from his fingertips.

"Have a taste," he told the boy.

Too frightened to refuse, little Zu walked up sheepishly, and licked the cocoa from his fingers. Golgol twirled them in the boy's mouth, teasing him until they were clean.

Golgol sucked loudly on his moist fingertips, relishing the taste the boy had left behind. He closed his eyes and waved his head like a blind man.

"More?" he asked kindly.

The boy made a half smile and shook his head.

"Oh well." Golgol shrugged his shoulders, "More for me."

"Well let's get started." He looked overjoyed. "Are you ready to get started?"

Zu's eyes were blank. "Yes."

"Good."

Golgol opened the icebox and stroked his chin. The shelves were lined with beautiful fruits from all around the world, brightly colored and dripping wet. He scanned the shelves and his eyes lit up when he found them. He turned to the boy. "For you, I have *just* the thing." He pulled two coconuts from the shelf, one in each hand. Then he danced as he closed the icebox with his hip.

"These are called *coconuts*," Golgol said. "Have you ever eaten a *coconut*?"

Silent, the boy shook his head.

"It's a pity," Golgol said, rolling the heavy fruits in his palms. "You can do so many things with a coconut. They are my favorite, aren't they sweet?"

Padibatakal glanced at him, but only briefly. "Yes, your favorite," she nodded, before turning back to her reading.

Golgol set his coconuts on the floor and smiled then. He loved looking down at the girl. "And you? You are also my favorite, my sweet. Did you know that?"

"Yes. I know it, " Padi said, never looking up. "I am your favorite."

"My favorite one. Mine and mine alone."

He watched her and waited.

"Yours and yours alone," she echoed.

Golgol held his smile and turned smugly to the trader. "It's true she's mine and mine alone."

"Very true," the trader answered.

"Mine and mine alone," he said to the boy, punching him playfully in the shoulder. "But I would let the cow of hindi mount her if the pay was right. Yes?"

The trader chuckled, his hands still on the boy's shoulders.

Golgol let his smile slip away and turned back to his coconuts. The boy was watching them with fear.

"You have two sisters, yes?"

The boy nodded.

"And I have two coconuts. Yes?"

"Yes."

"And for our game this morning I will give you my coconuts. Nice, yes?"

The boy nodded.

"Hold out your hands," Golgol said.

The boy did as he was told.

"Palms up," Golgol ordered as he handed over the coconuts, one to each hand. They wobbled awkwardly on the boy's palms.

"Heavy, aren't they?"

"Yes."

"Now what are your sister's names?"

The boy looked at their faces. For a moment he couldn't remember. His mind was empty. "Arya and Sasha."

Golgol smiled at the girls. "Which is Arya and which is Sasha?"

"I am Sasha," the older one said.

"And that makes you Arya?" Golgol said sweetly.

The tiny girl nodded.

"Good. I like those names. I like our game today."

Golgol turned back to the boy whose eyes were wide with fright. "It's a very simple game," Golgol assured him. "Hold the coconuts high above your head."

The boy hesitated. Then his arms wobbled as he lifted the fruits.

"For the sake of our game let's say the coconut in your left hand will be Sasha, and the coconut in your right hand will be Arya. Do you know your left from your right?"

The boy looked terrified now, his eyes down at his feet. "Yes," he hissed through his teeth.

"Good. Good. If you didn't know left from right the game wouldn't be very fun would it? No. Not at all. Your job Zu is to hold up the coconuts as long as you can. Hold them high and hold them steady. You wouldn't want to drop Arya and Sasha, would you?"

The boy shook his head, though only a gentle shake, not forceful enough to jiggle his arms.

Golgol's tone grew serious. "You know what will happen to the first one you drop, don't you, Zu?"

The boy was beginning to cry now. He dare not open his eyes.

Golgol stood and nodded. "Good," as he returned to the icebox.

Golgol began singing to himself as he pulled out a platter of chocolate-covered strawberries and banana slices, pomegranates, figs and dates. He slid the tray from the shelf and danced the icebox closed again. Then he sat down beside his Padibatakal and began feeding her the fruits.

Ineffectually Padibatakal nibbled on the treats, trying to ignore the scene in front of her. She had watched it so many times before. Sometimes Golgol gave the guilty child a pistol of their own, unloaded of course, and the two would have a duel in the kitchen. Other times he opened a chest under lock and key and brought out six revolvers, loading each with a single bullet, and asked the child to choose. Once chosen Golgol aimed at the child and pulled the trigger once, and if it didn't fire, he asked the child to choose again and again - until the game was over. But these variations were meant only for Golgol's amusement, Padi knew. The outcome was always the same. After years under Golgol's roof the only thing she knew for certain was that if a guilty child was brought in to Golgol's presence, they were brought out wrapped in carpet.

In the beginning Padi had tried to comfort the children, offering each of them an empathetic gaze. She had hoped for them to see some kindness in her eyes in the moments before they died. But always her head had grown faint and dizzy and eventually she turned away.

Now, after years and years, she didn't even look.

An eternity seemed to pass as Golgol slowly fed her. His groans of satisfaction filled the room, drowning out the tears and the whimpers of the girls.

"You eat so well, " Golgol told Padi, "The food is nice, yes?"

"Yes, the food is nice."

"You would not eat this well with anyone but me," he told her and then he was whispering. "*Look at those girls over there. Look how hungry they are. You would be starving if not for me.*"

"Starving. Yes."

"You will never go anywhere. You will never do anything. You will never be anyone's. . ."

"But yours and yours alone," she whispered.

Golgol smiled at her, and tickled her legs. He seemed in the lightest of moods. But in the next moment he turned and faced the boy curiously, as if he had forgotten he was there. He fed Padibatakal another strawberry and licked his fingers as he stood.

Zu was shaking now, the coconuts wobbling on his palms. His arms were growing heavy and both of his sister's were sniffling.

Golgol walked over to the boy and leaned down to face him, "I am the King on the mountain," he said. "I am the Lord on the hill."

The boy was sweating profusely, his two sisters frantic as they watched him. His right arm shook and the sisters held each other's hands.

Golgol chewed. "Whichever one dies," he said. "The cost of her funeral rights will be added to the other's debt. And it's soooo expensive these days. So, one will be dead, and the other will be a slave forever. So chooooose wisely, my friend."

The boy was gritting his teeth now. He felt his sweaty palms going numb as his elbows shook and shook. Now one of the sisters was wailing, the other stood dumb-faced, waiting for one horrible end or another. She had done the math in her head, knowing truly that her life was over no matter the fallen fruit. Golgol scooped out another glob of chocolate pudding and offered it to her. Apathetically she shook her head.

Padi didn't look up when she heard Sasha's coconut fall to the floor. She had turned completely around now, staring blankly at the pillow.

Instantly the trader let go the boy's shoulders and shuffled away.

Golgol turned to Padibatakal.

"I am the King of the mountain," he said. "I am the Lord on the hill."

He waited, his eyes on Padi.

"Yes. You are," she told him.

"Say it."

Padibatakal could hear the boy's breathing, heavier and heavier with every moment. She could hear the cock of the pistol, and the sniffling cries of the girls. She forced her mind to dwell on the pillow, only the pillow and nothing else. The pattern on the pillow was all that was real.

No sounds or smells, no screams. She blocked out the whole world and even her words as she spoke them.

"You are the King on the mountain. You are the Lord on the hill."

III.

Otsov Kolschen had always said that men are made by their choices. "Every decision, no matter how tiny, carves you and sands into who you will become." From time to time he would pull aside one of his disciples and whisper, "How you choose is as important as what you choose. What you choose is as important as the attitude you carry in your choosing. But nothing tops the who. The who makes all the difference.

For the Lord is merciful but the tighter you grip the devil, the closer you see his face."

One winter's morning an astonishing piece of news reached the Kaleos at Baiga Boksas street: Otsov Kolschen had finally chosen his doctor. It was a long-awaited event, one that the Kaleos were pleased to have resolved, but when the news came Tip wasn't there to hear it. All that morning Tip had been at market, shopping for the Kaleos for the coming week and when he arrived back at Baiga Backsas street he was greeted by Kolschen himself, who stood alone in their kitchen.

"I have something important to tell you," he said. "Monumental, in fact."

Tip was not accustomed to such attention. "What is it?"

"I have chosen a man to take over our clinic. His wife passed away and he needs a new mission."

"Well congratulations. Where is he?"

"Have a seat," Kolschen said gently.

Tip nodded, but with a question on his brow.

"He is upstairs as we speak."

"That's wonderful."

"And he's waiting to meet you."

"To meet *me*?"

"Or rather to *reunite with you*. I've told him your story, and he wants greatly to see you. I remember how you longed for reconciliation."

It was in that moment when Tip understood. His eyes closed. "It's *Unger*."

"It's *Unger*," Kolschen said. "I hope this isn't too difficult. But if it is, so be it. It *must* happen."

Tip stood to his feet, his heart pounding. "Should I go alone, or do you want to come with me?"

Kolschen gave the moment the briefest of pauses, knowing that Tip had grown much in his time away. "Alone would be better."

"I should have seen this coming."

"Yes, you should have," Kolschen smiled as he watched Tip climb the long staircase toward reconciliation.

The two men embraced as new friends, for neither felt like they truly knew the other. There was much made of their reunion - even among such men as the Kaleos, who couldn't deny the extraordinary nature of their relationship. And it was a relationship to be sure. For the pain that both men felt in the beginning was quickly replaced by the chance to define forgiveness with their lives, both by giving it and by receiving it.

In fact the receiving proved more difficult than the giving. For from the start Unger had no bitterness in his heart. What Kolschen had said was true, the boy had undergone a radical change, and Unger Soski knew that that kind of change was birthed in the soul.

Tip, however, allowed his guilt to linger. No fuss was ever made about the crimes he had committed. Sometimes the Kaleos even went as far as to joke among themselves about the two men's violent history, jokes that Unger himself could already laugh at. Tip knew the jokes were made in the spirit of forgiveness, and that all men are selfish beasts. But over time the words filled him with a strange guilt. He didn't believe he deserved such friendships.

Nothing I have ever done should have brought me to this, Tip thought. I didn't earn this mission or these men.

Every Kaleo told Tipper that there was nothing he could ever do to earn that kind of love. It was a gift given freely. But despite the truth of their words the weight of Tipper's sin drug behind him like an anchor.

Yet his work continued, and he was sharpened every day. He served alongside Derealdjon as before, playing the role of janitor, and assistant, but when the crowds began to overwhelm the new Doctor, Tip was moved to the clinic at Unger's request.

Throughout the day the children came like a continuous stream, and it wasn't long before Tip found himself in a rhythm, fetching supplies and checking temperatures and with every patient he learned something new. It was a fresh experience, and one he enjoyed, until late in the day when a certain patient walked though the door.

The color was driven from his face the moment Tip saw her. She looked to be in her third trimester, and her injuries made it difficult to walk. Her face and neck, and other patches across her hips and knees were badly bruised. One of her eyes was swollen shut.

But through it all it would have been impossible not to see her beauty. Her skin was golden and she had lavish rings in her nose and ears. Her hair shimmered like no other child in the slums and her clothes were covered with sequins. Tip felt certain he had never seen her before. A girl like this he would have heard about. To him she looked like the princess of the city.

Behind her stood a man against the window, his arms folded, and his eyes were locked on the girl. Tip and Unger noticed the stranger's rings and his gold watch, and both knew instantly that he was a trader.

She shifted from one leg to another, swaying in pain as Unger called her over.

"Please have a seat."

She seemed nervous to them both, curious and afraid of every new face.

"We want to thank you for coming in."

The girl nodded.

"I am Unger and this is Tip. Could you tell me your name?"

"It's Padibatakal."

She spelled it for them and Tipper wrote it down.

"Before we talk about your baby do you want to tell me about these bruises?"

The girl turned to look at the trader but whatever answer she was seeking Padibatakal didn't get. The trader stood stone-faced, watching the three intently.

When she finally spoke, it was clearly loud enough for the trader to hear.

"I can't answer any questions," she said. "I just need to know about this baby."

Unger knew that the girl's life was in his hands. He didn't change expression as he spoke.

"Sounds good," he told her, putting on a pair of gloves. "Can you pull up your shirt for me?"

The girl did as instructed and Tipper let out a gasp when he saw her belly. The bruises were so purple and pronounced that it looked like nothing human. Unger showed no reaction. He ran his fingers gently across her stomach.

"I'm going to move my hands like this and ask you some questions. Simple yes or no questions about the baby. When I speak just answer 'Yes, right there," or "No, nothing," and always point to your belly. Do you understand?"

The girl hesitated, her eyes darting back and forth. Then she moved her palm across her navel, "Yes, right there."

Unger's hand went where the girl's had gone, "Is your baby kicking?"

"Yes, right there."

"Did someone throw you down a flight of stairs?"

The girl shot him a painful stare. Unger shifted in his seat, trying not to face the trader. "It's alright. He can't hear us. Just keep your eyes on your stomach," Then he opened his eyes wide, leading her. "You're in a safe place, now."

"Yes. Right there," she told him.

"Was it the man who owns you?"

She gritted her teeth. "Yes, right there."

"Now keep your eyes on me. Was he trying to kill your baby?"

She nodded painfully, wincing, "Yes, right there."

Unger put both hands on her now.

"The man across the room, is he the man who owns you?"

She shook her head. "No. . . nothing."

Unger hesitated, generally surprised. "Does the baby kick you regularly?"

"Yes."

"I smell liquor on your breath. Is he keeping you drunk to kill the baby?"

Her eyes filled. "Yes, right there."

The trader took one step forward. His eyes never left her.

"Not to worry," Unger said. "The baby will prepare for birth in the next few weeks. When he does you will feel contractions slowly mounting."

Unger explained what she could expect in the coming days. He urged her to give birth in the clinic if she had no other place. When the trader wasn't listening Unger whispered of a different life that she could find if she broke away, but the girl seemed not to hear him.

When they were finished the two men helped her to her feet and Tip remained standing as he watched her go. The trader took her by the shoulders and her wince came again as she limped away.

"The hardest thing is to never become attached to a child," Unger said, rubbing his eyes. "As much as our hearts cry it isn't about *one* child. It's about the mass of children. If you get emotional then you'll break the law, or you'll buy a child outright and expose us. Then even if you save that child this clinic is finished and the masses of children will suffer. So don't let your guard down. Don't ever leave the reservation. *Never* strike out on your own."

"I won't," Tip said.

"No matter how much you might want to."

The truth was that Tip had often dreamed of saving one child, just one from the depths of the slums. It seemed so simple in his heart, to steal one away and find a home and never look back. But Tip knew of Unger's truth. He shouldn't sacrifice the many for the one.

"Are all the days like this one?" he asked.

"No," Unger told him. "That girl was special. In more ways than one."

In the coming days Tip found it difficult to push the girl from his mind. Where was she? he wondered. In whose dungeon was she kept? He pondered her fate constantly and questioned the locals at every turn. A girl named Padibatakal. A radiant child, bejeweled.

Two of the women he spoke with remembered a girl by that name, but both believed she had been sold years ago, as a payment against a long standing debt. The trail ran cold and for weeks there was nothing.

But a month later, while Tip was away helping Emerick load lumber for the next clinic, Padibatakal returned to Unger with her baby. She was there only briefly, but Unger remembered her the moment she arrived. He gave her some formula and advised her in every way he could.

Of course when Tip heard the news he was exasperated, asking a dozen questions. Unger reported that her bruises had all but disappeared and by some miracle the baby was healthy.

"She was watched the whole time by three traders," Unger said. "Different men from the first time. As soon as she could walk they led her away."

I will find her, Tip thought. She will come down for a checkup this week and I'll find a way to take her away.

But it wasn't to happen that week, or the week after that or the month after that. Tip Holland was twenty five years old now, away from home those seven years, but the tiny princess from the slums was always on his heart.

Nothing happened until late that autumn when a free dental check-up was offered to the public. Derealdjon and Yancey had been organizing the event for weeks. They gathered dozens of volunteers and a new stock of supplies were ordered, all of it under the name of modern dentistry. But in truth the event was a baptism in disguise.

The crowds gathered before sunrise and waited for hours. The line stretched a full city block and the Kaleos and their volunteers passed out food to the masses. Soon the Kaleos were consumed, examining patients, whispering questions, and for a few, leading them upstairs to perform their baptisms.

When the crowd was thickest near the end of the day the beautiful Padibatakal walked up to where Tipper was working, her babe held tightly to her chest.

When Tip saw her he sprung from his seat. He wanted to hold her in his arms, to fight the traders that surrounded her. But he quickly saw that there were no traders. Not behind her, or in the background. She was alone, except for the babe, and there was a glorious freedom painted on her face.

"If I believe, then I can never die?" she asked.

Tip was taken aback, stumbling on his thoughts as he soaked her up. He tried to catch his breath.

"Your body will die, but your soul will live forever."

"In heaven? Far from this place?"

"Yes, in heaven. Like no place you've ever seen."

"That's what I want."

Tip was so surprised he could hardly steer his thoughts. His anger boiled at the thought of what this little one had endured, but at the same time his heart rejoiced at her arrival.

"We need to take some time to talk about this," he said. "You won't regret it, but it's the most important decision of your life."

"I don't have much time. But I know it's what I want."

"But you must *believe it*. You must believe in His death and that He rose again to save you. "

The girl squinted and looked around the room. The crowd had grown thick in the clinic and each of the Kaleos were hard at work.

"Each of you men have Jesus?"

"Each one."

"Then that's enough for me. You are the only Jesus men I know and the only *good* men I know."

So Tip led her upstairs where Ruffino was waiting.

They had prepared the baptismal on the second floor and a dozen children were already waiting. Ruffino explained the scriptures and answered their questions and when they understood the covenant Ruffino stepped forward with a wooden bowl and proceeded to wash their feet. Tipper joined him, serving the young girl and her baby too.

"Can she be baptized?" Padi asked.

"There's no need," Tip told her. "She isn't yet accountable. I only wash her feet as an act of service."

Along with the others, Padibatakal made her covenant with God, believing in her heart and confessing with her mouth that the Christ had risen and delivered her from sin. When it was over Tip approached her, a great joy on his face. She was already standing to leave.

"Where are you going?"

She smiled. "I'm going to tell my owner everything I've done."

Instantly Tip's smile was wiped clean. "*No! Don't do that*," he pleaded. "Stay *here*, with me. He'll hurt you again if you go back."

She shook her head. "But he can't hurt me now. *I've been saved*."

"Your soul, yes. But this life, this body can still be broken. It still has a purpose. We'll find you a safe place."

Calmly she shook her head. "If I don't return he'll have my parents killed. He'll kill my sisters and my brother. I *must* go back. I must face him with the truth and there will be no more debt."

Tip pleaded with the girl, arguing with all of the passion in his heart. Yet despite his pleas the girl gathered the babe in her arms and turned to leave. She thanked him repeatedly and assured him that nothing was owed.

"I knew I would find you," she said. "I knew I would be saved and now I have been."

She wept joyfully and without another word she walked down the stairwell. Tip followed her downstairs and watched as the crowds swallowed her up.

She moved through the crowd and into the street. Tip looked to the Kaleos but Unger and Ruffino were still upstairs and the two dentists were overrun. She was slipping into the chaos now and in a moment he would lose her. As he saw her tiny shape disappearing Tip called out to the men but they didn't answer.

Tip gave little thought to what happened next. He felt his heart racing as he pushed his way through the crowd, his eyes fixed on the girl. Soon his legs were taking him out into the street, down one block, and then another, and soon he was moving up the forbidden hillside. He never looked back, never watched to see how far from home he had strayed. A dark cloud of shadows swallowed him as he broke into the slums for the first time.

The mysterious streets unfolded like a dream and all the while he kept his eyes on the girl, who marched steadily up and up with the babe in tow.

There were dozens, no hundreds of crazed faces, many of whom he had never seen. They looked at him wildly, their eyes seemed to flicker as he passed. Tip knew that his venture wouldn't go unnoticed and he cursed his choice of clothing. He pulled his hat down and lowered his eyes as he fought through the crowd, always gaining ground.

But the streets were dark now, as were the characters that surrounded him and he couldn't wrap his mind around what to say when he reached her, only that he must reach her, he must stop her, or he must die trying.

If I die up here then let them know why. Let my life be for someone other than myself, he prayed. Tip was determined to repent of the sins of his youth, to stop this one girl from falling to whatever fate awaited her.

He reached the top of the hill and the last bit of sunshine blinded him between the buildings and it was then that he realized she was gone.

He had seen her reach the hilltop and had been right behind her when the sun blocked his view but in a flash she had disappeared.

He spun in circles. She couldn't have gone far.

He ran to the next street and the street after, peering up and down the alleyways. He searched the fire exits and the sidewalks. Maybe she had stopped. He retraced his steps to the crest of the hill, went down a block then back again. He was sweating and furious now.

He wished for someone to ask. But what would he ask? *Have you seen a girl with a baby?* There were hundreds of them. Every night on every street.

His heart willed him to keep moving, ducking behind rickshaws and cattle for any place she might have stopped. He was twirling slowly, his hands on his head, when he heard raised voices from an open window above him.

Tip looked up. The shouts were coming like thunder from the third floor, though he couldn't understand a word. In that instant there were likely dozens of shouting matches in the slums but Tip had nowhere else to search.

He found the stairwell and scaled both flights and when he reached the top the voices were still ringing, but only angry hums to his ears.

Tip was breathing heavily as he pressed his ear against the door.

". . .is *saved*?" a heavy voice called out. "*Only I can save!*"

There was the sound of loud crying, and of heavy laughs like thunder.

". . .nothing you can do now," came a girl's voice, calmer than the other. Then the laughter came again.

". . .could ever do," the girl continued and Tip knew it was Padi.

He reached for the doorknob and was shocked as it turned open.

The voices came clearer now.

". . .amount of feet washing can ever change what I can do!" came the big voice again. "There is. . .ways something Golgol can do!"

Tip stood like a stone. *Golgol!* Tip thought. *He had broken into the den of the devil himself!*

There were more cries coming from the baby, and the sounds of a struggle. The room seemed to swell and turn all around him. On the table before him he saw a heavy candelabra, leather furniture and rolls of loose carpet. A corridor was before him, and the room he sought behind it. A single ceiling light flickered off the wallpaper peelings.

He searched for a weapon, anything he could use, but before he had time to think he heard two quick gunshots, coming in succession.

Tip's blood ran cold. Quickly he slipped the candelabra off the table and took two steps toward the corridor. Then he saw Golgol.

The man was standing near the sink, a heavy butcher's blade in his hand and the babe wriggling on the cutting board. As Tip looked across the room his breath went out of him. Padibatakal was dead on the couch.

Before he could move Golgol lifted the heavy blade above his head, "Washed her feet!" he hissed and swung down with all his strength, chopping the babe at the ankles.

A wild rage filled the place, a rage made of cries for mercy and screams of injustice. The screams of another world, bellowing out through the lungs of a babe. Tip's eyes watered with fury and for an instant he scanned the room. There was a cutlery set beside the sink, a fry pan on the countertop nearest him, an open window, but no, the window had bars.

Just seven minutes before Tip had been looking after the needs of the children, but now he was alone, alone with Golgol and he knew that if he wanted to save the child he would have to kill this man. Kill the man or be killed himself and he knew he must act quickly.

Golgol turned and saw him. His face was wild and flushed, now turned in confusion. He tossed the butcher knife into the sink and gripped his pistol. The babe was wailing for all to hear.

"Were you a suitor?" Golgol said smugly.

Tipper didn't hesitate. He heaved the candelabra at Golgol's head, who covered himself with his arms, and Tip followed the heavy weight as it flew. He took two quick steps across the room, grabbing the fry pan by the handle and Tip would have broken the man if Golgol hadn't shot him. The bullet sliced him open above the collarbone and Tip fell back on his elbows. Golgol aimed again but as Tip scrambled to his feet his boots slipped across the linoleum and the next shot missed him. The stumble that saved his life.

Tip was on his feet now, quick to grab the gun, and once they were locked together he was amazed by how easily he overpowered the big man. Tip could feel that there was nothing solid about him, just loose flesh, and in two quick tugs he broke the gun free, sending it flying out the window.

Golgol watched in disbelief as the gun clanked through the bars.

Tip backed up, watching from the side of his eye as the babe flapped on the cutting board. He grabbed the fry pan and took one quick breath.

"I am King of the Mountain!!" Golgol said. He cursed loudly and in a flash he pulled a knife from the cutlery block and began swinging it wildly.

Tip had never been in a fight in his life, but you wouldn't know it. With his first swing he flattened the man's nose with the pan. Golgol's greasy hair hung across his face, and two of his teeth sputtered out between his hair lip. One of his eyes went sideways in his head. But to Tip's great surprise Golgol sprung back up, slicing him across the belly and again across the ribs before Tipper dropped the pan and grabbed the big man's wrist.

Now the pair was locked together, both bleeding on the other. Each man's breath grew violent and labored, and all the while the child was wailing. Golgol bent the blade away from him, struggling to overpower the boy, but Tip easily turned his wrists. Now Golgol's mouth was clinched in a grimace. "I am. . . Lord on the Hill!"

What happened next was instantaneous. Golgol released the knife and lunged back for the block to grab another. He pulled the weapon and turned, his arm raised, but before he could strike Tip grabbed Golgol's shirt and drove the warm steel of his knife up through his double chin all the way to the hilt, sealing his jaw to the roof of his mouth.

Golgol gripped the knife with both hands and Tipper stepped back. The man stood wide-eyed, his face turned in a horrible grimace. *The tighter you grip the devil, the closer you see his face.*

Golgol's gums began to hiss as he struggled to speak. There was a wild rage in his eyes, as if a great injustice had been done. He fell to his knees and then the floor and all the while Tipper was shaking as he watched him, knowing he should remember the taking of a life. But he didn't linger.

As Golgol flailed Tip worked around him, pulling a pair of folded towels from the baker's rack. The babe's tiny feet were resting on the countertop and Tip wrapped the ankles as tightly as he dared. He tore off his shirt and began to fold a swaddle and as he did Golgol kicked him repeatedly with his flailing legs. Tipper ignored the kicks, shushing the babe and singing to her gently.

When she was swaddled Tip cradled her and turned to leave. Golgol's blood was covering the floor now and Tip had to tiptoe through the puddles and the spray and over the dying man.

"It's alright," he told the babe. "I've got you."

A dark chenille blanket was crumpled on the couch and Tip grabbed it as he moved toward the door. He covered his chest and his head and hid the baby in the folds of his arms. He gave Padibatakal one final look, her hair still wet from the baptism, and as he left he could hear the kitchen cabinets thumping with the sound of Golgol's kicks.

He descended the stairwell and moved into the street. The child's cries were like nothing human. Though he was a ghostly figure: a wild man in a dark cloak harboring a child's scream, the people around him hardly seemed to notice. Tip raced downhill through the crowded slums dodging through the livestock and the cluttered masses, moving swiftly among the sloping sidewalks and alleyways until he came to Baiga Backsas street.

As he burst into the station Tip held the child high above his head despite his wounds and maneuvered through the line, blood dripping onto his shoulders. He was bleeding badly now, his eyes glossy as they rushed the child across the room.

When Unger saw the boy, bloody and frantic, he jumped from his chair and took the baby. Ruffino settled the crowd and the dentists took over as he and Unger rushed the victims up the stairs.

They unswaddled the baby and examined her wounds and when they had her settled they tended Tipper, laying him down on the gurney. Soon the station was emptied and each of the Kaleos were called, even Alexei and Pietre, and all hands gathered as Unger began to stitch him up.

It was some time before they could get any answers, for his tears made his words unintelligible. Of course when he did calm down the men had a host of questions but nothing, not even their wide range of experiences could have prepared them for the answers. As Tip gave an account of what happened on the hill, many of the Kaleos looked on in astonishment.

"You *killed* him?" Ruffino asked.

"I was trying to do *something right!*" Tip said, shaking. His tears flooded him.

Alexei laid his hand on the boy's shoulder, trying to keep him calm. But he knew there wasn't a calm heart in the room. Without a doubt this was the most astonishing piece of news he had heard in his life. All of the men could feel it. A great cloud hung over them. Each of the Kaleos held grave questions in their hearts, Unger especially, who was uncertain how to feel.

Ruffino was the first to speak. Over the years he had given Tip Holland little thought. But he was thinking hard about him now. "You're *certain* he's dead?"

Tip nodded, wringing his hands. "As certain as I can be."

He thought of the look in the man's eyes, and the sight of him writhing on the floor.

"Yes. I'm certain," he told them.

The Kaleos took their leave and let him rest, his sobs heard throughout the building. He tried to sleep but only managed to weep, dwelling on his heartbreak and his anger. It wasn't until the middle of the night when the door finally opened again. Tip saw Alexei approaching him, the babe held tightly within his arms. The sight of the babe sprung him to life.

"God, Alexei, what is it? Is she alive?"

"Yes, Tip. She's alive. But you must listen carefully. My father has prepared a plane for you. We have to get you out of here right away."

"A plane?" Tip asked. "To where?"

"I don't know where. Someplace far from here, I'm sure. With Golgol dead there's no way to know if his men are loyal. But if they are, and if they find you. . ."

"What about the baby?"

"She'll live. It will be a hard life, but you saved it."

Tip's eyes filled again. "Where will you take her?"

"Don't worry about that. My father has a place. My father has many places. If she stayed here and someone saw her, and if they told someone who knew—"

"I understand."

Without hesitating Tip began to dress himself for his flight. He didn't know where he was going but he felt certain it would be a long ride. As he packed up it occurred to Tip then that the last time he had ridden on a plane was beside Unger Soski, on their ill-fated fishing trip. The thought rolled round and round his head.

When he was dressed he opened his drawer and began to stuff his weathered pack with everything he owned. He had accumulated nothing in his time in Uttar Pradesh. No photos, or mementos. Nothing to mark his time except his journal entries every night. He stuffed the journal in his pack and when he was finished he stepped up beside Alexei and looked down at the baby.

"Tip?"

"Yessir?"

"I'd say you've earned the right to name her," Alexei said. "You saved her life,"

To Tip the words came as a great shock. His heart couldn't handle such a thought. "I wouldn't know what to name her."

"An old friend maybe. Or an aunt? A girlfriend?"

"No."

Alexei rocked her in the swaddling towel. By some miracle she was sleeping now. Her face gentle and unblemished. "Then we'll name her after her mother."

5. Arrivals

There was a great stillness in the air, as if Act One of their lives had ended.

"*Our* grandfather?"

"Yes, Jack. You and Henry are first cousins."

The two looked upon each other with sudden interest, examining one another's features, but finding few similarities.

"Ah, well that's explains all the fanfare," Henry said. "Everyone here loved Kolschen. Now they get to meet the grandsons he never knew."

"And Henry you look just like him," Ruffino said. "So much so that it chills my bones." And the others nodded in agreement.

Throughout his years on Tenpenny Hill Jack had wondered why he had been chosen. It was a question that plagued him day and night, especially in the first years, when he felt the wings of Tip Holland mysteriously wrapping around him and his brother. Oh, Tip loved all the children that lived on the hill, but Henry and Jack were special and everyone knew it. Yet until now no one told him why. It was a great relief to Jack to know that there *was* a reason, although the reason itself brought on a great many questions.

"If Kolschen was our grandfather - then who were our fathers?" Jack looked at Tip. "Our *real* fathers I mean?"

"They were fearless men," Ruffino said. "Like their father before them. And that same wild freedom is pumping in your veins. A hunger for life that sent Henry roaming across Tenpenny since he was a child. The kind that led Jack across the sea to Tipper's door."

"So you knew them?"

"Very well," he said. "Worked alongside them. They were our dearest friends. Lifelong friends. The kind you'd do anything for."

"Even adopt their children," Henry said flatly.

Tip nodded, "If the need arose, yes - I was willing to do that. We all were."

"Then why you?"

"Your father's died suddenly and there were many factors to consider. Many things you still don't know. It wasn't an easy decision. I was chosen from a group of men but each one of them could have handled the job, likely better than I did. But in the end it fell to me."

Jack's head was racing. More than ever he wished he hadn't left his storybook back in the forest. "Our father's died. Then our mother's took us away? Is that right?"

"That's right."

"What about Kolschen? Why weren't we kept with him?"

"Because from the time you were babies, up until four days ago, Kolschen was in prison."

"In prison for what?"

Ruffino leaned in, "This will be a fine day for telling tales. And you'll learn a great deal. But there are some things that are better told later than sooner. It's best to begin with the tale of your fathers. The *whole* tale as we saw it unfold."

Jack was bursting with anticipation. Henry remained watchful and still.

It was then that Ruffino gave a full account of each of the boy's fathers - from their young years through their time at Uttar Pradesh. Everything they lived and worked for was mentioned and discussed. There were moments when both boys had a hard time listening, and other times when each of them swelled with pride. The account of their legacy went on for over an hour, and not another man among them hadn't both cried and laughed in the telling. By the time Ruffino had begun to wrap up his story the men were spread around the room: Tip was seated on the floor, Indian style while Unger stood by the window, to stretch his knees, which had grown arthritic in his later years. LaMont was standing too, leaning against the door frame and breathing in the scent of the sea.

"You see, even though you were orphaned," Ruffino said. "The two of you have been given some very rare gifts - gifts known to very few. Not another man among us had a worthy father. But you've been handed *a legacy*. Nothing is earned with more intention."

Ruffino paused and gave them both a thorough glance. "I wonder if either of you have any questions?"

"Is there nothing buried up in the hills?" Henry asked.

"There *certainly is*," Tipper told him. "And this very afternoon I'm leading you across the cove to find it."

"But it's only part of your journey," Unger said.

Jack raised his hand casually. "I have a question."

"Yessir."

"What do you *do* in this place?"

Each of the men turned to Unger, who raised his coffee, breathing in the steam as he sipped. He looked out the window at the work being done. From where he was standing he could see a headstone behind the barn.

"You boys ever seen a wrecker clear a roadway?"

"No, sir."

"Wrecker gets a call, strings out the cable, pulls the wreck onto the ramps and hauls it off." He took another sip. "My father drove a wrecker for thirty-eight years."

Old Unger smiled slightly, facing the runway. "Thirty eight years. And cars aren't the only things that need towing. Around here a man has more use for a horse than he does a truck. But if he wants to get anywhere substantial, he needs a plane."

Unger turned around. Something about the man, particularly the way Tipper watched him, made the boys take careful aim at his words.

"Planes crash too," he said sitting down again. "And with planes the wrecker has the same job he has with a car. Pick it up and haul it out. However car crashes can be soft. Often the damage can be mended. But plane crashes are harder. Statistics don't favor them. Most times the pilot and the passengers are all lost. Most times the family doesn't want what's left of the plane."

"All across this wild countryside there are crashes. Once every few weeks I get a call that one needs sorting out. So we fly the chopper in. A team collects the bodies, we gather all the scrap and bring it here. And now to your question, Jack. What do we do here? *Then* we train up mechanics to build planes out of the wreckage. *Then* we train those mechanics to fly those planes, to fix them, and once they're ready we train them in the gospel of grace. What we do here is ranching. We ranch airplanes from the wilderness and pilots from across the sea. We prepare them for where they're going, and then we load boxes of translated Bibles into the planes and the new pilots take them across the sea, and spread what they've learned. And through us God ranches believers with his gospel."

The two brothers sat dumbfounded.

"You're missionaries," Henry said.

Unger nodded. He walked to the window and motioned with his mug. "Across that ocean, in lands unlike any you've ever seen there now stand thirty-seven shining lights. You'd call them churches, orphanages, aid stations. They were all built by pilots and mechanics who came to study the gospel of grace right here at Tenpenny West."

"Where did the people come from?" Jack asked.

"Same place the children of Tenpenny came from. All around the world. The aid station that Kolschen built in Uttar Pradesh, a homeless shelter he funded in Guiyu. The big man laid out the fabric of a network that reaches to villages you can't even find on a map. Now there's a place just like this one across the water. An old bush pilot built it once he learned what Tipper had done. We send him some of our best pilots and they train others – and bring people back with them, some of them orphans. I've stood in this very room with many of your young friends back at Tenpenny."

"When did you start?"

"Tip and I started building this place while you were still with your mother and while Henry was under the Sister's care. At the same time that work crews were laying putting greens for the children of Tenpenny Central your father and I were clearing trees for a runway on what would become Tenpenny West, and we rebuilt our first supercub and your father and I sawed logs, drew up plans for a hangar that got delayed, and I oversaw a federal crew towing wreckage."

"Now you've done it," Henry said. "So what now?"

"Before long we'll need another place just like this one, only bigger, on the other shore to the south where there are more lost souls than you can count. And it won't stop there. Someday Tenpenny Central will have too many children to run successfully. There will have to be others then."

It would have been easy to see the wonder in both of their faces. Even Henry, who was rarely impressed with his fellow man, sat wide-eyed with approval, knowing first hand how many children these men had blessed. More questions came, with more surprising answers, and it grew and grew until the boys could hardly believe their ears - the scope of the mission was so immense.

"So why weren't we brought here sooner?" Henry asked. "Why not draw back the curtain?"

But before Tip could answer, the echoes of urgent shouts were heard through the open doorway. Each of the men looked up in alarm. LaMont, nearest the door, stepped outside, but just as quickly he stepped back in and turned toward the men, a look of concern on his face. "Someone is coming," he said, pointing toward the eastern field.

All of the men kept their seats until he added, "Coming quickly!"

Even before they had reached the door the men could hear it growing: the clear clutter-thud of hooves barreling down on the village. The sounds came like drum beats on the muddy road, and as they stepped outside they could instantly see what made them.

The horses were three in number, dark, strong mounts every one, and on their backs were riders hunched over or small in stature. The men in the doorway were certain from their coloring that the horses were not from Luleo - but none could make out the riders. All they knew was that an urgent haste was swiftly approaching; a haste that carried the moist scent of danger.

Henry stepped back inside and pulled a rifle from off the wall, kept nearby in case of bears, he later learned. He found a box of bullets and loaded in quickly.

All of the men were huddled in the doorway now, watching as the line of horses grew closer. They began to see that all three of the riders were awkward in the saddle, weaving in and out along the muddy trail like some ghostly apparition.

Ruffino, who still had the keenest eyes of the bunch, turned to Tip and said plainly, "That's your man."

Tip squinted. "My *man?*"

"The one in the middle there."

The rider at the center was a small figure leading the party of three. He was a dark man - shirtless and hatless with his brow shining. They could see now that he was holding the reigns for all three horses. As Tip spoke the sound of his own voice surprised him. "*Wonderboy?*"

To their bafflement the other two horsemen appeared to be prisoners, riding with their hands bound and slumping in their saddles. But what they saw next gave their hearts a shock. For across the bodies of the mounts, over the chests and legs of the riders was a thick splattering of blood, shining off the saddles and the horseflesh.

Every man stood bewildered as the wounded rabble arrived before them. Wonderboy pulled reign and reared in his saddle.

"*Help them!*" he called, breathing heavily.

In a daze the men surrounded the riders, pulling the prisoners down from their mounts. Each man had a host of questions but there was no time. One of the men had a bullet in his hip that bled across Jack's arms as he lifted him. He cursed and ranted as they tried to hold him steady. The other man was wordless as he winced. He was covered in sweat and a bullet had shattered his collar.

Wonderboy let go the reigns and Tip wore a look of wild confusion as he helped his friend to the ground. The feelings only grew when he realized that the little man was shot as well.

"Wh. .what happened? What are you doing here?"

Wonderboy's shirt had been tied in a crude tourniquet but he was still bleeding slightly. He held his upper arm. He didn't respond to Tipper's questions but led the men toward the galley and the two wounded riders were lifted high in the air.

They hurried across the short lawn and lowered them both through the door and Tip set the first man on the gurney, Putt asleep beside him.

"Move the dog to the floor," Tip said as he examined the man's wounds.

Putt was set down carefully in the corner while Jack, Henry and Unger laid the second man down on the gurney. He kicked and flailed as they tried to hold him steady.

Wonderboy was the last to enter, his arm tight against his body. His hands, trousers, and work boots all sprinkled with blood.

"*Why are you here? Why are they bound?*" Tip asked him.

"They tried to kill me. I wanted them to stop."

Every man but Henry wore a look of confusion. Henry just appeared frightened.

"Tried to *kill you?* Why? *Who are they?*"

But Wonderboy shook his head. He looked at Henry. "No time for that, Mister Tipper. They're bleeding badly now."

Tip could see that the little man was right. The wounds were treacherous if not treated quickly. He leaned over the face of the quiet patient, barely a man. He had bruises across his cheeks and his lip was split.

"What's your name, son?"

The boy was bleeding from the collarbone. He had to catch his breath. "*Danny.*"

"We're here to help you, Danny. Will you let us help you?"

"*Yes!*"

Tip looked at the boy fiercely. He didn't think he had the look of a killer. When he saw what he needed to see he pulled a knife from his belt and cut loose the man's bonds. The second patient kicked wildly and growled at no one in particular. He fought his bonds, his teeth clinched in a wild rage as his hip continued to bleed.

Tip considered him. "Danny, does this partner of yours have a name?"

Danny nodded, "Culpin. . . Stanley."

Tip looked over his wounds. "Well Culpin, Danny, I'm Tip Holland," he said calmly, "And if you both don't hold steady there's a decent chance you'll bleed to death."

Tip pulled a pair of scissors from the countertop.

"I know who. . . .you are," Danny said. His breathing erratic. "We met. . .on the Cutshank."

Tipper flinched, holding the scissors. He leaned in and eyed him carefully, searching back in time. "You're *Forsman's boy?*"

Danny closed his eyes and nodded.

Instantly a look of grave concern covered Tipper's face. "Then where's your father?"

"*He's circling around to kill you!*" Culpin called.

Ruffino was leaning over the man when he said it. "Kill who?"

"*That boy* and any man who holds him!" and Culpin spat in Henry's direction.

Tip felt like he was dreaming. In less than a minute a swarm of wounded men had arrived at his doorstep and now he was being threatened - by a man he was called to save, no less. He searched Henry's face for an answer but found nothing.

Danny's shirt was soggy with blood but Tipper began to slice it off. "LaMont?"

"Yessir?"

"I want you to go outside and ring the bell. Then fetch two rifles. While we operate I want you and Jack to keep watch on that field."

"I'll do it," Henry said.

"Not a chance. You aren't leaving my sight. LaMont, you understand?"

"Yessir."

"Then go," and LaMont disappeared through the door.

Unger was quick to cut open Culpin's pants, instructing the men to hold him steady.

He leaned in and whispered, "What's happening, Tip?"

"I don't know. But we have to stop this bleeding."

Ruffino was preparing syringes and bowls, towels and tools for surgery. "Who's this Forsman?" he asked. "Why the alarm?"

Just then the sound of the bell was heard across Luleo, ringing ominously for all to hear.

"Joe Forsman is a dangerous man," Tip said, sorry to speak such words in front of Danny. "And according to Culpin here, he's circling around to kill us."

"No, he's not," Danny assured him, his eyes closed. "He's not going to kill anyone."

Tip dwelled on the words as he removed Danny's shirt. The boy's collarbone was broken, but the bullet had passed right through.

When LaMont returned he and Jack did as instructed. They loaded the rifles and kept a lookout across the field as the others worked on the wounded.

Tip did everything he could to stop the bleeding, then he cleaned Danny's wounds and stitched him up while the other men worked on Culpin, whose injuries were not as simple to treat. Once his pants were removed Unger could see that the bullet had entered just below his hip and was imbedded deep in his thigh. They offered him anesthesia but he cursed them and continued to moan. What followed was a violent struggle as the men held him down, Unger forcibly treating his pain and opening the wound, digging deeper and deeper until the bullet was removed. They cleaned him and stitched him and the bleeding had slowed, but Unger was not optimistic.

"They're very weak," he told them.

"But the bleeding has stopped," Jack said.

"Yes. But anything could happen. It could start again, internally. Or an infection could set in."

Tip nodded. "Don't borrow trouble. You did all you could," then he looked across the room.

"Wonderboy?"

"Yes, Mister Tip."

"Why are you here? Why are these men wounded? Tell me what happened."

Culpin thrashed and kicked and continued to wail.

"Yesterday morning," Wonderboy told him, "The Bhotiyas arrived on the hill."

"Yes?"

"And when they reached us they said Forsman was following you."

Tip doused a cotton swab with alcohol and continued to clean Danny's wound. "Following us?"

"From the Cutshank."

Tip's eyes didn't leave his patient. "Why would he do that?"

Again Wonderboy looked to Henry, who was still holding Culpin down. "They didn't tell. But—"

Wonderboy closed his eyes. His head was shaking.

"Go on, man. Say it."

The little man breathed deeply, his heart racing. "They watched him kill the Pritchers."

Jack's heart sank and Henry went pale. His eyes dodged across the room, knowing that his sins had caught up to him.

Tip showed no sign of reaction. He worked the cotton swab into the boy's wound and dabbed the blood away. "Did they give a reason?"

"What?"

"A reason. A cause. Joe Forsman needs a reason to do something like that."

Wonderboy took another breath, again summoning his courage. "They said he took a beating."

Tip looked down at Danny's bruises and nodded, calmly handing the swab over to Unger. Then without warning Tip grabbed Henry by the wrist, yanking off his gloves, his knuckles still swollen. A ghostly fear shook across the boy's face, the kind Jack had never seen.

"I own up to it, Tip."

Tip Holland felt an anger rising inside of him, though he didn't raise his voice. "W*hat exactly*?"

"I went after Joe Forsman. Then his son here and another man. While you and Jack rode on from the Cutshank."

Tipper didn't seem surprised. He turned back to Danny, who Unger was tending.

"Danny is that how it happened? Is that where you got these bruises?"

"That's right."

"And you rode all this way to get your vengeance?"

The boy nodded, wishing for another father.

"And did your father ride here with you?

"Yes."

"And where is he now?"

"He's circling around to *kill you*!" Culpin said.

Danny shook his head, his eyes wide. "He's not gonna kill anyone." Danny told them. "If it eases your mind you should let him go."

"Why do you say that?"

"Because if you think you'll find him out there - you won't. You'll only waste your time."

Tip nodded at Wonderboy. "This man tracked you through the night at double speed, I imagine. We'll find him. We'll find him and we'll make this right."

"I don't mean he can't be found," I mean he. . ." and Danny lost his breath.

"Easy, son."

"I mean he's on his way home, or he's already dead. Your man there shot well."

Every eye turned back to Wonderboy, who was now seated in the corner holding his wound. They kept their eyes on the little man as Danny gave an account of all that had happened in the forest. Altogether Wonderboy had shot four men. Two were unhorsed and the others had fled. As the scene was described their hearts were filled with pride and wonder. The thought that the little tracker had gunned down four armed men, including Joe Forsman, was mystifying.

"Where was Forsman shot?" Tip asked.

Wonderboy shrugged. "I never saw."

"Through the hands," Danny said, sitting up. "He was shot through the hands. To ride he had to wrap reigns around his wrists."

"Around his *wrists*?" Tip continued to dress the wounds, his thoughts like a heavy fog.

"He wrapped them with his teeth. His hands were torn apart."

All of the men cringed at the thought, imagining what kind of shot could have robbed a man of both of his hands.

Then Danny told them, "Like I said, he shouldn't concern you."

Tip shook his head. "Danny, right now your father is my greatest concern in this world. Alongside you and your partner here. Do you know where he went?"

Danny winced in pain. "East, toward the Cutshank. If he makes it there he'll spend the rest of his life drinking whiskey through a straw. Which is just fine by me."

"You're a cowardly boy!" Culpin yelled. "He'll be here any minute. He'll be here to finish this!"

"No he won't," Danny said. "I know him. He's a quitter when his chips are down. He'd rather die than ride in here like that."

Wonderboy stood and approached the wounded. "From what I've seen this man is right," he said. "The big man tried to aim many times, but could never hold the rifle. I was out of bullets by then. If he could have fired he would have killed me."

Tipper considered everything he had heard. He looked over the men one last time and then turned sharply, facing Henry.

"LaMont, I'd appreciate it if you'd fetch two good horses," Tip said. "For me and my son here."

"Horses?"

"Unger will be in charge of the wounded. Everyone else will stay right where you are. Henry and I are riding out to find Joe Forsman."

LaMont seemed stunned by the news. "What? Why?"

"He's wounded and hurting. We're going to make this right."

LaMont looked out at the field.

"Do you want your rifle?"

"No."

"Anything?"

Tip shook his head, "When we find him he must know that we're unarmed."

"You won't find him," Danny said.

LaMont fetched the horses and soon Tipper turned to leave.

"Well I guess we'll see," Tip said, turning to his son. "Won't we, Henry?"

They rode into the trees and it wasn't long before they found Forsman's track. It ambled north and east, far from the Woodsies through the thick of the Wild West End. Forsman's horse was moving quickly across the forest, back the way he came and soon there were tracks of two mounts traveling together, both riders bleeding slightly.

As much shame as he felt in the saddle, Henry still held on to a part of himself that wanted to stare Forsman down. The man had been reckless with a young girl's heart, and with countless others that only God knew. Henry felt certain that Tip wouldn't allow it, but in his soul's dark corner he wanted to stand over the man as judge.

Tip could see from the lean of the prints that the riders were slumped in their saddles, weakened, but riding hard toward the Cutshank. From the steady pace Tip doubted that the man's wounds were fatal - but he did agree with Danny: Forsman would not be caught. He was hours ahead of them, moving steadily, and Tip's heart ached for the man's injuries, despite all that he had set out to do.

They gave up their search after hours of tracking. With no hands and a broken spirit - the people of Luleo had nothing to fear. The horses were watered and they turned back to the west.

"You may think you got off with something," Tip said, finally. "But everything has a consequence."

"Yessir," Henry said.

"Do you really believe that, or do you think yourself *above it?*"

"Tip I think-"

"Because after what you did," Tip gritted his teeth. "I don't believe you have the faintest concept of consequence."

Henry felt the weight of his father's words. He had disappointed the man many times, but never like this. Tipper's words caused Henry's heart to quake. His stomach turned and his eyes swelled. For the first time in many years Henry Snow was broken.

They found the campsite where they had fled the afternoon before and recovered their packs and rode the rest of way at a gentle pace.

"You have no reason to believe me," Henry admitted. "What I did was childish and self-serving. And I had no cause but my own enjoyment. I don't deserve all that's been handed me. No matter who my father was. I dwell on myself alone. In truth I feel like a villain compared to the men before me."

Tip was unmoved by Henry's words. "When you get back home - you're gonna go and see him, Henry. You're gonna walk straight up to Forsman's door and make this right. No matter what you're met with."

"Aren't you?" he added.

"Yessir."

Tip Holland kept his eyes straight ahead as he led them through the narrow path in the woodland. "Everything has a consequence."

Meanwhile, back at Luleo, Jack dwelled on the stories of his father as he helped the other men tend the wounded. They kept each of them hydrated, and Danny and Culpin were soon fast asleep, although both men appeared gaunt and fragile, having lost a great deal of blood. Jack knew their wounds were serious, even life-threatening if they hadn't arrived when they did. Unger had explained their treatment, and Jack had helped with every stage of their care throughout the long day at their bedside. Yet despite the violence spread before him Jack's thoughts continued to return to his father and Kolschen.

The thought of Wonderboy and Putt, and of Tip's anger were all still heavy on his heart, but the knowledge that his father and his grandfather were both respected men, even heroic men did much to lift his spirits.

For the second straight day Jack's heart struggled to contain all that he had seen. He still had many questions about the nature of this new place, and about Wonderboy's bold journey across the Wild West End. But despite all of the questions that spun around him, Jack still longed for conversation about the hill, and to his delight, Wonderboy was as joyful and talkative as ever.

"How are you feeling?" Jack asked.

"I'm feeling good, my friend. So good."

"You did a very brave thing coming after us," Jack admitted. "I imagine Tenpenny is falling apart without you."

Wonderboy gave Jack a wide smile. He shook his head in humility, but the truth was he took great pride in the boy's words.

"By now I'm sure that all the toilets are clogged," Jack said jokingly, "The roads are filthy, and your work crew is lost without you."

Wonderboy shook his head. "No, no," he told him. "They will be fine."

"Of course they will," Jack smiled. "But I wonder, do you happen to know if Padi ever get up on her horse?"

Wonderboy's smile disappeared. He had never enjoyed being the bearer of bad news. In fact he hardly knew how. The little man tried to answer the question in such a way that didn't seem one-sided, but it was impossible, he knew, and he forced himself to say, "Sissy wouldn't let her."

"Wouldn't let her?"

"She said riding was too dangerous."

"For Padi? Come on." The idea that Padibatakal had been denied her freedoms was disturbing to young Jack, but not altogether surprising considering who was now in charge. "Sometimes I think Sissy doesn't know anything - about any one of us."

Then Wonderboy surprised himself, "Or doesn't want to."

"Whoa!" Jack chuckled. "Easy there!" and the two shared a laugh at Sissy's expense.

The heavy laughter roused Putt from his sleep and he looked up at Jack in judgement. He licked his jowls and smacked his gums. "I gave this leg to save you," Jack heard him say. "The least you could do is keep it down."

"You're right," Jack told him. "You more than earned it, buddy," and he drummed his broken fingers across his fur until the old dog closed his eyes.

Jack turned back to Wonderboy but his heart was torn as he considered his next question. Greer had been heavy on his heart for days, even though the news of Kolschen had briefly driven her from his mind. It was true that his feelings for Greer were changing in her absence. But she's still someone I care for, he thought. Like any orphan on the hill.

The question of whether or not she had run away was one he had to have an answer to.

"Is there anything you can tell me about Greer?" Jack asked. "It must seem strange me asking like that. But has anything unusual happened?"

Wonderboy sat up. He turned serious in an instant. "How d'you know, Mister Jack?"

Jack nodded and gave a deep sigh. His eyes locked on the floor. *So Greer Ashby has run off and left us.*

"She told me before we left," Jack told him. "The morning the spring broke."

Wonderboy turned his head in confusion.

"I should have said something," Jack admitted, "But I figured she can do what she wants to do. No one should feel a prisoner in their own home."

Wonderboy shook his head, "I don't understand, Mister Jack."

"Did Sissy send you after her?"

"After her?"

"When she ran away did you follow her down the road? Use your bag of tricks?"

"She didn't *run away,* Mister Jack. She'll *never* run away."

But before Jack could speak Wonderboy added, "Pregnant girls are too scared for that."

Jack could feel his stomach rising in his throat. The words settled in and he began to choke on his anger. In an instant his confidence was shattered. Sweat began to swell on his brow.

"I suppose your right," Jack managed to say, covering up his surprise. "Who told you about her anyway?"

"The Doctor Zuni. But you couldn't have known, Mister Jack? She didn't find out until after you left."

"That's not important," Jack told him. "What's important is that she's taken care of." His heart was racing uncontrollably. "Have you told my father?"

"No, Mister Jack. I've been told not to tell Mister Tipper."

"That's a wise move. He's already upset about Henry. It wouldn't do to upset him again."

And Wonderboy agreed.

Jack could think of nothing to say. His head was spinning. The world swelled and receded around him. "D'you finish the pine haul?" he asked, just to break the silence.

Wonderboy was frustrated now. "No, Mister Jack. We couldn't. The lead hitch snapped and we didn't have another one. We'll have to fix it when we get back home."

Jack's eyes were dark, hollow pits, empty of feeling. He was holding back his tears. He kept his voice at a whisper, for fear of breaking, "Sure sure," he said to him. "If there's still a home left to fix."

6. Sissy's Hurdles

The foal died sometime in the night and by the time Padi discovered him he was already stiff. She didn't wake Momma Tom right away, but instead rubbed the neck of the tiny colt, whispering sweet words over his short life. For days Padi had enjoyed the feeling of a young thing in her arms and now that it was over she wanted to cherish that feeling as long as she could. The girl lifted her hairbrush from the bedside table and brushed his short mane in the dark of the morning, dwelling on the knowledge of life and death. For just the evening before there had been breath, she knew, and now the breath was gone; a present and a future, and now only the past remained. She thought it strange that a little foal could bring to mind such a powerful reflection. For the girl rarely gave a moment's thought to her parents death, and they had been people. But Padibatakal reminded herself that they were only faceless figures in her mind; ideas for her to wonder on, but the foal had been real.

When Momma Tom finally did come awake she took one look at Padi and instantly knew that the colt was gone. The old woman slid across the bed and gathered the girl in her arms and brushed her hair with her fingers, as Padi brushed the colt.

"I wanted to save him," the girl said. "I wanted him to grow strong and free and I wanted to ride him along the river."

Momma Tom knew the feeling well. She had been mothering other people's children for the better part of her life, and she had buried more than foals in her time. The sight of Padi's broken heart was tragically familiar.

"I know it, Mumsie. Life just comes and goes."

Padi's face seemed to sag with exhaustion. She hadn't slept well since Wonderboy had left, unable to escape the feeling that Jack and Henry and Tipper were in real danger, the kind she had never seen on Tenpenny Hill. Wonderboy wouldn't have ridden off so hard and fast if he hadn't feared the worst, she knew, and the uncertainty had robbed her of her sleep.

When she spoke she wore an empty, tired stare. "I like to think I'll grow old and wise, like you," Padi said, hugging the colt's tiny neck. "But who knows how long any of us have?"

The foals eyes were open, looking blankly at the ceiling. His little pale tongue rolled out to one side.

"All we orphans really have is *now*," Padi continued, in a soft whisper. "We don't know our ends *or* our beginnings."

Sadly Momma Tom shook her head. Of course she knew of the girl's beginning. She knew the story all too well. But she had always believed that if Padi knew the truth, that her mother had been a murdered slave and that Tip Holland had killed her father, it would have only served to confuse her. And Padibatakal didn't need any more confusion, not with Jack's heart dangling before her in the wind.

"That's right," she said. "You orphans have the *now*, and the prayers for what's yet to come."

For the past three days Momma Tom had been praying constantly for Tipper and his sons. She started praying the moment she woke and didn't stop until she fell asleep again, except to eat or talk to Padi. Always she kept the chessboard ready, in case Jack were to be standing there when she finally opened her eyes.

As the young girl continued to brush the colt's mane, Momma Tom prayed out loud. She prayed for Tip and Jack, Henry and Putt. She prayed for over an hour and soon Padibatakal became lost in the prayers, hearing only what she wanted. For there were so many dreams and truths dancing in her head.

". . .maybe he will come today or next week. But whenever he comes, Lord. I know he'll be different. He'll have learned something important and he won't be the same. I pray he'll walk in that door there, and he'll sit down to our chess game, and he'll be something different than he was before. . ."

Though Padi smiled at the thought, she didn't want Jack to be any different. There was nothing about him she would change.

". . .and I pray for the heart of Padi here. That it will heal quickly from the loss of the foal. . ."

To these words Padibatakal sprung awake. In the days since she was told that she couldn't ride all of her attention had turned toward the foal. Even though she didn't show it, her heart was crushed when she learned she wouldn't be allowed to race the horse named Duchess up and down the river, as she'd planned. She needed something to draw away her attention after the setback and the newborn colt had provided a perfect distraction, one she was thankful for. But now the colt was gone and her mind began to drift back toward her heartbreak.

Padibatakal had always been self-aware when it came to her frailties. She never lingered after a spell of disappointment, but instead began instantly to search for the next dream she might fulfill. Of course Jack Oakham was her grandest dream of all, and customarily the place where her heart dwelled in moments of heartbreak. It was impossible to deny that he had real feelings for her, but those feelings had never been defined, and her dreams were often wrapped up in the moment when they would be.

But as she sat with the colt in her arms, Padibatakal had reason to doubt that the moment would ever come. She had seen the letter Jack had written to Greer, and the look on Doc Zuni's face as he tried to conceal it. If Jack had time in the forest to write Greer a letter, then where was her letter, Padi wondered? What thoughts did Jack have for Greer that he didn't have for her?

The news of Greer's pregnancy had also set her mind to racing. Could it be Jack Oakham's baby? She shuttered at the thought. But it was a quiet truth known across Tenpenny Hill that at least part of Jack's heart was given over to the girl. And Greer was the most beautiful girl Jack had ever seen.

But beauty fades, Padi reminded herself. Life comes and goes and all we orphans have is now. But it was her future, with or without Jack Oakham, that she was thinking of when she interrupted Momma Tom's prayers.

"We need to bury the foal," Padi told her. She'd had enough praying for one day and knew surely that life was about moving on.

Momma Tom opened her eyes and there was a moment where her prayer world and her waking world blended strangely together.

"Of course, Mumsie. We'll bury him right away."

"And after we bury him," the girl added. "I'd like you to go with me. . . up to the bell."

Momma Tom sat up straight, her eyes only for the girl. She knew that Padibatakal was right, they had been in that room far too long, and now the scent of death was lurking there. It would do them good to breathe in the spring air. But that wasn't enough reason to ring the bell, Momma Tom knew and she said so right away.

"That's a big decision, Mumsie."

"I know it. But it's time."

"How long have you been thinking about it?"

"A long time. Years and years. But I was just reminded that life is short. I've had enough time to make a decision."

"Are you doin' this for you?" she asked. "Or for young Jack?"

"I'm doing this for me. Ringing the bell isn't the kind of thing you do for someone else."

Momma Tom smiled, satisfied with the answer, and soon the two ladies dressed themselves in fresh clothes for the first time in days.

When they emerged Momma Tom fetched the help of one of the new men, Chhedup, and the three set about their task. They carried the foal up toward Campbell Field, and Chhedup dug a grave. They set the foal inside and covered him up and Padi crawled around on her knees placing rocks upright as a headstone. They thanked God for the brief gift of life and for the reason to be so near each other for several days. After a sweet song the two made their way back down the hill, past the fountain and the washer pits, and when they reached the bell pole the girl didn't hesitate. She crutched herself up the steps and pulled the rope with one quick tug. The clapper struck and a joyful sound rung across the hills. It was a Tenpenny tradition that if any child wished to be baptized all they had to do was ring the bell.

Sissy Holland had never learned that there was more to leading people than telling them what to do. Despite all that Tipper had shown her, she saw leadership as nothing more than a system of expectations. And by the time the sun began to rise on her fourth day in charge, the power had been out to the courts for three of them, and the lives of the orphans and the staff had suffered greatly, all because of those expectations. She had fired their in-house electrician for "disrespecting her position" and then went about her day as if nothing had happened. What Sissy didn't understand, however, was that her expectations would soon have consequences.

The electrician, a man named Doyle Finney, was still a bit hesitant to leave once Sissy let him go. He was a fat man with red cheeks, loyal, with a loud laugh and a quiet voice. Tipper had hired him two years before to be the in-house electrician after his thirteen year-old son had run away and never returned. It was rumored that Doyle found women to be distrustful because he never looked Sissy in the eye, or spoke to her unless he was pushed into a corner. To Sissy that equalled sexism and for months she had searched for a way to prove it. When she told him to check the same bulbs in the courts that he'd checked the day before, just to keep him busy, he darted his eyes away and rested his chins upon his chest and when she didn't make another suggestion he told her, "That'd waste the whole dern mornin'."

His expression was one of distaste and he never looked at her, so she fired him, sighting the bigot for judging a book by its cover. The truth was that Doyle Finney had been lured by a strong-willed woman with red-hair when he was just a boy, had married two heavy-set brunettes, yet even in his fifties could not with confidence look Sissy in the eye because of his childhood fascination with redheads. Even when he was asked to leave he never looked at her.

Of course Sissy hadn't expected that one of the grounds crew would drive through the west gate of Campbell Field instead of the south, and that due to the sharp turn at that corner the logs that hung from the semi would clip the utility pole, uprooting it, and kill power to the courts indefinitely. She was then left with the dilemma of no electrician and dozens of expectant children to please.

Sissy was advised to beg forgiveness of Doyle Finney, but her pride killed the dream. She reasoned they could do without power to the courts until a new electrician could arrive, two days at the most. That meant that the dance they had planned for that evening would have to be postponed. With no courts to use for their evening activities Sissy had to bump up all of the plans she had for the following week. Soon the jobs the counselors and leaders were attending to were put on hold so that they could assemble a massive scavenger hunt to keep the children occupied. Before long every station on Tenpenny Hill was short-handed. The cooks couldn't get the food out in time, the counselors couldn't shower because there was no one in the cabins to watch the kids, even the infirmary had long waits because there was no one to police whether or not the children's injuries were serious enough to warrant a visit.

But her high expectations weren't the only changes Sissy was making. Once she saw how unhappy the children were about losing some of their favorite activities, she called off cabin clean-up for the next morning, and again the day after that. Then to take the children's minds off of the dances they were missing, and to curb her own exhaustion, Sissy set their curfew a whole hour earlier, which meant that shower time was shortened, Bible studies were cancelled, and the children lay awake in their beds.

In was a Tenpenny custom for the trumpet man to play reveille before lights out, but the only one among them who knew the tune besides Henry and Tipper was Doyle Finney, the recently fired in-house electrician.

With reveille gone the songs were soon to follow. What had been the staple serving of Tenpenny's table of fare seemed at once to be pulled from the menu. Little hummings that had been heard just hours before were like a sad memory, and no one dared break the mood with a merry belt. The joylessness of the hill could be felt by all and oh how the children grew to miss Tip Holland. They looked here and there for him to come to their rescue, like he so often did when the need arose - but there was no Tipper and no songs, nothing around them they could depend on but the certainty of spring, and the truth that this one would be nothing like the others.

Despite the walls falling down around her, Sissy couldn't distance herself from her own agenda, for in her mind it was the most important thing of all. It was the springtime now and for months Sissy had been making plans. For the past three years Sissy had tried, without success, to devote one entire afternoon in the springtime to making pies. Ever since she was a girl she had always dreamed of keeping a family tradition where her husband and children would make pies together across the long afternoon. She had envisioned that the tradition would take place on March the 14th - 3.14, or the day of "pie", as she liked to call it. But Tenpenny was still a frozen wonderland in the second week of March and to Sissy's mind, making pies called for warmer weather.

So every time the spring broke on Tenpenny Hill she had done her best to carve out an afternoon in that first week just for pie-making. But, like clockwork, every year she was interrupted.

But not this year, she told herself. In the dead of winter, when the children had all been huddled in their cabins waiting out the cold, Sissy had decided that from now on Pie day would take place on the first saturday after the melt. No exceptions and no excuses.

The suggestion that due to her mounting responsibilities she should postpone Pie Day until a future date never seemed to enter into her thinking. She had sacrificed more than enough for her brother. And even though the Hill was slipping further from her grasp each day, it was now the first Saturday after the melt. The day she had carved out for herself. And if she had it her way no interruptions would find her until the following day.

So when the sun rose Sissy Holland began to gather all of her ingredients. It took almost an hour to move everything from the mess hall to the chocolate house and she worked silently and alone. And without her nephews and her brother to keep her company, it was difficult even for Sissy to ignore just how lonely she had become. Although self-awareness was hardly in her nature, Sissy did experience rare moments of clarity where the curtain was drawn back. It happened only during times of personal stress and when the needs of her nephews didn't consume her. But in the days following their departure Sissy had no way to deny just how distant she felt from everyone around her.

It became clear that there was no one she could really talk to. The children saw her as their leader now, but in contrast to their treatment of Tip, each of the orphans offered her only silence, rejecting any notion of endearment. The workers too offered little in the way of support, choosing instead to avoid her when possible.

After several days at the helm, Sissy didn't claim to understand it or agree with it but she couldn't deny it: There was a great distance between her and the others on the hill.

In fact the only people she felt completely comfortable around were the Bhotiyas, who were adapting well to their new life on the hill. She enjoyed watching them work, imagining the journey they had taken to be there. Sissy especially admired young Immanuel, who had already learned a few words in English and used them constantly as he roamed about throughout the day, a great smile across his face. The Bhotiyas were good workers, always positive and steady in their task. They were put under Smithson's care once they arrived which of course led Sissy to ask the question: *Where was Wonderboy?*

Once she had gathered her ingredients and everything was in place Sissy moved up and down the hill, asking about the whereabouts of the little workman. She knew that if Wonderboy didn't return her chances of being interrupted increased with every hour.

She soon learned that he had disappeared the previous day around lunchtime and the only thing anyone knew for certain was that he had taken Monk, Sissy's blue roan, when he departed.

First she questioned Smithson, who himself was overrun with work and seemed flummoxed by the discovery, having not yet learned where his boss had gone.

"What do you mean, '*He's gone?*'" he asked.

Sissy went on to question the entire work crew, the cooks, even some of the children without learning a bit of useful information. It wasn't until she spoke with Doc Zuni that any of the pieces came together.

"So he was in here around lunchtime yesterday?"

The Doc nodded. "Yes. He was in here."

"And can you tell me where he went after that?"

Zuni believed that if Sissy knew the truth about Wonderboy nothing good would come from it. In his opinion it would only bring about a panic, causing the children's already fragile state to crumble.

"This is most difficult," he told her, sincerely. "I'm sure losing Wonderboy leaves you very short-handed. It's an unfortunate turn of events. And since Tipper left you in charge I believe you deserve answers. Unfortunately I feel no peace in giving them. Your problems are many and they will only grow if you dwell on Wonderboy. If I were you I wouldn't expect to see him for awhile, and know that all will be explained in due time."

Sissy had been worn thin waiting for explanations. Her brother hadn't explained his sudden departure, except to say he was leading his sons to their birthright, and what that was she didn't know. She had quickly learned that running Tenpenny required a great deal of explaining as well, although she had received none of it. Now Zuni offered her no explanation as to Wonderboy's sudden disappearance, though the man clearly knew what had happened.

"Due time?" she asked him. "How is it that I am required to wait for anything, Doctor? One of my staff members is missing and you dangle out riddles. Does that seem appropriate to you?"

"Not appropriate. But necessary."

"Ahh, well," She nodded. "Would it be *necessary* to keep secrets from *Tip* Holland if he was in my shoes?"

"No. It wouldn't be necessary."

"You must explain that, Doctor."

"You are not Tip Holland."

With that she turned and left, cursing the Doctor beneath her breath. The hill would remain in chaos so long as Wonderboy was missing. If she wanted any peace she knew she had to find him.

He had disappeared around mid-day, taking her horse and riding off to God knows where, and the last time anyone saw him was in the infirmary. Sissy knew that his departure had something to do with the Bhotiyas' arrival. She would have gladly questioned them but of course they spoke no english. Sissy needed answers and she needed them quickly but the Doctor wasn't willing to give them. Soon, as she marched down the hill, the only question that ran through her mind was "Who else was in the infirmary?"

Greer Ashby was seated in the shaded path along the river, smoking one of the last cigarettes that she had managed to smuggle on to Tenpenny Hill. She had taken up smoking after her family's funeral and made a habit of sneaking away at least twice a week to stay in practice. Yet despite her own depression she refused to inhale, letting the smoke drift down the river just close enough to smell. Greer knew that whatever else the baby was, it deserved a healthy start.

By now the news of Greer's pregnancy had spread across the hill and she was doing her best to keep out of sight until the brothers came back to her. She had little desire to spend another moment in the infirmary, for the smell of turpentine and filthy children flooded the place. However she had no option but to sleep there. Doc Zuni had been kind enough to leave her alone in her private room, knowing that loneliness was something she favored. But Greer reasoned that if she was going to be alone in the daytime, she could at least be outside when she did so.

That morning she had snuck away down to the river, far from the hustle and bustle of the spring. The idea of looking any of the children in the face was unsettling to her, even though she felt certain they were unlikely to judge. Most of the orphans of Tenpenny had themselves seen far too much heartache and disfunction in their own lives to ridicule anyone else's. Yet despite their forgiving spirit the idea of living among them gave Greer no comfort.

In fact the only comfort she did have came in the form of a letter, which she held against her chest like a treasure. She had already read it a dozen times, but as she sat on the shaded path with the cigarette between her lips, she was excited to read it again.

Greer,

I was wrong to argue with you before we left. No one should feel a prisoner in their own home so if you want to leave Tenpenny - you should go. Seeing what's out there will do you some good.

I should have said that before we left the hill. But the truth is I was afraid you might actually go. I'm not afraid of that now. You've earned the right to do what you want to do.

If you're still there when I get back I'll offer my friendship from a distance, but be careful not to lean on me for anything more.

I'm done lying to myself. You don't want any pity - so I won't give it. I won't offer you my heart because you won't receive it, and that is a relief to me.

If you're already gone when I return then I wish you a long healthy life.

- Jack

The note was not carefully written. Jack's words were barely legible. But as she read them Greer found new feelings swelling up inside her. Feelings she could hardly comprehend.

Her heart towards Jack Oakham had already begun to change with news of the baby, for Jack was no doubt the more responsible brother. But his letter had only served to further her feelings, leaving her confused and in need of a smoke.

She sat beside the roar of the river, thinking of him fondly, imagining him out west somewhere, and the perils he might be facing. The idea that either Jack or Henry were in mortal danger was a new reality for Greer, and one she didn't enjoy. It brought her mind back to the loss of her family, and drew her thoughts away from Jack's words, which were now foremost in her thinking.

She read the letter straight through very slowly, examining each word, and trying to piece together Jack's heart as he wrote them. For once his feelings are plain to see, she thought. For once he is telling it straight.

Greer had often criticized Jack Oakham for working too hard for her affections. She had never enjoyed lavish attention and had always resented Jack for giving it. But now, it seemed, something had changed and Jack no longer cared for her approval. He was going to say how he felt no matter how it may seem to her which served to seduced her all the more. She couldn't imagine what he had done and seen in the forest that changed him so suddenly, but whatever it was she liked it.

As she puffed on her cigarette Greer thought long on her present situation, about Henry and Jack and the baby and what the future might hold. Her options ran through her head, and always she returned to the words in Jack's letter. They echoed across her heart again and again until she heard footsteps approaching behind her in the grass.

"What are you doing down here?" Sissy said.

Nonchalantly Greer turned back to face her. "Sissy Holland, I'm smoking. Better call the cops."

Sissy wasn't expecting her conversation with Greer to go well, but she hoped it would start better than this.

"Smoking? With a baby in your belly?"

"I just like the feeling. I don't breath it in."

"It's still irresponsible."

Greer flicked the cigarette into the river and tossed her hair. "Well that's probably why I do it."

"How's that?"

"You see, Sissy, I don't really feel like a responsible person. And it takes one to move on from the loss of an entire family. And that's something I can't seem to do. It takes a responsible person to have a baby and raise it. So maybe that's why I smoke. I smoke because I don't measure up to what's coming."

Sissy covered her yawn. "And whose fault is that?"

"Who's *fault* is it?"

"You're pregnant, out of wedlock," then Sissy's voice took on a sing-song tone. "Blame must be assigned."

Greer shook her head, not at all surprised that the conversation had turned to blame. "Well Sissy, since you know everything why don't you go ahead and tell me?"

"It was your fault, Deary. That's your first lesson in being a responsible person: *taking the blame*. You played the broken heart for him. You lowered your eyes and you lured him in."

"Is that how it happened?"

"That's how it always happens, Deary. You acted a part in a play that's been running on repeat since the beginning of things. Since Eve of Eden."

Greer nodded contemptuously. "So what part did Henry play, exactly?"

Sissy sat down in the grass beside her. "Henry played the rugged hero, the part he was born to play. A man before his time. But he's still human. He still has weaknesses and you have preyed upon those weaknesses."

"I see. Your rugged hero is a victim."

"Of course he is. And you are his Jezebel. The strongest of men are nothing without a woman to guide them."

Greer's eyes began to swell.

"You see Henry Snow is a man of unusual talent and strength," Sissy told her. "But he needs a woman to teach him the high codes or he'll never be something great."

"And you're the one to teach him?"

"I already have."

Greer wiped her eyes, which by now were incendiary. "And the part about seducing a lonely orphan, did you teach him that?"

"Oh, Greer. My Henry never did that," Sissy said. "Someone else's child. But not my Henry."

Greer Ashby had a number of responses she wished to give, but before she could choose one there came a ringing from high upon the hill, as the clapper of the great bell sounded.

Sissy looked up the hill in annoyance, knowing that a baptism would ruin the plan for her day. She cursed beneath her breath before turning back to Greer. "I came down here to find you," Sissy said. "To talk about what happened with Wonderboy."

Greer smiled. "Doc Zuni wouldn't tell you."

"For some reason, no. We are far behind and there is work to be done. I must know where he is. I need your help."

"Well it's a bit late for that. Zuni kept his mouth shut for the same reason I'm gonna. The less you know about on Tenpenny Hill, the better it is for all of us."

Greer pulled another cigarette from her pocket and let it hang from her lips. She didn't look at Sissy, but instead watched as the river rushed on by.

"Young lady, I-"

But Greer shook her off. "Best take your holy self up the hill, Miss Sissy. Some child is waiting."

Sissy pitied the girl in silence. The idea of performing a baptism tugged further at her resolve but she could see that she was getting nowhere with Greer. Suddenly she turned back to the path.

"And when you get there," Greer continued. "Try not to judge whatever poor soul needs sanctification."

Sissy said nothing and never looked back. Judgement and admonishment are two different things, she said to herself. I have the right to admonish whoever I choose, she thought, as she marched back up the hill.

The morning was steadily advancing, much to Sissy's dismay. The sun was now bearing down on the rooftops and warming the branches of the great trees. Patches of snow glistened in the early light and what little remained would melt in the coming days. Sissy was no closer to finding Wonderboy and she knew the longer it took, the more turmoil it would bring her. She still had electrical issues to deal with and the evening activities to tend to as well. So, needless to say, as Sissy approached the top of the hill the ringing of the bell was the last thing on her mind.

Momma Tom and Padi were seated on the short stone wall beneath the bell, waiting patiently when Sissy arrived. The girl had a shy smile on her face and when Sissy saw her she couldn't contain her surprise.

Of all the unbaptized children of Tenpenny, Padibatakal was the last one Sissy expected to ring the bell. Not because of any overt belief the girl held to, but because Padi had been on the hill longer than all the other children, and it surprised her that she would make such a decision after so many years.

"Hello, Sissy," the girl said.

"Well hello, Padi." Sissy's eyes were wide now, her astonishment worn like a gift. "I came up as quickly as I could. Was it you who rung the bell?"

Padi nodded repeatedly. "Momma Tom helped me, but, but I pulled the rope."

Sissy knelt down beside he girl, her face wide with delight. "That's wonderful!" Sissy said, quite genuine. "A new life born in a new season!"

A moment later she added, "You know how proud my brother would be?"

Of course when Padi made her decision she had thought a great deal about what Tipper would feel. The thought delighted her, but she knew that with or without him the decision was the same, and she didn't want his absence to cloud her thinking.

"I'll be proud to tell him when he returns."

Sissy herself was wishing for Tip's return, if only to take the reigns of Padi's request. Whether she liked the role or not Sissy was their leader and Tipper had always made his stance clear in regards to leadership. "Leaders must be servants," he had told her as he washed the feet of an ailing child. "The last shall be first and the first shall be last."

Sissy knew that her role in leading the baptism was to serve the child from beginning to end, washing their feet and performing the entire ceremony by herself. Now truth be told it wasn't the feet-washing that bothered her, though she had no special taste for it. Instead what gave her pause was the embarrassment Sissy felt for Padi. The girl would have all the eyes of Tenpenny on her as Sissy bent down to wash her feet; feet that weren't even there. The very thought was the saddest she could think of. For Sissy had spent a lifetime concealing her scars and weaknesses and this girl was about to put her own scars on public display. In Sissy's way of thinking it would be better to never to be baptized at all.

"Tell me Padi, how did you come to this decision?"

The girl looked at Momma Tom, then down at her ankles.

"I've been thinking of it for years. But I wanted to make an informed decision."

"So what informed you?"

"A lot of things over the years," Padi said. "I've seen lives changed when the decision was made. But my actual decision came this morning, after we lost the foal."

Sissy looked to Momma Tom with sadness, "That's very sudden, don't you think?"

Momma Tom agreed. "That's what I said. But she tells me she's ready."

"Well I'm sure she is," Sissy nodded. "She's had plenty of time to make up her mind."

As she listened to Sissy's words, Momma Tom couldn't drive Padi's mother from her mind. She had never known the girl's mother, though she knew her story well. This baptism was a long time coming, she knew. The stories of mother and daughter had come full circle and she felt certain that Tip would be proud.

"Momma Tom?"

The old woman sprung out of her daydream and saw that Sissy had turned to address her. In fact Padi and Sissy both seemed to be waiting for an answer.

"I-pologize. What d'you ask?"

Sissy smiled. "I was wondering if Padi and I could have a moment to talk things over."

Though she thought the request a strange one, Momma Tom nodded. She kissed the girl on the crown of her head and silently slipped away to the stone wall by the fountain. When she was out of earshot Sissy started up again.

"I'm so proud of you, Padi. It takes a great deal of courage to do what you're doing."

"I don't think it does."

"Well I do. You are setting a wonderful example for the other children. And your timing is perfect. Tipper will return and perform the ceremony and it will make for a double celebration."

"I don't want to wait for Tipper," Padi said, quite firm.

"Oh Padi, of course you do. I'm so sure of it. As sure as I am of anything. Did you plan this for his homecoming? Oh how delightful! I know it's what Tipper would want."

The girl sat dumbfounded. She couldn't find a word to speak.

"Do you want to plan the baptism for the night he returns? Or would you like to do it later?"

Padi cleared her throat, "Tradition states that when you ring the bell you will be baptized that very night."

"Yes yes," Sissy answered. "*Old* tradition states that." Sissy scooted up next to the girl. "But we ladies can make our own traditions, can't we?" she winked. "There's no law stating that the old way is right." Then she draped her arm around Padi's shoulder. "It might be time for a change or two."

Padibatakal had no idea what Sissy was talking about. She didn't want to change anything, except her own public proclamation of baptism.

"But it's a Tenpenny tradition," Padi answered. "And I have my heart set on following tradition."

Sissy gave a heavy sigh. "Padi that's your choice to make, and I won't stop you. But if you'd let me I'd like to offer a bit of advice."

"Yes ma'am."

"Thank you, Padi. You may not be aware of how stressful this time is for many people. Were you aware of that, Padi?"

"No ma'am. I wasn't."

"But how could you? You've been nursing your foal. That's very sweet, but between you and me there have been some real problems on the hill. Many of the employees are exhausted."

"No, I didn't know that."

"Now I'm not talking about me, you understand? If it were up to me we'd shut down everything and have the celebration right now. But I've had my eyes open around here. I know the tone of the workers. And if I were you I'd think about all of them before I make your decision. Some of them haven't slept much this week. That can be very troubling when you work all day."

"I'd hope they'd forget their troubles when they saw the baptism."

Sissy shook her head, flinching "I wouldn't be so sure, Deary. Tipper assigned them quite a long 'to do' list before he left. Quite a long list. And with the spring beginning the children have it in their heads that they're going to do one thing tonight and now you're proposing that they cancel those plans and do another. And after a very long winter."

"I wasn't proposing anything."

"Oh but you were. You see that, don't you?"

Padi looked discouraged, for the first time. "It isn't just for me, you know? Many of the new ones have never even *seen* a baptism."

"But wouldn't they rather see one with Henry and Jack and Tipper beside them? For that matter wouldn't you? After all - they are your oldest friends?"

"I'm not doing it for them. I'm doing this because my heart is set on it."

"Padi, if I were you, I'd set my heart on a little patience. Think a little bit less about yourself, and more about the burdens of others."

Padi had a tearful look, but she held her tongue. "Yes ma'am."

Sissy smiled and stood to her feet. "I'm very proud of you, Padi. I know Tip will be too. You've done the right thing and God will reward you."

The girl barely looked at her as Sissy copied Momma Tom and kissed Padi on her head. Then without another word she was gone, heading down the hill toward the chocolate house. She wouldn't miss another pie day. They couldn't pull that one from her cold dead hand.

Momma Tom walked over, shaking her head as she rocked the girl. She could see from her face that disappointment had visited her, twice in one day.

"Easy there," she told her. "She put you off, didn't she?"

The girl began to shake. "Yes, she put me off."

"Shh now, shh. She don't know no better. You'll have your day soon enough."

Then Padi asked as the tears came. "What do I do til then?"

Momma Tom knew the answer. She knew it with everything she was. "The boys still need praying for, wherever they are," she told her. "And you can always do *that* without anyone's permission."

7. The Western Rim of the World

The brothers had gathered their belongings and were waiting for the sunrise, and for the last leg of their journey to begin. Jack was stirring the ashes with a green stem he had stripped from the overgrown barnyard. Henry was feeding the fire. The firelight blazed before their eyes.

Momma Tom had always called a fire "the caveman's television" and Jack could think of no other description to match it. He sat there, by the smoke house and the workshop, staring into the fires of Luleo, asking himself what kind of man he wanted to be. For now he had seen a great many things that remained fixed in his mind. It was hard for him to remember all of them at once. His mother had always said, "One thing at a time, little one. Boys are conquerors, but one thing at a time." And though the memory alone was like nourishment to young Jack, the advice he couldn't take. For what single thing could he think of? He was seated around a fire in a magical place where all the faraway people had come to. His heart was torn by love. His best friend Putt was cleaved and would never be the same. He was about to embark on the last leg of the great bittersweet journey. His broken fingers were sweating in their bandages. And his brother, or his cousin rather - Henry Snow, had betrayed everything he had ever been taught and now Greer was pregnant. Jack had thought about the girl for half the night, wondering to himself how the news would be broken. All of his thoughts rattled around in his head and he came to no clear answers. Not about Padi, or Putt, or how to deal with Henry. But the fire, the dying fire, aglow when the breeze came off the sea, was one simple thing he understood.

"Are you lonely, Henry?"

"Of course."

"Why?"

"We're incompleteable."

The two sat silently. Their faces glowed when the wind lit the embers. All around them the world was in shadow, but across the water, beyond the trees and the smooth green dales the snowcaps were lighted by the morning. The high ridge was filling with a golden light that raced down the pikes, revealing the rocky cut where they believed their journey would end.

"What's up there?" Henry seemed to ask himself.

Jack's eyes were locked on the coals. He grew somber and Henry could feel it. "I think it's an idea," he said. "Something's up there and we'll dig it up, but like you said it won't be no treasure chest. We couldn't lug out a bowling ball as worn as we are. I think it's an idea more than a treasure." Then he added. "How ya feeling?"

Henry shrugged. "Bout what?"

"*Bout what?* About the *Pritchers*. About *Joe Forsman*. About whatever Dad had to say." While Tip and Henry were tracking through the forest Jack had wondered the whole afternoon what his father would tell Henry when the moment arose.

"Oh that one. There are so many to think about. Well you know me, Jacko."

"Do I?"

Henry smiled. "You know I've never been what anyone says I am. And now least of all. And given the men who have walked before me - I have even less reason to fall back to the smallness of my ideals. But I am what I am. I shamed him. And after hearing what Tipper had to say I guess you'd say I'm whipped."

Whipped was right, Jack thought. In more ways than one. Their faces appeared bitter and beaten, their eyes drooping. But Jack knew that Henry wasn't speaking of anything physical. No, what Jack saw in his brother was different. Whatever Tipper had said had caused Henry Snow to stammer and he was still catching his wind.

The truth was that the knowledge of Henry's blood father had effected him greatly. He wasn't the man that his father was, or his grandfather either one. And it was hard for Henry to imagine that he ever would be. Neither of them would have done what he did to Joe Forsman, yet that action felt as true to Henry's spirit as any he could remember. There was a fire burning in his belly that his ancestors had learned to suppress. A fire replaced with gentleness. But Henry had little desire to replace it. Henry Snow was faced suddenly with the knowledge that his brother had inherited some very rare gifts, and he admired him for it. Oh Henry knew that he had been given gifts as well, the kind every boy desires, but if his journey had taught him anything it was that the strengths that seduced the world were of little use among men of character. Henry wanted to give Jack his due but before he could speak the door to the galley swung open.

"Good morning, gentlemen!" Unger said, more jovial than ever. "You two are looking fresh."

Despite their sagging faces the brothers did appear renewed in many ways. Their clothes were clean. The boy's hands, which had been filthy, were now scrubbed white. They had washed their hair and cleaned the film from their teeth and swabbed their ears of the leftover dust from the Rojo Prieta.

"Morning," they mumbled. Then Henry asked, "How are your patients?"

Unger had stayed up half the night with the three men and the dog.

"Wonderboy'll be fine in a week or so," Unger told them. "But the others lost a lot of blood. We'll see. They're pretty weak right now."

The thought of Danny and Culpin had been nagging at both brothers since they arrived. What would be done with these men? they wondered. Would they simply be put on their horses and sent home? If they were too weak to travel the thought of leading them back to the Cutshank was the only option Henry could think of, but thinking of it brought him no relief. For what laws had he broken on their behalf? The question of travel could also be asked of the old dog, who certainly couldn't walk back to Tenpenny on his own, and would have no part in being strapped down to a horse.

"What about Putt?" Henry said.

"Putt's old. He's breathing fine, but he's old. Surgery like that takes a lot out of an old dog. But it's the little man, Culpin. He's the one who took the worst of it. Say your prayers for him."

Jack did say his prayers, both for the old dog and for the wounds the three men had suffered. He prayed for many things that morning, things near to him and things back on the hill. Tenpenny seemed much further away than ever to him then.

He leaned over to his brother and slipped off the bear claw necklace from the black that Henry had made just four days before. Henry looked up at him curiously.

"For Putt," Jack said and his brother understood.

Jack stepped inside the galley where the dog was kept and knelt beside him and kissed him on his head. Then he unbound the strands of the leather necklace and tied it around the dog. Jack didn't know if Putt would know the difference between one bear claw and another. He wanted to go back to the forest and collect the claws from Esperanza herself, but these would have to do.

"You earned these more then we did," Jack said, tying it on.

The old dog huffed where he lay, "It's about time you said so."

Jack said his goodbyes and quickly rejoined the troupe. He felt mixed emotions about the parting. Oh he was happy to know that the dog would rest for awhile, out of harm's way, and yet a part of him was struck with a painful realization. Putt wasn't the same dog he had always been. The truth struck Jack like a hammer. Nothing lasts more than a moment, Jack knew. Even the mightiest whales will all sink to the bottom of the sea.

When Jack stepped outside Henry was still sitting by the fire, and Unger had drifted off to some unknown chore. But Jack looked beyond his brother, across the open fields, hoping to catch sight of his father somewhere.

No one had seen Tip since the night before when he sent them off to bed. They had made preparations all that evening to press on the following day, refitting their bandages, cleaning their wounds. Unger even checked Jack's fingers that had swollen to triple their normal size and a new metal splint was shaped to fit. Each of the Tenpenny three applied moleskin strips to their blistered feet, unpacked their bags, sorted their gear, and loaded it once again, this time tighter and sturdier than before. Then they hauled them onto their backs and refitted the straps to their bodies.

When Tipper had sent the boys off to bed Henry dozed immediately, but Jack stayed up for hours that night, scribbling notes in his story book that his brother had fetched from the forest. He tried to recall all that he had heard and seen in the past twenty four hours and when he was finished he slept a hard, consuming sleep, content as he dreamed of his father and grandfather.

Somewhere, beyond the thick of the forest, the sun was rising now and the grass shone wet with dew. The fog was clinging to the fields of Luleo, a cold wet morning, one the boys could only bear by hugging their bodies around the flames. But despite the bitter chill both of them caught sight of something they would always remember. Their father, having woken long before the dawn, was seen roaming barefoot across the grassy streets. His hands were out at his sides and his sons thought they heard him try to whistle, though his lips were too numb to do the job. He appeared to tiptoe, watching the sunrise and the village come awake and to his sons he seemed like a child whose chores were done, looking younger than they could remember him, as if the burdens of manhood had been lifted.

Jack stretched his arms behind his head and sat with the breeze, his eyes closed. Seeing Tip Holland meander through the streets of Luleo seemed strange and beautiful to his eyes and instantly his thoughts found, not for the final time, the distant features of Greer Ashby, who had been heavy on his mind.

"I really miss her," Jack said to his brother, hoping to draw him into a conversation. Wonderboy's revelation about Greer's pregnancy left Jack itching to talk about her, and especially with Henry.

"Ah yes," Henry said, as if he had been thinking the same thing. "Not a thing in this world excites me as much as making a pretty girl smile."

"Just smile?" Jack asked, a bit contemptuous.

"Well," Henry grinned. "A smile is where it starts and a smile is where it ends."

"You guys ready?" Tip said, walking up. By then the light was filling the treetops and the sound of work had started.

"Where are we going?" Jack asked, bitter at his brother's words.

"To chase down adventure."

"What more is there?"

"What more?" Tip chuckled. "The greatest adventure of them all. Your birthright awaits."

Tip swung his pack onto his shoulders and marched passed them, a strange new confidence in his eyes. Both of the brother's faces were turned with curiosity.

"Shouldn't we restock our supply?" Jack asked. "We're almost out of food."

"No," Tip answered. "We'll make do with what we have."

Jack sighed. "I can't take much more of this," he admitted. "I mean I need a day to wrap my head around things. It's been nonstop since we hit the forest. I can't live like that."

"We don't have another day," Tip said. "We don't have an hour to spare. Adventure doesn't wait. Vacations and holidays - those wait. But not adventures. They come whether you're ready or not and they slip away just as quick. In a blink you're an old man wondering where they've gone."

"Alright, alright," Jack said. "I don't need all that. I figure I know it by now."

Both Henry and his father looked on him curiously, for it wasn't Jack's custom to talk back to Tip Holland. Something was galling young Oakham, though neither man knew what it was.

"Lead on," Jack said right away, hoisting up his pack. "But don't blame me if my mind is elsewhere."

And with that Tip took up the trail at the same speed he had started the journey and all the boys could do was follow.

Those few workers who had already come awake were watching the boys closely. All at once they put down the tools they carried, stood in a line and offered the travelers a song of farewell.

"Down the Dagger to the broken road. . .
Across the Big Red Wind
Ne'er before have I heard told
The tales of the wild west end"

"Oh shut it up," Jack whispered. But the worker gang continued. . .

"Now break for sup and break for drink
And hear stories seldom told!
Salute the sentries with a wink
As you March to Watchmen's Cove!"

Their voices trailed off as the workers went back to their labors.

"Watchmen's Cove?" Jack wondered. "Is that where we'll find our birthright?"

"Almost," Tip answered. "It's buried just one leg beyond."

They marched north across the beachhead, watching the mountains to the west that would be their destination. It wasn't a ten minute journey along the sand before they saw, to their surprise, a second line of structures built against the sea. There were three more docks and half a dozen trawlers and skiffs tethered alongside them. There was a small workshop, and several men laboring, and nearby was the "wharf saloon" as Tip called it, where the swabbies took their meals and all of Luleo's citizens came for a drink.

"The longer we're here we need more boats for transport."

"Why build it here? Why not build it beside the others?"

"The shoreline off Luleo is shallow at places, especially at low tide. There's enough room for a few boats, but not for a wharf like this."

Briefly the brothers admired the workmanship as the wharf gulls squawked high above the trees and the sun lit upon their wings. But soon they had passed the wharf and followed the curving path of the sand, taking Unger's advice: "The beach bends to the northwest. Save your strength and follow it," he had told them. "When your father asks you to stop, keep your eyes to the North. You will hear them calling as they watch you. Then I'll know you're there."

Unger had told them that the night before. The callers he was speaking of were the eagles. And that is why the three walked silently over the sandy crests with their ears turned northward, hoping for the cry of the eagles.

They kept high on the beachhead with the sea to one side and the great woodland to the other. The ferns and the saplings grew to waist level and as they passed the wind shook loose the dew. All around them fallen hard gums and the moldered trunks of the big pines lay shadowed by the understory. For decades they had been hidden and would always be.

Sand dollars and broken clam shells, kelp stringers and solid bits of driftwood washed landward across the beach. The party could hear the rustle of the leaves in the treetops, high above where they could not see, and far ahead a squabble of gulls were shrilling as they danced across the sand.

In their long morning trek Henry Snow continued to scan the woods to the east and to look over his shoulder thinking that Forsman may still come rising out of the forest on his horse, but it never happened. In time he began to accept his disappointment. *Not all things come full circle*, he told himself. *Some stories don't have an end.*

After hours of marching the party emptied their packs and faced the truth that there was nothing left to eat. The dried moose steaks had been gone since two nights before and Tip's jelly was only a film on the inside of the jar.

Tip was quick to check his tide book, and when he found what he was looking for he pulled Jack's shovel from his pack. He instructed the boys to spread out across the beach, one on either side of him, and the three moved as one, every man searching the sand with their eyes.

They hunted methodically, looking for tiny "footprints" in the sand and there were many false alarms before Jack finally saw one. Tip passed Jack the shovel.

"Don't dig straight down or you'll break it," he told him. "Shovel next to the mark."

Jack did as instructed, plunging his shovel blade then quickly digging with his fingers. To his delight he pulled a razor clam from the darkness.

Each time they found one the party passed the shovel from man to man and one at a time they went to digging. Within an hour all three of our travelers had filled their hats with a fresh crop of razor clams. The brothers went to shucking while Tipper fixed a fire. Soon the old covered pot was boiling with sea water and the clams were steaming and Jack sprinkled the crop with garlic and each of the men devoured clams by the dozen, steam pouring out of their mouths as they swallowed.

They found a freshwater trickle that flowed between the trees and the party drank slowly from the hillside for the water was so cold it caused their heads to swim.

"Feels colder than ice," Henry said as he drank. "Hold these, Jacko," he said, passing his brother his hat of clams.

Henry ran his head beneath the bitter cold and shook himself wildly.

"How do you know I won't steal them?" Jack asked.

Henry's face shivered as he shook. "Because you're good. You intend to do everything you say and you never take the easy way."

The three men sat on the sand, finishing off their clams and after awhile Henry looked back at Jack and added. "At eleven when anyone was hurting you blamed yourself. Because Momma Tom asks for your advice. Does anyone want to fill my canteen while you're up?"

They gathered their belongings and turned to the north, belching loudly as they marched across the sandy breaks. They could see an endless shorefront, a line of grey dunes pressed against the beach, some rising out of the sea with great rocky shoals at their centers and others fledged with cane-like stalks springing from the sand.

The dunes lulled and drooped, wearing their ankles slick as they plodded northward. But it was only a short journey before the brothers noticed a shape emerging from the distant rises. It seemed to grow perfectly straight out of the grey sand and its color was like nothing that surrounded it.

They marched with their eyes ahead and soon, even from a great distance, each brother perceived the shape to be a thick wooden bollard, low and sturdy, sunk deep in the dune top, with thick lengths of rope clinging to its loops. The post had been placed there for some unknown purpose and neither of them could pull their eyes away. For it felt strange to see any sign of civilization in such a wild, untraveled place.

They walked quickly until they crossed the final dune, and there, tethered to the great bollard along the beachhead was a long shape draped in thick canvas. Both Jack and Henry watched the shape in wonder, for no doubt the thick drapery concealed something intended for the two of them.

Tipper marched ahead and when he reached the bollard he dropped his pack and walked toward the covered mass. His sons looked on in fascination as the old canvas pealed away, the seam ripping with every tug, until the mystery was brought to light.

It was a boat! A dugout canoe, long and extremely narrow, with wild carvings along the thwart, and others still, stenciled into the bow, like the face and neck of a crocodile.

Silently the brothers agreed that the dugout had been waiting by the beach for many years. The rope that was tethered to the bollard was threadbare and along the gunwales a nest of some tiny varmint lay abandoned.

The boat was set up across two great logs notched to hold it steady and when they turned it over Tipper wiped the seats down. Inside three sets of paddles were kept, one each of normal length and the other a short, stubby blade, built for some unknown purpose. The vessel was hand-carved in every detail, as long as a typical canoe but much more narrow, just wide enough for someone like Henry.

It took all three of them to lift the dugout onto their shoulders and place it on the beach but soon they had her in position and each of the boys were filled with excitement.

"I didn't know we would travel by sea," Jack said.

Tip smiled, admiring the vessel. He and Papon had carved the dugout across a long summer near the beaches of Luleo. It was a boat designed and built for one purpose, and other than a brief drift upon the sea it had never been tested. Tip faced the mountains and held on to his lingering smile.

"Just a shortcut," he told them. "But it will save us days. It'll be good to put our arms to work for a change."

The troupe left their packs behind, covered beneath the heavy tarp, and soon they each waded into the shallow surf. The surge of the current surrounded them, clear up to their hips, and their bodies began to shiver as they swung themselves inside.

When all was made ready Tip sighed. "And so comes the last land."

The treasure-seekers now turned what remained of their strength toward the sea. They pushed off with their long paddles, each of the men chopping at the surf and when they had crossed the breakers Tip Holland checked his watch for the first time in days.

"We have six hours to reach the shoreline," he told them. "Low tide will have come in by then. We'll make for the base of Watchmen's Eyrie."

The brothers looked out across the water. The cove spread before them all the way to the snowy peaks. Tip was right, they thought. It would have taken days to walk around the cove.

Whatever treasure awaited them lay high in the fog of the mountains, they figured; the great mountains that grew out of the distant trees. They appeared immeasurably high and mighty to both brothers, who hadn't a single experience with mountains between them.

But soon they would, Jack feared, feeling further and further from home with every paddlestroke. But despite his anxiety Jack kept his eyes to their destination. High above the cove, cradled between the two peaks was a bowl of fresh powder, like a nest scooped up between two stone pillars. The rim of the nest was lined with shallow hogbacks that weaved back across one another. Even from that distance they could see a host of eagles circling above their snowy nest.

"Why low tide?" Jack wondered.

Tip smirked. He had known the question would come. "What and ruin six hours of wondering?"

And so three men, in a boat carved for just such an adventure, cut a line across the cold waters of Watchmen's Cove and soon the boat was speeding westward, bound for the shore of the great peaks. The brothers each kept their eyes to the mountaintop, where high in the frozen reaches a far-off swirling wind seemed to be playing games with the snow.

They heard nothing but the slap of water on the hull and the sounds of tiny avalanches thundering through the spring afternoon.

The clouds were low, and soon came the shrill cries of the distant sentries. They would soon learn that it wasn't called Watchmen's cove without reason. Like white flags perched up high on the boughs an army of eagles honed in on the tiny boat as it passed. Jack turned to count the great birds as he paddled, their colors filling out against the sun. But their numbers were daunting and soon Jack gave up count.

Even though the brothers had spent little time in the water they pulled themselves for hours across the long arm of the sea. The stretched harbor was cool and peaceful and as feeble as they were, their weary senses still enjoyed the salty breeze.

Late into morning the team pointed their canoe at the rock swale that divided the peaks. When the rains fell the high treetops surrounding the cove vanished in an instant, as did the golden flowers of the distant shore.

They traveled those waters in cold silence, the brothers shivering as they held their thoughts close to their heart.

In fact it wasn't until Tip caught sight of strange shapes moving near the far shore that anyone spoke a word.

"What's that up ahead?"

Far away to the west a cut of land reached out into the surf, and slowly from those rocky shoals, swimming the cove, came hundreds of great beasts. They looked like rocks at first. But Henry shook his head, "They're moving."

Whatever they were, it was true they were moving, but so slowly the men could barely perceive it. Their heads laid back like ornamental treasures.

"Paddle faster," Tip said with excitement and the men doubled their speed.

"What are they?" Jack asked.

"Caribou. Hundreds of them. They're crossing the cove."

The birches and the alders shown silver and russet as the sun broke through the clouds and at once they could see the great antlered sets bobbing just above the waterline.

The three members of the party paddled with all of their strength. For it was a satisfying feeling, gaining on their prey. Of course Henry seemed to relish the experience more than anyone. For he could now see that his journey across the wilderness, and his ramblings as a boy, were both sequels to the adventures of his father and his grandfather, of a line of men who rushed adventure through their blood. He was a descendant of journeyman, and despite his overwhelming shame - that thought made him swell with pride.

The watertop swelled and shook as they dragged their paddles and Jack swore he could see huge shapes dart back and forth far beneath the surface. He looked over his shoulder, suddenly cautious of the giants that lived beneath him. For Tip had once told him of orcas hunting moose in the seas west of Tenpenny Hill.

But despite Jack's anxiety the moment never came. All three men were breathing heavily as they watched the herd break onto the shore.

They had never been closer than a quarter mile from the massive surge but the exhilaration was felt by all.

Henry and Jack faced each other, both wearing an expression of shocked delight, and then, to the brothers great surprise, Tipper began to sing. It was strange tune, unknown to both of them and sung in a language that neither had ever heard. Tip kept his eyes closed throughout the singing, as if trying to remember some long ago season of his life and the brothers listened carefully. Despite the exotic words both of them seemed certain that this was a song of the hunt and that they would remember the tune for the rest of their lives.

When Tip had finished Henry said, "I thought you'd be telling your stories all the way."

Tip opened his eyes again, having forgotten for an instant where he was. "No," he told him. "There are only two of my stories left to tell."

8. Six Pigs for the Big Man

by Henry Snow

They spared no expense to fly him out of the country. The plane was bound for Dili, though Tip didn't know who or what awaited him there. He feared that whatever his course, he would never likely find a purpose like the one he had known in Uttar Pradesh. But Tip Holland couldn't predict how the next stage in his journey would mold him into a man.

When he arrived Tip walked nervously across the tarmac and up the long flight of stairs and when he reached the terminal, waiting for him with open arms was Kolschen. The two embraced like father and son and Tip cried against his great chest. "I'm sorry," he said, sobbing. "For all this trouble."

"It's no trouble, son. We had to get you safe."

Tip pulled away. "Can I never go back?"

Kolschen looked over the boy's wounds. "Tip, you were wise to conceal yourself. But there's no way of knowing who might have seen you last night. Hundreds of witnesses crowded the streets. And in Uttar Pradesh your face is a hard one to miss. There are traders on every corner, and buyers as well, buyers who needed Golgol to do their business. My hope was to take you as far away from there as I could, and quickly."

Tip wiped his eyes, accepting his fate. "Are you worried they'll find me?"

"They won't find you," Kolschen assured him. "At least not where we're going."

That morning the two booked passage on a freighter bound for Irian Jaya and for a week at sea it was like old times between them. Kolschen picked up right where he had left off, teaching the boy something new at every turn, but for the first time their conversation resembled one that peers might share, for Tip had changed greatly since their journey on the road together.

"Tell me. What will become of the mission?"

Kolschen had been expecting the question. "Unger, Ruffino, and Derealdjon will stay where they are. But they'll withdraw to Baiga Boksas alone and wait out the pressure. My sons are taking over our efforts upcountry. They've already relocated. The others are spread to the wind, like us. Things needed to go quiet for awhile."

"Because of me."

Kolschen was particularly endeared to the boy in that moment. Even a giant like Otsov Kolschen could be moved to tears and the boy's conscientious ways had brought him to the brink. The big man looked down at Tipper proudly. They were on the top deck of the freighter, overlooking the open sea. "There is a baby girl now in my son's care. She has a whole life before her and there are no limits to a life. And before God if it had been me in that kitchen - I wouldn't have left either - until one of us was dead."

Tip nodded to thank him and broke the first smile he could remember. "Are you gonna tell me where we're going?"

"As you probably know I have interests throughout the world other than Baiga Boksas street."

"I know they exist - but I don't know where they are - or what you do there."

"Well I have an assignment for you - so you're about to see one of them firsthand."

Kolschen laid out their travel plans and spoke gently as he did, for Tipper was still shaken by the death of Golgol and the girl, and by the sudden changes to his life.

"I've been praying for years that great struggles would find you. That you would meet them as the man you were meant to be. For every stage of a man's life is an initiation. Most stages begin with a storm. And this is the next stage in *your* journey."

Again Tip nodded, awaiting his fate.

"In our years together you've learned to follow and to serve. But now it's time to lead. I'm going to put you in charge of something. Small at first, but important."

Before Tipper could respond Kolschen unfolded a map and laid it out across the deck.

"I need you to help build a school in this place *here*."

Tip scanned the map, then looked at Kolschen in disbelief. "Having never been there? Knowing nothing of the language? What language do they even speak?"

"Good. You know what questions to ask. That's what leaders do. *Now* seek the answers."

"But from who?"

"Once we arrive you will be joined by a small team of seasoned men." He pointed back to the map. "I have planted teams up and down this river for the past five years. They have lived among the villagers all that time. Your team will be positioned here, further down the river, deep in the jungle. It will take many days to get there."

"And when we get there?"

"I'm putting you in charge of the children. Basic schooling. Improve standard of living. Teach them the Gospel. Whether you know it or not you have a gift, Tipper. I believe children are your calling."

It was true, Tip knew. Children had won a place in his heart. If he had to move to the jungle he knew that no assignment would please him more.

The freighter arrived on the afternoon of the seventh day to a warm and boggy breeze. Tipper and Kolschen were picked up at the pier in a van and led through the wild city, up into the foothills and down soggy dirt roads and through filthy hamlets and checkpoints until they arrived at a tiny hut hidden in the jungle, miles from any other structure. From the looks of the little building it had been constructed in recent years for the paint had yet to peel in that rainy world. There were no windows but a large mail slot had been built into the door and as Tipper stepped inside he saw packages on the table before him, and photos of Kolschen's sons and maps on the walls, all arranged in a way similar to the other such stations that Tipper had seen.

Kolschen assembled the gear required for both men. He redressed Tipper's wounds and they took as much sleep as they could find and the next morning they hiked for hours through the jungle until they reached a wide and silent river. On the banks they found a native man, blonde haired and dark skinned who, in nearby pens, raised crocodiles for their skins and the meat of their tails to be sold at market.

Kolschen paid the man forty-two Kina for the use of one of his canoes, twice the value required, and they hauled their gear inside, strapped everything down, and embarked on their voyage downriver.

Kolschen did all the work, letting Tipper absorb his new surroundings. He paddled throughout the day, for Tipper's wounds were still too tender for him to be of any use.

"There are *four* things for you to know about this place," Kolschen told him. "The *first* is that pigs run the culture. They are the villager's only property. Here a man without pigs is nothing. A mature pig is considered equal to the value of any young child - more than a daughter in some cases - and often as much as a grown woman. So a pig killer is a murderer. If you want to marry you have to present a dowry of piglets, sometimes twenty or more for a bride in her prime. Some men don't breed enough pigs for more than one wife - so they have extramarital affairs. If they are caught in adultery, the payment is in pigs. If they don't have any pigs to pay, the matter may end in tribal warfare. Got all that?"

Tip nodded. "Pigs run the culture."

"The second thing is that protein is hard to come by and the natives are afraid of snakes. But they love to eat them - so if you want to make a good impression - start killing some snakes. The snakes here are some of the most poisonous on the earth."

"Piece of cake."

"This is also the worst area on earth for malaria and typhoid fever. And dengue fever. That's the third thing. It's always wet, always humid, and as you can see the mosquitoes are everywhere. So you're always at risk of getting sick. Most times it isn't fatal for men, but small children die often. Guard yourself any way you can."

"Repellant? Long sleeves?"

"If you can stand them. Sit close by the fires. Mosquitoes can't handle the smoke. And lastly this is a wildly promiscuous place. I've seen it all. Any two people might sneak away in a fit of passion - no matter their age or gender. Sometimes siblings are sleeping together. A brother and a sister. Sometimes two brothers. Rarely two sisters. And polygamy is everywhere. Men often marry two sisters and live with them both. But be careful how you deal with it. Years ago in the next village polygamy was declared a sin so a man killed his second wife so that he wouldn't be a sinner. You are entering into a wild, wild place," he told him.

"If you remember, I've been to some wild places."

Kolschen smirked. "Son, if you haven't been to West Papua, you haven't been to any place like West Papua. Where we're going there are no guns for five hundred miles, no electricity, or running water. Out here we're not in the 18th century like in some of our wild places. Out here we're in the stone age."

They traveled for days, and little was seen along the way. They stopped at night and made camp on the banks and at one point they came upon a small village where Kolschen purchased a parang and a whetstone to sharpen it. As he paddled he taught Tipper how to use it.

Another day passed before they reached the village of Kapalu but as it came into view Tip instantly understood what Kolschen had meant. From a distance he could see that many of the villagers wore nothing at all. Some of the men were burdened with slim quivers slung across their backs, while others wore cotton shorts imported since the mission was founded. The place had the look of wild damnation; the earth puddled and soggy with pigs, the villagers working without a sound. Wooden houses were built on high poles above the mud and surrounding them were raised walkways with coconut trees braced against them. Through the high doorways Tip could see small children tied to the pillars. To keep them from falling, he thought. One woman held her baby out at arms length to let him urinate - the stream dribbling onto a scrawny dog who slept in the mud below, her teats dragging the earth as she scurried.

But it isn't all dreariness, he observed. A line of trees behind the huts marked the edge of the jungle: rosewoods, red klinkiis and giant tauns, and the tallest among them were the aruka palms with their great fanning leaves sprouting like headdresses above the tops of the others. They shaded the edge of the village where small gardens were grown, built with mud walls to keep the pigs out.

Kapalu was built on the bend of the river, like all the other villages in the region, and as their canoe approached, a song of rapid shouts was heard from the high walkways. Men were soon beating on garamut drums and dancing as they sung. Up and down the beach, on both sides of the river, children began to run while others in canoes paddled with haste, and when Kolschen came aground the children embraced him in a swarm.

At the forest edge two of the natives were standing astraddle a hardwood log, hollowing out her belly with stone axes, and when they saw the crowd of children they dropped what they were doing and sprinted toward the beach.

Tip would soon learn that Kolschen was nearly considered a myth in their culture. Like all of the villages in the region the people were short in stature, with little variation and therefore Kolschen was believed to be a strange and wonderful giant, with huge features, a deep voice, and piercing blue eyes.

When they had completed their greetings Kolschen led Tipper down the beach to a small, newly constructed hut. The little building was the beginning of a schoolhouse, and although barely big enough to hold a meeting once Tip stepped inside he was introduced to four strange men seated in the corner. Their names were Dutch, Rigley, Papon, and Captain Tawling. To Tip the scene was strangely familiar; meeting in a secret corner of the world, with a team of specialized men. He missed the Kaleos dearly in that moment. But these new men were not the Kaleos, he thought. They were a much wilder lot than he was accustomed to.

Dutch was a lean, shaggy man well into his sixties who had been a military field mechanic before entering the life of missions. He was excessive in his disciplines, yet at the same time free of any rule but God's. He wore a hardened expression, and rarely smiled, but Tip predicted wisely that there would soon be lapses in his performance.

Although unkept and unfit, Rigley had a talent for exceeding expectations. He was as organized a man as Tipper had ever known and his knowledge of the jungle was universally respected. He was a man of forty years, bald on top, with long red curls growing shabbily round the sides. He revealed little of his past to Tip, or to anyone, but young Holland would soon grow to accept that where Rigley went, so went a feeling of responsibility.

Papon, who was the smallest man among them, but fierce and stoutly built, blessed the team with the invaluable gift of servanthood. He was a native bushman from a nearby village brought over for Kolschen's cause. A decade before Pietre Kolschen had saved his life and since then Papon had given his years to the whites. He spoke the native tongues and knew the local customs. He sung wherever he went and seemed particularly in tune with the natural order. But he was shy, not given over to conflict and it was clear to Tipper that the man had never been troubled by his inability to make a decision.

Lastly, Captain Tawling sat tall and lanky in his homemade chair. He was a proper man, too proper for his surroundings and yet not proper enough to return to the high life. He was a Captain in the truest sense, having commanded a skiff in Her Majesty's Royal Navy but had left behind his yacht club life after being misdiagnosed with cancer. By the time Tip had arrived Captain Tawling had been in the jungle for almost a decade, having tried on many occasions to build a proper mission in Kapalu. But it wasn't until Kolschen met him and funded his efforts that any real progress was made.

All that evening the team discussed their plans for the village, spilling over supply routes and topographic maps and sharing rumors of tribal warfare. The plans for the school were vague at best and Tip knew it would be an uphill battle. He asked questions and sought Kolschen's wisdom and a vision for the children began to form in his head.

As was their custom the locals opened up their homes when the new guests arrived, offering a room in one of their lofty huts. Kolschen and Tipper wrapped themselves in hammocks, and shared quiet stories and laughed into the night as their bodies were swarmed with roaches and fleas.

The next morning Kolschen rose before dawn and began teaching Tipper all he knew of the village, from her history, her beliefs, right down to her people. He gathered the team and offered a lengthy encouragement and said his goodbye's to each of the men, praying for their success and embracing them. When it was Tipper's turn he held him as close as a son.

"You will do well, Tovarisch. Remember what you have learned. Once you are established send word of your needs. In six weeks the next supply drop will arrive. I will make contact as soon as I'm free."

And the only two things Kolschen left him were the prayer and his blessing.

As his work began Tip couldn't help but realize how great a task Kolschen had given him. Other than building huts, the men of the village did little work, choosing instead to shade themselves with great leaves and brag about old war deeds while they watched the women in their labors.

The women spent their hours pounding sago mindlessly, and gossiping amongst themselves. Often Tip would hear stories of the world beyond the tree line, the "hinterlands" they were called, and strange whispers came of the people who lived there: Tribes with no names, no knowledge of country or history or governance. A people who had never seen a face unlike their own.

The favorite tribe of their stories was a band of cannibal women who were said to dwell beyond the mountains, living without men. They were known to raid villages once a year and kidnap young warriors, and use them for their seed before killing them and eating them whole. The women of Kapalu sat on the porches with their kinky hair, pounding sago and laughing at the thought, sometimes with approval.

The children too were put to work at a young age, skinning and cleaning food. Theirs was a culture without teachers, a world of no collective education, and few of the basic understandings that had enabled the west. Tip was wise enough to know that a great change would be foolish. But let them breathe, he thought. Let them know of the bars that surround them and pick their prisons for themselves.

At the end of his first day alone Tip stood alongside the river and looked out on the village with sudden clarity. This place is my penance, he told himself. This place is where I will earn my stripes.

Despite all that Kolschen had said to the contrary, Tip still believed that Golgol's death had been a great burden on the big man. The mission had drawn back its focus out of caution, and now the workers were dispersed, and Tip feared that the Kaleos of Baiga Boksas Street would never reunite.

But now I'm on the Mamberamo, he told himself. This mission is my chance at redemption.

He told the elders that first week, "I'll start by learning the language. Then I'll learn the names of the children. Beginning with the young ones."

Captain Tawling rubbed his temples. "The younger children don't have names."

"What?"

"Most don't get names until they are six or seven, because most of them die of fever."

So instead of learning their names Tip set his mind to first bringing health to the children. Most of the young ones were severely malnourished so he started with Kolschen's advice. He hunted snakes for the protein and reserved them for the leanest of the little ones. He organized a chart of the available foods and rationed out their benefits. He took stock of every mouth to feed and when he realized how numerous the dogs were, he personally castrated all but the eldest. A supply drop was planned for every other month and Tip ordered chickens and constructed a coop, and taught Papon how to harvest the eggs.

"I didn't know you were a farmer," Dutch said. "You were brought on to teach the children."

"If we meet their physical needs," Tip answered. "Soon the rest will follow."

From the beginning the white elders knew Tip to be a reliable hand, capable with children, and willing to do what was needed. But the qualities that they hadn't seen at first were persistence, imagination, and a fearless cunning that when given occasion to display caused those around him to be astonished.

Tip grew leaner and leaner as the months progressed. Gone were his softer portions, his slothful thinking, his narcissism, his ugly indecision. It was self denial that became his drug of choice. Now his voice had grown softer, his hair stained from the sun. He spoke kindly to everyone and had become an expert encourager. He rarely brought attention to himself, and the moments when it was forced upon him were when he felt the greatest discomfort. Soon everything around him, the river, the trees, the primitive tools, the smell and the sweat of the jungle all became absorbed within his flesh for Tip Holland was busy with the affairs of the village now; A man burdened with the survival of his people.

In the wet months of that first year many of the children were struck with fever, and Tip soon learned that it happened every season.

"When did it start?" He asked Captain Tawling.

"It started long ago. It's been happening for years."

"How many years?"

And soon Tip discovered that the spread of fever was introduced to the villagers at the same time as the gift of cotton clothing.

"Every night it rains," he told the elders, "and all their lives they've lived and worked in the rain. Their skin is made for it, it runs right off, but their cotton shirts are not. They get too cold at night and their clothing mildews."

Captain Tawling regarded Tip with sudden interest. "What do you suggest?"

"I suggest we take back their clothing."

"They won't like that," Dutch told him. "You may be risking our lives for the sake of fever."

But Tip had already considered the consequences, having prayed for a solution for days.

"I know they won't like it," he answered. "So we'll have to make it their idea."

With the next shipment of supplies Tip ordered an assortment of sweet and sour candies and when they arrived he went child to child and traded them for their clothes. Then he boxed up everything cotton, traveled downriver to burn the boxes, and sent a request upriver that no more cotton be sent.

For their next shipment he requested literature on the life of the mosquito and when the volumes arrived he read each of them twice.

"They breed in standing water. So we'll need to remove every bit we can find between here and the tree line."

They turned over pots, bowls, canoes. They filled in small pools near the village with topsoil and built trenches to the river from the bigger ones.

Rigley and Papon had established a draining system for the rain water many months before.

"The system works well," Tip told them. "But now the drums must be covered."

Tip ordered muslin mosquito nets for the children and screen doors for the huts, axe heads, tobacco, and candy to trade for the adult clothes as well. He mobilized the elders to teach their lessons around the fires, for despite the wretched heat the smoke drove away the roaches and mosquitoes.

"Where were you from?" Rigley asked him.

"I was from New York."

"And who were you back in New York?

"I was no one. I was lost."

"I can't imagine that."

"Well imagine it. I was a lost soul who believed in nothing."

Rigley smoked his pipe. "Well now you're not."

Often, in the dead of night, Tip would sit up in his bed and hug his knees, and listen as the innocent anthem of children's snores rang between the walls. He thought of his mother in those times, who had done nothing to deserve to be abandoned by her husband, or to be left with an unloving son who dodged the draft and disgraced her name. He often imagined the suffering she had endured when she heard the news of his cowardice. How strange it would seem to her now, he thought, to see her son living out his life in a jungle, for it was a jungle he had run from. It was sacrifice he had fled. And now he was living a life of sacrifice in the jungle, and the thought that his sweet mother would never see it brought tears to his eyes.

There were others too that he had grown to miss. He hoped that Wonderboy and his wife were happy together, that Unger and Kolschen and his sons were fulfilled in their endeavors. He even thought back to his sister, whose features he couldn't recall, yet he still prayed often that she would someday find the strength to forgive him.

But more than the rest Tip dwelled on the baby, Padibatakal, for she was the closest thing he had to a child of his own. He wondered where she had landed, and if she could crawl like the other children. The thought of her growing up and being cared for filled those dark hours. Often it was the last thing Tip thought about before he finally fell asleep.

One morning Tip awoke and was surprised to find six men sleeping on his doorstep. They were tribesmen from down the river, all of them exhausted, and in their carry was a huge store of mosquito nets and screen doors, axe heads and tobacco. Tip's order had been received three weeks prior and the journey had been a treacherous one. Their boats, overloaded with supplies, had nearly toppled in the rapids and two of them had come down with fever. But despite the dangers the men were sleeping soundly on the porch when Tipper awoke. Soon the sun crept up with the shouts of the morning, the supplies were unpacked and the work began.

They cut the screens to fit and fastened hinges to the doorways. For the children they placed a net over each of their beds and Tip spent the first night beneath one, in full view of the little ones, to show them there was nothing to fear.

They carved axe handles from the rosewoods and slipped on the sharpened heads, submerging them in water until the handles had swelled themselves shut. He traded tobacco for all of their outstanding debts, wiping away decades of blood feuds in one short hour.

And with the storehouse of supplies came news of Kolschen who had been months at sea for some unknown reason, moving cargo between lands beyond Tip's knowledge. With news of the world and encouragement to the team, he attached a note for Tip alone.

"Reproduce yourself." was all that it said. But Tipper caught his meaning.

The following day he picked the least willing of the children and began teaching them to read each morning. In the afternoon he told them stories of faraway lands and made strange faces and always they were laughing. After a few weeks he assigned each of them the duty of teaching a younger child their letters with his assistance and over many weeks he carefully began to withdraw. Soon a quarter of the children had begun to read and write.

In the evenings he met with the fathers in the village and walked them through the Gospels. Next he began training his leaders, all six of them now, to focus on one father apiece.

"I thought your job was the children," Dutch told him.

"When truth finds its way into the heart of a father, his children will always be blessed."

Rarely he preached to the whole village, preferring a more intimate group. His days were given over wholly to the people around him, and there was never more than the briefest of quarrels. Always he thought of the men who had poured out their lives for his benefit, and with each of his efforts he found he was thanking them, in the only way he knew.

Like the Kaleos he was intentional with every moment of his day. What hours he did allow for himself were spent reading or chopping away at the jungle, for his hope was to clear enough timber in one year to make room for a chopper to land.

One morning, after three years in Kapalu, Tip was chopping wood to his rhythm as the sun rose and when he looked up, Kolschen was there. The big man appeared well-rested, his clothes fresh, and though he was smiling gently, he looked older around the eyes.

"I see you've found a hobby."

"Yessir," Tip answered, his joy apparent. "It gives me some time to think. Some time to be alone."

The two men embraced and looked each other up and down.

"Men who take new ground are always alone. You've done well, Tovarisch," Kolschen told him, for he could see that all of his suspicions were true.

The two men walked along the perimeter of the forest as if no time has passed between them.

"How are you dealing with life in this place?"

"It's a challenge and I needed one."

"What struggles have you found?"

Tip had to stop and think. "Some days I feel like we're robbing them of their culture."

"Ah, their *culture*. Would you mind if someone robbed you of *your* culture?"

"How do you mean?"

"Is your culture important?"

"No. Not really."

"But theirs is?"

"I believe it is."

"Because its different than yours and you want to preserve it? Because it feels real?"

"Yessir."

"Some things are more important than culture, Tip. *This* is more important than culture. You aren't robbing them of anything. You are *giving* them a choice."

"A choice? For Christ?"

"Christ yes - but what does Christ sell?"

"Absolution?"

"Freedom, Tipper."

Tip Holland had given a great deal of thought to his freedoms during those years in the jungle. Thoughts he had never put into words. With Kolschen beside him he decided it was time.

"When I was younger I pictured it different," Tip admitted. "What it would be like to really be free. There were no disciplines, no commitments, only pleasures. Pleasures and instincts. And I would chase those instincts til my soul grew tired then I would chase others and then I would die. I pictured the life of a beast, and that we men were the same as beasts. I gave no thought to another conclusion. But I do now and it doesn't settle down as easy for me."

"Being a man is complicated."

"Yes, very complicated. Beasts are simple. I have to make up my mind which I want to be."

"And you'll be deciding that all your life. Some days your instincts will win. If it isn't every day, even if it isn't most days, you'll be a man. You'll be given over to every need but your own. That's how we break off from the pack."

"What pack is that?"

Kolschen smiled, "The heart of the boy cries out for freedom. He wants the animal life. But where is his fruit? Who does he bless but himself? The heart of the man is different - invisible as a child - to all animals misunderstood. The heart of the man is not for himself - it is filled with fruit. It is rare and precious and no vainglory lurks there. That's how we differentiate ourselves. The value of our lives are measured that way."

For an instant Tip Holland imagined that they were sharing the road again, as they had so many years before. He wanted to go back to that time, a time when he could follow and not lead, but Kolschen's words were still ringing in his heart, and he knew he would never have that time again.

"How are your sons?" he asked.

A strange smile spread across Kolschen's face. "*Married.*"

"*What*? " Tip looked stunned. "*When?* "

"A few months ago. A double wedding. You were an honorary groomsman."

Tip was smiling now, but in truth the news was such a surprise that he could barely keep a thought in his head."Well it's an honor to be honorary."

"True enough. And Pietre's first child is due in August."

"How about that. What month is it now?"

"March."

Then Kolschen added, "What is it?"

"Nothing," Tip answered. "I just missed a birthday is all."

"Which birthday?"

Tip shrugged. "Thirty."

The two men chuckled and Kolschen spoke up, "Well then I suppose congratulations are in order."

"For what?"

"When we met I wouldn't have thought you'd ever live this long."

Tip accepted the truth with a smile, but it was a truth he was afraid to face. "And congrats to you as well. What are their names? The wives I mean."

"Alexei married a tall girl, very shy. Her name was Lilliana Povisch before they married. She was working on your west coast before they met in the clinic. Pietre's wife is from your country as well. Sierra Jo Oakham - *Kolschen* now."

"Lovely."

They broke bread together that morning, and many days after, and talked well into the night about the affairs of the world, and the Kaleos, and the nature of men and boys. At one point Tip asked for news of Baiga Boksas street.

"For your own sake, Tip, the less you know the better."

Tip could sense an anxiety in Kolschen that he had never known before, but he didn't speak of it. Instead he focused on the needs of the village, asking questions regarding his vision for the people.

"Vision is like a polaroid picture," the big man suggested. "It must develop over time. Fall to your knees and the answers will come."

At no point in his visit did Kolschen rush the conversation, or imply that his time was short, but after a week he was off again, leaving Tipper with a prayer and a blessing. It was no secret that Tip Holland viewed Kolschen's family as *his* own family now, so naturally he dreamed of watching Pietre and Alexei's children grow, and someday meeting their wives.

It was almost a year later before the news reached them that a tribal war had begun. Three travelers, haggard and gaunt from their journey, stumbled in from the jungle early one morning and once they had been fed they told the white elders of the news they had gathered.

The travelers were all from different tribes and spoke various languages and the only man in the village who could translate them all was Papon, who spoke in Pidgin to the white elders. When he told the stories of the travelers he left nothing to chance, describing every word in detail.

All along the outliers, he said, in some villages Tip had never heard of, reports were coming in of headhunters in the hinterlands.

"There is a place in the highlands, an old place where the villagers still practice sorcery and speak to the dead. In this place a tribal war has started. The war has been waging for over a month."

Tip nodded. "What started the war?"

"This man is named Bohima, from the far north, Bohima says it started when pigs were stolen from the Big Man's tribe."

"Who is the Big Man?"

"He is known only as the Big Man."

"They are mostly lies these people tell," Dutch suggested. "The Big Man isn't real."

"Maybe so. But someone is doing the killing. Ask him to tell us everything."

And what Bohima told them filled their minds for hours to come. He had watched a war party from the highlands storm his village, their bodies covered in pig grease. They decapitating whole families and ate them where they lay.

"By all accounts many have been killed already," Papon told them. "Their spears are dipped with poison, he tells me."

"You have an army in this country?" Tip asked.

"Yes."

"Then why don't they do something?"

"What army could find them in the jungle? These are not the lowland rivers, these are the *highlands*. Impassable except on foot. And even then it would take a month if the army knew where to go. Would you march a month to be eaten by cannibals?"

Tip Holland felt a great burden rising within himself. It was as if everything he had learned was about to be put to the test.

"Not to be eaten," Tip answered. "But I would march a month for the chance to make peace. Papon - ask them what will happen next."

"The Big Man's tribe will likely make attacks all across the hinter-lands, on each of their enemies until their debt is appeased. If a tribe owes the debt of pigs to the Big Man and they can't pay it, they'll steal pigs from the neighboring tribe and that will spark more attacks. Soon the tribal war could spread in all directions. It may have already."

"How many pigs were stolen from the Big Man?"

"He doesn't know. Though it wasn't very many."

"And the war could end if he was given those pigs?"

"The Big Man isn't real," Dutch said.

"Fine. Let's say he isn't. But the war started with one tribe. What I want to know is will the war end if that tribe is given some pigs?"

"It could. Yes."

Dutch asked him. "What? You plan on taking them some pigs?"

And Tip nodded. "That's *exactly* what I plan to do."

The men discussed the matter long into the night, pouring over maps and debating the wisdom of venturing into the hinterlands. But Tipper remained convinced that there was no other choice.

"What do we believe in?" he asked the men. "Have we asked our-selves lately what we're fighting for? What we're fighting *against*? The debt owed is in *pigs*. We have pigs to give. Trade some men in the north a few pigs, and we might just stop a war. It will storm, Kolschen told me. Who will we be when it does?"

"Even if you succeed," Tawling said, "The lives you save you will never know. They will never know of you."

"Is that why we save people?"

Then Dutch answered, "Very well then. Who do you propose we send?"

Tip shook his head. "I'm not in the habit of sending men anywhere. The question is 'Who will join me?'."

"You mustn't go," Rigley said. "You're needed here. What about these children?"

"The children will have to wait. Kolschen asked me to lead and I will lead, but only from the front. Trekking to the hinterlands was my idea."

Dutch smiled with subtle indignation. "Where you want to go is a huge blank spot on the map, stretching for hundreds of miles. If you want to get there you'll have to cross swampland for two full weeks before you even reach the mountains. No one has ever done it."

"That's the spirit."

Dutch ignored him. "Listen, Sonny, the furthest north any white man has ventured is the Taku village. You're talking about going past Taku for another week just to get to the highlands. The headhunters are thought to be much further still - so far removed that the natives there believe they are the only true people in the world. And let us not forget that we don't know how to get there."

"Someone does."

"No one among us. The nearest man who even thinks he knows the way is in Taku Village. And Taku Village is a week away."

Tip folded the map, and he was never more certain of anything in his life. "Then we make for Taku village."

At first light the team assembled their supplies. It would be Tip, Dutch, Rigley and Papon. Captain Tawling agreed to stay behind.

All of the men in the party were outfitted with parangs and ropes and gear for the swamps and the highlands beyond. Lastly, on Tip's order, two pigs were placed in each man's care, while one man in the troupe was allowed to rest; Six pigs altogether. The pigs were the finest in the village and Tipper had bought each of them himself. They were tied together in pairs and led on a lead rope by their wrists.

Dutch pointed the men northward and almost instantly they were swallowed by the jungle. Everything they encountered, from the trees, to the stones, to the soil at their feet was wet to the touch, as if the jungle herself oozed with sweat. Soon their skin was beaded, their shirts dripping, their hair like mops atop their heads.

Even though Tip had covered every inch of his body with bug repellant the sweat soon washed it away. Within minutes the mosquitoes were eating him alive. Still the party marched on, squinting as they plodded through the thicket with their heads low until darkness fell, which came more quickly than Tip had expected.

The second day was no different from the first. They trekked from sunrise to sunset, and even with Dutch as their guide it was a slow, toilsome journey. In the coming days they forded a dozen rivers, building bamboo bridges to cross them and carrying the pigs in their arms. They hoisted their gear over the widest streams with pulleys and ropes. Twice they arrived at huge stone cliffs on the far bank and were forced to climb a hundred feet or more with the pigs pulled up one at a time. Harnessed and frightened, Tipper urged them on.

They entered into the swamplands and moved quickly through the water to avoid the leeches and the crocodiles but were only half successful. The nights were rainy and miserable, too warm for the fires that drove the bugs away, and too loud with the frog chorus to find any sleep. When morning arrived so did the incessant cries of giant parrots that squawked at them from the casuarinas.

It was the dark of night on the seventh day when they finally reached Taku village. Wild children began shrieking with terror when they saw them. A cloud of despair hung over the people, like their nightmare was about to begin.

"Why are they crying?" Tip asked.

Papon hesitated, looking high and low for evil spirits. "Because they are mourning their dead."

The dark corners remained lifeless and the wails sung from the secret hollows. The only men they saw were near the fire at the heart of the village. Eight men of fighting age, dressed in their colorful plumage, their painted faces shining in the light.

Seated beside the great fire was old Matthias Tiegel, bushy and shirt-less and apathetic, physician and white elder to Taku alone. When Tip and his traveling band arrived Tiegel hardly seemed to notice them.

As a boy Tiegel had found fault with his parents and escaped to the coast where he enrolled himself in university, paying his own way. But soon he found fault with his professors and his employers and fled to various stations throughout his homeland before he found fault with his homeland, thinking his malady an issue of culture. He found fault with one nation after another, and no woman could suit him for long, and by the time Tip arrived he had been finding fault with the most primitive land left on earth for over a decade.

Years before he and Captain Tawling had been partners but after their falling out Tiegel wanted nothing to do with any affairs outside of Taku. It wasn't until this young man, who he had never met, pressed him for answers that he gave the men anything of value. The young man was bushy and shirtless as well, but hardly apathetic. There was a passionate urgency in his questions, and an impatience for knowledge that reminded the old ragamuffin of vibrant younger days.

"These men are preparing for battle," he told them.

"With the headhunters."

"Yes," Tiegel said. "Strange men arrived here from the north two days ago. They were seeking compensation."

"How many pigs did they require?"

"One from us. At least one from each of the other three villages nearby."

"Four total," Tip counted. "How many did you give them?"

"None. No compensation could be given because all of our pigs have been poached. The headhunters left with threats of tribal warfare. They killed two of our men. Soon they will be back with a war party."

"To declare war?"

"To wipe out the village."

For a man on the verge of annihilation, Tiegel seemed calm and resigned.

Tip tightened his pack. "Sir, are you certain that no compensation can be offered?"

"Not to the men themselves. The order has been given."

"The order from whom?"

"From Apowazi. The big man of the tribe."

"*Apowazi?*"

"Chief of the Tree People. The greatest warrior in the highlands."

Tip turned to Dutch and cleared his throat. "We believed the Big Man was a myth."

"No. He's real," Tiegel assured them. "At least that's what the distant people say. I don't care one way or another. About Apowazi. About any of them. Is Tawling still alive?"

"He is," Dutch answered, surprised by the question. "Do you care about *him*?"

"No," he said flatly. "When he's dead I may start caring. But only for an instant."

The men regarded Tiegel briefly, but then turned back to the issues of the living.

"It's good they're only two days ahead of us," Tip whispered. "We'll reach them before they return."

"Reach them?" Tiegel asked.

"Yes," Tip nodded. "That's what we came to do."

They restocked their supply with whatever food they could scrounge and Tip gave Tiegel his word that they would pay off the debt of the pigs that were stolen.

"Tell your people not to seek vengeance for the poaching. When we return to our village I'll bring news of our peace. "

"You won't make it back," Tiegal told him. "If the Big Man is real he'll just slaughter every one of you. It's a fools errand you're taking."

Tip placed his hand gently on the man's shoulder. "For your sake, let's hope not."

As they turned to depart the young Taku warriors began whispering to themselves and Papon was close enough to hear.

"They say all of us will die," he told his team.

"No," Dutch argued. "That isn't what they said."

Papon flinched as Dutch continued. "What they said was, '*None of them will live.*'"

"What's the difference?" Tip asked him.

"There' s a difference, boy. Believe me."

They departed at dawn, following the tracks of the headhunters that ran like a broken trail through the forest. In the hours to come they would encounter scattered huntsmen from Taku passing like strangers from other worlds, their souls given wholly to primordial needs, their prayers spoken to gods long ago disproven.

All that morning the party crossed the Mamberamo hills and they had no way to know in what direction they had traveled. They could only follow the sign of the headhunters. Soon the rains came and frowned upon their pursuit and Tip led them quicker, keeping their fading path in sight. Occasionally he would stray down the road of some jungle dweller, a bandicoot or a possum, only to correct himself moments later.

As they crested the hilltops they came upon deep crevasses that opened suddenly at their feet and saw huge jungle valleys before them, stretching out for miles without the works of man in sight. When they stopped to rest the men boiled liters of tea in the rain and as the days passed they ate coconuts and pigeons and snakes when they could find them.

In the first week past Taku the jungle gave up no sign that men had ever walked the earth, other than the shallow tracks they followed. But on the eighth day they arrived at a ghostly place where a village once had been. Decaying homes were built high in the branches, all that remained of a once vibrant family, the most successful of the headhunting tribes a century before.

The huts had an emaciated, even supernatural look, their walls leaning and on the verge of collapse, with great holes in what once had been floors. The rope ladders, long and threadbare, appeared so fragile as they swayed that Rigley joked they could only be climbed by nimble ghosts, and even then with great caution.

"Why did they build them so high?" Tip asked, his head tilted as far back as it would go. "Was it for their enemies?"

"Not exactly," Rigley said. "They do it to get above the bugs."

As they entered their fourth week of travel the troupe soon wished for a similar solution - as the swampland grew thicker and the mosquitoes became intolerable.

Dutch was the first the fall ill, growing deathly cold until his fever spiked him into convulsions. They kept him hydrated while he sweated throughout the day but he took no food and grew anemic until the cycle of cold chills started again.

They traveled in pairs, always in sight of one another, but sharing nothing but their words and prayers. Papon was chosen to administer care, for he had been malarial many times as a boy and didn't fear recurrence.

After two days their progress slowed to a snails pace for Dutch didn't have enough strength to climb or to swim, but only to plod on one step at a time.

During the third night the symptoms started for Rigley. He was bitter cold that evening, in violent sweats at daybreak, and dead the following night. Dutch died soon after and they buried the pair side by side in the soggy earth, speaking kind words over their lives.

Tip and Papon gathered whatever excess gear they could carry, food, clothing, parangs and made a line northward through the primeval forest. Their going was slower with the extra pigs in tow but the trail was still visible and they both prayed fervently that the village was near.

Tipper was certain his symptoms would arrive at any time, but it never happened. Except for his feet which were badly blistered he felt as strong and ready as ever,

They pressed on in the rain for three more sleepless nights, speaking little and eating less. But in the morning of their twenty-ninth day they crossed a shallow stream, no wider than their leaping, and when they saw the muddy bank on the far side each man stood frozen like a stone.

All along the northern shore were footprints, naked prints and those of men. A path had been cut through the jungle, coming to an end at the creek. A watering hole, Tip thought.

They watched the trees, their eyes darting, their fists tight on their parangs. Both men held their breath, listening for the headhunters deep in the jungle. Only after minutes of waiting did they follow the path.

It ambled through the forest leaves, pounded by centuries of bare feet. At the edge of the trail, to their left and right, they noticed fresh sign of human scat. The two men began to see smaller prints as the trail continued, those of children, and soon the path opened up before them, ever brighter, until they found themselves staring out at a clearing in the jungle.

Tip Holland was breathing deeply now. His heart rested on the thought that he would do everything in his power to make Kolschen proud. The only thing he trusted were the scriptures. With great fear he tiptoed into the light and this is what he saw:

High before him stood a line of great tree houses belonging to a people that stretched back to the dawn of time. He could see dark shapes moving along the limbs and soon he could make out that the shapes were those of men, walking barefoot from tree to tree. The trees themselves were banyans, great smooth-barked towers that shaded the villagers from the nightly rains, and planted beneath them were rows of taro fields and yams. The longer Tip stood there, the more his eyes allowed him to see.

The men of the village could be spotted easily now: all were short and brawny with bushy beards, and each was mostly nude, some with small strips of breechcloth or tanket leaves draped over their buttocks, while others wore nothing.

Many of the men were adorned with huge headdresses, their feather plumes arranged wildly, and their skin painted as if for battle; an assortment of red ocher, white lime, and yellow. Each man among them had their noses pierced through the septa, some with quills and shells, others with huge pig tusks that shown white against their skin.

The elders were seated near the doors of the towering huts, their heads shaded with large leaves as they looked down over the women as they worked.

The women too were nude, their breasts sagging flat against their chests, with laplap skirts tied around their thighs and their buttocks bare. Some had ears pierced through with heavy bone, weighing them down so low that their lobes grazed the tops of their shoulders. They wore cassowary quills vertically through their nostrils and worked with their babies slung across their backs.

With Papon breathing heavily beside him Tip Holland stood like a statue. He looked out upon the world like he was seeing a window back through time. The scene at the base of the towers had the look of a great feast in the making. The carcasses of three pigs, cut into quarters, were hanging from crude gambrels and their blood was draining. A woman, old among her people, stood beside a deep hole in the ground and was filling another carcass with vegetables. Tip could see that the hole was smoldering, as if they intended to bury a pig inside and cook it slowly.

"I think they've been expecting us," Tip whispered. "They've already started to eat."

The thought of becoming a meal for these villagers was never far from Tipper's mind, and now that he saw what appeared to be a feast unfolding before him, his fears only multiplied. However Tip was soon to learn that he and his companion couldn't have arrived at a better time.

Suddenly a great horn sounded across the clearing, long and deep, and in the next moment a bowman high on his perch was shouting down at Papon, whose shorts could be seen even in the shade. The entire village responded, her children clambering up ladder huts, the women close behind, while each of the men on the ground shouted and hopped on bare feet, before rushing the strangers with bows and spears. They had the look of the lowland tribes, although there was a wilder, more enigmatic glare in their eyes, and until Tip Holland stepped further into the light not one among them, in any century, had ever seen a white man.

The sight of him was followed by more whooping and hollering and loud cheers. The villagers gathered in a wide circle and surrounded them, their shoulders rocking to and fro. Papon raised up his parang, welcoming his attackers.

"No," Tip told him. "If we must die, we'll take none of them with us."

The chief bowman, a sickly man bloated with Elephantiasis, gave Tipper a long look before calling up to the trees. His voice echoed across the clearing, louder than their panting. A moment later a dark figure appeared in the doorway of the high tower. The man was too far away for Tip to see but he knew that the man was a person of high standing. He stood straight, his hands above his head, looking long at Tipper.

"Tell him we want to make a trade," Tip said. "These pigs in trade for peace. An offer of compensation. Tell him."

Papon cleared his throat, which was tight with fear, and addressed the chief, calling out his offer in humility.

For a moment there was nothing. A crowd of men gathered behind the chief and there was hooting and chattering and then silence again. Tip and Papon stood swarmed in anticipation. For some time there was nothing - then the sounds of argument - then silence again as the chief looked down. But then suddenly his voice rang out with shouts and the beginnings of a song.

Tip would later recall that in that moment fear engulfed him. The warriors that circled them stepped closer. He believed the order had been given. But to his surprise when he looked upon them he saw no hostility in their faces, but rather their eyes were gentle and inviting, as if Papon and Tip were now a pair of welcomed guests.

The archer lowered his bow and pointed toward the tower huts. Then another pair of men, younger and lean, sprinted across the field and waved them on.

The warriors opened a path and half waking, half sleeping, Tipper and Papon followed their guides toward the base of the trees. When they looked up at the tower the figure that had stood in the doorway was gone. Only women and children were waiting on the high porch. It felt strange to both men to walk upright after so many days of bending through the jungle but their comfort wouldn't last. The great ladder awaited them, swaying gently like a dare.

Tip looked up the length of it, over one hundred feet to the branches above. When he reached the ladder he and Papon were forced to hand their pigs over to the bowman, Papon giving the men instructions, and it was then that he finally saw the warriors up close, their noses pierced grotesquely through the septa with stacks of bones, their faces hard and quick.

Tip sprung off the ground and made a steady go of it, slowing only to keep Papon in sight. As they ascended the women high above them screamed in fright and fled along the narrow porch. All around the world grew and grew, the jungletop opening for their eyes to see and their fears seemed to melt from one rung to the next. Tip found that he was now carefully balanced between two worlds, one of primal freedoms, and the other, the one he had left, was one of burden and responsibility. As he reached the top of the ladder and slipped inside the hut, he knew those worlds were about to meet.

They were now in a great dark hall, lit by a dozen fireplaces that lined the borders. Tip didn't know where they were, or what to expect, but he knew he had never been to a stranger place in his life. The floor was made of long chutes of bamboo, bound together with sago leaves, and as the two men tip-toed across the room they half-expected it to collapse beneath their feet.

Soon their eyes adjusted to the darkness and the great room stretched out before them. On the walls were war shields and human skulls, stone axes and hourglass drums.

At the center of the great hall was a blackened figure, a withered man-shape whose head was eyeless and whose fingers had broken free. He had been placed upon a stump at the heart of the hall, his embalmed figure bent and twisted like a contorted statue. Some of his hair still clung to his head and on his chest a necklace of tusks was shining.

Papon had heard stories of the highlanders embalming their dead, but he had never seen one himself. It was a practice reserved for the most courageous of warriors. For the men of the highlands believed that if they kept the body of a great war chief in their halls then his spirit would always be with them, giving them strength.

As Tip and Papon moved beyond the mummified remains they could see before them the shapes of twenty men standing in a huddle, swaying to and fro at the far end of the hall. A low humming poured from the crowd and roaches scurried underfoot as the two men crept closer.

It was the war party, Tip thought. The men's faces could be seen with crazed smiles, their eyes wide, and as the two men approached the warriors began humming loudly and singing and slapping their thighs.

At the head of the war party was a man set apart both by his age and his ferocity. The two men watched him carefully. He was no taller than the other men, but broad and powerfully built. His great arms were furry up to his shoulders, his feet wide and flat, and across his body a wild assortment of scars was marvelously displayed. He had thick stripes over his face and his forearms, and puncture wounds near his navel and his ribs. One of his nipples had been torn away long ago and his left eye was dead in his skull. Unlike the men around him he stood completely naked, except for a cord around his waist. There wasn't a hint of uncertainty in his face for he knew himself to be superior to all other men because of his fierceness and success in battle. He was Apowazi, the Big Man. He stared them down with a force that could have possessed weaker men.

Tip believed Papon to be a fierce opponent himself, but when standing beside Apowazi, Papon had the look of a child. The mans cheekbone's alone could reign over most men, Tip thought, for they seemed chiseled against his flesh.

Apowazi spoke one word, "Huhan," and at once the humming stopped.

But his war party continued to sway behind him. All of the men's teeth were stained red from the betel nut they favored, some of them sharpened to a point. To Tipper they looked like loyal demons. Every one of them wore pig tusks around their necks to represent the heads they had collected and many had open wounds across their shoulders and chests. One man, who appeared to be the son of Apowazi, wore a long rat tail as a headband. It seemed to twitch on his sweaty brow.

"Why are they wounded?" Tip asked.

But before he received an answer a woman appeared with a pair of bowls, filled to the rim with dried termites, and set them down at the strangers feet.

Papon nodded to the chief and received the gift. When Tipper hesitated his friend was quick to warn him, "If you don't want to be eaten - eat what you are offered."

So Tip consumed the termites by the handful.

As the war party watched the two men eat they didn't turn or whisper amongst themselves and there was little expression on their faces. When they had finished Papon nodded his thanks, never taking his eyes off of Apowazi.

"The termites were a gift. For some reason he has welcomed us. To show good favor we must offer him a gift in return."

Tip agreed, carefully opening his pack. He unrolled the sago leaves, revealing a mound of dried tobacco.

Apowazi watched with sudden interest. He stepped forward and his movements were gentle, revealing none of the sudden violence for which he was famous. He stripped bits of sago leaves from a nearby bundle and spread them out for all to see. His men were huddled close around him, their hands firm across his body.

The tobacco was divided according to the importance of the men, Apowazi taking most of it for himself. He knew how to count at least, Tipper thought, for soon he had filled the exact number of leaves for each of his men.

The war party was chattering now, whooping and humming and hopping on their toes. So excited were they that many of their hands were shaking as they tried to roll the cigarettes. From the looks of things, Tipper had given the proper offerings.

The soft-wood logs were crackling in the fireplace as the men lit their cigarettes. They stood over their guests and smoked with great pleasure.

"Now what?" Tip asked, after a long silence.

"Now we must begin a conversation."

"How do we do that?"

"You must give another offering. It must be a worthy gesture."

Tip paused. "We could spare two of the parangs. Offer him those."

"Iron is not known here."

"All the more reason."

Papon was whispering now, as gently as he dared. "They could turn them on us. They could use them to kill us."

Tip offered a smile to his friend, "Brother, they don't need a parang to do that. They could kill us with their teeth."

"But—"

"Offer the parangs," Tip said firmly. "Dutch and Rigley would want it."

Papon hesitated, but when Tipper urged him on he pulled out the long knives, showing them to his hosts. The members of the war party were still smoking, and none of them seemed to comprehend.

Slowly, Tip stood to his feet and pulled a coconut from his pack. He set it on the floor before him and the war party looked on in wonder as he split it open with one clean slice. The men were chattering again, their hands gripping one another as Tip placed the blades at the feet of Apowazi.

At once the great war chief held one of them up, looking at it closely. Then, to Tipper's horror, the Big Man ran his thumb down the length of the blade, splitting it open. Tip could see the blood running through the man's fingers, but Apowazi gave no expression. He seemed to accept the gift, for he held it high above his head and began speaking in quick shouts.

"He wishes to tell the story of their deeds. He wishes to trade their story for the blades."

"Will that get him talking?"

"I hope so."

"Tell him I accept."

One of the warriors stepped forward, a squat, fierce little man with eight fingers and relayed the story of their battle. When he spoke all of his words ran together.

"It began with war cries and insults," Papon said. "They were fighting a chief named Fire, a big man from the next village. They battled for a short time and each of Fire's men were terrified. When all his men were dead Fire and Apowazi fought in the middle of the field. Apowazi disemboweled him, but before Fire was dead Apowazi sawed his head off slowly with a bamboo knife while his war party held him down. Then he sent his headless body floating down the river. They collected the heads and the thighs of the worthy dead and marched back this morning. And now, 'The blood feud with Fire has ended,' he says."

"What started the feud?"

"He says that Fire sent a warrior on a quest to poach three of their pigs but they killed him after only two."

"How did they know it was Fire would sent the man?"

"Because it was a warrior of the next tribe. They knew it by sight. And when he was dead, they asked him many questions, and his spirit told them everything."

"His spirit told them? After he was dead?"

"They asked him questions for hours until his body jumped. When a body jumps at a question the answer is always yes."

"Of course."

Papon would go on to explain that the war party had returned from the raid just hours before, and that Tipper's arrival was a gift.

"They say you are the reason for their victory."

"Because I arrived today?"

"Yes."

The thought of being associated with such violence gave young Tip a shiver. But he knew he was no less a sinner then these men.

"And if the raid hadn't been a victory?"

"Then they would have blamed you for the defeat. They would have hacked both of us to pieces."

Tip Holland was sadly aware that some portion of himself still admired the chief. There's wasn't an ounce of phoniness within him. Parts of my soul will be a boy forever, Tip thought. In some ways might will always matter.

Apowazi stood suddenly, walking up to Tip and stomping his feet. He spoke a long incantation, in some tongue that Papon did not understand. But when he was finished he shouted a command to his men and all fell silent. Then his voice rung out in a whisper.

"He wants to know why you have come."

"Why?" Tip asked.

Apowazi rubbed his fingers along Tipper's scars, and when he spoke it was as if he was addressing the wounds themselves.

"He wants to know if you are a great warrior."

"Come on."

"He says you must be or you would not be here. He says you have killed a humbug man. That you are a warrior who has slain a great spirit of evil. And you have the scars to prove it. He calls you 'humbug killer' and offers you his friendship."

Tipper looked up in surprise. This man was bewitched with knowledge he shouldn't have, but the offer of friendship seemed the strangest thing of all. "I wonder what his friendship would look like."

"It is a precious gift."

Tip thought back to Golgol, of how he looked when he had died. He wondered if Apowazi was killed if these people could be freed of their bondage. But Tip knew he was no match for the man. He couldn't imagine that Apowazi could be defeated, even if he were attacked by ten men at once.

"Tell him I accept."

Apowazi gave no sign that he understood. He instead looked down at Tipper's boots and his face was hard as stone. Then he walked between them, his thighs brushing each of their shoulders as he crossed the hall toward the blackened figure. Tip noticed that there were no scars across the backside of the Big Man's body, only a tiny bag tied to his lower back.

The mighty chief placed his hand on the head of the mummified remains and began to shout and sing. Behind him the war party was humming again, their bodies rocking.

To Tipper's great surprise Apowazi reached behind him and removed a polished human skull from the bag on his back. He held it before him and repeated the same three phrases over and over for minutes on end.

"What's he saying?"

Papon leaned in to whisper, "The skull was his father's. He keeps it with him everywhere he goes, even in battle. His father was a fearless chief. The mummy was his father's father. The bravest warrior this tribe ever knew. Now Apowazi is asking their spirits for guidance."

"Guidance for what?"

"For his decision. Making peace is against their custom. Headhunting is a demand of their ancestors. He is asking permission to make peace with their enemies."

The mighty chief continued to repeat the incantation again and again until finally he rested. He put the skull away and called out with his full voice to some unseen servant. Out of the darkness came two women, one his loyal sister, the other a young woman, lean and sharp of feature. Her hands were bound with course twine and when she stood near the fireplace her eyes reflected the flamelight like a bridge lantern to realms unknown.

"This is to be Apowazi's new wife. She was taken this morning from the village of Fire. She was the only survivor."

Tip nodded a greeting but the young woman's eyes remained fixed on the chief.

Apowazi was yelling now, his feet stomping as he waved his hand violently.

"He says she is touched by a spirit. She speaks of the maker of the moon and the stars. He wants you to trade for her."

"*What*? Trade for her?"

"He says she is no good for him. She is touched by a spirit. If you don't trade - he will kill her. His fathers have said you were sent to decide her fate."

Tip looked at the woman, who seemed unlike any of the villagers he had met. She could not have been older than twenty but in her eyes shined a blinding light.

"We'll take her."

Papon lowered his eyes, looking down at the bamboo floor. "She is a highlands woman," he said. "A Walwasi. Walwasi women are always crazy. If we take her we might all die."

"If we die it won't be because of her."

"Apowazi will ask a great price in trade."

"Greater than a life?"

Papon shook his head in frustration and then Tip repeated himself.

"Tell him we'll take her. Tell him to name his price."

When Papon gave his answer Apowazi smiled for the first time. His voice was light and playful as he looked down at Tipper's feet.

Papon's chin sunk against his chest.

"What is it?"

Then Papon told him. "He wants your boots."

"*My boots?*"

"I told you the price would be great."

Quickly Tipper unlaced his boots and pulled them off before he was able to dwell on the implications. Apowazi sat down beside them, placing his hands on his knees. He was whispering now, and there was a burden in his eyes.

"He agrees to take the pigs as compensation."

"He does?"

"Peace has been given because it is you who have brought it. The feast is thanks to you. He thanks you, great warrior, for the victory his tribe has received. And his father thanks you and his grandfather as well. He says you must go, for the feast is beginning and only the slayers of the dead may participate. If you meet again you will see him dancing in your boots."

Everything seemed to happen too quickly for Tip to comprehend. The young woman was handed over, her bonds cut as the three of them were told to make their departure. Tip thought to say goodbye, but Apowazi did not appear to be in need of such considerations.

They descended down the long, ominous ladder to the earth below where the pigs were received after the Big Man's shouts. When the deal was made all three of them turned back to the south, still frightened, and Tip and Papon both rubbed their wrists where the pig ropes had scarred them.

With the cries and shouts of the ancient tribe calling after them the three travelers broke into the thick of the forest, retracing their steps, and soon Tip's feet were growing tender. They crossed the watering hole where his footprints now matched those of the natives, and continued a short ways until he called them to stop.

They were standing beneath a grove of banyans, huge in size, and near their path a mighty boulder, as large around as the trees, was resting in the shade. Tip dropped his pack and searched the soil at his feet until he found two small stones, nearly identical in size and shape, and held them up, eyeing them carefully. Papon looked on silently, questioning Tipper with his eyes.

"These are memorial stones," Tip said, as he began to dig a hole. "I have buried many of these around the world."

"What for?"

"Each one represents a turning point in my story. A watermark on my life. Long ago a great man taught me how important it was to mark my journey. I keep one and bury the other and along with the one I bury I leave a clue for others to find."

"Others? What others?"

"Maybe I'll have children someday."

Papon thought back on the journey they had taken, and the one they had yet to complete. "You would want your children to come back here?" he asked.

"Back here and to many other places. They will go further and see more than I could dream."

When his hole was dug Tip took a yellow envelope from his pack and buried it in a plastic bag along with the stone, and covered it neatly and swung his pack on his shoulders.

Through Papon he explained the long road ahead to Pasismanua, who seemed undaunted by the task. They descended the high country for days, growing thinner and more gaunt and always Tip's feet were bloodied. The days were followed by nights of anguishing toil, slow and hungry nights, nights of delusion and thirst, of boiling sweats and fits of fever.

Tip wondered often if his penance had been earned, if he was now forgiven for the sins of his youth, even though he knew there wasn't a way to earn such a gift. He longed to see Padibatakal, something he felt he *had* earned, and he dwelt on the thought through his long, painful journey. When they reached the graves of Rigley and Dutch, Tipper contemplated digging out their shoes, but out of respect for the dead he left them where they lay.

They pressed on at their dogged pace, seeing their home on the river like a prize to be won. Pasismanua enlivened the troupe with stories of her people, singing songs as they traveled and lending a hand at every turn. Papon couldn't help but be blessed by her presence. Sometimes they spoke for hours in a language that Tipper couldn't understand.

They arrived at Taku early one morning and Tip found Tiegel right where he had left him, alone by the fire. The man hardly even looked up when Tip approached him, never seeing the bloody scars on his wrists, his bare feet swollen and red.

"Your debt has been paid," Tip told him.

But old Matthias Tiegel simply shrugged him off.

Word soon spread throughout Taku of the white savior who had bartered a trade. Tip was given the nickname "Nogat Bikpela Su", which means "Mister No Boots" and Papon was referred to as Tip's "Wan Wokabaut", or traveling companion. They were celebrated and a great feast was prepared in their honor and that night Papon and Pasismanua were married. The following day the three of them set out for the south.

They faced struggles and setbacks and little adventures on their way home. The jungle was still the jungle, and through it lived the quick and deadly strength of wilderness. The rain pushed them onward, and slicked the rocks, and the wretched heat accompanied them through the shallow swamps, and across the range of the lowland people, to the skinny, still-worn path that led home.

By then their cache of supplies had dwindled down to half-rotten fruits gathered from the forest floor. The wounds on Tip's wrists and ankles had dried but even outside the covering of bandages his flesh had grown sore and purple around the lesions.

He limped doggedly across the path. Both of his feet were cracked by stress fractures and his blisters bled as his souls scraped across the trail.

But the moment came at last when they saw distant trees that held shadows they remembered – where the canopies were well-known and the path well-worn and it was then that their stumbling came like dancing and dim eyes brightened big as the sun.

The people of Kapalu rejoiced at his arrival, hungry for stories of the expedition. To Tipper's disappointment, every man among them looked to him as their leader.

But when he found Captain Tawling alone in his hut, there was little sign of rejoicing on the old man's face. He was seated on his bedside, his hat in his hands, and his eyes were bloodshot as he turned to face them.

"This is Pasismanua," Tip told him. "She is Papon's new wife. We have accomplished—"

"Tipper."

"Yes, Captain?"

"I've just received word from Kolschen."

"Yessir?"

"I have some terrible news."

And Tip knew from his face that his suffering had only just begun.

9. Secrets of the Mountain

Henry and Jack had been told that their birthright was hidden somewhere on the mountain, and after hours of paddling, the mountain was growing close. Before them they could see the far off shoreline clouded in fog, with great snow-capped peaks rising through the cloudcap.

Tip Holland kept one eye on his wristwatch, as he had all day, and the other on the land that unfolded before his eyes. For the better part of the morning Tip and Henry had been talking constantly, about Luleo and Taku and the fate of the Woodsies, mostly to keep things fresh. Now that Luleo was behind them Tip's mood had grown lighter and he proved it with easy conversation.

"So you brought them back with you?" Henry asked. "And what - stuck them in the woods?"

"No," Tip chuckled. "Nothing like that. They tried to adapt to the life in the west village. Pasismanua took right to the language, surprising us all. She's actually quite a phenomenon. But in the end it was too rigid for them to adapt to, and they made their lives in the West End, like they wanted."

"Did they build that house themselves?"

"I helped them," Tip said. "And in return Papon carved out this canoe. For this very purpose."

Henry paused to admire what a job that must have been, and then paddled on, knowing he would have loved to have trekked to Taku all those years ago. Of all Tip's stories it was the one that stirred him most.

In the coming hour Tip shared more of his adventure but before long the conversation turned to Tenpenny and both Tip and Henry shared what they missed most from home.

"For me it's the children," Tip told them. "I was put on this earth to care for children. And I deeply miss seeing them in the springtime."

"I miss the food," Henry admitted. "And some of the feminine companionship. What do you say, Jacko? What's the first thing you'll do when you get back?"

But Jack was slow to answer. By then his mind was completely consumed by Greer's pregnancy and he had little desire for conversation. Jack had hoped that the quest for their birthright would take his mind off of the shocking news that Wonderboy had given him. But the silence of the sea had only served to fuel his anger. He watched the back of Henry's head as he paddled, wanting to pick a fight with his brother right there on the water.

Growing up on Tenpenny Hill Jack had been taught to rassle and scuff and Henry had been his only opponent, other than when Tipper engaged him in a friendly contest. The pair had boxed in their brother brawl for years, and only once had either one of them tried to hurt the other with any real intent. And then it was Henry, whose nose had been broken by a lucky jab. Once, too, Jack had decked his brother after Henry claimed Putt as his own, but they were only boys then, and their anger was short-lived.

But even the slight against Jack's old dog had not stirred him to anger the way the news of Greer had done. What he was feeling now was new, and steadily as their journey progressed Jack wanted to call their excursion to a halt and make his brother answer for his actions.

But how am I to do it, Putt? Jack asked himself, still thinking his conscience was traveling beside him. How can I make this day about my anger?

For although Jack didn't know the entire story, he knew enough to be certain that Tip had been planning this day for many years, and that the news of Greer would surely disrupt their adventure, or even worse.

So Jack paddled on in silence, doing his best to carry his share of the work, and trying to keep his mind focused on whatever was buried high on the mountain.

"Oh, I'm more interested in what lies ahead," Jack said finally, ending the conversation.

For that of course was heavy on all of their minds. They could see before them a beach of black sand, and the land beyond that ran up and up into the foothills of the forest and further on to the tree line, merging with sheets of white cloud and higher still where they spotted the tips of snowcapped mountains.

"When we come to the beach head, what will we eat?" Henry asked. "Why did we abandon our gear?"

Again Tipper checked his watch and paddled on. "We aren't going to the beach head," he answered.

"We aren't?"

"You see those islands out ahead?"

Before them, like guardians at the gate, were three huge island towers standing against the shore, each capped with a crown of evergreens. The sheer walls were of bare rock, dark and shiny from the drizzle, and at the base of the great cliffs were jagged spires rising out of the sea. Each brother squinted into the wind.

"Yessir."

"We're aiming for the middle one," he told them. "There's an entrance at the base."

"*An entrance?* To what?"

"Your birthright, of course. We must reach the island within the hour. If we don't our chance will be lost."

You can be sure neither brother had any idea what Tipper meant by that. How could there be an entrance onto an island, they wondered? A beach perhaps, but not an *entrance*. But no beach seemed possible in such a place for the great heap of land swelled straight out of the sea, its rock walls rising hundreds of feet up to the trees. And what kind of entrance appears and disappears from one hour to the next, they pondered? Tip's words didn't just seem illogical to the boys, but fantastical as well.

Henry scanned the face of the great cliffs for some clue to their destination, but the only doorway he saw was a large cavern, hundreds of feet above the water whose entrance was circled by a swarm of gulls. We won't be going that way, Henry knew, unless the old man expects us to fly. But he could see no other pathway, and the closer they came, the more doubt was cast on the sincerity of their father's words. However Henry continued to work at double speed, for regardless of his skepticism his curiosity drove him on.

In the next hour the weather changed quickly and soon the long shadow of the islands darkened as the sky grew heavy and cold. Then came the rains and as the winds whipped across the watertop the canoe was beaten off her course. Soon they were steering treacherously through the maze of jagged rocks with one great island on either side of them, but their eyes honed on the middle one, with her high rock spires growing as they paddled.

Jack felt a great weight pressing down upon him, one he was eager to shake. But no matter how much he tried to focus on their present adventure he found that his anxiety held him firmly within her grip. He felt compelled to call out, to scream, to cry injustice, but the reality of the moment held him back.

They were now paddling with great intention, fighting the wind and the rain as they slipped through the narrow course between the rocks. Their path was slow and treacherous, and several times they almost capsized from the pull of the current, but suddenly their path opened before them and they broke free of their rocky labyrinth. It was then that they had their first clear view of what lie beyond.

"Look there!" Tip said with sudden excitement. "There it is! At last!"

Before them the black rock of the island rose out of the sea like a tower, and at the base, just above the water's edge, a small tunnel had been carved in the face of the rock. Both brothers could just barely see the opening, for it appeared to be no wider than the boat they were steering. Surely this couldn't be the entrance that Tipper had mentioned, they thought.

"A tunnel?" Jack wondered.

"More of a *cave* than a tunnel," Tip told him. "It doesn't bridge to the other side."

There was a great silence among the party. It lingered until Henry said, "You're telling us our birthright is buried underwater? In that tiny hole?"

Tip Holland chuckled loudly, shaking his head. "Did you hear me say that, Jack? That your birthright was *underwater?*"

"No sir."

"Good. Well do me a favor while you're back there and teach your brother how to listen."

Jack nodded, knowingly, but Henry said nothing in his own defense. He was leaning forward now in their little canoe, paddling steadily with all of his strength. For Henry had found a sudden interest in his family story, and now that the end was near he could think of nothing else.

"The gateway can only be seen at low tide," Tip explained. "It won't last long. We have to go in, get your birthright, and head back out as quick as we can."

Both brothers stared out in disbelief. The width of the passage looked to be no more than three or four feet at its widest point. How far it reached into the face of the rock they could not see for the tunnel stretched on and on into blackness. But stubbornly they paddled.

Now the doorway in the mountain was unobstructed before them, black and inviting like a yawning mouth. They watched it grow and grow. As the long canoe approached the stony entrance Tip removed his tiny paddle from the ribs of the boat. "Put away your paddles," he told them, and the brothers hid them and gripped the gunwales. Each member of the party lowered their heads as the boat slipped neatly inside. The little boat rattled against the gunwales.

As they were drawn into the darkness, a golden finch fluttered from the cave and passed over the troupe. It was shimmering and bright and far away from home, having traveled many months from the jungles of the tropical south to its spring nesting in the north. And although it would never matter in the slightest to anyone involved, this bird would lay eggs that would hatch into more finches and those finches would fly south with the winter and seven years later Jack and a huge friend he had yet to meet would be seen crossing a lush valley on the bottom half of the world with machetes in their hands by the great-grandson of that very finch.

Their heads nudged the sheltering rock and their going was slow. The heavy winds rattled the boat against the cavern walls as Tip used the short paddle to move through the tight enclosure, deeper and deeper into the blackness. Soon there was only a faint light behind them, fading the further they ventured.

But in the next moment they reached a domed chamber where the ceiling opened just enough for them to stretch their necks and Tipper turned on his headlamp.

They were now at a dead end, a small room with a rock shelf running alongside them, parallel to the canoe. At the far end of the room a heavy rope had been moored to a jagged stone ages ago and when the bow struck the far wall Tipper tied them down.

He instructed his sons to make a careful exit, using the rock shelf as a bracing. Once cleared the travelers were now seated side by side, facing one another for the first time in hours.

Henry was breathing heavily with excitement, but Tip noticed that Jack appeared unmoved by their adventure. More than that there was a fire burning in his eyes, as if he wanted no part of their little adventure. *This may have been too much for him all at once*, Tip thought. He considered how much the boy had seen and how quickly he had seen it, thinking back through their long journey, and the funeral, and all the secrets of Luleo. But more than the rest of it Tip knew that Jack Oakham was a young man burdened with the pain of others, and that it was likely the injuries to Wonderboy and old Putt that left him unsettled.

"Where do we go from here?" Henry asked, and the question was the right one at the time. The dark room was lit only by Tipper's headlamp, but it was easy to see that the canoe had nowhere to go.

Tip smiled at his sons and laid on his back, scooting along the rock. He pointed his light up at the ceiling and took an excited breath.

"We go *up*," he told them.

At once the brothers ducked their heads, following the path of their father's light. Under the lip of the rock a dark passage led up and up into the blackness. The opening was no larger than a manhole at the widest point, but any more than an arms length into the blackness was too dark for their eyes to see.

"It's called the *birth canal*," Tip explained. "Your birthright rests at the top of this passage. We have to climb up and retrieve it, and return before the rising of the tide."

"Or what?"

"Or we'll be marooned. When the tide rises the boat will be crushed."

Both brothers considered their predicament, one they felt certain that Tipper enjoyed.

"Henry, you're the biggest. For safety's sake you should go first."

Suddenly Henry Snow looked nervous, an expression Jack had rarely seen. "Go first?"

"If you got stuck beneath us, we couldn't pull you out."

Henry was quick to move into position. He looked up through the long chute in the rock and reached inside for a handhold.

"How did you find this?" Henry asked, pulling himself inside.

"I didn't find it."

"Well who did?"

Tip cleared his throat. "A man named Thaddeus Parnicca."

They ascended the passageway one man behind the other - Henry going first, as instructed, then Tipper encouraging from the middle, and finally Jack, silent and grim, bringing up the rear. Jack's spirits had lifted briefly when they had reached the cave but now he could see that there was still another stage in their journey and his uneasy feeling quickly returned, no doubt aided by the fact that climbing up through a tunnel proved particularly strenuous with two broken fingers.

They pulled themselves through the twisting, winding vein in the mountain, each man short of breath, as they groped in the blackness for the next rock to grip. All the way through the passage was tight, especially for Henry, who was unable to take a deep breath at most places, for his ribs swelled against the jagged walls.To make matters worse small pieces of rock would often dislodge underfoot and drizzle down the steep pathway, thumping the shoulders and heads of the travelers beneath. They passed by small, secret tunnels that trailed away into the rock - and when they spoke their voices echoed to places no man would ever see, into tiny chambers where gloomy creatures could be heard stirring from their sleep.

It's not important to go into all the ins and outs of the mountain tunnel, the dangerous crags and twists that the cold blackened caverns provided our travelers. By now you are well aware that this is a story of wild places and with them came many perils. No it's enough to say that they traversed the steep, and often slippery tunnel without much difficulty, except that the weary bones that carried them grew more weary and their eyes grew heavy for rest. There's no need spending time on all the conversations the party had amongst themselves for you know their concerns by now and that would only delay the telling of the final leg of the journey, which is the most important part of our tale, of course. It is enough to say that their travel was strenuous, yet steady. That is until the weather broke.

When the storm struck, the walls of the mountain rattled our travelers like oversized birds in their cages. The wind could be heard howling through distant chambers and in an instant a great gust pressed upon their faces. Mist drizzled down from some high passageway, and then droplets of rain, and it grew and grew into a quick stream that flowed into the tunnel from all sides until their bodies were drenched. Henry could see lightning above him as it flashed through tiny fissures in the rock, illuminating their passage upward to where he did not know. Then came the thunderstrikes, sudden and violent, and when the roar sounded it shook them so violently that each man struggled to keep a grip on the rock, for everywhere they reached was wet to the touch.

But Tip urged them to keep moving, for the tide wouldn't wait for a storm. They pressed onward into the high places, the cold water biting them deeper with every step. Their arms were like rubber as they pulled themselves up through the icy winterbournes and the braided streams that seemed to gurgle down from above.

The storm grew and grew, as if some dark and meddling force was trying to bar the brothers from their prize.

"How high do we go?!" Henry asked finally.

"To the top!"

"And how far is the top?!"

"Keep going, Henry! You'll know it when you get there!"

Henry had been uncertain before of their journey's end, but this time, he knew that his destination was near. He could no longer feel his worn-down limbs that had been pleading for a break, or his tongue swollen from thirst. His eyes were as a bird's, alert and deadly serious.

Then suddenly Henry felt it, a change in the air. Somewhere in the darkness an open door let in the aroma of spring. The passage was widening now and soon Henry spotted a pale glimmer of light. But more than the light he could feel the air filling his lungs as he climbed the last few rises, groping for the space to stretch his body out. Suddenly the passageway was flooded with light and he pulled himself up through the last of the dark tunnels. In the next moment he found himself in an open stone chamber.

The room was larger than Henry had expected, light filling the space from end to end. It poured inside from a huge, outfacing cave that looked down upon the lands to the east. As Henry rose to his feet a pod of seagulls fluttered from the cave face, escaping toward the rocks below. It was then that Henry realized he was standing in the very cavern that he had looked up at from the canoe, just two hours before.

Henry helped his father and brother out through the passageway, and soon both brothers stood side by side taking it all in. What had been a dark, lifeless passage was now a brilliant view stretching on to the eastern shore. They could see the black of the water, stretching out for miles to the beach where they had launched the canoe that morning. The brothers each marveled at the sight.

The last thing either of them had expected was that his birthright would be left behind in an empty cavern. But this was no simple cave. Displayed before them was a collection of rocks set side by side along the southern wall. They were wildly assorted; of various sizes and shapes and textures, some with the glimmer of precious metals. And on the floor before them, in the heart of the cavern, rested three small chests.

The room was still and quiet, until finally Tipper said. "Here we are," as he began to cry. "Here at last."

The brothers studied the rocks displayed at their feet, and the three small chests intently.

"This is the site of your birthright," Tip explained. "Here your fathers were brought when they were near your age. And Otsov Kolschen was brought here long before, by his father."

There was a long pause. "But Tenpenny wasn't built then," Jack stated.

"No it wasn't. But it had to be built somewhere."

"So *that's* why you built Tenpenny? To be close to the *birthright*?"

"That's why I built it *where* I built it. When the time came to bring you here, I wanted to make a journey of it."

The brothers were pondering this new revelation when Tipper asked them to take a seat. He crossed the stone chamber, wiping his eyes, and when he saw that they were listening he knelt before them.

"Are you ready to hear the story of your ancestors?" he asked.

"Yessir," came in unison.

Tip opened the first of the three chests at his feet. And from within he removed a heavy pair of antique shackles, rusted and well-used. He handed them to the brothers, who examined them closely.

"In 1753," Tip began, "a man named Thaddeus Parnicca, a fur trader born in Greece, sailed East from Kamchatka for five weeks until his sloop made berth along these shores. He was a man pursuant of new worlds, having already planted two missions in his short life, and within him breathed a desire to share the truth of his God."

In his keep, Tip continued, he commanded a half-dozen skilled sailors, navigator, boatswain, quartermaster and the like, many of whom had been with him for years. They were a hardy crew, and of one accord, having all been recruited by Parnicca himself. He made a point of training up ragamuffins - lost souls, men hardened by the world, for he found that broken men were the most malleable, and for them his heart beat with compassion.

They made berth near a native settlement on these wild shores, and set about the task of hunting and trapping and when the furs were gathered they were preserved below deck for the long journey home. The crew worked for weeks on end until their storehouse was full but as they made preparations to return they were delayed by an unusual request.

A second convoy of fur traders arriving from Kamchatka had arrested a man wanted for crimes against his navy. He was a petty thief, a murderer, and having been a ship's cooper once had sought employment among the fur traders once he had absconded. The convoy was weeks at sea before they discovered his identity and upon arriving in the east wanted little more to do with him.

"Do us the service of hauling him back," they asked of Parnicca. "We can't spare the men to watch him while we go to collect the furs."

Of course Parnicca was drawn to the prisoner for the same reason he was drawn to anyone - he was broken and in need of a savior. He agreed to the duty and was led below deck where he met the prisoner under lock and key, a man his own age - named *Luka Kolschen*," Tip said heavily. "The father of your family line."

'Luka was a selfish man, given over to his flesh. He cursed his former captors as he was led away, and cursed his new captors as he was clapped in irons and imprisoned below deck.

With their mission complete Captain Parnicca and his men sailed for the west, and on their long journey home Parnicca spent as much time with his prisoner as he could spare. Although captain of the vessel, Parnicca was the man who fed Luka daily. He brought down his meals and treated him kindly, and slowly he broke through with questions of his life. Luka answered none of them until Parnicca shared of himself. But soon the details emerged and an understanding was reached. He began to teach Luka his letters in the mornings, and poured over the scriptures in the evenings and always prayers were given and extra rations offered when they could be spared.

"One morning, at low tide, Parnicca's crew set anchor in this very cove," Tip explained. "Having traveled five weeks at sea they were in short supply of wood fuel and fresh water so the crew boarded a tiny skiff, steering landward through the jagged rocks.

On their way inland, Parnicca spotted a cavern extending deep into the rocky cliffs. Being an explorer by nature, Parnicca removed his outer garments and swam deep into the cavern, and discovering a passage through the rock he climbed it, without torch or lantern, until he arrived in this stone chamber. He called out to his crew below, who had nearly given up on him, and the men cheered and beckoned him back.

That night, in the cell with Luka he promised, 'Someday I will bring my children to that cavern.'

He shared his dream for their lives, for the legacy he wanted to bestow, and he spoke with a grace and a vulnerability that Luka had never heard. "I will leave their birthright for them to find there."

'Why are you telling me this?'

'I must tell someone. And you and I are friends.'

They sailed into the open sea, on their long journey home but within the coming days an outbreak of scurvy struck the crew. They lost one man every three nights until only two survived. Either due to his own physical resilience or his separation from the other men, Luka was spared their fate. Parnicca was also saved, due either to his own physical resilience or God's sweet mercy.

The Captain recorded the dead in the ship's log and buried the men at sea. He released Luka from irons, knowing it would take the two of them to man the ship, and they sailed together for a full month without complication.

In that time Luka became receptive to Parnicca's principles, knowing that without him all would be lost. He studied him, and heard his words, and their friendship deepened beyond any Luka had known.

But after that month, when they were only days from home, Parnicca too fell ill, and Luka made berth on the northern shores of Kamchatka, hoping to nurse his friend back to health.

"They set up camp on the beachhead where Luka hunted and fished and did everything in his power to protect his friend. Prayers were spoken and laughter heard, and for the first time in his life Luka Kolschen provided for the needs of someone other than himself.

"But one morning at dawn, a ship of the fleet arrived off the coast and anchored near the sloop. The sailors came aboard and reviewed the Captain's Log and the only two men unaccounted for were Parnicca and Kolschen.

"Captain Parnicca awoke and scanned the shoreline. He saw the flags of the fleet and their skiff moored to his sloop. Having spent years at sea Parnicca knew the sailor's procedures, and he considered it a great blessing that he was first to notice the ship. He rose with what strength remained, moving quickly to their storehouse and when he found Luka's irons he snapped them on his own wrists.

The young criminal awoke, his face turned in confusion.

"'You must tell them I'm you,'" Parnicca urged him.

"'What?'"

"'If you don't, they'll kill you.'"

Luka shook his head in anger. "'If I *do* they'll kill *you*.'"

'I'll die anyway in a few days. What good would that be for either of us?'

Luka argued and pleaded, and wept on his friends behalf, but in the end there could be no reversal. Spotting their camp on the beachhead the sailors made berth and questioned the men and Luka said nothing against Parnicca's wishes.

They expedited the trial. There were no drums or readings or any ceremony to mark his life. They hung Thaddeus Parnicca from a knotty alder, his body pale and withered.

In the midst of his sorrows Luka asked that the man's shackles be handed over and kept as a remembrance, and although he considered it a strange request, the Captain obliged him."

Both Jack and Henry looked down at the shackles.

"Luka traveled westward with the crew toward Kamchatka, and when he reached home he began a life of service. He visited Parnicca's family, telling them his story and offering his life as a sacrifice. He began his trade and was generous in all his affairs, living by Parnicca's principles, and soon his businesses grew and his children were blessed.

Since that time every man and woman in his line has followed in his footsteps. Parnicca set a path for Kolschen's family and not one of them has strayed. Each generation was given a series of traditions, one being to travel back to the origins of their ancestors. That tradition began here, in the birth canal, a cave discovered by Thaddeus Parnicca. For Luka returned here to mark the forking point in his life. He scaled the passage in the dark, and he laid down Parnicca's shackles and his memorial stones for his children to discover. He claimed this island as his own, so his bloodline would mark their story here."

"Why not bury it inland?" Jack asked him. "Somewhere simpler to reach?"

"Because adventure is alive and well. Because men finish the things they've bled for."

"What does that mean?"

"It means that if your birthright had been buried in your backyard no scars would remind you of what you had to do to get it. A birthright is a powerful thing. Something that should be earned and bled for. Men finish the things they've bled for and Luka bled for many things.

In Kluchi he built a school for the villagers. A school that still stands today. These rocks here are *his* memorial stones," Tip pointed. "They mark the beginning of that tradition."

Henry and Jack examined the stones, four simple rocks clumped together on the far end of the wall. Then Tip stepped up and pointed to the next pile beside it.

"This man here was his eldest son. He built a hospital in the desert - the first ever known to those people. He saved the lives of hundreds over the years."

And again Tipper moved down the line.

"These stones were from his daughter, who bore nine children, survived three husbands, and planted a dozen churches throughout the Maldives."

Tip bent down and picked up the next two stones.

"And these two were father and son. They each died as martyrs in one of the darkest corners of the world."

One after another Tip told the stories behind the stones until finally he came near the end of the line and lifted up a brick-shaped rock of solid alabaster and held it before him in his hands.

"Which brings us to Uri Kolschen," he said. "Luka's great, great, great, great grandson. This man began his work early. He was raised in Kluchi, and was a lawman, a marshall of the district. Determined to bring pride to his ancestors he set a rigorous schedule of generosity, using his knowledge of his citizens to better bless those in need. Uri had two daughters before his wife died, and later in life his second wife blessed him with a son. Your grandfather, Otsov Kolschen.

Uri brought each of his children here to receive their birthright, and told them the same story I am telling you. They too had memorial stones left to find around the world and when they came of age they went to find them, and discovered their missions in the process. The two sisters were bold in their travels, reaching deeper into strange lands than any of their fathers had done. By the time Otsov had come of age both of the sisters were well established throughout the world, sharing their inheritance with children and pursuing a life of service. Both of them married, though neither had a child that lived, and the mission of passing on their family line fell to Otsov, their baby brother.

Otsov, or simply Kolschen, as he was commonly known, was blessed with a vast array of talents suited for such a life. As I have told you he was an enormous man, which unto itself is nothing, but when added to his other gifts enabled many doors to open. He had an understanding of people, broken people in particular: their hearts, their dreams, their fears, and though he never preyed on those understandings, he did his best to embrace them, like a father would for a child. Throughout his life even grown men saw him as a father figure. And his time was never short with anyone. He reproduced himself, delegating everything that didn't fit within his giftings, and keeping little for himself. But the practice of giving all to others doesn't exactly work itself out, as his forbearers had proved. For wise men can recognize generous hearts. Wise men know visionaries when they see them. And by the time Otsov Kolschen was my age, he was known to many wise men, and everything he touched turned to gold.

He was brought here by his father and given his birthright and as soon as he returned home the first thing he did was buy a boat for a young fisherman. The man had been out of work for some time and Kolschen had inherited a fortune from his father, one he was ready to give away.

Kolschen told the man he was looking for a place where he could charter a boat for his children to fish someday. And although he had no children at the time, he bought the man a new trawler, fresh off the line, with the agreement that the Captain would take Kolschen and his family fishing one week a year when his children came of age. Kolschen quickly realized that it would be wiser to buy the man a boat and make their arrangement then to charter a boat every year, but the real bonus for Kolschen was that the new Captain could now make a living."

"And that man?" Henry wondered, "That new Captain? Was his name *Mushkin*, by any chance?"

"Yes, Henry. The man I stole from all those years ago."

Jack nodded, enjoying the story immensely.

"Next Kolschen set out to uncover his father's memorial stones. By that time the world was shrinking and a man could hope to see every corner of the globe in his lifetime. Kolschen used that to his advantage. He didn't establish one mission, but many. He set up safe houses throughout the world where he received his mail, always near places in need that his father had encountered, and always headed up by someone who had been broken once, and who Kolschen came to love and understand.

"How many were there?" Henry asked.

"It doesn't matter. Too many to count. It isn't a contest. But every continent was known to him. He ranged far. He built camps where camps had never been seen. He dug wells, and brought crops to new fields. He couldn't spend his money fast enough, and yet his fortune only grew.

It went on like that for years and then he found a wife and fell desperately in love. He settled in Kluchi for a time, taking over his father's duties as Marshall of the District, and soon he was blessed with two sons. Two fine sons filled with laughter and many of their father's qualities. They were your fathers, of course, and I knew them for my time, and I could see how their strength together would calm the waters of the world.

As young men they were brought to this very place, on Mushkin's fishing charter in fact. They too were given the task of retracing their father's travels and their inheritance was great. Each of them discovered their mission together, on Baiga Boksas street, setting the captives free. Like their father before them their opportunities grew with each generation, and more could be done because of the groundwork that had already been set. They died young," Tip said looking down at their stones. "But their impact would have been tremendous," he sighed. "If they hadn't been snatched away."

Now both brothers locked eyes on Tip Holland, waiting for what came next. But Tipper shook his head, "I won't tell you how they died. Or of the events leading up to the two of you being spread out to the wind. That story is for your journey home. What you need to hear was that you have a proud line of sacrifice laid out before you and that this place is here for your children, when you choose to bring them here."

"So will we follow our father's path, like the rest of them?" Henry asked. "Did they have time to leave their stones behind?"

"It's the right question, Henry, and one that Kolschen and I discussed long ago. They *did* bury stones, *a few* that is, and those are certainly left for you to find. But once Kolschen and I went on the road together I started burying my own stones as he instructed me, so that my children could know my story and follow me down that path. But the two of you are my children now. There will be no more. So you will each have two trails to follow. Where your father's ends, mine will begin."

Tip opened the second chest and resting inside were two yellow envelopes, folded neatly with the boys names on the face.

Tip handed them over and the brothers opened them, reading their instructions. The clues seemed cryptic to both of them, though each felt certain that the answers would unfold when their journey developed.

"Those words were written by your fathers - intended as guideposts to lead you on."

"So Kolschen asked you to look after us," Henry asked. "To take us to our birthright?"

"No. Even though Kolschen was arrested it was always his intent to bring you here himself. He did ask me to find you, and to care for you in his absence." Now tears filled his eyes. "But it was always his intent to know you and raise you up."

"But he couldn't?"

"No. He never got out. The great heartbreak of my life. But he thrived in prison, changing their culture from the inside. It was some years ago, when he knew that he would never be released that he wrote me asking if I would bring you here in his absence whenever the time was right."

Tip knelt down on the cave floor and hauled up the third chest, it's bottom caked in earth, and he set it on his lap. He gave Henry and Jack a calm, yet excited look and when he opened it there came a satisfying creak.

Inside, wrapped in plastic, were two thickly bound stacks of hand-written letters. Tipper unwrapped them carefully, handing one to each of the brothers.

"He wrote you these from prison," and Jack and Henry looked on in awe.

"He may not have known you in person, but he certainly wanted a say in how you were raised."

The brothers held the stack of letters before them, unsure of what to say.

Then Tip suggested. "Read them when we get back."

"So your job was to keep watch over us until Kolschen showed up?" Henry asked. "But instead you became our father."

"My job was to honor his wishes. To raise you under the principles and traditions of your ancestors. Each of you have a calling on your life passed down through your forbearers and I was charged with the task of ensuring that those traditions live on to your own children, whenever they will come."

Jack lowered his eyes, his thoughts drifting to the babe in Greer's belly.

"There are three questions that must be answered in life," Tip said. "Truthfully there are only three. 'How did I get here?' What is my purpose? What will I to do to fulfill that purpose?" For both of you - now two of those questions have been answered."

The three men talked for some time, of Parnicca, and the great journey they would some day take. "When you're older and settled," Tip said. "When the time is right to break away - your memorial stones will be waiting."

Both brothers had much to consider as they sat before their birthstones. For once it was Henry, entranced by the great adventure that awaited him who didn't want to leave.

But the hour was late and it was time to begin their long descent down the tunnel to the sea.

Tipper closed the chests and looked over the stones one last time. He was the first to lower himself down, gliding his hands playfully across the boulder tops and his sons soon followed. Years later a monument would be erected on the site, after another lengthy adventure. But those stories belonged to boys and girls that had yet to be born, to the next generation of Tenpenny journeymakers and their tales would far exceed any of the ones contained in this book.

Time was short and the three travelers were quick to shimmy through the narrow passageway, which was much easier to navigate without the water rushing around them. They scrambled through the winding vein and when they finally dropped into the stone room they could instantly see that the water had risen. They boarded the canoe and were forced to keep their heads down as they paddled along, this time toward the light. At some places their necks and backs scraped the rocks above but soon they had pushed themselves through the shrinking tunnel and into the open sea.

Sitting at the back of the canoe Jack remained silent, trying to make sense of his life. He cherished the letters that he had received, and the knowledge of his legacy. But despite all of the excitement and anticipation he felt that he didn't belong on any adventures. He still wanted nothing more than to be home, to attend to the needs of those around him, instead of being out on some island where he could serve no ones needs but his own.

It seemed strange to him that Henry Snow, descendant from the same line of men, could see his world as nothing but a bold adventure, waiting to be discovered, when Jack himself wanted nothing of the sort.

In time they began to paddle as one and all were silent for some time.

"Did you ever see your father again?" Henry asked.

"You mean Kolschen?"

"No, your real father."

"No. I never did," Tip said. "He died long ago. Though I would have loved to have brought him to Tenpenny. Who knows what would have happened."

Then Jack asked, "So you're an orphan too? Like we are?"

"You're no orphan, Jack."

They paddled through the sunset and into the dark of night and Tip steered them by the stars to the place where they had disembarked that morning. By the time they reached the beachhead and stowed the canoe there was very little romance left in them at all. They were beyond fatigue, their food cache had become merely a small stash of honey that Unger had left them. Their arms were swollen, their fingers raw. Jack looked the strongest of them all but in his eyes still swelled the colors of anger.

That night Henry watched as the moon drifted out from beyond the forest, following it as it climbed the sky and filled the land with a pale lantern light of silver and white, shining on the sea like a watertop flame. And even though he would tell himself to do so for many years, Henry Snow would never again visit that island claimed by his forbearers.

10. Departures

When he woke the next morning Jack decided it was time to confront his brother. With the birthright found, and the long trek ahead, he knew that the moment had come to bring the truth to light. It had been awkward, waiting to speak his mind during their long journey across the channel, but out of respect for his father Jack had held his tongue.

But now it was a new day and when he woke Jack hoped to resolve the matter first thing, around their morning fire, for he knew Henry was more even-keeled at first light than any other time of day.

But when Jack sprung from his sleeping bag he soon realized that Henry wasn't there. In fact neither was Tipper. Jack quickly discovered that he was all alone at their campsite. No fire, no breakfast sizzling in the fry pan, only silence and the sound of the ocean through the trees.

They had spent their evening a short walk off the beach, tucked away in a cluster of tamaracks to keep out of the wind. They had stowed the canoe for the next visitors and made a crude camp in the sand before falling asleep, exhausted. Jack could see that the fire had not been fed that morning, and there was no sign of breakfast. It was still first light, but bright enough to see that each of their packs were missing. In fact all that was left of their camp was his sleeping bag, his mat, and his dirty leather boots.

Jack laced them quickly and gathered his gear and the moment he broke through the trees and saw the ocean, he stopped like a stone. A short distance off the beach was a float plane, anchored in the sand. While he was looking at the plane - who should come stumbling out of the trees but Henry Snow. He stretched his back and buckled his pants.

"What's going on?" Jack asked.

"Dunno. That plane flew in awhile ago. Now she's just sitting there. Tip's on the beach with our stuff."

In the dim light Jack hadn't noticed him, but on second glance he could see his brother was right. Tip was near the water with their three packs stacked beside him. "I wonder why," Jack said.

Henry yawned, "I guess we're off to an early start."

When he heard their footprints Tipper turned to see. "Look who it is?" he said to Jack. "We were letting you sleep."

"I didn't know we moved the party. What's the plane for?"

"I'll get to that soon enough. You awake, Jack?"

"Not really."

"Then we'll give it a few minutes." Tip patted the ground and his two sons sat beside him. "That way we can enjoy the sunrise."

Tip Holland had a distant look about him. And yet he seemed free somehow, free of some burden that neither brother could see. Jack in particular was puzzled by the change, having expected a great anticipation to sweep over his father once their mission had been revealed. But strangely Tip no longer had the look of anticipation in his eyes. He barely even raised his head to look at them, choosing instead to fumble with a blade of grass in his fingers.

For some time he sat idle, shivering within his coat. But then he told them, "At the risk of sounding preachy I have one last lesson to teach you."

"Let's hope it's a lesson on how to fly a plane," Henry said. "I've walked enough for one trip."

And despite his deep frustrations, Jack managed an "Amen."

"I know this will be difficult," Tip told them. "In fact I can't really imagine given all you've heard and seen. But before we go home I must tell you of your fathers. Tell you how it ended, because the end of my story is the beginning of yours."

For the last time Henry and Jack opened up their storybooks and readied themselves for the approaching truth. Tipper fixed a fire and as it was growing he told them the final tale of their journey. Henry and Jack were thankful for the warmth, thankful for their history after so many years - but soon Tip's words proved true, for both brothers cringed as they listened.

When it was done Tip left them to their writing, wandering up and down the beach, for he wanted to give them room to breathe. The boys scribbled their thoughts for several minutes, overcome with emotion, and when Jack had finished he sat throwing sidelong glances at his brother. He still had a certain topic to address, one he was ready to be done with.

Jack knew they would have a long journey back together, but he didn't want to wait any longer. As soon as Henry had finished writing Jack planned to confront him.

"Are you two ready to go home?" Tip asked. "To be the men you were called to be?"

Both brothers looked out at the sea plane.

"I don't know about all that," Henry admitted, jokingly. "But I know I'm beat."

"Me too," Jack said. "I'm ready for home."

"It's a good place, isn't it?"

"Yessir."

"A fine place to grow up."

"It is."

Then Tip sighed. "That's good. Because it's yours now."

The brothers looked up.

"I'm giving it to you."

"Giving what to us?"

"Tenpenny. Luleo. The whole dream. I signed it over to your names the morning we left. That's your birthright."

Henry and Jack sat frozen in place.

"The others will help you," he added.

Henry pursed his lips. He seemed to drift away.

"Well what does that mean?" Jack asked.

"It means it's yours to run now. Your lives were made for hardship."

"What do we do?"

"Nothing really. At least not today. It isn't as if I expect you to take the reigns of every detail on the very first day. If you knew every corner of the globe that this place touches, it would likely overwhelm you."

Then Tip told them. "And from the looks of things you are already overwhelmed."

"Yes. Thank you," Jack said.

"But every year more and more will be handed over. Every year your burden will grow. Kolschen mapped it out that way for his own sons, and we've followed it to the detail. The two of you are men now and it was his wish that your lives be filled with struggle."

The brothers looked off at nothing.

"I believe you can make it work," Tip added. "If you do it together."

Jack refused to face his brother.

"What does it mean," Henry squinted. "'*The others will help you?*'."

"It means you'll have good men beside you. You won't be left to the wolves."

"What *else* does it mean?"

Tip leveled his eyes at them. "Well *that* is the lesson I have to teach you," he admitted. "This will be difficult. But there must always be consequences. Every man must pay for what he's done."

Jack felt a chill crawl up his back.

"No matter how far you run," Tip said. "Truth always catches up with us. Isn't that right, Henry?"

"Yessir."

"It's good you learned that. Now it's time *I learned it*. First hand."

Jack stood to his feet. "Hold on. What are you saying?"

With his hand Tipper calmed him. "You know what I'm saying. I'm turning myself in," he said. "I'm a fugitive, remember?"

Jack's heart went racing. He thought of Greer's baby. "No you're not. You wouldn't do that."

"Jack, listen."

"No, Tip. Fugitive or not you *won't* go. You won't just up and leave us. I know you. You've got it in your head that you have to, but you won't."

"Jack—"

"He's right, Tip," Henry said. "You're the *one* man who never leaves. You're there for every skinned knee. Ain't no way you won't be there for us now."

"I'm sorry, son."

"*You're sorry?*" Jack repeated, "You've got to be kiddin'. You worked all those years to build a dream and now you're gonna watch it crumble in the hands of two *boys?* No - any minute you're gonna wake up and realize that you can't leave because there's too much for you to do."

Tip sighed, "The two of you will have to get by without me."

569

Jack was fuming now. "Is that your plan? *'Get by without you?'* You know what you're doing, don't you, Tipper? You're making us orphans again."

A sadness crept across Tip Holland's face. He had never seen Jack so angry. "You're not an orphan, Jack, cause I ain't dead. But what I'm doing is long overdue. LaMont will fly me south and escort me to the police station in Soldotna - where I will *turn -my-self- in*."

Henry looked at Lamont, waiting in the plane. Then he looked at Jack, who was red with frustration. "Mr. Soski knows about this?" Henry asked.

"Course he does. They all do." Then he added, "Unger would be flying me there himself if he didn't have the wounded to tend to. And Henry I hope you've been praying for Danny and Culpin. Because if one of them dies - its still on you."

Henry ignored the warning, "So Unger agrees with you - about turning yourself in?"

"At first he didn't. But I've had years to work on him. There's really no argument a man can give."

What about a boy? Jack thought to say, but now his bitterness was silent.

Henry leaned in, and he counted on his fingers as he spoke. "Your crimes happened almost thirty years ago. Unger harbors no grudge. You built the whole place together. And he *forgives* you. Did I forget something?"

"Yep."

"What's that?"

"*His* forgiveness doesn't set me free. There is a consequence for every action. And I've dodged mine long enough."

Jack was numb. He shook his head in frustration, but Henry wasn't finished, "You'll lose your freedom, Dad."

Tip chuckled. "My *freedom* was given to me by your grandfather. It exists only to serve the two of you. Kolschen asked me to care for you until he came back, or he died. He asked me to take you to your birthright if he couldn't. So I've fulfilled my promises - and I've cheated justice long enough."

The boys said nothing.

"Now I'll have a new mission in a new place, with new people. You must see that."

"But why now?" Jack said. "For God's sake why did it have to be now - *of all times*?"

"There's *never been* a better time."

"What? Why?!"

"Because the spring is on. Because my work is done. Because my sister, God love her has no idea how to lead. When the two of you get home you're gonna inherit such a mess it'll force both of you to rise to the task."

Tip stood to his feet. "My hope was to bring hardship straight to your door. It was never intended to be easy."

He motioned for his sons to follow as he took long, playful strides toward the water. "Unger has prepared his two best horses for your journey back," he told them. "March down that beach toward Luleo and go see him when you get there. Then go home and get started. Before long Unger will arrive to help you. D'you understand?"

Henry nodded gently but Jack was still. He was barely listening now. Despite his birthright he wished they had never left Tenpenny Hill, for any reason.

"How long will you be gone?" he mumbled.

"Don't wait on me, Jack. I've already taught you everything I know. Just lead like you followed. Live your life on your knees." Then he smiled. "What am I saying? You've got this stuff in your blood."

Tip turned and nodded toward LaMont and like a death rattle came the sounds of the engine firing up. With it went any hopes the brothers still clung to.

Tip placed his hands firmly on Henry's shoulders, "Son, I'd like to think you'll wake up a bit because of this. But I can't know for certain. You've got a fine brother who will look after you. And more talent than a man has ever earned. So go earn it."

"Yessir."

They embraced as father and son and much was said in their gentle tears. Tip held him tight and began to chuckle and in his arms Henry seemed to shrink back into the child he once had been.

Jack began to plan out what he wanted to say but he could hardly collect his thoughts. It had all happened so quickly. He knew at least that he had to thank the man - for the commitment he had shown, for their years together, for every gift great or small. Suddenly Jack was frightened at the thought of what he wouldn't get around to say.

But soon Tip let go of Henry's shoulders, and grabbed Jack in the same way. The two rocked and cried until Jack knew it was time for words. Tip looked at him tenderly. "And for you, Jack, I have but one piece of advice."

"Yessir?"

Then his father leaned in and whispered, *"Let her into your heart."*

The words surprised Jack Oakham so much he forgot all of the things he had planned to say. He stood speechless as Tipper turned around. Then like a dream Tip handed Henry his pack and waded out into the sea.

The rest happened through their tears. They watched as he swung himself onto the pontoon and opened the door and strapped himself in, leaning his head back. Neither brother said a word as the little plane turned slowly in the current and sputtered down the beach. Both of them felt their bodies go numb as the engine picked up speed little by little. The plane was at the surf break, and then beyond, speeding up gradually until finally it lifted. They watched it rise until the humming of the engine was a gentle whirl against the sound of the sea. And then it was gone.

By now the color in Henry's face had all but withered away. It was springtime, and a host of challenges awaited him, none that he was ready for. The wounded men back in Luleo weighed heavily on his heart. He thought back on the Wild West End in that moment, of the great anticipation he had felt for many years. But what had begun as a thrilling chance at adventure was now a fog in his mind. He couldn't even remember why he had ever saddled up in the first place. His father was gone, and despite his carefree ways, Henry felt old as he turned back to look for his brother.

Jack had drifted down the shore, and every move he made was uncertain. At one point he stumbled on his own feet, which were cold and numb by then. He finally knew who he was and what he was meant for, but now he knew it without Tip Holland at his side. The man who had devoted his life to his raising was gone with the sound of an engine humming against the sea.

In time Jack loaded his belongings in his pack and the two boys set off down the beach. As they plodded toward Luleo it seemed to both of them that their adventure had ended, and their childhoods along with it.

They moved at a dogged pace, not feeling the push to go anywhere just yet, but lingering at each opportunity. Twice Jack called them to stop, dropping his pack on the sand and looking out at the sea, for his head was filled with weighty thoughts too heavy for his legs to carry. There was much for them to discuss, but the brothers simply sat in silence.

Ordinarily Jack would have considered such lingering to be wasteful, but he knew that Luleo was peopled, and that people ask questions, and Jack, for one, wasn't certain his heart could take any questions at the moment. When he reached Luleo he wanted nothing more than a warm meal and some time to think, seated alone in the mess hall, but answering no questions.

Henry too had no wish to talk. The thought of their journey home ran round and around his mind. But to him Tenpenny seemed different now. It wasn't filled with the same freedoms he had known before he left, but with conflict, and burden; more than he could conceive.

But regardless of what awaited them there both brothers rose and marched toward it, through the thoughts of Tipper, far away now, through the story of their fathers echoing in their minds with the sounds of the sea.

A wave came in high above the soft sand, drawing Jack's attention out to the water, where pieces of glacier could be seen floating in the distance.

"The ice is almost blue," he said, just to break the silence.

Henry Snow breathed into his palms and rubbed them together. "It *is* blue," he answered. "And pure. The pressure from the ice above pushes out all the oxygen. You can hold it in your hands and it's still blue."

It frustrated Jack that his brother had an answer for everything. He didn't care much about the ice, or what it meant, all he wanted to do was break the silence. But in the next moment, his gentle nature overtook him.

"Does it stay that way?"

"Eventually it changes," Henry yawned. "Even if it melts a little they can never make it blue again." Then Henry hummed a little tune and took the lead.

Jack marveled at the sight of his brother. The pair had been on the same journey from start to finish and although Jack was weighed down heavily by his brooding thoughts, Henry appeared unfazed. It was as if the reality of Tip's departure had paid him a brief visit, and then had drifted off on its merry way. Men like Tip Holland don't come and go every day,

Jack knew, or even once in a lifetime and he found the carefree presence of his brother to be unnerving.

Somewhere on that beach Jack decided that freedom was Henry's only true companion. Without it he'd be lost. His brother liked to feel that he was free from the weight that came with living, and that people who became bogged down by life were fools, every one. Jack believed he wouldn't waste a minute's time thinking about his birthright, or Tipper's advice if he could help it.

The thought of making decisions alongside him left Jack unsettled. All he could picture were the two of them coming to blows. Jack had enough battles to fight with his Aunt Sissy, he didn't need another adversary. But there it was, his life had been planned out without his permission, and he would do right by his ancestors.

As he marched down the beach he began to hear a host of voices speaking to him and around him, like a chorus in his mind. It was as if a great curtain had been lifted, a light had been cast upon his forbearers and he was crowned with their reassurance. He smiled a dreaming smile, imagining the line of men who had come before him as he walked the great line toward responsibility.

For hours they moved in silence, their heads heavy with grief and confusion. But finally, as clouds fell upon the land, Henry and Jack approached the wharf just north of Luleo. They stumbled toward the building that Tipper had called the "Milk Tavern" though from the outside it looked little like a tavern. Henry winked at every lady he passed, young or old, and went to humming a sweet tune.

All Jack wanted was to pass through and be on his way. He went as far as to plan his cold response to anyone fool enough to engage them in conversation. But as the two brothers moved among the buildings Jack was pleased to see that no one rushed to greet him.

"I'd like to stop if we could," Henry said. "To wrap my head around things. Once we reach Luleo everything will start."

Although surprised by the suggestion, Jack agreed immediately. His brother was right. This was the last moment they would have before their burden was upon them. He nodded and the two entered the tavern, drifting off to separate tables, sullen and quiet.

Briefly they sat in silence, looking off at nothing - but then just as quickly as he had entered Henry sprung up again and walked over to a far wall cluttered with pictures. Foremost among the frames was a painting, dusty and poorly lit, showing six flathead Indians as they stalked across a river with their bows down. Henry looked deep into their faces, so long in fact that the small crowd of patrons began to take notice. Henry leaned forward on his toes, seeming to search for some answer in their eyes, and when finding it, he turned and left the room. He stepped outside to roam across the wharf to some unknown purpose, perhaps to grieve in his own subtle way, Jack thought.

Whatever the reason Jack was pleased with the privacy. He didn't want any talk to muddle his feelings, which were weighty and full of tears. Instead what he wanted was to sit silently and think about the story of his ancestors, and of Tip's sudden departure, and his brothers irresponsible acts; one in particular he had yet to face.

Already Jack missed the wisdom of his father's council. When he thought about the heavy decisions that awaited him Jack's heart grew tired. He removed the stack of letters from his pack that Kolschen had written him, and he read them in order by date, one after another.

In the coming hour he felt his heart being mended as he reflected on his grandfather's words. He read them in disbelief as the breadth of his story came into focus.

Jack found that he was hungry, for he'd had no breakfast, but deep down it wasn't food he was after. It was truth, and Kolschen's words granted him a much-needed supply.

In his time reading in the tavern Jack stopped only once, out of sheer thirst, approaching the bar.

"Can I have some coffee?" Jack asked the barkeep. "I don't know how this works. I don't have any money."

The barkeep hesitated. "You just came back from the mountain, didn't ya?"

"Yessir."

"Then you can have anything you like, Jack. This place is yours, you know?"

Jack sat down to finish the letters, but there were too many and his heart was full. There will be more time when I get home to Tenpenny, he thought. I best be getting on down the road.

Jack stood and stretched and when he stepped outside he went searching for his brother. But a search wouldn't be necessary, for Henry

Snow was seated outside under the near trees, his pack beside him, and his eyes were closed as he rested his head against a trunk.

"Well, brother. It's come upon us," Jack said.

Henry surprised him when he snapped awake and hauled up his pack. "Yes it has," he said kindly. "Wake up time." Henry stood and stretched and turned toward the sea. "Do me a favor and walk with me."

"Where?"

Henry pointed toward the dock. "Just over here. That trawler belonged to Mushkin. Mushkin the Captain. Dad bought it when he heard Mushkin had died."

"No kiddin. How'd you know that?"

"Those fellas up there told me."

Henry walked toward the dock and Jack moved beside him.

"Kinda funny, thinking about Tip dodging the draft on this boat. A boat that we own."

Jack watched what appeared to be the crew working on deck, loading cargo and shuffling about.

"What are they doing?" Jack asked him.

"They're packin up and headin' back. Some urgent business across the sea."

The thought of the world across the sea overwhelmed young Oakham. He couldn't yet imagine the breadth of his burden. "This business with Kolschen's will is a lot to think about," Jack said.

His brother nodded, "It will be when I think about it."

"Well those wheels of yours are spinning, Henry. So I know you're thinking something."

Henry wouldn't disagree. He took a deep breath. "Jack has it been hard all these years, living in my shadow?"

Jack faced his brother, "You don't really cast one."

"Good," Henry chuckled. "You don't deserve that."

Then he added, "What about debts? Is there anything I owe you? Any debt I haven't paid?"

Now Jack's curiosity was growing. "You don't owe me anything, brother. There are others you owe, but you and I are square."

Henry took another breath. "I'm only concerned with you."

They walked in silence, closer and closer to the dock and all the while Henry was shaking.

"It's just that you don't deserve that from me," Henry told him. "Living in my shadow. You don't deserve to be less than anyone. To be drug down by anyone."

Jack walked a few more paces before he turned to his brother with a knowing glance. The trawler, the intentional conversation, all of it was happening for a reason.

"You're leaving," Jack said.

"I'm leaving," Henry admitted. "Adventure awaits."

Once again Jack could feel the pieces of his life changing all around him.

"You don't have a passport, Henry. Where do you plan to go?"

Henry nodded to one of the nearby buildings. "Turns out passports are a specialty in this place. We've already sorted it out."

Jack smiled. "So just like that?"

"No. I've been leaning that way for awhile. But I only just decided. Once I knew the truth about my father I gave up any thought of going home."

Jack watched the crew make ready for their departure. He looked tired when he asked, "So you're off to dig up those stones?"

"Among other things."

"When do you depart?"

"Within the hour."

"You picked a fine time to tell me."

"Like I said I just decided."

Henry Snow, the unbreakable wielder of charm and prowess, with all of his legendary talents, who had speared a bear the week before, shattered the ego of Joe Forsman; and after all of it, he's just a scared kid, Jack believed. He could shatter a hundred egos, kill a thousand bears - but he doesn't have the appetite for sacrifice.

"What do you hope to be over there, Henry?"

"I hope to be free, brother. Don't you ever want to be free?"

"It doesn't matter what I want. What matters is what's been asked of me."

"Well I'm not like you, Jack. I'm not like anyone. Somethin beats inside me that I can't shake."

"I see."

"And what you and Tip are asking for is years. The very best years. Helluva thing when big adventures are beginning."

"Your damned adventures."

But as he said it Jack could almost hear his brother being called to sea, could nearly watch the winds trying to claim him as their own. Oakham had half a mind to forget the whole business, let his brother disappear and preserve their friendship. But Jack knew no matter what he said, his brother's friendship was in its 11th hour.

"What of the children?" he asked. "With Tipper gone their worlds will be shaken. And without you their hearts will break in two."

"They aren't my children, brother. I've served my time on Tenpenny Hill."

Again Jack's thoughts ran back to the unborn child.

"Is there no one you feel responsible for? Nothing you'll miss? "

"I suppose I'll miss Wonderboy. . . and Greer. But they'll be fine. They'll have you."

"Greer has me?"

"More than she has me."

"How's that?"

"You listen. That's what she really needs. In truth I barely know her. I doubt she'll shed a tear."

Jack kicked his boot against the sand. "You're a coward, Henry."

"Careful now."

They were close to the dock and Jack turned to face him. He felt his brother shrinking before his eyes. "All that talent and I get to watch you run and hide."

"Talent is nothing without the character to wield it. And I'm in this world for myself."

Then he added, "And don't act so disappointed, Jack. I know you, remember? I know you didn't really see us teaming up. Fighting the good fight side by side, did ya?"

Jack hesitated.

"Of course you didn't. You know better than to start putting your hopes in Henry Snow."

"Do I?"

"Can you imagine *me* - a *responsible man*? Me as a *leader,* and a *father*?"

Jack Oakham was slow to arrange his answer. "I *have* imagined that."

"And how'd that look? Did I change my stripes completely? Did I cut off my wings?"

Jack sighed. "Maybe it wasn't what I saw, but what I *wanted* to see."

Henry closed his eyes and smiled, "People do what they want to do, Jack."

"Some people."

"No, brother. Everyone does *exactly* what they want to do. You want to stay. You want the struggle of it. It's who you are. But I'm built for other things. I'm built for liberties. I'm built to charm the crowd."

Jack scanned the field, the dock. Of course it was true. The place was filled with silent admirers. To the masses *might would always matter.*

"It's true, Henry - those who see you, stare at you. They want to be you," Jack said. "But they're foolish that way. They're not like me, brother."

"How so, friend?"

"They still ponder your fate."

As he always did when he was finally listening, young Henry seemed to disappear right before his brother's eyes. He could feel his ship was sinking. "You really believe me a coward?"

"Yep."

"Then what am I afraid of, Oak?"

"A whole lot."

"A whole lot, huh? Well I'll bet—"

"Almost everything."

The ship shimmered in the sun like a golden ticket, like a key to a faraway life. Henry fell quiet as he turned to face it. He didn't appear nearly as strong as he had the moment before.

"The world out there is magic," he said.

Jack ignored him. "You gonna go back and make things right with Forsman? Before you disappear?"

Henry never looked at him. "Jack if I go back to see Forsman - I'm gonna finish what I started."

"I see."

"But you'll handle it. You always do. I'm certain you'll find the right words and fix the *whole* business."

Henry seemed to be laughing to himself now, like he was the recipient of some private joke.

"And that reason right there is why I'll be lost without you, brother."

"What reason?"

"Without Jack Oakham, who would clean up my mistakes?"

Jack gave his brother one final look, to remember him. "Well I should count myself lucky I guess. If you're gone, there won't be any mistakes left to clean."

Then Henry grew serious. He seemed to hold the weight of the world in his eyes. "No no," he told him. "I think the ones I've already made should keep you busy for awhile."

Henry could hear the wolves howling in his heart as he walked away. Jack watched him, his heart pounding. He felt the urge to tell him about the baby, but he was certain he already knew.

As he approached the trawler Henry was singing a song, one that Tipper had taught him long ago, and unknowingly one that Kolschen had taught Tipper and his father had taught Kolschen. Leaving behind his life on Tenpenny Hill was as easy for Henry as walking down the dock.

Jack turned and left before his brother reached the trawler. He could hear the men helping him aboard while others clapped him on the shoulders and toasted his arrival. His brother's life lay across the sea, and it would be much like the forest had been. But Jack's life lay back on Tenpenny Hill.

*   *   *

Jack hauled his pack onto his shoulders and pointed down the beach with no one to talk to. He didn't even look back at the wharf but turned instead toward the south, his eyes watching blankly as the buildings of Luleo grew out of the distant trees. He imagined for a moment that he could see Tipper's plane still flying over the water, and then he imagined that the plane was stopped just off the beach at Luleo, and that Tipper had changed his mind and decided to stay. Everything will be just as it was, Jack thought. We'll go back together and work side by side and I'll ask every question I never got around to asking.

The thought lingered in his mind and brought about a whole host of regrets. For there were a great many questions that hadn't been answered, a deep reservoir of wisdom that hadn't been tapped. Jack's mind turned back to his memories, and his own actions over the years. Had he ever truly known who Tip Holland was? Had he ever really appreciated the price that had been paid?

Good fathers fight daily battles for their sons, Jack thought, and when they are old and sick, those sons are there to return the favor. But now Tip was gone and the boy realized he had done nothing to repay the man for his years of service. Now he feared he never would.

It was then, as he approached the barns of Luleo, that Jack realized his loneliness in full. He needed someone to get back to, someone to talk to. His thoughts were of the women in his life.

The morning was cold and the fires of Luleo were burning before him as he crossed the last stretch of beach and moved among the workers. The scene was similar to the one he had witnessed two nights before. Men and women everywhere were laboring in workshops, some riding horseback pulling carts, and others on scaffolds or over chopping blocks and songs could be heard in the distance.

But then, quite unexpected, Jack's eyes were drawn across the field to a scene unfolding beneath the alders. There were three men that he could identify, all citizens of Luleo, standing beside the trees, and for some reason Jack's heart began to race as he watched them. Something about the way the men were standing there, with their heads down, struck a nerve in the boy. A moment later, a fourth man stepped out from behind the trees with a shovel in his hands, and when he went to work Jack realized that a grave was being filled in the shady grove.

Jack tensed up. He had forgotten about the three wounded men they'd left in the galley. Instantly he dropped his pack and raced across the field. If one of the men had died, Jack knew that the consequences for his brother would be severe. He felt his life unravelling with every step. His throat was swelling shut.

Despite the little man's strength and determination Wonderboy was foremost on his mind. Jack held a strange fear that it was him they had lost. A blood clot maybe, or something else. But in that moment Wonderboy stepped out of the galley, his arm bandaged up and down, and when he saw him Jack breathed a sigh of relief.

As he approached the scene the men beside the grave turned to face him, Unger Soski among them.

"Which one was it?" Jack asked, stiff with fright. "Was it Culpin, or the boy?"

Unger shook his head, a heavy expression. "It was your dog, Jack," he told him. "He died this morning. Just died in his sleep."

Jack's eyes danced up at the trees. For a moment he stood frozen. Then carefully the boy sat on the grass, cradling his face in his hands.

"Better him than the others," he said.

Wonderboy sat beside him and waited. But the two had nothing to say, not for a long time. The nearby villagers were silent and Wonderboy simply patted him on his boot. The wind blew and the sound of life rung across the fields and Jack soon felt his stomach turning, thinking he was going to be sick.

After a long spell Wonderboy broke the silence, humming the tune that Putt had always dozed to. It was a sweet song, with a simple melody, but the little man was only halfway through before the memories choked him up. He stood to his feet and fetched a shovel and went to tossing dirt.

Young Oakham smiled up at him but shook his head, "No sir," he said, and clambered to his feet.

Jack took the shovel from the little man and cautiously approached the grave. As he looked down the boy felt his stomach turn again, for through the dark soil one of Putt's ears could still be seen.

"How are the others?" Jack asked, working the shovel. "Danny and Culpin?"

Unger flinched, touched by the question. "Culpin is sleeping. He wakes only to cuss us. Danny is walking around somewhere."

Jack plunged the blade into the soil. "We sure that's a good idea?"

"Yes, yes. It's perfectly safe. In fact he loves it here. I'd be surprised if he doesn't stay."

Jack nodded at the news, but in truth his mind had drifted. All of the thoughts of their great adventure passed before his eyes like a wave of pictures, like he was seeing them for the first time. He could hear the bears snoring in their icy den, could see Henry as he shivered high in the treetops, could feel the water rushing over him as he slithered up to his birthright. But none of them equaled the sight at his feet.

In silence Jack shoveled the rest of the dark mound into the grave and when it was finished he turned toward Unger Soski.

"I'll need to get back to Tenpenny," he said. "As soon as I can."

"Where's your brother?"

And Jack relayed the choices that Henry had made. All of the men who heard the news were dumbstruck, especially Unger, who seemed wounded somehow by the turn of events.

"So, like I said," Jack told them, "I need to get back."

Unger was slow to respond, still sorting out the direction that things had turned.

"Take some rest for a few days. There's really no hurry."

"There is for me."

Unger searched the boy carefully, and could see that he wouldn't be persuaded.

"You had any breakfast?"

Jack shook his head.

"Then go to the mess hall and get some. Meet me at the lots when you're through. If you have to go you have to go."

Jack did as instructed. He walked across the great lawn and each of the workers gave him a wide berth to pass. Then he entered the mess hall and filled up his plate.

Eating alone, Jack thought long about his old dog. He rubbed his knee against the table leg, just to pretend that Putt was doing it, and with each bump came a sentence or two about the food, or some other request that the old dog had, usually things luxurious or unreasonable. Over the years most of Jack's meals had been taken with Putt's nose nuzzled against his knee - as the two argued about who should get what and why. The thought made him smile, for he had yet to feel the pain of losing his friend. Putt's voice, the one Jack had heard since he was young, had the sound of a weathered old man when he spoke, and there was always wisdom in the rasp of it, like the voice he imagined his father would have when he was still a boy.

"They had halibut steaks just the other night," The old dog told him. "Big and thick and freshly cut."

"Halibut's too good for you," Jack whispered. "What you need are some cold beans and yesterday's gravy."

"*Yesterday's gravy?*" Jack heard Putt say. "Without me you wouldn't have lived to *see* yesterday. That old bear would have eaten you alive."

Jack chuckled. "That old bear was a cub at best. A runt too. I wouldn't even bother with a bear like that," he smiled.

"You'll be fine, you know."

"What?"

"You were born for what's comin'."

And those words, wherever they had come from, reminded Jack that Putt was gone forever. That Tipper was gone too. The feeling made Jack so lonely that he wanted to cry over his meal, but there were children across the room, watching him, and he was careful not to let them see.

He cleaned his plate and thanked the cooks and as he moved toward the door he saw Danny Forsman sitting beside the window, his arm in a sling. Jack's eyes were gentle when he nodded to the young man, who seemed alive with possibility.

"I'm sorry about your father," Jack said.

"I know," he chewed, "But I'm not angry. I'm finally out from under his wing."

Jack thought of the grand chasms that exist between one father and another. "When I get home - I'm going to see your father," Jack said. "Make peace if I can."

Danny shrugged. "If you must."

"I must," Jack told him, ending the conversation.

He stepped out into the morning and marched across the field, finding the old farmer sitting on the bench beside the lots. When he reached him Unger's sympathetic eyes gave him comfort.

"I've picked out my best horse for your journey home," Unger said. "Go on and pick out a saddle."

Jack thought of the Pritchers and nodded his thanks. He went inside the saddleroom where the wrangler set him up with Unger's gelding. Or was it *his* gelding now, Jack didn't know. According to Tipper, Jack now owned everything around him.

He walked his mount around the lots and gave the place a good long look, thinking of the work that lay before him.

Once he had readied his gear, he met Unger and Wonderboy on the great lawn and the men parted as equals, though Jack didn't feel it yet.

"When Wonderboy is strong enough we'll travel to the hill," Unger said. "It shouldn't be a few days."

Blankly Jack nodded.

"Or you can stay here with him," Unger suggested. "It wouldn't hurt to wait a while."

"No. I'm goin," Jack told him, for all of his questions had been answered. "I'm gonna say goodbye to Putt and then I'm going."

Unger embraced him and Wonderboy overshook his hand. Each man spoke kind words over him and he moved on, proud to be his father's son; proud of the call placed upon his life. Jack thought long on his father's death, dwelling on what it had meant. For as strange as it sounded to his heart, the burden of his legacy was the single thing that gave him comfort.

11. How Tenpenny Came to Be

By Jack Oakham

When Tip received the news from Captain Tawling he could barely stand, having just trekked barefoot through the jungle for thirty-three days. By that point in his journey Tip had seen enough of good and evil to know their effects on men when he saw them. And the look on Tawling's face could only mean one thing.

The message had been delivered to the Captain with the greatest possible speed - and the curriers were paid accordingly. Tawling handed over the envelope. It simply read: *"Urgent Request for Tip Holland."* and Tip could see that it had already been opened.

"I read it the day it arrived," Tawling admitted. "I didn't know if you were coming back. "

As Tip unfolded the letter the old Captain sat heavily upon his bed, careful not to watch the look on Tipper's face as he read it.

"My Dear Tip,

I regret that I must be the one to share such devastating news. Yesterday morning a great tragedy struck the Kaleos in the northern camp - and all of our dear friends there have lost their lives to our cause. They have made the ultimate sacrifice. There is nothing that can be done for the dead - but please make your return to the Faisal Street Encampment immediately. Much will depend on your arrival. We recognize the difficulty with which you must travel - bearing such news. Our prayers are with you.

In Christ, Unger Soski"

Tip sat down beside the old Captain, his head clouded with the weight of the news. Both of Kolschen's sons were dead. As were Brett Myles Emerick and Yancey Lamont. The entire north team was gone and Tip was left to wonder how such a thing had happened.

There was a dead silence about the place. All of the honor that Tip had felt just moments before was gone in an instant. He imagined it was the worst news he had ever heard. Or will ever hear, he prayed.

The Faisal Street Encampment was one of the old places; an abandoned warehouse that Kolschen had used decades before - as the mission was beginning. It was nothing, Tip knew, but a rotting shell; no place for refugees and children. Tip feared that if the men were forced to use it - it was because they had no other place to go.

"When did this arrive?" he asked, hardly breathing.

"Two weeks ago," Tawling said. "Two weeks ago this morning."

Tip sighed. "I hate to leave you all alone, Captain. But it seems I must. I'd be grateful if you would help me rig the canoe."

"Don't you intend to sleep a bit?"

"Not at a time like this."

So Tip laced up his spare set of boots and took the canoe upriver with great haste, sleeping only in the hull in the dead of night and even then only briefly. His thoughts kept him awake even as he lay there.

All during his journey he felt sick with worry and grief. By what means were four men - capable men - taken from us? he wondered. What evil would rid the world of such treasures? And where was Kolschen? For news like this should have come from Kolschen himself. But questions would continue to run through his mind in the days to come, as he paddled hour after hour toward the answers that awaited him.

He reached the trail after four long days and on the roadway near Kolschen's hut a driver was waiting for him. In the city a private plane was prepared, and alone and uncertain Tip was flown across the sea.

Once he landed he took a train south and another west through the hills and on still tender feet he walked twelve miles through unfamiliar burrows until he reached his destination. It had been six long days since the message was received, but almost three weeks since it had been sent.

The Faisal Street Encampment was just as Tip remembered it, and he had seen it only once. The street was quiet - the lot overgrown and littered with debris. There was no sign of life, no sound of children. The high windows were shattered and the dirt path to the doorway had little sign of wear.

Tip approached the only entrance, scanning the street, and the door creaked ominously as he stepped into the warehouse. The great room was empty and quiet, save for a few toys scattered about.

A little woman was cleaning when he entered the room. Instantly he knew her face. She was Risa, a volunteer from his days on Baiga Boksas street, and she hadn't changed a bit. But when she saw him, Tip Holland knew that the same couldn't be said of him.

"Is that Tip?"

"It's me, Risa. How good to see you."

"Lord blessed us, you've come. We'd almost given up."

Given up? he thought. *What was he here to do?*

"Is Unger here?" he asked. "Or Kolschen?"

"No, I'm sorry," she looked at him wearily. "Unger and Derealdjon and Ruffino are on a food run. It happens every day. They should be back within the hour. They will be delighted to see you."

"Kolschen isn't here?"

Again a frightened look, "He isn't."

"And the children? Where are they?"

"The children are safe. They are in the back lot. The second warehouse."

Tip's heart began to race. "Little Padibatakal? Is she among them?"

"She's in the second warehouse. Upstairs with Momma Tom."

Tipper cocked his head. "Who is *Momma Tom*?"

"Oh yes, yes. I forgot you haven't met. She's like the mother figure to these children now. She's been here for years. Her name is Judith Walters but everyone calls her Momma Tom. "

"Why?" he asked. They were walking now.

"Her husband was called Tom and they had a son named Tom too. And when they had their son her husband started going by Pappa Tom to keep them apart. Strangers, everyone called him Pappa Tom and eventually everyone thought is was their last name and then everyone started calling her Momma Tom. And it stuck."

Then she added. "But she lost her husband and her son years ago and Kolschen helped her. In time he brought her here and now she loves on the children."

"Kolschen's pretty good at that, isn't he?" Tip said.

"Widows and orphans," she told him.

Risa escorted Tip through the grounds of the encampment, but in truth the place was nothing more than a holding ground.

He was led through the yard, past a group of young girls, all of them joyful. They were playing quietly in the grass, so quietly in fact that his heart was unsettled by their silence. Why the secret hideaway, the food runs? What were they hiding from? He wanted to ask her questions but he knew the answers would come. And from the looks of things when they did come his heart was due for a jolt.

When they reached the second warehouse he could hear the sound of hushed voices, dozens of them, leaking out through the gaps in the walls. They were young and old and everything in the middle. A single staircase outside the building led to an upper room.

"Momma Tom is just upstairs," Risa told him. "And little Padi with her. I'm excited that you're here. It's nice to have good news."

"Yes, thank you. Tell me, Risa - what is she doing up there?"

"Momma Tom has spent each and every day in prayer ever since it happened. All day some days. She prays for you and for Kolschen, and the men and the children and all those left behind and all those on the run. Padi likes to pray with her."

Although confused and with many questions Tip said, "Thank you," and headed up the stairs.

When he reached the top he could only hear whispers through the door but he decided not to wait. His heart was thriving on the thought of seeing her once again.

The door creaked open and before him he saw the girl on the floor, crawling quickly. At first glance he was certain it wasn't Padi, for she appeared so quick and mobile. Then he noticed that her woolen socks were folded down and that there were no feet beneath them. She looked up at him and crawled away to the corner.

Seated in the dim light was a frail woman, dark-skinned and plainly dressed. Her face was in her hands. To Tip's eyes they were the wrinkled hands of a survivor, cradling her hopes as she prayed.

He waited in wonder, watching as the tiny girl, little Padibatakal, who looked nothing like her mother, began to warm up to him. She was about to speak when Momma Tom ended her prayer. The old woman opened her eyes and drew back her hands and when she raised her head to look at him, Tip could hardly keep his eyes upon her. For even in the dim light her face was aglow, radiant and clear, bright with understanding.

"How you do, Mister Tipper?"

"You know me?"

"I know you the wonder done saved little Mumsie here. Know what Mister Otsov tell me. They say you done some more savin' too. That jungle is sad now that they done lose you."

Tip shook his head. "What were you praying for?"

"Just then? This little Mumsie. I pray she find a husband."

Tip looked at Padi, clinging shyly to the woman's leg. "A little early, isn't it?"

"No Sir. Not for something like that. It's never too early to pray for that."

"Risa tells me you've been praying for days and days."

"Yessir, Mister Tipper. It's what I do in times like these."

"Well for that I'm thankful. And for you taking care of Padi here. I wondered every day where she was and who was with her. It's strange to say but I'm glad to see it was you."

"I'm glad too," she told him.

"Would you show me how you prayed."

Momma Tom bent down over her knees and cradled her face in her hands again.

"I pray for the right man at the right time, Father," she whispered. "I pray for a man who will take those scars of hers and see right past em - see right past the devil that dealt those wounds and into the heart of a great lady. I pray for a man of quiet strength."

Then she raised her head. "That's how I see him when he appears in my head. Is that the kind of man you always were, Mister Tipper?"

But before he could answer the door creaked open behind him. It was Risa and her eyes were bright.

"They're here," she told him. "They're downstairs waiting for you."

"Why didn't they just come up?"

"They wanted to give you some time with Padi."

Tip excused himself, brushing back the little girl's hair before he left. He followed Risa downstairs through the second warehouse where more children stared at him and into another room where the food was stored.

In the room were Unger, Ruffino, and Derealdjon Polle. When they saw Tipper each man rose and embraced him. As they did he could see the brokenness in their eyes.

Unger pointed for Tipper to sit and when all of the men were settled he finally broke the news.

"So tell me."

"Three weeks ago one of our volunteers saw four men enter the aid station on Baiga Boksas street. It was during the Kaleos' weekly meeting. The next morning, when we hadn't heard from them, we sent someone to check. They called back to tell us that the Kaleos had been killed some time in the night."

Tip laid his chin on his chest. "Martyred."

"By a group of men hired for the job," Unger told him.

Tip could hardly lift his head to speak. It was a long time before he found the words.

"So what they walked in, tied them up, and killed them. Is that right?"

"No," Ruffino told him. "The witnesses didn't see the men leave until the next morning."

"Why?"

"Coroner said they worked on them all night."

Again Tip put his head down.

"I know this is impossible to hear," Unger told him. "But the good news is we think whoever did this wanted everyone. Kolschen's whole team: his sons, his son's wives - even his grandsons."

Tipper shook his head, disbelieving. "What makes you say that?"

"Because a second group of men tore into Pietre and Alexei's home that same night. And a third group broke into our place on the south end."

Tip leaned forward in his chair, "Lord, where were you?"

"It was little Padi's birthday party. All of us were at the orphanage to surprise her."

Tipper was shaking his head in disbelief when Unger added. "The other Kaleos were supposed to come down the next morning - after their meeting."

"So when you got back - your homes were broken into?"

"They were torched. Some of our neighbors saw the break-in. But when we found them they were burned to the ground."

"And you've been here ever since."

"That's right. Three weeks right here."

"Then I imagine by now you have some idea who it was."

"We do."

"Well?"

Unger hesitated. "Tip listen to me. Evil men cannot be understood by you and me. They twist and they poison and it's best that we don't engage them on their turf. We shouldn't have made any inquiries. It would have been better if we didn't know who it was."

"Just tell me."

Unger sighed and looked at the others.

"There's no way around it," Tip added. "You're gonna have to tell me."

But their silence was deafening. Now Tipper boiled with anger. He sprung to his feet. "*Who* for God's sake? Tell me *who it was.*"

But before they told him anything Tip Holland already carried the answer in his heart.

"Golgol was a little fish in a big pond," Ruffino told him. "But somebody loved him."

Now Tip was breathing heavily. There was a long quiet across the room until Unger spoke again. "We've learned that Golgol was a part of a powerful family."

"A *crime* family?"

"We don't know much, but it looks like his father orchestrated everything."

"How do you know that?"

Unger sighed. "The slave trade is big business and to pull off a job like that takes money. Money talks in this part of the world. It talks and it gets talked about. And Kolschen owns more than a few banks around here. With more than a few employees. Many of whom are willing to die for Otsov Kolschen."

"So who is he, this father to Golgol?"

"We don't know his name, or his whereabouts. In fact we don't want to know. All we do know is that Golgol was the man's only son and his name died along with him. From what we can tell he wanted the same thing to happen to Kolschen."

Tipper sat back down.

"It's known as a blood feud," Unger told him.

"I know what a blood feud is."

"Well in this kind of blood feud," Ruffino explained, "It's not enough to kill off a man's family. He had Kolschen locked up so he would live to know that his line was wiped out for good."

Tipper wrung his hands. "So he wanted little Sasha and Viktor too."

"We believe he did," Unger told him. " But you shouldn't call them that. Those aren't their names anymore."

"What are they?"

"Sasha's new name is John Joseph Oakham - after his mother's ancestors. For the same reason little Viktor is now called Henry Snow."

"To keep them hidden?" Tip asked.

"That's the idea. Their wives were hysterical but after they settled down we decided it was best."

"Are they here?"

"No. We were planning to move them upcountry but then the next day both of them were gone, with their children. They left notes behind to explain their reasons but they didn't tell us anything. We assume they went together but we don't really know."

"So where are they?"

"We think they got the boys out. Both women were from the states. But no one knows where they went. I fear we'll never know."

"But they could be safe?"

"They could be. Both of them are strong," Unger told him. "But evil is patient. It endures. And sadly it only needs a single victory to succeed."

"Whereas goodness needs a lifetime."

"Yes it does."

Tipper looked angry again, rolling his neck and breathing heavily. "I want to know how he found us? He couldn't trace my fingerprints so I want to know how he did it. How did he tie Golgol back to Kolschen?"

"Of course we don't really know, Tip. But according to your story all that was left in Golgol's home were two dead bodies and-" Now Unger choked on his words.

"What man? Say it."

"The feet of an infant."

Tipper looked at the floor.

"We believe that was what did it. For all we know Golgol's father may have spent years searching for an orphan without feet."

"Has Kolschen been seen with her publicly?"

"Just once. But we think that if someone was looking hard enough those roads would point to Kolschen."

"But why didn't he steal Padi away?" Tip added. "She's his grand-daughter. She's a means for his line to continue. He could have stolen her back."

"Maybe he wanted to," Deareldjon suggested. "But he missed the opportunity."

"I for one don't think he knows," Ruffino said and Unger agreed. "If he did know she would have been top priority. In his eyes she was likely just another slave to Golgol. He wanted vengeance, messy and quick. But he didn't get it. Not all of it. My feeling is that until he does Kolschen will be stuck."

"So what was Kolschen charged with?"

"He wasn't charged. He was arrested and detained, never questioned, now he is incarcerated and his release will be delayed indefinitely."

"You can't just lead a man off in chains. When is his arraignment?"

"Tip I need you to understand that Kolschen's in a place where none of that matters. *You are* a living example that Kolschen breaks the law all the time. Phony documents, forged papers, human trafficking. He's a wanted man. But they didn't arrest him for any of that. They arrested him because someone wanted it done."

"Someone with power."

"Yes."

"Then can we even see him?"

"*You* can," Unger nodded. "The day after the killings Kolschen got a message out through the walls - asking for only you. Ever since then we've been waiting for you to get here."

Tip rested his face in his hands. He wore a burdened look, "That doesn't make any sense. I'm nobody. I was half-way around the world."

"He didn't explain himself, Tipper. He didn't need to. He just told us to get you here as soon as we could. We were told to brief you and send you on your way."

The men spoke prayers for his safety and gave him instructions. Tip moved across the city using only public transport, and then took a train south across the country, and when he arrived he was mindful that the streets surrounding the prison were likely being watched day and night.

He followed the instructions that were given him, which appeared to come from Kolschen himself. He entered the dank and eery place, and a great uneasiness overtook him as he was led past the lock down. He was taken to a room with two chairs and a pair of guards where he saw Kolschen draped in heavy chains.

The big man squinted as Tipper approached. "What happened to your feet, Tovarisch?"

Tip was surprised by the joy that still lived in Kolschen's eyes. "You wouldn't believe me if I told you."

"Of course I would. Tawling wrote me. He told me what you set out to do."

Tip leaned in to respond but Kolschen stopped him.

"Tip I had to pull some strings to get a visitor, so I doubt we'll get much time. I know you've traveled far, and the news must have hit you hard. But I must know that you are clear-headed."

"Yessir. I am."

"Good. I have a tale to tell you - one that no one else knows. And I need you to hear it, and remember it, and pass it on if the time ever comes."

"Yessir."

It was then that Kolschen told the story of Thaddeus Parnicca and the birthright that awaited his heirs. Kolschen explained every detail, described the location, and Tipper sat in awe as the story unfolded. When Kolschen was finished he asked Tip a dozen questions, testing him on the fine points until he had memorized every one.

"Until I get out of here, Tip - I'm leaving you in charge of everything."

"What?"

"I'm charging you with the task of finding my grandsons and keeping them safe. I'm empowering you to continue the work we've started."

Now Tip instantly burst into tears. He wept and wept and when he spoke the words barely came. "Why me?"

"Because you have what it takes."

"No."

"You've walked through fire and you've been refined."

"But I'm *not* ready. I'll *never* be ready. Not to do what you do."

"I wouldn't have chosen you if you weren't."

"You have other men. *Wiser* men."

"But none as bold as you, it seems. Or as young. And none have your gift with children."

But Tipper continued to shake his head. His mind was racing. His heart conflicted with the honor he'd been given.

"Tip no one has seen your face in years. Your name can't be followed. Who better to protect my grandsons?"

Tip's tears were flowing now. He choked off every word, "What do I do?"

"You gather everyone and move out of the country. Get to some temporary shelter and hold up."

"But Unger says he'll find us eventually."

"He'd be right if you were headed to one of the old places. But you're not. You're going to some place new. And you're going to build it from scratch."

"Where?

"Wherever you choose. Allow the others to advise you. But make it a new place. Out of sight and hard to find."

"What about assets? How do we fund a new place?"

"That's one area where you have a great deal of freedom. My holdings are *vast*."

Now Tip was deep in thought. "What does *vast* mean? *Vast* enough for what?"

"Use your imagination."

"Well can we access them?"

"Unger can. Years ago I signed over power of attorney. Just in case."

"But what about you? We can't just leave you here."

"I'll be fine. They feed me three times a day."

But tearfully Tip shook his head. Imagining Otsov Kolschen without his freedoms was too much for him to consider. But Kolschen watched the boy weeping and reached his hand up to comfort him.

"Tovarisch do you remember that pimple-faced thief who stole from Mushkin all those years ago?"

Tip raised his head to listen.

"He was a lost soul. A drifter with no father, no name, no purpose. Only aimless misery, and lonely misdirection. Do you remember that kid?"

"Yessir."

Now Kolschen chuckled, "Well, Tipper my best years may be right in front of me. Because this prison is *full* of kids like that. "

And even though notes would be smuggled out for years to come, notes for Tipper and Henry and Jack, those two men who truly saw each other as father and son would never meet again in this life, and for Tip Holland the glory of Kolschen lived on only in the promises he had made.

He smuggled papers and passports and they moved the children out in the dark of night. They traveled north, and found a refugee camp. For days they studied maps, debating their final destination, and as soon as they were in agreement Tip set out to gather a larger team, searching the world for people he trusted.

He found Wonderboy a widower and recruited him immediately. He met Doc Zuni in a library and offered him what he wanted most, the American dream. When he returned to the Mamberamo he found that his partners in the long jungle trek were more than willing to begin a new life.

In the coming months Unger and Derealdjon Polle would move with the host of children from one refugee camp to another, waiting for a place to call home. Ruffino took to the sea once Tip had gathered his team, towing the entourage in a small skiff across the great Pacific. All of them were gathered now, Momma Tom and little Padi, Tip and his friends from around the world. Everyone was there that he needed - except Henry and Jack, who were across the sea somewhere and Tip's search had yet to begin.

In their travels Tip was soon endeared to Momma Tom. "You knew Otsov's grandsons?"

"Yessir, Mister Tipper. They grew up right in these arms. Little Mumsie here would look after em good."

"We have to find them, you know?"

"*You* have to find them, Mister Tipper. But I'll just look after em as soon as you do."

When they landed on the western shores he contacted Unger who wired him the money to buy a plane. They hired a pilot and set out across the country, the motley crew, and when they landed Tip explained, "I haven't been home in fourteen years. There's someone I have to see. Just one last thing and then we're on our way."

He booked each of them rooms in a local hotel, just a few blocks from his home,

and when he arrived at her door the others stayed behind. He knocked and she answered and the look on her face could have knocked the wind out of a weaker man.

"Hello, sweet sister."

12. The Pickleman

Jack stood over the grave of the old dog and watched as the new light flooded the pastureland. The morning was cold, the coldest of the spring so far and he blew into his palms as he whispered to Putt.

In his heart his mother was there with him, and now she walked alongside the old dog - and both of them were like shadows trailing behind. Although his heart was aching Jack didn't find any tears that morning, but instead nodded his goodbyes to Putt, and to Luleo and mounted his gelding and turned to the east and rode from the village without any of the fanfare that his brother had enjoyed.

He rode across the forest through the morning, thinking long on the story of his life and he didn't stop until he reached the carcass of the old bear. It was a short ride by horseback, not long enough to wrap his mind around his new circumstances. He was still dwelling on the old farmer, Unger Soski, and what his friendship meant when his eyes fell upon the bear. She was bloated horribly, and Jack's mount knickered and turned from the smell.

The violence of the past days had numbed his heart to the scene, which was as gruesome as any he had ever observed. He clambered down from his horse and saw by his feet spent shell casings and two arrows broken by the fall. A black stain still shown on the earth: Putt's blood he believed. Jack was surprised to see that the bear's flesh had been ripped away, for days it seemed. It was torn from her legs and shoulders and in some places down to her bones, by wolves, no doubt.

For several minutes Jack knelt quietly by the bear, looking over the scene, until suddenly his eyes were closed and his breathing quickened. He thought of Putt with all his strength tilting toward the great bear. Both had looked mighty just days before, ferocious in the face of the other, and indestructible to him. Now both were dead.

"Whether it be time, or lives or love we must always make it count," Jack thought. "Friendships should mean something. Those we love should know it."

He peered into the bear's dried sockets where her eyes had been. Her mouth was open, her tongue gone, but she looked ready to speak. He stared into the hollow sockets and waited.

Finally he rose to his feet and nodded to the great bear and when he did a pair of figures moved through the trees, just out of sight. Jack saw instantly that they were the orphan cubs.

They had watched when the bullets struck her and heard the long chase through the woods. By the time they reached her all that remained was her scent, for her hide had already been stripped.

Jack cringed as he realized that it must have been them who were feasting on her flesh. He shook his head and mounted quickly, giving the cubs little time to rush him in the clearing.

"May she sustain you," he said out loud. "As mine has sustained me," though he felt silly speaking to the bears.

Jack followed the same trail they had sprinted down just days before. He rode across the afternoon until he reached the window in the meadow, remembering to tether his horse in a secret spot that Tip had shown him.

He greeted the Woodsies, announcing his arrival from a distance. Pasismanua was gentle and Papon carried his casual demeanor. They offered him lunch and weakly he told stories of Kolschen's funeral, and the fate of his father and brother.

Twice in the first hour Jack began to stand and leave but both times Pasismanua settled him with her eyes and eventually convinced him to stay until the evening passover, she called it, when the bears would receive their feeding. The children agreed. They tried to get him to stay longer but at dusk, while Papon was feeding the bears, Jack saddled his gelding and headed east across the great forest and rode until the last light.

He camped alone that night and dreamed of his long journey to Tenpenny as a child. Of how frightened and tired he had been. How uncertain he was for his future. Whether or not he had what it took.

He awoke an hour before dawn, covered in his rank-smelling saddle blanket, the shadows of the moonlight shafts dotting the forest floor. He called out to Putt, to Tip, even to Henry. He tried praying, even singing, but nothing could drive him back to sleep. He thought of building the fire back up but he was too restless to sit any longer. Finally Jack kicked out of his blanket and slipped on his boots and his hat and saddled his mount in the light of the moon and pointed her east and pinned his chest to the saddle horn to avoid the unseen hazards.

Within an hour he could hear the birds chitter and briefly it rained, a frosted rain of early spring, but rain still, and the cold stung his neck and earlobes and made Jack weary of his road.

He broke out of the forest in the cold light that afternoon and could still smell the burnt wood left in the fire pit that he and Henry and Tip had shared. The bones of the fish they had caught had been scattered and he said to himself, "God for all I've seen."

Jack didn't know which story he was supposed to think on from one moment to the next, Tipper's or his own. He could hardly recall all that had been told to him in the past days. On one occasion he pulled reign just for a chance to flip through his storybook and read all that he had scribbled. Why had Tipper decided to tell his story? And why had he waited until now? And now that Jack knew the story of his blood father, he couldn't decide who Tipper really was anymore.

He was every bit the man Jack thought he was when they had left, but he was not his father in the same way. He was a steward now in his mind, a steward of Henry and Jack, of Tenpenny.

Jack couldn't deny that the thoughts he had for his blood father caused a pride to swell up within him, but he still struggled to reconcile the whole of his story, as he would for many years.

When he broke out of the forest he trotted the mount across the long frontier of the Rojo Prieta, pointing for home. The snow had melted little in the time since he crossed the valley, almost a week prior. If anything the plain seemed colder and whiter now than it had the first time. He could still see the faint indentations of a trail of horses heading into the unknown of the west end. He could barely recall the anticipation they had felt as they crossed it.

The sun scaled the open sky and Jack didn't stop for lunch or to rest his mount. He rode steadily across the broad plain, and stopped only hours later, when his eyes made out a figure on a faraway knoll.

In the distance Jack could see a single tree towering over the plain, and beneath it a dark shape. As he rode closer Jack watched to see what unfolded beneath the shadow of the tree and when he did the hair on the back of his neck stood on end.

Beneath the single tree, shaking in the wind, was the shape of a man, and nearby a dead horse, slit open down the belly. The man was laid out flat on his stomach, a great hulking figure with no hat.

Young Oakham readied his pistol and rode up cautiously, not knowing what action to take. He announced his arrival and when there came no answer he dismounted, and cautiously knelt beside the man. The face was windblown and covered with snow, but even pale and disguised as it was, Jack knew it was Forsman. At close look an array of bruises still covered his face.

Beside the man were a few small branches, taken from the tree, and a knife and a tinder box. Meant for a fire that never caught, Jack knew. These branches are too green for burning.

Balled up near his shoulders, the man's hands were wrapped in long bandages, likely stripped from the wounds on his face. Jack surprised himself when he unwrapped one and peered beneath it, seeing the palm of his left hand, pale blue, a great hole blown through it, likely rendering it useless.

Jack breathed heavily. He had seen many wounds but none like this one, and never a dead man, not in all his life. The only corpse he had ever seen was his mother, on her bedside, and there was a peacefulness about her then. But there was nothing peaceful about the big man lying mangled in the snow. The entrails of the horse had been dragged a short distance from the cavity, blood pooled nearby, and Forsman himself appeared ghostly and tragic.

Jack was overwhelmed by his feelings. What he was seeing couldn't be pushed inside a box, like he wanted. The end of a life was laid out before him. A story's end. There would be no redemption for Joe Forsman. No chance now to make things right with his son. Jack looked long at his face. This man who had set out to kill his brother, and Putt, this man who had intended things on Greer that he couldn't imagine, who had bush-wacked dear Wonderboy, was dead before him. His life had ended on a bare patch of snow beneath a single tree on the plain and no words had been offered, and now Jack had found him.

Despite himself, the sight of the man, a lone corpse on the plain, suddenly moved Jack to tears. He thought of Danny, the angry boy he had known only briefly and how little the news of his father's death would effect him.

Oddly, young Oakham felt a strange responsibility for the corpse. He carried no spade and could imagine no way to move the body, accept by dragging it, which would be a disgrace, he knew.

Jack Oakham wiped the tears from his eyes and gave Forsman a long look. It was true that his brother had worked the man over, even beneath the thin layer of snow he was horribly disfigured. Jack surprised himself when he brushed the snow from the man's face, but was even more surprised when a gentle breath whispered from his lips.

Instantly Jack scrambled away, crawling backwards on his elbows. He watched as Forsman's fingers fluttered. There came one long steady breath before he was silent once again.

Jack stood to his feet, breathing heavily. He kept his eyes locked on the big man, pale and broken, but alive! He had only a gentle pulse, and his skin was colorless but he had breath, a breath that young Oakham was watching.

Jack stood to his feet and thought long, for all of them, for every man, woman, and child he had ever met and would ever meet. Jack knew that a moment before he had been just a boy on his way home but now he was staring down the great question of his life. Somewhere other boys his age were playing tennis in the sun, or sweeping sawdust off of cellar floors, and others still were singing in great choirs, their voices reaching out to girls who'd love them or hate them eventually, but none of that mattered in the end. Those were just moments, that everyone, anyone could have. They chose no one and were never fought over, never remembered, never regretted or relived. Those moments found no significance, no audience. They were, and then they were again, without consequence. But not this moment, Jack thought.

His mother was there watching, with Tipper, with Putt, with the four children Jack would raise someday, the eldest of which would die in infancy. And Momma Tom and Padibatakal were there, two women who loved all, and they were suckling the foal beside Greer, who hated this man more than anyone. And Greer's babe was watching and waiting, and Danny too, and all the bitter hay farmers on the Cutshank, and Wonderboy holding his wound. Sissy was there, ready to criticize and Kolschen beside her, smoking his pipe. The great war chief Apowazi stared him down and Golgol too, smiling through his hair lip. All had become one, one voice yes or no. Jack Oakham listened through the muddled chorus and just as clearly as he could see the dying man, so too could he hear their voices on the wind.

In an instant Jack began rubbing Forsman's shoulders and speaking his name.

"Get up, man!" he said. "You'll die if you don't get up!"

But Forsman looked as still and lifeless as he had the moment Jack arrived. There was no movement, no color, just the slightest breath trickling from his lips.

Jack sprung to his feet. It took all of his strength, but with great care the boy rolled Forsman onto his back. Jack could see his front coat and shirt, covered with dried blood where he'd wiped his hands, a crimson stain now covered with frost.

Jack stripped his coat and laid it across Forsman's chest.

"Wake up, man!" he said with his voice cracking. "Wake up or you'll freeze to death!"

Jack felt certain that if he didn't do something Forsman would die, likely within the hour. His skin was pale, his breath gentle, and his face bitter cold to the touch. Jack stood and spun around nervously.

His first thought was to fix a fire. He looked the timber over again, but knew with certainty that the green branches would never burn on their own. Jack turned in a circle, looking across the wide prairie for any tender he might use, but finding none.

I could ride back to the west end, he thought. I could gather timber and bring it back. But in a moment the thought was run off from his mind. Jack had nothing but his arms to carry timber with, not even saddlebags to store a few loose branches. That much timber wouldn't heat the man for ten minutes, he knew, and then where would he be?

It was a frightful thought, but Jack knew he had to get Forsman on his horse, one way or another. If he could stand him up perhaps he could drape him across the saddle.

He knew the situation was all but impossible. Forsman could awake suddenly and try to kill him, though he thought it unlikely. The man's hands appeared useless. Still, Jack pulled Forsman's rifle from the saddle, unloaded it, and tossed it away. Then he opened the big man's coat and did the same with his pistol, and removed a knife from his hip and searched his pockets. Jack's movements were quick but steady.

He led his mount alongside the man and tied her to the tree. Jack took several deep breaths and with all his strength he heaved the big man up, hoping to stand him on his feet, but his attempts were useless. The dead weight proved too much for Jack to carry.

In that moment more than ever Jack longed to have Henry back. With his brother's strength the two could have easily loaded the big man onto the horse. But Henry wasn't there, Jack knew. No one was there. It was the first time in his life, the first of many, when all of it rested on him.

Jack tried to haul the man up a second time but all of his effort was in vain. Not on his best day, after a full night's rest in his own bed could be hope to lift a man like Joe Forsman into the saddle. Carefully Jack set the man's body carefully onto the snow pack and looked up at the tree above.

Her limbs were sturdy. Her base was thick. Jack thought of moose hunts he had been on with his father and brother, of times when they had quartered the big animals. Jack looked to Forsman's saddle, then his own and immediately rose back to his feet. Quickly he hauled the rope from his saddle horn and tossed a length into a fork in the high branches, guiding it back and forth to make certain the drag wouldn't tear the rope.

Once the whole length of it was fed neatly through tree, Jack sat the big man up, and ran one end of the rope round his chest and carefully through his belt and up again looping it through his shoulders. He pulled the loose end of the rope as far as he could stretch it, and tied a taut line hitch a few feet from the end. Jack tried to stretch the loose end to run through the saddle, but the rope wasn't long enough for his purpose.

Without hesitating Jack pulled a second length of rope from Forsman's saddle and tied the two strands together. He ran the slack line beneath the horse's neck and around the saddle horn and when it was secure he took the reigns of his mount and led her on.

As the horse tugged on the pulley line, Jack thought back on the long journey through the Wild West End. He had done everything he could to deliver Putt to safety from the den beneath the lake, and to kill the great bear days later and save Putt's life. He had said all he knew to say to Henry to keep him from leaving, but Putt was dead and Henry had left him. Jack felt the weight of his failures bearing down on him, but here was Forsman, alive for the moment, with but one course to take.

Silently Jack prayed for the man's safety, which was held within his hands, as he marched his mount one slow step after another. When the slack was spent a creak sounded in the branches and the rope, now tightly stretched, hoisted the big man into the air. Jack felt certain that the strain of the rope would wake him, but Forsman hung limply, his red hands slapping against his legs.

Jack led the mount several paces more, watching Forsman rise until his hips were at eye level. With a "whoa" Jack stopped the mount and tied the reigns off on the low branches.

For a moment Jack watched as Forsman swung slightly in the breeze, his breath still drifting from his lips. The tree was holding and so was the rope, but Jack knew the next stage would be treacherous, with little time to overthink it.

A few feet up the trunk was a stub branch that had broken off years before. Perfect for the hitch, Jack thought. He turned the horse as wide as she could reach. Jack strained, his teeth chattering, as he tugged on the taut line hitch and tied the slack loop round the stub branch. With all of the weight on the tree, and none on the horse the whole trunk creaked as the big man swayed.

Jack separated the two lengths of rope, removed the reigns from the branches and led the mount away.

Had a stranger approached the scene from a great distance it would have appeared that Jack had hung the man, as his dark silhouette dangled freely from the tree.

Jack loosened the rope from his saddle and quickly led his mount up to Forsman, whose chin rested on his chest. Jack circled the horse around so that she approached him from behind, and jerked down firmly on the reigns, guiding the horse's head smoothly between the man's knees. When Forsman's body was hanging directly above the back of the saddle Jack tied the reigns off on the tree.

Then came the moment he was dreading most. Carefully Jack scaled up onto the horse, facing Forsman. He knotted the rope around the big man's wrists and tied the slack into a lasso. Forsman was broken, the frostbite coloring his nose and his ears and he wouldn't have long to live, but to Jack's eyes he was secure.

The boy dismounted and then mounted again, facing forward, and tied the lasso around his own chest, pulling it as tight as he dared.

He sighed heavily. There was so much that could go wrong. At any moment Forsman could come awake and surely he would shake himself loose and all would be lost. However Forsman didn't wake, but hung like dead weight, a weight that still filled Jack with doubt.

From where he was sitting Jack couldn't untie the rope from the branches so he braced himself as he drew out his knife. The rope, still taut, broke cleanly with one quick swipe and in an instant the weight of the big man bore heavily upon the boy, Forsman's great head slumping across his shoulder.

Jack righted himself on the saddle and put away his knife. He breathed deeply, adjusting to the sensation. "I'm breathing for two, now Putt," he said aloud.

Now Jack was in quite a pickle, he knew. Once mounted he could never dismount, not without a tree to hoist the man up again, and jarring his memory Jack couldn't recall a single tree big enough to stand the burden between him and the hogback, a short ride west of Tenpenny hill. He feared he was embarking on a fool's errand.

On the other hand, now that he knew there was a slim chance for the man, Jack had no intention of leaving him behind.

Carefully he reached down and took the reigns and set a line for home, planning to cross the Prieta in one steady ride, nary too quick or too slow. He could feel the breath of the big man swelling against his back as he led the mount steadily across the plain.

His eyes were tight to the wind and the bitter cold shook him to the bone, but he had done it! He was riding steadily now, covering seven good miles an hour over the uneven country and his mount was sound.

At one point Jack slowed to check Forsman's pulse, and spoke softly to the man, assuring him they had only a few hours yet to travel.

Suddenly Jack smelled a wild scent in the air but soon realized that Forsman had only wet himself in his sleep. Jack felt the need to do the same, but held it in.

"Come on, Sancho," he said. "Only a short ways now."

The mount needed to relieve himself as well, of his burdens and to stop for a feeding, but Jack pressed on, knowing well how late the hour was growing.

"Danny?" Forsman asked. His voice was only a shallow whisper.

Jack's throat tightened up. He slowed his mount and spoke over his shoulder. "No. I'm not Danny, Sir. Danny's not here."

Jack waited and listened but heard nothing so he rode on, as quickly as he dared. His mount barely raised her head.

"Where's Danny?" Forsman asked finally.

Jack stopped the horse. "Danny's fine," he assured him. "He's in a good place. We left him in a good place, Mr. Forsman."

Jack heard one long wheezing breath, a straining to speak. "Who are you?"

"I'm no one," Jack said as he adjusted the rope on his chest. "I was just on my way home when I found you."

"You wore this coat into my bar. . . a week ago," Forsman said. "You are the smaller brother."

Jack gave a half smile. "That's about right," he admitted. "I *am* the smaller brother."

Forsman asked no more questions, but rested his head against Jack's shoulder. They rode across the windswept afternoon and into the dusk light, over bear tracks hardly visible, over Wonderboy's trail and the tracks of the small posse as it weaved across the snowmelt. Within a few hours the horse was over-burdened, shuffling along with its head hung low.

The evening came quickly and after some hours Jack began to fade in and out of consciousness himself, his arms numbing to the weight of his cargo.

They found Wade's body that night beneath the moonlight, laid out flat on his back. Jack pulled reign and took a long thoughtful look at the body, pondering if anything could be done.

"Don't bother," Forsman told him, his head still resting on Jack's shoulder.

Jack turned back and shook his head. "It matters."

"He's long dead," Forsman whispered. "He tied himself down and died in the saddle. . .days ago. His horse must have finally tossed him."

They rode on as the clouds darkened the sky, and twice Forsman shook so violently that Jack thought he had passed away. But a short while later, when they reached the Pritchers, Jack rode wide around them, not wanting to see. But a strange southern wind whipped across the forlorn valley and in an instant the stench overwhelmed them. Forsman raised his head and saw against the snow three dead horses, half eaten and bloated, their halters shining in what little light remained.

He sighed and fell back asleep.

With each passing hour their conditions deteriorated. Forsman was soon too weak to speak, and his hands began bleeding through the bandages. Jack's mount was raw to her fetlocks, her head wagging and her eyes closed by the time they reached the hogback. Jack himself was feeling poorly, his eyes drooping, his arms swollen and numb.

In the dark of the morning, just hours before dawn Jack began to see the outline of his home on the saddleback, the alders and the hemlocks of the long-awaited Tenpenny Hill. He had never seen it from the west, but he knew it instantly. His heart gave a jump as he passed the old wooden sign facing east along the path. *No one passes but the Picklemen.* He turned back and read it.

"I need you to hold on a bit longer," Jack said to Forsman. "We're gonna fix you up. Get you warm at the top of that hill."

Even in the moonlight Jack could see that the grounds were much greener than they had been when he left, and despite the snowy valley to the west, the trees of Tenpenny Hill were starting to bloom. He noticed the coffee-brown mud along the bank of the Nippintuck where he could clearly see the footprints they had left the week before. Putt's paws could still be seen scraping across the bank and Jack went as far as pause for a moment to hold back his tears. They approached the worn path and slowly tread through the alders toward the saddleback.

"You should have left me out there," Forsman whispered, his teeth clacking. "No one would have known. You should've just ridden by."

"I would've known," Jack told him.

And as they trotted up the hill he added, "And somewhere so would you."

13. Hands and Feet

It was spring by the time he crossed the threshold of the stone steps, struggled up the hill with his back tender and his eyes heavy. Jack longed for a chimney fire and a porch, the bubble of stew and a warm bed. It was spring in his home at Tenpenny and Jack had much to speak of, and wounds to heal, a fire to feed. He would think hardy thoughts of who he was now, instead of who they would someday be. But first he had a mission to complete.

Smithson sat on the porch of the little workman's cabin, warming his hands by the fire. He looked troubled and exhausted as he sat there, and his eyes only raised slightly as he heard the clippedy-clop of shod footfalls approaching up the road.

Jack spotted the porch fire and the huge shadow of the big man. His left arm had fallen asleep at the shoulder and when he waved he did so with his reigns in hand.

Smithson lumbered down the porch steps, a strange, confused expression on his face.

"Once I cut him loose you'll need to catch him," Jack said.

Smithson saw the slumping figure draped across Jack's back, the ropes, the wounds and he nodded, but with questions still on his brow.

Jack pulled the blade of his knife up against his chest and sawed the rope, cutting through one strand and then the next until Forsman's body slumped to one side and Smithson supported him. Quickly Jack dismounted, clumsy in his steps, his legs failing him. He was light-headed as he helped Smithson lower the man down from his horse.

"Stay with him," Jack said.

"Who is he?"

"It doesn't matter," he sighed. "Just stay with him until I get back."

He found Zuni sleeping in the infirmary. He plugged the tub beside him and ran the warm water.

Zuni sprung awake. "Is that Jack?"

"That's right, Doc. It's me."

"Lord. When d'you get here?"

"Just now. I need your help."

"Did Wonderboy find you? Where's Tip?" Zuni looked down at the bloodstains on Jack's pants.

"He found us," Jack said. "I'll tell you everything. But right now I need towels and some hot tea and whatever else you can give me. There's a man outside almost dead from the cold."

They carried him onto the bed and stripped him down to his under-clothes and when the tub was ready they loaded him in. The water pinked from his bloody palms.

Smithson boiled a pot of tea as Zuni carefully examined the man's hands, crippled and stiff, then his gums and his cheekbones. He stood looking down at the tub.

"We'll need to feed him, too," Jack said. "He hasn't eaten in days."

"That's Joe Forsman, isn't it?"

"It is," Jack nodded.

Smithson turned from the tea kettle, letting out a gentle gasp.

"He was shot through the hands," Jack told them. "Coming on three days ago."

"Three days?

"Yessir. Saturday morning."

Zuni leaned in. "Those bruises are older than three days."

"He got those earlier."

"From Henry?"

Jack looked sharply at the Doc. "Yes, from Henry. The Bhotiyas told you."

"And where is Henry?"

As they cleaned Forsman's wounds Jack told the story of his adventure. As he chronicled the crossing of the Wild West End Zuni could hardly contain his excitement, but as Jack described the events of Luleo and Tip's departure, Zuni's expression grew heavy and grave.

The old doctor sat back in his chair. "He went through with it?"

Jack squinted. "You knew? How did you know?"

"Tip wrote me a letter. He wrote both of us a letter."

Just then the cry of the teapot sounded and in an instant Forsman sprung awake. The big man's legs splashed through the water and Jack and Zuni were quick to settle him down. They grabbed his shoulders and pressed against his knees.

"You're safe now," Zuni said. "You just need to hold still."

Forsman was wide-eyed, his eyes bloodshot. He cringed as he opened and closed his hands. It wasn't until he set them in the water that he realized the rest of him was numb.

"Where am I?" he asked.

Smithson looked away. Forsman's bloody gums and missing teeth proved unsettling when he spoke.

"You are at a place called Tenpenny Hill," Jack said. "About ten miles south of the Cutshank."

Suddenly Forsman remembered what had happened, and who Jack was. His eyes honed in on the boy.

"I want to speak to that father of yours. About your brother. I expect repercussions."

"I'd say you took your penalties when you shot our horses."

For an instant Forsman liked the boy. His tone outweighed his years. "And that man of yours who shot me?"

"He was shot too, don't forget. Shot first. And then I saved you from certain death. No, Forsman what happens to you isn't up to my father anymore. My brother's gone and my father left this place to me."

Zuni and Smithson faced each other, their mouths open.

Jack leaned down beside the tub. "We're gonna feed you and patch you up. I'd say that's pretty generous. Nothing at all will be asked of you. There are no debts to pay. The Doc and I will decide when you're strong enough to sit a horse, and then you'll make your journey home. Until then you are here. This place and these children know nothing of violence so I ask you, blindly, to keep it that way. Later today Smithson and I will ride back and bury your man."

Forsman said nothing.

For some time Zuni watched the boy, wondering if what he had said was true. They salted the water and tended his wounds and after he finally took some tea Forsman fell back asleep.

Of course once his patient was unconscious Zuni had a slew of questions for Jack, and the boy's answers came reluctantly.

"How is Wonderboy?" Zuni asked, after a long discussion.

"He'll live," Jack assured him. "Unger Soski is with him."

They reheated the tub with fresh water, and Jack began to prepare a meal. He had heated some soup on Zuni's stovetop and while he was stirring the pot the door creaked open behind him. He turned and saw Greer standing in the shadows.

"Jack?"

"It's me," he told her, growing more perturbed. His heart was scattered. The last thing he wanted was to explain himself to Greer. "I'm sorry we woke you. I'll be in to see you after sunrise."

But despite his words Greer stepped forward, her eyes on the tub.

"Greer, please. I'll see you after—"

"Is that *Joe Forsman*?"

Jack sighed. "Greer, I'm asking you kindly, and patiently to go back to bed. When we're finished here I'll—"

"Lord *God*! What's *he* doing here?"

Jack's temper was rising. "He was shot. He was dying when I found him."

Greer shook her head and spoke slowly."I don't care what happened to him. That's Joe Forsman. God Jack, he'll *kill* me."

Jack stood to his feet and pulled Zuni aside. "Watch him. You and Smithson both. Don't let him within reach of anything sharp."

Zuni gave Jack a curious look, not for the last time. "Of course," he told him. Then he watched as Jack led Greer back through the door.

Just as surely as he knew himself, Jack Oakham knew this to be a day of reckoning, a day he would stare the truth in the face. They reached her bed. "Have a seat," he told her.

"What happened to your hand?"

"Greer have a seat."

"I don't want to."

Jack had no stomach for an argument. He crossed the room and sat in the rocker, his legs still aching.

"There's really nothing to be afraid of," he told her. "He doesn't have the strength to wipe his nose."

Greer seemed to relax, a gentle smile spread across her face. "He was shot, huh?"

Jack leaned his head back and closed his eyes. "Through the hands."

"It's so strange to see you. It's seems you've been gone so long."

The change of her tone struck him. Instantly her fear and anger were gone.

"So long," he agreed.

"Oh, Jack. There's so much I need to tell you. I have to think where to begin."

"No," he told her. "Don't begin."

"What?"

Jack leaned towards her and held her gaze. "*I* have something to say."

Greer flinched when she heard this, surprised by his tone. She rested back on her elbows, and blushed. "Go ahead."

But before he could utter a word, Jack Oakham fell asleep. It was only a passing moment, no more twenty seconds, but long enough to clear his head. And then, just as quickly as he had passed out, Jack sprung back to life.

"My chief concern is this baby," he told her, wiping his eyes. "That's what I needed to say. We will care for your child as long as you need."

"Who told you about the baby?"

He waved her off. "Greer if you can't find the strength to raise this child, then we'll do it for you. But I believe you have the strength. What you should do is crystal clear. Running off somewhere shouldn't cross your mind."

"What about Henry?"

"Henry did exactly what *you* wanted to do. He went across the sea."

Briefly she thought what this meant for her baby. In a moment the thought was gone.

"What about how I feel?" Greer asked. "For you?"

Jack yawned. "This isn't a season for feelings, Greer. Your feelings change with the winds. This is a season for burdens."

"I lost my whole family. I don't want any more burdens."

"But you have them already. You and I and the others, we won't get any hand-outs because we're orphans. Life won't get easy all the sudden. It doesn't matter what you want any more, Greer. Your life won't feel like any of the hopes you had envisioned for it. But there will be a new child at the end of it. A chance for a new family."

To that the girl had nothing to say. She watched Jack patiently, hoping he would keep talking. Hoping he had more to say so she wouldn't have to. But Jack was already weary of speaking. His body ached and a great anger was swelling up inside him, though he couldn't decide who he was angry with.

Finally she said. "What are your burdens, Jack?"

He had almost drifted off again. "From now on, what's on this hill is all I will think about or care about. There's no room for anything else."

"And what about your mother?"

The mention of Jack's mother made him quiver. He suddenly felt the need to shake her loose. Seven years before, in a tattered sun dress and a hat one size too big she had walked barefoot across their lawn and arched her back, her smile pointed down at him, and she was painfully beautiful even to a boy. It was a fine cold day, and he could still smell the pinyon on the fire, and hear the crackle of the embers, in their simple lawn just a short drive from where she had died. Jack watched her look down at him, one last time, but in his dream his mother didn't smile. Her eyes were turned in a question, as if she no longer knew his face.

"She's gone," Jack sighed.

The two of them sat together in silence.

"What am I to think about?" she asked him.

"This baby for one. That's more than enough. But you have me, and you have other friends - like Wonderboy and Padi."

Her eyes locked on the floor. "I've thought a lot about Padi lately. She wasn't allowed to ride, you know?"

"I know."

"And then Sissy cancelled her baptism."

"She what?"

"Padi asked to be baptized and Sissy refused her."

Jack stood and circled the chair, now standing behind it. He gripped the back boards of the rocker. "Why would she refuse her?"

"Sissy thought it was for the best. She told one of the cooks that she thought the feet-washing would be too difficult for Padi."

Now Jack's anger had a home. He looked to the ceiling and breathed deeply. "Sissy Holland prevented Padi from being baptized because of her feet?"

"I know. It was a new low. She did the same thing about her riding the horse. And to me about the baby."

"The same thing?"

"Shamed us, Jack. She shamed us both."

Jack checked the clock on the wall and turned to leave, the dawnlight creeping in.

"I have to go," he told her. "I'll bring you breakfast later this morning."

She turned to look out the window. "You aren't the same," she said. "What's that?"

Her eyes were vacant and small. "You aren't afraid of me."

Jack kissed his fingers and laid them on her head. His heart didn't quicken. "It's funny to think I ever was," he told her. And then he left her to her bitterness.

But as he opened the door a new sound caught his attention and he turned an ear to listen. From the infirmary Jack could hear, gentle but clear, the sounds of Zuni snoring, and the muffled sounds of Forsman, still in the tub, sobbing through the walls.

By the time he finally stepped outside the first light of morning was beginning to break across the rooftops. He moved past the great fountain and the mat flat and down the hill toward the lots. Jack could hear the cabins stirring with anxious children awaiting their day. In just a few minutes Tenpenny Hill would come awake.

I have time, Jack thought. Just enough to see her.

The street was silent. He could only hear the Godsounds rising around him: dew dripping from the treetops, the wind rustling across the leaves, or the birds stirring for first light. He had longed for this moment for so long, to be back on Tenpenny Hill, that the realities of smelling his home in his lungs underwhelmed him. Still he thought how nice it was to be a silent part of something, to hear nothing but the waking world.

Yet despite how much silence Jack had earned, the feeling wouldn't last, of course. In the next moment he heard footsteps trailing down one of the side paths, with gravel crunching underfoot. Aunt Sissy was storming across the road, a desperate expression on her face.

"Jack?"

"Yes, Sissy. It's me."

"Have you come back to me?"

"To Tenpenny."

For a moment she seemed at a loss. Her eyes danced around. "So soon?"

So soon? he thought. What was she expecting?

"Not soon enough," he said. "Is there anything you need this morning? I'm sure you must be tired. With all that responsibility."

"Are those fingers broken?" she said with contempt in her voice, judgment in her eyes.

"They are."

"Figures," she smirked. "Only a fool would cross that forest in the springtime. You boys and that dog are lucky to be alive. Where are the others?"

"Yes, lucky," he admitted, straight at her. His voice was heavy now. "*I am a lucky fool to be alive.*"

Sissy cocked her head. "Jack!"

"Aunt Sissy I asked kindly if you needed anything. If you do, then point the way. If you don't the sun is on the move and I have loved ones to talk with."

"That old mutt of yours?"

Jack approached her, leaning in until their eyes were locked.

She shivered. "The dog of yours I meant to say."

"That dog of mine is no longer part of our conversation."

"Don't forget yourself, Jack. I'm your Auntie. What we talk about is for *me* to decide."

"No ma'am, Sissy. Your decision tree just withered and died."

"Jack!"

"You have but one leaf left."

She couldn't contain the fury on her face. "And what *leaf* is that, Jack *Oakham*?"

"You can humble yourself before the strength that surrounds you," Jack counted on his fingers. "Or curl up down that hill somewhere."

A great terror flooded her face. She couldn't contain how appalled she looked.

"Now listen here! I don't care one bit for the way you're speaking to me."

"I'm devastated by that."

Her jaw dropped. But when she recovered she shook her head in judgment. "Your poor father would be so *ashamed of you*, Jack. Just *ashamed*."

Jack chuckled. The thought of his father shaming him was enough to make him laugh. "It's embarrassing how little you know about your brother."

"Well I know this much: When he hears how you spoke to me he won't like it. And I'll make sure you see the look on his face when I tell him. I'll tell him this very morning. Every word. Oh to think of what he'll do when he hears what I have to say."

Jack Oakham raised up his tired eyes. "Tip Holland can't be swayed by words from weaklings and neither can I. No, Sissy, it's *you* who should be ashamed."

"For what, Jack? Oh please tell me."

"You denied a girl her freedoms, and have done your best to dash her dreams. You robbed her of her liberty in the name of safety."

She disregarded him. "Well, I disagree. I only protected that girl."

"She doesn't need your protection. She's a bird with wings. If you loved her you'd have the strength to let her fly."

This time she stuttered, "Well. . . I disagree."

"Clearly. Then you shamed an orphan girl in a time of great distress. I use my words carefully. *Shamed her* into believing that her baby was a black stain."

"What difference does it make if she's an orphan? All *I see is orphans.*" Her eyes were afire now. "And Greer had no business seducing my Henry! Someone has to be the *light.*"

"Sissy Holland. . . mother of nothing. . ."

"How *dare you*?!"

"The only time you see the light is when you drop your heel to snuff it out. How long did it take you once we were gone? To be reckless with the hearts of two young ladies. To dash their hopes and shamed their hearts. How long did it take you?"

"I did no such thing."

"There are scars to prove it, Sissy. Cause and effect."

"I disagree."

"God be praised that doesn't matter."

"What?"

"Do you see your brother here? Has he returned? Or Henry, either one? Do you even know why we went to the Wild West End? Do you know what's out there? Do you know the story of this place?"

"Jack? Where—"

He leaned in further, "Sissy, you want to live in a fog about who your brother is? About what he's made of. You wanna miss the point until the day you die? Be my guest. That makes you the butt of the biggest joke of all."

"Where is my brother? Where is my Henry?"

"Sweet now, are we?"

"Jack. I've been misunderstood."

Young Oakham found that he was smiling now. "No ma'am. Cause and effect is something I fully understand. What you did to Padi. What you did to Greer. These things have consequences. You've dealt them wounds. Now *that* I understand."

An evil smile spread across her face. "The only reason you're defending them is because you love them and you can't mount the courage to tell them yourself. You need to fight for them from the sidelines to feel like a fighter. It's all about you. You men. You love them both from a distance because a distance is safe."

Jack Oakham was calm when he answered, his eyes searching hers.

"There isn't room in my heart for the love of two ladies," Jack told her. "Is that right?"

"And love doesn't live *at a distance*."

Then he added, "Does it, Sissy?"

With that her eyes drifted to the ground at her feet. The differences between men and boys, the lonely and the loved, struck her like a bolt and in a moment she was shaking. Jack watched her turn and amble up the hill, as if she didn't know where she was going. She seemed to stumble on her own feet, her own thoughts, as she buried her face in her hands.

That was the first of many, he thought. There are many more to come.

One week to the hour had passed since the last time Jack Oakham had traded words with his Aunt Sissy, but it seemed like a lifetime to the boy. His mind drifted then, to a place it often rested. Despite his long journey, and the distance he felt from his old life, Jack Oakham was still able to recall the four constants he had known on any given day: Momma Tom's love, his father's wisdom, Putt's friendship, and the Biblical struggle between his Aunt and his brother.

Of course now his brother had left him, and with him went the struggle. Putt was buried beneath the branches of a bald cypress, and his grave would be walked over day and night. Even Tip himself had left him, although Jack was hopeful that his wisdom remained. But the only thing that Jack still clung to from his old life was the love of Momma Tom.

It's time for a new list of constants, Jack thought, while I hold tight to the one I have.

Like a fish held within his hands so too was his heart longing to wring itself free, to burst out through his fingers, to hold her hair, her hands, to wash her feet. He could feel the warm swelling in his throat, the need to say anything and everything with a full heart.

Jack walked quickly, a heavy breath filling his lungs. He grabbed a wooden bowl from the lots and filled it with warm water. Wouldn't want her to be cold, he thought. Then he found the braces that Tipper had built for her and took them off the wall and a bridle and hung them over his shoulder.

He drifted across the yard and through the open corral with the leather smell. He brushed the fetlocks of the horses that were waiting to be fed, and opened the door to the parched bedroom.

Padibatakal looked up at him through the doorframe, her eyes ablaze. He cradled her with his look, held her and rocked her with his trembling eyes.

As he stepped inside Jack glanced up at the dim light, withered by the dusty glass but shining clearly on the bed. Beside the leather Bible, flapped open with faded yellow pages, Momma Tom sat with her legs folded across the linens and a smile. There was a wooden chessboard turned to the door and she said, "Ah, there you are."

Acknowledgements

F or aiding him in the creation of this book the Author wishes to acknowledge:
Dr. Dudley Delffs, Dr. Phyllis Klein, Josh Pierce, John Morgan, Chase Epley, Brett Myles, Joy Young, Michelle Johnston, Tim Walker, Dr. Richard Morgan, Harry Chavanne and his beloved wife, Andrea, for her years of endurance and encouragement.

CPSIA information can be obtained
at www.ICGtesting.com
Printed in the USA
LVHW030243191022
731045LV00001B/7